To
Peter John Anderson
and
William Douglas Simpson

this book is dedicated by one
who is proud to have been
amongst their friends

Cab

A Thousand Years of
ABERDEEN

A Thousand Years of
ABERDEEN

—

ALEXANDER KEITH MA LLD

Aberdeen University Press

First published 1972
Reprinted 1980
© Mrs Lewella Keith 1972

Drawings by Gordon Henry and Ian Munro

ISBN 0-900015-29-2

Printed in Great Britain
at the University Press
Aberdeen

Preface

In the Introduction to one of his books A. E. W. Mason remarks that his Preface is really an appendix to what follows. The description may quite aptly be applied to this Preface.

In this book the story of Aberdeen during a thousand years unfolds itself. The ostensible author is little more than the medium through whom the tale is developed. And without any effort or direction on the writer's part, the character of the community has built itself up within the biography of the burgh. It has got to be admitted, with regret, that that character has not improved with more recent years. In the middle of the second half of the nineteenth century there becomes discernible a deterioration in civic quality which increases at the turn of the century and still more after the Kaiser's War, and obtrudes itself blatantly after Hitler's War. Aberdeen, save in a few quarters nowadays liable to be regarded as decadent, is no longer Aberdeen. With the bright lights of the city's achievements behind us we stand confronted by a darkening and deepening gulf.

It will be observed by the most casual reader, who has only to scan the titles of the chapters, that this book is not actuated by any strict plan. This is done, or not done, on purpose, for two reasons. One is that in the last few decades in the world around us we have had enough of planning and its awful consequences. The other is that the writer considers that a local historian should be a gossip, rambling on with his tale, full of old saws and ancient and modern instances. This also explains the repetitions, which to the scientific mind may be tiresome, but which help to make both situations and personalities more comprehensible. It does not explain the ragged edge of the end of the book. Change is all the rage, not merely in the city's physical presence, but also in the direction of its component bodies, and it has been quite impossible to keep up with them, while to cut the narrative short, say at 1950, would have left far too much untold.

A lot has been omitted. There has been no room. There is a crying need for thorough studies of Aberdeen's industry, which has enjoyed half-a-dozen romances; of Aberdeen's contribution to national defence — so substantial that in this book an attempt to give a reasonable account of what Aberdonians did in the First World War had to be abandoned; of its place in the arts and architecture, which one commends to Mr Fenton Wyness while there still remain untouched by the vandals some specimens of the town's fine buildings, and while we are stil near enough to the days of the classics to appreciate the far from insignificant legacy by Aberdonians of pictorial and sculptural art.

This history has, for reasons mostly outside the author's control, taken a very long time in the writing. For essential assistance in many more ways than the merely mechanical, he wishes to record his utter indebtedness to his wife, Lewella, who has never — or at least not often — lost patience with him and certainly never lost faith in the book. It is almost unnecessary to congratulate the illustrators, Gordon Henry and Ian Munro; their end pieces speak for themselves.

Contents

Part 1

The Burgh Taking Shape

Background to A.D. 84–1329

If Britannia indeed 'arose from out the azure main', Aberdeen emerged from the cold grey North Sea, a daughter of the foam like Venus, but unlike her grey and cold as her native element. There is no record of Aberdeen's origin. Where in the neighbourhood its first settlers located their huts, and when their huddle of rude dwellings acquired the status of a community, we do not know. We even do not know, beyond dispute, from what physical feature the name Aberdeen is derived. The very source of its motto Bon-Accord is obscure, and its communal fortunes are legendary stuff for twice as many hundreds of years as they are minuted in history — and Aberdeen's civic archives are the oldest in Scotland.

Little by little, in ways that can be imagined though not described, Aberdeen grew into a community with some degree of recognisable civilisation, progressing from separate families to groups of families, held together by the co-operation necessary to extract a precarious livelihood from an undernourished soil and a stormy sea. From the remains of pottery, ornaments, dwellings, weapons and tombs unearthed from time to time archaeologists have reconstructed the civilisation of those vague ages in the territories corresponding to modern Scotland before it felt the impact of a new cultural influence when the first century of the Christian era was three-quarters spent.

The coming of the Romans meant war, and war then as always meant the speeding up of the processes of construction as well as the invention of destructive devices. Whether the Romans introduced the bagpipes and 'the garb of old Gaul' to Scotland is a question upon which a Lowlander may beg leave not to intrude.[1] The Romans must, however, have caused the inhabitants to draw their scattered settlements somewhat closer, and to try to improve whatever rough organisation they possessed for promoting social discipline and communal existence. When the Romans for a season established themselves between the

1 The bagpipes probably. The modern kilt was improvised by an Englishman in the early days of the eighteenth century. The word 'kilt' is Norse.

Solway and the waist formed by the firths of Forth and Clyde, they showed the tribes within their jurisdiction the advantages of ordered village life. The rest of the people north of Antonine's wall that connected the two estuaries must also have been in less degree taught by Roman expeditions into their territory, that greater unity and larger numbers increased the measure of their security. Perhaps, too, the Roman occupation and the Roman invasions gave the Caledonian tribes opportunities of learning arts of tillage and crafts of manufacture that improved their prospects of extracting a better livelihood from the relatively scanty resources of their own wild country. No doubt Aberdeen in its comparative isolation from the centre of this fermenting influence felt the impulse to develop itself. Indeed it may have been then, as it certainly was later, somewhat ahead of the rest of the country, since from earliest records of its condition the town was considered important and regarded as big and wealthy, all three adjectives in those days being understood to signify very much less in size and substance than they mean now.

For seven centuries after the withdrawal of Roman civilisation, Scotland was abandoned to a precarious and tumultuous existence in which the only gleams of light emanated from the fitful and often temporary creations of Christian cells, where peace and order dwelt, throughout the land. These religious influences promoted social sense, coherence and a rudimentary culture within the circle of their jurisdiction. Aberdeen had reached that stage in its development when, in the first half of the eleventh century, Malcolm II, 'destroyer of foreigners', succeeded in unifying the Picts and the Scots, the Britons of Strathclyde and the Saxons of the Lothians, into the nation and within the boundaries that are still recognised as Scottish. Aberdeen's experience of its religious colonies had been auspicious. It was in a fit shape to benefit from the luck of being selected by David I as a principal centre for the Flemish craftsmen whom he encouraged to settle in Scotland. It had, of course, like the rest of the land, to suffer from civil strife and Viking forays, but no part of the nation was so well prepared to enjoy the benefits of the reigns of the second and third Alexanders, who gave their people the largest lease of freedom from mischance that the Scots were ever to know in independence.

CHAPTER ONE

From Darkness to Dawn

There is no record that a Roman foot ever trod the soil of Aberdeen. Aberdonians there may have been, and very likely were, in the native army that Agricola defeated about A.D. 74 at Mons Graupius, probably in Angus. In 209 the Emperor Severus, as the traces of his camps reveal, marched by Peterculter (Normandykes), by Echt (the Barmekin), Kintore (the Deer Dykes), Glenmailen and Inverkeithny perhaps as far as Burghead. One place, known to Agricola's troops as 'Devana', which name appears in an equivocal position in the first of British maps, that of Ptolemy, who lived in Alexandria, in Egypt, some seventy years later, has come to be popularly identified with Aberdeen, although the scanty circumstantial evidence suggests Culter, where the Romans crossed the Dee, or Loch Davan where the presence of a necropolis indicates there was a large native community in Roman times.

In one respect Devana makes a bid to be accepted as identical topographically with Aberdeen. Some Gaelic scholars have professed to recognise in Aberdeen the words 'Aber' and 'da-aevin', as meaning 'the outfall of two rivers'. If their supposition was indeed fact, Roman soldiers might easily have corrupted 'da-aevin' into 'Devana'; and, as it happened, in Roman times the Don flowed into the sea about a quarter of a mile north of the estuary of the Dee. But the most modern philologists seem to be agreed that Aberdeen means the mouth of the Don. That ascription may be accepted for the nonce, always bearing in mind the warning of the late John Fraser, Professor of Celtic at Oxford, that a Gaelic place-name is not necessarily to be taken as the original title, which may have been in a word or words in a dialect antecedent to the Gaelic which had by Celtic incomers been translated or converted into Gaelic terms.[1] Ville de Aberdon or de Aberdein, popularly called Old Aberdon or Old Aberdein, is a common phrase in charters relating to what we usually nowadays term the Aulton or Old Town, and the Norse version Apardion is near enough to Aberdon to support the latter name. At

1 There are amusing mistakes where Saxon names have superseded Gaelic titles — Auld Maud for Allt Maud, Peeled Egg for Peltaig, and so on.

least we are sure of 'Aber'. As for 'Old' Aberdeen as distinguished from Aberdeen or 'new' Aberdeen, the solution offered is that when Edward III burned down the latter in 1336, he spared the other, which thereupon became 'old' whilst the more southerly community was setting up house again. Unfortunately for this idea, 'Old' Aberdeen had been mentioned in a Bull of 1157.[1] For a century or two around that time, 'old' Aberdeen was alternatively known as the Kirktown of Seaton, which in itself complicates matters again. Given the proximity of Don with Dee in the Celtic era, the Aberdon interpretation for both Old and New Aberdeen is perfectly feasible and logical.

In any case, to begin with there were between Don and Dee not two but five clusters of huts or hamlets that were eventually to coalesce to form the modern city. A mile south of 'Old' Aberdeen, wedged between the mouths of Dee and Don, there were a half dozen of hillocks, later to acquire the names of St. Katherine's (west of the Shiprow), Castle, Heading (across Commerce Street from the Castle), Broad or Cunningar (rabbity), Gallow (now partly Trinity Cemetery, partly Errol Street), Port (Seamount Place), School or Woolman Hills. In the shelter of these mounds — whose number caused Aberdonians to boast that their city, like Rome, was built on seven hills — and on the links, haughs and inches to the south between St. Katherine's Hill, the Den burn and the Dee, arose the clachan of rude hovels that formed the nucleus of modern Aberdeen. When, there is no means of knowing; the hamlet 'just growed'. South-east of that there developed another hamlet associated with a shrine to St. Foty or Fotin, corrupted quite naturally into Futtie, and then, since that was deemed vulgar, into Footdee. West of the Denburn and no doubt dotted along its right bank, there came to be a string of huts that acquired the name of Gilcomston, and further south and west another elementary village called Ruthrieston. Gillecolaim son of Muredach and Ruadri, Mormaer or Earl of Mar, appear as witnesses to a deed of gift in the Book of Deir, at a date around A.D. 1100. About the same time the Saxon tongue began to be spoken by the literate classes. These two townships could, of course, have been founded earlier; both 'old' and 'new' Aberdeen may be assigned to a period perhaps 500 years before that.

These primitive communes would have had little (except religion) in common save their topographical proximity, but their situation was sufficiently exclusive to endow them in their earliest, most malleable

1   It is only fair to say that the authenticity of this document has been challenged.

years with some of the attributes associated with a race apart. To the east the sea, difficult and dangerous for ungainly cobles to cross; Don to the north and the Dee to the south, both unbridged; and to the west the great Stocket forest, dense with timber and brushwood — on every hand these natural limits marked off what was to be Aberdeen from the rest of the country. To that isolation may be traced something of that Aberdonian humour which tends to differ from others, accentuated no doubt by Aberdeen's early association with incomers like the Saxons and the Flemings, who from the twelfth century onwards took an increasing share in the commercial and municipal development of the town.

Until about A.D. 1200 we have to do a great deal of groping in a search after facts in Aberdeen's history. Apart from some early events associated with religion (of which in more detail later), the first real gleam of light comes suddenly from a rather unexpected source. In 1153 a Norse chieftain called Eysteinn, on a foray which is recounted in the *Heimskringla* of Snorri, 'spread his sails to the south, and steering along the eastern shores of Scotland, brought his ships to the town of Apardion, where he killed many people and wasted the city'. Snorri then quotes from a contemporary saga:

> I heard the overthrow of people,
> The crash of broken arms was loud,
> The King destroyed the peace
> Of the dwellers in Apardion.

From another saga we learn that in 1162 Swein, one of the last Viking leaders, spent a month's holiday in Apardion with the then King of Scots, Malcolm IV, 'the Maiden'. By inference, Aberdeen was then a considerable town.

In the long dark interval of 700 years between the departure of the Romans from Britain and this Norse interlude, we have little that is authentic about Aberdeen itself. But some assumptions we are entitled to make. Donald, Mormaer of Mar, with a band of Aberdeenshire men, fought in the greatest of all Ireland's battles against the Norsemen, at Clontarf, near Dublin, in 1014. If there were not men in the contingent from Aberdeen itself, Aberdonians would have heard something about it. Just two years before Clontarf, the Danes under young Prince Cnut, who later became King of England, were heavily defeated at Cruden Bay. In 1058 Malcolm Canmore defeated Macbeth and slew him at Lumphanan, and within a few months Macbeth's stepson

Lulach, actually the true heir to the Scottish throne, came to his death with much slaughter at Merdrum, on the hills above Rhynie. Contemporary Aberdonians must have had some knowledge of these events, for the merchants of the town traded with the people of the hinterland in a variety of commodities. These merchants, no better than packmen, must have taken their lives in their hands and left their fortunes at home when in summer they ventured forth to seek business in the country. Petty chieftains took toll of travellers, and their perpetual interference with peaceful pursuits sent many a stout peasant into the wilds to become a masterless man and to join with others in brigandage.

CHAPTER TWO

Church and Charters

─────

From A.D. 1200 onwards we can see Aberdeen with a clarity which, at first intermittent, becomes steadily greater as the years go on. Indeed, the history of Scotland itself before that date is not very clear as to detail, although outstanding events and the course of certain broad tendencies have been established. Of these tendencies the most important was the change wrought through the expanding influence of religion. In this Aberdeen participated. It is now generally accepted that Christianity was introduced into Scotland from the south by St. Ninian at the close of the fourth century A.D. From his headquarters at Candida Casa, or Whithorn, in Wigtownshire, he seems to have travelled as far north as Aberdeen. About 450 St. Palladius may also have done so; he is believed to have died at Fordoun.

One of Ninian's immediate successors as head of the Whithorn community was St. Ternan, from the Mearns, one of Ninian's personal converts. Nearly a hundred years after his time, another of the Whithorn fraternity, St. Drostan, came to Aberdeenshire and founded in Buchan the monastery at Deer, in which in due course there was written Scotland's first example of national learning and culture, the Book of Deer. About the same time as Drostan, St. Mochricha, whose name has been corrupted into Machar, appeared on Donside and built the first rude church on the bluff of Tillydrone, near the mouth of the river. The legend that he set his church there because St. Columba instructed him to plant his community where he found the crook of a shepherd's staff is rather vitiated by the fact that Machar preceded Columba by a hundred years; but the original monastery of Deer was placed in a bend of the Ugie closely resembling the Don at Seaton, and probably those early missionaries felt that in such a location there was a symbolical appeal which they could not resist. St. Machar is reputed to have died in France in 594. It is assumed that about St. Machar's time a church was founded in Aberdeen itself.

The missionary activity in the North-East — if we accept the legends — during the two centuries or thereby covering the Ninian and Columba

periods is, according to the accounts of religious foundations then made
in the area, so extraordinarily great that we can only conclude either
that the North-East was an exceedingly populous district or that the
missionaries were almost as numerous as parish ministers today.
The case of Aberdeen suggests that the proportion of clerics to population was in those early days far higher than at present. In addition to
the churches at Old Aberdeen and in Aberdeen itself, with their
extensive properties and buildings in both town and country, three,
or perhaps four, religious orders were established in the burgh by or
soon after A.D. 1200. In 1211 William the Lion handed over his palace
and garden in the Green to the Trinity, Red, or Maturine Friars.
Thence by a strange sequence of events we have the Tarnty Ha' of
today, while Trinity Lane and Quay help to identify the boundaries of
the monastery. In 1222 Alexander II founded on the Schoolhill a
monastery for the Fratres Praedicatores, the Dominican, Black,
Mendicant, Preaching Friars. The building he assigned to them is said
to have been a palace (let us call it a residence) of his. Blackfriars Street
today records the gift and situation. About twenty years later the
Carmelite or White Friars erected a house on the south side of the
Green (near Carmelite Street now). Besides these, the Knights Templar may already have been established in their chapel, which stood
on the north side of the Castlegate (roughly St. Peter's Chapel now).
The Franciscan or Grey Friars in the Broadgate did not appear until
1471.

These orders and the churches had drawn to themselves the main
wealth of the city. Large parcels of land and holdings in the villages of
Aberdeenshire were bestowed upon them by Crown endowment or by
sinners hoping for absolution and admirers seeking reputation. These
benefactions maintained numerous clerks and canons; in 1508 the
number of chaplains, clerks and singers connected with St. Nicholas
Church had to be cut down to sixteen. The Templars, whose hold
was not very extensive, owned a house or more in the Under or Nether
Kirkgate, one in Schoolhill and two in the Shiprow. Kinkell was a
Templar church. At various times they acquired Auchterellon in
Buchan, Leslie in the Garioch, lands in Turriff, Aboyne and Tulloch,
and in Culter, where on the site of Maryculter House they had a
preceptory, they held no less than 8,000 acres.

The Church of St. Nicholas had a regular income of 1,800 merks[1]

---

1   The merk was rather more than 1s. 1d. sterling, when a shilling went a good
     deal further than our pound.

and the 'seise boll', a boll from all cargoes of grain, coal and salt coming into port if carried by strangers, half a boll if by Aberdonians. Little wonder it was esteemed the 'finest parish church in Scotland'.

> St. Nicolas' stately structure here doth stand,
> No paroch church can match't in all the land.

Gifts, mortifications, other donations and fines, drawn from the fruits of the work of the people, substantially augmented the annual income, while at the same time retarding the expansion of output and trade of which, even then, Aberdeen was capable. Between 1277 and 1524 the Church of St. Nicholas received from wealthy citizens no fewer than thirty-one chantries, with altars, near their family burial-places. It was this drain upon enterprise, the vast wealth it represented, and the multitude of idlers that inevitably came to be supported by it that explains much of the excesses committed at the Scottish Reformation as in the French Revolution. There is reason, too, for the belief that the various orders and the Church itself gradually degenerated into mere machines in the administration of their property, the human touch was lost, and their tenants saw with relief lands and houses passing to new and, temporarily at least, more considerate owners.

So much for religious foundations. The first serious attempt at political and economic co-operation was made when four burghs in southern Scotland, Berwick, Roxburgh, Edinburgh and Stirling, founded a sort of parliament, the forerunner of the Convention of Royal Burghs. But very early, if not as soon as these, there was a hanse or economic league of the larger communities of the North-East — Aberdeen, Banff, Elgin, Forres, Nairn and Inverness. This is indicated in Aberdeen's first extant Royal Charter. It was granted about 1179 by William the Lion to his burgesses of 'Aberdoen', and to those of Moray and north of the Mounth, that is from the Dee to the Moray Firth. It confirmed to them rights which it states they had enjoyed in the time of David I, his grandfather, who reigned 1124–53. Minus the seals, this charter is still in Aberdeen's archives, the oldest extant, says Kennedy, to any Scottish burgh. It was granted at Perth, is written in the quaint abbreviated Latin of its time, and it bestowed on the burgesses the right of trading 'when and where they pleased, as freely, fully and honourably, as their ancestors in the time of David'. Before this royal warrant, there was, it is vaguely rumoured, a charter granted about A.D. 800 from Dunnideer by Gregory the Great. If

Gregory ever existed, which is doubtful, his charter is lost. Less vaguely, Alexander I is said to have given a charter somewhere between 1107 and 1124. It is lost. Lost too is the charter from David I, the existence of which is inferred in William the Lion's grant.

Besides the 1179 document, William gave the town two charters, which are preserved with the seals. Dated from Aberdeen with the month but not the year, they belong somewhere about 1196, and confer upon the goods belonging to burgesses of Aberdeen immunity from all tolls and customs in markets and fairs throughout Scotland. As every royal burgh in Scotland had the right to levy toll on all goods brought for sale from other places unless that place had a charter like this one granted to Aberdeen, the privilege bestowed by it was invaluable. Further indulgences came from Alexander II in a mercantile charter from Alyth, undated but somewhere between 1214 and 1222. This extended the town's trading rights, established a weekly Sunday market, regulated the extent to which merchants not burgesses from outside the burgh might do business in the market, and in particular reserved the cloth-market to burgesses except between Ascension Day and Lammas. This reservation indicates that thus early Aberdeen's trade in woollens, which has never been quite lost, was in a thriving state.

The most interesting feature of this charter is the establishment of a Merchant Guild. 'I . . . grant to . . . my burgesses of Aberdeen that they have their Merchant Guild, the waulkers and weavers being excluded'. The Guild was destined for centuries to provide the rulers of the burgh. Significant also is the distinction between merchant guild and craft guilds, the latter being associations of makers rather than sellers, of producers rather than traders. The waulkers (fullers) and weavers were expressly debarred, although or perhaps because the weavers were early agitators for a craft guild (not unlike but not quite a trade union) to protect their interests. In this rivalry between merchants and manufacturers, Guild and Crafts, middlemen and producers, Aberdeen was not different from any town of the Middle Ages. The interests of the two classes were often at variance, and we shall in the next three centuries come on evidence of much bitter strife as the Crafts struggled for a share in the government of the burgh.

Alexander III granted Aberdeen two charters, one from Kintore in 1274 confirming the earlier privilege of holding an annual fair in the fortnight after Trinity Day; the other from Kincardine in 1277 extending his protection to the burgesses, their lands, servants, and

belongings. The series of charters and their contents present us with
the picture of a burgh steadily acquiring character, prestige and wealth.
Indeed, the reign of Alexander III was the period of Scotland's greatest advancement since the kingdom was brought together by Malcolm
II, and of its greatest prosperity until long after the Union of the
Parliaments in 1707. In no other reign while it was independent did it
enjoy the blessings of prolonged peace. Alexander's death, followed
by sheer bad luck, then English cupidity and a long period of governmental incompetence, deprived Scotland, and Aberdeen with the rest
of the country, of the progress which the nation's native abilities,
given full scope, could have achieved.

CHAPTER THREE

The Medieval Burgh Reconstructed

In 1244 Aberdeen was destroyed by fire. This was a common occurrence in those days of wooden houses: in the same year Forfar, Haddington, Lanark, Montrose, Perth, Roxburgh and Stirling had a similar experience. Actually the fire was a godsend. The houses were hovels, the closes and narrow streets indescribably filthy, and the flames consumed a vast accumulation of dirt and debris that had been a fertile breeding-ground for disease.

The fire, unfortunately, could not cleanse the persons of the citizens. We can picture men of the wealthier sort, perchance with the king among them when William was residing in the Green or Alexander II in the Schoolhill, gravely pacing the open expanse of the Castlegate or strolling in the King's Meadows east of the Porthill or on the slopes of Castlehill. Habituated as their noses were to potent smells, they must have been glad, on a hot summer's day, to leave the foetid atmosphere of their homes. Even the King's 'palace' would have a single low door and tiny windows stuffed with any material that would keep out the air whenever darkness fell.

Their affection for their spouses has never been sufficiently appreciated or adequately extolled, for the ladies bathed themselves half a dozen times in their lives and never changed their underwear. Their reciprocal feelings for their husbands triumphed over an aroma that probably an annual 'dook' or plunge in Don, Dee or sea would dissipate as temporarily as would a whiff of south-easterly gale drive northwards into Formartine the odour of fish guts that clung to the city. Even out of doors a modern Aberdonian, could he be in the company of his ancestors, would be well advised to plant himself firmly to windward. The poorest inhabitant of the worst slum today lives in less squalid surroundings than the city fathers of the thirteenth century. Their streets were deep in mud in wet weather, in dust when the days were fine. Their houses let in wind and water through a hundred chinks. The smoke of their peat or wood fires, when it missed as it usually did the orifice in the roof that did duty for a chimney, remained inside.

Not a house in Aberdeen was built of stone and lime until after 1500. St. Machar's Cathedral and the Church of St. Nicholas had, before that time, been at least in part constructed of more durable material than satisfied the domestic needs of the citizens. Many of the dwellings were of clay, or clay and wattle, and thatched with heather or straw. The streets were very narrow, the houses separated by vennels or lanes, and usually equipped with backyards bounded by low walls of turf, 'feal-dykes' that were all the ramparts the burgh possessed. Aberdeen never seems to have rejoiced in fortified boundaries like Berwick-on-Tweed or Londonderry.

Living room and bedroom were the same, except in a few cases of unusual wealth. The hens and pigs shared the apartment. The sanitary arrangements can be appreciated from the garderobes of our ruined castles, which, primitive though they were, must have been many times superior to conditions in crowded towns. Sties, middens and hen-hutches filled the closes and were heaped into and across the streets, on which pigs, dogs, cats and poultry were as numerous as human beings. If the 'gardez-loo' deluge from the upper windows that made Edinburgh notorious were absent in Aberdeen, it was probably because Aberdeen had few upper windows. Instead of liquid shrapnel over head and shoulders, the unwary traveller was liable to a watery machine-gunning round the legs from doorways. 'The clartier the cosier' was the slogan of our remote ancestors, and with some it is not forgotten today. The fire of 1244, by no means Aberdeen's only visitation of that kind, left the ground bare and clean, and in 1244 rehousing was a simple matter. There was timber in plenty in the Stocket and in a few weeks a new town would be knocked together, with houses a little bigger and more pretentious and with closes less confined. As a consequence, the town boundaries crept outwards — up the Gallowgate over the shoulder of the Porthill, southwards from the foot of St. Katherine's Hill towards the Inches and the Dee, westwards to the abrupt ravine in which the Denburn flowed.

What defence the town had is not quite clear. In 1264 we first hear of the castle of Aberdeen. Money was expended upon some building there in that year, and there is mention of an account of 10s. for carrying ten casks of wine from the shore to the castle. That it was not constructed wholly of wood is evident from the name of one of the tradesmen employed on the buildings, Ricardus Cementarius (Richard Mason, Masson, or the Mason) — of whom more later. Doubtless there was mason-work of sorts in the larger public buildings by this time.

But Aberdeen at Alexander's death was a very small place indeed. There could not have been more than 1,500 people in it. It was a village the size of Ballater or Alford. It clustered on the Castle Hill, on the now vanished St. Katherine's Hill between the Shiprow and the Green, and along the ridge of the Porthill over which the Gallowgate climbed. The burgh boundary did not reach down to the present line of St. Nicholas Street until centuries later. There were mussel beds at the end of our Constitution Street, beside the estuary of the Don. There may have been a few huts at Foty or Futty. Between the base of St. Katherine's Hill and the Dee, there were haughs and a marsh, intersected by streams like the Denburn. In 1242 a chapel to St. Katherine was erected upon, and gave its name to, St. Katherine's Hill. The pious donor was Kennedy of Kermac or Kermuck in Buchan, Constable of Aberdeen, whose arms can still be seen upon the gable of a house in the Square of Ellon.

Part of what is now Ferryhill lay under water, owing probably to lack of drainage. North and west of the Gallowgatehead stretched The Loch (Loch Street commemorates it). The Loch burn draining the Loch made its way to the Dee along a line just west of Market Street. The rising ground from Schoolhill and Woolmanhill towards Rosemount was covered by thickets of gorse and heather chequered by cultivated patches. Beyond that, sheltering the city between north and west lay the forest lands of the Stocket. Foresterhill was part of this expanse of self-sown woodland, which stretched down the slope as far as the stone circle that was a feature of the landscape at Gilcomston.

About 1200 the main concentration of better-class population was probably to be found in what would now be regarded as a few mean huts on the banks of the Dee, south of the Green. From the fact that there were royal residences there and on the Woolmanhill, we may assume that both the Green and the Woolmanhill were the wealthier localities — the West End, but outside the town, whither those who could afford a country cottage withdrew in summer.

East of the Porthill lay what came to be called the King's Meadows. Stretching westwards towards the Denburn and southwards towards the Dee there were tilled plots. A few cultivated patches were also being wrested from the heather of the surrounding higher ground. Aberdeen, in fact, was in 1200 acquiring the environment of tillage which persisted until the city began to expand 400 years later. The whole of the land between the two rivers from the sea to the Justice Mills, and along the Denburn valley down to Gilcomston came to be dotted with crofts, the names of which have been preserved in records, and a few in our modern place-names.

Away out by the Don at the Kirktown there was a little church, not yet a cathedral, which was the centre of the bishopric. There may not yet have been a bishop's palace. Outside the burgh's boundary, a stone's throw from one of the town gates, stood Aberdeen's own church of St. Nicholas. Within the town there were the monasteries of the three religious orders already mentioned. There was a small chapel on the Castle Hill which was to have a rather unusual future. The monasteries were each a little centre of healing, and the sick of the town were constantly about their gates. There was no regular hospital, nor as yet a lazar-house for the lepers whose increasing numbers were beginning to cause concern, and who for the next three centuries were to be a prominent feature of both the history and literature of Scotland.

Probably at this time, certainly very soon after, the frontiers of the burgh were defined by the presence of bows, ports or gates. These gates, six in number, were astride the principal streets. At one time there were only three, symbolised by the three silver keys presented to the Provost on his election. Then there were four, evidence of this number being contained in the old saw, 'There's nae sic anidder in a' the four bows o' Aiberdeen'. But which were the original three, or four, cannot be determined. Probably the Gallowgate or Causey Port (which was regarded as very old in 1518) was one. It stood about the east end of Spring Garden. The Justice or Thieves' Port, built in 1439, and so called because it gave on an alley leading to the Heading Hill,[1] behind the Castle Hill, where malefactors expiated their offences, was at the north-east end of the Castlegate. At the south-east corner, at the head of what was then Futty Wynd,[2] was the Futty Port. The Trinity or Shiprow Port crossed the Shiprow near the head of Shore Brae. The Netherkirkgate Port stood between Flourmill Lane and the Well-house which is corruptly commemorated by the Wallace Tower. The Upperkirkgate Port was situated slightly below where Drum's Lane now debouches on the street. We hear a great deal more about the ports in the fifteenth and sixteenth centuries. As has been indicated, probably there were only three at the end of the thirteenth century,

1 Heading is supposed to be 'Beheading Hill'.
2 Whether Futty Wynd was the same thoroughfare as the Foty Gate mentioned in a document of 1391 we have no means of knowing. Foty Gate left the Castlegate about where the head of Marischal Street is now. It is not clear if it followed the same direction; probably it bore to the south-east.

of which the Gallowgate, the Shiprow, and the Netherkirkgate ports are the most likely.

The more venerable of the burgh's streets first receive mention in the following order: The Castlegate (*vicus castri*), 1107; The Green (*vicus viridis*)[1] 1273; The Shiprow (*vicus navium*), 1281; Gallowgate or Thieves' gate (*vicus furcarum*), and Futty (*vicus de ffoty*), 1350; Exechequer Row (*le chekery*), 1350; Upperkirkgate and Netherkirkgate, 1382; The Quay, 1400; Justice Mills (*molendinum justiciarii*), 1400; Guestrow (*vicus dict le Gastrow*), 1450. There was a Tolbooth built in 1191, north of where Weigh-house Square is now. There is no reference to a Market Cross at this time.

The first allusion we have to a Common Seal occurs in 1271. That seal has disappeared, although the charter to which it was appended is preserved. There are several extant impressions of a Seal of the burgh, the first of them in the year 1350. The description[2] of this Seal is as follows:

Obverse St. Nicholas mitred and vested, his right hand raised in benediction, his left holding a pastoral staff. On his right is a crescent (symbolising a ship), on his left a six-pointed star. The legend is

SIGNUM BEATI NICOLAI ABIRDONENSI

Reverse A wall of masonry with a two-leaved banded gate in the centre and three spires rising above the coping of the wall, the tallest in the centre and each with a terminal cross. The legend is

SIGILLUM DE COMMUNI ABIRDONENSI

The last example of the use of this Seal was in 1423–4. In 1430 a new Seal was made. Its description is as follows:

Obverse The armorial bearings of the Burgh (a tower surrounded by a battlemented under structure) on a shield with the double tressure of the Royal Arms of Scotland, counter-flowered with sixteen *fleur-de-lis*. The shield is supported by two animals, with manes and tufted tails like lions, passing down behind their legs, their faces in profile, and their

---

1   G. M. Fraser (in *Historical Aberdeen*) pertinently emphasises that the Green was always a thoroughfare, not a stretch of greensward.

2   It will be observed that this description differs substantially from Kennedy's. For materials about seals, see *The Armorial Ensigns of the Royal Burgh of Aberdeen* by John Cruickshank, 1835.

mouths supporting the ends of a scroll on which appears the motto BONACCORD.

Reverse   In the lower foreground a wall of masonry, with an open gateway in the centre, the portcullis suspended, and beyond the wall in the middle St. Nicholas standing under an ornate canopy, mitred and vested, his right hand raised in benediction, his left holding a pastoral staff; and to his right, behind, is his special emblem, three children in a tub. On both obverse and reverse the legend is

SIGILLUM COMUNE DE ABERDEEN

The use of the tressure of the Royal Arms of Scotland is rare on civic armorial bearings. Only Perth has it besides Aberdeen, and its presence indicates that it was a royal grant. The animals supporting the shield, though they look like lions, are probably meant to be leopards, another sign of a royal grant. Only five other Scots burghs have the royal leopards in their bearings. Indeed, the supporters, the tressure and the general setting of the shield almost exactly counterfeit the Privy Seal of James I, and it is perhaps no far-fetched assumption to attribute the armorial grant to James I, not to King Robert I. His grant, if he made one, has not survived. The 1430 Seal, according to an inscription on the back of the extant matrices, was cast in the provostship of John Vass. 'Ye.zer.of.grac.M.CCCC.XXX. jon.ye.vaus. was. alderman. and yes.sel. mad.'[1]

About the same time a second seal appears on the scene, the Seal of Causes or Privy seal. It is inscribed SIGILLUM SECRETUM BURGEN-SIU VILLE *Abierdanensis ad Causas.* Shield and lettering are like those of the 1430 Common Seal, but the supporters are absent and the bearings are three towers. In 1537 a new seal of causes was prepared, the interesting feature of which is that it presents a clear representation of the three towers which are defaced in the extant examples of its predecessor. A third privy seal is mentioned as being ordered in 1670.

In 1272 we find Richardus Cementarius as 'aldermanus',[2] as Aberdeen's provost was originally called, and a year later we come upon the first reference to the baillies (ballivi) of the town. They were four in

---

1   'The year of grace 1430 John the Vaus was alderman and this seal made.'
2   In Aberdeen 'praepositus' did not signify 'provost' until 1640. A 'praepositus' originally was a ballivus or baillie (incidentally, Aberdeen's use of two ll's in the spelling is etymologically correct), and the provost was 'aldermanus', which term in the seventeenth century was for a time applied to past provosts.

number: Ricardus Cementarius, who was the mason employed on the Castle in 1264; Walterus de Malemuk; Duncanus de Lasceles; and Thomas Filius Alicii. Masson, Lessel and Alison are common enough names in Aberdeen still. Cementarius heads the list of provosts in the vestibule of the Town House; Mathew Greatheued was alderman in 1281, and Malcolmus de Pelgouenie (Balgownie) is mentioned for 1284. Cementarius has the distinction of being not only Aberdeen's first recorded provost, but also the first identified Aberdonian. He does not come quite alive, but we know he founded a chantry or altar in the Church of St. Nicholas in 1277 for the repose of the soul of his wife Elene. He gave, for the support of a chaplain to the chantry, the income from certain property, including St. John's Croft, a piece of ground west of the Denburn on the road leading to the Crabstone. The name Cementarius appears as a witness on several local charters of that time. He died in or before 1294.

We are without much data as to civic and municipal procedure at this stage. At the end of the thirteenth century the alderman seems to have been first among equals in a quartet of baillies. After Bannockburn we find an alderman distinct from the four baillies. The town for administrative purposes was divided into four 'quarters'. They were Futty and the Green, which explain themselves; the Even, which was the part lying west of the Guestrow and Gallowgate and north of the Green; and the Crooked, which comprised the town north of the Castlegate and east of the Guestrow and Gallowgate. Each baillie was in charge of one quarter. There was also a common council drawn from the burgesses of guild. The municipal government in fact was in the hands of an oligarchy, who voted themselves into power and kept themselves there, if not continuously, at least recurrently. Kennedy says: 'It may be granted, that originally the magistrates and counsellers of boroughs were chosen by a poll of the burgesses, perhaps without much form or ceremony.'[1]

As regards industry, we have mention of a windmill (*molendium ventilarium*) in 1271. Its position appears to have been on the Porthill; there was one there, shown in Gordon of Rothiemay's map, of 1662. That which gave its name to Windmill Brae was built in 1678. From the windmill may have come the citizens' meal. But fish-curing, by sun and salt, was the main industry; and, of course, you must catch

---

1 Munro (*Memorials of the Aldermen, Provosts and Lord Provosts of Aberdeen*) does not go back beyond the Act of 1592. Elsewhere he remarks, 'we have been unable to discover anything having a resemblance to a popular election or an election by the suffrages of the burgesses'.

your fish before you can cure it. In 1281 the English bought a hundred barrels of pickled Aberdeen salmon, 5,000 salt fish, and some dried fish for their army. Pickled salmon was exported to the English Billingsgate of those days, Yarmouth. Aberdeen cured fish became so popular on the continent as to receive in the sixteenth century the distinctive name of 'Habberdine', which may derive from the Low Dutch pronunciation of 'Aberdeen'. Fishing was conducted in small boats little better than hollowed-out logs, which on calm days bore their fortunate owners sluggishly a few hundred yards out to sea or along the coast. The mention in the 1222 charter of fullers and weavers is direct evidence of cloth-making, and there must have been domestic crafts.

Trade, as we understand it, was not brisk. Perhaps half-a-dozen daring skippers in a year would take to foreign parts a ship that was a little larger or less clumsy than the fishing cobles. The voyage would be along the coast, or in favourable conditions across the North Sea to the Low Countries. We have very little information as to how often or how far these hardy mariners made their trips, but we learn (in the next century) of an Aberdeen cargo vessel, bound for St. Omer in Flanders, which was seized off Yarmouth by a gentleman pirate from Winchilsea who appropriated a cargo that included 56½ sacks of wool, 5½ dacres of oxhide, 150 salmon, 200 'bords' of oak, and a 'trussel' of deer hides and lamb skins. Continental seamen also occasionally entered the port of Aberdeen. Trade for the most part was by barter, and so it continued for nearly three centuries. In the Castlegate there was a *hostilagium* or official customs and clearing house, while in the Chakra Wynd or Exchequer Row stood the *Skakkarium*, where originally the King's dues were collected, but which also, it is claimed, performed the function of minting coinage from the time of William the Lion: the earliest Aberdeen coins preserved are those of the reign of David II.

Aberdeen's biggest business, however, was with the people of its own hinterland. Countryfolk brought in food and fuel — peat and wood; they brought in the skins of their domestic animals and of the wild creatures they slew in their hunting. They sheared their sheep, and packed the wool, along with those hides, in panniers slung across the backs of ponies. These commodities they exchanged for the fish caught by the Futty folk and the cloth woven all over the town. This inland trade ranged wider than Aberdeenshire and Kincardineshire. Its existence explains the formation of the Hanse of the north-eastern burghs, and it explains also the terms of the royal charters granted to the town. It was its mercantile and market privileges that made the royal burgh so important and powerful in medieval economy.

CHAPTER FOUR

The Wars of Independence: 'Bon-Accord'

The death of Alexander III in 1286 was the end of an epoch for Aberdeen as for the whole of Scotland. During the next twenty-eight years Aberdonians fought, suffered and endured with the rest of the nation, and participated in the triumph at the last. But because, more than once, at critical junctures, the burgh was in the forefront of the struggle for independence, more of the rewards of victory accrued to it than to any other part of Scotland.

The English appeared in Aberdeen in 1290. The death of the direct heir to the throne of Scotland, the Maid of Norway, soon after her grandfather, Alexander III, and the ensuing strife among the claimants to the succession presented Edward I of England with the opportunity for which he had been hoping. By a combination of threats and promises he got himself accepted as Lord Paramount of the Scottish Kingdom and umpire in the succession. The first thing he did was to occupy all the strong points. The castle of Aberdeen was one of these. When Edward had awarded the crown to John Balliol, he sent instructions to his lieutenant, John de Gildeford, to hand over these castles to the quisling King of Scots. That was in the late autumn 1292. While he had the authority, Edward kept the whole country up to the mark, much as Cromwell was to do some 350 years later. He saw to it that Aberdeen paid certain dues owing to the Bishop of Glasgow, and he insisted in 1293 on the unpaid balance of the dowry of Margaret, Alexander III's daughter being sent to her husband, the King of Norway.

But even worms turn, and so in 1296 did Balliol. Why and how matter little. It is sufficient here to record that in the summer of that year Edward invaded Scotland, routing the Scots in the first battle of Dunbar, as shameful a defeat for the vanquished as Cromwell's victory at the same place in 1650. He accepted Balliol's submission and resignation, and proceeded on a triumphal progress through the country. In the English translation of the French diary of his tour we read: '14 July, 1296. The Saturday to the city of Aberdeen, a good castle and a good town upon the sea, and tarried there V days.' Homage was being exacted, and Friar Hugh, of the Trinity Friars, was one of those who put his signature to Ragman's Roll, as by a contemptuous parody the parchment engrossing the submission of the Scots was called. It was during this visit that Edward is said to have appropriated the local charter of the Knights Templar in Aberdeen. For once he did not steal any civic documents.

Soon after Edward returned to London, advices reached him that Scotland was in a blaze. During the winter of 1296-7 there was serious trouble in Argyll and Ross, but there never was a time between the dawn of history and 1745 when disturbances were not endemic in those regions, so that disorder there had no serious significance. Reports of resistance to authority elsewhere were of much graver importance. They seem to have begun to reach the English Court in May 1297 but, allowing for the speed of communication and other delaying factors in those days, they must have referred to risings which had begun early in the year. They came from the south-west, from Moray, Aberdeen and Central Scotland.

At this point it is necessary to take Carlyle's advice and clear our minds of cant. The history of Scotland, as retailed in almost all the history books and as taught in Scottish schools has been deplorably garbled in its references to the Wars of Independence.[1] As regards Aberdeen, it was on 11 June 1297, that Edward sent orders from Kent

---

1   The Wallace legend has completely obscured the history of the period. The commencement of the resistance in 1297 has been ascribed to him when he clove an Englishman to the brisket in a street fight in Lanark; and the subsequent conduct of the war on the Scottish side, the victory of Stirling Bridge and the rest of it, have been laid to his credit. It is not only the earlier historians who have fallen into these errors, which were probably due to reliance upon English accounts that understandably seek to lay all the blame for the rising upon the man whom Edward murdered. Later historians — Hill Burton, Fraser Tytler, Hume Brown, Herbert Maxwell, Sanford Terry, Andrew Lang — all with greater or less fidelity follow the will-o'-the-wisp of Harry the Minstrel. Only Agnes Mure Mackenzie and Sir James Fergusson, following after Evan Barron's *Scottish War of Independence*, which blew the myth sky high, have endeavoured to rectify the error. Barron's masterly analysis almost wholly clears the ground of pitfalls, but even he, in his Invernessian anxiety to give the Celts the credit for the resistance, ignores the fact that the Highlanders, who were the congenital foes of all Sassenachs, whether Lowland Scots or Englishmen, took very little part in these wars, which were fought under the leadership of Anglo-Norman, Saxon and Flemish barons or gentlemen by the partly Celtic and partly Saxon-Flemish-Norse common people of the North-East, the Scottish Midlands, and Clydesdale and Carrick.

to the Sheriff to suppress the malefactors who had been reported to him as being active in Aberdeenshire. The report must have been sent off in the middle of May, and the events that gave rise to it must have been antecedent to the report by some weeks. They may have been connected with similar outbreaks a few miles to the north in the Province of Moray, which then extended from the Deveron to the Great Glen. The resistance there was led by a young noble of Flemish extraction, Andrew de Moray, whose short but brilliant subsequent career suggests that he co-ordinated the efforts of the Moravians with those of the Aberdonians. It is pretty certain that these preceded the act of violence in Lanark which has for so long been regarded as marking the rise of the curtain on the first War of Independence. It should be noted that while in Aberdeenshire there were one or two ancient noble families, such as the Forbeses and the Fergusons, who were Celtic, there were several Scot-Norman houses like the Cheynes, the Comyns and the Barclays, while the urban aristocracy of Aberdeen were Flemings, who were craftsmen and merchants, and Saxons, who were seafarers. All these, in addition to the already traditional Aberdonian habit of having their own way of looking at things, were deeply interested in the possibilities of the situation, the Celts, Flemings and Saxons being inclined to resent English domination, whilst the Normans, holding fiefs in England or related to vassals of the English king, would be disposed to await developments until they could rise in safety. These circumstances may go some way to explain the 'malefactors' of 1297, the fact that the Earl of Buchan, a Comyn, was busy suppressing disorders that summer, and a Wallace legend.

According to his versifying chronicler of 150 years later, Harry the Minstrel, Sir William Wallace was in Aberdeen that summer. With a wealth of gory and picturesque detail, Blind Harry relates how Wallace captured Dunnottar, where the English garrison leapt into the sea to escape death by fire and were drowned. Next he came to Aberdeen. The English set the town alight and retired into the castle. Finding himself unable to take it, Wallace set fire to a hundred English ships in the adjacent basin, and slew all the English he could find, sparing only priests, women and children. The prose historian, John of Fordun, adds that he put to death a number of citizens who displayed anglophile sentiments.

In this story there seems to be not one word of truth. During the summer Wallace conducted a series of raids in Central Scotland. He was then joined by Andrew de Moray, whose name thereafter in the documents of the period takes precedence of Wallace's. It is conjectured that Moray's were the tactics that defeated the English at Stirling Bridge, that he was mortally wounded there, and that the Scottish defeat at Falkirk and the subsequent guerilla warfare reflect the absence of his direction and control. It is possible that before Stirling Bridge Moray may have been in Aberdeen on his way south, and there were no doubt Aberdonians in the Scottish army. But as regards Wallace, the biographer of Bruce, John Barbour, a most accurate recorder, who was much nearer the time of Wallace than Blind Harry, is silent as to the Aberdeen exploit. No English writer and no independent Scottish historian mentions the burning of the English fleet, although a hundred ships were a big armada to lose. The tale is on a par with the romantic glamour cast on the star near the east gate of St. Machar kirkyard as the spot where one of Wallace's limbs was buried. His limbs were sent to rot at Newcastle, Berwick, Perth and Stirling. As for the Wallace Tower, the name is a corruption of Well-house, for there was a well at the foot of the Nether Kirkgate; the house itself was built for the Keiths of Benholm at the beginning of the seventeenth century.

Edward invaded Scotland in 1298, when he defeated Wallace at Falkirk, and in 1300 and 1301, on none of which occasions did he penetrate by land beyond Perth. In 1303, however, he came again and reached Elgin, being in Aberdeen from 23 to 28 August, although the dates are all we know of his visit. In 1304 the Comyns, who had been defying him, came in at Stirling, where he was besieging the castle, the last stronghold to hold out against him. He took it that summer. About that time a couple of English civil servants, James de Dalileye and John Weston, who were 'making an extent of all the King's lands in Scotland', visited Aberdeen. No doubt Aberdeen in May 1305 sent delegates to the meeting at Perth which chose representatives to go to Westminster to receive Edward's plans for the government of the country. Thirteen months after this deputation, in which Aberdeen was probably represented, met in London, Bruce slew the Red Comyn at Dumfries, and the whole country was in a ferment again.

Buchan was dominated by the Comyns, who for family and other reasons were bitterly hostile to Bruce, but Aberdeen appears to have adhered to his cause from the first despite the presence of an English garrison in the castle, the occasional sight of the English fleet on the sea, and the proximity of the dour Celts of Buchan licking their paws at the prospect of plundering the rich community within a few hours' march. Bruce was crowned at Scone, surprised and routed at Methven Wood on 26 June 1306 and took to the hills. In the three months between his coronation and his defeat at Methven, he had according to Barbour been 'over all the land' seeking the support of the nation. We have the names of 135 of his followers, twelve of them from Aberdeen and Banff, three from Aberdeen itself. Whether or not there were Aberdonians with him at Methven, it was not long before he took refuge in Aberdeen. Barbour says first of all he made for the hills. There he lived on the country till the most of his little company was 'riven and rent', without shoes save what they cut out of hides. 'Therefore they went to Aberdeen' where Bruce's brother Nigel and the Queen and some ladies joined them.

> A gud quhile thar he sojournyt then
> And esyt wondir weill his men;
> Till that the Inglis men herd say
> That he thair with his mengye lay
> All at ese and sekyerly.

So they attempted to surprise him, but Bruce took to the hills again, later sending Nigel with the ladies to Kildrummy Castle, where Nigel eventually was slain and the Queen taken prisoner. When Sir Aymer de Valence entered Aberdeen on 3 August 1306 he found his quarry gone.

More than a year passed, during which in Lorne and Carrick and Galloway the King experienced that famous series of adventures which, on Barbour's authority, every Scottish schoolboy knows, or ought to know. Then, having won the battles of Glen Trool and Loudon Hill, the King with a compact little force in good heart

> Toward the North has tane the way
> Richt stoutly, into gud aray.

Hearing that Sir John Comyn, Earl of Buchan, was moving towards him, Bruce made straight for Inverurie. There, however, he was stricken with sickness and it was judged advisable to retire to Slioch, where the Comyn faction were repulsed after a three-day skirmish. The Comyns withdrew into Buchan, while Sir Edward Bruce went to Strathbogie, the king still being carried in a litter. As Bruce began to recover, they returned to Inverurie, upon hearing which the Earl of Buchan gathered his adherents again, 'a full gret company of men arayit jolily', and

> Til ald Meldron thai held the way,
> And thar with their men lugit thai,
> Before Yhoill-evyn ane nycht bot mair.

Bruce, who had about 700 men, moved out towards Old Meldrum and defeated his enemy on what is now the farm of North Mains of Barra, on Christmas Eve, 1307. Comyn fled to England, Bruce wintered in Aberdeen, leaving his brother Edward to chase the remnant of the Comyn's men into Buchan, where they were again defeated at Aikey Brae, near Old Deer. The King

> Gert his men burn all Bouchane
> Fra end till end, and sparit nane;
> And heryit thame on sic maneir
> That efter that, weile fifty yheir,
> Men menyt the heirschip of Bouchane.

Barbour goes on to say that the whole of the North-East gave in allegiance to Bruce, who then marched to Perth.

This episode in Bruce's career has been related at length because, while it is obvious the King resided in Aberdeen when the herschip of Buchan was going on, and he there recovered his health before moving southwards again, there is not one word in Barbour of an exploit which has been retailed with minute detail and much gusto by several of Aberdeen's historians. According to the accounts variously given, after the Battle of Barra, the Aberdonians stormed the castle of Aberdeen and put the garrison to the sword. The Aberdonians' password was 'Bon-Accord'. Why did not Barbour, an Aberdonian writing in Aberdeen while men were still living who could recall those days, and presenting to the world a full-length picture of his hero against a background of the events of the time — why did he not include this glorious and exciting feat of arms in *The Brus*? He mentions so many duller incidents, and waxes eloquent on so many deeds that could not have stirred his Aberdonian blood as this gesture was calculated to do. Are we to take his silence as proof that the castle was not taken? Was the Bon-Accord story a myth?[1]

It is quite impossible to give an absolutely dependable answer.

[1]   Sir Charles Erskine of Cambo, Lyon King in 1674, announcing the matriculation of Aberdeen's coat of arms with the motto Bon-Accord says: 'The word Bon-Accord was given them by King Robert Bruce, for killing all the English in the night, in their town, the word being that night "Bon-Accord".'

Never was there such an elusive castle as the building that stood on, and gave the name to, Aberdeen's Castlehill. We have documentary evidence that King Edward saw the castle, which was described as 'bon'. We read of wine being carried to it. We first meet with Aberdeen's earliest civic head, Richard the Mason, in connection with the castle in 1264. We know John de Gildeford was Edward's governor of Aberdeen's castle. But there is no record, save the reference of 1264, of its being built and no contemporary mention of its being destroyed. Indeed, the Castlehill — unless there was a Pictish fort with mud walls and wooden fencing around it in Aberdeen's dim and distant youth — was named after a building whose ghostly existence extends over no more than forty years.

It is further on record that while Edward Bruce was harrying Buchan, Edward II sent orders to his fleet to succour Aberdeen's castle, but so far as authentic history knows, nothing happened. There is, however, a story, with as little authority behind it as the other, that the English made an attempt by land to retake the castle. They were met by Bruce's men in the burgh and by the citizens under 'John Fraser' (a suspicious name in itself, for it was not until after Bannockburn that the Frasers came to the North-East), completely routed and the prisoners hanged. The canons of Aberdeen, the story goes on, tried in vain to save the lives of the unfortunate Englishmen. All they could do was to bury them in consecrated ground in the town's kirkyard, between the church and the Schoolhill. The massacre story, it should be added, is rather contradicted by yet another and equally unsubstantiated statement, that the Aberdonians were able to exchange some of their more important prisoners for the King's sister, Mary Bruce, who had fallen into English hands.

CHAPTER FIVE

The Great Charter

When the Battle of Bannockburn wiped the English — if only temporarily — off the Scottish map, King Robert had leisure to study the needs of the nation he had saved and reunited. The north-eastern corner of his realm saw him more often and for longer periods than the rest of the country. In this, indeed, he was only following the precedent set by his forerunners, who, even in an age when the Court was nomadic and there was no formal capital, spent much of their time and gave much of their attention to Aberdeen. This personal care had arisen out of the necessity for keeping watch upon the north, which under Norse influence was a constant source of menace to the kingdom until Alexander III finally broke the Viking power at the Battle of Largs in 1263. But after that for a century and a half the Celtic Highlanders demonstrated that they needed no Scandinavian tuition in the harrying of the Lowlands. The most practicable route for a Highland inroad was through Aberdeenshire. Consequently, in the county the Scottish kings gradually established a system of defence in depth, with strong castles deployed on a framework to which the fortress of Kildrummy was the key. And in the Middle Ages, when military necessity demanded the royal presence in an area, relaxation had to be provided in a hunting estate. First Kindrochit in Mar was the King's lodge, and later Hallforest, outside Kintore, which tiny hamlet was a royal burgh perhaps even before William the Lion's day.

Like William the Lion and Alexander II, King Robert spent a lot of time in Aberdeen. Several of the charters he granted were prepared at Hallforest, but upon Aberdeen he lavished gifts in excess of any bestowed upon other communities. The Aberdonians had been 'different'. They had been amongst the first to rise in defence of Scotland's freedom; they had been almost his only friends in time of dire trouble. The burgh had offered him a refuge in illness, and its people had shared with him in the joy of victory. He, and his son David and his whole family, regarded Aberdeen as their own romantic town, and

Robert's grants to the community in consequence far exceeded in number and value those he was moved to give to other places like Edinburgh and Perth which might be deemed more eligible recipients of his grace and favour.

As soon as Scotland's independence and Bruce's ascendancy were assured, the spoils of victory were shared out. The Crown and Comyn lands in the neighbourhood of Aberdeen were extensive, and they were divided amongst Saxon and Norman families from the Borders and Lothians — the Gordons, Keiths, Frasers, Hays, Burnetts, Johnstons and Irvines were among the most prominent beneficiaries. Their descendants were to play a big part, for good or ill, and some of them for both, in the future of the Royal Burgh of Aberdeen. To Aberdeen itself the King granted no fewer than six charters. Royal it became now in every respect, and not merely in name. Throughout the whole of its previous existence, despite the granting of so many commercial charters from so many kings, the town had never received for its own proper use any property. All its revenue, if any, consisted of whatever difference to its benefit there might accrue from the royal dues collected by the town from the citizens and the valuation put upon the collection by the Crown. The customary procedure was for the Royal Chamberlain to agree to accept, probably in advance, a lump sum rather less than the actual assessment. The Crown, being always needy, preferred to get money in bulk promptly instead of a larger aggregate in smaller amounts scattered over a period. But the margin can never have been great, and without an assured substantial income, the burgh could make no real corporate progress. King Robert I changed all that at a stroke.

Only four months after his victory at Bannockburn, from Dundee on 24 October 1314, King Robert gave the burgh the office of keeper of the Royal Forest of Stocket, which carried with it for the benefit of the burgesses all the liberties and privileges pertaining to the forest save the ownership of the growing wood and the right of hunting, which were reserved for himself. A second charter confirmed the privilege bestowed by Alexander III in 1274 of holding an annual fair during the fortnight after Trinity Sunday.

Five years later on 10 December 1319, from Berwick-on-Tweed, he amplified his grant into the Great Charter of the burgh. This time, in presence of the General Council of the nation, he bestowed upon the burgesses and community of Aberdeen the ownership of the burgh itself and of the Stocket forest in free burgage on consideration of an annual payment of £213 6s. 8d. Scots.[1] The lands, mills, river fishings, small customs, tolls, courts, weights and measures, and all other liberties, commodities, and usages were theirs. They could build and develop within the boundaries of the forest — the Freedom Lands, as they have come to be called — and only the game and growing timber and the right of hunting in the forest were reserved. No other Scottish burgh was so favoured until ten years later, when the King, almost on his death-bed, alienated an equivalent portion of the Crown's property to Edinburgh. The Great Charter had other uses for Aberdeen. It enabled the town to reserve for its own use a substantial proportion of the dues hitherto collected from the citizens to be paid into the royal treasury. It also confirmed to the burgh its right to be represented in the parliaments of the nation.

One other very considerable benefaction to Aberdeen is ascribed to Bruce, for his three aforementioned charters are either routine confirmations or conventional grants, and the gift of £13 6s. 8d. Scots for ten years to help meet the cost of a fire in 1326 was doubtless a customary means of showing the royal solicitude for citizens anywhere. About 1320 the Brig o' Balgownie was built across the Don. The funds for the work were provided either by Henry Cheyne of Inverugie, then Bishop of Aberdeen, at Bruce's instigation, or by the King himself.[2] Three hundred years later, when Sir Alexander Hay of Whytburgh mortified certain small crofts of a yearly value of £2 5s. 8d. sterling for the maintenance of the bridge in good repair, it was expressly stated in the deed that the original structure was erected by King Robert 'at his orders and expense'. Incidentally, Sir Alexander Hay's bequest is one of Aberdeen's proudest exhibits. It now amounts to over £56,000. It has paid for the upkeep of the old bridge, built the original new bridge further east at a cost of £16,000, and made in whole or in part a number of roads and bridges in Aberdeen and its neighbourhood.

Doubtless the King had the Brig o' Balgownie built with an eye to

1   This feu-duty of about £17 sterling is still paid. In 1818 Kennedy estimated the income of the possessors of the Freedom Lands, from the property given to the burgh by the King, as £18,000 sterling. It would be twenty times that now.

2   Boece says Cheyne, who was a nephew of the Comyns, was restored to his see by Bruce, and 'out of joy that he was received into the King's favour, upon his return home, he applied all the rents of his see, which during his absence had accresced to a considerable sum, towards building the stately bridge over the River Don, which it is said, is 72 feet wide and from the water to the top of the arch 60 feet high.'

Buchan and any remnants of disaffection that might smoulder there. A bridge so near Aberdeen would increase the mobility of a royal army ordered to move northwards. But the bridge also facilitated trade. The town at all times was assured of supplies from the Mar area lying between the two rivers. The country north of the Don, however, was more populous and probably richer in agricultural produce. In the absence of a bridge — for wooden structures could not be relied upon to withstand an Aberdeenshire winter or a thorough-going Don spate — communications and commerce were vexatiously hindered. The country people would simply refrain from bringing in bulky goods for sale. The building of the bridge at Balgownie dispensed with all such obstructions to free commercial intercourse between Aberdeen and the districts of Buchan, Formartine and the Garioch. That meant a very great deal in those days. The nearest bridge over the Dee was at Durris; Edward I used it on the way to Aberdeen in 1296. The Brig o' Balgownie, however, is Aberdeen's oldest authentic man-made link with its beginnings; and although nature is responsible for much of its charm, it has claims to be regarded as not less lovely than the most beautiful of its kind.

In 1319 Aberdeen made its true start. By the grace of King Robert, and thanks ultimately to the stout hearts and sound judgment of its own citizens, it became a burgh of power and substance, important both in politics and commerce. That Wallace, who was little more than a name to the town, and almost certainly never set foot in it, should have a statue in the heart of the modern city — and the biggest statue in the city at that — while its true and first and most magnanimous benefactor, the King of its own choice, Robert the Bruce, should be forgotten, is one of the minor mysteries of Aberdeen history.[1]

Aberdeen's communications and trade with the north had been greatly improved by the building of the Brig o' Balgownie. To the south the approaches were less convenient. There may have been a bridge over the Dee nearer than Durris, but the usual crossing was by ferry at the Craiglug, whence the name Ferryhill. We may anticipate the course of events here for convenience sake and bridge the Dee as well as Don. About 1488 it was decided to have a bridge built, and churchmen being jacks of all trades then, Mr. John Livingston, vicar of Inverugie, was chosen as architect and superintendent. The cost

---

1   When in 1945 the suggestion was made that some memorial should be erected to commemorate King Robert, the Town Council showed little enthusiasm and public opinion, in so far as it was vocal, was hostile.

was to be defrayed by an annual grant of £20 for ten years from the public funds. But the scheme fell through. Among his numerous projects for the improvement of Aberdeen, Bishop Elphinstone included a bridge of seven arches over the Dee, where the present old Brig stands. He seems to have made a beginning but the bridge was not completed until 1527, in Bishop Dunbar's time. On 17 December 1529 Robert Elphinstone, Parson of Kincardine, and Maister Alexander Galloway, Parson of Kinkell, met the Council on behalf of the bishop and 'exponit and shew openlie in plane court how ye said reverend fayther, out of his grit exorbitant and sumptuuss expens, had bigit of new ane nobill and substancious Brig, dotit and finsait with all necessary, oer ye watter and ryver of Dee'. The negotiations for handing over the bridge to the town took a long time, on account of stubborn opposition by a small group of burgesses who objected to the transaction for some reason that is not divulged. The Council sent the bishop a handsome letter of thanks: 'of the quhilkis guid deid and mynd God eternall revard you, for we ma nocht.' A money chest was made to hold the Brig of Dee fund, the 'kyst' having originally three keys — one for the Bishop and Chapter, one for the Provost and Council, and the third for one of the principal deacons of the Crafts of Aberdeen; but later the kyst was equipped with four locks and keys, 'of the quhilk the provest sall have ane in keiping, and the merchandis ane wthir, the maisteris of the kyrk wark the third, and the deikynnis of craftis the ferd'.[1]

Having once taken over the bridge — 'the greatest and braivest brig now to be seen in Scotland', wrote Parson Gordon of Rothiemay in 1661 — the Council took good care of it, at least while the novelty lasted. But to begin with they had their worries. No sooner was it in their possession than the laird of Abergeldie demanded 'ane esy gait and passage betwix the brig of Dee and Chappell of the samyn quhairthrow thai mai eselye without impediment wyrk and labour thair watteris'. On getting no satisfaction, Abergeldie drove a passageway through at the north end of the approaches, so that the Council had to take out a summons against him in Edinburgh 'for hewing of the bulwark of the brig of Dee'. As no more is heard of the action, the laird probably desisted. Another danger was flood water. From time

1   The device of multiple locks was used by the Crafts, each of whose strong-boxes had three keys held by office-bearers who had all to be present when the box was opened. The same practice is understood to have been resorted to in our own day by an Aberdeen kirk session.

to time the master of the brig work was instructed to 'prowyd remeid' from the threat of spate. When Alexander Monypeny was appointed the handyman, a kind of rudimentary police workshops of a man, one of his duties was that he should 'daylye intend and advert to oure brig of Dee bulwarkis and chappell of the samyn, and sall reform all small faltis that sall happin in the saide warkis'.

When the bridge was in commission it became clear that other improvements would have to be made to the approaches of the town. In 1541, therefore, the master of brig wark was instructed 'to big ane bryg of tre over the pot burne' or Ruthrieston burn. In 1556 Robert Lumsden, master of brig wark, was ordered to erect a suitable bridge 'of twa bowis sufficientlie with stane and lyme' over the Den Burn, paying for the materials 'with the reddiest of the money that he hes of the mailes of Ardler'.

Thus did Aberdeen get its first convenient access from and to the south. A braw brig it was, with its ribbed arches, then unique in Scotland; indeed, as it was then described, 'ane substantious bryg of fyn aislar stane and lym, with pillaris, pendis, doubill brasis, battaling and cawseis', with a flat roadway and above every arch recesses in the parapet to give pedestrians room and safety. It had the royal arms, those of the Duke of Albany (Protector during James V's minority), of Elphinstone and of Dunbar. It had at the north end its chapel dedicated to the Virgin Mary, for the convenience of travellers desirous of performing their devotions at the beginning or end of their journey. The chapel was destroyed at the Reformation. And finally, at the south end, there was built a port or porch, with a tower over it, to be manned in time of war or pest as the town's first defence against invasion or infection. The architect, Alexander Galloway, was honoured by being asked to submit a scheme for the fortification of the town.

The Middle Age. 1320–1559

The 250 years that elapsed between the War of Independence and the Reformation were for Scotland a period comparatively static in trade and industry and of something closely resembling anarchy in politics. From 1314 to 1559 there were only two strong kings, Robert the Bruce who could handle men, James I who could not. Robert died in his bed, James was assassinated. James II might have proved better than the rest, but he was cut off early. For the second half of the period, Scotland, under kings who either led her into foolish wars or had not the force of character to control their nobles, never had the chance to settle down. In the last twenty-five years the religious and economic revolution we know as the Reformation, fermenting in society, made confusion worse confounded, and the country did not regain its balance for nearly two centuries after the change of faith was effected.

So long as King Robert lived, and indeed until the death of his son David II, Aberdeen presents the normal appearance of a Scottish town. Displaying its traditional individuality and reflecting its privileged position in the affections of the sovereign, it was just another Scots burgh. With the coming of the Stewarts the atmosphere changed. Perth, which for long had claimed to be the capital by virtue of being the usual, though not the sole, meeting-place of the Scottish Parliament was superseded by Edinburgh, by far the largest town. In wealth, however, as indicated by its customs dues and other payments, the northern city had no cause to fear comparison with any town, not even the capital itself. Aberdeen in fact, because of its civic endowment and its trade, felt strong enough to go its own way. Thus for fully two hundred years it exhibits a curious detachment, an almost exotic appearance in a Scottish setting.

Civic states, even at their worst, have engaging qualities — the classic Greek, the Renaissance Italian, the medieval Flemish. Basically similar, they present an infinite variety of development and conduct. Aberdeen has been called the Athens of the North, and in some respects it resembled Athens. Both were cities prolific of exiles, although the

Greek exiles were mostly driven out, whereas Aberdeen's went of their own free will. In the quarrels of its leaders, there was more than once a touch of Attic ambition. But its intellectual energy had a Renaissance quality, something of Florence in its aesthetic colour and the spirit of adventure in its pursuits. It gave Scotland its first poet, its first historian, its first considerable painter. Hardly had Greek become known in Scotland when Aberdeen University was employing the language on formal occasions. It was a pioneer in the arts of pageantry, display and advertisement, and so brilliant and competent in such productions that William Dunbar, himself a showman of no small distinction, could not forbear to praise. Nowhere in Scotland was architecture studied to better purpose than in Aberdeen, and the crafts of the carver and the needlewoman were not neglected. In Scotland today there are no finer examples of native medieval architecture and design than the Crown of King's College, the bridges of Balgownie and Dee, the oak screen and canons' stalls in the university chapel, the heraldic roof of the Cathedral of St. Machar, and the tapestries of the Church of St. Nicholas.

But when we come to the more strictly intellectual achievements of medieval Aberdeen's sons, and consider also the political and commercial vigour of the inhabitants of the burgh, we are conscious of a hard bourgeois temper, like that of some Dutch or Flemish city of the same period. It was said of one celebrated Aberdonian then, in compliment to his capacity, that he was 'a gude, trew, stowt man, lyk a Dutche man'. The scholars who went from King's College to instruct their contemporaries on the Continent in theology, philosophy, medicine and mathematics were sure-footed and sound like their fathers who bought wool and sold cured fish and traded with any country that would do business with them. The University of Aberdeen was not launched until it was amply endowed in sharp contrast to the colleges of St. Andrews and Glasgow, which had a long struggle to rise above their initial poverty. In religion, Scotland and the Netherlands both took their Protestantism from Geneva and found their brand of democracy in its uncompromising creed. But like Brabant in the Low Countries, Aberdeen was always inclined to be more Laodicean when it came to a religious revolution, and while the Scottish city never relapsed as the Brussels region did from the new deal in spiritual matters, it was the stronghold first of the old faith and later of the episcopal compromise for 150 years.

Behind all this variety of eager intellectual aspiration which made the burgh's cultural adventures possible were a thriving commerce and steady application to manufactures and business. Both trade and industry naturally suffered from the disorders of the Kingdom, from the depredations of 'our auld enemies' the English and from the periodic cycles of economic depression. But throughout the two centuries and a half we can hear in Aberdeen the constant bustle and noise of productive work. Its contacts with the Continent broadened, and as they did so, the range of its products was increased. Not only the Low Countries and the French Atlantic ports were familiar with Aberdeen ships and the Aberdeen accent. They could be seen and it was heard along the coast of the Mediterranean and on the quays of the Baltic and Scandinavia.

Despite the distances of those times, Aberdeen never failed to be sensitive to events that only indirectly concerned it. The disaster of Neville's Cross in 1346 when David II was taken prisoner, the palace revolution that culminated in the Battle of Sauchieburn and the sordid murder of James III in 1488, the overwhelming disaster of Flodden in 1513, the disgrace of Solway Moss in 1542 — all these sharp events keenly affected Aberdeen, and caused reactions almost as emphatic as those which the burgh displayed in connection with the much closer threat that was dissipated by the Battle of Harlaw in 1411.

In almost every case, when national losses had to be repaired, Aberdeen men had a part in the deliberations and the actual steps that were taken. From time to time Aberdeen's representatives in the national councils were among the most practical and respected of the advisers of the Government. This ready and frequent participation in affairs was something that no city State ever experienced, and to that extent there is a distinct duality in the development of Aberdeen's civic character.

Part 2

Scotland's Principal Trading Port

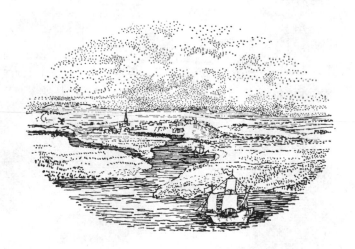

CHAPTER ONE

Trade and Industry

From our earliest glimpses of Aberdeen we can deduce that it was, for those days, a considerable trading centre. When the War of Independence was won, it was by the standards of the time a rich town whose commerce yielded a large revenue to the Crown — much more, many a year, than Edinburgh with its 16,000 inhabitants and Perth with its 8,000, the two chief burghs in the kingdom. In 1368, for example, ten vessels entered the harbour and paid dues amounting to £1,960 7s. 8d. Scots (about £163 7s. 6d. sterling) and in the middle of the century we learn of eight vessels entering or leaving in a year. These, it should be said, were poor years. The exports were natural produce — wool and woollen cloth, hides and skins, tallow, salted salmon and other cured fish. We can visualise its market as not unlike a Hudson's Bay Company trading post today. Uncouth men clad in skins, speaking the Gaelic, would bring in their loads of pelts, somehow making themselves understood by burgesses already using the Doric. Travelling merchants would lead back to town a string of garrons carrying panniers packed with skins, hides and fleeces. Fishermen from the Don, Futty and the Inches beyond the Green would offer their catches of salmon, whiting, codling and perhaps herring and mackerel in their season, all salted or smoked or semi-cured. And the exports must have been profitable, for the little ships that carried them to England, Flanders, the Low Countries and the towns of the Baltic Hanse — Danzig was the furthest port of call in that direction — brought in linen and fine cloth, claret, white wine, oil, salt, spices, soap, dye stuffs, iron, tar, wheat, barley and peas; and sometimes arms and armour. Aberdeen's standard of creature comforts, though not high, was well above the primitive.

All, however, was not plain sailing. We saw a case of piracy in 1273. In 1302, 1365 and 1369 there is mention of depredations, and they were not isolated cases. So bold did the buccaneers become that commissioners were appointed to treat with them. And the intermittent hostilities with England gave the auld enemy opportunities to exercise their inborn talent for appropriating other people's property and to intercept legitimately the merchantmen of their northern neighbours. The Scots, however, had themselves little to learn in piracy. In 1410, the year before Harlaw, the Earl of Mar seized a Prussian vessel over which Aberdeen was involved in a great deal of trouble.

Behind the trade, there was an astonishing variety of industries in a medieval city. If people's wants were simple, the processes of manufacture were slow. Work was well done. An artificer could afford to spend a long time over his job. His customer was so seldom in haste in the ordinary business of life that there was nothing odd in waiting. Handicraft is of its nature very nearly allied to art, and artists will not be driven. So, in the Aberdeen of the fifteenth and sixteenth centuries, although there were not more than 400 to 500 households all told, we find scores of trades. The survival of the medieval craft guilds in our Incorporated Trades has preserved for us a great body of material bearing upon the society and economics of half a thousand years ago. Today there are in Aberdeen seven Incorporated Trades. There were at one time ten. Edinburgh and Glasgow have, or until recently had, fourteen each — the number in the Capital is now twelve. Stirling has seven, Perth eight and Dundee nine. The Craft Guilds or Crafts were an integral part of medieval civilisation, and the backbone of industry for several centuries.

The old Aberdeen Crafts were the Hammermen, Bakers, Wrights and Coopers. Tailors, Shoemakers, Weavers, and Fleshers — these are the seven Incorporated Trades today; the Dyers, Masons and Barbers. In the eighteenth century there is one mention of Bookbinders. The Hammermen consisted of goldsmiths, blacksmiths, skinners, pewterers, glaziers, potters, armourers or sword-slippers, saddlers, cutters, glovers, braziers, hookmakers. The presence of glovers is explained by the fact that in the early days they made gauntlets of steel. The skinners were also claimed, more logically, by the Shoemakers. The Bakers, or Baxters, had no associated trade. They, with the Weavers, were the oldest of all. With the Wrights and Coopers went carvers. The Tailors included all whose trade demanded the playing of the needle;[1] thus in the eighteenth century they took in upholsterers. The Shoemakers — then called Cordwainers or Cordiners — maintained a line of distinction between themselves and common

---

1   Until the Restoration, needles were skewers of bone or boxwood, or clumsy pieces of iron or steel.

cobblers. They also controlled the trade in hides and skins. The Weavers or Websters are the first trade to be mentioned in the charter of 1222, along with the Fullers, otherwise known as the Litsters or Dyers. Both crafts, but particularly the Litsters, regarded themselves as above the other trades, and the Litsters attempted to have themselves accepted as eligible for inclusion in the Merchant Guild. The last of the Litsters died in 1886. The Fleshers as tradesmen, if not as a trade, were mentioned early in the sumptuary regulations of the burgh. The Masons gradually became submerged by Freemasonry, and the craft eventually disappeared in the Aberdeen Mason Lodge. The Barbers included the Leechers or Surgeons and the Periwig-makers. They lost the Surgeons when these became professional, and the Craft faded out during the nineteenth century.

All the Crafts devised regulations for the social, moral and industrial conduct of their members. All craftsmen were expected to repair to church timeously every Sabbath, and not go to sit or stand in the fields. They were supposed to remain at church 'until the sermon be ended and the blessing said'. This was a post-Reformation ordinance. Swearing, slandering, or giving the lie 'in ane fenced court or meeting' had to be expiated by a fine. Members were liable to a fine for not attending meetings and burials, and there was to be no turning up in caps or blue, black or grey bonnets; if they had not 'hatts on their heids' they had to pay for the omission.

Servants and apprentices, then as now, presented many problems. Masters were instructed not to play with them 'at no pastyme' on work days. Servants and apprentices were to attend divine service with their masters, and not to play at 'golff, fute ball, kyills, bowllis, cairts, or dyce'. There were many complaints about apprentices of the Hammermen 'visiting and drinking, neglecting their due time to come to their work, and to rise early in the morning for entering thereto, intolerable to be suffered in a civil burgh'; with the masons it was 'drinking and debauching', with the shoemakers plain 'lowsness'. Baker apprentices were forbidden to marry or 'spouse them ane wyff', and generally to keep clear of the girls during their apprenticeship, on pain of having 'to begin of new again'.[1]

The craftsman had to be an artist at his work. The mastersticks or essays — the specimens of his manufacture — which a candidate for membership of his craft and for admission to the ranks of the free-

1 Ebenezer Bain, *Merchant and Craft Guilds*, should be consulted for the Craft regulations.

men had to produce were extremely exacting. The Hammermen regulations prescribed the following:

Saddlers   A man's stock and a woman's stock of a saddle.
Armourers   A mounted buckler sword, together with a rapier mounted.
Gunners   A pistol with a hagbut.
Smiths   Two pieces of work of such as is wrought in the town.
Pewterers   A basin with a stroup.
Skinners   A pair of gloves for a man and a plain chevring for a woman.

In the Middle Ages and for a long time thereafter there was no absolute freedom to buy and sell. The fixing of the prices[1] of necessary goods and of raw materials was one of the principal functions of the magistrates. Upon them too developed the duty of seeing that all commodities made for sale were of a reasonable standard of quality. As the deacons of the Crafts came to be recognised, much of this responsibility was passed over to them. Between the Council registers and the Craft records there is ample data regarding the cost of living and other sumptuary and trade regulations in Aberdeen.

As early as 1399, we find that four *appreciatores carnum*, or meat inspectors, were chosen after the election of the magistrates to keep an eye on the quality of the flesh exposed for sale. The shambles at an early period were at the great cross in the Market-Place known as the Flesh Cross for that reason, a smaller cross, where fish was sold, being termed the Fish Cross. The Flesh Cross, in appearance similar to the Market Cross, supporting a platform and surmounted by a crucifix, stood at the east end of the plainstones, almost opposite the entrance to Lodge Walk. The Fish Cross was near the site of the present Cross. Between the two crosses, and opposite what is now the end of King Street, stood a gibbet where some of the town's malefactors were dispatched by hanging.

For many years the fleshers were also fishmongers. Until the middle of the seventeenth century they had booths for the sale of meat on the ground floor of the Town House, which was erected west of the

---

1   There is no lack of data respecting the prices for food and other commodities. Kennedy gives a long list, with the comparative sterling values in the first half of the seventeenth century compiled by Thomas Ruddiman. But even these were inaccurate, though far less so than any translation into approximate values today would be. The whole style of living as well as the meaning of money has changed. To quote the prices and to attempt to evaluate them would, therefore, be quite misleading.

Tolbooth. They had also shops throughout the town. The bakers were watched as intently as the butchers, the weight of their loaves and the quality of their cakes being a frequent subject of regulation. As early as 1457, when there were twelve master bakers in the burgh, each had his mark, which was impressed on the loaf like signs on old china.

The coopers too, who were noted far and wide in the thirteenth century for their handiwork, had each 'his own merk to his own wark'. Their barrels also were carefully inspected as to their measure and paid for at fixed rates. The cordiners were often in the black books of the magistrates, while the Crafts themselves usually laid down the penalties for industrial misdemeanours. The Council register contains many little prohibitions and trivial cases which indicate the alertness of the magistrates. In 1505 Philip Belman was fined for selling an apple for a penny instead of three apples for a penny. In 1521 the baillies charged the inhabitants of Futty not to pull, gather or take away mussels or cockies on a new bed at the north water (the Don) beside the Cunningar Hills (Broad Hill). In 1531 fines were stated for allowing horses, cattle, sheep, swine and other beasts to stray in the kirkyard. Things being no better two years later, George Annan was appointed pundlar (impounder) of the kirkyard, and if "he tholes ony beasts to come in the kirkyard thenceforth unpundit, his crag (neck) to be put in the gouchf (jougs)'.[1] About the same time steps had to be taken to prevent the casting of turf or divots on the Links and Inches and the stealing of sand from the Castlehill and Woolmanhill. In 1561 a shambles of wood was made at the Fish Cross to lay the white fish upon, and in the same year the Greyfriars Place was set aside as the centre where all malt and meal coming to the town should be 'sett, sauld, mett, and mesourit'. In 1555 it was ordained that tailors should sell only 'maid breikes and boxis of tartane or grose cloth and lynningis for cleything'. Forestalling — buying up the whole supply before it came on the market — and regrating — buying and selling again in the same market — were visited with very heavy punishment, as they forced up prices and rendered the official price-list inoperative.

In 1557 the Town Council had to dispatch an agent to Edinburgh to solicit a remission of taxation on account of the 'great exorbitant charges, taxations, damages and skaiths, by sea and otherwise, sustained by this poor town of Aberdeen and inhabitants thereof within the Queen's last immediate years, and of the indigence and poverty

---

1   This may or may not be a mistake. Our ancestors used gofe, goif, goyff, gwff, gowcht, gow — all in Jamieson's Dictionary.

therethrough of the poor commons thereof'. The same year the Council sent 'ane wryting' to the town of Dundee warning Dundonians that they come nocht here with their creamery and merchandise at St. Nicholas Day, because it is nocht fair, but against the privilege and infeftment of the town'.

On several occasions in the sixteenth century the magistrates, in order to ensure a fair distribution of merchandise, bought all the incoming cargoes. The burgesses were then expected to buy portions commensurate with their needs. Failure meant loss of citizenship. Sometimes when a ship came in there was not enough goods to go round. In that case those who were served did not participate in the distribution of the following cargo. On the other hand, there were occasions when purchasers could not be found, and a species of bribery was resorted to: those who bought were told they would get preference next time.

As commerce went in those days, Aberdeen plied a busy trade in the fifteenth century with both the Netherlands and the Baltic ports, Danzig and Poland particularly. The Danzig business developed sharply after 1500, and during the next 200 years the number of Scotsmen trading in Poland was so large as to become proverbial. Several observers put them at 40,000. In those days Aberdeen merchants were paying 40 merks for the privilege of trading with Danzig, and in 1410 Aberdeen's Council spoke of ancient friendship in a letter to the Baltic city. The profitable character of the Baltic ventures may be reflected in the double charge exacted by Aberdeen from Aberdeen merchant cargoes out of Danzig for the upkeep of the town's early 'lighthouse'.

After 1500 there were Aberdonians of the name of Skene with cloth mills and sugar refineries in Poland. There was, however, trouble occasionally. A good deal of gentlemanly piracy went on, and at the end of the fifteenth century when some Aberdeen merchants paid a Danzig exporter with spurious coin, the Danzigers diverted their cargoes to Leith and Dundee. So heavy was Aberdeen's loss that the magistrates went the length of offering to make good any shipping losses the Danzigers might suffer through Scottish pirates.

The older and steadier commerce was with the Low Countries. Bruges, Middleburg, and Campvere were in turn the Scottish staple there — the clearing-house for all Scottish imports. Aberdeen, which had taken a prominent part in getting a Scottish Consul or Conservator — 'host and receiver' — appointed in the Netherlands, never fully acquiesced in the recognition of a single staple. Skippers from the town went to Antwerp or Flushing when they thought they could find a readier market or a more acceptable return cargo than at Middleburg or Campvere.

Merchants were fined if they did not carry back in merchandise a certain proportion of the amount of their outgoing cargo. There were about half a dozen great Aberdonian shipping families — the Cullens, Blindseles, Rattrays, Fiddeses and Pratts. Greatest of all the town's merchants were Andrew Cullen and Andrew Buk. Cullen was Provost in 1506 and 1535. He was the first Alderman to be regularly termed Provost in the records. A fragment of stone on the wall of Collison's Aisle bears his name. Andrew Buk was commended by James V in 1540 for commanding Aberdeen's ship of war during the King's expedition to Orkney and the Western Isles. Even Bishop Elphinstone engaged in the overseas trade, though as a priest he must have procured a special licence to do so. When he was building King's College he sent abroad wool, salmon, trout, and money, receiving in exchange carts, wheelbarrows, and gunpowder — to quarry and transport the freestone from Elgin which he was using in Old Aberdeen.

As trade increased the Council had to pay greater attention to the harbour. In 1511 berthing was regulated in an elementary fashion. Vessels had to lie in the 'gawpuyl' and not between the ferryhouse and the mouth of the river. This was in order, evidently, to keep the channel clear. A skipper who dumped his ballast within the flood-mark was liable to a fine of 40s. Scots. Later one Robert Lindsay got 40 merks for presenting the magistrates with a sea-chart. The only mason work in connection with the harbour appears to have been a bulwark built in the first half of the fifteenth century south from the Shiprow along the line of Shore Brae, and a pier constructed by the inhabitants themselves on the south side of the channel. When the St. Nicholas silver work was sold off at the Reformation, the proceeds were applied partly to the building and reconstruction of the pier and the quayhead, as the seaward end of the bulwark was called.

CHAPTER TWO

The Reid Harlaw

Robert the Bruce's death hit Scotland, and Aberdeen, hard. The burgh had had another fire in 1326, which in itself was a benefit rather than a misfortune. But when the six-year-old heir to the throne, David II, was sent abroad for safety and education, Edward Balliol, the unhappy John's nephew, with English aid and the inevitable handful of Scottish malcontents, asserted a claim to the succession. Randolph, Sir Robert Keith and other survivors of Bruce's paladins were either slain at Dupplin Moor, where Balliol triumphed, or died about that time, and the country lapsed into a familiar state of turmoil. In 1333 Edward III invaded Scotland. In 1336 he sent Sir Thomas Roscelyn to the North-East, which was typically lacking in appreciation of English superiority. Landing near Dunnottar, Roscelyn marched upon Aberdeen, where he found the inhabitants drawn up in the Green to dispute his entry. A bloody battle ended in the rout of the Aberdonians. Roscelyn, however, was slain, and his men not only put to the sword all the people they could lay hands on, but they supplemented the massacre by setting the town alight. It burned for six days. It was regarded as the worst calamity the burgh had suffered. At the beginning of last century, when St. Nicholas Street was being constructed, charred beams and other blackened evidence were excavated bearing testimony to the catastrophe.

But the tide was on the turn. That same year the Patriot cause got the necessary stimulus when Sir Andrew Moray defeated an army of pro-English Scots on the slopes of Culblean in the shadow of Morven. Edward found himself powerless to overcome the moral resistance of the nation, and when David II came home at the age of eighteen, he enjoyed his own again as king as a matter of course. At once Aberdeen began to figure prominently as it had done in his father's day. David's first parliament was held in the burgh in 1342. In Exchequer Row he re-opened a mint for the encouragement of trade. He frequently resided in the town. The Bruce family, indeed, seem to have regarded it as their home. Christina, King Robert's sister and widow of Sir

Andrew Moray, lived in Aberdeen for several years, and died there. So in 1353 did David II's sister Matilda, who was the wife of Thomas Isaac, clerk and burgess of Aberdeen. Of her John of Fordun ungraciously remarks that she did nothing worth remembering. David's English queen Joanna and the two princesses had their dresses made in Aberdeen in one year at least, 1342. David himself, as a lad in France, had Aberdeen salmon regularly sent to him.

David the Unlucky in the autumn of 1346 was taken prisoner at the Battle of Neville's Cross, and as the English put a stiff ransom on his head, his bad luck dogged his country. Aberdeen was one of the four burghs that undertook to help discharge the ransom, part of which was paid in Aberdeenshire wool. At the parliament at Scone in 1367 it ranked next to Edinburgh amongst the burghs. In 1388 the first parliament after David's death met at Aberdeen and concerted the measures leading to the invasion of England culminating in the Battle of Otterburn, which gave us two of the earliest of our great ballads.

At this time, indeed, Aberdeen not only was taking precedence of most of the kingdom, but was also laying the foundations of future distinction for itself. In municipal development it was well to the forefront, and the careful habits of a long succession of public men and public servants have preserved to us a treasure unequalled in extent in any other Scottish town. The Burgh Records are almost complete from 1398 onwards,[1] as well as the notes of proceedings in the courts; we have five and a half centuries of written local history in the city's archives. This solicitude for its corporate documents was almost contemporary with a vital reform in the government of the town itself. The election day for alderman, baillies and common council by the burgesses was the Monday after Michaelmas. On this day in 1394, besides going through the process of election, the meeting sanctioned a code of rules regulating municipal procedure and customs which was endorsed in 1436 and continued for generations. These laws provided for the strict surveillance of the alderman's financial intromissions on behalf of the burgh; confined the handling of the town's rents to the baillies; limited the term of office of alderman, baillies and all officebearers to one year; reserved the election of the burgh's parliamentary representative to the whole council; and generally tightened up the financial system and the council's supervision of the markets and food shops.

1   There is one blank, 1412–33.

But a town council at the turn of the fourteenth century had to take cognisance of other problems than merely domestic ones, problems indeed much more serious than any that fall to their modern counterparts. We may fail to appreciate the virtues of the close corporation, but by and large the medieval council did just as good a job as its twentieth-century descendants. In the unsettled condition of the country, Aberdeen's situation was such as to cause its administrators constant and more than a little anxiety. It was one of the three richest cities in the kingdom. The nearest town of any size and strength was four days' march away. What royal power there was lay at a distance now that the King — Robert II and III — proposed to reside in Edinburgh or Stirling or Perth. The barons of the North-East could call on plenty of fighting men but could little afford to keep them under arms. And beyond the barons were the wild and rapacious Highlanders of Badenoch and Ross, to whom burghs like Elgin and Aberdeen represented wealth beyond the dreams of avarice. The town's civic heads had, therefore, to work out a policy of defence. It was not perhaps done, at least to begin with, of set purpose, and it took a long time. But by the mid-fifteenth century it amounted to a dual strategy of armed diplomacy. The council and magistrates insinuated themselves into the society and good graces of neighbouring lords and lairds, to whom they from time to time committed the protection of the burgh, whose male inhabitants they kept in a state of armed alertness.

The first big threat came from one who was destined to be regarded as its greatest protector. Robert II was not much of a king, but he was a prolific parent. Every true-born Scot today will have a lot of difficulty in proving that he is not descended from Robert II. One of his sons by Elizabeth Mure, his morganatic wife, was Alexander Stewart, the 'Wolf of Badenoch'. It was one of the tragedies of the Stewarts that their sons on the wrong side of the blanket were better men than those begotten with benefit of clergy. Alexander Stewart was the first example. His father gave him Comyn lands in Badenoch and Buchan, but for all that he developed into a brigand on a grand scale. Gaining the earldom of Ross by marriage, he secured control of the whole of the North and North-East of Scotland. There was this to be said for him, that though he was the terror of the land, no one in his dominions was permitted to be lawless but himself. In the course of a quarrel with the Bishop of Aberdeen, he sent at least one host of ragged Highland caterans to beat up Aberdeenshire, who ravaged the county to the very gates of the burgh. His son Alexander carried on the feud.

He occupied Aberdeen with his plundering 'tail' of Celts. The Bishop, unarmed, persuaded him to withdraw peaceably, and although his Highlanders continued their forays in the west of the county, no one in the burgh minded that so long as Aberdeen was spared.

Alexander Stewart, natural son of the Wolf of Badenoch, Earl of Mar, Lord of the Garioch, Lord of Duffle in Brabant, made a scarlet splash on a drab page of history. Strong-minded and high-handed, he had all the Stewart love of ostentation and much more than their share of brains. He became the Earl of Mar, so the story goes, by besieging the widowed countess in her castle of Kildrummy and threatening to burn the place about her ears unless she gave him her hand. She married him. That was in 1404. In 1408, the year the countess died, Mar made a hectic visit to England and France. He and Sir Walter Lindsay crossed the border to tilt with Lord Beaumont. The Scots won, for once. 'For gret pris and renoun', says Andrew de Wyntoun, the historian, 'the Scots won gret commendation'. Mar then sailed to France 'with a nobyl company, well arrayit and daintily, knichts, squires, and gentlemen sixty'. In Paris, at the tavern of the Tynnyn Plate, for six weeks 'he kept open house and table. He was commendit of all nations for wyt, wertne, and larges'. On his way home he got mixed up in a civil war in Flanders. Unable to resist a fight, though he had only four knights and twenty-eight men-at-arms, he was given the post of honour in the vanguard during the campaign.[1] His four knights, all Aberdeenshire men, appear to have been Sir Alexander Forbes, who as the first Lord Forbes re-established the greatness of his house; Sir Alexander Irvine of Drum; Sir Alexander

---

[1] The Earl of Mar's young men so distinguished themselves at this battle of Liege on 23 September 1407, that they found honourable mention in an old French poem of that time:

> Nouveaux chevaliers escossoys
> Furent ce jour, j'en scay levois,
> Pour leur prouesse, en grant renom.
> Sire Alexandre on son droit nom
> De Commech, qui ot cuer entier,
> Ce jour y fait chevalier, . . .
> Sir Alexandre d'Iervin
> Qui le cuer ot humble et benin,
> En ce jour monstora hardie chier;
> Et cil qui porte la baniere
> Dia conte qui est tant frisiez
> Ce fit Sir Johan de Miniez.

Commech is Keith, Iervin is Irvine, Miniez is Menzies; other Scots knights not of the North-East, are also mentioned.

Keith of Grandhome; and Sir John Menzies of Pitfodels. Mar got lands and a not very tractable second wife as his share of the spoil in this little war, and from his Brabant property he imported Flemish stallions and mares whose blood greatly improved the breed of Aberdeenshire horses.

These fighting dandies were familiar visitors to Aberdeen. Any day one or more of them would come cantering in by the Netherkirkgate or Gallowgate port, along the Braidgate and down the Shiprow to their favourite public house, kept by one Robert Davidson, a good fellow and substantial citizen who had for three years been provost of the burgh and was to fill the chair once again. Davidson was a frequent guest[1] in the country houses of his friends and it is no far-fetched assumption to attribute to him the conjunction of diplomacy with alertness upon which Aberdeen's safety was to be based for some generations after his death.

In 1411 a dispute arose between Donald, Lord of the Isles, and the Regent Albany, uncle of the Earl of Mar. The dispute threatened Mar's own possessions, which may have been an added stimulus to his energy when Donald swept through Ross, Moray and Strathbogie with a Highland host behind him. The whole country rose at Mar's call — Buchan, the Garioch, Mar, the Mearns and Angus. Aberdeen furnished its contingent — not a very large one, about the strength of a modern platoon, it would seem — under Provost Robert Davidson. With him was Laurence Leith of Barns, son of a previous provost, and doubtless other men, adventurous all, whether notable or not. Mar had his knights of Liege with him. Sir Andrew Leslie, the robber baron of Balquhain, who when hard pressed used to retire to his fortified eyrie on the Mither Tap of Bennachie and glower upon the Garioch till it was safe to come down — he and his six stalwart sons, all of whom were carried home feet first that night, were there; Sir Robert Melville of Glenbervie, Sheriff of the Mearns, attended, who some years later was caught by his enemies and boiled to death in a cauldron[2] — 'sodden and suppit in broo' was the technical term for a

1   There is one recorded occasion of a house party at Kildrummy Castle at which Davidson and William Chalmers were both present, along with the Chancellor of Scotland and other notables of great eminence.

2   At least one other instance of this highly utilitarian method of liquidating obnoxious citizens had been recorded in Scotland. One of the de Soulis family, laird of Hermitage in Liddesdale, was similarly disposed of on a ridge which is still pointed out by the natives with characteristic Border satisfaction.

popular form of lynching in Scotland, for the participants partook of the soup boiled out of their victim. Gilbert de Greenlaw, whose sculptured tomb may still be seen within the ruined church of Kinkell, fought his last fight there. The Lowland army, greatly outnumbered but very well armed, barred the advance of the caterans on the 'muirs beneath Harlaw' on 24 July 1411, and on the meadows of Balhalgardy, then as now farmed by Maitlands. The struggle lasted all day, and victory, as in the case of the other two battles fought between Aberdeenshire men and Highlanders, remained with the Lowlanders. The slaughter was great, and many notable men fell on either side.

> Gude Sir Alexander Irvine,
> The much renownit Laird of Drum,
> Nane in his days was better sene,
> When they war semblit all and some;
> To praise him we should not be dumb,
> For valour, witt, and worthyness,
> To end his Days he ther did cum,
> Whose ransom is remeidyless.
>
> And thair the Knicht of Lawriston
> Was slain into his Armour schene,
> And gude Sir Robert Davidson,
> Wha Provost was of Aberdene.
> The Knicht of Panmure, as was sene,
> A mortall man in Armour bricht,
> Sir Thomas Murray stout and kene,
> Left to the World thair last gude nicht.

Davidson's body was brought back to the city and interred in St. Nicholas Church, before the altar of St. Ann founded by his father, and endowed with gifts by the Provost himself, 'that potent man'. In the wall of the church, above his tomb, there was placed the inscription

> Sir Robert Davidson, Slain at Harlaw.
> Eques Auratus.

In 1740 during rebuilding, Davidson's grave was opened and his remains found, with a small silk skull cap that had been on his head when he was buried. The cap, unfortunately, was given away. The tombstone was in existence in 1811, and the inscription was still legible, but in 1874 no trace of it could be discovered. The Harlaw Standard, however, is preserved in the town's armoury.[1] Of this, Aberdeen's most romantic provost, the Chartulary of St. Nicholas says 'he built the town-house on the north side of the market-place opposite the cross, at the cost and charges of the community. And he was a man brave and bold, who prospered in all things, and died in the war of Harlaw, and with him many praise-worthy burgesses, staunch and steadfast, rooted in honest principles . . . in defence of the town, and for the liberty of their fatherland'.

1   The armour in the Town House said to be Davidson's is not his. The Incorporated Trades have his sword. Why the inscription should title the worthy Provost 'Sir' and term him 'the golden knight', no one has explained. He was not a knight.

CHAPTER THREE

Watch and Ward: The Forbes Feud

As its conduct in sending its own detachment to the Harlaw campaign indicates, Aberdeen had already a deep sense of its autonomous status and the need for instant defence. Nevertheless the citizens were startled by the narrowness of the town's escape. At once measures were taken to strengthen its position. In the following year, the Earl of Mar was given a post of privilege in regard to it, the citizens being instructed to acknowledge no lord or lordship save the King, the Regent Duke of Albany, and the Earl. In this relation to the burgh Mar continued till his death. In 1440, we find Sir Alexander Irvine of Drum, son of the burgh's old friend, described as 'captain and governor of the town', apparently not for the first time. In 1462 the community bound itself in manrent 'til a noble and michtie lord, Alexander Earl of Huntlie'. This was the first Earl of Huntly. He was a Seton, not a Gordon, his mother having been the heiress of the Gordon estates, who conveyed them with her name to Alexander Seton when she married him in 1408. This Alexander Seton rewarded with a portion of meal all-comers who consented to take the name of Gordon and the oath of fealty to him. They were known as the 'Bow o' meal' Gordons, the real (but illegitimate or collateral) original Gordon stock being known as the 'Jock' and 'Tam' Gordons, from the Christian names of the sons of the first Aberdeenshire Gordon.

The arrangement in no sense implied subservience on the part of the burgh. It was a free agreement, a treaty between equals, and it subsisted with remarkable goodwill for two centuries, although its stated duration was ten years. Huntly on his side undertook to keep the burgh in its 'freedome and infeftments for certain terms', while the town promised to be 'leal and true', to aid him in counsel, and whenever he should reside in Aberdeen, 'to take such part with him in his defence as we would do for the defence of our own persons, keeping (i.e. 1eserving) our allegiance to our Sovereign lord the King, and the freedoms of our said burgh'.

The last phrase was the most important one. It was not a mere form, as was proved in the summer of next year. Huntly, intending an expedition to the Highlands, summoned his dependants and vassals, Aberdeen among them, to muster 'this Monunday at evine' in the Cabrach. Richard Kyntor, the Provost, respectfully but firmly declined. 'In gude fathe, we hafe na hors, na may we get nane to come', wrote the head of the town. Moreover, he said, Aberdeen had been charged by its sovereign lord 'to kepe oure toune' because the King had information that an English fleet was on the way to destroy the burgh. No Aberdeen contingent served under Huntly's banner unless he was acting directly as the King's representative. In 1519 the then Earl, founding on the old bond, summoned the burgesses to help him in the siege of Dunrobin in Sutherland, but again they refused, although they sent him on loan three pieces of artillery, with powder and stones.

That was, as it were, the diplomatic aspect. The burgesses made other arrangements of a more martial character. They trusted in the lord — Mar or Drum or Huntly — but they also kept their powder dry. At all times they were prompt to attend to the immediate defence of the town. The cause of their solicitude might be news of another war with England or another Highland foray or a piece of dangerous horseplay by neighbouring lairds. In particular, an English landing was always a possibility. The city fathers had to be soldiers and civilians both, and their deliberations on local politics and trade were frequently interrupted by discussions upon military dispositions and the provision of weapons. Several of the burgesses seem to have applied considerable thought to the problems of soldiering, and whenever alarm was given they were detailed to form a council of war or to supervise the defensive preparations that were undertaken. The citizens were expected, under pain of banishment and loss of goods, to serve when circumstances demanded in the local defence force. Seldom did a decade pass without a call to arms, and although the citizens who saw active service were few, the rest were always ready to show their mettle. Twice they had to deal with serious raids from the county in the streets of the burgh. In both cases they routed the invaders, not without casualties on both sides. In a third incident, in which fighting is not reported, the Provost had to requisition the town's artillery to defend his house. During the 150 years that elapsed between the Battle of Harlaw and the Reformation, there were eighteen occasions on which Aberdonians considered it necessary to look to their arms — an average of once every eight years.

The measures taken did not alter greatly over the whole period, although there was a certain amount of development on the artillery side. The first step by the Council invariably was to issue a warning to all 'indwellers' to be on guard and to be ready to take their turn in the watching of the burgh 'for to keep the common profit of the town and the freedoms of it, and their neighbours also from skaith and surprise'. 'Every craftsman' had to have his 'dense aix[1] or halbert beside him in his working house', and to carry the weapon when he went out ('passes to the gait'). The penalty for failure to share in the town's defences was 'banysing and tyttyn doune of his huss', and those who had no houses to be pulled down were to be banished and their goods confiscated. This severe punishment does not seem to have been imposed often. After 1500 the penalty for evading watch duties was the payment of a pound or two of wax to 'the haly bluid licht'. The danger signal was the ringing of the common bell, at which tocsin every man was expected to rise in readiness to go on duty if and when ordered by the officers of the town. The watch sometimes consisted of thirty men who did patrols, sometimes of observation posts of four men, the usual sites being the Cunningar hills and at St. Fitticks beyond the water. All-round observation was kept, for not only were the ports 'stekit and closit' every night, but anyone who perceived any suspicious person or circumstance was expected to give warning. A sentry in St. Nicholas steeple was to knell the bell once for every stranger he saw riding towards the town. If there were more than he could count, he was to 'knell ay continual', whereupon the watch in the tolbooth would 'jow' the common bell. Strangers were viewed with suspicion. Country men were for years inhibited from being members of the watch, although in the sixteenth century they might be brought in as labourers on the fortifications.

A fine of 8s. was imposed on any citizen who did not carry his weapons with him. Periodically, on the links generally, but sometimes on the Woolmanhill (perhaps in the square field where the Craft miracle plays used to be staged), a wapinschaw was held, when the men turned out in 'their best deray', with 'jaik, spear, sword and knapshaw, and other gear'. The arms, it will be observed, were strictly defensive. a wapinschaw was at first what the word signified, a parade of weapons and kit inspection, although later it came to include a shooting contest. The spear was the traditional weapon of the Scots schiltrom, $5\frac{1}{2}$ ells long; the 'other gear' usually included a targe. In 1525 young and able

---

1   A dense or Danish axe was a Lochaber axe. The Danes introduced it into the West Highlands.

men are to be armed with culverines, cross-bows and long bows, and to practise shooting with them. Wapinschaws are to be held once a week or twice a month as the provost and council think expedient.

Scotland was well to the forefront in adopting cannon for its wars, and Aberdeen had artillery as early as 1497, and probably for some years before that, the first reference being casual enough to suggest that cannon were familiar equipment. From time to time orders were given to buy artillery, powder and shot, and to fee gunners — one was a Fleming imported for the job. During the Flodden scare, emplacements were made for the cannon, but while frequent and urgent orders were given by the council for the construction of earthworks, the public seem to have been remiss in attending to the matter. There are several entries in the Council register about making 'fossis' and 'strengths' (trenches in modern times and, *mutatis mutandis*, pillboxes), and committees were appointed to make arrangements and select sites. Such walls as the town possessed were not formidable, and were mainly the back-dykes of gardens, yards and closes. These the owners were ordered to keep built-up.

The chief fortifications, actual or intended, were a 'blockhouse of great strength' at the Sandness mentioned in 1493, and a trench and parapet stretching from the south to the north haven — from the harbour to the mouth of the Don, then much closer to the Dee. In 1497, on paper at least, this was an undertaking of the greatest urgency. The whole resources of the town were mobilised for work. 'All pynours,[1] stablers and carters having horses' had to repair to the links; a list was drawn up of those in possession of carts — twenty-three are enumerated, of which eight belonged to single individuals, three to crafts, and twelve to groups of two or more persons; labourers were brought in from the country; and even the booths of the shopkeepers were closed until the trenches were completed.

As a complementary precaution to the earthworks, the harbour used to be closed and locked 'in all goodly haste', a boom being thrown across the entrance constructed of masts and iron chains. On one occasion, for speedier communication between Torry and Aberdeen as well as for a boom, two lighters were moored end to end across the Dee, and the fishing boats of Futty laid beside them to form a rough pontoon bridge. The blockhouse at the Sandness was 36 feet long, 18 feet broad and 6 feet thick in the wall. The fort was built of stone

1 Shoreporters. The Shore Porters' Society was established in 1498 and has been in existence ever since.

and lime, with loopholes and doorway of ashlar. Subsequent to 1497
the building was altered, for when it was removed late in the nineteenth
century, it was circular in shape, with a smaller building raised in the
centre of the larger one for holding ammunition and maintaining a
look-out. Findlay's buildings were erected on the site in 1878 as a
fish-curing establishment. They now belong to the Harbour Commissioners.

The people of Aberdeen kept in mind the safety of the little village
of Torry and of the seat of the bishopric at Old Aberdeen. After one
alarm the town's amateur soldiers worked out a scheme of defence
which consisted in the defenders lying low while the enemy landed, and
thereafter taking them in flank and destroying them. Part of the plan
referred to the defence of Old Aberdeen. 'All manner of men, with
their carts of war, with horses, gunnery, artillery, and all other de-
fensible weapons,' were to be ready to march against the invaders
'for the safety of our cathedral kirk, my lord of Aberdeen's palace, our
masters the canons, and their servants and habitations'.

Aberdeen also took its part in expeditions that went, or were intended to go, beyond the Border against 'our auld enemies of England' —
no phrase occurs more frequently than that in the records. In 1495,
Aberdeen, which had already undertaken to entertain eight members
of the entourage of the imposter Perkin Warbeck,[1] was excused on
payment of £100 the duty of sending troops to the Scots army that
was about to invade England on behalf of his claim to the English
crown. In 1513 the town raised £400 to provide twenty spearmen, three
riding and three draught horses for the campaign that ended in disaster at Flodden. There the little body of Aberdonians fought in
Huntly's battle and doubtless several fell. In 1540 the town provided
James V with a ship of war, manned by twenty-five citizens (some
of them of the best burgess families), for his expedition to the West
Highlands. As illustrating the principles of sixteenth-century economics,
it may be mentioned that a committee of the council decided the fee
each seamen should get on this occasion, 'ilk man according to his
degree, because thair is better and war'; while the King himself ordered
that Andrew Buk, the redoubtable mariner who commanded the ship
of war, should get the first available cargo of the town's merchandise
that was to be exported on his return. The burgh several times fitted
out a warship.

1   This 'Duke of York' was married to Lady Catherine Gordon, daughter of
the 2nd Earl of Huntly.

At the shameful debacle of Solway Moss a hundred Aberdeen men, chosen by the provost, were present, the canny Council ordaining that if they did not pass beyond the Forth they should refund a proportion of their expense money. In 1544 when the English invaded Scotland, many citizens fled from the town. The following year the Earl of Huntly became provost, apparently because it was felt that the times demanded a soldier at the head of affairs. Huntly ruled for two years mostly by deputy. No doubt his influence was responsible in 1547 for the town raising £300 on behalf of the Government as well as eighty pioneers with pay and provisions for a month. At Pinkie Cleugh, on 'Black Saturday' that year, there were thirty Aberdonians, including four members of council, among the ten thousand Scots who were left dead on that unhappy field. On this occasion the town borrowed a cannon, 'the laird of Drum's falcon', for the campaign. The Aberdeen contingent was, as usual, under Huntly, then Chancellor of Scotland, who tried in vain to stem the disgraceful rout of his countrymen, and who was himself taken prisoner in a gilt and enamelled suit of armour that must have been a windfall to his fortunate English captor.

The long years of unsettlement that succeeded the accession of the Stewarts tended to strengthen the authority of the ruling bodies in the burghs. In such conditions men do not desire change in administration. They agree to postpone reform and innovation to a more peaceful and, therefore, more appropriate future. It was substantially so in the evolution of Aberdeen's civic government. The pattern was like that of any other Scottish royal burgh. The system was not democratic until the Reformation and Calvinism breached the fortresses of privilege. Neither was it altogether autocracy. The town was in fact ruled by an oligarchy, by a small circle of wealthy burgess families who preserved for themselves as a jealously guarded and vigorously defended birthright the function of electing annually so many of their own members as aldermen, baillies, treasurer, dean of guild, and common council. The choice was openly made but the franchise was closed to the majority of the inhabitants.

The system was twice assailed before 1600, once abruptly from within, while the other attack came from outside and was prolonged. The internal trouble came about in a rather curious way. In a close corporation like a Merchant Guild such as ruled Aberdeen, it was naturally desirable and generally insisted on that every member of the electoral body should be an indweller of the town. If outsiders to any number should be permitted to take part in the control of affairs, it was but a step to the transference of the whole power outwith the bounds of the corporation, which, of course, was an intolerable idea. There is one instance of a provost being elected who resided beyond the Dee at Torry. Instructions were at once given by the Council that a house within the burgh should be found for him. He could not, it was considered, exercise his functions properly if he resided a mile distant from the centre of affairs.[1]

At the beginning of the sixteenth century there had, however, been a little laxity. The rich burgess families bought estates, or 'baronies', outside the town, and their sons and daughters married into 'the county'. The county lairds who were thus connected with the burgesses frequently became the owners or tenants of subjects within the town, or contrived to get themselves accepted by the Merchant Guild as members or associates. Once adopted, they had no difficulty in attending the annual convocation of the 'hale community' of burgesses which chose the provost and baillies for the ensuing year. The practice, however, had become obnoxious to the burgesses, and in 1525 'the haill body of the guid toune' took measures to put a stop to it.

Why the question should have come to a head at this time has not been explained. It may have been that the burgesses were aware of the intention of one of their number, John Collison, who had been provost in 1521–2, to run for election again at Michaelmas 1525; and it may be that they were against his candidature. This, however, does not seem probable, for despite the ill-advised high-handedness of his conduct on this occasion, he continued to be entrusted by the burgesses with responsible duties. It may have been that the intrusion of the lairds into the electoral body had just become a serious threat and was being promptly resented; or it may have been that the objection was to the persons of the particular lairds who at that time happened to have intruded into the guild. At any rate, the meeting of the burgesses decided that no landward gentleman, even though a burgess, should have a vote or be entitled to come into the tolbooth to stop election proceedings, unless he resided in the burgh, paid taxes, and participated in the normal civic duties of an indweller. Anticipating trouble as a result of this ordinance, the meeting instructed the provost and baillies to keep and defend the tolbooth during the election of the new provost.

1   These deplorably bigoted capitalists had the same idea as the socialists of the 1960s, who have insisted on every town councillor residing within the town.

Everybody present concurred 'except John Collisone elder and certain of his complices', who contended that landward gentlemen like the lairds of Drum, Wardes, Balquhain and Meldrum should be allowed to vote. Now 'ane ambesowus proud man was this John Colesoun', as someone wrote in the margin of the 'Buk of Statutis', one of the great manuscript sources for Aberdeen history; and this incident bears out the aspersion. Collison's daughter was married to Drum's brother; the Leslies of Balquhain and Wardes were his wife's sons by an earlier marriage; and Seton of Meldrum was his wife's brother. So at least says the same anonymous scribe of the 'Buk of Statutis'.[1] Collison in fact was a pushing and progressive citizen, a landowner in the Lochfields (which covered the district at the northern end of Loch Street and the west end of Innes and what was Berry Street), the tacksman of several half-nets in the Dee fishings. Arthur Johnston of Caskieben, the great Aberdeen Latin poet, wrote an epitaph on Collison a hundred years after his death, in which he described him thus: 'A man he was worthy of Saturn's golden age; a citizen like Sparta's; a magistrate worthy of the city of Romulus.'

But in 1525 Collison over-reached himself. He concocted a scheme with his county relatives to frustrate the decision of the burgesses and by a *coup de main* to prevent the next election, or secure his own election to the chair. The Michaelmas election was fixed for 2 October. On the night of the 1st, Alexander Seton of Meldrum, John Leslie of Wardes, William Leslie of Balquhain and Alexander Leslie of that ilk, with eighty spearmen, burst into the town and began to lay about them among the inhabitants. The long-ingrained habit of living on the alert stood the citizens in good stead. They rushed to arms and a stubborn fight developed, the assailants eventually being driven out of the town. The struggle in the darkness, however, cost the Aberdonians about eighty casualties, dead or wounded. Next morning the Council named Collison as the instigator of the outrage, and, while discussing leases of town lands and fishings, declared that they were to be let to no one 'art or part of the cruell murther, slauchter, mutilatioun, and hurting of their nychtbours'.

The sequel was not up to the standard of the incident. The citizens

---

1   But A. M. Munro says 'Collison married Elizabeth Leslie, only daughter of Alexander Leslie, first baron of Wardis, and the widow of William Seton of Meldrum. The issue of this marriage was, so far as known, a son, John, who married Margaret Seton, and a daughter, married to a brother of the laird of Drum.' The relationships hardly matter, but they illustrate the interlacing of the burgess and county families.

were ordered to stand to their arms as if an English war was on, and the burgh complained to the King and Privy Council. But the assault was not repeated, and apart from vague hints of a settlement of the outrage by arbitration, history records no end to the episode. Collison regained his place in the esteem of his fellow-citizens, and in 1532 was one of Aberdeen's Parliamentary Commissioners. He died before 27 February 1535 and was buried in the North Aisle, then known as the Aisle of the Haly Blude, in St. Nicholas Church. Today significantly it is Collison's Aisle[1] and in the recess of the rounded arch below the north window there used to be the stone figures of the provost and his wife, over what no doubt was the site of the family tomb.

Seton did not long survive his escapade. In 1528 he had paid a composition, along with William Leslie of Balquhain and others, for the slaughter of Gavin Murray, Andrew Stratton, and William Forbes. Whether these men were killed in the assault in Aberdeen does not transpire. It has been conjectured, though there is no evidence, that the killing of this William Forbes was the cause of Seton's own death. At any rate, in January 1527, Seton was most cruelly murdered by John, Master of Forbes, a violent and disputatious person, in the house of the then Provost, Gilbert Menzies of Findon. This house was itself ill-fated. It was burned to the ground in 1529, and on its ashes arose the first dwelling-house in Aberdeen to be built of stone and lime — the celebrated Pitfodels Lodging (the Menzies family being the owners of the estate of Pitfodels), which stood on the Castle Street, next door to the Earl Marischal's house. Pitfodels Lodging saw much history ere it was pulled down in 1766 when the Council decided to make a new approach to the harbour. The head office of the Aberdeen Bank was built upon the site. It was a large ornate building, three storeys high, with ornamented but loop-holed turrets. In 1639 the Marquis of Huntly resided in great state in the house, and in 1650, when Charles II passed through on his way south from Kingston-on-Spey, where he had landed from the Continent, it harboured royalty. That faithless monarch might, as Joseph Robertson bitterly remarks, have seen from the window a limb of his faithful Montrose blackening in the air. Lucy Walters was with the King, in rather compromising evidence, and the city ministers had to request the already Merry Monarch to keep his curtains drawn.

The murder of Seton was but one knot in a tangle of family feuds —

1   But it may be named after John Collison's great grandson, John Collison of Auchlunies, provost in 1594.

Forbeses and Leslies, Forbeses and Gordons — which crossed and intertwined until at this distance of time it is sometimes a conundrum to discover who was foe to whom — and why. Into this dangerous measure Aberdeen could not avoid being drawn. Irrespective of the matrimonial alliances of its leading burgess families with the county lairds, and in addition to its bond of manrent with Huntly, it had had, in defence of its own economic interests, to make a composition with the Forbeses. The House of Forbes, then at the height of its power, controlled in particular the middle and upper reaches of the Don, and the lands of its cadets lay within easy reach of the town.

The salmon fishings in Don and Dee were very valuable sources of revenue to the burgh, and the depredations of riparian lairds and their vassals during the close (or 'undue') season had in the opening decades of the sixteenth century reached proportions that threatened the solvency of the Common Good. In 1526 an arrangement was reached with Lord Forbes in terms of which his lordship, in return for a yearly propine or gift of a tun of wine, undertook to protect the town's interests in respect of the fishings. But either Forbes did not intend to honour his bond in this 'gentlemanly blackmail' or he found that he could not control the poaching propensities of his friends. Soon the Council of Aberdeen is found lamenting that 'they who should be keepers are principal destroyers and fishers of the waters in undue time'. Accordingly the tun of wine was countermanded by the Council. When Forbes remonstrated, he was informed that if he would faithfully perform his part of the bargain the citizens would send him his wine again; but he had to give his word under seal and superscription and to punish the poachers. The town, in fact, was very much upon its dignity. Upon his lordship further requesting a half-net's fishing, the douce burgesses dispatched a letter to him which still stands across the centuries as a fine example of plain and honest rebuke. 'My lord, in good faith we know not that ever your lordship had any title or right thereto, and as for us, we are o'er small men to hold (withhold) anything from your lordship ye have a right to. And for us, will never give you anything for any title or right your lordship has to any waters among us, and where you desire us to be kind to your lordship, as ye have been to us in time bygone, we thank you of kindness bygone, and pray your lordship to persevere in time coming.'

Infuriated by such bourgeois hardihood, on 30 July 1530, led by Forbes of Pitsligo and Forbes of Brux, the Forbeses broke into the town. The citizens were not, however, as in the Leslie raid caught napping. The Forbeses came down the Gallowgate to the north end of the Broadgate. There they were met by the men of Aberdeen with brows as black as their own. A stiff combat ensued, swaying back and forwards in the narrow street, and with several casualties on both sides. At last the invaders were driven into 'the place' of the Grey Friars, where they were cooped up for twenty-four hours. Apparently by that time they were glad to have the permission of the burgesses to depart, but whereas they had entered on horseback, they went home on foot. Then, with a forward cast to more modern procedure, both parties went to law. For once the law supported the rough-and-ready method. Provost Gilbert Menzies, his four sons and nineteen Aberdeen citizens were charged at Linlithgow and acquitted. Even the horses had not to be returned. For some time the lawless Forbeses refused to desist from maltreating the inhabitants, and in December the King instructed the sheriff of Aberdeen county to exact sureties for good behaviour from a long list of Forbes lairds and their abettors. The same month, at Perth, Lord Forbes became surety for his sons that the provost, his family, the baillies, council and community of Aberdeen should be 'harmless and scatheless of me and my said sons, and our servants'. This, unfortunately, was not the end of the quarrel. The Master of Forbes, who had secured remission for the murder of Seton of Meldrum, broke the truce and reverted to his old practice of molesting the citizens. His father was called upon to pay £2,000 for the misdemeanour and had to pledge part of the lands of Forbes to the King for payment.

Thereafter the town and the Forbeses existed on happier terms. But the Master seems to have been a violent and unbalanced man. In 1537 James V with his new wife, Mary of Lorraine, visited Aberdeen. The Master of Forbes, according to information (which may have been false) laid against him by the Earl of Huntly, was arrested along with his father on a charge of conspiring to assassinate the King 'by shot of culvering' while the royal visitor was passing along the streets. The Forbeses were tried in Edinburgh and his lordship was acquitted. The Master was found guilty and sentenced to be hanged at once like a common felon. At the solicitation of his friends, the sentence was altered to one of beheading and quartering. This treason charge, a Forbes historian vehemently asserts, 'was one of the blackest forgeries that Hell could plot — to take away his life, so that all our Writers unanimously agree that he fell a victim to the malice of a subtle and formidable enemy'. However that may be, while the Forbes feud with the Gordons continued and indeed grew in intensity, the family's differences with Aberdeen disappear with the death of the choleric Master. Lord Forbes got his wine again, and when his successor came to erect a town residence, the citizens gave him some timber and other help to build it.

Past experience, however, made the Aberdonians wary. The lands of Ardlair, in Clatt Parish, mortified to the town by Bishop Gavin Dunbar for the upkeep of the Bridge of Dee, were coveted first by a Leslie and later by a Forbes. In both cases the town stoutly refused to grant a lease, even though the King put forward the Forbes request and Huntly the Leslie application. Replying to the King, the Council mentioned that the lands in question lay between the estates of the Forbeses and the Leslies. If either got possession, 'they should in short time appropriate the same to them and theirs, and should be occasion for renewing of the old displeasure done among them, and we be called the occasioners thereof'. Wherefore, the King was informed, the land had been set to 'husbandmen, labourers of the ground, that would give maist therefor, to the uttermost profit of that common work'. This combination of shrewd political sense, thrifty economics, and sturdy independence deserves to be remembered. In 1592, however, Ardlair was sold to John Leslie of Balquhain for 4,000 merks, which were used to redeem the town's four mills that had been pledged for security of a debt. Kennedy says 'this money was afterwards accounted for, by the treasurer, to the Bridge of Dee funds'. It was then laid out in the purchase first of Hilton (then called Cuprastoun) and later Gilcomston.

CHAPTER FOUR

The Auld Blood of the Town: The Mess of Pottage

Like an Italian city state, in the Aberdeen of 500 years ago, the civic chair was the spoil of struggle between the leading families, the Vasses, the Scherars, the Marrs, Fyfes, Fichets, Kintores, Chalmerses, Collisons, Blinseiles, Menzies, Rutherfords and Cullens. These merchant princes ruled the roost and could ill brook the appearance of others beside them. As late as 1635, when Alexander Jaffray became Provost, the first provost of a family that was to have a long and honourable connection with Aberdeen, we learn that 'mony lichtlied both the man and his electioun', for he was not of 'the auld blood of the toun', being but 'the oye (grandson) of ane baxter (baker)'.

In the first half of the fifteenth century, a new family appears upon the scene. The Chalmerses were still at the height of their influence when the first member of this house, which was to rule the destinies of Aberdeen for 200 years, made his appearance in the provost's seat. This was Gilbert Menzies, surmised to have been a son of Sir Robert Menzies of Wemyss. Gilbert came from Perthshire to Aberdeen about 1408. In 1412 he was a baillie. He bought and sold land a good deal, and in 1423 he was elected provost. When the last Menzies was elected provost 211 years later, the family had been in the chair during 114 years, one member holding office for twenty-nine years at a stretch.

No more brilliant autocratic family than the Menzies ever resided in Aberdeen. They held their heads high before royalty; they lived side by side with the most opulent of the nobility; even the Cock o' the North could not browbeat them. They were, on the whole, capable administrators, showing as time went on less sign of conservatism than might have been expected from a family endowed with power for so many generations. They were moreover never afraid to be on the losing side, a test of greatness that few families can pass.

The first Gilbert of this remarkable race was four times provost and three times the town's commissioner to Parliament. His son and heir Andrew was the first to be of 'Badfothalis' or Pitfodels, the greater part of which, however, was brought into the family by the marriage of a descendant to Mariote Reid, daughter of the laird of Pitfodels and tacksman of Rubislaw, Alexander Reid, who is noteworthy as being the first provost of Aberdeen to have his portrait painted.[1] Pitfodels was for more than three centuries the principal estate of the family. Andrew was twice provost and once Member of Parliament. Then came his son and heir, Alexander thrice provost, and it was in his lifetime that the first representative of a great rival family appeared on the scene in the person of Sir John Rutherford of Migvie and Tarland, whose mother probably was a Menzies. Rutherford was eleven times elected provost, and represented Aberdeen in Parliament. His third election was disputed by yet another Menzies, David, who brought the King into the dispute, alleging that Rutherford had procured election by the votes of his kinsmen. Rutherford, who stood well enough with James III to secure from his Majesty a declaration that the antagonism to 'our lovet fameliar servitour is richt displeasant', was otherwise charged with being 'a masterful oppressour of the lieges, ande for his oppressione thar may nay merchante live within the burgh'.

During Sir John's term, James III was murdered, and it would seem that the supporters of the patricide James IV were in the ascendant among the town's electors. At any rate, David Menzies became the next provost, and when Lord Forbes, carrying aloft on his spearpoint the dead monarch's bloody shirt, tried to arouse Aberdeen to avenge the assassination, he got from Council and burgesses fair words but no support. Rutherford was back in the two following years. 'Masterful' he seems to have been, though not altogether an oppressor. He was always at the service of the community, or accepting with the Provost of Edinburgh the task of going as 'two burgess merchants of fashion' with a cleric to the Archduke of Austria to arrange about more favourable terms for the import of Scottish goods into Flanders. On the other hand, he had probably too many irons in the fire to be altogether exact with his finances, for in 1498 he handed in his accounts with a statement that as the Common Good was exhausted, the Council would have to find the money it required. In the end, he seems to have found it himself, but the auditors three years later refused to give him a clearance. Perhaps the common people had as little liking for the

1 The portrait stood 'above the session-house door' in St. Nicholas Kirk until 1640, when 'the session, understanding that some capitanes and gentilmen of the regiment of sojerie lying in this town had tein some offence at the portrait of umquhill Alexander Reid, sometyme of Petfoddels, as smelling somequhat of poperie', ordered it 'to be tein doun and not to be set up again'. Reid was provost in 1492 and 1493.

Menzies family as for the Rutherfords. We find one stout citizen from the Gallowgate saying (in hyperbolical phrases not unfamiliar in our own day) that Provost Alexander Menzies had found the boll of meal at 4s. and would leave it at 20s. This was esteemed to be 'perturbious' language, and the critic was cast, as befitted such a devil, out of the town.

The sixteenth century, the period of almost complete Menzies supremacy, began with a Menzies in the chair, but ended with a Rutherford. Gilbert Menzies, son of David, and known as 'Banison Gib' in recognition presumably of his command of language, was laird of Findon, and the owner or tacksman of many estates round Aberdeen, in Buchan and in the Mearns. Between 1505 and 1536 he occupied the chair twenty-three times, and established such commanding influence that he could enjoin upon the councillors to obey his son Thomas during his own absence, despite the fact that Thomas was not even a baillie. Thomas himself, after trial trips in the civic premiership in 1525 and 1533-4, settled down to the most remarkable autocracy in the city's history.

His first spell in the chair was from 1537 to 1544, when the Earl of Huntly, whose influence in Aberdeen, as throughout the north, was enormous, intervened, perhaps as the result of representations by a baillie of the name of John Gordon, between whom and the Menzies family no kindness was lost. The course of the quarrel it is — as in most cases of the kind — impossible now to follow. Menzies appears to have been disposed to temporise, but Gordon was implacable. Halfway through the term in 1545 Menzies resigned and Huntly took the chair, only (as might have been expected) to rule by deputy. For some time Menzies acted for him, but as a partial cause of the civic crisis had been the growing sympathy of Menzies for an alliance with England, and as Huntly vehemently supported the Papist regime and the auld alliance with France, other arrangements had soon to be made. Huntly appointed four of his friends, with John Gordon the chief, to deputise for him, and in 1545 the list of members of the new Council was dictated by the Earl. There is a flash of temper in this election meeting. Menzies, who besides being a practical administrator was deeply imbued with the traditional spirit, protested against the Council being elected in any fashion except that 'as use has been past memory of man', whereat John Gordon broke into raucous expletive, with the jeer that all Menzies' 'buching sall not make it, nor yet your stone house'. Apparently Gilbert Menzies, Thomas's brother, had grinned at this sally, for at him Gordon roared out, 'Weil, are ye lauchand, I sall gar you greit'.

But as usual, he laughs longest who laughs last. What happened to Mr. John Gordon does not seem to have been recorded, unless he be, honourably, the 'Maister Johne Gordone' in the list of twenty-nine Aberdonians slain at Pinkie in 1547. Another of Huntly's deputies was William Rolland, and two men, 'elder and younger' of the name of 'Wilyem Rolland' also fell at Pinkie under Huntly. Huntly, the resplendent and magnificent, died among the peat bogs of Corrichie Hill in 1562, not in fair fight but by murder, and if we may believe the rhyming chronicler of that doleful battle:

> Then Murray tried to tak auld Gordon,
> An' mony ane ran wi' speid;
> But Stuart o' Inchbraik had him sticket,
> An' out gush'd the fat lurdane's bluid.

While the balladist credits Stuart of Inchbreck with the slaying of Huntly, some contemporary chroniclers assert that he died during the battle from natural causes. His body was conveyed with little ceremony to Aberdeen, thus fulfilling the prediction of his lady's principal witch called Janet, who according to Knox had foretold that Huntly should be in Aberdeen the night after the battle without any wound. When the victors reached Aberdeen, the earl's body was thrown on the Tolbooth pavement to be seen by all the people. 'Lady Forbes, among many others', says Knox, 'came to see the body; and seeing him lying upon the cold stones, having only upon him a doublet of canvas, a pair of Scots grey hose, and covered with an arras work, she said "There lieth he that yesterday in the morning was esteemed the wisest, the richest, and a man of the greatest power that was within Scotland". And in truth', Knox goes on, 'she lied not; for in man's opinion, under a prince, there was not such a one these three hundred years in the realm produced'.

Menzies returned to the provost's chair in 1547, and remained there continuously despite the Reformation and the upheavals connected with civic administration until he retired in 1576 to die two months later. Forty Michaelmas elections had seen him returned to the Provost's seat. It should be added that both Thomas and Gilbert, his father, held the office of town clerk also, filling it with a deputy. Gilbert may have taken it over from his cousin, also a Gilbert Menzies, for whom the office was purchased by his father Alexander for forty merks in 1502.

The venerable Thomas was succeeded in 1576 by his son Gilbert, of Cowlie (Cowie) and Pitfodels, who reigned until 1588. Unlike his father, who had trimmed a bit in the matter of religion — probably because he was pro-English in politics though his creed was Catholic, — Gilbert wholeheartedly supported Rome. This may have accounted in part for the constant municipal turmoil during his twelve years of office, while the Crafts were pressing to extend their electoral rights. He was too worn out to seek office in 1588, when his younger brother, Thomas Menzies of Kirkhill (of Nigg) and Dun was properly elected. He also demanded that he should succeed his brother as town clerk, and after some demur he was confirmed in that office for one year.

In his term the Menzies gift for ostentation had one of its finest opportunities to display itself. In the spring of 1590 the good town of Aberdeen furnished a ship 'the Nicholas to pass to the parts of Denmark, for conveying and hame bringing of his highness (James VI) and the queen, his dearest bedfellow in this realm'. Baillie John Collison, afterwards provost, was chosen to command the ship by the Council, with a supercargo by name David Indeaucht 'to oversee the vivers and all other necessaries, that they be not unprofitably bestowed or devastated'. The commander got £100 to buy his uniforms and £320 for incidental expenses, while a piece of artillery called a falcon was sent aboard in addition to an armament furnished by the owners of the ships James and Andrew. The Nicholas sailed with a crew of twenty men on 16 April 1590, all streaming with flags and 'taffety' bunting.

That was almost the last public gesture of Provost Thomas. Serious trouble at length boiled up uncontrollably in the Council. Led by John Cheyne of Fortrie, an advocate, who reached the chair in 1593, the opposition protested to the Privy Council before the 1590 election. The indictment of the Menzies party was compendiously drawn. It claimed that for eighty years past the liberties and privileges and free election of Aberdeen had been 'pervertit and abrogat by the unlauchful usurption of the provostrie by the race of Menzies'. The charges are thereafter piled high in a sentence of 350 words. How strong the Menzies interest was in the Council may be gauged by the fact that the names of no fewer than six Menzies appear in the complaint. That interest was, indeed, still too strong. The action was lost and Cheyne found himself out of the Council at the next election. He succeeded in winning the chair in 1593, but only for that once. He deserves notice as the first outstanding champion on the Council of the craftsmen's rights.

The century drew to its close with the four families — Menzies, Rutherford, Chalmers and Cullen — alternating in the provostship. To Alexander Rutherford of Rubislaw, a Menzies on his mother's side, falls the uncommon distinction of being mentioned for his eloquence. He was Aberdeen's Commissioner to the Parliament of 1605 that first considered — over a century before the actual event — a legislative union of Scotland and England. Rutherford during the debate spoke in Latin, French and 'Scottish', to such purpose that James VI who was present with the English Commissioners, drew a diamond ring off his finger and gave it to the provost in commendation for his oratorical effort. The last Rutherford in the chair was David, brother of the eloquent Alexander and husband of a daughter of Provost Alexander Cullen. For the closing moments of its history 'the auld blood of the town' was coursing strongly.

Of the last three Menzies provosts two were knighted, Sir Thomas Menzies of Dun and Cults in 1617, Sir Paul Menzies of Kinmundy at the coronation of Charles I in 1633. Both worthily upheld the traditions of their family. Sir Thomas was in the chair when in 1596 the Convention of Burghs bestowed on the craftsmen the right of two seats on the Town Council and ten votes in the election of magistrates, while the Merchant Guild had thirty-one votes. He was provost when a new jail or Tolbooth was built east of the Town House — its remnants can still be seen from Lodge Walk. He also, by an irony of fate, was one of the burgh's commissioners to the General Assembly at Aberdeen in 1616 which considered the stamping out of the Popery to which so recently the Menzies family had adhered so steadily. In 1620 Menzies went to London and presented James VI with a fine Ythan pearl found in the Ebrie burn. He also carried with him some silver ore from a mine in Sutherland to have an assay made. For the pearl James gave Menzies lands at Dunfermline and the custom of merchant goods within the burgh of Aberdeen. But the Provost died at Wooler on his way home. His grave is lost. So also is the secret of the silver mines: 'he concealing in what part of Sutherland the same was found, and dying upon the way at that tyme in his return from London towards Scotland, the State is hitherto depryved of the benefits of these mynes.' Sir Paul Menzies, twelve times elected by the unanimous vote of the citizens, was one of the few of his family to remain in the chair and the good graces of the burgh simultaneously. He died aged 80, in 1641, and with him came to an end an auld sang indeed.

On the eve of the Reformation, in the heyday of the Menzies ascend-ancy, a great disaster overtook the burgh. The Freedom Lands granted to the town by Robert the Bruce and hitherto let on lease were feued out in order to wipe off current indebtedness. Aberdeen's patrimony was exchanged for a mess of pottage.

In the early burghs every burgess held of the Crown: 'ilke burges sall geyff to the kyng for his borowage (i.e. holding in the burgh) at he deffendis, for ilke rud of land vd the yhere.' This yearly rent the burgher paid to his baillie and the sum of the rents was remitted to the Royal Chamberlain. But when first of the Scottish burghs Aberdeen received a gift of land in 1319 from Robert the Bruce, the system was naturally altered. The town was now landlord and entitled to apply for its own uses all the rents and customs, saving only an annual feu-duty to the Exchequer of £213 6s. 8d. Scots. Thus began on a proper footing the Common Good of the burgh. In later years this great pro-perty of the town was augmented by the grant, purchase or private gift of the lands of Rubislaw, the Cruives, right of markets, assize of ale, white fish, and the Justice Mills. At the beginning of the sixteenth century the town's landed estates covered an area of about thirty square miles. The boundary ran roughly along what is now Great Western Road and the North Deeside Road, keeping north of Cults House and south of Dalhebity, as far as Mill of Ord, where at the 'Ringing stone' it turned north, passing just west of the junction of the Alford and Echt roads at Bishopsford, and taking in Cloghill and Brimmondhill. North of Brimmond at the 'Douping stone' near Greenwell Tree it swung south-east and returned towards the sea in a long slant that touched Newhills Church and Dancing Cairns quarry. From Middlefield it turned north again to the Don, followed the river bend round Woodside House, and thereafter proceeded erratically through what is now Hilton to Ashgrove, Powis Place and the foot of the Gallowgate at Mounthooly.

The first burgh accounts we have are for 1398 and are probably incomplete. They show a revenue of about £29 from the outlying lands, almost £138 from salmon fishings on Dee and Don, and £70 from mills and crofts in and about the burgh. This left a surplus over the King's feu-duty of less than £20 to the Common Good. But by the 1430s the revenue was £453 8s. 8d. One of the main expenses was that of sending commissioners to Parliament. One year they cost £66. Another year a contractor required £40 for building a new port or burgh gate. To supplement the resources of the Common Good and cover the cost of extraordinary expenditure, taxes or stents were imposed on householders: for 1408 we have a stent-roll of 344 householders, representing a population of about 2,000.

There was indeed unending trouble about money. A provost at the end of his term would find the burgh owing him a few merks. The auditors were not very conscientious and the provost seldom exacting. The burgh's deficit would be carried forward, gradually increasing, from one provost to another till it became too big to be overlooked. In 1491 Sir John Rutherford, for example, had to draw attention to a debit balance of 66 merks apparently due to him but actually accumulated over his own and several preceding provostships. The result was that the Council enacted that whenever the Common Good was exhausted, the provost should inform them. This became the custom for a time. On the other hand, a provost might claim monies that the Council were reluctant to acknowledge. The Scherars, two of whom when Provost presented such demands, seem to have been shearers by nature as well as by name. One, in 1449, was not paid, the other, thirty years later, had his outlays refunded on condition that he repaired the Castlehill beacons and removed a Spanish wreck from the harbour entrance.

In 1447 the burgh accounts were in a very bad way. The Council were due a gentleman of London of the name of Thomas Beruwale (or Berowald, doubtless) a considerable sum. As security they had pledged the burgh's common seal with him. The English financier, however, not being a collector of curios, felt that the bargain was hardly in his favour, and seized the goods of several Aberdeen merchants to cover his debt. Whereupon 'the hale counsaile ripely avisit has fundit and concludit that John of fife for a quarter, John the Vaus for a quarter, Gilbt meignes for a quarter and John blyndseil and Thom blyndseil and Adam hill for a quarter sal ansuer and Red the toune of the det aucht to Thomas beruwale of londone and sal freith (ransom) and bryng hame the commoune seel and content the nyghboris of the toune that thar gudes war tane tharfor'. A more common device was to anticipate the yield of the town's properties, of course involving an eventual loss to the burgh. Thus land or a fishing would be let at a longer lease than normal — three, five, seven or even nineteen years — at an almost nominal rent in consideration of the lessee paying at the outset of the tack a grassum or ready money fine. The losses to the municipal exchequer could be very heavy, and it was hard to return to economic leases, because the extraordinary expenses of a royal visit or a war with England, which were met by such grassums, were of frequent recurrence.

The Freedom Lands and Privileges of Aberdeen were enormously and increasingly valuable. They were jealously guarded by the burgh. Time and again the town's right was challenged, either by individuals anxious to improve their personal estate, or through the forgetfulness of authority. Only one example need be mentioned. In 1493 James IV, no doubt oblivious of his great ancestor's gift to Aberdeen, generously bestowed the Stocket upon Sir Andrew Wood, his adroit and successful pirate sailor. At the beginning of 1494 the citizens were called to arms. The alderman, baillies, council and community, 'warnit be the hand bell throw the haile toune, gathreyt, and circualy inquerit by Philip Dumbrek, officiar, grauntit and oppinly schew that the wald ayfaldly defende thair landis and heretage of the Stockat, bathe with thair personis and gudis, at ale thair possibilite, quhilkes is purchest be Andrew Wod, as thai er informit'. In May, Alexander Reid the Provost, Sir John Rutherford of Tarland, Alexander Chalmers of Murtle, Alexander Menzies and John Collison were appointed commissioners to defend the town's rights before the Privy Council in Edinburgh. They and the text of Robert Bruce's charter triumphed. Of the Scottish nobility an imposing retinue was present. The Council, having seen the 'infeftment maid by King Robert Broiss, of maist nobell mynde' and being as usual 'riplie avisit, decretis and deliveris that for ocht that thai have slt sene the said aldorman, balzea, and commuintie, sal breuk and joise the said burgh of Abirdene, with the pertinence as thai breukit abefor, because they clamyt the said laundis and places be wertew of the said charter'. Many years later the same performance had to be repeated before King James VI at Dunnottar when a nephew of the Earl of Morton, the late Regent, to whom his uncle had conveyed part of the Freedom Lands, was dispossessed.

But property that was safe from the assaults of the stranger was less fortunate at the hands of those who would have defended it stoutly against encroachment from the outside. Aberdeen had much to be grateful for to the family of Menzies, but for posterity their good service was nullified by one short-sighted mistake. In the middle of the sixteenth century, while the greatest of the family, Thomas Menzies of Pitfodels, was Provost, the financial stringency of the burgh became insupportable. Menzies devised, and being all-powerful on the Council carried, a scheme for the feuing out of the town's lands. For this purpose a licence was sought from the Crown, and obtained on payment of 2,500 merks. The plan consisted in substituting for leases that were usually annual a system of perpetual feu-duties coupled with an initial payment of a heavy grassum. In general the sitting tenant was successful in becoming the feuar. A section of the burgesses, however, were not satisfied. They were in a minority, but at the beginning of 1557 they forced a compromise. By its terms all those who had tacks of lands or fishings were to continue to hold them as feuars at the rates laid down for the feu-duties, and those who had acquired feus over the heads of the tenants were to relinquish them to the old tenants on being repaid the amount of their grassums. From this composition we can deduce that the objectors to the original arrangement did not oppose it on grounds of economic principle but because they and their friends considered themselves unjustly treated in the disposition of the subjects.

The actual amount of the feu-duties and grassums are not without interest. The sums are, of course, in Scots money.

Subject	Feu-duty			Grassum		
Fishings from Bridge of Dee to Sea ⎱ Fishings from Cruives of Don to Sea ⎰	£329	3	4	£1,847	0	0
Lands of Gordon or Kepplehill	40	0	0			
Lands of Shedocksley	53	6	8			
Lands of Tulloch	4	0	0			
Lands of Kingswells	26	13	3			
Lands of Foresterhill	20	0	0			
Lands of Cruives of Woodside	40	0	0			
Lands of Kingshill	1	6	8			
Lands Bogfairly	44	13	4			
Lands of Rubislaw	20	0	0			
Lands of Hessilhead	13	6	8			
Total for lands	£263	6	7	£194	13	4

The feuing thus secured to the town, besides a lump sum of £170 sterling, an annual income of some £50 sterling. Further feuing brought the total income up to about £70 sterling, but the whole transaction came in the long run to represent a tremendous loss to the community. In 1887 the revenue of the lands and fishings thus alienated was in the neighbourhood of £40,000. In 1920 the Town Council bought back Hazlehead alone for £40,000. In 1943 the small estate of Raeden cost them £19,434 10s.[1]

---

[1] It should be added that these were fair market prices. In neither case was the community held to ransom.

Opposition to the feuing 'pley', as it was called, acquired a new character shortly after the Reformation. The Crafts took up the running, probably more for the sake of annoying their natural antagonists, the merchant electors and members of the Council, than through any passionate desire to improve the finances of the burgh. They served a summons upon the provost and baillies for disposing, dividing and sharing among themselves the lands belonging to the town: for sharing out the plate, furniture and plenishing of the church of St. Nicholas at the time of the Reformation; for applying to their own uses eight great oak trees in the kirkyard; with a great many other items alleged to have been improperly handled. Nothing more came of the accusations. In 1591, when John Cheyne launched his thunderbolt against the Menzies family, part of the complaint to the Privy Council craved the restoration of the old tack system on the town's lands — 'that the small customes, commoun landis, takkis and utheris casualiteis, commoun rentis and gude of the said burgh, micht be yeirlie roupit and sett to the best availl, conforme to the use and consuetude of utheris burrowis'. That petition also failed and there the matter was dropped.

The annual municipal balance sheet would be somewhat like this:

INCOME

Feu-duties of salmon fishings and common lands	£718	10	0
Ground annuals, including Vicarage of St Nicholas	52	0	0
Nine mills, with multures	1,293	0	0
Bell, toll and petty customs	888	13	4
Dues from flesh-house, meal-market, etc.	447	5	4
	£3,399	8	8

EXPENDITURE

Maill duty to Crown	£418	0	0
Stipends	1,678	0	0
Town Clerk	14	13	4
Schoolmasters	213	6	8
Treasurer	20	0	0
Clock minder	22	6	8
Town's Adviser	10	11	0
Other items	10	13	4
	£2,387	11	0

The credit balance of over £1,000 Scots, or about £84 sterling, probably worked out at a higher figure by reason of the burgesses' entry money and other small fees.

Up to 1531 the Provost was also Treasurer, but in that year the first Treasurer was appointed, although the first burgh account extant is for 1559–60, the eve of the Reformation, and the first full rental of the Common Good is not available until 1629.

CHAPTER FIVE

Crafts and Council: Pomp, Pageantry and Poetry

The Aberdeen of the Middle Ages and the Reformation period was, as we have seen, governed by an oligarchy composed of a handful of families belonging to the Merchant Guild. It was substantially the same as mercantile fraternities elsewhere. To begin with the burgesses seem to have been simply indivdiuals with privileges in the burgh. Later the burgess class came to be limited to merchants, members of the Merchant Guild. Naturally traders accumulated the means to acquire property. Finally it would seem that the ownership of property was a sufficient qualification for membership of the guild, plus the payment of certain fees, plus the performance of certain functions — 'Scot and lot, watch and ward', the duties of paying taxes and defending the town.

The situation of a man who plied a craft or trade was very different. No craftsman could be a member of the Merchant Guild unless he renounced his Craft. From very early times — we saw the dividing line in the charter of 1222 — there was a distinction between the merchants and the craftsmen, between the middlemen and the manufacturers. Both were freemen, both could be burgesses upon taking the oath of loyalty to the constitution of the community. But no craftsman member of a trade could exercise two trades at once, nor could he change his trade without consent of the Council. Far less could he be a member of the Merchant Guild,[1] and consequently he could not as an individual exercise a vote in the affairs of the community. In Aberdeen, however, it seems clear that from very far back the Crafts were allowed representatives to vote at the election of the provost and baillies, although these representatives could not be members of the Council.

The craftsman, it should be noted, was not a man of straw. Many craftsmen were not employees, for in those days the manufacturer

---

1 An Act of James III stated that every craftsman must 'either forbear his merchandise or else renounce his craft'. This was repeated in an Act of the following reign.

or maker by hand worked either in his own house or his own booth. As the inventories of such tradesmen prove, he had to be a person of some substance,[1] whether he employed a staff of freemen who lived at home and apprentices who lived with him, or apprentices only, or worked alone. And as a man of substance he was regarded. By a curious anomaly he could not be an auditor of the town's accounts, in the disbursement of which he had legally no say; whereas in the affairs of his own craft he might rise to duties connected with the very considerable property owned by the Trades which would fit him admirably for the discharge of functions in the civic administration to which he was not permitted to aspire.

From the commencement of Aberdeen's written history we find the Craftsmen rebelling against their position of political tutelage. To this unrest, impatience with a financial injustice contributed. As individuals[2] and as members of a Trade, craftsmen burgesses subscribed to the Common Good of the town. The collector, the Dean of Guild, had a seat on the Council by virtue of his office, and took part with the provost and baillies in administering the fund; but the craftsmen had no share in it. In short, they were useful citizens — according to modern standards probably more useful than the merchant burgesses; they shared in the upkeep and defence of the community,[3] of which they numbered the greater part, but there their interest ended.

For a century and a half the craftsmen agitated without much success for recognition of their importance. At last, in 1424, by an Act of James I, one of their practices, hitherto illegal, was recognised. For each Craft it was ordained that 'a wise man of the craft' should be chosen, with the approval of the alderman or provost of the burgh, to be 'Deacon or master over the rest for the time, to govern and essay all works that be made by the craftsmen of that craft'. But give an inch, take an ell, the Trades seem to have presumed too much upon this licence, or — what is perhaps more probable — the influence of the merchants had been too strong at Court. Three years later, the grant was annulled, and instead of the Deacon chosen by the Craft

1 Except as regards underclothing. 'Ane sark' was generally ample.
2 Craft burgesses, like merchant burgesses, were liable for stent or tax to keep up 'the commin warks of the town', and until the Reformation for the maintenance and repair of an altar in the parish church.
3 They fought in bodies according to their Crafts at Harlaw, and there are weapons in possession of the Incorporated Trades today that are believed to have been taken from the Highlanders on that occasion.

and approved by the Provost, there was substituted a Warden chosen by the Council and imposed upon the Craft. As this official's duties were mainly sumptuary and consisted in regulating the workmanship and prices, the hand of the Merchant Guild that dealt in these goods may be shrewdly suspected in the overturning of the 1424 Act.

Not only were the deacons made illegal; the act of assembly for transacting the domestic business of the Craft was also prohibited as resembling 'meetings of conspirators'. In Aberdeen the Council objected to the dues[1] paid by the craftsmen upon becoming members of their trade corporation, alleging that these payments conflicted with the composition paid to the Common Good by a person on admission as a freeman or burgess. The times, however, were troubled, the authorities much occupied by other matters, and after a little the Crafts proceeded to ignore the law and resumed the election of deacons without so much as consulting the Council.

By an Act of 1469 burgh councils were made self-elective bodies, the authorities being moved thereto 'throu multitud and clamor of common sympil persons'. It was laid down that 'the Auld Council of the town shall choose the New Council in sic number as accords to the town. And the New Council and the Auld of the year before shall choose all officers pertaining to the town, as Alderman, Baillies, Dean of gild and other officers.' Authority stepped in again in 1491, the Fstates abolishing the trade diaconate, on the ground that the election of such an office-bearer led to the Crafts 'making laws of their craft contrary to the common profit, whereby when one leaves work another dare not finish it'. At the same time craftsmen who demanded wage 'for the halie day as for the wark day' were indictable as 'common oppressors'. There are in this Act traces of objections to practices not unlike those of modern trade unionism. It should, however, be emphasised that the craftsmen were not associations of employees, but of all freemen who were fully trained in one or other of the various trades embodied in their Craft, whether working 'for their own behoof' or for a master.

Imperceptibly the Crafts grew stronger. Their burgess members, as freemen, paid 'Scot and lot' as the common taxes were called, and had no intention of losing the ground gained. They had responsibilities as citizens of the nation, let alone the town which bore hard upon them, yet these responsibilities as citizens at the same time were

---

1 One of these dues was bancate or banquet money, a small sum paid to provide entertainment when a man was admitted a member of his Craft.

evidence that they were considered capable of exercising the essential duties of citizenship. Thus the Aberdeen craftsmen complained with a humorous pathos to the Queen Regent that they were often called upon 'to pass upon Assise in actions distant fra us fourty, fifty and lx myles, that we know nothing thairof mair nor thai that duilles in Jherusalem'. Perhaps it was the style of their complaint that secured them the exemption they sought. Trouble between merchants and craftsmen in Edinburgh led in 1555 to the abolition, or rather reiteration of the abolition, of the deacon, but soon the craftsmen acquired from the Regent the right once more to elect their deacons, and two craftsmen 'of the most honest and famous' became eligible to sit on the Council.

In 1560 the Crafts were empowered to send a representative — in practice they sent their Deacon — to vote in the election of the town's office-bearers. These and all previous privileges were confirmed in a charter granted to craftsmen in 1581 by James VI on representations from the Crafts of Edinburgh, Aberdeen, Dundee and Perth. So wroth were the Aberdeen Merchants at this piece of independence on the part of the Crafts that two dozen of the Trades' leaders were summoned before the Provost, Baillies and Council, and forced to forgo the privilege they had so lately won. Not only did they promise obedience to the town authorities for the future, but they also pledged themselves to renounce what they had gained by the charter, 'and all other privilege and letters purchased or to be purchased by them perpetually in all time coming'. Such a submission could not be binding. The next year the deacons refused to take part in the civic election.

All this while the craftsmen were making trouble in the streets of the town as well as in their places of meeting. One of the effects of the Reformation, introducing as it did a spectacle of unfamiliar licence as well as the democratic principles of Calvinism, was to encourage demonstrations of freedom on the part of those who felt they had injustices to liquidate. It was while the Reformation was still fermenting in Scotland that the Parliament banned the annual saturnalia associated with the names of Robin Hood and Little John on the First of May. No doubt the celebrations had grown outrageous with the years, and Scotland was always a queer mixture of piety and profanity. In Aberdeen as elsewhere, despite the prohibition, Robin Hood and Little John continued to perform their yearly games. But their appearance in Aberdeen was used as a screen for demonstrations and disorders by the craftsmen in protest against the unfriendliness of the Council.

The town, in self-defence, secured a writ from the Crown ordering submission to the authorities of the burgh by 'all seditious craftsmen such as cutlers, baxters, saddlers, sword slippers, cordwainers, blacksmiths, goldsmiths, coopers, barbers and others' — evidently all the Trades were defiant. The royal displeasure stilled the tumult for a decade or more, but the disturbances broke out afresh at Yule in 1579, with feasting and playing and much disorder, when the craftsmen bluntly declined to work on Christmas Day.

Shortly afterwards matters came to a head, since the Crafts' representatives were part of the legally constituted electoral body and their absence rendered an election invalid. Accordingly in 1587 the Council, the Merchant Guild, and the Crafts, on the invitation of the two former, sent delegates to a conference or 'commonsing' in St. Nicholas Kirk, under the chairmanship of Mr. Alexander Cheyne, minister of Snaw (i.e. the 'Snow Kirk'), Commissary of Aberdeen. There agreement was reached, and the Common Indenture, otherwise described as Aberdeen's *Magna Carta*, was ratified by the community in formal meeting, on 6 August 1587 — an important date in the political development of the burgh. It fixed the scale of fees for entry into a Craft and for admission as a burgess. The whole dues exigible from a candidate for entry to a Craft and as a freeman were to be delivered, along with the 'bancate', to the deacon of the Craft concerned. He kept the 'bancate' and one-third of the dues for the use of the Craft, and handed over the remaining two-thirds to the Dean of Guild for the town's purposes.

The craftsmen succeeded in making good a large part of their pretensions with regard to trade and municipal affairs. They were allowed the privilege of buying and selling Scottish goods within Scotland, certain staple commodities excepted. These included fish, hides, skins and wool. The Merchants retained the monopoly of seagoing traffic and of shipping. Some of these staples the craftsmen got leave to deal in by retail. The Weavers won, after three hundred years of struggle, the right to sell, either wholesale or retail, the produce of their own labours. Rather less progress was achieved on the political side. The Crafts could choose six of their members yearly to be on the leet from which members of the Council were elected, and two of them were to be upon the board of auditors chosen by the Council to examine the accounts. No craftsman, however, until he had been admitted a burgess of guild, was to be eligible for the offices of provost, baillie, dean of guild or treasurer.

Only one bone of contention remained. For a considerable time the Crafts, to promote co-operation amongst themselves in matters of common interest, had been in a habit of appointing a Deacon-Convener, who presided over joint meetings of the deacons and other officials of the individual Crafts — the Convener Court as it was and is called. In the Common Indenture we have mention of George Elphinston, saddler, the first Deacon-Convener whose name has come down to us. In 1591 the Council objected to the appointment of such an official and demanded to see the Crafts' authority for making it. As there was no legal sanction for the office, no answer was forthcoming, but from 1599 (except for the period 1602–11) there is an unbroken series of Deacon-Conveners.

In 1587, however, the Crafts (or Incorporated Trades as we call them today) had gained beyond all cavil the status in their own affairs which the Parliament or the Crown had from time to time bestowed upon them and then withdrawn. Their autonomy as associations of craftsmen was not in future seriously challenged.

In their political capacity, the end of the sixteenth century saw the craftsmen gain very valuable ground. Their success came unexpectedly. Arising out of quite another municipal dispute, King James VI at the request of the parties concerned gave directions as to the election and composition of the Council in 1592. By his Decree Arbitral, as it was called, two craftsmen were included in the Council. They were James Robertson, goldsmith, and Alexander Steven, baker, the Deacon-Convener for 1591 to whom the Council had taken exception. Immediate peace was not forthcoming. The Crafts still resented Council interference in what they regarded as their domestic concerns. Moreover the electoral procedure was falling into a nullity, the issue of an election being settled before it was held. So, on the eve of the Michaelmas election in 1592, 'it came to blood before the Greyfriars Kirk', craftsmen and merchants at loggerheads once more. A few days later reconciliation was effected at the Woolmanhill playfield.

The Decree Arbitral had dealt with a special case. The community felt that a principle should be established, a form governing the election of office-bearers and Council and regulating the composition of the executive body. This, known as the 'Set' of the burgh, was laid down in an award given, at the request of the community, by the Convention of Royal Burghs which met in Aberdeen on 5 July 1596. The finding recommended 'that two craftsmen of the old council, and two of the new, with the six deacons only, being ten persons, were to have votes

in the election of provost, baillies, and other office-bearers; and in case
any of them happened to be absent on that day, it should be lawful
for the remaining members to elect another in his place. That the
provost, baillies, and other members of the old and new councils,
who were burgesses of guild, should not exceed the number of thirty
persons . . . and, in the event of an equality of votes, it was expressly
declared that the provost or chief magistrate present should be entitled,
not only to a deliberative but also to a casting vote.' Until the Burgh
Reform Act two and a half centuries later, Aberdeen elected its municipal office-bearers according to this 'Set' of 1596.

There is some warrant for the assertion that the century and a half
between 1400 and the Reformation was the most picturesque period
in Aberdeen's history. Not only did the century open with the Earl
of Mar and his gallants frequenting the town, when the partnership
was broken up there were several royal visits which occasioned displays of great pomp and ceremony by the citizens, culminating in the
most famous and magnificent of all when James IV's queen came to
the burgh in 1511. Proficiency in pageants and processions, however,
was easily acquired and maintained in Aberdeen, which for many
years had devoted its fast days and holidays to that very popular form
of amusement.

The functions of the craft guilds were not originally intended to be
recreational, but they developed in that way through the close connection between the guilds and the Church. In the Middle Ages as
now, the regular churchgoers were in a minority, but the Faith had
to be kept before the eyes of the people, and to that end the priests
devised pageants and dialogues which were performed out of doors for
the very good reason there were no halls in which to stage them. The
performances required casts, and the casts were found in the organised
guilds of workmen. The crude plays were presented at various festivals
of the Church — Yule, Easter, Corpus Christi, Whitsun, Candlemas.
Of these Candlemas seems to have been the favourite in Aberdeen,
where there was a longer and stronger tradition in favour of the 'auld
lovable consuetude and rite of the burgh' than in any other Scottish
town with the possible exception of Edinburgh: in England, York,
Chester, Wakefield, and Coventry were noted for similar activities.
We unfortunately have no script of the great Aberdeen pageant of
the 'Halyblude', customarily given at Candlemas. But we do know
certain facts about it.

It is in 1440, in the Town Council registers, that the Candlemas celebration of the Halyblude is first recorded. In 13 May of that year it is stated that the Council appointed as a burgess, one Richard Kintore, then Abbot of Bonaccord. Two years later the Council allocated to the respective Crafts parts in the performance thus:

The Litsters	The Emperor and Two Doctors
The Smiths and Hammermen	The Three Kings of Cologne
The Tailors	Our Lady, St. Bride, St. Helen, Joseph
The Skinners	Two Bishops, Two Angels
The Websters and Waulkers	Symion and his Disciples
The Cordiners	The Messenger and Moses
The Fleshers	Two or four Woodmen
The Brethren of the Guild	The Knights in Harness
The Baxters	The Minstrels

In addition, each craft was expected to supply 'alsmony honest Squiares as they may' — except the Tailors, who were asked to find merely 'Squiares', and the Brethren of Guild, whose allocation was 'Squiares honestely arait'. Besides the Abbot of Bonaccord who was in charge of the proceedings and received a fee for his services from the town, there was a Prior of Bonaccord who acted as his principal assistant. In 1508, for no obvious reason, Robin Hood and Little John were substituted for the Abbot and Prior. By 1531 the pageant leaders are called the Lords of Bonaccord, and held duty — as probably the Abbot and Prior did — for a year. This no doubt reflected a change in the character of the pageant, which indeed could hardly be expected to remain without alteration over nearly a century.

There came to be a considerable dispute as to the precedence of the various Crafts, and in 1531 the Town Council laid down the following order and apportioned the pageants at the same time:

The Fleshers	St. Bestian and his tormentors
The Barbers	St. Laurence and his tormentors
The Skinners	St. Stephen and his tormentors
The Cordiners	St. Martin
The Tailors	The Coronation of Our Lady
The Litsters	St. Nicholas
The Websters, Waulkers and Bonnetmakers	St. John
The Baxters	St. George
The Wrights, Masons, Slaters and Coopers	The Resurrection
The Smiths and Hammermen	The Bearmen of the Cross

It does not appear, however, that familiarity with those saintly personages bred respect for religious observances or decorous conduct among the celebrants. Indeed, in 1445 the Council had to take strong measures because of 'divers enormities' committed in previous years by 'Abbots of this burgh called Bonaccord'. They stopped the Abbot's fees, and assigned to the Provost the duties of the obnoxious functionary. This sharp lesson had its effect. By the end of the century the official attitude was the other way round. Members of the Crafts were encouraged to turn out and to make a standard for their Craft. Those who failed were to lose their civic freedom for a year. In 1539 the two Lords of Bonaccord petitioned the Council to restore the old usage (which had been falling into neglect) and to order 'all the young and able men within this gude town to convey us every Sunday and holyday, and other needful times' arrayed according to custom, 'and aged men to meet us at the Crabstone or Kirkyard'. This indicates that at the beginning of the sixteenth century, performances were given at or near the Crabstone or in the parish churchyard; and at other times we read of plays at the Windmillhill (the Porthill) in the early days and at the Schoolhill, doubtless at the Woolmanhill end, where the ground on which the old Royal Infirmary buildings are was a square flat field that made an admirable stage.

When the first signs of the Reformation were already visible, if not recognised for what they were, the reputation of the Lords of Bonaccord stood very high in the opinion of the authorities. Lordship of Bonaccord was considered to be an 'office of honour' in the community, a status which aggravated the offence of a certain Mrs. Alex. Kayn, whose unfortunate husband was in 1542 'convict and put in amerciament of court' because the lady had called the Lords of Bonaccord and their company 'beggaris and skafferis, their meltyd was but small for all thair cuttit out hose, with mony oder injurious words unlawful to be expressed'. It is unlikely that the lady had no cause for her criticism. We can imagine a wardrobe and props that became steadily more dingy and ragged, and in the course of years the company that attended the Lords of Bonaccord would tend to drop to the level of lewd fellows of the baser sort. Ten years later, indeed, the Council had to reprimand the Lords of Bonaccord in general for wasting the town's money and corrupting the morals of its youth by 'ower mony great sumptuous and superfluous banqueting'. The Lords, it was stated, had come to vie with their predecessors in the splendour and riotousness of their feasts, and were neglecting their true duty, which was to hold the

4

'gude town in gladness and blythness with dances, farces, play and games, in times convenient'.

The blow fell in 1555, that is, before the Reformers were in full control. An Act of the Scots Parliament ordained that 'in all times coming no manner of person be chosen Robert Hude nor Lytill Johne, Abbot of Unreason, Quenis of May nor otherwise neither in Burgh nor to landward. . . . And if ony wemen or others about simmer trees singing make perturbation to the Quenis lieges in the passage through Burrows and other landward towns the wemen perturbators . . . shall be taken handled and put upon the Cuckstool of every Burgh or towne'. The prescription of 'wemen perturbators' refers to the celebration of May Day that was generally performed with dewy ablutions and inno- cent merrymaking by the girls.

The Crafts in Aberdeen did not accept the Parliamentary decree without resistance. In 1562 John Kelo, the bellman, was accused with others of having passed 'through the rews (streets) of the toun, with the hand bell, to convene the haile communite, or as many thairof as wald convene, to pass to the wood, to bring in symmer upon the first Sunday of May'. The charge held that this procedure was an attempt to raise tumult and engender discord between the craftsmen and the free burgesses of guild. The accused stated they had acted in conformity with the old usage and by command of John Grant, a free burgess and brother of guild. On this occasion the fault was confessed and amendment promised. Three years later the same bellman, now better advised of the law of the land, went through the 'rewis and gettis' (streets and gaits) warning the inhabitants on behalf of the authorities not to take part in any Robin Hood or Abbot of Unreason festival. This he did to discount the efforts of some craftsmen who, with a minstrel playing before them, paraded through the Gallowgate in contempt of the Town Council's proclamation and of the Act of Parliament. There were five of these craftsmen and they were punished by being 'discharged of their freedome, and from all exercise of their craft'. Perhaps for Aberdeen history the most interesting feature of the case is that one of the accused was a certain Matthew Guild, armourer and sword-slipper, father of Dr. William Guild, the 'father' of the Incorporated Trades and in his day Principal of King's College. During those sixteenth-century years we frequently encounter a familiar name. In 1554, in connection with a dispute over precedence in the pageants, the deacon of Masons was William Jamesone, grand- father of George Jamesone, Aberdeen's first prominent artist: while in the person of David Anderson, 'master of St. Nicholas wark' in 1525, we may be in the presence of the grandfather or great grandfather of Aberdeen's most celebrated character, David Anderson, who has come down through history as 'Davie do A'thing'.

Visits of Royalty are as a rule of merely temporary interest. They fill the picture for the time, and in the olden days they never failed to empty the treasury of whatever town had the honour to entertain them. The propine or present which it was the town's custom to give to a royal visitor consisted, usually, of a sum of money, with sweetmeats added if the visitor was a queen or had a sweet tooth. When it was learned in 1511 that James IV's young Queen, Margaret Tudor, was to visit Aberdeen, it was determined to make the occasion something for men to talk of for their lifetime. In this the Aberdonians succeeded to admiration, and though they were lucky in having in the Queen's train William Dunbar, the most brilliant Court poet in British literature, to immortalise their efforts, there is no doubt that the burgh presented a sumptuous entertainment. The Town Council resolved to 'receive our sovereign lady the Queen as honourably as any burgh of Scotland, except Edinburgh allenarly, and to make large expenses thereupon'. Orders were given to remove all middens from the streets, to empty, redd and clean the same, and to clear away from them all swine cruives.

The most permanent result of this universal scavenging and public will to please was Dunbar's fine poem, 'The Queen's Progress at Aberdeen'. The Queen was met outside the town by the burgesses in their Sunday best. Four of the handsomest of them, dressed in velvet, carried her into the town under a pall of 'velvet cramase', with guns going off all round. A procession of girls greeted her at the port and the streets were hung with tapestry, and there were pageants at every corner. Three of these were Scriptural — the Salutation of the Virgin, the Wise Men of the East and the Loss of Eden — two of them not very appropriate for a young bride. A fourth was a champion representing Robert the Bruce. One depicted the Stewarts. There was a combined choir and orchestra of young ladies, 'all clad in green of marvellous beauty' and 'with hair detressit' hanging like golden threads under white embroidered hats. They played on timbrels and sang 'richt sweetly'. At the Cross wine ran abundantly and the crowd convoyed the Queen to her lodging. In short, Dunbar made out a good case for the high panegyric of his celebrated opening stanza:

Blyth Aberdeene, thow beriall of all tounis,
    The lamp of bewtie, bountie, and blythness;
Unto the heaven ascendit thy renoun is
Off vertew, wisdome, and of worthiness;
Hie nottit is that name of nobilness,
    Into the cuming of oure lustie Quein;
The wale of welth, guid cheir, and mirrines;
    Be blyth and blisfull, burgh of Aberdein.

Some of Dunbar's verses are written into the Aberdeen Minute Book of Burgh Sasines, 1503–7. This dry-as-dust compilation also contains fragments of two local songs, one of which, 'Adieu dear hert of Aberdeen', inspired later and better singers.

Copying verses more or less competent into registers and minute-books seems to have been a convention in Aberdeen. The Convener Court Book of the Seven Incorporated Trades contains a number of pious lines, some of which may have been in the old register of 1599 to 1677. Two of them, one familiar, and one not so well-known, may be quoted:

Our life is but a winter's day
    Some only breakfast and away;
Others to dinner stay and are full fed;
The oldest do but sup and go to bed.
Long is the life that lingers out the day,
    Who goes the soonest has the least to pay.

All mortal men of death are sure,
    But houre or tyme they cannot tell;
To watch and pray we should take care,
    And with no wrongous matters mell.

Such sombre sentiments were more in the tone of the seventeenth than of the sixteenth century.

Contrary to common belief, while the Reformed Kirk laid a heavy hand upon excess in public festivals, it did not deprive the nation of dramatic displays. In 1580, when James the Sixth was expected in Aberdeen on his first visit, the Council decided to welcome him in the 'lovable consuetude' that the burgh had used towards 'his grace progenitouris Kingis of Scotland of gud memorie'. In addition to a propine, decoration of the town, and the furnishing of the royal lodgings, the Council minute appears to indicate that there were to be theatricals

— 'farscies, playeis, historeis, antikis'. Moreover, every opportunity seems to have been seized upon by the authorities for public merry-making. There was a celebration in thanksgiving for James VI's escape from the Gowrie Conspiracy. The birth of his first-born, the short-lived Prince Henry, in 1593 occasioned a prolonged jollification. Following the afternoon sermon, the Council ordained 'ane tabill to be coverit at the mercat cross . . . for the magistrattis and bayth the counsallis, with twa tunnis of Inglis beir, to be placed and run at the said mercat croce, the vyne to be liberallie drunkin in sic reasonabill quantities as the deane of gild sall deuyse, four dussoun buistis of skorchettis, confecttis, and confectionis to be placed on the said tabill, and cassin amongis the pepill, with glassis to be brokin'.

James's accession to the throne of England was received with extravagant transports of joy. The inhabitants were immediately summoned 'be sound of trumpet and drum', to the church to 'prais God for his gratious and mervellous providence . . . and efter the ending of thanksgiving, and of the exhortatioune', the order was for 'bon-fyris to be sett on throcht all the streittis of the towne, the haill bellis to ring, the croce to be deckit and hung, wyne and spycerie to be spent abundantlie thairat, a number of glassis to be cassin, and the haill youthis of the toune to tak thair hagbuttis and accumpanio thair magistrattis throcht the haill rewis of the towne, pas the tyme in schuting thair muskattis and hagbuttis til lait at nicht, the townis haill munitioun and artailzerie to be chargit and schott, and all godlie mirriness and pastyme vsit, that may express the joy and glaidness of the hartis of the pepill'.

CHAPTER SIX

Provosts and a Poet: The Chronicle of Aberdeen

In the fourteenth century individual citizens, hitherto vague and shadowy units in a mass, stand out in some relief against the background of their times and circumstances. They are still far from clear and sharp — they are human figures seen at 600 yards, not 60; but they are recognisably human, they are coming nearer, and even at their distance some of them show distinctive characteristics.

The first recorded Provost we have glanced at: he was little more than a lay figure. But about half a century after him we meet three men — one notable on the national stage, the other two leading burgesses of the town. When King David was taken prisoner at Neville's Cross, and the country got together to arrange in 1357 for his ransom and release, Aberdeen was represented by three commissioners, Laurence de Garviach or Garioch or Garvock, William de Leth, and John Crab. Garvock became Provost in 1366. He is believed to have been a member of the family that then held Caskieben and Balnacraig, and his seal, which is in existence even today, indicates that he was a person of importance. But he was nothing like so important as the other two.

John Crab was the man — or if not he, the son of the man — whose engineering skill prevented the English from recapturing Berwick in 1318. Not only did he construct fortifications and engines of assault which quite baffled and parried all the English endeavours to win back the town; he also deserves to be regarded as the man who taught the Scots to be engineers. Lord Hailes mentions another John Crab who was a sailor and during Bruce's wars played havoc with English shipping. This privateer, or Scottish Drake, may have been the same person as the engineer of Berwick. One thing is certain: the engineer had his Aberdeen connections, for a charter of David II's reign conveys to Donald Piggottis 'all lands which pertained to John Craib, in the counties of Berwick and of Aberdeen, both inside and outside the burgh' But whether Crab was a native of Aberdeen is undetermined. The Crabstone we met with long before the siege of Berwick, but it could well have got its name from association with a member of the Crab family. Part of John Crab's reward for his Berwick exploit was the grant by Robert I of the lands of Prescoly (Persley), Granden (Grandhome), and Auchmolen (Auchmill) and Auchterrony. Auchterrony included the lands of Waterton and Walton and covered the present estate of Craibstone, which takes its name from John Crab. That was about 1322, and near the same time he also received 'the lands called the Puddlepace, where the Cuckstool stood' in Aberdeen. This vivid if slightly noisome glimpse of medieval Aberdeen, the site of the public pillory, requires no explanation, but why John Crab received it is much less obvious. In 1342 he was witness to the gift by William Meldrum of a chantry in St. Nicholas Church. In 1376 there was a grant to John Crab — but this must have been the son or grandson of the Berwick Crab — of the lands of Fichlie, Drummallochie and Sinnaboth, near Kildrummy; and in 1382 John Crab was tenant of the Bishop of Aberdeen in the barony of Murtle, and had a dispute with the churchman. The first notable member of another very famous Aberdeen family, William de Camera (Chalmers), took a lease of the same subjects in 1388, so either Crab had died or the Bishop had got rid of him.

The third commissioner, William de Leth or Leith of Ruthrieston, was Provost in 1352–6 and again in 1373. He is given as marrying in 1350 a daughter of Donald, Earl of Mar, and became the ancestor of the Leiths of Leithhall, Freefield and Glenkindie and of the present baronet of Fyvie. In 1351 he slew or accidentally killed a baillie named Cattanach, at a spot on the Barkmill moor which was marked by a cairn. In remorse, Leith, besides presenting the town with the Justice Mills, 'adorned and decored the Parish Church of St. Nicholas of Abirdene with two large bells of great price, hanging in the bell-tower, at his own cost and expense, whereof the name of the one is Laurence and the other Mary. To whose soul may God be gracious'. The big bell, 'Auld Lowrie', was recast at Middleburg in 1634, its original inscription being preserved. A translation of the Latin runs:

Lo, I the bell do not proclaim the praise of that which is unholy,
I glorify the Creator,
I draw away the fear of thunder,
I mourn in solemn tones the departed,
I tell of the recurrent rites of faith,
I move the heart of man that is joyful.
 Behold me, I am Laurence.

The smaller bell was also recast. Both perished in the fire of 1874.

Leith enlarged the choir of the church and founded an altar of St. Laurence and St. Ninian there, before which he was buried at his death in 1380. Almost at that very spot, on the west side of Drum's aisle, there is still a decaying stone built into the wall. A brass tablet inserted below it in 1836 by Leith's descendant, John Leith-Ross of Arnage, states that the stone 'represents the Chauntry or Annual Mass to be sung for the soul. Founded by William Leith of Barns, Provost of Abdn. in 1351, who with many of his descendants is interred underneath.'[1] Besides Ruthrieston, Leith held the estate of Barns, in the parish of Premnay. For several years he was collector of the King's customs at the port of Aberdeen.

Later in the century there were two other Provosts interesting for their descendants rather than themselves. Alexander Bannerman of Waterton and Elsick, son of Donald Bannerman, physician to David II, bought Elsick in 1387. He was a progenitor of the Earls of Aberdeen, the present Earl of Southesk, the present Duke of Fife, and several Bannermans whom we shall meet fairly prominently later. He was Provost in 1382. The other Provost (1391–4) was William de Camera, or Chalmers, of Findon, son of Robert Chalmers of Balnacraig and Kintore, who got Robert III's permission to build a Town House anywhere except in the centre of the market place. The result was the first Town House, erected when Robert Davidson of Harlaw fame was Provost, very much on the present site of the Tolbooth tower.

From these facts we get an impression of competent, gear-gathering, bustling men, who mixed freely with the aristocracy and lairds of the surrounding country, and who were busy acquiring estates for themselves. This impression is intensified in the next century. The nobility were then just as friendly with the burgesses as the kings had been two centuries before. William Chalmers, jun., son of the William Chalmers of Findon who was Provost in 1391–4 and who was himself Provost in 1404, in that year was present at Kildrummy Castle and witnessed the deed which made Alexander Stewart, Earl of Buchan and son of the Wolf of Badenoch, the lord of the widowed Countess of Mar and master of the historic earldom. Another interesting transaction which not only illustrates the easy terms on which the town lived with its neighbours, but also introduces us to a famous site, concerns the exchange of subjects in the Abbey of Deer lands for a tenement and land in the street called Foty Gate. This tenement is believed to have become the town residence of the Abbot of Deer. It stood where the

1   This, however, is really a Blinsell monument.

Earl Marischal's house, Marischal Hall, was later built, the site being partly on the present Marischal Street, and partly the present Bank of Scotland (formerly Union Bank) building, where once the Aberdeen Bank had its office.

It was not, however, granted to any provost or burgess of Aberdeen to secure the immortal fame that descended upon one of the town's churchmen of that century. For one man who has heard of John Crab and his petronels, a hundred are aware that John Barbour wrote *The Bruce*. Barbour was a native of Aberdeen, born there about 1325,[1] and he may have been educated in France. It is conjectured that he had already been Archdeacon of Aberdeen for some years when we first meet him in that position in 1357. Before getting that appointment he may have been an official at Court. He was a scholar and man of business as well as a priest and poet; and above all he was a historian whose account of his times, as we have it in *The Bruce*, is now accepted as the most accurate of contemporary or later records. He was evidently well thought of by the Royal Family; he several times audited the King's household accounts and those of the Exchequer; he twice when well on in life went to Oxford to study: he twice travelled in France. Both David II and Robert II gave him pensions.

When he began to write we do not know, but he was almost certainly the translator of two old French romances in *The Buik of Alexander* and the author of the *Ballet of the Nine Nobles* before he embarked seriously on his masterpiece. After he had completed *The Bruce* he wrote a poetical history of the then reigning family which the historian Wyntoun calls 'The Stewarts' Original', but which is lost. It is further conjectured that he wrote the lives of St. Ninian and St. Machar in *The Lives of the Saints*. If this is so, if he began to translate *Les Voeux du Paon* into *The Buik of Alexander* in 1366, he successfully challenges Geoffrey Chaucer for the distinction of being the first British poet to write in the modern fashion. He is acknowledged as the Father of Scottish poetry and history; he may be the Father of English poetry too, for his Scots would be perfectly intelligible to the Englishmen of his time. *The Bruce* is a remarkable achievement. With some of the later Latin classics for models, Barbour contrived to avoid superstition and the miraculous, and to present plain fact in simple and

---

1 'According to our information, was the son of Andrew Barber, a citizen and proprietor of a tenement in the Castlegate' — Kennedy. Whence came 'our information' Kennedy does not say. Perhaps it was a charter of 1350 which mentions an Andrew Barbitonsorus in the Castlegate. Also he puts Barbour's birth about the year 1330.

authentic poetic guise. To youths educated to avoid intellectual difficulties, Barbour's Scots is doubtless occasionally obscure, but if
read with intelligence it offers no insuperable obstacles to comprehension, and it rewards the reader with several passages of deep, if
unaffected, beauty and many that stir and excite. The celebrated
interpolation in praise of Liberty,

Ah! Freedom is a noble thing

is part of the canon of Scottish national philosophy. The passages that
describe incidents are first-rate; indeed, until Walter Scott, Scotland
had no greater story-teller; while the lines in which, for example, he
recounted how the Scottish patriot women joined their fugitive husbands in Aberdeen are elegant both in form and sentiment.

His first visit to Oxford in 1357, with three students under his wing,
and his second in 1364 'for purposes of study' probably with a convoy
of young pupils are evidence of the extensive intellectual curiosity
of the Scottish youth of his day. His own career is proof of the same
adventurous spirit. The charge against him that he borrowed a book
from St. Machar's Cathedral and failed to return it has fallen to the
ground with the discovery that the delinquent was John Barbour,
'cantor', who was still alive, and unrepentant, in 1413.[1]

Barbour died in 1395. He dates his great poem 1375. One of its
most searching readers would have been his contemporary in the
Church's service in or near Aberdeen, John of Fordun, author of the
first five books of the Latin history of Scotland called *Scotichronicon*.
It brings the story of Scotland down to the death of David I in 1153.
Fordun himself is thought to have belonged to Fordoun, and to have
died in 1384. He was diligent in the collection of his data. Like Macaulay
he would travel 'a hundred miles to make a line of description'. 'So
on foot', we read, 'making his way like a busy bee through Britain
and Ireland, through cities and towns, churches and monasteries,
among historians and chroniclers, handling their books of annals, he
travelled, and by some means of this tedious investigation discovered
many things which he knew not, and collected them together in his
book.'

Once the knights of Harlaw were dead or had declined into old age,
individuals for two hundred years of Aberdeen's history count for far
less than families. With some of those predominant families we have

1   For the main feature of this summary of Barbour's career, I am indebted to
    Dr. R. L. Graeme Ritchie's *The Buik of Alexander*, Scottish Text Society,
    1925.

dealt elsewhere. Of two individuals we could bear to know a great deal more than the next to nothing we have concerning them. One, certainly of Aberdeen, was a poet; the other, probably an Aberdonian, was an artist. One of the most famous and frequently quoted of medieval Scots poems, from the reign of James IV, is Dunbar's *Lament for the Makars*. In it Dunbar gives a list of Scottish poets who have died, and one verse runs:

> He (Death) hes tane Roull of Abirdene,
> And gentill Roull of Corstorphine;
> Two better fallowis did no man see—
> Timor mortis conturbat me.

Roull (or Rule, as we have it still) was not an uncommon Aberdeen patronymic and of French derivation — Raoul.[1] One alderman came from the family, Thomas Roull, who was provost in 1416, and he may have been the Thomas Roull who with John Roull was in the Aberdeen contingent that fought at Harlaw. In 1424 he witnessed a charter at Kildrummy Castle. What special claim he had on the citizens' grateful remembrance has not been indicated, but nearly two hundred years later the St. Nicholas Kirk authorities were still maintaining in good preservation the inscriptions 'to keep the memorie of Fyffe, Roull, and provost Davidson'. John Fyfe was several times provost between 1437 and 1457. He was in the chair when rules were introduced controlling the magistrates' term of office and the alderman's intromissions with the burgh funds. He also secured the abolition of all customs on exported skins and imported salt, a very valuable concession to Aberdeen. Fyfe in fact never held a term as provost without promoting some reforms. With him and Robert Davidson, therefore, Roull was in excellent company.

The shadowy artist was one Alexander Chalmer, who is mentioned in the Royal Treasurer's accounts thus:

'July 23, 1515. Item, deliverit to Alexander Chalmer, Paynteour for ane hundredthe and xl Payntit Armys to the Obsequys of our soverane lord King James the Fred, price of ilk pece twelf pennys, summa viij lb'.

Chalmer, Chalmers, or de Camera — it is French again, Chambre — is another distinctive Aberdeen surname. Aberdeen had three provosts of the name of Alexander Chalmers, one of whom was artistic and interested in architecture, and might have been the painter's father. For several generations the Christian name of the eldest son in the

1   There was a Bernard de Roule who resigned the lands of Follarule in 1365.

family of Chalmers of Murtle (and later Cults) was Alexander. The first of these Alexander Chalmerses to be provost (in 1443) was son and grandson of provosts. He had a faculty for coming into court. In 1452 he had a dispute with one Baillie Malcolm Forbes, who later absconded with moneys belonging to William, Lord Keith.[1] In his tablet in Collison's Aisle Chalmers is described as 'providus et honorabilis vir' — a prudent and honourable man. The next Alexander Chalmers, who succeeded to his father's estate in 1463, died in 1497, was appointed chief master of works — that is architect — 'of the biging of Saint Nicolace queyr for two yeris to cum'. He was provost for the eighth time in 1495 when King James IV erected the village of Torry into a free burgh of barony. One of his sons was the first laird of Strichen. It was a hundred years — in 1597 — ere the third Alexander Chalmers filled the provost's office. His year at the head of affairs was notable for the burgh's destruction of no fewer than twenty-six witches, for the burning of whom the Dean of Guild received £47 3s. 4d. In that year also a Flemish weaver of grograms, worsets and stamings, was allowed to carry on his trade outside the jurisdiction of the Weaver Craft. This Alexander Chalmers was the grandfather of General John Hurry or Urry or Ury of Pitfichie, whom Montrose so soundly defeated at Auldearn in the Troubles, and who changed sides as easily as he altered the spelling of his name.

In addition to the Chalmerses, there were at least four eminent civic families — the Kintores, the Rutherfords, the Menzies and the Cullens — of which the first and last provide characters somewhat outside the civic circle. Two Kintores, William and Richard, held the provostship for over twelve terms between them in the first three quarters of the fifteenth century. Two hundred years later we find an advocate of the name practising in Aberdeen, but the surname has died out. The Kintores doubtless took their designation from Kintore, of which Provost Richard was certainly a burgess and both he and William were perhaps natives. Richard is noteworthy as being the only provost to have been also Abbot of Unreason. He did not gratify the humour of posterity by holding the two offices together. It was in 1440 that as Abbot of Bonaccord the Council voted him a burgess' admission

1 This was not the only occasion on which a Keith had lost money at the hands of an Aberdeen 'doer' or factor. There was another case just 400 years later, when the then Lord Kintore suffered through the defalcations of an advocate, who absconded. Amongst the papers destroyed were, it is believed, all the early documents relating to the Royal Burgh of Kintore, of which he was Town Clerk.

fee to cover his expenses in producing the Halyblude play at Woolman-hill; it was not until 1458 that he first took the chair at the Council. His interest in the popular plays indicates that the whole town parti-cipated directly or indirectly, for the Kintore family took an important part in municipal affairs at that period.

The Cullens round about 1500 were one of the most opulent merchant families of Aberdeen, one of them, Andrew, being bracketed with Andrew Buk at the head of the great traders of the burgh. They dealt in everything and were paid in a variety of coins that nearly equalled the diversity of their merchandise. Andrew, himself a provost, dealt in 'gyngar, pipper, cloys, massis, fin succour, saip, venykay, madir, allom, blak bonetis, fostian and gren chamlet' among other commodities. His brother, Provost John, in return for a cargo of Aberdeen salmon and wool, received '13½ ald crounis, a ducat, three Hary nobillis, and an angell'. A clerk in a counting-house then required a liberal financial education.

To the Cullens fell, in the municipal field, two unsought distinctions. Andrew was the first provost to be described regularly by that title in the minutes. Alexander, a descendant who was several times Provost in the years around 1600, had the experience of conferring the free-dom of the burgh, on 23 October 1601, upon Laurence Fletcher and others, players, designated 'His Majesty's Servants', but actually one of the London theatrical companies. An entertainment to them and their expenses cost the town £126 3s. 6d., they got £28 to themselves, and a further charge was of £5 'for the stageplayers' support that nicht they played to the town'. This seems to have been Aberdeen's first visit from a touring repertory company. Much ink has been wasted in trying to prove that William Shakespeare was one of the strolling players. He belonged to Fletcher's company in London, and one of his editors, Charles Knight, thinks the visit suggested *Macbeth* to the dramatist and even argues that he visited Forres and the blasted heath (but not Lumphanan and the site of the last battle) for local colour. It is a pity Aberdeen cannot claim Shakespeare with Johnson and Scott in its Burgess Roll, but the fact that no Will Shakespeare signed with Fletcher and the others in 1601 is almost conclusive proof that he was not with them.

The most celebrated of the Cullens, however, was neither merchant nor provost, but grandson of the wealthy Andrew, and Vicar of Aber-deen. Walter was his name. He was born in 1526, son of that Baillie Walter Cullen who was 'maister of wark to the glass wark' of St.

Nicholas Kirk at his death in 1561. Young Walter apparently was not intended for the Church, since he was a burgess and married while the Reformation was still pending. But about 1570 he was appointed Reader in St. Nicholas Church, an office in the Reformed Kirk that corresponded to that of deacon in the Church of England today; he was a member of the staff, read prayers and lessons, he catechechised and might even be permitted to administer the sacrament, while he could, if he cared, proceed to fit himself for the full ministry. Cullen got £20 Scots for his salary. In 1577 he became Vicar of Aberdeen by a curious arrangement elsewhere described which sharply reveals how lacking in bitterness the Reformation was in Aberdeen itself.

Walter Cullen is the 'author', if we may dignify him by that title, of 'The Chronicle of Aberdeen', in itself a rather ambitious name for what is no more than a very imperfect diary and obituary. It consists of more or less random notes relating to contemporary events, and of a fairly large number of brief obituary paragraphs beginning with the election of John Cullen as provost in 1491, and ending in 1595. These notes were inserted in the earliest volumes of the burgh's register of births, marriages and deaths. After Cullen's death, the volumes were handed over to the town by his heirs. They had been in his possession because as Reader of Aberdeen he had the duty of receiving notices of marriage and proclaiming the banns. In the main, the entries refer to the Cullen family, of which Walter was amusingly proud. He even went so far as to make a 'Cullen' of Coligny, the great Huguenot Admiral of France, who was murdered in 1572 after the marriage of Henry of Navarre, as if the Aberdeen burgesses were scions of the French nobility. The reference to Coligny's murder and to the massacre of St. Bartholomew are the only ones that take us outside Scotland and England, and almost the only ones that reveal a literary style. They contain a malison upon Rome that comes incongruously from one who, albeit a Protestant, had accepted his religious office at the hands of a Roman Catholic bishop. Reduced to modern English, the Coligny entry runs thus: 'The 24 Day of August, the year of God 1572 years, Jasper of Cullen, great Admiral of France, was cruelly murdered in Paris under colour of friendship, at the King of Navarre's bridal, and under night, by the most cursed King of France, Monsieur his brother, and by the device of the pope, cardinals, bishops, abbots, priors, monks, friars, canons, priests, nuns, and whole rabble of that devilish sort of papists, devised at the Council of Trent, whose cruel murder we pray God to revenge. So be it.' Walter, however, had plenty of murders to record in Aberdeen itself. It was an age when men's minds, having burst the bonds of ancient religious beliefs and cultural limitations in the Reformation and the Renaissance, were still too enamoured of freedom to consider that liberty itself might have its limitations nevertheless. There was Gilbert Knowlis, elder, burgess of Aberdeen, slain with his son at the Causewayend going to the Cross by James Gordon, brother to the laird of Abergeldie. There was Alexander Menzies, son of the provost, slain at the Loch of Loirston by William Forbes of Portlethen. Alexander Keith of Owchorsk (Aquhorsk), who had married the aforementioned Alexander Menzies' sister, was slain in Aberdeen by the goodman of Balbithan, John Chalmers. The slaying of William Guild, son of Mathew Guild, armourer, in 1584, made way for another William Guild who was to be one of the city's chief benefactors. There seems to have been grades of manslaughter, for John Keith of Clackriach was 'cruelly slain' in Aberdeen at the Justice Port, by William Gordon of Gight. There is, however, no mention of punishment, except in the case of the man whose job it is to kill people: 'John Wishart, cordiner, departed the 18 day of March, year of God 1588 years, wha was slain by James Paterson, hangman of Aberdeen, and the said James hangit, and his heid set on the Port therefor.'

Death might even have come in scriptural fashion, to a man sitting in his own house, for on William Strachan, stabler of Aberdeen, the loft fell 'and felt him and he departed . . .'. Death by drowning and shipwreck was common. One dreadful catastrophe Walter records in 1541, when 'departed Thomas Brechin's ship, on the coast of England, at Skerisburgh (Scarborough), with the merchandise within her', and twenty-eight men were lost. A double drowning in 1590 in the Pocra burn introduces what seems to be the first instance of the corrupt spelling of Futty. Cullen calls it 'Fuitde', which probably reflects what had come to be the prevailing pronunciation.

Although his main interest was the Cullen family whose advancement and domestic concerns he faithfully chronicles, Walter Cullen was an individual of wider tastes and sympathies. He kept an eye on events throughout Scotland — James V's marriage, the 'Fedyll' or 'feidell'[1] of Pynke or Peynky, Aberdeen's casualties at which he mentions by name; the murder of Darnley, the birth of James VI, the assassination of the Regent Moray, all these and other happenings are set down. Among local events he says, unfortunately, not a word about

1 We still have the word, e.g. 'the snod-dykit feedle', but it has a different meaning.

the burning of 'Towie's House', and so fails to give us a contemporary testimony to the identity of that disputed stronghold[1]; but he mentions the battles ('fedylls' again) of Tullyangus and the Crabstone in the same year 1571, at both of which Adam Gordon of Auchindoun defeated the Forbeses.

He recorded the event as a rule with little more comment than a 'So be it', sometimes not even that. We could have enjoyed an occasional expression of opinion like that quoted from his reference to Coligny's murder. He diverts us with his recipes, and with his plain tales of storms and natural phenomena; 'On Wednesday the 13th day of November, the year of God 1577 years, was seen at even ane blazing star, which stood in the west, and continued that night, to the great admiration of the people'. Most of all we are grateful for the poems he copied into the registers. Whether he was the author he does not say, for one which he introduces as 'collected and written' by himself may have merely been found and transcribed. One poem, which is imperfect, he described 'quod Nicolsoun', a poet not elsewhere encountered in the realm of Scottish verse. Of the other poems, five in number, 'Ane Godlie Ballett of Any Synnar Cryand on God for Merce in Tyme of Trowbill', which is in the same style as Montgomerie's or Hume's devotional effusions, is not without merit in stanzas like these:

> Thy swerd is drawin, thy bow is bentt,
>   To plaig ws in thy ire.
> Thy wrythe on ws is kindlitt bauld,
>   As hoitt consumyn fyr.
> Hald up thy hand, and spair us, Lord,
>   Maist hummelie we desyre.
> Haif grace to ws, we pray,
> Nocht for our saikes, bott for thy lufe.
> O Lord, O Lord, O gracious Lord.
> Lord, twrn thy wrathe away.
>
> Manasses, Paull, and Maigdaling,
>   War hewe synnaris wyld,
> Yett quhene thay turnitt onto the,
>   Thow did thair synnis exill.
> Thy mercy hid thair wikitnes,
>   Quhilkes did thayme so defeile,
> Haif grace, etc.

1   It was either Towie Castle or Corgarff Castle, probably the latter, but there has been much dispute on the subject.

We might have had more cause to be grateful to Walter Cullen had he been less curt and more explicit in his jottings. Another half century was to pass ere a historian of our town and region arose whose main theme was the domestic life and state of Aberdeen and its hinterland. Cullen, in his long life from 1536 to *c.* 1610, could have told us much that he does not even bother to record: a tantalising scribe.

CHAPTER SEVEN

The Grammar School: Public and Private Health

Aberdeen from very early times paid attention to the education of at least a few of its prospective citizens, although we do not know how or when the Council came to take charge of education within its sphere of influence. In 1256 statutes enacted by Bishop Ramsay mention the schools[1] of Old Aberdeen, and enjoined upon the chancellor of the diocese the duty of providing a master to teach grammar and logic in the schools of Aberdeen. At that time it would seem that the ecclesiastical jurisdiction in this matter was not yet challenged by the town. The bishop's injunction, moreover, is a reminder that Scottish elementary education did not begin with John Knox.

In 1262 we come across a Thomas de Bennum (Benholm) rector of the school of Aberdeen, but the first specific mention of a grammar school is in 1448 when the chancellor of the diocese collated John Homyll as successor to Andrew de Syves (Schivas) in the post of 'Master of the schools of the burgh of Aberdeen', Homyll having been examined and found 'of good life, praiseworthy conversation, and skilled in literature and science'. In 1479 Maister Thomas Strathachin (Strachan) was appointed master by the Town Council 'at the instance of our sovereign lord's letters, my Lord of Aberdeen's letters, and of Maister Alexander Inglis, Chancellor of Aberdeen's letter of request'. Strachan was to receive £5 Scots until such time as he got a chaplainry in St. Nicholas Church. Such preferment then was a common device of a corporate body evading its financial responsibilities.

In 1509, Strachan having died, the town appointed John Marshall as Master 'be gift of ane pairt of bedis' (beads). In 1521, Marshall, 'inquirit be the provost quhome of he had said scoyll of Abirden', is presented as having 'grantit in jugment that he had the samyne of the said guid toun offerand him . . . and ranuersit his compulsatour (disclaimed any control) of the Curt of Royme in all poyntis. . . . And that the town keepand to him ald wse (use) and wont, liik as they did to the maister of the samyn in all tymes bigane.' Marshall, whom

1 'Schools' in the Latin and Middle Scots, but meaning 'School'.

we meet in another connection, died in 1529, and was succeeded by Mr. John Bisset, who is the first to be styled Rector. Bisset having become a regent at King's, the Council in 1538 appointed Mr. Hugh Munro 'on his good bearing', and ordained him to pass to the Chancellor of Aberdeen, and desire his admission thereupon, 'conform to our sovereign lord's request maid to the forsaid provost, baillies and council'. Council and Church were in fact at variance, for that very day the Chancellor announced that he had chosen 'an able, convenient, discreet man', Mr. Robert Skene, to be master of their grammar school, 'because the admission and presentation of the said master pertained to him, as he alleged'.

The immediate upshot of the dispute is not clear, although the provost, three of the baillies, and the majority of the Council were for resisting. But the next mention of the master, in 1544, reveals that he is Mr. Hugh Munro. He resigned in 1550. He must have given acceptable service for the Council granted him a pension of 40 merks. There was no further trouble with the Chancellor, who, of course, disappeared after the Reformation. During those years the school had come through bad patches. In 1527 the buildings were 'decaden and abill to fall down'. The master of kirk wark was ordered to attend to the repairs immediately. The school then stood to the east of where Gray's School of Art was, but west of Harriet Street. The ruinous condition of the building may have been a cause of the prolonged decline in the popularity of the institution at this time. In 1529 the town agreed 'to give Master John Bisset, Master of the Grammar School, the sum of £10 Scots to help pay his board, because now their said school is desert and destitute of bairns, and will be a long time ere it come to perfection that he may get meikle profit thereof'.

The curriculum of the school may be deduced from the Latin grammar, *Rudimenta Puerorum*, compiled in the first half of the sixteenth century by John Vaus, of King's College, for the Grammar School. On entering the school, the boy 'shall prostrate himself on the ground and with bended knee shall salute Christ... and the Virgin Mother of God with a short prayer...'. At 7 in the morning work commenced and at the end of the period the teacher came in and punished by tongue or cane those who were not proficient. After the punishment, there was at 8 a.m. a public prelection of all the lessons by the teacher, and after that, breakfast. Assistant masters did private prelection with the boys from 10 to about 11 or 11.30 a.m. when the boys were allowed into the town. There was a prelection on Terence,

Virgil or Cicero at 11.30 a.m. by the rector for all who cared to attend. The afternoon was similarly spent until 5 p.m., when there was an hour for disputation. 'And when that is finished, they will hasten to sing prayers to God.' Subjects taught besides Latin, were counting, and Greek, Hebrew, French, Irish (or Gaelic), but there was to be no speaking in the vernacular tongue except by those who knew Latin.

There were some curious customs and perquisites attached to the school. In 1542 we learn of the strange play of the Boy Bishop. On St. Nicholas Day it was the custom of the rector to visit the houses of parents of his pupils. He was accompanied by one boy, known as the Boy Bishop, who was dressed in episcopal vestments and equipped with the insignia of a bishop. It was actually ordained by the Council that the master on such a promenade was to receive 4s. Scots 'of the sobirist (i.e. poorest) person' that entertained him, and every other honest man to give him at pleasure; but anyone who refused had to pay 4s. to the master and 8s. to the baillies as a fine. This Boy Bishop mummery was common all over the country. The Bishop of the boys at Eton College performed divine service on St. Nicholas Day, and at Winchester on Innocents Day. In Salisbury Cathedral the ceremony was abolished in Henry VIII's time.

The rector could also claim special fees from parents at Candlemas, and those who gave liberally thus ensured a good place in class and special privileges for their sons, who were termed (according to the paternal munificence) kings or princes. Yet another exaction was Bent money, a small fee paid by the boys for liberty to play on the links, among the bents, one afternoon a week. In this connection there emerged a strange story a few years after the Reformation during a trial for witchcraft. Certain boys had been caught stealing green growing bere. Afterwards they had gone to play at the links, and the accused, who rejoiced in the name of Janet Wishart, was alleged to have bewitched two of the boys so that they drowned themselves in the Auld Watergang.

The boys could be wild enough. One January day there was a stand-up fight — no unusual occurrence — in St. Nicholas Church between Gilbert Kintor and David Anderson, rector (or under-master) in the Grammar School. Anderson and a friend thereupon fetched the boys from the school, who proceeded to attack Kintor and his brother, the latter being clouted 'with ane tre' by a pupil named Skene. After the Reformation the authorities frowned upon the old fun and pageantry of the holy days. The rector applied the necessary discipline. In 1569, in response to a complaint, couched in Latin, from the boys that they were no longer permitted to 'skale' at the times and terms when they used to have liberty, the Council gave them holidays 'from St. Thomas even before Yule until upon the morning after Epiphany day'. This privilege was withdrawn by the Council in 1575. Five years later the Council had to take stronger measures against 'the enormities committed by the disordered bairns and scholars of the grammar school of this burgh and other schools within the same'. The lads whether gentlemen's sons to landward or burgesses' sons, had to be presented to the provost and baillies and find cautioners for their good behaviour before being admitted to the school. Even this did not suffice. A year later the boys seized the school and held it against the masters. The Council refused to permit Yule holidays, but conceded three days at the beginning of each 'raith' or quarter, making twelve days off in the year. In 1589 the Council are again demanding guarantees against disturbances by the scholars at 'the superstitious time of Yule'.

There are happier glimpses of the school. One is of it being thatched and glazed and generally done up with 'the first and readiest silver' that came to hand. Another is of the generous patronage of the town to those who deserved well of it. Thomas Cargill, the rector, was a facile Latinist, and did not neglect fit opportunities for the exercise of his talents. He got £3 from the town for printing a commendation of the Earl Marischal's establishment of the new or town's college. Some years later, he was inspired by King James's escape from the Gowrie conspiracy to a Latin treatise of congratulation, into which he providently contrived to insert 'some commemoration of this burgh's antiquity and privileges'. For that the Council gave him £20.

In the contemporary notes that have been called 'The Chronicle of Aberdeen', Walter Cullen records in 1580 the examination of five candidates for the office of master of the Grammar School. The board of examiners consisted of the bishop (Protestant, by this time), the principal and sub-principal of King's, the Commissary of Aberdeen, an advocate from Edinburgh, and his brother. Thomas Cargill was adjudged 'the best clerk', and was accordingly presented to the office by the town. It is clear that the examiners judged well. His salary of 50 merks at his election in 1580 had risen to £80 by the time of his death in 1601. The latter sum was divided between his joint successors, both destined to be very eminent men, David Wedderburne and Thomas Reid. With them a new phase in the history of both town and school opens which may conveniently be left for later consideration.

Mastership of the Grammar School was a monopoly as regards the teaching of grammar. That was part of the bond. One of the first effects, as it was one of the prime causes, of the Reformation was a desire for more knowledge, and the tendency was a strong inducement to men of the clerkly type (probably done out of a vocation by the collapse of the Roman Church) to turn their attention to pedagogy. It was difficult to maintain the old monopoly in face of the spirit of the age, but the change was made very gradually. In 1583 the Council recognised the justice of the claim of John Phinevin, teacher of young children, to a house for a school, and granted him for that purpose the annual rent of a house in the Schoolhill at the north-west corner of the Kirkyard (which must have been next door to, not the house of, the Song School). This school for young children became the English School, and still later the Town's School. There was also permitted a few years later a dame's school, but only for 'mayden bairns', in which woman mistresses were to have no 'man doctor (teacher) under them'.

A school for teaching grammar was ordered to be shut in 1594 for want of permission from the rector of the Grammar School. In 1597 it was further decreed that, except the Sang School, there should be no other school within the burgh but must be 'subaltern' to the rector of the Grammar School and have his licence and goodwill. It was not until after the Union of the Crowns that one of 'our auld enemies the English' came forward with a scheme for a writing school, which the Council accepted. Even then it was made perfectly plain that 'the town are only obliged to find ane grammar school and ane sang school, and noways to find any English schools'.

Medicine in Aberdeen seems to have been first practised, in accordance with modern notions, by Gilbert Skene. He belonged to a county family, the Skenes of Wester Corse, and his father James was a notary in Aberdeen. In addition to Gilbert, several of James Skene's sons rose to eminence. One was Commissary of St. Andrews and Dean of the Arts Faculty there, one studied in Paris and became a lawyer in Edinburgh. Most distinguished of all was another lawyer brother, John, who as a boy got into trouble both in the Sang School and in the Grammar School. He studied at King's, graduated at St. Andrews, taught in the University there, travelled in Scandinavia and Poland, returned to practice law in Edinburgh, and eventually became Lord Advocate and Lord Clerk Register. He went with the Earl Marischal to Denmark, as one who could 'make them long harangues in Latin'.

Later he was ambassador to The Netherlands and he was also a commissioner at conferences which considered the question of legislative
union after the Union of the Crowns. He compiled the legal classic
entitled *The Lawes and Acts of Parliament made by King James the
First and his Successors Kings of Scotland* in 1597, and wrote an equally
valuable *Exposition of the Termes and Difficult Words contained in . . .
Regiam Majestatem*, the same year.

Gilbert Skene was not (as the historian of the Skene family has
stated) the first mediciner of King's College. The first was James
Cumine, who had the Chair of Medicine from 1505 until his death in
1521; the second was Robert Gray; and Skene, who probably was raised
to the Chair in 1556, was the third. Eventually he was appointed a phy-
sician-in-ordinary to James VI, not the first and very far from the last
Aberdonian to receive this mark of royal favour. He died in 1599 in
Edinburgh, where he had resided and practised for twenty years.

Skene was not only the author of the first Scottish medical tract,
though not the first Scotsman connected with Aberdeen to write a
medical treatise[1]; he was also an extremely realistic practitioner in
medicine. Two brief works of his are extant, the first, printed by
Robert Lekprevik in Edinburgh in 1568, entitled *Ane Breve Des-
criptioun of the Pest*, and the other much shorter, a description of the
qualities and effects of the Well of the Woolmanhill, Aberdeen 1580.[2]
This well, still known as the Well of Spa, though its much controlled
waters now issue forth in a different spot from that of Skene's day, has
long been an object of scientific interest and poetic affection.

As for the dissertation on the pest, Skene had ample opportunity
of studying the plague without stirring out of Aberdeen. His first predecessor in the medical chair had received in addition to his college
fees, 10 merks and a fishing from the town of Aberdeen. His municipal
functions were to 'mak personale residence within the saide burghe,
and cum and vesy tham that heis seik, and schow tham his medicin'.
Skene no doubt held the same or a similar post, and his tracts indicate

1 This distinction belongs to Bernard Gordon, apparently of the Gordon-
   stoun branch of the family, who is stated by David Buchan to have studied
   in Aberdeen. His book *Lilium Medicinae* is said to have been finished in
   1305, circulated for nearly two centuries in manuscript, and was first printed
   in 1480, for use in the medical school of Salerno (a locality not without
   fame in our own day). Gordon was 'publick professor of phisick at Montpelier'.
2 Skene's authorship of the Well of Spa tract has been contested. There is not
   much evidence either way.

that in the elementary way that was the only way to be expected in those times, he was observant and could make deductions from the symptoms which he was able to note.

Plague, or 'the pest', was a frequent visitor to Aberdeen, as to every town in the Middle Ages. The Black Death reached Aberdeen in 1350, and the plague is first recorded in 1401. That may not have been the first outbreak, it was merely the first after the date from which we possess written evidence of events in the burgh. We hear of it after that a dozen times in 200 years. What the disease was we have no precise evidence, but as it was caused clearly by the insanitary conditions that prevailed, it may have been typhus or paratyphoid.[1] In the last plague epidemic which occurred in 1647, no fewer than 1,760 persons, one quarter of the population, died within four months. Both prevention and cure were simple. All the gates were locked and watched, so that no traveller might enter without inspection and licence, the host with whom he was lodging having to stand surety that he was clean. An armed post was established at the Bridge of Dee, and another at the Bow Brig over the Denburn. Each baillie had to select reliable men to supervise his own quarter of the town, to see that no strangers were harboured secretly, and that there was no ingress through broken walls. The baillies further had to give forty-eight hours notice to quit the burgh to 'all manner of codderers, vagabonds and puir bodies, quhilk are not natives of this town born that have nothing to live well on their own'. Beggars native to the town received the 'town's token', which enabled them to remain within the burgh. Even as late as 1585, the gatehouse at the Bridge of Dee was manned to deal with incomers. Infected visitors and townspeople harbouring them were actually liable to be hanged. Two Aberdonians were sentenced to death for this crime of harbouring, but were reprieved on influential representations. Burning on the left hand for breach of statutes against the pest was for long a normal punishment. Concealment of infection previously had been punished by expulsion from the town, and in this connection there may be a hint as to the character of the disease in the fact that it left its mark upon the body, for the town's officers examined 'nakit' those who were suspected not to have notified that they had the disease. Notification had to be made within six hours.

Infected citizens of good standing had to remain with their whole households indoors until their houses were 'clengit'. Others were

1 In 1539 the Council Register described it as 'the contagious infecting pest called the boiche'.

'put to the links', where huts or lodges were erected for the segregation of the wretched sufferers. Persons entering the port by sea had to stay on board unless and until they got the magistrates' licence to land. Occasional instructions were given to have the calsay or causeway cleaned, and in 1539 we read of a 'cassay-makar' being engaged to relay the streets. But although much has been said by patriotic Aberdeen historians about the exceptional cleanliness of the town (by the standards of those times), there is little to support their assertions. In 1494 a rate of a penny was imposed on every firehouse and booth 'to halde the haill common gaitis and venellis of Abirdene clene and weill dichtet'. In 1507 'every fyrhouse within this burghe sale furnis and sende ane sufficient work servand with spaide, schwile, or barrowe, to help to rede the common loche'. The streets were usually swept clean of their middens and purged of their habitual domestic fauna only when distinguished visitors like royalty were expected, not from sanitary reasons. To the pynours or shore porters fell this duty. Until about the middle of the sixteenth century the fleshers had to 'dicht the fleshhouse at the great cross every Friday'. Thereafter the duty of seeing that 'the mercat and causay about the corce' were kept clean was assigned to the bellman. Any person found 'gadderand myddinges on the yett', or throwing 'mwk (muck), yerd, aise, or ony sic filthiness' on the streets was liable to be summarily fined 8s. A variant of this penalty was confiscation of the midden — a very serious matter for the culprit, since even then the value of such refuse in tillage was recognised. Swine wandering at all hours of the day and night on the thoroughfares were a perpetual nuisance. Their rooting propensities were somewhat curtailed by their owners' obligation to ring snouts. After the Reformation, swine found on the common streets could be 'expelled' or slain.

Agriculture was primitive. If winter lingered long in the lap of spring, sowing was apt to be too belated, or was neglected altogether. At best the yield was not high, for crop after crop for a dozen or more years was taken off the same ground, which was not recruited by manuring or rested by fallowing. Cattle were starved through the winter, all their food being green broom or whin; the value of hay was little understood. Only animals that died from natural causes were likely to be eaten. Fish supplies were dependent upon the season and the weather. In 1356 the provost had actually to travel to England to buy grain. That was not an isolated incident.

It is perhaps remarkable that we have such scanty evidence of precautions against epidemics and expedients to deal with disease.[1] The pest was always at the gates ere the gates were shut, and such provision as was made in the form of hospitals was for old age rather than sickness. Whereas there was a priest to every hundred inhabitants, we hear of only one doctor before the founding of King's College, and the Barbers, or Leechers, who were the medieval representatives of Galen and Hippocrates, were very late in reaching sufficient numbers to warrant their organisation into a Craft.

The first hospital of which we have record is one whose impress remains on the topographical index of the town. Bishop Matthew Kininmund, who occupied the see from 1172 to 1199, founded the Hospital of St. Peter on the hill between Old and New Aberdeen. Its name lives on in the Spital and in the cemetery of St. Peter.[2] It was not, however, wholly a house for the treatment of the sick. That was probably its last and least function, except in so far as the infirm and indigent who were its inmates were stricken by active disease.

With our ancestors, thought for the future safety of their souls was a far more potent incentive to charity than provision for the immediate preservation of their bodies. Or perhaps it would be more accurate to say that they had little voice in the matter, since the priests who had the direction of their lives took care that any spare cash would be safely bestowed upon some spiritual object that would ensure for at least one deserving clerk a comfortable existence in this world lest conditions should prove less tolerable in the next. And so the endowment of St. Peter's hospital was earmarked in part for the saying of masses for the souls of William the Lion and his successors and forebears, and also of the pious episcopal founder. How little these reverent usages meant in the estimation even of bishops is illustrated by the fact that Bishop Henry Lychtoun in 1427 diverted the revenues partly to the support of his own table.

The hospital's misfortunes did not end there. Only the lands around it were left for its support by Bishop Lychtoun. A hundred years later they were taken into the patrimony of the Cathedral and their revenues absorbed into the common funds of the church, while the master of the hospitals was promoted to the rank of prebendary. The final blow

1   The tradition that the bellman used to perambulate the town on horseback with an onion impaled upon a spear to attract the infection is, alas, no more than a legend.
2   The burial vault of the Moirs of Scotstown eventually covered the site of the building.

was dealt by the last Catholic Bishop of Aberdeen, William Gordon, *after* the Reformation. He had already alienated the hospital's lands and feued them out, and in 1565 he conveyed the last remaining piece of ground, that of North Spital, to his girl friend Janet Knowles, and to her son George Gordon. From this illuminating document we learn that the bishop had three sons and three daughters. When Bishop Gordon was done with it, nothing remained of the institution but its site, its graveyard, and the feu-duties of the alienated lands. In 1574 the Crown gave to King's College the whole of the property that remained.

Both Aberdeen and Old Aberdeen had bedehouses, or hospitals for indigent and decayed men of good character. In 1459 John Clatt, a canon of the Cathedral, granted his lands and tenements in the Nether-kirkgate, and certain other revenues and properties, from the lands of Mondynes and in the burgh of Kintore, to erect a hospital for that purpose. It came to be called St. Thomas's Hospital, and it was built in Correction Wynd, about the spot where Melville Free Church used to be. A few years after its foundation it reverted to the Town Council, who quite illegally applied it to the reception of destitute brethren of guild and members of the trades. In 1574 it could only support four burgesses, who received £10 each for their board and lodging in the house. About 1600 the last of the lands with which the hospital was endowed were disposed of, but the burgesses of guild undertook to contribute to the maintenance of the institution. In 1631 the house was repaired and enlarged to accommodate six decayed guild brethren, who each were given £100 Scots a year for their maintenance, and to provide their uniform which consisted of a russet gown. In course of time the old men grew quarrelsome, and at last the bedehouse was shut down, and the beneficiaries received a sum to find board and lodging outside. Hospital and garden were sold in the middle of the eighteenth century and the proceeds added to the hospital funds.

A similar house, founded in Old Aberdeen by Bishop Gavin Dunbar in 1531 and known by his name, was one of the show places of the Aulton, with its quaint doll's house frontage, until about a century ago when it was pulled down. It sheltered twelve old men, who received 10 merks pocket money, the same for fuel, and 1 merk to procure the white coat which was their distinctive habit. At the end of the seventeenth century the control of the hospital passed to King's College and the minister of Oldmachar. About a century later, house and grounds were sold, and the proceeds, with accumulated funds, were sufficient to supply a charity to be shared amongst eighteen old men.

One other hospital which partook far more closely of the true character, in modern usage, of such an institution, there was in Aberdeen. That was the Leper House, or Sick House, surrounded by a croft to which it gave its name, and standing between the Gallow-hill and the Spital road. It was probably erected about the middle of the fourteenth century, and its last patient entered in 1604, after which it gradually fell into decay. Its endowments were always poor; at one time it depended for its upkeep upon one peat from each load of peats brought into Aberdeen. When the subjects were sold the price was intended to be applied to the support of a mental hospital — which was never built.

The eight followers of Perkin Warbeck whom, as we have seen, King James IV apportioned to Aberdeen for entertainment paid scurvily for their upkeep. They brought and left syphilis. The Aberdeen magistrates at once recognised it for a disorder to be dreaded. Warbeck's gentlemen were in Aberdeen in 1496. On 21 April 1497, the Council emitted the first public regulations made in Britain against venereal disease, otherwise designated 'the strange sickness of Nappilis' and 'infirmity of Franche'. The decree ran: 'It was statut and ordainit . . . for the eschevin (eschewing) of the infirmitey comin out of Franche and strange partis that al licht wemen be chargit and ordainit to desist fra their vicis and syne of venerie, and al thar buthis and houssis skalit (emptied), and thai to pas and wirk for thar sustenacioun, under the payne of ane key of het yrne on thar chekis and banysene (banishing) of the toune.'

With the knowledge at their disposal there was not much the authorities could do beyond isolate infectious patients and leave nature to kill or cure. Walter Cullen, Reader of Aberdeen, although an educated man, could set down in the latter half of the sixteenth century, as serious cures for various ailments, the following recipes:

TO GAR ANE SLEIP

Tak egromonie and put it under thair heidis that thai waitt nocht of.

TO CAUSE ANY BYILL BRAIK OR GADDER ANE HEID

Tak ane onyeoun and rost waill and tak wormewood and syne bra them in ane mortar and la to the byill or tak surrakis and rost thame in ane dockane and la thame to the byill.

AGANIS THE HEID AIKING BY TO MEIKILL DRINKING

Tak rue levis and bray thame (in) wynager and put roissis to thame and bitter almoundis and with this rub your heid and ye salbe eisit.

The last simple was probably in frequent use. It was an age of hard drinking, so hard that the Council had to threaten with a heavy fine anyone, in private or public, who compelled a companion to take more liquor than he wanted.

Yet in an allied matter the Council was very much a pioneer. In 1595 it took steps to ensure the purity of the seeds sold within the town — at least of the onion seed which was then in wide demand. In that year the Council being informed of various cases of inferior seed being sold, ordained that merchants buying the seed 'in uther realmes' should bring 'hame a ticket of the merchand fra quhom he byes the said seid of the sufficiencie and guidnes theirof'.

As late as 1596 there was but one medical practitioner in the burgh. He, Maister Quintine Prestoun, professor of phisick, asked the Council's permission to take an apothecary, 'in respect of his debilities, being sumquhat stricken in aige, and sua not abill to accomplische the deutie without ane coadivtor'. With the apothecary was to go an 'apothecarie chop, for the better furnesing of this burght and of the cuntric, of all sorts of physical and chirurigicall mendicamentis'. Where the 'chop' was we do not know.

CHAPTER EIGHT

Cathedral, Churches and Sang School

With the growth of an atmosphere of comparative security following the victory at Bannockburn, Aberdeen began to show a constructive interest in its own development. Bishop Cheyne, besides playing a part in the building of the Brig of Balgownie, devoted some of his time and energy to the raising of a worthy monument to the patron saint of the Kirktown by the Don. Long before the wars of independence there had been a church of sorts. Cheyne took this shanty down, no doubt intending to erect a more seemly fane, for he was evidently given to architectural exercises. Bishop Alexander Kininmund I, who received the mitre in 1329, the year of King Robert's death, built or improved the Bishop's palace near the east end of the church site, and provided residences for his subordinates in what is now the Chanonry. But soon after their construction in 1336, the English, as will be told presently, after burning Aberdeen, set fire to the Bishop's new buildings. Nothing seems to have been done to replace them for over a century, but the bishops themselves may have had a residence at Loch Goule, to the north-west of Aberdeen. They had a summer seat at Fetternear, which fell to the Leslies at the Reformation, and which, from a fable that Wallace lodged a night there, was called Wallace's tower.

The cathedral site was cleared again about 1356 by Bishop Alexander Kininmund II, who laid foundations and built about 9 feet of the walls of choir and transepts. Bishop Adam Tynninghame (1382–90) erected a large part of the choir. A more energetic occupant of the see, Henry Lychtoun, found the building only about a quarter finished, but by 1424 he had almost completed the nave in granite from now forgotten quarries[1] at Tarves, and the seven windows and twin octagonal steeples of the west front. By 1430 he had St. John's aisle on the north side built, the foundations of the great central tower laid and the two small towers completed. His successor, Bishop Lindsay, put on the roof and laid a pavement of freestone for the floor. Bishop Elphinstone's contribution was to put the finishing touches to both nave and choir.

[1] The granite may have been gathered from the fields.

Finally Gavin Dunbar, most enthusiastic architect of all the bishops, completed the west front with its battlemented flanking towers, added on the south side Dunbar's aisle about 1522, and was responsible for the rare and magnificent carved fir ceiling. The cathedral was then complete.

Unhappily it did not long remain so. Little damage was done at the Reformation, but Monck's troopers, in the half-dozen years before the Restoration, purloined the buttresses, along with the stones of the bishop's palace of 1329, to build a short-lived fort on the Castlehill. In 1688 nature took a hand, when a gale blew down the central tower, weakened by the loss of the buttresses. In its fall it overwhelmed the two aisles and the choir. Thus today, apart from the ruins at the east end, we are left with the west entrance known as the marriage porch, with the fine west front and its steeples and graceful septet of windows, and the nave. But even the nave has been despoiled. In 1867, despite protests by responsible architects who knew that restoration was possible without substitution, the priceless heraldic ceiling was removed, the almost unique (and sound) fir roof taken away, and a new one laid in. The ceiling Dunbar so gloriously decorated 400 years ago is not the ceiling that still wins our admiration today.[1]

Nevertheless, although we cannot undo past mistakes, we may rejoice in what is left. In Old Aberdeen the community possesses priceless assets of art on no trivial scale. There is the old Brig, its site surely chosen as its span was proportioned with an artist's eye. There is the cathedral, which, while it has none of that soaring quality, or the elegance and stateliness of such as Ely or York, displays a serene, firm nobility, a human and friendly atmosphere despite the austerity of its masonry. The ceiling is paralleled only in St. Albans. It is long since men grinned appreciatively at an emblazoned Roman Catholicism brooding over a Presbyterian congregation. The ceiling and the great crown surmounting King's half a mile down the street represent an age when Christendom was one unit with many parts, not many parts existing separately. In the cathedral the Princes of the Church are in procession, from the Vicar of St. Peter at their head to Aberdeen's episcopal incumbent; the temporal Princes of Europe line up under the Emperor; the King of Scots and his nobles are in the same company as the sturdy burghs of Aberdeen and Old Aberdeen — the

1 See *The Heraldic Ceiling of St. Machar Cathedral* by Sir W. D. Geddes and Peter Duguid, New Spalding Club; and Dr. Kelly's paper in the third Spalding Club Miscellany, Vol. 1.

whole array a microcosm of medieval civilisation. And over the trees of the Chanonry the Crown of King's proclaims now the memory, as it proclaimed then the reality, of the Holy Roman Empire.

Of Aberdeen's religious houses at the Reformation the monastery of the Dominicans on the Schoolhill had no separate church. Owning land at Kintore, Banchory-Devenick and Dunnottar, as well as town property, they became wealthy and dissolute until they were taken in hand, 1503–8, by Friar John Adams, later Principal of the Order in Scotland and the first graduate in theology of King's College. The chief patrons were the Earls Marischal, whose family tomb was in the monastery. Like the Carmelites' church and convent in the Green, the building was razed on 4 January 1560, by the Reforming invaders from Angus. The property, like that of the Carmelites, fell to the Earl Marischal, all being applied to the endowment of his college. The wall of the Carmelite churchyard was ordered to be repaired as late as 1648.

South of the Carmelites the monastery and chapel of the Trinity Friars were also burned that day, but the blackened walls remained in possession of the Order until 1587, when they reverted to the Crown. In 1631 Dr. William Guild purchased them and presented them to the Crafts for a meeting-house and hospital. It was in the burying-ground of the monastery that in 1606 Aberdeen's first shipyard was situated. In that year Alexander Davidson, 'timber man in Sanct Androis', who had purchased enough timber in Drum to build 'ane bark', received the magistrates' permission to build his ship in the old cemetery, which was then 'filthily abused by middens'.

The ancient chapel on St. Katherine's hill had disappeared by 1660. On the Castlehill St. Ninian's chapel was used to support for the guidance of mariners 'ane gryt bowat or lamp' on the east gable, 'with three gryt flammand lychtis to byrne continewallie thairin' in winter. This light, installed in 1566, is last mentioned in 1627. In Futty the small chapel of St. Clement erected by the Council for the use of the white fishers about 1498 fell into decay after the Reformation. In 1631 the citizens raised £4,000 Scots to have it repaired. In 1787 the old building was pulled down and the present St. Clement's Church built. The Templar chapel in the Castlegate was in ruins. Besides these, we must not forget the chapel at King's, the Snow Church (which was Old Aberdeen's parish church), a chapel at the Brig o' Balgownie and another at the Bridge of Dee, these two for the benefit of travellers.

The Church of the Franciscans or Grey Friars survived the Reformation by the intervention of the Council. With it went a monastery
and garden, the site now occupied by Marischal College. The ground
was given to the Franciscans in 1469 by Richard Vaus, laird of Menie,
who belonged to an Aberdeen burgess family. After the Reformation
the subjects fell to the town, which made them over to the Earl Marischal
who applied the buildings to house his college. The majority of the
brethren went to the Continent. The Prior of the Order in Aberdeen,
Thomas Gray, lived to the age of 137 in exile, the secret of his longevity
being a stout stomach and excellent appetite. The joint vandalism of
the Town Council and the University at the beginning of the present
century deprived Aberdeen of this, its sole complete pre-Reformation
church. Greyfriars was built, as we have seen, by Bishop Dunbar from
the design of Alexander Galloway, Parson of Kinkell.[1] It was in Greyfriars that Aberdonians signed the Covenant on 3 April 1639. And
it was there that in 1640 the General Assembly held one of its most
critical sederunts.

Of the original church of St. Nicholas in its complete state there
remain only the arches supporting the steeple in the centre of the
transept, Collison's Aisle on the north transept, and portions of St.
Mary's Chapel, once known as 'The Lady of Pity her vault', under the
choir or East Church. The first church dated to about 1060. There was
a nave in the thirteenth century. By the end of the fourteenth transepts
and chancel had been added, with St. Mary's Chapel east of the chancel
on a lower level. In 1477–1507 the Council, who never forgot they
were the patrons of the church, built a great choir in place of the
chancel, and extending beyond it over the chapel. This made the
church complete. In the centre where the transepts met, a square tower
rose. For 12 feet it was of stone, which supported an oaken octagonal
steeple, covered with lead, soaring 140 feet above the ground. It
carried a clock with four dials and the famous peal of bells. This was
the steeple that was burned in 1874. In 1598 the choir was divided off
by a screen of wood, for which masonry was substituted later.

The building of the choir took far longer than seems necessary.
References to 'St. Nicholas wark' become incessant in the Council
records. St. Nicholas, patron saint of mariners, made a special appeal

1 Dr. William Kelly argued that Galloway was merely the bishop's agent, and
   that the architect was the master-mason, Thomas French. But, most
   uncharacteristically, Dr. Kelly seems to forget that in those days an educated man could, and often did, turn his mind to any science or art. (See
   William Kelly: A Tribute.)

to those living by the sea. In 1449 the Council ordered all merchants exporting goods to Bruges to pay a tithe on their cargoes for the repair of the church. In 1518, once the choir was built, the merchants un-animously taxed themselves for the upkeep of the church to the extent of two shillings great Flanders money on every sack of merchandise consigned to the Netherlands and the Baltic. In the actual building of the choir the citizens voluntarily contributed £44 4s. 2d., one French crown, and two English groats; 80 barrels of salmon; 287 dozen stock fish, 13 dozen sheepskins ('futefell'); and their own labour in some cases. Many fines were applied to 'St. Nicholas wark'.

Within, the church was embellished by much carved work, by elegant stalls for members of the ecclesiastical college, and by its thirty-one altars endowed by the pious liberality of the citizens. After the Reformation, a certain impatience with funeral ostentation becomes discernible. The carved work, stalls and altars disappeared, and the congregation had to stand during the interminable service. The church walls were by this time covered by memorial tablets, coats of arms, and elegiac inscriptions. Even the great pillars were similarly decorated. With such a concourse of ghosts commemorated above ground, it can be imagined that the ground beneath the floors, unlike the heaven of Byron's 'Vision of Judgment', was full to inconvenience. 'Through the multitude of deid bodies buried therein', we read, 'few places is to be found thereintill but green graves, albeit the kirkyard be ane honourable place of burial, if they would content therewith'. There was a curious funeral custom in Aberdeen. When a 'man of guid' who had borne office in the town died, the segister (sacristan) rang all that day. When any 'substantious freeman' died, his 'mening' was rung but thrice. When a craftsman died he got a single ring. Before the Reformation the bellman every Monday passed through the streets naming and praying for the souls of those who had died the previous week.

In Aberdeen, Old Aberdeen, and in all fairly populous communities with some ecclesiastical status, a Song School was an indispensable adjunct to the church. The ornate and elaborate music of the Mass and other services required competent choir work as well as trained voices, so that a musical seminary became necessary for every abbey and church with pride in its own performance and a population large enough to draw upon. Aberdeen's school taught music, and music only. In England a song school corresponded to our primary and a grammar school to our secondary department. We do not know much about the Old Machar school, whose activities before the Reformation are very dim to us.

Aberdeen's original Sang School was housed somewhere in or near St. Nicholas Kirkyard. In 1559, before the Reforming mob invaded Aberdeen, the building had become ruinous. In 1586 a small house was built for the keeper of the kirk door 'where the Sang School was' wherever that was. A few years later great stones were taken from there, which may suggest that this house was not the same as that known as the Kirk lodge at the corner of Schoolhill and Back Wynd which became the local habitation of the school in 1605. Between times the school had been housed on the Castlehill and from 1601 in 'Thomas Nicholson's new biggit hous at the burnheid'. From the pupils of the Sang School the Council supplied the singers for the parish church. Boys and men who could undertake the choral work were rewarded with clerkships, the fees of which were drawn from one of the four quarters of the town. Some of these clerks proceeded to the Grammar School and University, leaving substitutes to keep their clerkships warm.

In 1483 Richard Boyle succeeded Sir[1] Andrew Thomson as Master. But he could not play the new organ which the Council had installed in the church, so he was superseded by Robert Huchonsone, who could, Boyle continuing to teach under him. The organ, it may be remarked, was paid for by an impost on the swine and sheep brought into the burgh. The Master had a variety of duties. He was organist and choirmaster, for which he got 24 merks. In the school he had to teach the bairns in his charge, and particularly those of burgesses, to sing and to play on the organ. His fees he collected from his pupils or their parents; the endowments are described as 'scolage and duties'. At the beginning of the sixteenth century the choir was augmented, the extra choristers being drawn at least partly from the school; to one of them was assigned a rota of citizens to feed him day about. In 1533 it would seem that the artistic temperament had been at work: all the paid singers were discharged for 'demerits bygone done to God and (the Council) except Sir Andrew Couper that is an agit man'.

In 1544 Sir John Fethy was appointed Master and as a prebendary of St. Nicholas Church. Fethy, who later became master in turn of Dundee and Edinburgh Sang Schools, was a composer and poet well-known in his day. A song, 'O God Abufe', in a collection[2] of airs and

1   'Sir' is 'Rev', a member of the secular clergy, otherwise 'Pope's knights'.
2   The manuscript is in Trinity College, Dublin.

sonnets made by Thomas Wood, Vicar of St. Andrews, in 1592, was written and composed by Fethy. Of him Wood says he 'was the first organist that ever brought into Scotland the curious new fingering and playing on organs'. Fethy also wrote two poems preserved in the Bannatyne MS. of 1568 — 'Pansing in Hairt with Spirit opprest', and 'My Trewth is plicht unto my Lufe bcnyng'. Soon after his appointment Fethy had a dispute with his assistant John Black, in which the Council supported the Master. Later there was trouble with the choir, whose fees were suspended. When Fethy left Black succeeded to the mastership and as 'Chorister and Master of myd lettroun'. He was in charge at the Reformation, and left the district. Later he returned and in 1575 we find him Master again.

In the next twenty years the school had a precarious existence and several heads. In 1592 a double seat was made in the kirk for the pupils. In 1596, when the East Church was partitioned off, it was arranged that the Master should 'uptake the psalm' in one church, his assistant in the other. In 1598 the mastership fell vacant. There was no suitable candidate. John Leslie in Kintore was appointed locum tenens 'being a qualified musician, albeit he cannot instruct his scholars in playing'. At this point we may take temporary leave of the institution, by now called the 'Music School'. It had a century and a half ahead of it and some distinction to earn.

From the middle of the fifteenth century references are frequent to the minstrels of Aberdeen. The burgh employed several pipers. They were used on State occasions, as when they were sent to Holyrood for James IV's marriage. For that event they were provided with badges, containing an ounce and a half of silver and with the city arms engraved upon them. They were made by Davy Theman, keeper of the 'common horologe and knock'. A more prosaic duty for the minstrels, who included a fiddler and a trumpeter, was to act as knockers-up and to announce bedtime. They marched 'through all the rews and streets of the good town at five hours in the morning and betwixt eight and nine at even'. This peregrination seems to have been conducted partly for the discourse of music after the common bell had awakened the citizens in the morning and warned them of curfew at night. In 1566 we meet a sweschman or drummer in a coarse scarlet coat. A few years later he took the place of the minstrels in perambulating the burgh. At 4 a.m. and 8 p.m. playing on the Almany quhissle (German whistle) and accompanied by a servant beating a tambourine, he went round the town, 'whereby the craftsmen, their servants and all other laborious folk being warned and excited, may pass to their labours, in due and convenient time'. The equivalent of trade union hours was rather more than double the modern allowance. In 1569 the Council decided that once a wheel had been made for the easy ringing of the great bell called Nicolas, the sacristan of the parish kirk should ring it every morning at 4 a.m., and the little bell called Skillat at 8 p.m., to warn the craftsmen to begin and end their labours. The minstrels all lived in the burgh, being assured by the Council of 'reasonable diets' from the householders. The equivalent in cash was twelvepence. As time wore on, bringing changes in values, each burgess householder when his turn came to feed them, had to give them 16 pence, and each craftsman 12 pence. Once the sweschman got £5 and the piper 10 merks from the town for their 'extraordinar pains' in discoursing music while the inhabitants were building a pier on the south side of the harbour.

CHAPTER NINE

Lamp of the North

In 1483, the year of Martin Luther's birth, William Elphinstone came from Glasgow as Bishop of Aberdeen. He was a scholar, a priest and a lawyer, he had lived as a student in France, at Paris and Orleans, and been a lecturer in Paris University; he had diplomatic experience and served on missions to England, France, Burgundy and Austria. Less than five years after coming to Aberdeen he was appointed Chancellor of Scotland under James III, and although the murder of that King deprived him of both patron and place, he was soon to rise in James IV's favour. In 1492 he became Keeper of the Privy Seal. He attended Parliaments and took a leading part in the business of the nation, so that his influence with the King was very high. But it was not high enough to enable him to dissuade James from his wanton and foolish campaign against England which culminated on the doleful hillside of Flodden in the greatest military disaster ever suffered by Scottish arms. Having striven in vain to avert calamity, Elphinstone, with the King dead and the whole nation mourning, was endeavouring to restore the damage when he died worn out in Edinburgh in 1514 at the age of 83.

Few men have deserved better of Scotland, and none of Aberdeen and the surrounding country. Very soon after he came to the North-East Elphinstone began to identify himself with its work and its aspirations, as if he were a son. In the thirty years of his sojourn in Old Aberdeen he did much for his adopted town and he planned more than he lived to accomplish. He greatly advanced the building of a more dignified cathedral of St. Machar. He founded the University and College of St. Mary, now known as King's, and saw to its proper endowment. He persuaded James IV to licence Scotland's first printers, Walter Chapman and Andro Myllar, in Edinburgh in 1507, so that the *Aberdeen Breviary* might be worthily printed: and he projected the building, though he was not spared to see it begun, of our present, but now the 'old', Bridge of Dee. He also made arrangements for building a church for the Grey Friars.

Elphinstone's name, of course, is chiefly remembered by the college he founded. Aberdeen's was the third University to be erected in Scotland: St. Andrews in 1411 and Glasgow in 1450 already attesting Scotland's desire for learning. Aberdeen, thanks to Elphinstone's practical good sense and skill in getting money out of people, never suffered from lack of funds. In response to petitions from both King and Bishop, the Pope Alexander VI issued a Bull on 1 February 1494/5, sanctioning the erection of a University. Alexander VI was the Borgia Pontiff whose sins, for those who like that sort of thing, make as diverting reading as the lapses of any medieval secular prince; but to Scotsmen his founding of Aberdeen University will atone for much. The Bull itself, beautifully written and in an excellent state of preservation, is still to be seen at King's College. It begins by expatiating upon the value and power of learning, passes to a concise survey of Scotland, alludes to the remote regions cut off by mountains and inhabited by ignorant and almost barbarian people, and points out that the city of Old Aberdeen, being situated close to those savage territories, could fittingly supply by means of a university the religion and culture that the North of Scotland so much required. Then, after a rather surprising compliment to King James, whose obedience to the decrees of Rome it extols, although in fact he was as often contumacious, it formally gives permission to found a university. The Bull next proceeds to lay down the constitution of the university and it ends by conferring all the privileges of existing universities upon Aberdeen and laying the curse of St. Peter and St. Paul on those who seek to interfere with the enjoyment of these privileges.

Two years later Bishop Elphinstone published this Bull from St. Machar's Cathedral. The delay may have been due to the Bishop's desire to have his foundation placed upon a sound business footing from its inception. A year after the issue of the Bull the Pope assigned certain revenues. Next James IV assigned the revenues of the churches of Arbuthnot, Glenmuick and Glengairn, and later of Slains, with certain Banffshire feu-duties specially earmarked for the support of a professor of medicine. Elphinstone himself joined the vicarage of New Aberdeen to the university, gave a feu-duty from the lands of Petty for the support of the students in theology, and founded the Church of St. Mary ad Nives[1] (St. Mary of the Snows), the revenues of which were received by the Grammarian of the University. Aberdeen

---

1   St. Mary ad Nives stood where the Snow Churchyard still is in Old Aberdeen. It was for long the parish church of Old Aberdeen.

burgesses were not to be outdone in generosity by Popes, Kings and Bishops. Robert Blinseile made a deed of gift of a Castlegate feu-duty as early as 1500.[1] Duncan Scherar, prebendary of Clatt, made over feu-duties in Aberdeen and Kintore.[2] Others outwith the burgh, and even the county, contributed gifts more or less substantial.

As soon as Elphinstone was sure of his funds he went ahead with his buildings. Very soon after this proclamation of 1496-7 he had secured temporary houseroom for his college. This should not have been very difficult. Long before Elphinstone's time — according to Boece as early as about 1157, but certainly from 1240 — there was a College of Canons at Old Aberdeen for the training of priests. It naturally was connected with the diocese, and there may have been a habitation that could be used for the new college, in which, after all, the real emphasis was still upon the teaching of theology and canon law. Probably the University got going about the summer of 1497. It was in operation in 1499, and by 20 August 1500, when Hector Boece, its first Principal, appears on the scene, its office-bearers were all at work. Over the west door of King's College chapel it is stated that the masons began to build there in the spring of 1500, and the charter issued by Bishop Elphinstone himself on 17 September 1505 is considered to have marked the virtual physical completion of the college.[3] In 1505 John Knox was born. Both college and child were to alter the shape of future things.

Hector Boece was a Dundonian, educated at St. Andrews and Paris, where he was a professor when Elphinstone invited him to Aberdeen. He has won a reputation quite at variance with his character. His close friend Erasmus, the celebrated Reformer, with whom he corresponded for many years, said of him that 'he knew not what it was like to make a lie'. Yet his *History of Scotland* might have been written by the Father of Lies himself.

> If you should bid me count the lies
> Of Hector's history,

1   Provost of Aberdeen, 1482, and a great benefactor of the Church. His seal is still extant, attached to his deed of gift of St. Ninian's Chapel on the Castle-hill, 1504.
2   William Scherar, Lord of Kinellar, and Alderman of Aberdeen in 1447, had lands in Kintore. The prebendary was his son.
3   The master builder is nowhere specified but J. M. Bulloch ingeniously argues that Thomas Franch (or French), a Linlithgow man, who was Elphinstone's master-mason on the cathedral, may have had a hand in the construction of King's. The tower of St. Michael's, Linlithgow (taken down in 1800) was by Franch and very similar to the Crown Tower of King's.

I might as well essay to sum
The stars or waves of sea.[1]

Nevertheless his Latin is excellent, the style of his History elegant. Moreover he was a thoroughly good fellow. The Aberdonians clearly liked him. Soon after his arrival he was presented to the altarage of St. Ninian in the parish church, so that he was brought at once into close association with the Town Council. Evidently nothing he did served to create division between town and gown. Indeed in 1528 we find a very pleasant minute of Council which records the decision to give Boece (his name is spelt Boyis in this case) a propine or present of a tun of wine 'gif he will bid quhill (wait until) new wynnis cum hayme, or thane (or alternatively) with tuenty lib Scottis to help to by him banatis (bonnets), quhilk of thame he thinkis maist expedient, at his awin plesour'. Propines were usually reserved for kings and queens and distinguished visitors; inhabitants and neighbours seldom participated. Bocce, therefore, was favoured and he must have earned the gift by his conduct towards the town. For propines cost money, and on this occasion, the council having decided to make the gift, had to meet again in the afternoon 'to se and devise quhar this mony salbe esiast gottin'. To the fact that Boece had the rudiments of medicine has been attributed the appointment of a Mediciner in the first years of King's College. Doubtless he would have favoured the presence of medicine in the curriculum, but King's, taking its character from the University of Paris on account of Elphinstone's own connection with the French seminary, could hardly have excluded such a chair. What smattering of science Boece had cannot be told, as James Cumine, the first Mediciner, and Alexander Galloway, both of whom displayed an enthusiastic if not very discriminating interest in scientific subjects, are credited with having guided their Principal in the passages of his magnum opus which trench upon science.

The first Principal had a salary of 40 merks or £26 13s. 4d. Scots or £2 4s. 6d. sterling. It appears to be, but actually was not, inadequate to the appointment. Dr. Johnson, whose ignorance could at times be appalling, jeered at a country and a university that paid such a stipend, but a much more capable commentator, Cosmo Innes the historian, gave it as his opinion in the middle of last century that no Scottish Principal in Victoria's time was so well off. He may have been passing rich on £20 a year, but he had a great deal more. He was canon of Aberdeen and the rector of Tyrie. The King gave him an annual

1   Dr. James Moir's translation of Leland's Latin epigram on Boece.

pension of £50 Scots, later raised to 100 merks. Besides his Latin *History of Scotland* he was author of the *Lives of the Bishops of Aberdeen*. We may say of him that he conscientiously tried to encourage learning in the North-East, and he had a Churchillian taste in headgear. Boece died in 1536.

Besides the Chancellor (Elphinstone himself) and the Rector, who were unpaid, thirty-six persons were to reside within the college and receive emoluments of some kind from its endowments. The Principal, who had to be a master of theology, was the administrative head, lectured on theology and preached. The Canonist, the Civilist and the Mediciner, who were doctors respectively of canon law, civil law and medicine, were expected to lecture on their subjects. They had to wear the academic costume suitable to their degrees. The Mediciner was the first professor of Medicine to be appointed in Britain. Cambridge did not have one until 1540, Oxford till 1546. The Sub-Principal, a Master of Arts, deputised for the Principal and lectured on the liberal arts; the Grammarian, also a Master of Arts, instructed in grammar. These, the six teachers or professors, were, with the exception of the Mediciner, to be prebendaries, and all were elected by the Chancellor. There were five students, already Masters of Arts and proceeding to be Bachelors of Theology, who assisted the senior staff by acting as lecturers to the students of Arts. These students of Theology, who combined their studies with the teaching of the Arts bursars, each took a class through its whole course of three and a half years. This was known as regenting, and they were called regents. The subjects were: First year: Logic; Second year: Physics and Natural Philosophy; Last year and half: Arithmetic, Geometry, Cosmography and Moral Philosophy, the last-named covering 'ethics', that is to say politics and economics. The students in Arts were thirteen in number, all bursars.

Lectures for long consisted in the dictation of the prescribed book, more likely than not in manuscript to the students; hence we get the title Reader for a University Lecturer. Grammar was, of course, taught at the Grammar School, and there seems to have been another school for the same purpose connected with the University. The Grammarian taught Latin, and at a remarkably early date, for the teaching of Greek was not introduced into Scotland until 1534, he or one of his colleagues instructed in Greek. We first hear of Greek at King's in 1541, when during a visit by King James V and his Queen the students entertained the royal guests by 'disputations in all kinds of sciences' and by 'orations in Greek, Latin, and other languages'. It was by disputation that students were examined for their degrees.

There were twelve other members of the College. Eight were prebendaries: one the Organist, one the Cantor, to lead the singing, one the Sacrist, to supervise ceremonial. An ordinary member was Procurator, in charge of certain duties of management. Finally, there were four choristers or choir boys. Above all there was the Chancellor, who by the foundation was the Bishop, and who as supreme head of the University received all reports and advised upon all disputes. The Rector inspected the work of the College annually and reported to the Chancellor. How he was elected is not detailed in early documents, but doubtless, following the practice at Paris, which was Aberdeen's model, he was chosen by vote of all members. All the members had to live in except the Canonist, Civilist, Mediciner and Grammarian, who had manses outside. The students were recommended by the Rector, the Dean of the Arts Faculty, the Principal and the Sub-Principal. Those who took Arts alone stayed three and a half years, those who proceeded to Theology twice that period.

The College gates opened at 5 a.m. in winter and 4 a.m. in summer, closing at 8 p.m. in winter and 10 p.m. in summer, the keys being held by the Principal or his deputy. The appropriate robes and hoods had to be worn and the service in the chapel had to follow the correct canonical lines. Elphinstone seems to have been very insistent upon such matters and an enthusiast for music. He revived the Gregorian chant in the Cathedral services, installed a peal of thirteen bells in the Crown Tower of the University,[1] and we know he took a close interest in the Sang Schule. He furnished the Chapel sumptuously. A great glory of King's (and of Aberdeen) is still the beautiful carving of the oak of the canons' stalls. Stained glass windows he had put in: they are lost. There were three altars, images of saints, the great screen, chairs of brass, tapestries, carpets, and bells of gold and silver. Of the original building only the Chapel and Crown Tower, the wing that was first built, remain; and the Crown itself was blown down in 1631. Boece's proud description is worth quoting:

1 The peal is described as 'an musicall harmonie of thirteen costlie and pleasant bells, pleasing the ear with sweet and holy melody'. Trinitas, the biggest, measured 5 feet 5 inches; the next largest were Maria, Michael, Gabriel and Raphael. Five smaller bells sounded the half hours. The chapel had three bells. Some of them seem to have been broken up and perhaps recast in 1700, the rest were sold in 1823 when the University was in financial straits.

'In the college there is a church, floored with polished and squared stones, with windows, fine carved work, seats for the use of the priests and benches for the boys, made with wonderful art, marble altars, images of the saints, statues and pictures gilt and gold; chairs of brass; hangings and carpets to cover the walls and floor, that the whole might appear more splendid. It was also magnificently decorated with much other precious furniture. The furnishings used for sacred functions consist of fifteen vestments of cloth of gold, known as capes, chasubles and tunics (dalmatics), and twenty-eight of velvet. All these were embroidered with a warp of golden threads, and had pictures of the saints woven into them, the colours used being scarlet, purple and blue. Seven of fine linen were inter-wrought with palm leaves. These had fringes of golden threads with golden stars scattered over them. Other twenty, also of linen, showed palm branches and a watered pattern. These were for the use of boys in their sacred duties, that their attendance on the priests might add to the dignity of the praise of God. Besides these, for everyday use there were many sacred vestments of scarlet and watered linen.

'There were also a crucifix, two candlesticks, the same number of censers, an incense boat, six altar cruets, eight chalices, a textuary, two monstrances for holding the Host . . . another of the same, two cubits high, of incredibly fine workmanship. Besides these were a finger basin, a receptacle for water, a vessel for carrying the holy water, along with a sprinkler. All these were of gold and silver. There were also several cambric cloths, embroidered with gold and various figures, and other of the finest linen, interwoven with flowers of various colours. With these the altars were covered in time of service. There, too, is a casket of cypress-wood, set with pearls and jewels, and of beautiful workmanship. In it are kept for veneration the holy relics of the saints set in gold and silver.'

Dunbar presented to the Chapel the 'Altar of the venerable Sacrament, built by the Rector of Kinkell, with a place for the sacrament of pyramidal form, given by the same donor. Amongst the gifts of Bishop Gavin Dunbar to the high altar was a veil, most magnificently embroidered with gold, together with wooden supports and rods, beautifully painted, with iron keys to guide these supports to the sacrament house, with balls decorated with gold; together with a table for carrying the venerable sacrament, with antipendia decorated with letters of gold and scriptures, embroidered as befits the House of God.'

This is not the place for a detailed history of the University, but in certain respects the state and fortunes of the College belong to the history of Aberdeen. The men who sustained the Lamp of the North were also benefactors of the city. Elphinstone's projects we have glanced at. His immediate successor was a relation of the Earl of Huntly, forced upon the canons by that powerful magnate. 'The canons', says Boece, 'yielding to the evil times, lest they should have to submit to even harsher treatment, unanimously conceded his demands.' Fortunately, Bishop Alexander Gordon died in three years. Then followed one of the most progressive of all Bishops of Aberdeen, Gavin Dunbar (1518–31). He continued Elphinstone's extension to the Cathedral and completed his plan of the College buildings. Near the Cathedral he built a home for poor men, known as Dunbar's Hospital, whose quaint frontage (the house has long since disappeared) is familiar from the illustration in Orem's *Old Aberdeen*. Dunbar erected the black marble tomb over Elphinstone's grave in the College Chapel, and surmounted it with an elaborate jewelled effigy which was lost at the Reformation. His own tomb is in the Cathedral. Bishop Leslie in his *History of Scotland* says of him 'while he was thirteen years bishop, what he gathered of the bishopric, ilk pennie he spendit upon these three — the kirk, the country, and the poor, and put not one farthing to any private use or to the profit of his own'. It is a noble tribute, perhaps implying that other bishops were less scrupulous.

Dunbar's successor, Bishop William Stewart, built a library, which he endowed, and a jewel-house for the college. He also brought to King's his pulpit from the Cathedral, and in the chapel it remains. He was followed in 1546 by the last and worst of the Catholic Bishops of Aberdeen, William Gordon, whose excesses were notorious amongst his contemporaries. He paid no heed to the college, which was saved from complete spiritual collapse by that very remarkable man, Alexander Galloway, rector of Kinkell. He was architectural chief of staff to both Elphinstone and Dunbar, and his accomplishments in that art and its cousin of design entitle him to a position of honour, almost comparable with Barbour's in literature, as a pioneer in Aberdeen. He was an official of the college from 1516, four times Rector of King's, a very sound man of his business as his report on his famous Visitation shows, and a dabbler in science albeit to modern ideas a credulous one. He accompanied Hector Boece on a trip to the Hebrides, and it was Galloway, according to Boece, who on that occasion opened some mussel shells and found in each 'ane perfect shapen fowl' — in other words he discovered that barnacle geese grew from shell-fish.

Galloway in his capacity as Rector conducted a Visitation of the College in 1549. Such was the condition into which the institution was sunk that he recommended no fewer than fifty-one alterations and improvements in the conduct and regulation of the establishment. The finances had to be tightened up, the buildings repaired, the lamp kept burning before the Holy Sacrament, the members of the University had to resume residence in the College, perform their religious duties, and wear their appropriate garb. The students in Theology had to take holy orders. Only Latin was to be spoken in conversation within the College (formerly it was Latin or French), no boys (garsiones) were to be employed as waiters lest they should tempt the members to use the vernacular, no women were to be admitted except to service in the Chapel, and that only by the west or outer door. These suggestions indicate pretty sharply how lax the conduct of Elphinstone's institution had become. In 1529 Bishop Dunbar had granted a charter promulgated in 1531, which increased the number of members of the College to forty-two and altered in some respects the constitution as laid down by Elphinstone.[1] Galloway's reforms of 1549, which were immediately ratified by Bishop Gordon, in several particulars reverted to the spirit if not the letter of Elphinstone's deed.

At that time, on the eve of the Reformation, the college as regards its stone-and-lime existence was on much the same plan as now although, apart from the Chapel and Tower, the actual buildings have changed. The south side of the modern quadrangle was then occupied by Dunbar's buildings — the residential part of the College. It consisted of seventeen or more living-rooms or studies, each with a bed-closet, and named after the planets and other heavenly bodies. The Principal had two rooms, one of which may have been used to house distinguished visitors. Two Arts bursars and one student of Theology were supposed to occupy each suite. The cooking and feeding accommodation was at the southeast corner. Where the Ivy Tower now stands teachers and students dined together. Under the Library projecting from the Chapel, there may have been class-rooms, but the Canonist and the other doctors

1 Elphinstone was engaged in revising his charter at the time of his death, and some or all of the changes effected in the charter of 1529 may have been his, not Dunbar's. One of Dunbar's ordinances of 1531 directed that the procurators of the nations (i.e. the students' representatives) should take part in nominating and electing the principal and also in appointing the canonist, civilist, mediciner and grammarian.

lectured in their manses. Of these we know the site of only one, the Mediciner's, which was originally between the west front of the college and the High Street. On the north, where there is now the lawn in front of the Elphinstone Hall, there was the college graveyard.[1]

1   The discovery on the north side of the quadrangle in 1937 of the old well is an interesting reminder of the collegiate character of the original institution.

Order Out of Chaos. 1560-1745

The two centuries that followed the Reformation were the most turbulent in Aberdeen's history. During no single decade of the period could an Aberdonian count on living other than dangerously, for although several decades did elapse without serious incident, the shadow of civil war always impended over the town. The Reformation itself might have been expected to produce a long and arduous conflict, but actually its direct military consequences were soon disposed of. The Catholic Church had, however, while its supremacy was unchallenged, at least the one virtue of elevating religion above the plane of physical strife. Protestantism, essentially an assertion of man's right to think for himself, naturally did not tend to preserve religious homogeneity or concord within itself.

Scotland began the Reformation by selecting the most extreme form of Protestantism, which embodied the largest possible measure of freedom to the individual conscience and imposed the heaviest load of responsibility within the church upon the individual member. Such a system, whether of Church or of State government, represented then a revolutionary experiment in democracy; indeed, even today the Presbyterian order is further advanced in democratic practice than anything in political procedure. The pace, accordingly, soon proved too hot for many who were otherwise quite content to accept the Reformation in principle.

The first reaction to the Reformation was that of those who preferred to remain Papists. Their natural leaders, in the absence of the Sovereign who was promptly put out of harm's way by the Reformers, were found among the great lords. The North-East was the principal stronghold of the Roman Church, and for the first thirty years of the Reformation — from the Battle of Corrichie to the curious affair of the 'Spanish Blanks' — we have Aberdeen at the very centre of civil conflagration. Foiled in their attempt to restore the old religion, the Popish lords naturally threw their weight in with the prelatic party within the Church of Scotland who were far more likely to tolerate their presence than the

Presbyterians. As the King also had allied himself with this party, on the 'No bishop, no King' principle, the Popish lords and their descendants developed into the staunchest supporters of the monarchy.

Three decades passed in the putting down of the pretensions of these Catholic lords. Then came the Union of the Crowns, with its consequent enormous strengthening of the King's authority over Scotland, and the first three decades of the seventeenth century were spent in consolidating that authority, mainly by extending civil control over the Kirk through the medium of the episcopate. When Charles overreached himself, the Civil Wars began. In Scotland, however, they were religious rather than political, and the parliamentary issue was little more than an irrelevance.

In the history-making of those days Aberdeen played an important part. Indeed for a town so far north of the centre of things its experiences were remarkably direct and positive. It was less influenced by the early stages of the sectarian strife which developed when the young King James decided that Presbyterianism was too democratic to be a fit setting for a monarchy, and successfully employed his not inconsiderable skill at intrigue to secure the introduction of Episcopacy temporarily in 1584 and on what promised to be a permanent footing in 1610. Probably because its own last Roman Catholic Bishop had continued to function for nearly twenty years after the Reformation, Aberdeen was less disposed to cavil at retention of a title and an office that it had never been without during its recorded existence.

But this easy acquiescence in the episcopal compromise was paid for by Aberdeen in blood and tears and treasure from the year of the signing of the National Covenant in 1638 until the defeat of Charles II at Worcester in 1652. The Civil Wars were much more bitterly fought in Scotland than in England, and no Scottish town was so often and so deeply ravaged as Aberdeen. The Great Civil War began in Aberdeenshire, and with the exception of a respite from 1642 to 1644, and again from 1646 to 1650, Aberdeen was under the harrow of Royalist or Covenanter or Cromwellian Independent for all those years, and when in 1660 the Restoration came there is evidence enough that the memory of rule by Montrose, whether as a soldier of the Covenant or paladin of the Crown, of Aboyne and Burleigh, Argyll and Kinghorn, Gordon and Ancrum and all the other garrison commanders and conquering soldiers it had known, had quenched the martial ardour of its citizens for a season.

But the convulsions of the Killing Time that shook the South-west of Scotland from 1666 until the Revolution of 1688 left Aberdeen undisturbed, and although Dundee's rebellion of 1689–90 came nearer to its gates, nothing at all resembling the suffering of the Civil Wars was visited upon the city. During those years the principal impression produced upon Aberdeen by outside events and conditions was that of commercial frustration. The Navigation Acts of Cromwell, continued under the Restoration and after the Revolution, bore as hard upon Scotland in the seventeenth century as the ignorance and indifference of the bureaucracy of Whitehall in the twentieth. Aberdeen then, however, suffered more in proportion than now, for it was the chief exporting community in the Kingdom.

The Union of the Parliaments in 1707 helped to undo the evils of the Union of the Crowns in 1603, and once the Jacobite risings of 1715, 1719 and 1745 had been suppressed, the application of scientific discovery to industrial development for many generations made amends for the loss of national independence. But as in the Civil Wars, Aberdeen had to endure more than most Scottish burghs in the two major attempts of the Stewarts to win back their own again. In all the history of the city, indeed, no fact is more striking than the blossoming of the community in every branch of its existence as soon as the insurgent clans and conscripts were scattered at Culloden. Whatever may have been the shortcomings of Cumberland and his lieutenants, as far as Aberdeen is concerned their misdemeanours were a small price to pay for the period of prosperity that immediately followed.

During the years of turmoil the aspect of Aberdeen had gradually altered. It was not so much a physical change, although between 1600 and 1750 the wooden houses gave place to houses of stone, and single-storey dwellings were supplanted by buildings of several floors; but the boundaries were scarcely enlarged; the streets remained much the same, and a baillie of 1530 revisiting his old haunts in the Bon-Accord of 1740, would have had no difficulty in finding his way about. The change was social and psychological rather than physical. In 1560 Aberdeen was still a medieval city state, a community to all intents and purposes independent; static, picturesque, and looking rather to its past than forward. By 1746 Aberdeen was an integral part of the United Kingdom, taught by adversity to remember that it no longer belonged to itself and that it must always bow in major issues to a stronger will outside its own small political economy.

Some of the change was due to its own efforts. It had always had a flair for commerce, being well-situated in a productive hinterland and

convenient for overseas or coastal trading. But too many of its adventurous sons had gone abroad as students, soldiers, or merchants for the
community to remain unaffected by new ideas. Aberdeen's export of
brains had begun before the Reformation, but the liberation of spirit
which the Reformation effected tremendously increased the traffic.
In the beginning of the seventeenth century no city of the Old World
was better or more favourably known throughout Europe than Aberdeen. There was hardly a Continental university of note that had not
an Aberdonian professor. The seaports of the Baltic and of the Low
Countries swarmed with its sailors and traders. Germany, Poland,
France and Holland were the happy hunting-grounds of its martial boys.

Never before had Aberdeen occupied so eminent a position in
international renown. Never since has it achieved the same international
significance. For its success as a breeder of cosmopolites had the effect
of diluting its own aggressive native characteristics. This unexpected
result, however, was not apparent during the particular period under
review. The city had still enough of intellectual resources to supply
its own needs and to keep its exports of brain at a high level. And its
contacts abroad gave its rulers hints and ideas. They began to experiment in industry. They tried municipal enterprise and found it wanting.
They tried a municipal encouragement of private enterprise and found
that this was a policy that paid. Possessed of a toun's college and a
grammar school and a song school, they encouraged all manner of
educational undertakings, and they began to consider the advisability
of extending the community's services to the community. They had a
town's printer, whose ways they minded very carefully. They kept
an eye upon 'fancy religions'. On the other hand, the failure of their
industrial House of Correction project coupled no doubt with the
passing of the plague, caused the Town Council to leave public health
in the main to public-spirited private individuals.

A certain amount of regulation affecting the community's convenience and decency there was, and towards the end of this period we
find it growing. There was some control of the town's mills to secure
the food supply; there was more active and gradually increasing interest in the town's water supply; and more attention was given to
sanitation and cleanliness. But upon private individuals devolved
the task of instituting the infirmary, and the numerous private bequests to schools and universities and the founding of Robert Gordon's
Hospital reveal that while the individual was prepared to be generous
to the community whenever he could, the community still felt that

its responsibilities towards the individual were few. The Council, like any prince or baron of the Middle Ages, was happy to reward those who, like Dominie Wedderburn and Parson Gordon and Printer Forbes, deserved well of the town, and initiative on the part of the citizens in any legitimate enterprise was encouraged. But the time had not yet come when men had thought so much that it was no longer possible to think logically and originally at the same time; and so development was very gradual and showed no serious departure from the tradition of centuries.

Because of its Episcopalian leanings, Aberdeen had a peaceful time between the Restoration and the Revolution of 1689. The exceeding rigours of the Covenanters before the arrival of Cromwell had alienated the sympathies of many of the Presbyterian nobles, who were not in the habit of being treated as 'God's sillie vassals'. They accordingly veered away and eventually slipped into the ranks of the Episcopalians. The remarks of George, the fifth Earl Marischal, or of his successor William who held Aberdeen for the Covenant, upon the immuring of the Covenanting prisoners in the Whigs' vault at Dunnottar would have been illuminating. But the Revolution and the accession of William III made the return of Presbyterianism inevitable. Had it not done so, there would have been no Jacobite Rebellions, which were just as much a phase of the religious struggle as the Bishops' Wars had been. The issue was probably never in doubt, however strongly sentiment may advance the legend of Jacobite virtue. It is profoundly significant that between 1638 and 1745 Aberdeen changed over from Episcopalian to Presbyterian: and the community that had defied the Covenant for the love of Charles was ready to welcome even such a bounder as the Duke of Cumberland because he was its liberator from the Jacobites.

While, therefore, religion played a great, though dwindling, part in Aberdeen's as in Scotland's development during those two centuries, other forces were at work which are today much more familiar to us. The opening up of Aberdeen's harbour by David Anderson in 1612, and the small experiments in the establishment of corporate industrial concerns during the seventeenth century were the tokens of a new form of productive endeavour.

On the whole, however, this phase of Aberdeen's history, from the Reformation to the end of the Jacobite Rebellions, is dominated by religion. Reformation and Renaissance both made themselves felt in a culture which was assured where it was classical and was tentative on its more speculative side. Both were strengthened, the one by the treasures made available by the Renaissance, which gave us the fine Latinity of Arthur Johnston and the abundant romantic genius of Sir Thomas Urquhart, the other by the independence and individualism incalculated by the Reformation, and we have testimony to its liberating force in the genius of the Gregories. It was an age that was occupied by the creation of order out of chaos.

Part 3

Trials of a Presbyterian Revolution

CHAPTER ONE

The Reformation

The Reformation no more took Aberdeen by surprise than it did the rest of Scotland. For many years this, the greatest of the revolutions in European history, simmered in men's minds and bubbled up in national politics. Scotland was slow to change. Germany, England, and the Low Countries had all gone over, in whole or in part, to one of the several forms of the new religion before Protestantism was established in Scotland. In the actual event, Scotland adopted the most uncompromising, the most logical, and the most democratic of all the Reformed creeds. Calvinism suited the Scottish temperament as Lutheranism with its less emphatic insistence on the individual's freedom of judgment could never have done; and a variant of the Anglican style, which for long disputed with Presbyterianism for the supremacy, was eventually by its relegation to a subordinate position in public opinion proved to be lacking in the qualities that attract the Scot.

Compared with districts like Fife, Angus and Perth, where passions ran high at the time of the overthrow of Popery, Aberdeen escaped lightly as regards its sacred fabrics and their furniture. When the religious revolution was over, there still remained in the North-East a larger residue of Catholics, including many influential individuals like the Earls of Huntly and Errol, the Principal of King's College, and the (almost) hereditary Provost of Aberdeen, Menzies of Pitfodels, than in most areas of Scotland. In addition, even the Aberdonians inclined to Protestantism had an inherent objection to the destroying of good property, especially when it was theirs or likely to revert to them. Thus many of the principal monuments of the Roman Catholic regime were preserved in Aberdeen into the era of the Reformed Church.

Kennedy seems to be responsible for the tradition that the first sign in Aberdeen of the coming religious revolution was the assertion of his professional independence of the Church of Rome by the Master of the Grammar School, John Marshall. That was in 1521, and actually just before Martin Luther nailed his thesis to the church door in

Wittenberg. But the incident is capable of the interpretation that Marshall was simply declaring his preference for the Town Council rather than the Bishop as his superior, and endeavouring as best he could to escape from the uncomfortable necessity of having to choose publicly between two employers who could seriously influence his future. Aberdeen could not well escape contact with the new faith, for its trade with the Baltic and the Low Countries was bound to result in the importing of opinions as well as of goods. This fact was fully realised, and in 1525 an Act made it unlawful for a ship to bring any Lutheran books into Scotland, which was described as 'clene of all sic filth and vice'.

Had the princes and clergy of the Church of Scotland been 'clene of all filth and vice', the Reformers might have found the Scottish nation unfruitful soil for their tenets. But the Church had waxed rich, its ministers too sure of their own immunity from immediate retribution to be as upright as public men should be, and they had overlooked the fact that Scotland had now three universities. The higher education would not predispose men to oppose the Church because it was the Roman Church, but it did make such men aware that a corrupt clerical administration was bound to involve the nation sooner or later in similar disorders. As regards men of education there was, of course, the further fact that the Church of Rome discouraged the adventurous mind as much as a twentieth-century Government Department dislikes private initiative.

The contrast between doctrine and practice was apt to be striking at times. In 1524 the Council had to apprise even so good a Bishop as Gavin Dunbar that 'their Kirk had stood lang desolate of divine service' — as if he were not aware of what was happening within a mile of his palace. It seems chaplains of St. Nicholas, having nothing else to do, were squabbling among themselves, and duties were neglected. The bishop tried without success to improve matters, and the baillies had to discharge all the clerks over whom they had jurisdiction. At the same time the bishop communicated to the King information that there were strangers within the diocese of Aberdeen in possession of heretical literature; and the King passed on the message to Aberdeen with orders to seek out the heretics and confiscate and dispatch their goods to Edinburgh. James was understood not to be blind to the errors of the church, and the penalties he suggests for heresy are not severe.

For the next twenty years Aberdeen was untouched by the religious convulsions that were tormenting Scotland farther south. Not until

1543 do we get another memorable item of news. James V had died, and the Earl of Arran, the Regent, a man of liberal views, had permitted the use of the Scriptures in the vernacular. Two friars with reforming opinions were appointed to preach and teach 'the true word of God' in St. Nicholas Church. The Church, however, was still too strong. Arran had to recant, and in 1544 we find two substantial citizens, Thomas Branch and Thomas Cussing, paying for their hatred of idolatry. At the instance of the Earl of Huntly, they were thrown into the tolbooth for hanging the image of St. Francis. As to Cussing's subsequent career there is no information, but Branch died in 1574 and was buried in St. Nicholas Kirk: 'the very image of honesty', said his epitaph.

Huntly now became Provost. Himself Hereditary Baillie of the diocese, as well as Lieutenant of the North, he had secured the election of his brother as Bishop. His power throughout the area was therefore absolute. No emissary of the Reformed doctrines could enter easily, and if he succeeded in entering, his hopes of survival for even a short time were remote. The Reformation did not reach Aberdeen until the rest of Scotland was controlled by the Reformers. Knox returned to Scotland early in May 1559. That summer, aware no doubt of the fate of Church property in Perth and St. Andrews, the chaplains of St. Nicholas delivered the silver work and ornaments of the church to the magistrates for safety.

Six months passed and nothing happened. Then on 30 December, Provost Menzies, himself a staunch Catholic, informed an assembly of the burgesses that certain men from Angus and Mearns 'are to be in this town this present day to destroy and cast down kirks and religious places thereof, under colour and pretence of godlie reformation'. Either on that day or within a week the storm broke. It proved to be short and not particularly sharp. The Angus and Mearns men, on crossing the Denburn, would have made for St. Nicholas Church, the most prominent and patently ecclesiastical piece of architecture in sight. They attempted, no doubt finding the interior bare of loot, to strip or tear down the spire, but the citizens interposed to protect the town's church, which they regarded as their property.

Foiled at the church, the invaders spread over the town on 4 January 1560, led by inhabitants who knew their way about and had an inkling of the relative riches of the several orders of friars. They despoiled and demolished the monasteries of the Black Friars on the Schoolhill, the White Friars in the Green and the Trinity Friars a little to the south-east. A monk perished in the flames that devoured the old palace of William the Lion. The iconoclasts next bethought themselves of the Cathedral and King's College. On their way thither, they stopped in the Broadgate to pillage Grey Friars' church, but had to break off while they were stripping the roof on account of the opposition of the citizens. The Council Register says the magistrates interfered 'to preserve the said timber, slates, and stones, for the public works of the town, and specially for the furtherance of God's glory and his true word and preachers thereof'. The mob attempted to rush King's College, but the Principal had removed the valuables to safety and he defied the despoilers. They, therefore, continued along the Chanonry to the Cathedral. Huntly had carried away the precious furnishings and plate, so the baffled visitors fell foul of the building, wrecked the chancel, tore the lead off the roof and cut down the bells. The lead and bells were shipped to Holland, but the boat — by the judgment of God, according to the Catholics — sank off Girdleness.

That was the rough-and-tumble part of Aberdeen's Reformation. There was no more looting — except by landowners, merchants and the Council; the town's people saw to that. Joseph Robertson, Aberdeen's most erudite historian, avers that many of the ornaments were in existence a hundred years later. The fate of at least part of the Cathedral plate and ornaments that Huntly took away for safety to Huntly Castle was curious. After the battle of Corrichie in 1662, when the stronghold of Strathbogie was emptied by the Earl of Moray's orders of all its valuables, some of the ornaments and hangings found their way to Kirk o'Field, where they decorated the hall until Darnley's death. Those furnishings of St. Nicholas Church preserved by the town deserve a paragraph to themselves. Much that was lost in the flames or the sea or the confusion was of trivial value. Of nothing rich and gaudy is the proverb 'all that glisters is not gold', so true as of church ornaments. Nor need we deplore a breach in the continuity of learning or a loss of books or knowledge. The friars were not learned. King's College was at almost its lowest intellectual level. The library of one monastery contained but thirty volumes. The dispossessed brethren were scattered but not maltreated. Some took service in wealthy families of Catholic persuasion. In 1576 the death is recorded of a servant of Provost Menzies 'sometime ane quhit freir in Aberdene'. Within a fortnight of the entry of the Reforming rabble, the Council had decided to pull down the fabrics of the monasteries, use the materials for public works, and sell the silver and brass and ornaments of St. Nicholas Church for the Common Good. Soon the community bound itself to defend the liberties of the realm, and dispatched forty men for the service of the Congregation, as the Reformers' party was called.

On 6 January 1561 the citizens of Aberdeen, for the second time within a year and a week, were spectators of a unique event in their history. On that day 'the haill toun being lauchfully warned' gathered to 'hear and see the silver wark, brazen wark, cups, and ornaments of their parish church roupit'. Patrick Menzies of Pitfodels, the Provost, bought the lot. He gave £142 Scots for the 'kuppis' (cups, chalices, etc.), and silver fetched 21s. the ounce, brass 16s. the stone, the whole amounting to £540 'money of Scotland', or about £45 sterling. The silver work thus sold was only a fraction of the full inventory of the church's effects before the Reformation. It is surmised that amongst those who made away with its effects were its own servants, no doubt with the highest motives at the time. Alexander Anderson, Principal of King's College, is accused to having 'sold the books, ornaments and other furniture belonging to the College', but he was not so bad as all that. Provost Menzies and his associates had dissented from the decision to hold a roup. The Provost, however, did not resign office, any more than he changed his religion. But a month later we find him riding to Edinburgh to arrange about the taking over of the friars' crofts by the town. The money he paid for the St. Nicholas plenishing was applied to the repair of the harbour, the upkeep of the Bridge of Don, and the maintenance of the town's artillery and defences.

CHAPTER TWO

The Church Reformed

The Reformation in Aberdeen involved no victimisation by the Reformers, and in the town itself no seditious plotting by the remnant of the old faith for a return to Popery. The picture that presents itself, indeed, is one that might confound those whose conception of the Reformation is based upon highly coloured legends of the religious revolution. In Angus, Fife and Perth there were tumults and destructive orgies. In Aberdeen the whole disturbance was over within one week, perhaps even one day. There was one casualty, a single monk accidentally cremated. Three monasteries were levelled, of which one at least was better out of sight. Spoliation was limited, and the friends of Rome probably pocketed as much as the other side. Even the Roman Bishop kept his job. The canons of the church handed over the revenues of their altarages to the town and received the life-rent of them for their complaisance. The salvage of the destroyed monasteries came in handy for burgh repairs and construction. 'There never was a better bargain driven.'

Certain aspects of the bargain are almost too good to be true. Not only was William Gordon recognised as Bishop until his death in 1577, but he had control of Church property and dealt in it as he pleased. Even more remarkable, that very pronounced Calvinist, Walter Cullen, Reader of Aberdeen in 1570, accepted the post of Vicar of Aberdeen at the hands of the Catholic Bishop, as if it were the most natural thing in the world: 'The said Maister Walter Gordone demitted the said vicarage, in my Lord of Aberdenis hand, by ane ryng; and thairefeter, the said lord geyf the said Walter Cullen collacioun, be the said ryng on his fynger, in Alexander Chalmeris, youngeris, howise.' Tolerance could hardly go further, unless in the case of Sir Thomas Menzies, the Provost, who was an elder of the Kirk without forswearing the faith of his family in which he was brought up.

Fanaticism in religion was in Aberdeen of late growth, when Episcopalian and Presbyterian in the seventeenth century regarded one another with far greater venom than ever poisoned the relationship of Catholic and Reformer in the Aberdeen of the sixteenth century. No Reformed

Bishop of Aberdeen was appointed until after Gordon's death. Three months later, 'Maister David Cunyngayme, sone to the lord of Cunyngaymeheid, was consicratt biscoip of Abirden in the said Kirk (St. Nicholas) be Maister Patrick Constance, biscoip of Sanctandrowse, quha maid the sermond. Maister John Craig, minister of Aberden, Maister Andro Strayquhan, minister of   ,[1] collatraris, and that in presense of the haill congregatioune of Aberden, with oderis of the cuntre present for the tyme.' This description of Bishop Cunningham's 'consecration' is the only notice extant of the Scottish ceremony introduced in 1572 and superseded in 1606 by the Ordinal then in use in the Church of England. Thanks to Walter Cullen, we have it, brief though it is.

Aberdeen's first minister of the 'true faith' was Mr. Adam Herriot, who was appointed to the charge of Aberdeen by the Reformed Congregation in 1560. Herriot, who was born in 1514, had been a canon regular in the order of St. Augustine at St. Andrews. Early in his career he had begun to entertain certain doctrinal doubts, but being a man of deep learning and integrity of mind, he did not reach a decision until 1559, when providentially on the very eve of the Reformation he publicly bore witness to his conversion. The Congregation, considering that Aberdeen had a strong residuum of Catholics, felt that Herriot, 'learned in scholastick divinity, and for his moderation', would be well fitted 'to reclaim men from their errors'.

From the first, Aberdeen took to him. When he arrived, the citizens presented him with a doublet, bonnet and hose, all of black — an even more substantial 'propine' than the customary modern gown. The suit was renewed annually, he got £10 in cash to cover house-rent and £30 to purchase other necessaries, all in addition to his stipend of £200 from the revenues of the town. At no time, however, was the Council of Aberdeen more careful than in the enlightenment of the Reformation. In 1562 the Council minuted that the annual sum of 300 merks should no longer be paid to the minister out of the Common Good, as his stipend ought to be sustained out of the monies received by the bishop from the dues to the church. Whether the Catholic bishop thereafter found the Protestant minister's stipend we are not informed.

In 1564 John Knox paid his only visit to Aberdeen. He remained in the town for six weeks, but that is all we know of his stay.

Of the first Protestant staff at King's College James Lawson, the sub-principal, is outstanding. He founded Edinburgh's High School,

1   Blank in the original.

he introduced the study of Hebrew at King's; and when, having been chosen by Knox as his pastoral successor, he died in Edinburgh, 500 mourners composed his cortege. Lawson, in addition to his college functions, was appointed minister of St. Machar, with a stipend of £100 — the first of a distinguished list. Before Lawson's pastorate, the charge had been filled by John Erskine, an 'exhorter'. It would seem that Lawson undertook some work on behalf of Herriot, whose health was failing. Even that assistance was insufficient and in 1570 Walter Cullen was appointed Reader. In 1573 Herriot resigned. In 1574 he died, 'greatly beloved of the citizens for his humane and courteous conversation, and of the poorer sort much lamented, to whom he was in his life very beneficial'. His elegy was composed, in Latin, by the celebrated Aberdeen humanist — not the only one of the name — John Johnstone, Andrew Melville's friend, Professor of Theology at St. Andrews. Johnstone, whose father Robert was a merchant and burgess of the town, was the founder of a bursary in Marischal College.

John Craig succeeded Herriot. He had been a wanderer over the face of Europe for his faith. Born in 1512, a product of St. Andrews University, he joined the Dominicans but left for England in 1537 after a spell in prison on suspicion of heresy. From England he crossed to France, from France to Italy, where he entered the Dominican Monastery at Bologna. In the library he found the *Institutions* of Calvin, which converted him to the Protestant faith. He was seized, taken to Rome, cast into a dungeon, and finally condemned to the stake. The day before he was to become a martyr, Pope Paul IV died, and in conformity with custom, the prisons were opened. Craig escaped; after adventures that recall the experiences of the Hebrew prophets, he reached Vienna. There the Emperor Maximilian protected him, and when the long arm of the Pope was stretched out after him, gave him a safe conduct through Germany.

In 1560 Craig found himself in Scotland again, so much a stranger that he had forgotten his native idiom and had to converse in Latin until it came back to him. In 1563 he was appointed Knox's colleague, in 1571 he was sent to Montrose, and in 1573 he was translated to Aberdeen. But he did not stay long. In 1579 he left for Edinburgh, having been selected as King James VI's own minister.[1] Craig's

---

1 Walter Cullen says he 'departtit, with his wyfe and barnis and haill hoissell, owit of the said burght, and left his floik onprowyditt of ane minister to be preachour to the Kingis grace, as he allegit' — a sentence which seems to embody a certain lack of amiability.

influence over the boy King may have been good or bad; the product of it was certainly nothing much to boast of. Few Scottish monarchs left a bigger legacy of misfortune to their subjects and their subjects' posterity. During the ascendancy of the subtle and unscrupulous Esmé Stewart, Lord of Aubigny and Earl of Lennox, Craig compiled a document which had much to do with the subsequent religious disorder in the Kingdom, the Negative Confession of 1580, upon which it is unnecessary for a history of Aberdeen to expatiate.[1] Craig died in Edinburgh at the end of 1600.

On the ecclesiastical side Aberdeen was less inconvenienced than the rest of the nation by the innovations of the Regent Earl Morton, although in other respects Morton proved himself the reverse of a friend to the town. In an age when uprightness among the rulers of Scotland was conspicuous by its absence, and when cruelty and rapacity flourished amidst political and religious turmoil, Morton's malignant countenance lowers in the company of his none too comely contemporaries. He was not alone in his ambition to press forward the dynastic union of Scotland and England; such a merger was in any case inevitable. His opinion that identity of ecclesiastical government in the two countries would promote that union had some support in logic if not in national psychology. But there is little doubt that this introduction of episcopacy was due to his desire to line his own pockets, and there is no doubt that it was obnoxious to the people of Scotland, as their two great religious leaders, Knox and Andrew Melville, testified by their deeds and declarations. For nearly ten years, however, the new dispensation in the church did not affect Aberdeen, where the Catholic bishop still flourished.

When Craig departed, Alexander Arbuthnot, who was the first Protestant Principal of King's College, appears to have officiated as *locum tenens* if not as actual minister[2] until 1582, when Peter Blackburn was appointed. Blackburn had been associated with the great Andrew

---

1   Hill Burton, Hume Brown, Andrew Lang and Sanford Terry hardly do more than mention the Negative Confession. A full analysis of it will be found in Professor G. D. Henderson's *Scots Confession, 1560*.
2   Kennedy calls David Cunningham, the first Protestant bishop, 'Minister of St. Nicholas Church'. Rait, *The Universities of Aberdeen*, quotes from the report of the General Assembly of 1581, 'Maister Alexander Arbuthnot transportit to the ministries of Aberdeen, and ordanit to demitt the principalitie of the college in favour of Nicoll Dalgleish'. Cullen, who must have known, says Arbuthnot was the minister. When the Church was divided in two Cunningham certainly officiated in the nave, now the West Kirk. Spottiswood calls Cunningham 'a grave wise and learned man'.

Melville as a professor in Glasgow and James Melville, Andrew's nephew, and Wodrow both speak highly of him; but Calderwood accuses him of meanness: 'he was said to be ever mindful of a purse and five hundred marks in it, which he keped in his bosome, than anything else.' Blackburn succeeded Cunningham as bishop and died in 1616. His colleague at St. Nicholas was Robert Howie, first Principal of Marischal College, who became Principal of St. Mary's College, St. Andrews, a few years later.

In 1596 the magistrates decided it was time to make a big structural change in the parish church. For some time two congregations had worshipped in it, one in the nave and one in the choir. They had had to stand during the long service, and a leaky roof did not add to their comfort. While the religious upheaveal was on, some lead from the roof had been stolen. At another time a great gale tore off strips of it; and we constantly read of divots being applied to hold the place water-tight. But in 1596 the Council 'ordanit the haile carvit tymmerwark betwixt the pilleris in the queir to be removit and placit convenientlie quhair the same salbe thocht meit to be placit to the effect that ane stane wall may be biggit betwixt the said queir and the bodie of the kirk that the said queir may be maid ane preiching kirk for preiching of the word of god and ministratioun of the sacramentis'. Thus did the West Kirk, the nave, then known as the Auld Kirk, and the East Kirk or choir, then called the New Kirk, attain to separate existence. For some time the bishop ministered in the Auld and Blackburn in the New Kirk. The Auld Kirk catered for the Green and Crookit Quarters, the New for the Even and Futty Quarters.

A curious light is thrown upon the conditions of existence in those days by an edict of the Town Council of 12 July 1595 to the effect that 'thair was wrang dane the nicht immediatelie bygane, in erecting and bigging up of ane little faill house on the north syd of the kirk yard, under silence of nicht, quhilk obefoir was demolischit by virtew of ane act and ordinance of consale' and that the house should therefore be 'cassin doun'. The kirkyard even at that time was inconveniently full of dead, without adding tenements for the living; in fact, the constant unearthing of human remains was becoming somewhat of a scandal.

One remarkable superstition became popular at the Reformation. While so many primitive beliefs and practices were discarded, it is strange that one of the most savage of all, credulity in witchcraft, should have sprung into prominence. In the last decade of the sixteenth century, fanned by the ardent approbation of King Jaimie himself, the fires that consumed the poor wretches found guilty of witchcraft burned more furiously than those that a generation before had released the Protestant martyrs at the stake. Aberdeen suffered from an epidemic of witch-doctoring for a few years from 1594. Several miserable women were burned in that year, but in 1596–7 no fewer than twenty-four women and two men died under or after the most cruel torture. Confined in the steeple or basement of the kirk, branded and 'brodit' (prodded with sharp stakes) and starved, two women died before they expiated their offence. The others were burned, and their funeral pyres apparently pleased the good people. Such things were all in the day's work, as this entry in the Council Register of 21 September 1597 shows: 'The quhilk day, the prowest, baillies and counsell, considering that William Dun, dean of gild, hes deligentlie and cairfillie dischargit him of hes office of deanrie of gild, and hes painfullie travellit (laboured) theirin to the advancing of the commoun gude, and besyddes this, hes extraordinarlie takin panis on the birning of the gryt number of witches brint this yeir, and in the four pirrattis, and bigging of the port on the brig of Dee, reparing of the Greyfreris kirk and stepill thairof, and thairby hes ben abstractit fra hes tred of merchandice continewallie ... theirfoir in recompence of hes extraordinarie panis and in satisfactioun thcirof (not to induce any preparative to deanes of gild to crave a recompance heirefter) but to incurage utheris to travell als diligentlie in the discharge of their office, grantit and assignit to him the soume of fourtie-sevin pundis thrie s. four d. awand be him of the rest of his compt. of the unlawis (fines) of the persons convict for slaying of blakfische (kelts), and dischargit him theirof be thir presentis for ever.' Others profited by similar good works. The town's common servant got 40 marks for 'awayting on the witches' and Thomas Mollysoun, the common town clerk, £40 for his 'pains and labours' in the whole matter.

CHAPTER THREE

The First Religious Wars

Once the change of religion had been accomplished, Aberdeen might well have prayed to be rid of its friends. The citizens themselves, except for a small minority, settled down to a regime of toleration which did more credit to their human sympathies than to their enthusiasm for either the old faith or the new. But in the hinterland there was no question of live and let live. Huntly the resplendent failed to gauge the trend of the times, and because of him, for nearly forty years the town was doomed to be the cockpit of contending factions.

It began as soon as it was known that Mary Queen of Scots intended to return to Scotland. While Lord James Stewart, James V's natural son, acted as the strong arm of the Reformers, the Catholics looked to Huntly as their champion. Huntly sent an emissary to France to inform Mary that if she put in at Aberdeen he would have 20,000 men awaiting her with whom she could bring the rest of the kingdom back to the old religion. Mary ignored Huntly's suggestion for the time and went to Edinburgh. But Huntly's offer to her became known, and from that time Stewart, Argyll, Athole and other Protestant nobles formed a band against him. Lord James Stewart, by virtue of his marriage with a daughter of the Earl Marischal, aspired to be an influence in the North. Mary gave him the Earldom of Mar, and soon after made him the Earl of Moray, which put him in possession of territory on Huntly's own doorstep.

We may imagine, therefore, that it was not solely a question of a trip to the north that moved Lord James, now Moray, to persuade the Queen to make a progress in the area of his new dignities. Mary arrived in Aberdeen in August 1562 along with the great Protestant lords, Moray and Morton and Maitland of Lethington — the last said to be the only statesman of his time, and known by compatriots who could not get their tongues round Machiavelli as Michael Wylie, which was neat. With them was a guard of Lothian spearmen. She was heartily welcomed by the town, and Provost Menzies presented her with a propine of 2,000 marks. Huntly, out of favour, lay close in

Strathbogie, but his countess did her duty at Old Aberdeen, where the Queen was residing with the Gordon bishop. Lady Huntly, however, failed to persuade the Queen to visit Huntly Castle. The royal retinue trotted north, by-passing the castle by a few miles to Inverness. Sir John Gordon, ordered to come in, refused. Directed to hand over the castles of Findlater and Auchindoun, he saw to it that the gates remained shut, although his more politic father forwarded the keys to the Queen. The tacit rebellion of the son involved the father. Huntly was summoned to Aberdeen to meet the Queen on her return journey. When he failed to arrive, Moray had him denounced as a rebel and called upon the Protestant families of Angus and the Mearns to help enforce the royal mandate.

Huntly with about a thousand men was at the Loch of Skene on his way to Aberdeen when he heard of the muster against him. He retreated into the amphitheatre of the Hill of Fare, and there, by the side of the Corrichie burn, Moray with a superior force came upon him. The charging Gordons flung themselves in vain upon the disciplined spearmen of the Lothians. Huntly, with his sons Sir John and Adam of Auchindoun, were among the prisoners, and apparently Huntly died of apoplexy in the excitement of the capture. The royal troops returned to Aberdeen in triumph. The Queen may have been a spectator of the skirmish, although 'the Queen's chair' pointed out as her vantage point has only legend to associate it with her presence. On arrival in the town the principal prisoners were summarily tried and convicted and several of them hanged. Sir John Gordon was sentenced to be beheaded, and was dispatched in the Castlegate. Tradition, which loves to lave its hands in blood, avers that Sir John was the Queen's lover, that Moray forced her — 'not without tears', says one writer — to witness his execution from the window of the Earl Marischal's house, and that the headsman's axe was blunt. There is no historical warrant for any part of this romantic embroidery, but even if the Queen saw both battle and execution, there was in those days nothing extraordinary in it. Lord Gordon, heir to the earldom, was warded in Dunbar Castle until 1565, and when in the following year the Queen broke with Moray he was appointed Chancellor of the kingdom. He remained loyal to Mary while she was in Lochleven Castle and later, and so he, like his father, found himself on the wrong side of the wall when Moray was able to assume the office of regent.

Once the Regency was established the Gordons began to harry the lands of the Protestants in the north, but desisted on an agreement being reached between Huntly and Moray, whereupon Aberdeen was made the centre for the reception of those who came in to answer for their offences against authority. Moray himself sat to receive them in the tolbooth and assessed the compensation that was to buy them escape from punishment. Never, it was said, had 'such mean gentlemen paid out such great sums of money'. The pacification did not last long. On the assassination of the Regent in 1570, Mary from her English prison sent Huntly her commission as Lieutenant-Governor of Scotland, and he issued a call to arms from Aberdeen. His military effort was unsuccessful. Meanwhile an attempt to bring to an end the ancient feud between the Gordons and the Forbeses had been made by means of a marriage between the Master of Forbes and Huntly's sister. But the union was a failure, both sides were more than ever embittered, and after a running fight at Tullyangus in the Correen hills above Alford, at which Black Arthur, the great champion of the Forbeses, was slain, the Master of Forbes went south to look for allies. While he was away, the troops of Sir Adam Gordon of Auchindoun, the victor of Tullyangus, burned down Corgarff Castle, with the wife of Forbes of Towie, its tacksman, and over a score of women, children and servants. This dreadful deed, conspicuous even in that dark age, has been for ever held up to reprobation in the great ballad of 'Captain Car, or Edom o' Gordon'.

The Master of Forbes in the south won the support of the new Regent the Earl of Mar, and with his own and some men of the Mearns advanced northwards to Aberdeen. The town was occupied by Adam Gordon, who drew up his Badenoch archers and spearmen across the south road beyond the Crabstane — about where the Hardgate crosses Bonaccord Terrace — posting an ambush of musketeers at the dip now known as Union Glen. The Forbes force manfully fell upon the Gordons, but were caught in the flank by the musketeers, and after the battle had been 'cruelly fochten for the space of an hour', they withdrew, leaving sixty dead and their leader a prisoner. They were used with such consideration by Sir Adam that the atrocity of Corgarff falls out of character with his methods, and may therefore have been due, as some versions of the ballad allege, to his man-at-arms Captain Kerr or Car. The Battle of the Crabstane was fought on 20 November 1571. For eighteen months thereafter Aberdeen was the base of Huntly's operations in favour of his imprisoned Queen, but in the beginning of 1573 he made his peace with the third of the Reformation Regents, the Earl of Morton. Sir Adam, who seems to have been something of a fire-eater, left for France. Even there he only narrowly escaped falling a victim to the vengeance of his enemies, for the Forbeses made a daring attempt to assassinate him in Paris.

Meanwhile it was a sign of the times that the Aberdeen Council was veering from its reliance upon Huntly to closer relations with the Earl Marischal. To his palace-stronghold at Dunnottar the town's title-deeds were sent for safety in 1572, and a little later Huntly was given 600 merks to evacuate the burgh. These two developments may have become necessary as a result of the hostile attitude of the Regent Morton. He held the citizens to be art and part of the Gordon rising and particularly in the Battle of the Crabstane. During a visit in 1574 he demanded a fine of 4,000 merks and assurances that the burgh would be ruled by sincere adherents of the Reformed faith. Of the impost three-quarters was raised within a few weeks, while the remaining thousand was applied by direction to local hospitals and public works. Later he raised an action before the Privy Council for the disfranchising of the burgh and the payment of a further fine of £20,000 Scots. Fortunately, this issue lapsed with his own fall in 1578. About the same time his grant of Balgownie and the fishing of the Lower Don to his nephew George Auchinleck of Balmanno — an infringement of Aberdeen's freedom rights — was also quashed.

King James several times visited the town when he grew to manhood. On one occasion he besought and was given a loan of 2,000 merks which he omitted to repay. Some of his visits were warlike, like that of 1588, when the new Lord Huntly intended to dispute with the King the passage of the Bridge of Dee, but disbanded his men before the armies made contact. Another visit in 1592 arose out of the affair of 'the Spanish Blanks'. One of the Kers, a close confidant of the Gordons, was caught on his way abroad with certain documents in his possession believed to be addressed to the King of Spain and bearing the signatures of the Earls of Huntly, Erroll and Angus, and Patrick Gordon of Auchindoun. Under torture Ker confessed that the intention was to bring in Spanish troops to re-establish Catholicism and invade England. He retracted his confession later, but there were other signs in the North of a renewal of Papist activity, and the lords concerned were outlawed. James, when he reached Aberdeen, bound the citizens not to confederate with Huntly, Erroll, Angus and other barons, or 'with jesuits, priests, papists or declared rebels'. Aberdeen remained the centre of attention for at least two, perhaps three, nations. In 1594 three suspicious strangers landed at Aberdeen. The magistrates at once put them in ward, but before the Government could be communicated with, first Angus and Erroll demanded that they be released, and three days later, the magistrates standing firm, Huntly threatened fire and sword to the burgh unless the trio were set at liberty. The peril was at the door and help far away. The magistrates complied.

That autumn the Earl of Argyll, with a Highland host of seven thousand men and the King's commission to bring Huntly to book, invaded the Gordon territories from the west, the Forbeses being ready in arms to assist when the punitive expedition should reach Donside. But Huntly and Erroll with a couple of thousand retainers and six cannon met the Celts at the Allt-a-Coileachan burn between the Cabrach and Glenlivet. The cannon scared the Highlanders and when charge after charge failed to break the Aberdeenshire lines, the invaders retreated. Immediately thereafter, however, the King arrived in Aberdeen with a Lowland contingent, the Protestant magistrates rallied to him, and his indignation, fanned by Huntly's reported description of the expedition as a 'Gowk's storm', was only allayed when the royal eyes saw the destruction of Huntly's castle of Huntly, of Erroll's castle of Slains, and of sundry smaller keeps in Aberdeenshire. For the reduction and demolition of the castles, the town supplied masons, pioneers, gunpowder and tools. Both Huntly and Erroll retired out of harm's way until 1597. Then Aberdeen witnessed one of the most brilliant spectacles in its history, when the two Catholic lords were received into the Protestant faith in St. Nicholas Kirk.

The scene is vividly recorded in a lengthy letter from Thomas Mollisone, the Town Clerk, to his 'luffing gossip', Robert Paip, Edinburgh, 'advocate before the Lordis', 'throchtis of paper would not contene all that is to be wretin hereon'. The proceedings occupied the three days of the week-end 25–27 June. On Saturday a fast was proclaimed and a sermon preached in the old, now West, Kirk by George Glaidstanes. Before the sermon Huntly and Erroll presented themselves in the session house, where, in the presence of Patrick Murray, the King's Commissioner, the Bishop of Aberdeen and several ministers, Huntly subscribed a peace pact with Lord Forbes, 'berrying all quarrellis and deadlie feadis betwix thame twa'. While this was being done Forbes remained in the church. The document with Huntly's signature was taken through to Forbes, who also signed, then entered the session-house with 'gryt humilitie'. There the two lords shook hands, Huntly declaring: 'This I do at hes majesty's desire and at command of the Kirk.' Huntly was also reconciled with young Drum at the same time.

On the Sunday the Bishop of Aberdeen preached, the two earls being at the marriage desk with the King's Commissioner, a panel of ministers and most of the town council being present, and 'of nobillmen, Baronis, gentilmen, and comoun pepill sic a confluence that the lyke was nevir sein in that kirk'. Thereafter, before the pulpit, the earls having made full confession of their defection and apostasy, the bishop absolved them, and while Huntly got pardon for the slaying of the bonnie Earl of Moray, another Gordon, the laird of Gight, craved absolution for 'ressat' of the Earl of Bothwell. Finally the earls, gentlemen and other official personages partook of communion.

On Monday the Cross at the Castlegate was covered with tapestry and the earls sat in chairs beside it. At the Cross 'ane litell house' also draped with tapestry sheltered fourscore young men of the town, musicians in their best finery. A table was laid out with 'sirfootfeattis, cumfeattis, and vtheris confectiounis with a gryt numer of glasis: wyn in gryt abundance'. After the King's Commissioner had delivered a wand of peace to the earls and received them back to royal favour, the ministers and town council embraced them, toasts were drunk off, and sweetmeats scattered in the causeway for all and sundry to scramble for. The musicians sounded their hagbuts all the while so energetically 'that day nor dur could not be hard'. Last of all, earls and ministers adjourned to the tolbooth to receive the freedom of the burgh, and Mr. Mollisone concluded, with evident appreciation of many copious libations, 'at evin nothing bot wauchting (drinking)'. Thus did the lieges celebrate on the slightest provocation in the spacious days.

Aberdeen may have been a spectator of one, and some of its citizens undoubtedly took part in another, warlike expedition. Some of the scattered remnants of the Spanish Armada in 1588, driven north by tempest and fear of Drake, may have come close enough inshore to be seen by the inhabitants. One galleon apparently foundered fifteen miles north just beyond Erroll's castle of Slains, and the incident is recorded in the name St. Catherine's Dub given to the spot where the vessel sank. About the same time, the Earl Marischal's younger brother, Robert Keith of Benholm, seized the Abbey of Deer, which the Earl had inherited. Fraternal expostulation having failed, the Earl got the King's warrant to call upon the lieges for assistance and forty hagbutters were supplied by the town of Aberdeen. With these and others the Earl manoeuvred his brother out of the abbey into Fedderate Castle, where, after a siege of three days, terms were arranged.

Apart from these events which may be termed 'historical', the days of the reign of James VI and I were exciting in Aberdeen, but the excitement often sprang from happenings that conventional history is inclined to overlook. Yet they unquestionably affected the lives of the townspeople far more sharply than the Reformation and the Union.

During the sixty years from 1560 to 1620 Aberdeen continued to be disturbed by domestic brawls and by the forays of the Aberdeenshire lairds. Much blood was shed, several lives were lost, property was continually being stolen or destroyed, and the Town Council, despite numerous edicts, never quite mastered the disorders. There was a very bad instance in March 1588 in which highway robbery was aggravated by barefaced perjury on the part of the perpetrators. In that month several Aberdeen merchants passing on their lawful commercial occasions to Trinity Fair on Lower Deeside were set upon by the Leslies of Balquhain 'all bodin in feir of werr with Jakis steil bonetis pistolls lang gunnis bowis and vther armour invasive of sett purpois provisioun preconceavit malice and foirthocht fellonye and laitrent'. Led by the eldest son of the laird of Balquhain, the well-born robbers set upon the merchants on the King's highway, 'maist crewallie and awfullie invadit thame bi way of deid for thair slauchtres with schott of gun, arrowis and straikis of swordes and hes hurt and woundit sindrie of thame baith in thair heids and bodies to the grite effusioun of thair bluid and maist apperand danger of thair lyves besyd mony bawche and blay straikes gevin thame quhairof thai are nevir abill to recover thair helthis and thai alsua by way of manifest and oppin reiff maist schamefullie cuttit fra the saide personnes thair haill pursis reft and spoilzeit and awaytuik thair haill silver and packis . . .'.

The account of the outrage thus given, with much more in the same strain, in a letter from King James's Privy Council vibrates with indignation. Their lordships' wrath became all the more virtuous when certain Leslies resident in Aberdeen and in league with the Balquhain marauders 'forgeit and inventit' a 'sinister information' against the baillies, several councillors and some burgesses of the town. Their lordships indeed came to the conclusion that the information had been laid against the citizens of Aberdeen 'to draw thame being peciabill men living under our obedience furthe of oure said burghe to the effect they may execute thair cruell myndis and intensiouns aganes the said complenaris be the way'. The cause of the Leslies' enmity seems to have been that the burgesses thus assailed had been chosen to adjudicate upon the conduct of one of the Leslies in Aberdeen whom they had found to have violated his oath of burgess-ship, and whom accordingly they had sentenced to be deprived of his burgess status.

'As the auld cock craws the young ane learns.' In 1612 twenty sons of substantial persons, mostly county lairds, and mostly scholars at the Grammar School, were by ordinance of the Town Council 'presently excludit and put furth of all the scuilles of this burghe and nevir ane of thame to be admittit nor ressauit in ony schuill or colledge of this burghe in any tyme heirefter'. On 1 December they 'had tacken the sang scuill, keippit and hauldin the same, with hagbuttis, pistollis, swordis and lang wapynnis' for three or four days until the magistrates were 'compellit be resson of the great insolencies, ryottis, and oppressiones committit be the saidis schollaries', to throw them into the Tolbooth.

The Town Council lived in continual fear of skirmishes between partisans. In 1603, the Council decided to petition the Privy Council to impress upon 'all and sindrie erlis, lordis, baronis, gentilmen, thair men, tenentis, servandis, dependaris, and all vtheris our soverane lordis and lieges' resorting to Aberdeen to behave themselves and keep the peace. A vivid picture is drawn in the petition of the tumults raised by these occasional visitors and 'clannit men', and of the fate that in the seventeenth century as in the twentieth awaited those who sought to give 'the redding straik'. Four years later the Town Council again felt it desirable to approach the Privy Council 'that they may be frie of any charges to be gevin thame be letteris of captioun for taking and putting in ward of clannit gentilmen resorting to the burght denuncit rebellis for sclauchter and vther capitall crimes'. As late as 1619 we learn of the town being 'trublit' by the feuds of outsiders who used their weapons within the burgh boundaries.

Fear and detestation of the Celts lay heavy upon Aberdonians. In July 1595, 'the disordourit and lawles helandmen in Birss, Glentannar, and thair about', grew bold enough to extend their depredations to the near vicinity of Aberdeen, 'nocht onlie in the onmerciful murthering of men and bairnis, bot in the maisterfull and violent robbing and spulzeing of all the bestiall, guidis and geir of a gryt pairt of the in-habitantis of these boundis'. The Town Council ordered the citizens to stand by their arms, arranged for the alarm to be given if need be, issued instructions for the ports to be closed, and undertook to send 'exploratouris' to certain country lairds to learn the Highlanders' whereabouts.

The Aberdonians were not alone in their dislike of the Highlanders. In 1602 there was sent down to Aberdeen one of several royal proclamations calling for men to serve in a punitive expedition against some refractory region. As usual, Aberdeen compounded by a payment in cash. The 1602 expedition was against the Islesmen and James's proclamation was wroth 'with the detestabill and barbarous behaviour of the inhabitants of the Lewis, quha being woid of the fear and knowledge of God, and misknawing thair alledgeance and obedience to vs, ar occupeit in nothing ellis bot in bluid, murthour, reif, thift, and oppressioun, ewerie ane of thame exercising monstrous and beistlie cruellties upon vtheris, as hes not bene hard amangis Turkis nor infidelis, and with that they ar plantit and possessit with the maist fertile and commodious pairt of our haill realme, quhilk being inritcheit with a incredible fertilitie of cornis, and plantie of fisches wald render maist inestimabill commodities to oure realme, gif the barbaritie of the wyld and sawaige inhabitantis thairoff wald suffer and permitt a paciable traid and traficque amangis thame . . .'. The fertility, assumed or real, of the Isles in 1600 has a strange ring in the ear today.

As well as extraneous peril there was an imminent danger of rioting within the burgh itself. In 1604 the Council, 'with consent of the communitie', forbade the selling of 'ony wyne, aill or beir . . . efter ten houris of the nicht', and forbade also both the citizens and visitors 'to be fund nor sene vagand nor gangand on the streitis of this burgh efter the said hour, bot that all persones sall contene thameselffis in thair houssis and ludgingis fra that hour furth, and that for eschewing of the undecent and ungodlie use of night-walking, carting, dycing, and drinking, over frequentlie usit in this burgh in tymes bypast, quhilk hes bred gryt disordour and dissoluteness off lyfe in sindrie inhabitantis . . .'. To keep the peace a watch of eighteen men was empowered to patrol the burgh during the long dark nights. This system of combined curfew and proctors or police was for long maintained, although at times found to be inadequate. In 1607 'the insolencies of a number of deboschit and disorderit persones, als weill inhabitantis of this burght as extranearis, leving edillie and louslie, without anie calling or vocatioun, daylie trubilling this toun and nichtbouris thairof' were such that an appeal for powers was made to the Privy Council, and the citizens undertook to have their arms by them and to supply a nightly patrol of twelve persons, 'to begyn at nyne houris at evin, and to continew till fyve houris in the morning, with hagbut and lang wapoun'. Thereafter for some years nothing is heard of such troublesome conditions, the only tumults being an occasional assault, curiously often by some landed gentleman upon a school teacher, or an instance of insubordinate conduct by pupils in the grammar or song school.

The inhabitants were well fitted to play their part in repelling a Highland foray, resisting a country laird, or arresting 'disorderit persones'. They had a long training in the use of arms and their instruction was renewed in periodical musterings and wapinschaws. In May 1599 the Dean of Guild was ordered to pay Thomas Ballantyne a rose noble for his pains in 'instructing certane young men and nicht-bouris of the toun to handill thair hagbuttis and pickis in the Linkis'. Under penalty of £20 the lieges on the days of a public wapinschaw were expected to present themselves, 'ilk persone with his awain armour ... sic as corslet, jack, pick, spear, muskattis, hagbuttis, halbertis and twa handit swordis'. There were other weapons, such as the ancient 'dens aix'.

The muster was in the Links, the roll of inhabitants was called by the baillies of the four quarters, and 'the absentes wrettin and vnlauit'. Thereupon the whole parade was 'put in ordour and discipline' by the magistrates and the appointed commanders, one half of the hag-butters leading the procession, followed by the half of the spearmen and pikemen, then the rest of the hagbutters, next nine spearmen and pikemen, with halberdiers and those armed with Lochaber axes, and last 'in the end and taill', the men of Futty. The line of march from the Links was "by the lang gett' on the north side of the Castlegate or Justice Port, down the Gallowgate and Broadgate to the Castlegate. On reaching the Great Cross, there was 'som little forme of skirmishing maid be the hagbutteris, ane and halff againis the vther, betwixt the croces'. The proceedings closed with a proclamation warning the citizens to be prepared to turn out the next time a wapinschaw was ordered. Non-attendance at musters was expiated by a fine except in cases of absence on necessary business and 'the poore sort of people quhilk had nather armis nor apparell fitting for musturing'.

CHAPTER FOUR

The Toun's College

We left King's College in 1549 at the point where Bishop William Gordon ratified the reforms recommended by Alexander Galloway as a result of his famous Visitation of that year. But Galloway died in 1552 and nothing seems to have been done. The College which in 1534 was described by a foreigner as the most celebrated of the three in Scotland lapsed into stagnation. Out of its decline, although happily not from its ashes, there was to rise in due course the rival, and now allied, institution of Marischal College. But the gestation and birth of the Protestant University occupied half a century.

The last Catholic Principal of King's, Alexander Anderson, had been Galloway's vicar at Kinkell and was for many years connected with the College as regent and sub-principal before he became its executive head in 1554. Anderson, who according to Knox was 'a man more subtil and craftye than ather learned or godlie', did not lack knowledge of his own mind. In 1560, when the Reforming mob would have pillaged the College, he armed the students and drove the intruders out of the precincts. Just before the Reformation that 'great scholar and subtil disputant' went to Edinburgh along with some of his Professors as the champions of Popery to dispute with Knox and other Reformers. Even a Catholic writer admits that the Papists had the worst of it, but the debate, as given by Wodrow, is much less intellectual than the Admirable Crichton's with the doctors of Padua, and much less entertaining than Panurge's with the doctors of Paris. In fact, Anderson, although ordered to be put in ward, snapped his fingers at authority. He even secured from Queen Mary a written injunction that the College should be 'unhurt, unharmit, unmolestit, inquietit' by any of her subjects. This was during her visit to the North in 1562, but Randolph, the English ambassador, who was with her stated that only 'fifteen or sixteen scollers' were in attendance.

His eventual overthrow, however, was inevitable. In 1569 Adam Herriot, the minister of Aberdeen, drew the Assembly's attention to the state of affairs at King's. A commission was appointed, under John

Erskine of Dun, Superintendent of Angus, to investigate. The contumacy of Anderson must have been notorious, for the most powerful man in Scotland, the Regent Earl of Moray, came North with the commissioners. Anderson and four of his colleagues were summoned to attend an inquiry in the Kirk of St. Nicholas. When they appeared, they were ordered to sign the Confession of Faith, and of course refused, despite the exhortations of the Regent: 'most obstinately contemning his grace's most godly admonitions.' The Commission could do nothing but clear them all out. Anderson himself lived on in Aberdeen until his death eight years later, 'excommunicatt contrayr the religione and at the Kyngis horne', but not molested.

Anderson was succeeded by one of Andrew Melville's greatest friends, Alexander Arbuthnot, 'a man of singular gifts of learning, wesdome, godliness and sweitness of nature'. Few men have earned greater praise for their character, while accomplishing less to sustain their reputation. The son of Andrew Arbuthnot of Pitcarlie, in the Mearns, where he was born in 1538, he died while still in his prime in 1583. On all sides elegiac tributes were paid to his memory. Andrew Melville celebrated him in verse, James Melville in prose, while Spottiswood pronounced this eulogy: 'He was greatly loved of all men, hated of none. Pleasant and jocund in conversation, and in all sciences expert: a good poet, mathematician, philosopher, theologue, lawyer, and in medicine skilful.' With such impressive academic qualifications, it was probably as difficult then as it would be now for an electoral body to get past Arbuthnot. But he was a complete failure in his job.

The greatest of Scottish Churchmen and educationists, Andrew Melville, intended that his friend should introduce at King's College the modern methods and discipline by means of which he himself had restored Glasgow University. But for three or four years nothing happened, and in 1578 the Parliament appointed a commission to examine King's. It was three years ere the report reached Parliament, only to disappear. At once the General Assembly stepped in and sent its own commission of inquiry — one of whose members was the fifth Earl Marischal. On this occasion the report was ready in six months, but there was still an influential party around Aberdeen who did not favour reform, and King James was induced to intervene, which he roundly did. For various reasons he was annoyed with Arbuthnot, whom he censured, and the Assembly was ordered to desist. The Nova Fundatio, or new charter for King's, which was the outcome of the

Assembly visitation, remained for many years a dead letter. Arbuthnot himself was of too gentle a nature to suffer harsh treatment, and it is not unlikely that the royal displeasure was responsible for hastening the death of one whose mild enjoyment of life was already being frustrated by the satires of circumstance. Arbuthnot's 'Miseries of a Pure Scollar' is an interesting early example of subjective verse, and a good deal sounder both as philosophy and as poetry than most of the exercises in the same style in our own day. But more remarkable is his 'Praises of Wemen' coming from the principal of a college and a pillar of a Kirk credited with hostility to the graces of life. The delicate compliments in this poem, delivered with just the slightest suspicion of the tongue in the cheek, are delicious. In the *Bards of Bon-Accord* William Walker pointed out Arbuthnot's anticipation of one celebrated sentiment of Burns:

> Quhen God maid all of nocht,
> He did this weill declare,
> The last thing that he wrocht,
> It was ane woman fair.
> In workes we see the last to be
> Maist plesand and preclair,
> Ane help to man God maid hir than!
> Quhat will ye I say mair?

The year after Arbuthnot's death Parliament appointed another Commission. It spent thirteen years patiently re-examining the accumulated evidence, or in doing nothing. Eventually in 1597 the Nova Fundatio was ratified by the Scots Parliament.[1] The changes were, for all the bother, rather insignificant. Instead of regents taking a class through its whole curriculum, there were to be specialist teachers confined to one subject. But this reform was not put in force at King's until 1628, and was abandoned for the old style in 1641. It was incorporated in the original academic system of Marischal College, and struggled on until 1642, when the new seminary reverted to the old method.

Other changes effected by the New Foundation included the elimination of all the Theology students, prebendaries and choirboys, the abolition of the Canonist, the Civilist, and the Mediciner, and the

---

1   At least I hope so. R. S. Rait, *The Universities of Aberdeen*, says it was the first Commission that submitted the *Nova Fundatio*. J. M. Bulloch, *A History of the University of Aberdeen*, says it was the second.

reduction of the bursars by one. Thus within the college only sixteen members of Dunbar's foundation remained, with the addition of an Economus (who was quartermaster and cashier), a cook (who kept the garden) and two personal servants, one for the Principal and another for the Sub-Principal. The Principal became also professor of theology and minister of St. Machar's Church, and his salary was fixed at 23 bolls of corn and 200 merks Scots. He was to be elected by the Chancellor of the University, the Rector, and other officials, assisted by such strangers as the Principals of St. Andrews and Edinburgh, and the minister of St. Nicholas. The bursars were to be chosen by examination, but the fixing of fees indicated provision for students who did not require financial assistance. The Rector was to be elected (as now) by four 'nations' — called in the document Mar, Buchan, Moray and Angus (also as now); but in practice from 1634 to 1856, the divisions were Aberdeen (Mar after 1640), Angus, Moray and Lothian.

The subjects to be taught were physiology, geography, astrology, history and Hebrew by the sub-principal; one regent was to 'propound the principles of reasoning from the best Greek and Latin authors, with practice in writing and speaking'; another was to take Greek and the elementary Greek and Latin authors; the last regent's share was arithmetic, geometry, and philosophical passages from Aristotle and Cicero.

But the Reformers could not wait for the New Foundation. They were profoundly sensible of the need for controlling the instruction of youth in the way it should go; and for their educational purposes orthodox universities were an urgent necessity. Edinburgh University was accordingly founded in 1583, and ten years later George Keith, 5th Earl Marischal, presented Aberdeen with its own college whose religious tenets were above suspicion. Aberdeen University's second founder was a man outstanding in the Scotland of his time, and he was a fit representative of the nobility to live in the same age as Aberdeen's most remarkable group of citizens during its whole history. The fourth Earl, who had favoured the Reformation and collected a great deal of valuable property thereby, was the slightest bit of a scoundrel. The 5th Earl was his grandson. He had a liberal education and did the Grand Tour. A sojourn for study at Geneva brought him in contact with Calvinism and secured him the friendship of the illustrious scholar Theodore Beza. In Germany he is reputed to have stayed with the reigning Grand Duke of Hesse, and the two traced their ancestry to its common source — Arminius, the German robber prince who slaughtered the legions of Augustus. On his return to Scotland he succeeded in

1581, at the age of 27 to one of the most renowned titles and the richest inheritance in the land. He could travel, it was said, the length of the country and never miss a night in his own castle. The Marischal estates were not insignificant before they were enormously augmented from Church spoils, and there was naturally a good deal of feeling about the Keiths cornering so great a share in the distribution of the rich domains of the religious houses. More than one curious legend connects the eventual downfall of the Earls Marischal with these transactions. The fifth Earl, however, gave as well as took, and there is a refreshing contempt for public opinion in the motto which he assumed and which he transferred to Marischal College to be perpetuated as almost the only original legend in heraldry — 'Thay haif said: Quhat say thay? Lat thame say.'

No sooner had he succeeded to the earldom than he became immersed in public business. He was a member of Assembly Commissions and of the Privy Council. He, and he only of all the nobles in the North-East over a period of nearly 300 years, was strong enough to defy the power of the Gordons with impunity. So long as he was alive the Gordons might defeat Protestant armies but they could not do as they pleased in the North. In 1589 he was sent to Denmark to bring home the King's bride, the Princess Anne. He was, however, frustrated by storms, and eventually James himself braved the hazards of a North Sea crossing and brought his consort over in person. But he appreciated the Marischal's services (and outlays) by confirming him in the possession of the Abbacy of Deer, 'in perpetual monument of the said service'. In an age when most of his class were engrossed in extending their estates, he had other ambitions, and it is significant of his character that of all the great lords who were associated territorially with Aberdeen, he alone gave substantial benefits to the town. But in his chief benefaction as the giver of its Protestant Lamp to the North-East he was almost anticipated.

In July 1592 Sir Alexander Fraser, who had first erected the little village of Faithlie into a burgh of barony called Fraser's port, later Fraserburgh, contrived to persuade the King to give him permission to establish a college. It was opened in 1600[1], only to be closed down five years later. But the buildings during the pest in the next century were made available to the students of Kings', while those of Marischal are said to have found a temporary lodging in Peterhead.

The foundation charter of Marischal College is dated 2 April 1593.

[1] Where the Alexandra Hotel now stands.

The preamble states that learning in the North of Scotland is still 'generally deficient', and that accordingly the Earl desires to establish 'a public Gymnasium ... where young men may be thoroughly trained and instructed, both in the other humane arts and also in Philosophy and a purer piety, under the charge of competent and learned teachers, to whom shall be given from our endowment such salaries as may be required'. The endowment consisted of 'the manse and offices, glebes, yards, cloisters, church and wells' that formerly belonged to the Franciscan or Grey Friars — these having been conveyed to the Earl Marischal by the Town Council for this purpose; 'the lands, crofts, roads, rigs, orchards, barns, dovecots, tenements, houses, buildings, yards, acres, annual rents, feu-duties, kilns, offices and others whatsoever' belonging to the Dominican and Carmelite Friars in Aberdeen, and the estates and lands belonging to the Earl in Bervie, once the Chaplainry of Bervie, and also the Chaplainry of Cowie.

The University was to consist of a principal, three regents, six alumni or bursars, a steward and a cook, all living in, and provision was also made for students not bursars. The scheme of education laid down in the charter was practically identical with that contained in the New Foundation for King's. As regards the regulation of the student body, however, Marischal is exceptionally interesting because the rules laid down by the founder were observed up to the union of Aberdeen's two universities in 1860. The ancient right of students in Continental Universities of electing their Rector was preserved in Marischal's charter. At King's procurators of the student 'nations' (otherwise the students' representatives) were originally appointed by the principal and professors, but for many years the functions of the procurators were assumed by principal and professors. About the second quarter of the nineteenth century, however, the procurators came to be elected by the masters, not the undergraduates, in arts. In Marischal, not only was the Rector elected by all the students, but the election proceeded by each nation choosing a student as their procurator who gave and recorded their votes at a meeting of the Senatus Academicus.

By the Universities (Scotland) Act of 1858, which brought about the union of the two colleges, provision was made for 'a Rector to be elected by the matriculated students, voting according to the present usage in Marischal College'. This enactment has earned for Aberdeen University one unique distinction. W. M. Alexander sums it up thus:

'Only in the four universities in Scotland do the students today possess the right, once widespread amongst their forerunners in continental Europe, of electing the rector. Only in Glasgow and Aberdeen do the student nations — four in number as in medieval Paris — make the election. And only in Aberdeen do they do so through the procurators of the nations. The practice in Aberdeen is thus the closest approximation now existing to the original usage; and it is the only instance where the original procedure is still intact.'[1]

1   W. M. Alexander, *The Four Nations of Aberdeen University.*

CHAPTER FIVE

Education under Difficulties

During the three half-centuries after the founding of Marischal College, Aberdeen's two universities were, on the whole, little more than the equivalent of our secondary schools; indeed, for a period around 1700, they were scarcely so advanced as that, since it was quite customary for children of 12 and 13 to matriculate in them and beardless boys of 16 and 17 to graduate from them. King's in one respect had pulled itself together from its languishing state of the last years of the Popish ascendancy, for in 1604 thirty-eight students entered and in 1612 twenty-five; but on the eve of the Civil Wars the number fell again to about a dozen. At the beginning of the seventeenth century, all the private benevolence that accrued to Aberdeen's seats of learning was directed towards Marischal College, which benefited to the extent of 26,000 merks all told, or to the Grammar School, and the portion of King's was a solitary feu-duty of 50s. That meagre benefaction, happily, was sumptuously overshadowed when in 1620 Patrick Forbes, the Protestant Bishop of Aberdeen, raised 10,000 merks to endow a chair of divinity[1] for his second son John, and the fund, applied in 1626 to the purchase of the lands now known as the Kirktown of Kinellar and Cairntradlin, secured a substantial revenue to the College.[2] But one chair does not make a new university, as Bishop Forbes was to discover. He had to labour hard to restore King's to a status approaching its original virility under Elphinstone and Dunbar and it is an admission of his success that he is known today as the second founder of the college.

In 1619, on his own suggestion, Forbes was instructed by King

---

1 The bishop provided that the appointment should be by examination, the board to consist of the moderator of the Synod of Aberdeen, two commissioners from each presbytery in the synod, the principal, one professor, and the dean of the faculty of Divinity. The examination, like many another sensible custom, has recently been discontinued.

2 These lands were sold by the University as recently as 1945, when it was discovered that the rents were insufficient to maintain the farm cottages at the standard demanded by the housing authorities.

James VI to conduct a visitation of both Colleges. King's he found in 'miserable estait'. Its funds were in a condition of 'abominable dilapidation', and its resources handled with as little skill as if 'nather a Gode hade been in heaven to count with, nor men on earth to examine their ways'. Raitt, the principal, quite unconstitutionally was acting as procurator, and so had charge of the funds. He alleged that the college was due him 'thrie thousand pundis'. At matriculation every bursar paid the college a silver spoon or its equivalent in cash, yet the inspectors counted in the college 'but sex silver spoones and no moir silver wark of ony kynd'. Even the kitchen was ill-found, with 'two dossen of plaittis and als many trencheris, no naperie but tua breid clothes and fyve servittes'. There was 'no ministrie of the gospell in the kirkis of the deanrie, but lamentable heathanisms and sic lowsnes as is horrible to record, albeit evin about the cathedral kirk of the dyocie'. The visiting commissioners instructed the principal to free the college from debt, provide new table-cloths and other linen, and put the fabric in proper repair, 'leid whair leid wes, sklaittis quhair sklaitt wes, aik quhair aik wes, fir quhair fir is'. A rector, canonist (whose appointment was nominal and carried no salary), civilist, mediciner, and grammarian were appointed, and thus the New Foundation, if it had ever been in force, was set aside. Forbes indeed is said to have thrown the New Foundation into the fire, although those who favoured it were later to produce what they professed to be an authentic copy. Four years later the Commission made a further inspection, and must have been satisfied with Raitt's performance, for he remained principal until 1632 when he died.

Bishop Forbes conducted another visitation in 1628, when, in response to the plea of parents of the students (who then as now usually objected to spending money on education), he abolished the practice whereby graduands gave banquets to the professors, substituting an arrangement permitting the students, at 'the tyme of their examination and tryallis and graduation, to bestow upoune the saidis maisteris and examinatouris ane drinke upoune fute for recreatioun allanerlie without anie forder additioun'. But the parents were not altogether absolved, and part of the margin of price between the banquet and the drink, to the amount of four pounds Scots, was claimed by the college to provide books for the library.

By the time of the next visitation in 1638 circumstances had radically altered. Forbes had died, and his successor, Bishop Bellenden, was soon confronted not only with a reanimated Presbyterianism rising to a new ascendancy, but also by a demand from within King's College itself for the restoration of the New Foundation which the great Presbyterian leader Andrew Melville had intended that the college should adopt. There was a new king, Charles I, on the throne, who did not know enough about the regulations made by his father to be able to check the mistakes of his Civil Service, even then replete with inhibitions. In 1633 the king confirmed the original Foundation of the College, but in 1637 the Presbyterian party, as a test of its growing influence, attempted to have the New Foundation resuscitated, and the king was persuaded to eat his own words and order that it be re-established. The mediciner, William Gordon, and the canonist, his brother-in-law, James Sandilands, flew if not to arms at least to Archbishop Laud, under whose pressure the king appointed a Commission which effected nothing of importance. His Majesty also wrote a letter re-establishing the New Foundation, and six months later produced another and completely contradictory epistle upbraiding those who had abandoned the 'ancient and treu foundation' for one of 'thair awain forgeing'. The aggrieved ones had the temerity to reply in sarcastic vein. The Commission heard evidence and arguments and decided that everything should remain as it was until it should please His Majesty to give fresh light and leading. The Bishops' Wars prevented such guidance from being communicated.

When Bishop Bellenden was removed from office, the university lost its chancellor and in May an Assembly Commission visited the College, deposed Principal Leslie and Alexander Scroggie, discharged the cantor as 'ane unprofitable member' and the canonist, who was later reinstated with the sensible proviso that he should teach the law of marriage, wills and teinds only; and received the signatures of the sub-principal, two regents, the grammarian, the sacrist and the mediciner to the Covenant. That autumn only eleven students matriculated but Spalding says that the 'scolleris' after some initial uncertainty settled down, and 'ilk man fell to his owne studie and charge calmlie and quietlie'. In July 1640 the General Assembly met in Greyfriars Church, replaced Principal Leslie by Guild, deposed Dr. John Forbes after giving him the opportunity to change sides, and divided up the revenues of the diocese between King's and Marischal, King's getting two-thirds.

During this period Marischal College — whose first M.D., incidentally, was a graduate of Harvard — had on the whole conducted its affairs at a greater distance from the public eye. Robert Howie, the first principal, left for St. Andrews in 1597 and was succeeded by Gilbert Gray, who died in office in 1614. After him came Andrew Aidie, who resigned in 1619 following a dispute with Bishop Forbes. When the Bishop's visitation reached the gates of Marischal College, Aidie refused entry and referred the commissioners to his patron the Earl Marischal. William Forbes, later Bishop of Edinburgh, was principal for a year and then Robert Baron, who died shortly after his tulzie with the Covenanters. All the while Marischal College was being steadily enriched and extended by endowments. Several bursaries were founded; the famous mathematician and doctor, Duncan Liddel, gave bursaries and a Chair of Mathematics, of which the first occupant was William Johnston, brother of Arthur the humanist. Liddel's lands of Pitmedden, upon which his monument still stands, were bequeathed to the College. The first of the Aberdeen botanists, Dr. James Cargill, gave bursaries, and a Chair of Divinity was erected out of a bequest, subsequently supplemented by the Town Council, from Patrick Copland, 'preacher to the Navy and Fleet of the East India Company'. Copland explained his pious gift in a few phrases the substance of which has been in the minds of many other Aberdonians who have striven to improve the city of their birth — 'For as mekle as I being a borne citizen of the burgh of Abirdeen within the Kingdom of Scotland, and being brought up from my childhood in their grammar school and College untill I passed my course in Philosophie, I acknowledge myself hereby bound and obliged to benefite their communwealth and to advance their Schooles and College so farre as lyes in my possibility.'

In 1641 the Scots Parliament, by this time of course under Presbyterian control, passed an act 'to uneit and erect the tue colledgeis of Aberdeen, viz. the old colledge thairof and the new callit Marischellis Colledge, in ane joynt universitie to be callit in all tyme cumming King Charles' Universitie'. The Act, however, never took practical effect, for Marischal College would not co-operate, perhaps because in the apportionment of the revenues of the diocese King's got the lion's share. In 1661 the Act repealing all the legislation of the Scots Parliament during the Civil War and Protectorate swept away the Universitas Carolina which had for twenty years existed only in name.[1]

Despite the political tumults of the first sixty years of the seventeenth

1 It may have been in connection with this union that Aberdeen was visited by William Harvey, the discoverer of the circulation of the blood. He was made a burgess.

century, the buildings of both colleges were not neglected. In 1623 Dr. William Guild, then minister of King-Edward, mortified to the town a house in the Broadgate for the purpose of constructing a commodious gateway into Marischal College, which had become obscured from the street by the building of high houses in front of it. The entrance was completed in 1633, and lasted until the structural alterations in 1893 caused it to disappear. Before the Marischal gate was completed, the Crown of King's fell in a tempest in February 1633, whereby, says Spalding, 'both the roofes of tymber and lead and other adjacent workes, wer pitifullie crusched'. Bishop Forbes and Dr. William Gordon the Mediciner led the movement for its restoration, which was accomplished by George Thomson, mason, whose name is carved upon one of the keystones of the Crown. During the Cromwellian occupation in 1658, the square tower in the north-east corner of the quadrangle, known as the Cromwell Tower, was built by public subscription. Principal, professors, graduates, students, and ministers contributed side by side with the 'Lord General George Moncke', who gave £120 Scots, and a large number of his officers. The building had not been completed by the Restoration, and it is gratifying to know that when the Episcopalians returned to power they made up the deficit in the building fund. Within the chapel a picture of the Virgin on the organ case was removed at the instance of the Assembly, which held that 'a pourtraicte of some woman, nobody could tell who' was 'a thing very intollerable in the church of a college'.

Guild, who had come under suspicion of being too royalist, was deposed in 1652, and was succeeded by one of the most vigorous of the principals of King's College, John Row, son of the historian parson of Carnock. Row was himself a grammarian, poet and historian, whose academic accomplishments did not abate his capacity for administration. In 1653 he prepared a code of rules to regulate the students' day. Morning prayers, at 6 a.m. in summer and 6.30 in winter, followed breakfast. Thereafter the classes met to repeat the prescribed lessons. Then the whole college assembled for the reading of the Scriptures at 10 a.m. and at 11 the lectures delivered earlier in the morning were gone over by the students, with tutorial assistance from the regents. Dinner at noon was diversified by the reading of passages of secular history and crowned by a passage of Scripture. The afternoon was spent in hearing a Hebrew or a theological discourse or in recreation on the Links; at 5 p.m. the classes met for more lessons, followed by evening prayers and an exposition of a passage from the Bible. Supper was eaten at 8 p.m., then psalms were sung, and after a further hour of study, the college went to bed. The subjects studied included Latin, Greek, Hebrew, logic and mathematics (arithmetic the first year, geometry in the second, chronology and optics in the third, and geography and astronomy in the fourth). The students might converse in Latin, Greek, Hebrew or French.

Life at the university under Principal Row was not so stodgy as it may appear. He encouraged sport, although he deprecated such clownishness as the hurling of dinner-time volleys of bones across the tables, and 'some crymes were punished corporallie, others by pecuniall mulct, and grosser crymes by extrusion'. While he frowned upon golf, he had a billiard-room fitted up in the Cromwell Tower, and allowed one John Ross to take a lease of the College bowling-green. Ross got from the professors 'tuelve paires of boules and a rolling stone compleitlie mounted with two sythes', which equipment indicates that bowlers were as fastidious then as now about the condition of their green. Football was also played, the bajans having to supply the footballs for the other classes. An archery target was erected in the quadrangle, which may have resulted in a certain restriction upon the movements of the neighbours, for one resident near the college complained that he had been transfixed 'throw the breaches be ane arrow which did come over the Colledge yard dyke', while a baillie declared that he was 'in great hazard by the saide arrowes'. There is evidence too that even in those ultra-Puritan times the professors were not ignorant of the pleasures of the table.

But the best of good things come to an end, and in 1661, Row was dismissed. It was alleged that under him 'the fundations (were) violated, the youth trained up in principles of disloyaltie and schisme, discipline and order hath been neglected, and many other abuses to the prejudices of religion, the King's maiesties interest and interest of the universitie'. He opened a school in Aberdeen itself, but later went to live with his son-in-law, the minister of Kinellar, and he died there sometime after 1668. He was succeeded by William Rait, who reigned for a year, and then by one of Dr. Guild's colleagues, Alexander Middleton, who held office until 1684. Under Middleton a Chair of Oriental Languages (which meant Hebrew) was founded; Marischal had had a Hebrew Chair as early as 1642. The first holder of the chair was Patrick Gordon, who had learned Hebrew from a Jew. During the post-Restoration period there were five visitations, one of which renewed the regulation that regents should serve for no more than six years, and another enacted that 'there be no privat laureations in aither of the two colledges', where it had become a common practice for regents to confer degrees at their pleasure. In 1670 Parliament, to compensate for the loss of the diocesan revenues, which were naturally once more diverted to the bishop's use, granted the two colleges the stipends of all vacant parishes in the synods from Aberdeen northwards, eight-thirteenths to King's and the rest to Marischal. In 1672 tutors were forbidden to teach university subjects outside the colleges and steps were taken to prevent the regents of one college from poaching students from the other. Earlier in the century Marischal College library had got some excellent books from Thomas Reid, Latin Secretary to James I, including the only volumes, with one exception, of the library of old St. Paul's Cathedral to survive the Fire of London. Bishop Scougal and his son Henry augmented the library at King's. About the time of the Revolution in 1688 the canonist disappears from the records for good.

With the accession of William and Mary the universities of Scotland came much more closely under the eye of the Parliament. Middleton was succeeded as Principal by his son George, who took the oath of allegiance to the new regime in 1690 along with all the staff save the professor of Divinity, who, however, was allowed to remain for several years longer. In 1690 Parliament appointed a commission to visit the universities. This commission threw appointments to regencies open to public competition, the examiners to make trial of the applicants and 'to consider not only the abilities and learning of the said parties, but also their piety, good life, and conversation, their prudence, fitness for the place, affection for the government of Church and State now established, and their other good qualifications complexedly'. In 1709 James Urquhart, son of the mediciner, and John Gordon, son of the minister of Cluny, competed for a regency at King's. The Senatus 'put in ane hatt ten little pieces of paper, upon every one of which was writtine a distinct subject or head of philosophie, one of which the competitors was appoynted to draw, each of them one, and to have a discourse and sustain theses thereupon'. The Commission further made a beginning of the curtailing of the practice of regenting, by ordering in 1698 that the Greek chair should be kept separate from all other subjects at King's. A preliminary examination in Latin was made compulsory for entrants into Arts, and gowns had to be worn, black by professors and red by students, during the term. In 1700 the Earl Marischal founded a chair of Medicine at Marischal and in 1703

King's got its chair of Mathematics. In 1709 the Scots Universities received the statutory right to a copy of every book entered at Stationers' Hall — a right which Parliament bought back in 1836, Aberdeen then getting an annual compensation of £320.

When the 1715 Rebellion broke out Marischal College followed its patron and chancellor, the last Earl Marischal, in opposing the Hanoverian succession. In consequence, when the rebels were scattered in the following year, only one professor was left in his chair, all the rest being deposed; at King's the principal, the civilist, and two regents forfeited their places. Work was suspended at Marischal during the sessions 1715–16 and 1716–17, and ere its functions were resumed its principal, Paterson, was dead, and some of the professors had taken to the hills. Thomas Blackwell, the only professor who had remained loyal to the Government, became principal. In the same year the college instituted a professorship of Greek, and in 1727 a chair of Oriental Languages was founded. At King's George Chalmers, minister of Kilwinning, succeeded the errant Middleton. From 1725 for some forty consecutive years the office of mediciner was held by a member of the Gregory family.

The period from the Restoration to the last Jacobite rebellion in 1745 saw a good deal of change in the university buildings. In 1682 the Senatus of Marischal commenced to raise a repair and extension fund to replace the ruined buildings of the old Greyfriars monastery. The alterations went on for thirty years, and among the subscribers were Scots communities in the Baltic countries and elsewhere abroad. In 1698 the Convention of Royal Burghs meeting in Aberdeen gave a donation, in return receiving a banquet from the College which consumed '2 lib of cours biscat and six ounce of fyne biscut, 5 of rough almonds, 5 lib of raisans, 3 pints of claret and ane Choppin of ail, a pint of Canary, 7 pints of aill, whit loafs, pips, tobaco, and candle'. King's College found a munificent benefactor in Dr. James Fraser, who had matriculated in 1660, and after graduation went to England where he eventually became secretary of Chelsea Hospital. He died in 1731 and an inscription commemorating him may still be read in the chapel. Funds from him in 1775 replaced the old library which Bishop Stewart had built at right angles to the south face of the chapel. At the same time the dormitories on the south side of the quadrangle erected by Bishop Dunbar were taken down to make room for new buildings provided by Fraser. He also made gifts to the library, Bishop Gilbert Burnet of Salisbury performing a like service to Marischal.

Outside the universities the facilities for education in Aberdeen were considerable and constantly growing. The ancient Grammar School benefited from the fact that both it and Marischal College were town's institutions and so received favourable treatment from the Council. One of the school's most distinguished rectors, David Wedderburn, who was appointed in 1602, was in 1619 entrusted also with the duty of conducting the Humanity class in the university and twice received monetary rewards from the magistrates, once for a Latin poem in honour of King James and in 1639 for his grammar of the Latin tongue, which continued in use for well over a century. He was also retained by the town to write an annual piece of verse or prose upon the affairs of the burgh — the first and only example in Aberdeen's history of a civic poet laureate. Wedderburn's salary was £80 and the pupils' fees, fixed at 10s. the quarter in 1602, were raised later to 13s. 4d. This increase seems to have been sanctioned as a compromise with Wedderburn, whose exactions from parents had become too severe. Whatever his qualifications as a scholar, he seems to have been an indiscreet disciplinarian, for in 1612 some of the pupils mutinied, and armed with pistols and other weapons barricaded themselves in the Song School building. Twenty-one of the most insubordinate were expelled, and some of them imprisoned. The Grammar School boys, however, were for long afterwards noted for their obstreperous behaviour, and in 1700, by threatening violence, they caused the Council to modify an order that they should repeat the Shorter Catechism publicly once a week. After Wedderburn the rectors received as a rule a salary of 600 merks.

The great educational event of the first half of the Eighteenth Century was the founding of Robert Gordon's Hospital by a deed of 1729 executed by Robert Gordon, a merchant of Danzig, who died in 1732 leaving a fortune of £10,300. The building was completed in 1739 at a cost of £3,000. Owing to the political troubles of the time and to financial stringency, it was not until 1750 that the school was opened for educational purposes. Its inauguration will be recounted in a subsequent chapter.

There were various other educational establishments. A school instituted by the magistrates in 1607 for writing, arithmetic and bookkeeping, lasted for more than 200 years. In 1673 the magistrates gave patronage to a school for English grammar which latterly was localised in Drum's Lane. The Sang School flourished in the Back Wynd, particularly after the beginning of the Troubles in 1638, when the institution became very busy teaching singing as well as instrumental music on the virginal and the lute. Thomas Davidson, who was master at a salary of £100 Scots, was from 1652 to 1675 responsible for the first published book of Scottish music, the *Cantus, Songs and Fancies* issued by John Forbes in 1662. It is interesting to note that during the Presbyterian ascendancy masters of the Sang School were debarred from performing at lykewakes, a privilege which returned to them at the Restoration. In 1758 the school premises were sold by order of the Council.

CHAPTER SIX

The Troubles

Save for the war scare of 1626 and 1627 when a Spanish landing was feared and there was the usual bustle of wapinschaws and fortifications,[1] and for the rowdy presence of some of Colonel Mackay's soldiers bound for Germany, the years until 1640 were in sharp contrast to the following two decades. Charles I's accession had been received with great cordiality and his coronation as King of Scots in Edinburgh on 18 July 1633, was followed the next day in Aberdeen by rejoicings of more than common extravagance. But as Walpole was to say a hundred years later, 'they may ring their bells today, but they'll be wringing their hands soon'.

In 1634 Patrick Leslie of Iden (now Eden) was elected Provost. IIe had been a Commissioner to Parliament in 1633 when Charles was in Edinburgh, and as a Presbyterian of resolute character had displeased the King. No sooner had the news of his civic promotion reached Whitehall than steps were taken to annul it. A letter was dispatched forthwith to the magistrates through Patrick Chalmers, the Sheriff-Clerk. It is a sufficiently historic document to deserve reproduction:

Charles R. — Trustie and well-beloved, we greet you weel.
Whereas we are informit of some seditious convocatiounes practised among you, coming as we heir especiallie from the electioun you have latelie made of one Patrick Leslie for your provost, whome we are informit to have wrongit your trust in his careage at our late parliament and theirfoir to have deserved no such chairge, and in regaird we have always formerlie found you forward for our service and accordinglie have dispensed our favour to you in quhat micht concern your liberties and priviledges. Now being cairfill of that which may concern our service and the peace and weal of that of our citie, in redressing of the abuses past and preventing the lyke inconvenience, it

---

1 Captain Arthur Forbes 'quho is ane gentilman' and had served in the Low Countries, was chosen to train Aberdeen's 'Home Guard' of 1626.

is our pleasur for that effect that you remove the said Patrick Leslie from being your provost, and in his place we wish you to mak choice of Sir Paull Mengzes who was formerlie in that chairge. So not doubting of the performance of this our pleasur we bid you farewell. From our Court at Whitehall the 10th December 1634.[1]

The demand put the Council in an awkward predicament, for it was negotiating with the King for a reaffirmation of the burgh's charter of rights, and the royal letter contained a pretty plain hint that if Leslie continued in the chair the desiderated charter would not be forthcoming. There was nothing for it but to submit, which was done incontinently; even Patrick Leslie himself, like a twentieth-century prisoner of the Comintern or the Gestapo, confessing his acquiescence and demitting office. For all that, the Leslie party in and out of Council, having recovered from the shock was too powerful to remain long inactive. At the Michaelmas election nine months later the nomination of Leslie would again have gone through had not the Bishop of Aberdeen and the Sheriff of Aberdeenshire entered the council chamber, and demanded that the proceedings be sisted until the King was consulted. Seven of the Council were for acquiescence but nine stoutly refused to be browbeaten and objected to any invasion of their rights,[2] whereupon the Bishop dissolved the meeting.

A fortnight later letters from the King and Chancellor were read, the first ordering a unanimous (and of course complaisant) vote, the second requiring 'in his majestie's name that they suld not make chuse of the said Patrik Leslie to be thair provost, nor yit suffer him to haive woyce in thair counsall'. This produced a scene, for Leslie got hold of the official leets and would not surrender them, protesting that the majority of the Council was with him, and that he had the right to put his vote on the leets. Sir Paul Menzies the provost and two others of his party followed Leslie about the Council house, 'drawing of the said Patrik's hand and the pen frome the paper'. After much scrambling and bicker-

---

1   This vicious and unconstitutional practice initiated by Charles I was occasionally resorted to, but in a milder form, during the Protectorate, and frequently repeated in an exaggerated degree by both Charles II and James VII. After the Revolution it was discontinued until our own day, when in 1944 Herbert Morrison, Home Secretary, gave orders to Scottish burghs to rescind certain appointments they had made. Only Dunfermline had the courage to tell him to mind his own business.

2   Leslie and two others were absent: two baillies and the treasurer contested the attempt to intimidate them. One, Robert Farquhar, later became provost and a knight and laird of Mounie.

ing Leslie and nine others withdrew from the meeting, and the remaining nine proceeded to elect a new Council and provost. The alderman's mantle fell on Robert Johnston of Crimond, but owing to the turmoil attending it, the Privy Council pronounced the election void and recommended the election of Alexander Jaffray,[1] who was quite outside the controversy, as provost; which was accordingly done. It is rather curious that the new provost should have been as stiff a Covenanter as Leslie, several of whose friends were included in a second new council, but Leslie himself, despite promise of future amendment, was debarred by the Privy Council from being elected.

While this local squabble was running its course, greater events were brewing which more and more were to distract his Majesty's attention. His passion for interfering did not stop at local government and Aberdeen: he must needs also direct the religious beliefs and observances of all his subjects. Aberdeen was as Laodicean as regards Charles's innovations as it had been in the changeover of the Reformation. It was the only district in Scotland which the new Liturgy and Book of Canons failed to set in ferment; indeed the Book of Canons was printed for the Government by Aberdeen's town printer, Edward Raban, in 1636. For two years dissatisfaction seethed throughout the country, except in Aberdeen, in which parish church no voice was raised against the elsewhere obnoxious service-book.

In March 1638, the lairds of Dun, Leys and Morphie, all strong Presbyterians, came as a deputation to the Town Council to solicit aid in resistance to the new religious order. But Aberdeen was 'constantly abyding be the King', who wrote to thank the Council for its loyalty. In July the Covenanting party sent a further deputation to Aberdeen, consisting of the Earl of Montrose, Lord Coupar, the Master of Forbes, Burnett of Leys, Graham of Morphie, the Rev. Alexander Henderson of Leuchars, the Rev. David Dickson of Irvine and the Rev. Andrew Cant of Pitsligo. This was heavy metal indeed, and shows how important the adherence of Aberdeen to the Covenant was considered to be.

The visitation commenced inauspiciously. When the strangers reached the city the magistrates in accordance with long custom offered them the Cup of Bonaccord from which to drink prosperity to the town. But the Commissioners were men with a mission. They spurned the proferred hospitality saying that they would not drink until the Council had subscribed the Covenant. 'The like was never done in Aberdeen

---

1   This was the father of the more famous Alexander, one of Aberdeen's greatest provosts and characters.

in no man's memorie', ruefully comments Spalding. The magistrates
gave the wine to the poor men in the St. Thomas hospital, and took
counter-measures to show their displeasure. When on the Sunday the
commissioners would have preached in the city churches, they found
the doors closed upon them, and were driven for want of a better
pulpit and chapel to conduct three services during the day from the
forestairs above the great courtyard of the Earl Marischal's house in the
Castlegate. Later the three reverend visitors disputed with the celebrated sextet of Aberdeen Doctors — Dr. John Forbes of Corse,
professor of divinity at King's; Dr. Alexander Scroggie, minister of
Old Aberdeen; Dr. William Leslie, principal of King's; Dr. Robert
Barron, professor of divinity at Marischal; Dr. James Sibbald and Dr
Alexander Ross, ministers in Aberdeen. The controversy which ensued
in no fewer than eleven pamphlets was of the rapid-fire but long-range
variety, for the contestants did not meet to discuss their differences.
The general opinion of the public was adverse to the commissioners.

> From Dickson, Henderson and Cant,
> Apostles of the Covenant,
> Good Lord deliver us,

mocked the profane. Only 500, some with reservations like Dr. Guild,
were found to sign the Covenant, but amongst the magistrates who did
so were Patrick Leslie and his brother John, and Provost Alexander
Jaffray. The Council got another commendatory epistle from the
King, who in face of the threat implicit in the Covenant was dispensing
with the obnoxious regulations in religion; but these things availed
both King and Council little in the future.

In September 1638, probably just after news that the new charter
had been signed, Alexander Jaffray was again elected provost, and
ten days later, Huntly as King's Commissioner in the North presented
himself, read Charles's letter withdrawing the Liturgy and Book of
Canons, and desired that the Council subscribe the Confession of Faith
of 1580 and the General Band of 1589 for maintenance of the true
religion, these being Charles's reply to the National Covenant of 1638.
The Council and two of the town's ministers complied, with the
qualification that they did so only because the 1580 and 1589 instruments condemned popery. In the meantime word had been received
that the Covenanters were drilling in the south. Because of 'some
disorderlie and vnpeacable careage of the trayned band' in the city, the
Council had discharged the company and ordered that no inhabitants

should 'presume to tack vpoun hand to touch drumme, lift cullouris or armes' or engage in drill. This, however, was too much for the citizens to accept. In this as in other matters the community seems for some years to have been in the habit of giving the Council a lead, for measures of public safety were adopted in January 1639 at the instance of the brethren of guild and the deacons of the crafts, and in March, the toune being convenit' decided that 200 muskets with bandoliers, powder and lead, and 100 pikes should be purchased from Huntly to arm such citizens as could not afford to arm themselves[1]; it was 'the collective bodie of this burghe' which took the initiative in having a permanent council[2] of war appointed; and it was because of the arguments of 'a great number of nichtboures' that the Town Council decided not to send a commissioner to the Glasgow Assembly at which to all intents and purposes the nation broke with the King.

But despite the promptings of the citizens, only a few trenches had been dug on the north side of the town from the Gallowgate port to the Castlehill, with some timber sconces on the south side and eleven cannon in the streets, when the Earl of Montrose, at the head of a Covenanting army of 9,000 men,[3] entered the town on 30 March. Spalding described the brave show they made as they came in by the Overkirkgate Port, through the Broadgate, the Castlegate, and out by the Justice Port on to the Queen's Links. 'They came in order of battell', says Aberdeen's picturesque historian, 'weill-armed both on horse and foot, ilk horseman haveing five shot at least with ane carabine in hand, two pistols by his side, and other two at his saddle toir; the pikemen in their ranks with pike and sword; the musketiers in their ranks with musket staffs, bandolier, sword, powder, ball and match; ilk company had their captins, lieutenants, ensignes, sergeants, and other officers and commanders, all, for the most part, in buff coats, and in goodly order. They had five colours of ensigns, they had trumpeters to ilk company of horsemen, and drummers to ilk company of footmen; they had their meat, drink, and other provision, bag and baggage caryed with them.'

The Covenanting Army made a short stay to begin with. The troops

1 The Dean of Guild and the treasurer had to give the Marquis a bond for £3,685 4s. Scots to cover the cost.
2 Of sixteen members; Huntly called a muster of all the loyalists between 16 and 60 to meet him on 25 March, but only 160 from the Aulton and Spital presented themselves, and they were unarmed and untrained.
3 There were over 6,000 from the south, and Lord Fraser and the Master of Forbes brought in 2,000 from the north.

marched through the town to the links, pitched camp, a council of war was held,[1] and then, led by Montrose, the Earl Marischal and General Alexander Leslie all but 1,800 of them set out for Kintore. Those left behind to garrison Aberdeen were commanded by the Earl of Kinghorn. The citizens were at once set about filling up their trenches, dismounting their cannon and surrendering their arms and munitions. The soldiers were billeted at 6s. 8d. a day, repayment of which was promised, the intention being (Montrose had said) 'in no way to do the smallest wrong or injurie to any, nor use the meanest violence'. But that idyllic relationship did not last. The Covenanting ministers in the town had proclaimed that 'now the curse was alighted on Meroz, which came not to help the Lord against the mighty'; and they were right. The Doctors had taken wing and fled. Some other prominent anti-covenanters took ship along with sixty young men who were going to join the King. Kinghorn ordered the town to sign the Covenant. This being received with hesitation, Montrose returned to Aberdeen, and in Greyfriars Kirk the people were told they must fortify the blockhouse against foreign enemies, subscribe the Covenant and make common cause with the rest of the Kingdom; and contribute a tax of 100,000 merks plus the cost of the army since it came to the city, the original subscribers of the Covenant being exempt from these imposts.

The community met and accepted all the demands but the 100,000 merks; that it was unable to pay, and if the levy was insisted on, the citizens asked for a month's grace 'to remove themselves, wives and bairns, with bag and baggage out of the toun'. On 10 April they signed the Covenant. The levy was later modified, but four commissioners from Aberdeen nominated by Montrose to attend a meeting of Covenanting delegates in Edinburgh were put in ward there until security should be found for the fine. Soon after the Covenanting forces began to retire south. Before leaving, however, their leaders summoned Huntly to a conference under a safe-conduct signed by Montrose. The meeting took place in Marischal's house, but Huntly refused to resign his commission as the King's lieutenant in the north, and went home to his own rooms. In the morning he found himself under guard, and had to go with the Covenanters to Edinburgh, where he was placed in the Castle. 'You may take my head from my shoulders', he said, 'but not my heart from my Sovereign.'

1   Two deputations from the town to Montrose — George Jamesone was a member of one — got fine words but no satisfaction.

No sooner were the Covenanting leaders' backs turned than Huntly's son, the Earl of Aboyne, with the laird of Banff and sundry other Gordon chiefs, began to raise the country. In the first week of May, the lairds of Delgaty and Towie-Barclay attacked Balquholly (now Hatton Castle) where Sir Thomas Urquhart was residing, and lifted some muskets which had been collected there. On 10 May Urquhart and some Episcopalian friends laid siege to Towie-Barclay, where the stolen arms were stored, and one of the party was killed by a shot from the castle, his being the first blood shed in the Great Civil War. The local Covenanters, under Lord Fraser, and the Master of Forbes, had meanwhile assembled some 3,000 men at Monymusk, to which muster the Earl Marischal, who had assumed the office of governor of Aberdeen, ordered the Council to send eighty men. Fraser and Forbes having gone to Turriff to encourage the adherents of the Covenant in that district, had assembled 1,200 men there when they were surprised by the laird of Banff and Gordon of Haddo and put to an inglorious rout on 13 May 1639, which has come down in history under the nickname of the Trot of Turriff. Emboldened by their success the victors advanced upon Aberdeen, which, Marischal having withdrawn to Dunnottar, they occupied unopposed. The Royalists' first act was to plunder the houses of the townsmen whose Covenanting sympathies were known. Then they demanded of the Town Council that they should be quartered gratis on the Covenanting members of the community, but this was refused, the citizens, anticipating the corporate responsibility of much later years, answering 'all in ane voce that they wold not be separat nor divyde thameselffis frome the auld convenanteris, since they are all memberis of one bodie and incorporatioun with thame'. Nor would they agree to send soldiers to the King, on the ground that so many men had gone to the foreign wars and the King's service that an insufficient number remained to guard the town.

Aberdeen, in fact, in its extremity was bethinking itself that Aberdeen should come first. The Royalists remained in the city for only five days. When they retired, the Earl Marischal followed on their heels with 2,000 men, and not long after he had reoccupied the town, Montrose appeared on the scene again with 6,000 men. The bishop's palace was now pillaged and for a second time the citizens who leaned towards the King's side had to pay the price of their loyalty or leave their homes. Several made for Macduff, and there took ship for the south. They had not long put to sea, however, when they fell in with three ships bringing Lord Aboyne, with the King's commission of lieutenancy, and with military stores, to the north. Those they joined, the flotilla put in to the roadstead of Aberdeen, and their presence caused Montrose to raise his siege of the House of Gight and leave for the south in search of reinforcements. Aboyne landed on 6 June, was joined by his brother Lord Lewis Gordon, with 1,000 of the caterans from Birse that Aberdonians hated above all other mortals, and exacted a loan from the town. Then for ten days there was a comparative lull before the tempest broke which in its full fury caused Spalding to exclaim in an agony of mind, 'O woful Abirdene! by thy sins this heavie scourge is laid upone thee bye all the burrows in Scotland — much to be bemoaned and lamented!'

CHAPTER SEVEN

More Troubles

By 14 June 1639 the Earl of Aboyne had 4,000 men in Aberdeen, including the burgesses, who had been ordered by the Town Council
to assist him. They were under the command of Lieutenant-Colonel
William Johnston, a son of Robert Johnston of Crimond and a Scots
cousin of Arthur Johnston the poet. This Johnston had served in the
Green Brigade with Gustavus Adolphus, and is credited with setting
the trap for the Covenanters that caused the Trot of Turriff. He was a
much better professional soldier than a Colonel Gun whom Charles
had attached as military adviser to Aboyne. Having clapped Provost
Jaffray and his son in jail, Aboyne set off for Stonehaven. Marischal,
by now joined by Montrose, moved north to meet him, and though
much outnumbered, succeeded in putting the Royalists to flight at
Megray Hill. Aboyne retreated in some confusion, pursued by Montrose,
to Aberdeen. There the Royalists decided to defend the town on the
line of the River Dee. The townsmen, under Johnston, made themselves responsible for the custody of the bridge itself. The Gordons
seem to have arranged themselves farther back out of range of the river.
Aboyne's force was smaller now, for Megray Hill had been a dis-
couragement to his caterans, many of whom had set off for home with
such booty as they had collected from friend and foe alike. But of the
remainder, some were mounted, and that was a big asset in those days.

Megray Hill was on 15 June. On the 17th Montrose's Covenanters
were in bivouac at the place still known as the Covenanters' Faulds.
On the morning of the 18th, they opened upon the bridge with their
artillery; Spalding says their 'cartow', a quarter cannon throwing a
'bullet' of 20 lb., was 'veray feirfull', but it does not seem to have been
very deadly. Skirmishers crept up to the south bank of the river and
exchanged musket volleys with the men of 'both Aberdeins', who gave
fire abundantly. The casualties to the defence during the whole day's
work amounted to one townsman, John Forbes, 'pitifullie slayne',
and William Gordon of Gordon's Mills, 'rakleslie schot' in the foot.

Unhappily, the fall of Forbes proved the defence's undoing. The warlike citizens were essentially civilians and they lived in an atmosphere of peace. On the 19th, therefore, fifty of them — half of the bridge's defenders — insisted on returning to the town to attend Forbes's funeral. After they left, a new assault was launched, which was foiled by Johnston's dexterity. What Spalding calls 'the tynsall (loss) of the brig' came about in this wise. Seeing that a frontal assault would be either too costly a success or a failure, Montrose devised a feint. He sent his horse up the south bank of the Dee, and when they had gone so far, they pretended to attempt to swim the river. This quite deceived Gun, who with Aboyne and the Royalist horsemen set off along the north bank keeping pace with the troop on the other side, and leaving only Johnston and his fifty to hold the bridge. When the horse had been well drawn off, Montrose opened a tremendous fire upon Johnston, who was himself hit 'in the thie or leg by the buffet of ane stonn throwin out of the brig by the violens of ane schot', and was rendered unfit for service. Thereupon the townsmen withdrew and the Covenanters took possession of the bridge without more ado. Aboyne, returning too late, 'takis the flight schamefullie, but (without) straik of suord or ony vther kynd of vassalage'.

The Gordons' conduct filled Spalding, usually their eulogist, with unwonted censure. Aboyne and his horsemen, he says, 'lay vnder bankis and brayis, saiffring thameselffis fra the cartow, and beheld the Abirdeins men defend the brig'. But 'it is said our Abirdeins men wes praisit, even of thair vary enemeis for thair service and reddie fyre'. Four Aberdeen men were slain on the bridge and others wounded, and one, John Seton of Pitmedden, whose death is celebrated in the ballad 'Bonny John Seton', was shot while riding up the river with Aboyne. By 4 o'clock the engagement was over, the Gordons well away and unpursued, but while the ordered ranks of the Covenanters entered the burgh on the one side, the Royalist citizens with their wives and children in their arms and on their backs, fled by the other ports, 'weiping and murning most pitifullie, straying heir and thair, not knowing quhair to go'. By paying a fine of 7,000 merks and thanks also to Montrose's refusal to carry out the orders from Edinburgh to destroy the burgh, Aberdeen escaped systematic pillage, although some property was looted and forty-eight citizens who had taken part in the defence of the town were pinioned and thrown into the tolbooth. A few days later came the news that Charles and the Covenanters had reached agreement at the Pacification of Berwick.

So ended Montrose's first campaign that involved a battle, and so was the Battle of the Bridge of Dee fought for little result. A couple of commissioners sent to Berwick to lay before the King a statement of the town's losses in his service got Charles's thanks and sympathy. He had nothing to give that would reduce the town's debt, which stood at £19,954 8s. 7d. at Michaelmas 1639. One strange incident put the final punctuation to the campaign. A convenanting gentleman, Ramsay of Balmain, had been slain in the battle and was interred with military honours at the door of the Kirk of St. Nicholas. When the firing party discharged their last volley over the grave, a comrade, Erskine of Pittodrie, who was standing opposite, fell shot through the head. This assassination was believed to be the work of some private enemy in the town who had taken his chance of closing the account.

Whatever may have been the general opinion on the situation, the Covenanting leaders were under no illusion as to the durability of the Pacification. They had in their service many seasoned professional soldiers, whose talents they determined to keep within reach, so they formed these veterans into a special reserve of officers, of whom Aberdeen's quota, town and country, was a lieutenant-colonel, three captains and nine other officers, whom the district had to maintain at a cost of £400 a month.

The winter was quiet, but in the spring of 1640 the Covenanters began to take precautionary measures. A tithe tax was imposed for the defence of the country, and Marischal soon after requisitioned all the silver and gold plate and coin in the possession of the citizens. On 5 May Marischal having come to town and ordered that the citizens be mustered, 260 presented themselves at the Links; the rest had presumably left the town. On the 28th Major-General Robert Monro with 800 foot and 40 horse arrived at Aberdeen as a garrison and laid certain demands before the Council which were given the title of 'Articles of Bonaccord'. These involved the compiling of a roll of those who had not subscribed the Covenant, the levying of a stent or tax for the maintenance of the garrison, the restriction of preaching to Coven-anting ministers, and handing over of the keys of all the gates and public buildings, the surrender of all arms, cannon, ammunition and stores, and 'in testimonie of thair Bonaccord with the soldatists that hes come so farre a marche for their saiffities from the invasioun of forrane enimies, and the slaveries thay and thair posteritie micht be broct under', to supply 1,200 pair of shoes and 3,000 'elves of hardin tycking or saill canves' for tents. In August a company of 120 Aberdonians, under Marischal's brother, Robert Keith, marched to join General

Leslie's army which invaded England in the second Bishops' War. Monro himself remained in Aberdeen until 12 September 1640 living on the inhabitants and pillaging the hinterland. Between the Mercat and Fish Crosses in the Castlegate he constructed a court de guard and a wooden mare for inflicting military punishments. One citizen of over seventy who spoke against the soldiery was made to ride 'the mare to his great hurt and pain'. Still, Monro and his officers marched out of Aberdeen with burgess tickets in their bonnets, the first mention of the wearing of the insignia in that way.

To Monro succeeded Lord Sinclair with 500 men as ravenous as their predecessors. They were inflicted upon Aberdeen until 9 February 1642, 'daylie deboshing, in drinking, hureing, nicht-walking, combating, sweiring, and bringing sundry honest women-servandis to gryte miserie'. The Church courts dealt with sixty-five of those erring sisters, some of whom were inhumanly punished. 'Thus this ribald regiment heaped up sin to our owne numberless sinis, and did no more good, bot lying idle, consumeing honest menis viveris.' It left the countryside 'manless, moneyless, horseless and arms-less'.

From the departure of this garrison until the spring of 1644 Aberdeen enjoyed almost unbroken peace. The quiet was only disturbed when Gordon of Haddo, meeting Alexander Jaffray, then a baillie, and his brother John at Dalweary, near Kintore, assaulted and wounded them both. Jaffray in his magisterial capacity had had to sentence one of Gordon's retainers, and this was Haddo's high-handed way of showing his resentment of any limitation being put to the liberty of his household. The Town Council decided to take measures to bring Haddo to book, and the Privy Council fined Haddo 20,000 merks. But when an attempt was made to levy the fine, it was, as usual, the countryman who struck first. Anticipating trouble, the Council instituted a night patrol and placed four pieces of artillery in position to ward off an attack. But in the early morning of 19 March 1644, immediately after the watch was dismissed, Gordon, with the laird of Drum and other friends galloped through the Aulton into Aberdeen, seized Provost Leslie, Robert Farquhar (who was to succeed to the provostship that autumn and was one of the wealthiest men in Scotland), and the two Jaffrays, and by 10 in the forenoon, they were prancing up the Gallowgate again with their captives mounted on stolen horses. 'The like seldome hes bein sein', reflects Spalding, 'that so few men so pertlie and publictlie sould have disgraced sic a brave burghe, by taking away thair prouest and the rest men of not, without any kynd of contradictioun or obstacull.'

Haddo stayed in Old Aberdeen long enough to mount some of his children, who were at school there, behind his servants. Then the cavalcade rode through the Loch Wynd, had a drink at Kintore, lodged for the night at Leggatsden, and had the prisoners safely in Strathbogie the next morning. Ten or twelve days later they were lodged in Auchindoun, where they were kept prisoners until five weeks afterwards when the arrival of Argyll with a Covenanting force in the North-East caused the Marquis of Huntly, who had abetted the outrage, to set them free. Alexander Jaffray in his diary says they were by Huntly and his servants 'very cruelly used' during their imprisonment. Jaffray's wife was ill at the time of the raid and died within a week of it, but as she had borne her lord and master ten children in her twelve years of wedded bliss, we need not blame Haddo wholly for her demise. A good deal of false sympathy has been wasted on Haddo, who shortly after was captured, haled to Edinburgh and executed.

As had been noted, Huntly was deeply involved when Haddo was raiding Aberdeen. Montrose, with orders from the King to raise the Royalists in Scotland, was at Carlisle awaiting his chance to slip over the Border. Word of his intention proceded him. On 28 March Huntly was in Aberdeen with 300 horse and the same number of foot, demanding money and free quarters for his men. He lived on the town until 30 April when the approach of the Covenanting Army, 6,000 strong, under Argyll, Marischal and other lords, warned him to disappear. The Covenanters marched in without opposition, went rather better than Huntly in the severity of their exactions from the city, and after a few days took the road to the north, leaving the Earl of Kinghorn for the second time governor of Aberdeen. With Huntly gone to earth like the old fox he was, there seemed to be little prospect of a big man-hunt in the north-east, when Kinghorn was succeeded in his post by Balfour of Burleigh.

But by the end of the summer Montrose was playing ducks and drakes with the Covenanting pattern of an orderly and united Scotland. More by luck than by management he had got in touch with Alisdair (Colkitto) Macdonald, who at the head of 1,100 Catholic Irishmen sent over by the King's sympathisers to make trouble in Scotland was wandering about the Central Highlands with the Covenanting net closing about him. Montrose's commission as the King's lieutenant gave him command of those hard-bitten desperadoes, and won him the support of the Stewarts and Robertsons in Atholl and some Gordons and Macdonalds from Badenoch. In all by the end of August he had 2,200 men, of whom half were badly equipped and only three had horses, a heavy drawback in a century when cavalry was deemed essential to victory. But at Tippermuir Montrose got the weapons he required and proved that brains in the general are worth more than cavalry. Without horse or artillery he defeated Lord Elcho's 7,000 men, who included 700 mounted troops, in a few minutes. His casualties could be counted on one hand; the Covenanters lost hundreds. He took Perth without a blow, but was not strong enough to storm Dundee. He therefore turned northwards to Aberdeen, probably in the hope of securing Gordon help. Aboyne was with Charles, his younger brothers Lord Gordon and Lord Lewis Gordon were actually with Balfour of Burleigh, and only young Nathaniel of Ardlogie joined Montrose.

On 11 September Montrose reached the Dee between Banchory and Mills of Drum, having traversed the hills from the Mearns by the Cryne's Cross Mounth. He crossed the river at once, and occupied Crathes Castle. Next day he hastened downstream and camped for the night at the Twa Mile Cross, on the croft of North Garthdee, between modern Ruthrieston and Cults south of the railway. That night the moon rose over Aberdeen as red as blood two hours before her time. In the morning Montrose's scouts found the army of the Covenant under Burleigh well posted on the brow of the slope at the north end of the Hardgate. His left reached to about where West Craibstone Street is today, his centre ran through Strawberrybank, and his right wing continued in a line parallel with Justice Mill Lane to a point near the site of the Uptown baths and the Odeon Cinema. The lower Justice Mills, which gave their name to the ensuing battle, lay below the right wing, in a south-westerly direction. Skirmishers were posted along the course of the Howburn and in the houses and gardens on the banks of the stream and on the lower slopes north of it. Burleigh had about 2,000 infantry — mostly Fife levies but a good many from Aberdeen — and 500 horse, Forbeses, Frasers and Crichtons, besides eighteen under Lord Lewis Gordon. He had several pieces of artillery. His horse was disposed on the extreme right and left of his line, an arrangement which was followed also by Montrose, who came to the encounter with only 1,500 foot — many of his Highlanders having decamped with the spoils of Tippermuir — and seventy cavalry and a few light guns.

On the morning of the 13th Montrose sent a herald and a drummer to the magistrates summoning the town to surrender with an assurance of good treatment if that were done; and otherwise ordering that all old persons, women and children be got out of the place, those remaining to expect no quarter. The provost, on receiving the letter, convened the Council, 'at the Bowbrig in Alexander Fyndlateris house', where Lord Burleigh and some of his officers were. It was decided to fight, but the herald and drummer received a hearty cup as well as the letter, which ended, above the civic signatures, with the words, 'your lordship's faithful friends to serve you', erased in favour of the shorter and more equivocal 'your lordship's as ye love us'. Unfortunately, as the messengers were passing by the Fife regiment on their journey, a shot was fired, by a mounted man it was thought, and the drummer fell dead. This was at 11 a.m. Montrose 'fynding his drummer aganes the law of nationis, moat inhumanelie slayne, grew', says Spalding, 'mad, and became furious and impatient'. He had held back his men at the Twa Mile Cross until he should receive Aberdeen's answer. Now he set his army in motion, no doubt crossing the old Ruthrieston bridge as he advanced to the assault.

Just as the battle began a high wind arose out of the west-south-west and blew into the faces of the Covenant Army. Colkitto's Irish formed the Royalist centre, with Sir William Rollo and Colonel James Hay on the right wing, and Nathaniel Gordon on the left, the horsemen at the extremities, with a few musketeers and bowmen amongst them to give them greater striking power. Colkitto opened the battle by clearing the skirmishers out of the houses and yards on the line of the Howburn and then breasting the slope towards the main body of the enemy. Then the horse on Burleigh's left wing, when the Royalists came upon the open brae, charged in small troops, first Lewis Gordon, then Fraser and Crichton, quite without effect. At the same time, however, 400 of the Covenanter foot and 100 horse on the right wing, slipping down the sunken path that is now Justice Mill Lane and through the hollow past the mills themselves, suddenly assailed Montrose's left wing from the rear. Nathaniel Gordon just managed to hold firm until Montrose brought Rollo's contingent from the other flank, when the Covenanters were thrown back with heavy loss. The transference of Rollo seriously weakened Montrose's right wing, and Sir William Forbes of Craigievar, who commanded the rest of Burleigh's horse in that quarter, took advantage of the situation to launch and press home a stiff charge. The Irish veterans, however, merely opened their ranks and let the cavalry through, then wheeled, and poured in a volley at their backs. This disorganised the horsemen, who broke and drew off. Montrose, like Wellington in the evening at Waterloo, ordered a general advance, Burleigh's centre melted away and fled, and the swift-footed Irish and Highlanders cut down the fugitives in a continuous slaughter from the northern end of the Hardgate all the way to the Denburn.

There were no defences behind which the city's garrison might rally. The Irish, to whom Montrose had promised the town to sack, swarmed into the narrow streets cutting down the flying Covenanters without mercy, and then stripping them of their clothes (to preserve the garments unsoiled) before dispatching their victims. Old and young, armed and unarmed, male and female, were indiscriminately butchered, and the younger women violated or carried back to the camp. The battle lasted but two or three hours, the subsequent slaughters went on for four days, 'and nothing hard' says Spalding, 'bot pitifull howling, crying, weiping, murning, throw all the streittis'. The dead lay naked on the causeways, and none dared remove them for burial for fear of the Irish. 'The wyf durst not cry nor weip at her husbandis slauchter befoir hir eyes, nor the mother for the sone, nor the dochter for the father; whiche, if thay war hard, then thay war presentlie slayne also.' The jail was broken open, the prisoners set at liberty, many houses were entered and ransacked.

Montrose was not above profiting in person from the disorder. In January 1645 it was related to the Town Council on behalf of the partners who conducted the cloth factory in the Correction House how 'the Marques of Montroise did desyre and require thame to furnishe so much English cloth and baise (stockings) to the Irish officiars, with furnite for four sutes to four of the prymest of them; as lykewayes that they suld furnish, for himselff and Colonel Sibbald, so muche dropdeberry, London cloth, taffatie and other furnitur, vtherwayes they wald not be able to saiff the boothes of the toun unplunderit altogidder'. Matthew Lumsden, baillie; Thomas Buck, Master of Kirkwork; Robert Leslie, Master of Hospitals; Alexander and Robert Reid, advocates; Andrew and Thomas Burnett, merchants, and many more citizens, 'to the number neir of aucht scoir' (say the town records) lost their lives in this blackest week-end Aberdeen has ever experienced. Spalding gives a list of 109 Aberdeen names and nine unnamed casualties, adding, that they were slain beyond the town and after the battle, about Justice Mills, Foresterhill, Newhills and Sheddocksley, as well as in the fight and in the burgh. He adds that some country folk and some of the Fife regiment also lost their lives. On the Monday, Spalding himself 'saw two corpis cariet to the buriall throw the Oldtoun with wemen onlie, and not ane man amongst them, so that the naiket corpis lay onburiet so long as this lymmaris war ongone to the camp'. It was all the work of the Irish. On the day after the battle the rest of the Royalist army was sent on to Kintore and Inverurie, while Montrose followed on Monday, the 16th, after the customary proclamations made by a victorious general in a conquered town. And then, so swiftly did the scene change, on the 18th, the vanguard of Argyll's Covenanting army that was in pursuit of Montrose from the south marched into the town, and all the local Covenanting notables and ministers, who had fled on Montrose's approach, reappeared and 'cropis the calsey bravelie'.

Montrose may have been in Aberdeen again the following spring, for we learn that from 7 March to 14 May 1645 the Council did not meet 'in respect that Montrose and his army wer in thir fieldis, and daylie repairing to this burghe'. Actually he posted nearly 100 horse in the city, while he kept his headquarters at Kintore. Away from the eye of their master, his troopers grew careless, and on 25 March some of Nathaniel Gordon's friends were surprised by a body of Covenant horse under Sir John Hurry which broke into the town and killed or captured a few of the garrison, including the leader of the Farquharsons. The funeral of this important henchman brought Montrose into the burgh again, attended by Colkitto himself. Fortunately, the storm that attended his brilliant campaigns after the Battle of Justice Mills passed Aberdeen by. In May 1650, after his last defeat and capture at Carbisdale and on his road to execution in Edinburgh with a herald preceding him crying, 'Here comes James Graham, a traitor to his country', Montrose may have passed through Aberdeen. After his execution on the 21st of the month, one of his hands was sent to Aberdeen and nailed to the Tolbooth. On 7 July, Charles II, having landed at Speymouth, reached Aberdeen, and put up in Pitfodels' Lodging across the Castlegate from the blackened limb of the man whom he had rather callously sent to his death.[1]

There was yet another skirmish a year later. In January 1646 a

---

1   The limb was taken down there and then, probably at Charles's instigation, and decently interred in St. Nicholas kirkyard. After the Restoration the magistrates handed it over, in a coffin draped with crimson velvet and after lying in state in the Townhouse, to Harie Graham, Montrose's half-brother.

Covenanting garrison took over the care of the town. In April, on General Middleton's departure for the north, a regiment of foot and another of horse under Colonel Montgomery were left in charge. In May Huntly, who was, rather late in the day, again in arms for the King, assembled an army in Inverurie and Kintore, where Montgomery attacked him on the 13th but was repulsed with loss. Huntly then took the initiative and advanced towards the city. From a position north-west of the Loch, on the heathy common where Broadford now stands, he launched his attack. A section of the Gallowgate took fire, and Aboyne, breaking in there, swept down the street to the Broadgate. There he fought a hand-to-hand duel with the Master of Forbes, whom he slew, and Montgomery's men were eventually driven into the Castlegate. Those who could not escape 'by speed o' fit' shut themselves up in Marischal's mansion and the house of Menzies of Pitfodels, and finally surrendered. 'This was thought to be one of the hottest pieces of service that happened since this unnatural war began, both in regard to the eagerness of the pursuers and valour of the defenders.' But nothing came of it. The First Civil War was over before the skirmish was fought, and Charles had surrendered to the Scots army in England. Huntly was betrayed, captured and beheaded shortly after his Sovereign, while Argyll, who was responsible for the execution of both Huntly and Montrose, ended his own life on the block after the Restoration.

The citizens of Aberdeen seem to have reacted to the execution of Charles I much as the rest of Scotland did. They for the most part acquiesced in the Scots Estates' decision to bring home the young Prince Charles, and Alexander Jaffray, Covenanter though he was, went to Holland as one of the commissioners that interviewed Charles. They returned with him to this country, landed at Speymouth, and came to Aberdeen. The silver keys of the city were presented to him, and the town clerk, James Sandilands of Cotton, pronounced 'an eloquent and pertinent harangue'. The King on that occasion remained but a single day. Complaint was made by some of the old Royalists that 'very few persons of quality were admitted to him, being most either malignants or engagers'.

Between the Scottish defeats at Dunbar and Worcester, Charles was again in Aberdeen for a few days in the spring of 1651.[1] Thereafter some steps were taken to put the town in a posture of defence, but there was no gainsaying the disciplined soldiers of the Common-

1   This was the last visit of a Sovereign to Aberdeen for close on 200 years.

wealth, and Dundee having resisted and been sacked, Aberdeen surrendered at discretion when General Monck demanded its submission. On 7 September 1651, after arrangements had been made that no violence should be offered by the victors if none was done by the citizens, Monck marched into the town. Amongst the crowd that watched the Army of the Commonwealth defile through the streets was a student of Marischal, Gilbert Burnet by name, later to be Bishop of Salisbury and historian of the Revolutionary Age. He thus described the entry of the English soldiers:

'There was an order and discipline, and a face of gravity and piety among them, that amazed all people. Most of them were independents and anabaptists: they were all gifted men, and preached as they were moved. But they never disturbed the public assemblies in the churches but once. They came and reproached the preachers with laying things to their charge that were false. I was then present; the debate grew very fierce; at last they drew their swords: but there was no hurt done; yet Cromwell displaced the Governor for not punishing this.'

Having achieved an ambition that no Englishman before him had reached, that of conquering Scotland, Cromwell saw to it that Scotland was firmly but wisely and fairly governed. Monck laid an impost of £12,000 upon Aberdeen, but on the town's poverty being represented to him, he suspended the exaction of the levy, which was never made. Cromwell instituted a commission to inquire into the feasibility of a legislative union of the two kingdoms; and Aberdeen's two delegates to this inquiry, George Cullen (later Provost) and Thomas Mortimer, accepted the scheme. Of the five Scottish members of this Union Parliament, one was Alexander Jaffray, Aberdeen's most famous seventeenth-century provost. Cromwell ordained that it should be illegal to take or tender oaths or covenants; for several years during the Protectorate, the municipal elections were suspended, and when they were resumed in 1655 they were left free except for the injunction that no person likely to be dangerous to the Commonwealth should be chosen. In Aberdeen Presbyterian intolerance was curbed by the Cromwellian Governor; Monck appointed a board of five colonels who deposed the malignant Principal and certain professors of King's whose religious tenets were displeasing to the English authorities; but he and his officers subscribed to the building of what is still known as the Cromwell Tower at King's, and he and his deputies were in fact good friends to the city. It is true that the

buttresses of St. Machar Cathedral were used to erect a fort on the
Castlehill, as a result of which the great central tower of the Cathedral
fell and overwhelmed the aisles in its ruin; but in 1659 Colonel Fairfax,
the garrison commander, offered the fort to the Council for £50 — it
had cost £800 to build — and even when the offer was turned down
he did not demolish it according to orders, but left it intact.

CHAPTER EIGHT

Pulpit and Printing Press

King James was constrained in 1592 to agree to what amounted to the abolition of the episcopacy established by the 'Black Acts' of 1584, but he promptly proceeded to lay plans for its restoration. These had taken shape by 1597 and the extravagant demands of the more extreme clergy greatly contributed to the success of the royal tactics. When he left for England in 1603 episcopacy was to all intents and purposes restored. Some years elapsed, however, before the full system was formally engrafted upon the Kirk, and the King's ambition to dictate religion to his people realised. In that development Aberdeen happened twice to participate very intimately. It was in Aberdeen that the first General Assembly summoned to meet after the Union of the Crowns was held; or rather, since the regal, and as it turned out the legal, summons was not issued, it was a substitute gathering called by the Church leaders on their own authority, which met in the city. For various reasons, only nineteen ministers presented themselves on 2 July 1605. They elected John Forbes of Alford as their Moderator, but did little more apart from hearing an epistle from the King and having an argument with his Commissioner. They then dispersed after adjourning their proceedings to a later date, but before that time the Scottish Council of State, of which the then laird of Fyvie, Lord Dunfermline, was chancellor, summoned Forbes to appear before them and imprisoned him. He with some others was eventually condemned in a fraudulent trial to perpetual banishment. James proceeded to impose what amounted to full episcopacy on the Church of Scotland. This rebuff to the stalwarts of Presbyterianism put new heart into the Papists, and for several years the Jesuits were busy 'proselytising' in the North-East. In 1611 the consecration of Bishop Blackburn as head of the diocese was a further blow.

A decade or so later the first shots in a further skirmish between the King and the Kirk were fired at the General Assembly which met, legally this time, at Aberdeen in 1616. On this occasion most of the independent ministers who were disposed still to struggle against the ascendancy of the Crown were absent, Aberdeen having indeed been chosen for the meeting-place because of its reputation for compliance with the royal wishes. This assembly gave authority for the preparation of a Liturgy to supplant Knox's Book of Common Order, and a new Confession of Faith to take the place of the great canon of 1560. Various alterations which the King desired to see introduced were accepted, and they proved to be the forerunners of the celebrated Five Articles by which the King intended to assimilate the Church of Scotland to the Church of England. The fate of this, as it transpired hazardous, experiment does not concern us here, except that Blackburn's successor at Aberdeen intervened in the subsequent negotiations in a way which revealed the intensity of the struggle between loyalty to God and man engendered by James's policy in the hearts of the noblest of Scotsmen.

Aberdeen was indeed fortunate to find a bishop whose transcendant qualities have won for him as high a place in the history of Scottish Protestant Episcopacy as William Elphinstone fills in the history of Scottish Catholicism. Patrick Forbes of Corse (1564–1635), a landed gentleman and a student, received his education at Stirling and at Glasgow University, where he came under the influence of his relative Andrew Melville. When he had to take up residence at Corse as laird, he remained the student, and when, after the Aberdeen Assembly, the Presbytery of Alford was denuded of its Presbyterian ministers, the imprisoned incumbent of Alford itself being his younger brother, he tried to fill the blank by lay preaching. He was not, however, out of terms with the Episcopalians, although the Archbishop, Gladstanes, ordered him to desist from his ministrations. But in 1612 John Chalmers minister of Keith committed suicide, sending for Forbes on his death-bed and beseeching him to take over the parish. The appeal succeeded, Forbes became minister of Keith, and in 1618, having drifted apart from the extreme Presbyterians, he was appointed Bishop of Aberdeen.

Patrick Forbes's zeal for the cause of religion and culture had no limits. One of his first acts as bishop was to give the King a testimonial on behalf of William Forbes, minister of Monymusk and a High Churchman, who was then preferred to the principalship of Marischal College. In 1621 William Forbes went to Edinburgh as one of the city ministers, but enthusiasts like Andrew Cant, who was later to rule Aberdeen for nearly twenty years, drove him back to the north. In 1633 he preached before King Charles, and perhaps on the strength of that appearance he was appointed the first Bishop of Edinburgh.

He died within a year of that promotion. In Aberdeen Patrick Forbes kept the even tenor of his way. While by personal visitation he imposed strict discipline upon his ministers, he solicited the advice of his friends for the improvement of his own behaviour. By having the larger parishes divided into livings of more manageable proportions he did an administrative service of enduring value to the church of the North-East.

Forbes twice conducted a visitation of King's College and once of Marischal, and made several improvements in the administration of both. In the Colleges he encouraged theological inquiry and was the moving spirit behind the celebrated 'Aberdeen Doctors' who so famously waged wordy warfare with the Commissioners of the Tables in 1638. But though Episcopalian and a Royalist, Forbes was no sycophant, and when the King ordered him to favour the claims of one of two quarrelling rectors, the Bishop found for the other, declaring that while he had received his post from the Crown, his conscience belonged to God. Despite a crippling attack of paralysis in 1632 he would not desist from preaching or his episcopal routine and when he died the magnificence of his funeral and the sincerity of the tributes to his memory in prose and verse attested to his godly life and the veneration in which he was held.[1] The great historian of the reigns of James and Charles I, Samuel Rawson Gardiner, says of Forbes, 'he was one of those bishops who justify episcopacy in the eyes of men. If his advice had been taken by James and by his son, there would have been no civil war in Scotland.'

With the disappearance during The Troubles of the Aberdeen Doctors, the standard of pulpit performance in Aberdeen seems to have fallen considerably, and for a century thereafter it failed to improve sufficiently to produce any lasting effect upon the memory of history. In the period of the Civil Wars and the Protectorate the dominating figure in the church in Aberdeen was Andrew Cant, an Aberdonian, whose father on Deeside had married a Burnett of Crathes. Cant, when minister of Pitsligo, had been one of the reverend Commissioners dispatched by The Tables to convert the stiff-necked Aberdonians to the Covenant. Perhaps the failure of that mission in 1638 was responsible for the arrogance with which Cant comported

---

[1] Whether Presbyterian or not, Aberdeen likes a Churchman who is above paltry sectarianism. In our own time Bishop Deane, of the Episcopalian Church, who did not deem it beneath his dignity to sit in the assistant's stall at the Kirk of St. Nicholas, received a farewell dinner from the Presbytery of Aberdeen.

himself when in 1641 he was appointed one of the town's ministers. 'This Cant', as John Spalding, who detested him, contemptuously called him, was a vehement disputer, but no great preacher. He ruled his congregation like a tyrant and held the Town Council in slight reverence, being no doubt assured while his reign lasted that he would have the weight of Edinburgh behind him in any dispute with the magistrates. Yet he was not wholly intransigent, for in 1642 the minister of Drumoak, John Gregory, father of the great physicist James, 'teached most learnedly' upon the Presbyterian order of which he did not approve, and Cant, who was present, tried various means to stop him and finally challenged him to a debate. Two days later Cant himself preached and 'railed out' against Gregory, but eventually the baillies got the two divines together 'at a cup of wine' and they settled their differences.

Spalding tells a malicious story that 'Mr. Andrew Cant, the holy minister's son', and 'another holy brother's son in his company', were implicated in a theft and got off only because 'the two rich fathers' paid for their sons' delinquency. Spalding alleges that their 'spending, drinking and debauching' were a public scandal. Cant, however, was an honest man who wished passionately to make others as strictly righteous as himself. He insisted upon public baptism. He reprobated ostentation in the observance of religion. He set his face against the orgies that were in those days practised at lykewakes, funerals, baptisms, and weddings. He objected to excessive indulgence of the grosser appetites. Worst of all, in the eyes of his detractors, he believed that no person should be permitted to partake of Holy Communion who could not stand inquiry into his morals or his religious beliefs. His greatest drawback was no doubt his manner. He did not suffer fools gladly, and when at the Restoration power departed from him, there was nothing left to him but to take a quiet leave of the community which he had dominated for twenty years. He died in 1663 in his 79th year, unbending and true to his convictions to the last, and his bones lie under an undecipherable flat tomb below the west wall of St. Nicholas Kirkyard, almost opposite Little Belmont Street.

It has never been asserted that he was much of a preacher. Neither was the Reverend William Strachan of Old Aberdeen, his contemporary, whom Spalding singles out for praise among all the Presbyterian ministers, although he was responsible for the removal of some of the old wainscotting in the Cathedral. Yet Strachan's robust eloquence was efficacious. 'Mr. William Strachan', comments Spalding, 'teaches powerfully and plainly the word of God, to the great good and comfort of all his auditors; he takes strict account of those that come not to the Communion and keep not the kirk; calls out the absents out of the pulpit, which drew in such a fair auditory, that the seats of the kirk were not able to hold them.' In Aberdeen itself the difficulties preachers had to contend with were enormous. There were few seats or stools in the churches, and the congregations were continually moving about during the long sermons. People took their dogs to church with them and 'be the barking and perturbation of these dogges, the people are aftin withdrawn from hearing of God's word, and often Divine service is interrupted ane thing that is not to be comported with in a civil burgh'. The magistrates and kirk session had to prohibit the admission of dogs, 'whether they be mastives, curres, or messens', to the churches, and to make it 'lesome' (lawful) in certain circumstances for the 'scourgeris to fell (kill) these dogges'. It was also forbidden to leave the church before the service was ended 'except they be seik and may nocht endure as lang'. Another distraction was young children below school age, and 'not of sic aige and dispositioun as they can take thame selffis to ane seatt quhen they cum to the kirk, bot vaig throw the same heir and thear in tyme of sermone, and mak perturbatioun and disordour'.

When the Reformers took firm hold of Church observances and ritual, worshippers in the churches were expected to stand during service. Gradually stools were introduced, while the Council and other privileged persons had desks, and the Crafts and other bodies had lofts, in front of which there used to be suspended canopies or hearses. Ornamentation was thus not wholly excluded; indeed it was well into the seventeenth century when Mary Jamesone, daughter of the painter, wrought her fine tapestries for the church. Women in church were, however, a sore trial to the authorities. By 1660 they had persuaded or compelled their husbands to allow them to sit at the desks, which were intended for men only, the tradition being that women sat on the floor or in the body of the church 'in little handsome chaeris'. The Council, therefore, rebuked them but — the Restoration having failed to restore democracy — stipulated that the prohibition did not apply to 'the laidies of Earles, Lordes, Barrones, and other honourable women.[1]' A few years later another abuse crept in when mistresses

1   In 1683, understanding that he intended to reside in the burgh, and for the 'manifest great good will, kyndness and care he had shown for the weal of the town', the Earl of Aberdeen was presented with a 'seat and dask in decent forme' in St. Nicholas Kirk.

brought their maids and mothers their children into the pews. It was accordingly laid down by the Council that 'no bairnes nor young children be brought to the kirk till they be capable to hear the Word and attend the ordinances', and that 'no servant women sall enter within the tirlies or baras dores of the said pews'. In 1687 this scandal was still rampant, for mention is made of the great abuses caused on the Lord's Day by servant women 'thronging in the passage and mongst the pews for woemen, vpon pretence of carieing in and takeing out their mistresses books'. A misdemeanour for which women are not specifically mentioned was that committed by those who 'walk and discours in the isles of the Old and New Churches in tyme of divine worship'. This indecorous behaviour was another Restoration phenomenon. Before then the churches had their warden or sacrister, among whose many functions was the 'choping of sleiperis'; the 'removeing of meane men and boyis whae occupeis honest men's daskis, and will nather remove nor mak roume to men of better qualitie'; 'preserving the windowis unbrokin'; and 'they sall keip preceislie the magistratis dask fast shut, till the magistratis come thameselffis'. In those Presbyterian days, the kirk bells were rung on Sundays, the first bell at 8.30 a.m. the second at 9 and the third at 9.30 and on weekdays an hour earlier for service, and at 7.30 a.m. and 5 p.m. for prayers. The church doors in the winter months were to be open from 5 a.m. to 6.30 p.m. with two candles burning, and in summer from 4 a.m. to 9 p.m. In 1695, however, public morning and evening prayers in the Old Church were discontinued for want of attendance.

Outwith the church the sacrister and his assistants had to keep the churchyard free of horses and cattle straying or being driven in, to prevent anyone from drying clothes in it and schoolboys from playing games in it or from throwing stones at the church. The vigilance of the sacrister, however, did not prevent some evilly disposed person from stealing the provost's new cushion with the velvet cloth on it from the church in 1649.

During the extreme Covenanting ascendancy an Act of the General Assembly denounced 'hinging of pinsells and brods, affixting of hingers and armes, and suchlyke scandalous monuments in the kirk' and prohibited burials in churches. In pursuance of this act, the Town Council fixed a tariff for burials in the kirkyard. The north side was reserved for the poor who were unable to pay. Inhabitants of the burgh who could pay were accommodated in the south side thus — adults over

20, £10; between 14 and 20, £5; bairns 'haiving a kist', £3, 'wanting a kist', 20s.; strangers, barons or baron's wife, 40 merks; gentleman or his wife, £20 Scots. These charges proved to be too high, and in 1649 it was directed that everyone 'who sall be carried upon staves' be buried on the south side or within 30 feet of the wall on the north side and should pay £3, and those carried 'under men's arms', 20s., the rest of the north side being free. At the same time the hire of mortcloths which the town provided was fixed, the best velvet pall for adults being £3 and for children 20s., and the second best being £2 and 10s. Until this date the Crafts had mortcloths of their own, but these were now handed in to become part of the common pool. They seems to have been not very good mortcloths, as they ranked in the tariff with the town's old palls of black cloth at 20s. In 1666 the use of wainscot or oak coffins was prohibited, except under what amounted to licence from the Council.

Between the Restoration and the last Jacobite Rebellion in 1745 only one great religious book was written in Aberdeen, a classic of devotion which may still be read with profit, *The Life of God in the Soul of Man*. Published in London in 1677, it was composed by Henry Scougal, who died the following year at the age of 28, son of Bishop Patrick Scougal, and himself professor of Divinity at King's College. But there was much traffic in what the sergeant-major calls 'fancy religions'. During the second Stewart period the Quakers gained a great hold in Aberdeen.[1] Besides Alexander Jaffray, the Barclays of Ury, David the soldier with Gustavus Adolphus, and Robert 'the Apologist', were both stalwarts of the Society of Friends in the North-East, and Robert's masterpiece, from which he drew his nickname, *The Apology for the True Christian Divinity*, appeared in 1676. Robert collaborated in several Quaker publications with the most waspish and virulent of all the theological controversialists of that day, George Keith. An Aberdonian and an M.A. of Marischal College, 1658, Keith joined the Society in 1662, wrote incessantly and belligerently upon the Quaker faith, and did missionary work in Holland, Germany and London. In 1689 he visited New England, and while there a doctrinal cleavage developed between him and other protagonists of the sect which eventually led him to repudiate his former colleagues as emphatically as he had previously defended them. He joined the Church of England in 1700 and died rector of a Sussex parish in 1716.

1　William Dewsbury was the first to bring the tenets of the Society to Aberdeen in 1662.

In Aberdeen the Quakers suffered heavy persecution. Many of them were imprisoned in the Tolbooth of Aberdeen in conditions of the utmost degradation and squalor, packed, as one baillie put it, 'like salmon in a barrel'. The Barclays and Keith suffered with the rest. David Barclay said he found more honour in his imprisonment than in the entertainment he used to get from the city when the magistrates were wont to ride out to meet him on his entry into the burgh.[1] Robert Barclay, who died at the age of 42, and was a friend of Queen Elizabeth of Bohemia and Prince Rupert, married the daughter of an Aberdeen baillie, also a Quaker. Another Aberdeen baillie who was prominent in the movement was Alexander Skene of Newtyle, author of *Memorials or the Government of the Royal Burghs of Scotland*. His wife, Lilias Gillespie or Skene, also a Quaker, was Aberdeen's first poetess. Her hymns and lyrical devotions[2] are full of quiet strength and beauty, and no doubt reflect upon her own profound spiritual experience:

> The darkest houre is ever nearest day;
> And tryallis deep for mercies great make way,
> When powers of darkness, hell, and death assaille,
> When hope is gone, and human help doth faille,
> The Lord is neare, his present help appeares,
> Gives secret strength, our doore of errore cleares.

At the turn of the century several eminent Aberdonians became attracted to a form of mysticism known as Quietism, or sometimes called Bourignonism after a French lady who practised the philosophy in a rudimentary form until her death in 1680. Henry Scougal was a mystic, and he and his friend George Garden, author of *Comparative Theology*, which is full of Quietism, were disciples of John Forbes of Corse, an 'Aberdeen Doctor' and son of the great bishop. Grouped around Garden, who was a brother of the James Garden deposed from the chair of Divinity after the Revolution, were Forbes of Pitsligo,

1   Whittier has a famous poem on Barclay:—

> Up the streets of Aberdeen
> By the kirk and college green
> Rode the Laird of Ury.
> Close behind him, close beside,
> Foul of mouth and evil-eyed,
> Pressed the mob in fury.

2   Lilias Skene's verses existed in manuscript until comparatively recent times. William Walker had the manuscript and copied it while writing *The Bards of Bonaccord*, but when the papers were returned to their owner they were burned by a maid.

the 14th Lord Forbes and the 16th Lord Forbes, Lord Deskford, and, most eminent of all, a fashionable London physician, James Keith, M.D., son of John Keith, the old Episcopalian minister of St. Machar, who had gone on with his pastoral work in the usual way until his death without paying heed to the revolutionary convulsions that upset his church!

It was thoroughly appropriate that the substantial volume of 'Funerals' which represented the community's tribute to the great bishop Forbes should have been produced by Aberdeen's first printer, Edward Raban. For to Forbes fell probably more than a third share of the honourable responsibility for establishing a printing-press in Aberdeen. Along with him Robert Barron, the professor of Divinity at Marischal College, and Sir Paul Menzies, the provost, have been named[1] as the principal agents in bringing Edward Raban to the town. Raban, born in England of a German family, had practised his craft at the Sign of the ABC in the Cowgate of Edinburgh for a few months and on the South Street of St. Andrews for rather less than two years when he accepted the invitation to try his fortune farther north. Actually he seems to have come to Aberdeen first of all as printer to the university because his first volume published in Aberdeen, a collection of theses which were to be disputed at King's College on 22 July 1622, so styled him, whereas it was not until 20 November that a Town Council minute appointed him printer to the town.

The wording of this minute is an interesting illustration of the educational arrangements of those days and an indication that even then the Town Council was not unmoved by the cost of school books. One of the reasons for creating the position of town's printer was that it carried conditions reducing the prices of the books by one-third; but the pupils (or their parents) had to make some amends for the economy, since in addition to the £40 yearly voted by the Town Council to the printer, every child at the Grammar, Music and English Schools had to contribute 8d. quarterly for the printer's benefit 'to be payit with their scholage to the Maister of Schole'. At the same time the Council took steps to prevent profiteering in educational literature. 'A tabill salbe made of all suche bukes as ar requisite for the bairnes both in the grammar schole and Inglishe schole and the said tabill to be printed

---

1 Kennedy, I. 175, says Menzies and Forbes were Raban's sponsors. Forbes certainly was, but there is no record extant of the Provost's part. J. P. Edmond, *The Aberdeen Printers*, persuasively argues for Barron's participation, Raban having printed a book for Barron in St. Andrews in 1621.

and put on a brod and a copie yairof to be fixit in the clerkis chalmer
and ane vther in David Mailing's bueth quha sellis the bookis and the
third tabill to be affixit in ilk schole.'

David Mailing, or Melville, the bookseller mentioned in the minute,
appears to have been the printer's closest friend, acted as cautioner for
him and otherwise assisted and collaborated with him. When Melville
died in February 1643 Raban took over the bookseller's shop in Broad
Street. At the same time he adopted the title of 'Laird of Letters',
no doubt bestowed upon him by some facetious Aberdeen crony. The
printing-house, 'The Town's Arms', as Raban named it, was in a two-
storied building on the north side of the Castlegate, in the 'toun's foir
house above the Meill Mercat'. The rent was forty pounds, so that in
effect Raban as town's printer sat rent-free. His private life was probably not unexceptional then, though it would hardly be regarded as
unexceptional now. He had rows with the Council over his house,
which was new when he entered it but had fallen into disrepair within
ten years, Council houses then as always being liable to easy dissolution;
and for a breach of the peace on Christmas Eve 1639, he and his wife
were fined 54s. or twenty-four hours in jail.

Raban was twice married. His first wife Janet Johnstone, died in
1627, and within the next ten years he married Janet Ailhous, whose
charms may have inspired the prose work upon which his literary
celebrity, such as it is, principally rests — *The Glorie of Man, Consisting in the Excellencie and Perfection of Women*. From the dedication
to this remarkably eulogistic treatise we can gather that Raban had
been travelling outwith Scotland in the autumn of 1637 and the winter
of 1637–8. He appears also to have laid himself open, no doubt during
his bachelorhood, to 'the imputation of Sarcastic, bitter, too loose and
liberall speaches, agaynst the most noble worthie and transcendant
sexe of women', and by his panegyric he hoped to be 'pronounced
guiltless, quyte and free from all Aspersion' by the 'most glorious,
noble and gracious sexe'. Good wine needs no bush, but Janet Ailhous
(who later figures in the stair-head row already mentioned) was lavishly,
if inferentially, advertised.

Raban's excursions, as printer only, into the no less controversial
subject of theology proved more uncomfortable for him. The press was
not free. In 1634 King's College had requested of the King that it
should exercise control over printed matter in Aberdeen, and this
submission from Old Aberdeen may have given Laud the idea for his
edict of 1637 that all printing in England should be subject to licence

from himself or the Bishop of London, except that in Oxford and Cambridge the licensing authorities should be the Chancellors or Vice-Chancellors of those universities. Aberdeen University (for the two colleges were regarded as one institution from 1641 to the Restoration) never had much opportunity of exercising supervision over Raban except in his capacity as Printer to the University, but a greater power could and did summon him to account. In 1647 he was called before the General Assembly meeting in Aberdeen to explain why, in his print of a Psalm book and Book of Common Order, or Presbyterian Liturgy, in 1633 'he had marked (or shortened) ane common prayer'. An attempt was made to get him to confess that the abbreviation was done by design or at the instigation of some of the (Episcopalian) ministers of Aberdeen at the time; but Raban stoutly affirmed that the cause was want of paper and he was sorry he had offended. So the brethren let him go 'after a rebooke for his rashnesse in curtailing a prayer'.

The Assembly could hardly refrain from regarding the Laird of Letters askance in those troublous times. It was true that he had lent himself impartially to both sides in the celebrated controversy of 1638 between the three Commissioners of the Tables who came to Aberdeen to recommend the National Covenant to the inhabitants, and the ministers and divinity professors of the two colleges, the 'Aberdeen Doctors', who challenged and rebutted the arguments of the visitors. The 'General Demands' of the Doctors, the 'Answeres' of the Reverend Brethren, the 'Replyes' of the Doctors, the 'Answeres' to the 'Replyes', and the 'Duplyes' of the Doctors to the second series of the 'Answeres' all issued from the busy press in the Castlegate. On the other hand, Raban had printed 'With Royall Priviledge' in 1636 the 'Canons and Constitutions Ecclesiasticall Gathered and put in forme for the Government of the Church of Scotland'. This obnoxious document, which was intended to eliminate Presbyterianism and which contained the Service Book the use of which later provoked the historic and decisive riot in St. Giles's Cathedral, Edinburgh, was originally printed in Aberdeen because Raban's friend, Dr. Robert Barron, was selected to edit the edicts on account of his good standing with the King and Laud, and because religious sentiment in Aberdeen was mainly episcopalian. Raban does not seem to have been taken to task for his share in the business by the 1640 Assembly, but that body haled Barron's widow into custody and impounded some of her dead husband's effects, including the 'tailly du pierre' or wood block upon which was cut the royal arms that appeared on the back of the title-page of the Book of Canons.

Aberdeen's first printer appears to have had but one assistant, for his staff is usually mentioned as if it were singular in number. Yet he issued a great variety of publications, some of them of considerable bulk. J. P. Edmond lists 144, not including proclamations. In addition to official volumes and topical books, mainly of controversy, Aberdeen's printer provided an outlet to the public for the works of Aberdeen men like Arthur Johnston, William Guild, David Wedderburn and John and David Leech. Nor did he neglect the classics. Although Ovid alone of the Latin masters is represented in the list, he found time to set forth a reprint of a famous essay of the Middle Ages by an Italian savant, the *Bellum Grammaticale* of Andrew of Salerno, and Dunbar, Henry the Minstrel and Alexander Montgomerie (*The Cherrie and the Slae*) find places, and a curious item is a pamphlet, *A Godly Dream* by Elizabeth Melville, Lady Culros, younger, 'at the request of a special friend'.

As a printer Raban had a well-developed sense of balance and excellent taste. He had not many types, but he made skilful use of his woodblocks to improve the artistic effect of his productions. Some things are beautifully printed, for example a trifle in Latin verse by John Leech which was struck off before Raban left St. Andrews. But his most enduring monument is *A New Prognostication* of 1623, the first of the Aberdeen Almanacs, which were to become a byword and attained such prodigious popularity that James Forbes, one of Raban's successors, could count in 1677 on a circulation of 50,000 copies. The *Aberdeen Almanac*, published in an unbroken series until about ten years ago, was the oldest periodical in Europe. That Raban did not escape the economical tendencies of the city of his adoption is indicated by the fact that in 1625 the woodblock of the Aberdeen arms appearing in the Almanac got cracked, but it continued in use, with the printer's other blocks, until the time of James Chalmers's grandsons, when, in the middle of last century, an errand boy, anticipating the characteristics of his kind in our own day, used the whole stock to light a fire in 28 Adelphi Court.

Among other Raban publications which deserve mention are the Psalter of 1625, which is both the first Aberdeen Psalter and the first in Scotland with harmonised tunes; an item in a controversy between Dr. Barron and Professor George Turnbull of Pont-a-Mousson, which extends to 808 pages and must have imposed a severe strain upon Raban's types; the 1633 issue of the Psalms in prose and metre, this being the first prose version to be printed in a Scottish psalter; the

Funeralls of Bishop Patrick Forbes, Raban's masterpiece as a craftsman, which contains an epitaph in verse by himself that does not disgrace its subject or its author; a collection of medical graduation theses presented at King's College in 1637, which is the earliest of its kind extant; and that (to modern ideas) quaint compilation, *Pharmaco-Pinax, or a Table and Taxe of the Pryces of all usual Mendicaments, Simple and composed,* 'contayned in D. Gordon's Apothecarie and Chymicall Shop, within Mr. Robert Farquhar's high lodging, in New Aberdeen, together with certayne approved Remedies against Diseases, which now most reigne amongst the Commons, All for the use of the People; proportionate both to Rich and Poore, Learned and Unlearned; and profitable to all'. This final example indicates that the divine afflatus which inspires the modern advertiser of druggists' simples and compounds is of ancient provenance.[1] It should perhaps be added that 'D. Gordon' was Dr. William Gordon, Aberdonian, M.D. of Padua, Mediciner of King's College. The 'Mr. Robert Farquhar' was to become provost in 1644, a knight in 1651. He was among the earliest graduates of Marischal College, and his 'high lodging' with a close bearing his name was in the Upperkirkgate west of the Guestrow.

After 1644 the productions of Raban's press are few and references to himself curiously scanty. There is a grim entry in the Burgh accounts for 1648 of 'wool and ane skinn . . . to Edvart Raban to print the papers that is prined (pinned) on the bristis of thes that stand on the scaffold'. The next we hear of him is in the Town Council Records for 5 January 1650, when James Brown, son of William Brown, minister at Invernochty, is appointed printer to the burgh in succession to Raban. Eight years later, in the Kirk and Bridge Work accounts, under the date 6 December 1658, the burial is recorded of 'Edward Rabein at Wast Dyk', that is, under the west wall of St. Nicholas churchyard. With or in the wake of Raban Aberdeen's first bookbinder Francis Van Hagen came from the south, before 1628–9 when he is mentioned in the Treasurer's Accounts as having the 'southernmost of the choppis under the clerks chalmer'. He seems to have died about 1636 and was succeeded by his son Peter or Patrick, who combined his craft with the oversight of the town's clocks. He died in 1665 and was succeeded by

1   Much might be written about Aberdeen's connection with the history and development of pharmacy. A shadowy seventeenth-century alumnus of Marischal Colleges, James Keith, who went to America and became the ancestor of John Marshall, first and greatest of the constitutional lawyers of the U.S.A., was also the progenitor of the most notable pioneer of patent medicines across the Atlantic.

another Francis who continued in the shop for three or four years. Later there was a James Miller a bookbinder.

James Brown is not the first Aberdonian printer. That distinction belongs to Thomas Davidson, 'ane northland man borne in Scotland, upon the waterside of Dee', who was in business in Edinburgh by 1530, became King's printer in 1541, and was the first of his craft in Scotland to employ roman type. Brown was far inferior to Raban, he lacked an eye for the composition of a page, and he economised on his ink. Edmond lists 38 of his publications, all as uninspired in subject as the printing; but one commission to him from the Town Council may be recorded as memorable. In July 1657 'the counsell appoints ane weekly diurnall to be sellit for the wse of the inhabitants, and John Forbes, stationer, to furnish the samen weekly'. In the Burgh Accounts for that year there is noted a payment of £4 10s. Scots to Forbes 'for fyften diurnalls, at the magistrats ordor'. Unfortunately we have no further information upon this, Aberdeen's first newspaper. Forbes and his son succeeded eventually to the printing appointment on Brown's death in July 1661. His burial at the west dyke laid him beside his more illustrious predecessor. James Watson was an Aberdonian who set up as a printer in Edinburgh. He published a *Choice Collection of Comic and Serious Scots Poems* in three volumes in 1706, 1709 and 1711. He also wrote a history of printing.

The elder Forbes is first mentioned as a stationer in 1657, but it has been conjectured[1] that he succeeded Raban in David Melville's old shop in the Broadgate. With him was associated his son, John Forbes, Younger, as printer, when he applied for the office made vacant by Brown's death. As with Raban, so with the Forbeses, the Almanacs, or Prognostications, were 'the stang of the trump', in their business, and the Forbeses were much inconvenienced by raids upon what they no doubt conceived to be their copyright. In 1667 the Town Council censured Alexander Gray, a chapman, for having sold a thousand prognostications from the south in the burgh at a 'more easy rate' than Forbes, whose Almanac cost only a third of an English penny. In 1684 an Edinburgh printer and a Glasgow printer put their names to reprints of his publication, whereupon Forbes complained to the Privy Council, who ordered the offenders to desist. Before this, in 1671, Andrew Anderson in Edinburgh persuaded the masters of his craft in the Capital to apply jointly for a patent in his name vesting them with the office of King's printer, which, when received, prevented any

1   By J. P. Edmond. Brown does not seem ever to have sold books.

printer in Scotland from printing a book without licence from Anderson. The Edinburgh printers soon began to prosecute the other printers in Scotland, but Forbes at once took up the cudgels, and in a letter to the Town Council of Aberdeen in February, 1672, the Edinburgh printers came to heel, protesting that they had no intention of exercising the patent in respect of any Aberdeen printer licensed by the magistrates, bishop or clergy of the town.

On 2 December 1675, John Forbes the elder was buried in St. Nicholas Kirkyard. In the following year his son was reproved by the magistrates for printing a book for the Quakers, who were then out of favour with the authorities; and again in 1683 he got into trouble with the magistrates by printing a pamphlet of which some of the medical profession did not approve. In this case he was ordered not to print any publication in future without inspection and permission by the Council. A minor, but to us more diverting, worry to John Forbes was his 'flyting' or controversies with rivals elsewhere. For example, in 1683, a James Paterson, 'mathematician', accused him in rhyme in an Edinburgh almanac of making ridiculous errors in the Aberdeen Almanac, as for example:

Also he errs again in his Tide Table
At Leith, as if the Moon were not so able
To rule the Tides here, as at Aberdene:
Likewise he errs this year for Halloween,
Saying it falls upon the Munday night,
When Hallow-day on Thursday falls by right.

To these and other citicisms Forbes replied with asperity, alleging that Paterson's errors 'are more gross, making the Flood of Noah in his Chronologie in all his Almanacks three hundred years short. A very beastly error .... Truly I am heartily sorry that both Mathematician and Printer are so evil Principled in the Grounds of Christianity'.

Printer Forbes's most enduring monument is his famous *Cantus, Songs and Fancies*, which went through three editions, in 1662, 1666 and 1682, and for which the printer received £100 Scots from the Council in acknowledgment of a fulsome dedication to the magistrates. The *Cantus* is not only the first published collection that we know of which contains Scottish songs, it is also the only music book which presents to us the music then used and the teaching method employed in an early Scottish music school. Its very existence quite disproves the assertion that the Reformation drove song out of the country; indeed,

8

bearing in mind the 'Gude and Godlie Ballates', it might much more accurately be said that song drove the Roman Church out of the country. Forbes appears to have been the first Scottish printer to possess music types. The excessively ornate dedication is generally accepted as being the work of the elder Forbes, while the 'brief introduction to Musick as is taught in the Music-School of Aberdeen' was the work of Thomas Davidson, son of Patrick Davidson and brother-in-law of Andrew Melville, masters of the Music School respectively 1607–36 and 1636–40, who himself became Master in 1640 and held office until his death in 1675.

Aberdeen in those days had a reputation among Scottish burghs — which were then much more musical than now — for its devotion to singing, although it no doubt fell short of the heights of fame ascribed to it in Forbes's Dedication. It was rather overdoing local patriotism to allege as Forbes did that all Europe was aware of Aberdeen's musical eminence 'witness the great Confluence of all sorts of Persons from each Part of the same, who of design have come (much like that of the *Queen of Sheba*) to hear the sweet chearful *Psalms*, and Heavenly *Melody* of Famous *Bon-Accord*, whose hearts have been ravished with the Harmonious *Concord* thereof'; and flattery overstepped itself when Forbes says of the Baillies that 'it hath pleased Divine Providence, in the Persons of your Honorable Wisdoms, to Bless the Bench of Famous Bonaccord with such a Harmonious Heavenly Consort of as many Musicians as Magistrates'. The musical contents of the *Cantus* are more circumspect and more important. On the whole the music, judged by more recent standards, is dull. There is one traditional ballad, however, 'The Gowans are Gay', and one humorous old folksong; while the secular items include words by poets like Scott, Montgomery, Surrey, Dowland, and Sir Henry Wotton, and airs that are to be found in the earliest Scottish manuscript collection (the Skene MS.,[1] also of Aberdeen) and elsewhere, and are repeated in modern editions of early music.

Forbes the younger died in 1704, and after an interval during which the press was in the ownership of his widow, he was succeeded by his son-in-law James Nicol at the end of 1710. During the widow's tenure, the only book of interest was a curious contribution to the controversy over the Mysticism of that age, *Bourignonism Displayed*. Nicol, who retired from business in 1736 for 'onerous causes, good respects, and

---

1   William Dauney, a member of the Aberdeen Musical Society, published the Skene MS. early in the nineteenth century.

considerations', printed nothing of importance. His press and types, however, were commandeered by the Earl of Mar during the Fifteen insurrection, and ordered to be sent to Perth to print rebel proclamations there, the Town Council authorising that a sum of money be borrowed to transport the press thither.

The day on which Nicol resigned the post of town printer, 6 May 1736, also saw an application to succeed him by James Chalmers, son of the professor of Divinity in Marischal College, who had served his apprenticeship with Nicol and thereafter spent some years in London gaining experience. With Chalmers's appointment as printer to the town and the university there opens a new era in the history of Aberdeen printing, discussion of which may appropriately be postponed to a later time.

CHAPTER NINE

The Goodly Town

After 1600 we know the shape and physical character of Aberdeen from the description of contemporaries. Within a period of just over a hundred years four Aberdonians set down their observations and reflections on the city and its neighbourhood. Two of them, Robert Gordon of Straloch and his son James Gordon, minister of Rothiemay, make as it were a joint contribution. The older man wrote an account of the county, which was the subject of one of his famous maps. The son made an equally famous plan of the city, and no doubt drew upon his father's reminiscences for the 'Description of Both Towns of Aberdeen' with which he supplemented it. In the Town Council records of 16 October 1661 we find that 'Master James Gordoun, minister at Rothiemay, haid beine at great paines in draughting upone ane meikle cairt of paper, this burghe and fredome and other pairts adjacent neir therto which he haid this day delyverit to the counsell weell done'. Generous in those days to the intelligent and the deserving, the Council presented Mr. Gordon with a silver cup weighing twenty ounces, and a silk hat, with a silk gown 'to his bedfellow', all of which were no doubt very comforting to the recipients.

A quarter of a century later, Baillie Alexander Skene of Newtyle wrote his description of the city. It is much less detailed than Gordon's, the author having been more interested in local government than topography. Finally, in 1715 Sir Samuel Forbes of Foveran commenced an account of Aberdeenshire which he did not live to complete. It contains a short survey of the features of the city that does not add much to the facts contained in its predecessors. Besides the local commentators, one or two visitors recorded their impressions, of whom the most notable was the German Richard Franck, whose notes belong to 1658. From those sources we can compile a composite picture of the Aberdeen of the seventeenth century, being careful to make allowances for the change in standards of cleanliness and conception of space.

Whereas in 1500 not one private house was constructed of stone and lime, by 1600 a considerable number were wholly or partly, and by

1700 the majority were of that material. Gordon says that in his time the buildings were of stone and lime, with slate roofs, of three or four or even more storeys. To the street projected galleries of timber called forestairs, which were hung with tapestries and decorations on festive occasions. Franck gives the composition of the houses as stone and timber, and describes the streets as large and spacious. Gordon is enthusiastic over the cleanliness and beauty of the houses, both inside and out, and states that the streets are all neatly paved with 'a grey kinde of hard stone not unlike to flint'. These, however, are compliments that Aberdeen hardly deserved. In 1716, after a serious fire at the head of the Gallowgate, the Council had to forbid the thatching of houses with heather or straw. In 1721 a blaze in the Broadgate led to the establishment of a fire brigade, an engine being purchased in London for £60.[1] But the provision of appliances could not save obsolete houses. On 4 August 1741, a terrible fire on the west side of the Broadgate threatened to lay the whole of that neighbourhood in ashes. These houses were still of wood, and the rapidity with which they were destroyed inspired an act of the Town Council instructing that the outside walls of houses must be constructed of stone or brick and no timber used, that the roofs should be of slate or tile instead of thatch or divots, and that no chimneys of lath and plaster ('stake and rice') be erected. From this time began the custom of facing dwelling houses with dressed granite. Forestairs, too, were apt to be deathtraps in the dark or on festive occasions and several fatalities were recorded.[2] In 1640 a householder in the Green received permission to erect a stone forestair on payment to the town of a yearly duty of 26s. 8d. Scots or alternatively (the applicant being a causeway maker) to maintain in repair all causeways of the burgh free of charge. Against projecting shops and booths the Council waged continual war 'as being a deformitie of the King's hie streitis and a diminesheing of the same'. In 1628 it was ordained that all shops projecting beyond the gutter must be demolished or drawn within the line of the gutter; in 1632 a regulation was made forbidding the erection of any forestair or shop that should fall ruinous; and in 1640 the same causewaymaker in the Green, who had propped up the front of his house by trees set in the street, was peremptorily told to bring them

1   Protectorate troops put out a bad fire in 1657. Another outbreak which threatened to consume the head of the Shiprow in 1669, led to the Council ordering twenty leather fire-buckets from Holland.

2   For example, 'Thomas Urquhart, Chirurgeon in Aberdeen (being drunk) fell over William Watson's stair within Netherkirkgate about seven hours and immediately departed this life'.

within the gutter close to the wall. Lots of trees grew in the gardens and Gordon of Rothiemay says that when seen from a distance the town looked 'as if it stood in a garden or little wood'.

In the seventeenth century, with a population of between 6,000 and 8,000, the town consisted of thirteen major thoroughfares extending north to south from the Gallowgatehead to what is now Regent Quay, and west to east from the Woolmanhill to the Castlehill. There were still the same six ports[1] at the same places, but within them the town was getting taller, the houses adding storeys to accommodate the additional inhabitants, and there was just a faintly discernible tendency for more people to live outwith the traditional perimeter. The Green and the Schoolhill were still the only two residential suburbs, but some of the merchant princes had their small estates in the hinterland. The freedom lands extended between Dee and Don inland for about four or five miles, but the depth of the cultivated belt round the town was not much more than a mile. This arable area was divided into a large number of crofts, market gardens and pasturages, but even as late as 1746 most of the land west of a line joining the Brig o' Dee with Gordon's Mills on the Don was not broken in: there, Parson Gordon says, 'the country is barren like, the hills craggy, the plains full of marshes and mosses, the fields covered with heather or pebble stones, the cornfields mixed with these but few'. But the arable environs, the soil amply fed with the 'fulzie' of the streets and the burgh middens, were very fertile, growing oats, bere and wheat and abundant pasture.

Gordon and Skene include three hills in their urban area; Gordon says the city lies between, Skene says upon, the three. Both are right except as regards the number of hills, for by this time the Schoolhill had also to be included, with the northern half of the kirkyard lying upon its eastward slope, a line of houses running parallel to the north wall of the churchyard, and beyond the houses the Grammar School and, towards the time of the Forty-five, Robert Gordon's or Silverton Hospital occupying part of the land where the Black Friars' monastery had stood. None of the hills was very high. Gordon and Skene agree that from the streets their eminence was hardly discernible, and it was only from outside the city that their height was apparent. The highest was the Gallowgate-hill, otherwise called the Porthill and the Windmill-hill. The street we still know as the Gallowgate ran over the hill slightly west of the highest ridge, and had houses on either side backed by gar-

1   In 1669 the King's arms on the Gallowgate port were ordered to be renovated. In 1662 two houses on the port were allotted to the 'scourger'.

dens. Those on the east side extended to the brow of the ridge, at the northern-most end of which stood the town's earliest windmill; those on the west had their grounds running down to the Loch, which was more of a marsh with the Loch burn running through it than a sheet of water. In 1603 the Council decided that the Loch should be reserved for growing grass and serving only for that purpose, while the burn should provide water to drive the town's mills.[1] The grass was to be 'straitlie and diligentlie keipit', and to be 'yeirlie rowpit and putt to the grytest proffitt and availl'. This seems to have remained a pious aspiration for more than a century, until the Lochlands were made the scene of a celebrated agricultural experiment in the 1730s by Alexander Robertson of Glasgoego, who was provost in 1740–1. Robertson rented an acre and a sixth of the land for three pounds ten shillings. His first crop of grass was foul with weeds, but his treatment resulted in such excellent crops thereafter that when he let the land out in small plots the total rent came to £10 sterling.

At one time an extension of the Gallowgate, the Broadgate originally did not belie its name. But its very spaciousness was its ruin when the town's living space became congested. The temptation to make use of a street so broad to provide an extra double row of houses was too strong to be resisted, and so the Ghaistrow was built. The Broadgate's greatest glory was Alexander Galloway's beautiful church, built for the Grey Friars, which, after a generation in disuse and decay, was renovated by the Council when Dr. Guild offered to reglaze its windows, and a loft for the magistrates was put in. Its condition had been appalling, and in 1607 the Council had ordered the wood and other junk that people were storing in it to be removed. Behind Greyfriars kirk lay the Marischal college, and a familiar sound to Aberdonians in the later seventeenth century was that of the Greyfriars bell calling from the little spire of the kirk to the students to go to their classes. During part of the Troubles the kirk was used as a court de guard.

From each end of the Broadgate, as now, ran a street to the parish church. The Upperkirkgate was continued into the brae of the School-hill, at the top of which in 1595 there had been laid out the Westerkirk-gate, now the Back Wynd, which skirted the churchyard westwards and connected with the road that made towards the west and the Brig o' Dee. The Netherkirkgate ended beside the East or New Church, the chancel of the pre-Reformation parish church, below which the

1 People were debarred from pasturing horses, 'ky or other bestiall' and from shearing the grass of the loch.

vault of Our Lady of Pity was used for storing lead and timber to repair the church roof. The amount of public attention that was then bestowed upon the town's church can scarcely be appreciated now. It was regarded with boundless pride, ashlar-built as it was, with its towering steeple of wood, covered like its roof with lead. 'There is no church so neat and beautiful to be seen in Scotland', says Parson Gordon, while Skene called it 'a great and fair fabric' and enlarged upon its neat interior with its 'good desks and galleries of excellent workmanship of wainscot, and great and large lights and windows'. The bells of St. Nicholas and the clock in the steeple were much cherished by the community. In the rejoicings for Charles I's coronation in Edinburgh the principal or prayer bell, Laurence, was apparently overworked, a 'rift' appeared in it, and in 1632 it was taken down and sent to Flanders to be recast.

While the western and northern parts of the town were little different 300 years ago from the corresponding districts today, a great transformation had occurred in the central and southern portions. Union Street, St. Nicholas Street and Market Street did not exist. St. Katherine's hill, round the eastern and south-eastern fringes of which the Shiprow still winds, then rose to a summit at a point just within the pend entrance to the Adelphi now. The base of the hill can still be approximately traced by St. Katherine's Wynd, the Netherkirkgate and Carnegie's Brae, which was then known as Putachie-side from the fact that the town house of the Lord Forbes (whose country seat, now Druminnor, was then called Putachie), stood upon it on the western slopes of the hill. The western perimeter of the hill swept over what is today the junction of Union Street, St. Nicholas and Market Streets and thence followed an arc to meet the Shiprow where it debouched on the Green, about where Trinity Lane now enters Market Street. This old street, prolonging Putachieside, was known as Dubbie Raw; west of that, there being no Union Street then and consequently no artificial level, the ground sloped up from the Green to meet St. Nicholas churchyard. Aedie's Wynd also ran on the western side of St. Katherine's Hill, the houses on the east side of it with their gardens stretching eastwards up the slope. There was the same arrangement along the Shiprow.

The householders whose yards formed part of the hill were inconvenienced in the middle of the seventeenth century by people of mean station who frequented the slopes of the hill. They, therefore, in 1648 obtained the Town Council's permission to enclose the hill by a dyke, access being given by a door to which each honest house-holder in the town could have a key if he so wished. As the records contain no further mention of undesirables haunting the precincts of the long ruined chapel at the top, this device presumably had its effect.

The whole of the eastern end of Union Street, below Market Street, was then built over except for two narrow thoroughfares leading into the Castlegate and a third transverse breach where the Shiprow connected with St. Katherine's Wynd. Huxter Row lay at the extreme south end of the Broadgate, where it stopped short at the buffer formed by the block of buildings of the Round Table (no explanation of the name has ever been forthcoming) which all but enclosed the western end of the Castlegate, while on the other side of the Round Table, separating it from the buildings on the site of the present block in which the Athenaeum stands, ran the equally narrow Narrow Wynd. At the southern side of the Athenaeum block the Exchequer Row connected as now the Castlegate with the Shiprow. The Castlegate itself was the pride of the city. 'The Castelgaite', says Gordon, 'is a squair, about 100 walking paces in breadth and twyce as much in lenthe, nor can Scotland showe such ane other'. Says Skene, 'The Mercat-place is larger than in any town of the Kingdom, being an hundredth and twenty-four double space in length, and about a third part thereof in breadth where it is narrowed, so that two Regiments of foot souldiers may be drawn up in rank and fyle, tho in open order'.

Of several important buildings in the square, the Tolbooth, or Town House, sometimes styled the Mids o' Mar, was the most interesting. The original building on the site had been constructed at the end of the fourteenth century, no doubt mainly of wood, and by 1600 its pretensions to aesthetic and practical value had worn thin. It had been in two portions, the western half consisting of a few rooms for civic administration situated about the present entrance to the Sheriff Court, the eastern serving the purpose of a jail. At the beginning of the seventeenth century a great development in the judicial system had the unexpected effect of rendering renovation of the Tolbooth inevitable. In 1604 new powers were given to the justices of the peace. They had to meet four times a year to deal with offenders and to devise precautions against future offences. They were ordered to be vigilant in regard to Jesuits and Papists, to take note of any prospects of civil commotion, to concert measures for dealing with sturdy beggars, who were to be forced either to work or to leave the country, to find out about poachers and destroyers of trees and persons carrying unlicensed arms, and to keep an eye on the bridges, roads and inns of their area.

This multiple commission, in the opinion of the Town Council, was likely to involve a considerable increase in the floating population of the jail. By 1612 the civic authorities were quite certain of this, and resolved to take measures to rid the community 'of their great burding, fascherie, and truble that thai do susteine throche iniquities of this present tyme, in daylie and nichtlie watching, walking and warding' of prisoners committed to the Tolbooth. It was therefore resolved that all public works, even that of constructing a bulwark at the harbour, should give place to the building of the Tolbooth, all the money in the Treasurer's hands was voted for that purpose, and the community agreed to stent themselves as need be to meet any further charges. It was not, however, until 1616 that preliminary arrangements were made with Thomas Watson, mason of Rayne, to execute the work, nor until 1622 that the accounts were paid, and not until 1629 that the steeple was completed.[1] The new jail or wardhouse was called the High Tolbooth, the building west of the tower the Laigh Tolbooth, housing the civic apartments, the sheriff and other courts and a magazine for ammunition. To begin with there was no entrance to the Tolbooth from the front, but in 1755 the main door was made in the first floor, reached by a double flight of steps from the plainstanes or pavement below.

The new and larger Tolbooth with its vaults and its walls 5 feet thick did not, as it proved, discharge the citizens from their duties as warders. It might almost be said that open house was kept in the Tolbooth. One murderer who let himself and his fellow-prisoners out chalked on the door, 'Rooms to let'. In 1638, in the very height of the first excitements of the Bishops' Wars, the Town Council was distracted from considering matters of great national import by the escape of Alexander Keith of Balmoor from the Tolbooth in a trunk. The rescue was effected by his sisters and some other women friends, who had the trunk taken to the pier and put on board a boat which carried Keith to his castle at Boddam. The town had sixty men out for a fortnight vainly searching for him. The following year his creditors, at whose instance he had been thrown into jail, raised an action against the magistrates for the sum owing to them by Keith. In 1660 Viscount

1   The present steeple is a replica of the 1629 spire. When the new Town and County Buildings were erected in 1870 the old tower was refaced with ashlar, but from Lodge Walk there can still be seen part of the side and the corbells of the 1616 tower. The condemned cell on the top floor is the original, and the only one of its age in Scotland. The bar upon which the fetters ran is an interesting feature. The clock was replaced by the present one in 1726.

Frendraught and James Crichton of Kinaldie, also imprisoned for debt, escaped, and the magistrates having failed to find them took steps to exonerate themselves in case of actions by the creditors. In 1665 the keeper of the Tolbooth was dismissed for refusing to take into his house a prisoner who had broken his back and a leg in attempting to escape. A year or two later the town sergeants, who were supposed to be the warders, were ordered to make good at their own expense damage done to the fabric by escaping prisoners. In 1673 Francis Irvine of Hilton and some other prisoners for debt made a spectacular escape. In 1698 James Gordon of Arradoul, incarcerated for having slain Leith of Overhall in a duel, walked calmly out by the door, an exploit which resulted in the punishment and discharge of all the jailers, and the even more significant Town Council edict that in future 'no persons imprisoned be permitted to goe forth out of the prison house under the silence of the night without sufficient caution be given to the magistrates for their speedy return'.

All those enterprising gentlemen are, however, but shadows beside John Leith of Harthill. This landed desperado, whose brutality and insolence were almost incredible, kept both the city and the Garioch in a constant uproar for a number of years just before the Troubles. At Christmas 1639, however, he went too far, and created such a scene in St. Nicholas Kirk, abusing Provost Leslie and resisting the town's officers who sought to remove him, that the magistrates had him up before them immediately after the service. He then proved even more contumacious. He called the provost, who presided, a doited cock and an ass, snapped his fingers at the baillies, tore up the charge, picked up 'penner and inkhorn' from the table and threw them 'eagerlie' in the clerk's face, cutting him 'to the great effusion of his blood'. On general principles — for he had not long before broken into a private house, assaulted the householder and beaten his wife, and lifted some cloth that he fancied from a merchant's booth — the magistrates ordered him to be detained in the Tolbooth.

There he tried to burn the place down on the grounds that the chimney smoked. Then he broke down part of the stone wall of his cell 'with pick and gavelocke'. His friends smuggled in arms to him, and he attacked the jailers with dirks, knives and cudgels, and derived great amusement from taking potshots at the passing citizens from his cell window. Next he took possession of the jail, barricading the outer door with large stones so that the other prisoners got neither meat nor drink nor visitors. Finally, he crowned a hectic sojourn of nine months and fifteen days in durance with a wanton assault, 'casting ane stane out of the wairdhous window at Andro Robb,[1] calsay maker, and hiting him thairwith on the head, whaneas the said Andro desyrit him to come doon to the magistrates'. After that, they packed him off to Edinburgh, where he was warded for four years. Spalding, for whose likes and dislikes there is no accounting even by political prejudice, laments Leith's misfortunes: 'None would become caution for him', he complains, 'being a fierce man'! And again, 'Pitiful to see ane gentleman chief of ane clan, of good rent, so extremelie handlit'.

Being a true market-place, there was constant alteration in the commercial accommodation of the Castlegate. In 1595, to protect the meal that came to the market from rain and wind, 'common halls' were made of timber from the north 'cheek' of the door eastwards to the malt market. In 1613 a flesh-house was ordered to be built on the north side of the Castlegate, and again in 1631 we find the Council ordering a flesh-house to be erected at the back of 'the tounes new hous', on the north side of the square, the decision being accompanied by the order that no flesher shall in future slay 'ony nolt, sheip, nor wther gudes, nor bestiall, in the King's high streets'. In 1641 our persistent friend Andro Robb was instructed to 'calsay' the Green opposite the mid mill (which stood almost where the National Commercial Bank on the west side of St. Nicholas Street now is), and from the Broadgate to the Tolbooth, the gutter to be laid with flagstones.

There were still two market crosses in the Castlegate, the High (or Flesh) Cross in front of the Tolbooth, and the Laigh (or Fish) Cross some distance to the east. The Laigh Cross is believed to have been no more than a plain pillar (in the country it would be called a 'prop') on a low platform. The High Cross, which figures in all public celebrations of the city, was a true Market Cross bearing the royal arms, surmounted by a cross, and consisting of a platform high enough to raise dignitaries who sat upon it well above the heads of a surrounding crowd. As the burgh grew in wealth and its citizens travelled about and saw other cities, the cross ceased to satisfy them. They found that whereas it should be an ornament it was far inferior to many 'meaner burghes'. In 1664 and again in 1666 the Dean of Guild was instructed to have a new cross of hewn stones after the model of Edinburgh's set up. Nothing, however, was done until 1686, when the Council had before them, from that great seminary of masons, Old Rayne, 'ane

---

1 Andro Robb was our old friend who propped up his house in the Green with a tree.

moddell and frame of timber and paseboard' by John Montgonerie of a design for a new Market Cross, of hewn and ashlar work, with the present and eight earlier Kings' and Queen Mary's effigies engraved on the panels, with shops under the platform, and a great high pillar on the centre .. all for the sum of £100 sterling. This is the Cross as we have it today. It is hexagonal in shape, and each face of the hexagon is divided into two panels, presenting the effigies of the ten Scots monarchs from James I to James VII and, on the west face, the royal and the city's arms. The 'great high pillar', wreathed with thistles, carries on a Corinthian capital a unicorn bearing a shield with the lion rampant. That so artistic a piece of architecture should be the workmanship of a small mason in a remote hamlet in the Garioch is even more remarkable than that a rural parson like Alexander Galloway should design the Bridge of Dee and Greyfriars Kirk.[1]

Like St. Katherine's hill, the Castlehill was fringed with houses and gardens, but with the difference that the feuars on the Castlehill were not allowed access to the hill. The space not devoted to the Chapel of St. Ninian's on the top, which was mainly used as a beacon for mariners, although in 1635 the body of Bishop Patrick Forbes lay in state there, was reserved for burning at the stake. There, from 1590 to 1597, many witches were 'wirried', and there in 1647 was consumed the last malefactor to be dispatched by fire in Aberdeen. On the ridge to the east known as the Heading Hill the Scottish guillotine or 'Maiden' plied its trade, its last employment being on a murderer in 1615. In 1600 the Council had to administer a sharp rebuke to the inhabitants of Futty, a godless and refractory generation, for holding a fish market on the slopes of the hill on the Sabbath and not attending divine service. The more respectable members of the population also frequented the neighbourhood of the hill, but after sermon, because there were two walks, one gravelled, at the foot of the walls, the other grassy, on the top of the terrace, from which there opened out a pleasant prospect of the links, the roadstead, and Torry. Sir Samuel Forbes said (without much warrant) this custom was continued from the days of the Wars of Independence, when the priests ordered the citizens to repair every Sunday to the chapel of the castle to pray for the English soldiers whom they had slain.

The conformation of the harbour environs has also greatly changed. The Weigh-house or Pack-house, for weighing merchandise, is marked

1   Today, of course, the Corporation would have to go to London in a comparable case, and might be worse served.

by Weigh-house Square. All the Virginia Street area was reclaimed from the tidal basin in the middle of the seventeenth century and put into pasture. This was effected by raising a terrace built up with large stones, which provided a promenade between the harbour and the ships on the one hand and a flowery meadow on the other. Still farther on, and leading into the Links themselves, was the Carpet Walk, so called (in 1715) 'from the softeness and thickness of the wreathed green moss with which it is overspread'. The quay (the rudiments of our Trinity Quay), begun in 1526 and gradually improved and extended from the Weigh-house (built in 1634) until its length in 1659 was 500 walking paces, was faced with stones and filled in the centre with sand. Beyond it stretched the village of Futty, running along the firth for 400 paces to the channel of the Dee. It was a parish in its own right, with its own church, St. Clement's Chapel built in 1598. Beyond Futty was the fisher-boat haven, then the Sandness, with the Blockhouse near the point. Opposite the Blockhouse on the Torry side there was a little watch-tower, by 1661 in ruins. The largest vessels of that day could lie at Torry, despite the narrowness of the harbour mouth, which was further contracted by a pier. Inside the harbour and above high tide there were some inches on which salmon fishers had their bothies. North of the harbour mouth and east of the city lay 'many fair fields, fruitful of corns, quheat, beans, oats, pease, and pot hearbs and roots'. Next to them lay the Links where football, golf, bowling and archery were practised and where the citizens walked 'for their health'.[1] On the firm sands between the two rivers — after Gregory diverted the Don — there was a two-mile course for horse-racing.

Constant structural repairs were being carried out in and around the burgh. In February 1633, the steeple and crown of King's College was blown down in a tempest, and the Council subscribed 400 merks towards the cost of restoration. In 1598 the chapel on the Castlehill, 'quhilk is the townis commoun hous', was painted and a little stair of timber was built on it in place of an old stair that had decayed. In 1650 the Council, in view of 'the great necessity of the fabric' of St. Nicholas Kirk, and 'narrowlie eying the preservatioun thairoff from rwin', ordered lead to be provided for 'thaiking' and repairs. In 1648 Andro Rait 'master of impost' was instructed to buy a 'yoll' for 'easeing' the townspeople and ferrying them over the Dee, but a certain Alexander Reid was to have the use of the vessel for three months provided he

1   The Bool Road, now Albion Street, may have taken the name from 'the bools', the game having been introduced after the Restoration in 1660.

handed it back in good order. In 1670 Alexander Skene of Newtyle 'considdering everie blessing bestowit be God on any place should be improvin for the publict good', asked permission to rebuild the Well of Spa, which 'besides being renowned aforetime', had lately produced good effects in cases of 'the gravill, and stone in the kidnes and blader, the collicks in the stomack, when so violent that nothing else could, and despirat lyke hydropsies'. He also asked the Council to reprint Dr. William Barclay's treatise, 'which wold be about ane sheet of paper', adding modern medical testimony, 'whereby seeklie strangeris knowing of such ane free offer of health might make the more frequent resort to this burghe'.

In 1679, it was recommended that the town's arms and Bishop Elphinstone's arms should be hewn upon the porch at the south end of the Bridge of Dee. But in all the period the most permanent restoration work was that carried out in 1605 upon the Bridge of Don. In that year the community agreed to tax itself 500 merks for the repair of the bridge, but almost simultaneously Sir Alexander Hay, one of the Clerks of Session and later Lord Clerk-Register, mortified certain annuities valued then at £27 8s. 6d. Scots (£2 5s. 8½d. sterling) to be held by the Town Council for the maintenance of the bridge. The town tax was cancelled on the assumption that the Hay bequest would prove sufficient for its purpose, nor has the benefaction disappointed the town's expectations. It has paid for the upkeep of the bridge for nearly three and a half centuries, built the new Bridge of Don, supplied large contributions to the construction of various roads and bridges in the North-East of Scotland, and its capital value, which now stands at over £25,000, can hardly be said to have been impaired by the drains made upon it.

CHAPTER TEN

Introducing Economics

———

Wars and rumours of wars may bulk largely in Aberdeen's history, but its most continuous traditions are those of peace. While its communal endowment and its burghal politics go back to Robert the Bruce and before him, its industrial system in its modern form may be traced to the beginning of the seventeenth century.

Up to the early years of that century, Aberdeen's industry followed the customary medieval lines. Factories as we understand the word there were not. Merchants traded in various commodities, buying and selling abroad by barter mainly and at home collecting their wares from a host of individual and independent small producers. The modern multiplication of middlemen was unknown. The processes of commerce were simple and comparatively straightforward. One of Aberdeen's staple products was skins. The farmer — itself a term hardly to be endowed with its modern meaning — killed his cattle singly, or in small numbers either for the use of his own little rural community or for his own household, or he drove the beasts into town and sold them to the fleshers. Often there was no question of killing for meat; an animal died from 'natural causes' and was eaten, with no questions asked and no doubt without disagreeable effects on the health of the consumers. But whether the creature died or was felled, whether its demise took place in the country or in the 'fleshous' behind the Tolbooth, the owner of the skin got in touch with a merchant who dealt in skins and he in his turn, when he had accumulated sufficient to warrant their dispatch, sent them off by boat to the Low Countries or England or the ports of the Firth of Forth, or even turned them over to such cordiners or shoemakers in the city itself as had not been active enough to secure hides for themselves. Sheepskins were similarly dealt with and trappers and hunters brought their pelts to the same market.

The same principle applied to the trade in plaidings or tweeds, for which Aberdeen was famous from a very early date. The weaver craftsmen, of whom we first hear in 1222, were not permitted to trade in their own goods. These were assembled by merchants, who in turn sent them outwith the country. Salmon, yet another of early Aberdeen's staple exports, were caught in the numerous fishings at the mouths of the Dee and Don by the employees of the well-to-do burgesses who leased the fishings, and were exported in barrels made by craftsmen of the wright and cooper fraternity, the exporters sometimes being the tacksman of the fishings themselves who had more than one commercial iron in the fire.

But about the commencement of the seventeenth century the first signs of a subtle economic change can be observed. There was a distinct willingness to adopt new methods. In 1597 a Fleming of the name of Michael Wandail received permission to weave certain kinds of worsteds and woollen fabrics — 'grograms, worsets and stamings' — on condition that he adopted and instructed an apprentice. In 1599 we find the Aberdeen Council expressing a very shrewd economic sense as well as considerable independence when it turned down the suggestion of the King that a Scottish Conservator — he would be termed trade commissioner in our day — be established to further Scottish commercial interests in London. One reason for the objection was that there were other parts of England with which Aberdeen traded, and the establishment of a conservator in London 'will import ane gryt preiudice to the merchandis of this realme that treddis in the north pairtis of Ingland, and vther pairtis of the said realme, quha wald be compellit to change thair trade and pas to Londoun'.

By this time Aberdeen's seaborne trade had become so considerable that we find one authorlty estimating that the loss of one Aberdeen ship was more serious than that of ten from other Scottish ports. The town's exports of salmon, hides, pork and woollens had reached very substantial proportions. The high standards of the exports were very jealously maintained by both the Crafts and civic authorities. The craftsmen's work was examined from time to time, the salting and packing of the salmon were inspected, and the barrels, having passed muster by the 'auld gede and standart of Abirdene', were officially marked before shipment was permitted.

In 1612 there was unusual industrial activity in the burgh. Two foreigners named Fabian Fanton and Antonie Samboys received permission to make heckles and traps for catching rats and mice. That was a small affair in comparison with an unsuccessful experiment in another branch of industry which, curiously enough, has been several times repeated and until recently always failed. The Aberdeen magistrates purchased a Dutch fishing-boat, with full equipment and a Dutch skipper, at Amsterdam, the skipper being expected to train an Aberdeen crew in the best methods of catching and curing herring. In 1614 we learn that the Council 'had riggit furth ane bark callit Stella for the bushe fishing, the Maister thairof under God John Williamsone', and that both the 'maister and most part of the companie ar Hollanderis, quhome we have feit and conduct for the purpose'. Although the Dutch boats' constant presence in large numbers off the coast was bitterly resented by the Scots — who, however, seem to have done little or nothing to wrest the fishing monopoly from the Hollanders — Aberdeen Council actually presented the freedom of the city to certain Dutch fishermen, in the hope, no doubt, that their example would be an inspiration to Aberdonians. But the Aberdonians failed to respond, and we hear no more of the venture.

During the century Aberdeen mariners ranged far and wide over the old world. They started trade between Aberdeen and Leghorn at a time when Scottish ships seldom penetrated into the Mediterranean, and towards the end of the century at least one Aberdonian, Thomas Gordon in his ship the *Margaret*, made regular trips thither. It was, too, an Aberdonian who was the first Scots skipper to reach the New World, and in the thirties John Burnett took goods from Aberdeen to Virginia, and brought back a cargo of tobacco. An English attempt to divert the American trade from Scotland was prevented by Charles I, who with all his faults had a sound commercial sense; but Cromwell with his Navigation Act, which was perpetuated after the Restoration, for long restricted what was a perfectly legitimate branch of Scottish activity. At the end of the century Aberdeen Council invested £300 sterling in the Darien Scheme, and lost the whole sum when England succeeded in ruining the venture. Later, after the Union of the Parliaments, when the Darien Company was in part at least reimbursed, Aberdeen got back its share. In 1692 we hear for the first time of a West Coast ship in the port, a Glasgow vessel being the visitor in that year.

In 1636 there was a further expansion of industrial commitments. A brewery was established which from some reason did not last long — perhaps because people in their homes, in the absence of an excise duty, could brew better and cheaper ale. In that year, however, the magistrates contrived to combine social with industrial improvement by securing from the King a patent for the establishment of a House of Correction, a sort of Bridewell or reformatory, whose existence and location are commemorated in Correction Wynd. First of all the magistrates appointed two Englishmen, Robert and Nicholas Brastounes, who came north from Edinburgh, to advise upon the erection of such an institution. What their proposals were does not transpire, but a little later it becomes clear that it was decided to purchase 'a commodious tenement of land'.

When the whole cost of establishing the correction house was gone into, it was felt in the existing state of the town's finances that the basis of the undertaking should be broadened, and a remarkable form of co-partnery was devised. The brethern of guild — that is, the merchant burgesses — and the Crafts agreed to co-operate in finding the cost of founding the establishment, with the help of a special taxation of 2,000 merks from the community. The 'undertakers' were bound to supply a master and workmen for the respectable side of the institution, which was to be supplemented by the labour of 'ane sufficient prisone', whose inmates would be recruited by the magistrates from 'all vagabonds, strong and sturdie beggares, idle and maisterles persones, children disobedient to parentis, leud leivars, pyikers, commoun scoldes, and vncorrigible harlottis, not amending be the discipline of the kirke'. Of both the workers and the prisoners the master was to be in charge, and the two sides of the establishment were to be devoted to the making of 'bridcloath, carseyis, seyis, freiss' and other textile manufactures. No raw material for the house was to be bought from and no finished article from the house was to be sold to any but the co-partners. They for their part were bound to keep not more than ten delinquents at any one time in this employment, for the maintenance of which the collector of the kirk session would pay them an annual grant of £240 Scots for ten years. Further, they were to receive in the first year an apprentice nominated by the magistrates, and thereafter one every two years, without fee, until the ten years were up.

The company seems to have been quite prosperous until the Troubles, when the factory was subjected to pillage when either of the armies occupied the town. After the Battle of the Justice Mills, the partners are said to have lost nearly £2,000 worth of goods plundered by the Irish or handed over to the Royalist leaders to forestall further looting.[1] Somewhat later the partners bought a waulking mill on the Don, but thereafter their venture languished and in 1657, when the Council looked around to find a means of implementing the terms of the mortification of Robert Johnston who had bequeathed £600 to promote manufactures in which the halt and the blind could participate, it was

1   See *More Troubles*.

decided to buy over the Correction House and the mill. Municipal ownership, however, was no more successful than private enterprise, and in 1698 another group of business men approached the Council with a new scheme. They proposed 'for the encouragement of vertew and to supress idleness and several other considerations', to re-equip the house as a manufactory 'for makeing cloth, stockings, serges, stuffs, and other commodities, and the stock to be put in for advanceing and manadging the forsaid work is sex hundreth pound sterling'. The Council gave the petitioners the use of the building for seven years, 'maile free', advanced a sum to repair the house, and authorised a grant of £200 sterling from the Johnston mortification 'free of annual rent', also for seven years. But once more failure supervened, and in 1711 the undertaking was finally discontinued.

The mention of stockings is one of the first regarding a product for which Aberdeen later acquired international fame. Somewhere about the middle of the seventeenth century the knitting of stockings, or basses, as they were called, commenced. We hear of them incidentally in 1645, but a century was to elapse ere Aberdeen stockings acquired their full lustre. Even so, they began well, for once the Troubles were over, a burgess, George Pyper, was giving employment in their own homes to some 400 knitters and spinners. Other industrial pioneers in the meantime were busy in other directions. In 1696 Patrick Sandilands of Cotton started to manufacture paper at Gordon's Mills on the Don, and although his experiment was too far in advance of the times to last long, it is an interesting harbinger of what at about the same place was eventually to become one of Aberdeen's principal industries. It may have been the self-same mill that had been taken over about half a century before by the Correction House people, and it was probably this building that figures in 1703 in yet another Aberdeen textile enterprise. Despite the grant to the new Correction House company in 1698, the Johnston mortification had still funds to spare. In 1703 they were invested by the trustees in a joint-stock company floated by a member of the Earl Marischal's family and the second Robert Barclay of Ury to try to carry on a woollen manufactory at Gordon's Mills. Its fabrics were serges, damasks, plush and cloth of superior quality, and workmen were imported from France for the more difficult processes.

Aberdeen's chief manufactured export in the seventeenth century was plaiden or tweed cloth, of which in the year 1650–1 there were shipped to Danzig and Campvere 73,358 ells. Of lamb skins in one year 30,000 were dispatched to Danzig. In a single season, which then extended from 12 December to 19 September, more than 1,440 barrels, each of 350 lb. weight, of salmon caught in Dee and Don were sent to Holland, France and Spain. After the Union of the Parliaments fast smacks used to run lightly salted salmon to the London market; some even had tanks in which the salmon were transported alive. Pork went mainly to the Low Countries. Aberdeen butchers bought young pigs in the surrounding country and fed them to fifteen or eighteen months.

The main ports with which Aberdeen traded were Danzig, Campvere, the Scottish staple port in Holland, various places in France, Spain and as far round the Mediterranean coast as Leghorn. After the Union of 1707 London came into the forefront of the picture, although Aberdeen alone among Scottish towns clung for a long time to Campvere. A new trade was developed before the Forty-Five with North America and the West Indies. In 1744 and 1745 Aberdeen merchants appealed to the Government to permit them to send salmon to France, although Britain and France were at war.

Despite its flourishing and far-flung trade, Aberdeen's own fleet was very small. In 1626 the town had only ten small ships, three of them unseaworthy, and fifty seamen. In 1656 there were nine vessels, the largest eighty tons burden, the smallest twenty, and aggregating 440 tons. By 1692 the shipping was down to two galliots of thirty tons each. Most of the trade was done by Dutch boats, and it was that fact that made Aberdeen Town Council so reluctant to seize Dutch shipping in the harbour when ordered to do so on the outbreak of war with Holland in 1665. The roadstead was often the scene of lively incidents. During the wars at the beginning of the seventeenth century between Spain and Holland, men-of-war of both countries called frequently at Aberdeen; indeed, a merchant named William Laing was a kind of Spanish consul in Aberdeen. In 1623 a Spanish privateer was blockaded in Aberdeen by Dutch warships. About the same time an attempt was made to poison the captain of a Spanish warship lying in the harbour. During the Civil Wars English ships patrolled off Aberdeen. In 1651 they chased an Aberdeen barque aground opposite the Broad Hill and the whole town turned out in arms.

It was an Aberdeen master, John Strachan, who was chosen by Charles I in 1642 to convey the Queen, Henrietta Maria, to safety in Holland. On his return journey four Parliament ships tried to intercept him, but he reached the coast, ran aground, turned his guns on the enemy, and finally was rescued by Royalist troops. No doubt he was the 'Capitane Johne Strachan . . . residente at London' who in 1660 after the Restoration was expected by the Town Council to be 'verie serviceable to this burghe' and to whom accordingly the Treasurer was ordered to present a handsome cup of silver weighing 25 oz., and two barrels of 'good and sufficient salmon', all 'in tokin of the toun's respect to him'.

Although overseas and coasting trade was brisk, the harbour was never very convenient for loading and unloading cargo until the beginning of the nineteenth century. In the seventeenth lighters had to be used to carry goods between the ships and the quays. Yet the Council constantly undertook harbour improvements. At that time the quay extended from approximately the foot of our Market Street to James Street. The quay had been laid in what was the original channel of the Denburn, not a very firm foundation, and it frequently required repair — 1453, 1484, 1512, 1526 and 1549. A crane was set up at the quay head in 1582. In 1607–10 a breakwater known as the Bulwark was built on the south side by the inhabitants themselves, of stones and great timber baulks or stakes. We have a lively picture of this undertaking, which was carried out to the strains of the town's bagpipes and drums, a very early anticipation of modern opinion on industrial psychology — 'Music While you Work' if not, it may be hoped, 'Workers' Playtime'. In 1616 the erection of two corn-mills was ordered, the mills to be worked by the tides, and the Weigh-house was built. It served as a storehouse and then as a customs house. Its timber platform was added in 1708, and it stood until 1883. Aberdeen, after Davie do A'thing removed Craig Metellan, had two harbour problems. One was silt, which everywhere played havoc with roadsteads where there was a river channel, even to the extent in some cases, like Chester, of causing them to cease to be ports. The other was the extremes of tides, which were so helpful to Davie do A'thing, but often endangered ships both when crossing the bar or when anchored within the roadstead. Only smaller ships could come up as far as Futty and the Quayhead (opposite the foot of Shore Brae), the others had to lie off Torry.

Smuggling was a popular industry, and the white fishers of Futty, where the illicit landings were commonest, had in any case a reputation for brawling. Their conduct of a Sabbath on the Castlehill gave rise to Council enactments, and their free trade operations involved the maintenance of three preventive men, then called waiters, who kept a sharp eye for evasions of the Customs regulations.

In 1637 a great disaster befell four transports laden with soldiers in the harbour. Spalding relates how:

throw ane great speat of the water of Die, occasioned by extraordinar rayne, thir haill four schippes brak louss, for nather tow nor anker culd hald them, and wes driven out at the water mouth upone the night throw the violens and speat of the water, and by ane south-est wynd wes driven to the north schoir quhair thir schippes wes miserably bladit with lekis by striking on the Sandis. The soldiouris sleiping cairleslie in the bottom of the schip upone hether wes all in swoum throw the water that cam in at the hollis and lekis of the schip to thair gryte amasement, feir and dreddour. Alwais they got up ilk man with horrible crying and schouting; sum escapit, other sum pitifullie perishit and drount.

In 1648 the Denburn was diverted near the Weigh-house and made to discharge into a new harbour channel there. In 1656 one of the officials of the Protectorate, Thomas Tucker, reporting on customs round the coast, described the harbour, which he called safe with reservations, and he incidentally characterised Aberdeen as 'no despisable burgh either for building or largeness', and the Castlegate as 'a very stately market-place'. An embankment which Tucker mentions as in course of construction on the south side of the Dee was completed in 1659, and by 1661 there was a repair dock at Futty. Before that date the extension of the great quay from the Weigh-house to beside Futty Church had reclaimed many acres of ground which covered the present Waterloo Station, Commerce Street, Sugarhouse Lane, Water Lane, Mearns Street, James Street and the south part of Marischal Street. This area was converted into fertile corn land.

The two mills which were constructed to be driven by the tides seem to have been failures; even today the harnessing of the tides has not been productive. It is not, however, surprising that the experiment should have been made, for Aberdeen in those days was a city of mills. Of the oldest of which traces have been found, in the south end of two houses whose gables abutted on the Netherkirkgate between Broad Street and the Guestrow,[1] there is no historical mention, from which it has been deduced that the mill had ceased to work before 1398 when the town's records began. Probably it had been superseded by the mill, known as the Upper Mill, which has given its name to Flourmill Brae, and which was certainly in existence as a meal mill before 1400. The

1   These buildings, of course, were not those now occupied by municipal departments.

water which drove this mill came from the Loch, and went on to drive the Nether Mill, which was built about 1525, and which stood on the site of the block of buildings enclosed by Hadden Street, Exchange Street, Imperial Place and Stirling Street. In 1847 this mill became a malt mill, just as the Upper Mill became a flour mill. Both were discontinued in 1865. Between the Upper and Nether Mills there was built in 1619 the Mid Mill, about where the Commercial Bank buildings are at the corner of St. Nicholas Street. It was discontinued in 1798.

The first mills to be mentioned are the Justice (then the Justiciar's) Mills, which figure in a charter of 1349–50. The name probably derives from the early courts of justice being held on some mound in the vicinity. The site of the mills is fixed by the street name of Justice Mill Lane, on which the higher mill stood, the lower being in the dip below. Both were driven by the Holburn. There was a tradition that the first of the Justice Mills, both of which, like the Upper and Nether Mills, were town's property, was given to the burgh in the middle of the fourteenth century by Provost William Leith, in expiation of his murder of a baillie. By the end of that century the four burgh mills were let at £20 Scots. Provost Gilbert Menzies took them over as security for a loan to the town in 1575 and they were redeemed for 5,000 merks from his grandson in 1597.

There seem to have been three windmills. A windmill is mentioned in a charter of 1271: its site is unknown. There was one about the top of Bridge Street, which was let in 1501. In 1605, by order of the Council, a windmill was erected at the Gallowgatehead (on the northside of the stair that used to lead from Seamount Place to West North Street). There may have been an earlier one there. In 1678 a windmill was constructed on the south side of Windmill Brae.

The town had other mills outside its boundaries from which it drew meal. In 1616 the Council decided to build a mill at Maidencraig, also known as the Denburn or Den Mylne, on the north side of the Skene Road four miles out. A mill was erected at Gilcomston in 1613 by the proprietor of the land, who thus broke the town's monopoly of making meal. The Council threatened fines and double multure dues on any of its tenants who patronised the private mill, and gave notice to interdict tenants outwith the Town's control from getting burgh refuse for their fields. The mill was discontinued after 1679, when the Council purchased the lands of Gilcomston. There was in 1760 a lint mill and croft on the north side of Baker Street. These were bought in that year by a distillery company which changed over to brewing and built large premises with a big mill-wheel on the south side of Baker Street. The premises were taken down in 1902 long after they had ceased to function. Strachan's mill in Leadside Road was in existence in 1773 and was acquired by the Strachan family in 1849.

The Denburn drove another meal mill called the Stonyton mill about where the lane between Osborne Place and Carden Place would cross Albert Street. It was done away with in 1842. In 1661 the Pitmuxton Mill stood on the west bank of the Pitmuxton Burn near Allenvale Cemetery. It disappeared about a century ago. The Bucksburn Mill, also town's property, was built in 1616 — a big year of mill-making by the burgh. There was a mill at Ferryhill in 1667. After a fire it became a glove factory and was removed when new streets were built east of the Hardgate.

Gordon's Mills, near Hayton on the Don, were in existence in 1639 as meal mills. Then they were turned over to wool and later to paper. The Lady Mill built in 1832 on the east side of King Street by the Powis Burn was until recently a sawmill. One of the reasons given in 1603 for a complete scheme for drainage for the Loch was to supply a plentiful flow of water for the town's mills between the Loch and the harbour. David Anderson was put in charge of the undertaking, which involved the deepening of the burn channels draining the Loch between its eastern bank and the Gallowgate, whereas the stream between its western bank and the Woolmanhill was closed up. For labour the citizens were expected to turn to in person or to send their servants as they might be warned by the master of works.

But there was a further intention behind the scheme. At an earlier period the Loch had covered an area of a hundred acres, on the north along Fraser Road to Millbank Lane and down to the foot of Holland Street, but chiefly south of Hutcheon Street, its boundaries being, roughly, Kingsland Place, Maberly Street, Spring Garden, Loch Street, Crooked Lane, St. Andrew Street, Blackfriars Street, the railway and the slope to the east of Ann Street. It was at that time replenished by the Westburn and the Spital burns, and its outlet was at Gilcomston Steps. The burns had been diverted some time in the fourteenth century to supply water to the eastern part of the burgh, and for many generations the Loch was a filthy marsh in wet weather and an unsightly hollow in drought. To the west of it a mill-dam, also called the Loch, had been made, banked up to a slightly higher level than the bed of the marsh.

The scheme of 1623 provided that in future the Loch bed or marsh, which apparently had been let out on lease to be tilled, should be 'unlaborit or manurit' and be left in grass and 'serve onlie for that use'.

Probably the Council felt the abomination would be kept in check by grass, and in any case there was a sufficiency of arable crofts on the links, behind the new pier east of Shore Brae, and on the slopes west of the Denburn. Some thirty years later there is recorded a Council order to have geese kept out of the Loch 'considering the prejudice done to the grass by the loch by the dailie resorting of the geese belonging to sindrie of the inhabitants'. Another problem was the servant maids who emptied household slops into the nearest water they could see — and it should be remembered that the Gallowgate in those days housed all 'the best people'.

In 1644 a report made by valuators appointed by the Council of crops growing in the town's lands mentioned 'three bolls sowing' at the Hill of Faulds, 'a little quhet at Gilcomston, not considerable', and three bolls sowing near Wedder Craig. The same inspectors reported that the Auldtown people were being guilty of the offence of casting their peats on the town's lands. Eight years later the charges for loading peats and the price per load were fixed, the latter not to exceed 5s. Scots, or about 5d. sterling. At the same time people were debarred from burning the town's mosses and sowing corn there.

When the Jacobite Rebellions ended, Aberdeen was still like a modern village in its intimate possession of domesticated animals that public health prefers to keep at a distance from big centres of population. In 1693 the Council debarred all persons from feeding sheep on the links, the bent hillocks and the Denburn valley because the 'fermorers and others' keeping horses and kine within the burgh were thereby made destitute of grass. In 1700 one Agnes Geddes, relict of Alexander Kynach, cowfeeder, was continued in her late husband's post as town herd for keeping the town's kine on the links. But most illuminating of all is the Council's long war against swine in the streets and houses, a contest in which the burgh was not victorious until late in the century. The depredations of the pigs, 'being ane unseemlie kynd of beast', are picturesquely recorded: 'seeing by experience it is found they are werie prejudiciall to the yards (gardens) and sowin land . . . in digging and holling up the samen with their heads and snoutts, and that in the churchyard they have cassin up great graves and incoverit dead corpses, which is both dangerous and shamefull, and they noways being waitit upone, doe converse in all the filthie dunghills, middings, gutters and sinks of all sorts of excrements and by their working raise ane infectious and intollerable smell . . . and also they may prove dangerous to young children and others quhen they are going at random through the streets'.

CHAPTER ELEVEN

Genius by Inbreeding

At the Union of the Crowns Aberdeen was a city of personalities, richer in that respect than it had or has ever been. For half a century the number of its eminent men, either natives or graduates of one of its two universities, was out of all proportion to its population. Some were of international reputation, several of them still remembered, if not by every schoolboy, at least by anyone with normal historical equipment. The memory of others is engraved in local annals. There was a lot of brains in scions of the old county families like the Gordons, Keiths, Forbeses and Johnstons, but the most striking distinction belongs to a curious group of burghal families, long connected with the life of the city and its commercial and cultural development.

Until 1610 Aberdeen was handicapped in its commerce by the presence in the centre of the harbour entrance of a great boulder known as Craig Metellan or the Maitland Rock. This obstruction denied to larger vessels of the new age entry to the roadstead. In that year an enterprising Aberdonian, already favourably known in the town as 'the most skilful mechanick that lived in Scotland in his tyme', decided to make away with the monster. The story how 'by the renowned art and industrie of that ingenious and vertuous citizen David Anderson', Craig Metellan was removed, describes the birth of Aberdeen, the modern city. David Anderson of Finzeauch, known from his many undertakings as Davie do A'thing, had observed that whereas scarcely 2 feet of water covered the harbour bar at low tide, there was a depth of 15 feet at spring tides and nearly 10 at the neaps. He harnessed the sea to remove the obstacle. At low tide he attached a number of empty casks to the rock by stout tackle. As the tide rose the barrels by their buoyancy lifted the great stone from its bed and carried it up the channel, where the ebb left it well out of the path of sea-going traffic. Some accounts of the feat, which evidently and rightly bulked large in the imagination of contemporary Aberdonians, credit David with having seated himself upon the rock or one of the casks and been thus carried in triumph along with the uprooted monster. If we add to that embroidery a cheering crowd we shall be doing no more than justice to one of the most formative incidents and one of the outstanding men in Aberdeen's history.

David, who died in his prime in 1619, and to whose genius is ascribed amongst other exploits the setting of the sundial upon the Town House wall, belonged to a family long noted for its practical abilities. Early in the sixteenth century a David Anderson, 'one of the principall men' in the town, often a baillie, for several years 'maister of Sanct Nicholace wark' was constantly on committees for the burgh's defence. In 1527 as master of the pier work he went to Dundee to purchase stones for the new pier. In 1529 as a baillie he accompanied Parson Galloway when that versatile cleric toured the town preparing a scheme of defence. In the same year, with William Rolland and Sir Alexander Scherar, vicar of Nigg, he was in charge of the construction of the Bridge of Dee. In the closing decades of the century another David Anderson was master of kirk work. The relationship of a third David Anderson, a plumber described in 1599 as the common servant of the town, to Davie do A'thing is not known. He himself is said to have been the son of Gilbert Anderson, but so many mechanical Davids are suggestive of some kinship. Our information about this remarkable man is annoyingly vague. What relation was he, if any, to the Skipper Anderson (who will appear again in this history) who took the fifth Earl Marischal to Denmark to bring home James VI's queen? Was he, as seems likely, 'David Anderson, Elder', who in 1603 got a commission to drain the Loch? Davie do A'thing certainly served as dean of guild and baillie, he designed a steeple for the parish church and he made 'ane orloge in the common clerkis chalmer'. On that evidence we are probably justified in assuming that it was he in 1605 who was asked to repair the kirk lodge, who in 1606 was requested to send the brazen cock of St. Nicholas steeple to Flanders for renovation, and who was instructed to buy lead from Dundee. Him too in 1609 we may accept as the councillor in charge of the building of the new twin-arched Bow Brig over the Denburn, for which Andrew Jamesone, father of the greater George, was the contractor.

David Anderson's half-brother — some say, cousin — was Alexander Anderson, professor of the Mathematics at Paris, an academe highly renowned in his day. He was, says Sir Thomas Urquhart in his best panegyrical vein, 'for his abilities in the mathematical sciences, accounted the profoundliest principled of any man of his time. In his studies, he plied hardest the equations of algebra, the speculations of the irrational lines, the proportions of irregular bodies, and sections of the cone. He was excellently well skilled in the theory of the planets and astronomy; the optics, catoptricks, dioptricks; the orthographical, steriographical, schenographical projections; in cosmography, geography, trigonometry, and geodesie; in the staticks, music and all other parts and pendicles, sciences, faculties, or arts of or belonging to the disciplines mathematical in general, or any portion thereof in its essence or dependencies. Having a body too weak to sustain the vehement intensiveness of so high a spirit, he dyed young.' Little wonder, indeed! But it may be wondered whether a eulogium of some modern scientist by some modern scribe will not read as quaintly 300 years hence.

David Anderson married Jean, daughter of Matthew Guild, a 'sweird slipper' or armourer who for many years was a prominent figure in the struggles of the Crafts. We saw how he on one occasion temporarily lost his freedom as a citizen, following an act of defiance against an ordinance of the Town Council, but he was a substantial individual capable of fulfilling the responsible duties of deacon of the Hammermen for six terms in succession. Never has Aberdeen had a more pious family than the Guilds. Davie do A'thing himself had purchased from the Earl Marischal the manse, barns and yard of the Black Friars on the Schoolhill. After his death his widow and daughters conveyed the property to the Town Council as a fund for the education and maintenance of ten indigent orphan boys or girls of Aberdeen. Jean Guild left another bequest for the maintenance of poor widows of burgesses and of aged spinsters.

But her benefactions were far excelled by those of her distinguished brother, the Rev. Dr. William Guild, one of the great names in the city's history, although not always remembered with the respect which is his due. Born in 1586, Guild was educated at Marischal College, and was only 22 when he published in London in 1608 his first treatise, *The New Sacrifice of Christian Incense; or The True Entry to the Tree of Life, and Gracious Gate of Glorious Paradise*, which displays even in its title an acquaintance with the gaudy conceits of Mr. John Lyly. In that year he became minister of King-Edward,[1] and employed the leisure of a country parish in further literary exercises. In 1610 he married Catherine, daughter of James Rolland of Disblair, a lady who

1 It would be a pleasant gesture on the part of Clio were we to learn that Guild baptised at King-Edward the infant Thomas Urquhart, to be one day Sir and of Cromartie and the translator of Rabelais. The author of *The New Sacrifice of Christian Incense* would have been an appropriate literary godfather of the author of *Trissotetras* and *Logopandecteison*.

made several bequests to the town and university. Guild, although a rural parson, got around,[1] became acquainted with at least two English bishops, and secured an appointment as a chaplain to Charles I. In 1631, after several trials in the pulpit 'to the contentment and general applause of the whole congregation', he was selected as one of the ministers of Aberdeen. By this time Edward Raban, the town's printer, was his publisher, and from Raban's press in the years from 1626 onward there issued no fewer than thirteen of his works.

In 1631 Guild acquired the deserted monastery and chapel of the Trinity Friars. He presented the property to the Trades to be their meeting-house and chapel, and they severally levied themselves to put the buildings in tenantable repair. Their joint contribution of £2,200 Scots, which effected the reconstruction, represented 'the best pairt of the moneyes quhilk they hade to the foir in thair commoun boxes, swa that thair stok and rent for the present wll be but verye meane'. Accordingly in 1632 they approached the Town Council for assistance, and the Council allowed them, 'to the behoof of the decayit craftisman quho sall happen to be admitit in the said Hospitall as bedalls thairof', 200 merks annually for five years at interest. In gratitude for this aid, or simply out of natural munificence, Guild in 1633 undertook to reglaze all the windows of the Greyfriars Kirk, except the south-east gable window for which Alexander Stewart, merchant, made himself responsible. This act enabled the Church, then described as 'a pleasant and magnifick edifice . . . very convenient and easeful for the whole inhabitantis', to be opened for public worship after many years of neglect.

When in 1638 the ministers of Aberdeen were asked to sign the National Covenant, Guild did so with three reservations: he promised only to forbear the practice of the Articles of Perth, a group of ordinances passed by a dubious Assembly in 1618 and regarded by the Covenanting party as savouring of Popery; he refused to condemn episcopacy; and he stood by his loyalty to the King. But even in signing the Covenant with these limitations, he was more compliant than the majority of the divines in Aberdeen, who adhered stoutly to Episcopacy but refused to append their signatures. Two years later, when Dr. William Leslie was expelled from the Principalship of King's College for his refusal to accept the Covenant, Guild agreed to sign without reservations and was appointed to the vacant office. But he seems to have

1 Singularly enough, it was far easier for an unknown Aberdonian to enlist the aid of influential Englishmen than appears to be the case now.

been reluctant in accepting. At the General Assembly in Glasgow in 1638 which abolished the episcopate, he was present and fell in with the majority, with the result that feeling in Aberdeen on his return was so bitter that he had to withdraw to Holland for a time. He never was, however, a whole-hogger. After Cromwell took control of Scotland, he fell into disrepute with the authorities for his Royalist sympathies, and in 1651 was deposed by Monck. Retiring into private life, he continued his anti-Papist writings, and died in 1657. His monument in St. Nicholas Churchyard is still maintained by the Incorporated Trades of which he was the first patron and most renowned benefactor.

During his period and after his death Guild continued to promote the welfare of his native city, particularly through the university. But some of his efforts did not meet with unanimous approval. John Spalding, the Aberdeen historian of *The Troubles*, the principal charm of whose narrative lies in its frank prejudices, had never a kind word for 'Dr. William Goold'. Everything he did was found by the candid partisan to be deplorable, In his zeal, no doubt, for the honour of the university, Guild in 1642, 'began to preiche within the college ane weiklie sermon to be taught that day to the Old Toun people, studentis, maisteris, and memberis of the college'. This innovation annoyed Spalding because Guild conducted the service in English, whereas 'by the foundation he is bound to preiche or give out his lessons in Greik, Hebrue, and Latyne, except exercises and presbitrie dayes'. It was, however, in his building operations that Guild chiefly incurred the censure of Spalding. In 1641 Charles I gave Dr. Guild the Bishop's house in Old Aberdeen in a gift. It and the bishop's dovecot, which was in ruins, he had taken down, using the timber and stones for various constructional purposes in the college and for 'the bigging of ane song scool quhilk be som was not thocht sacrilegious; bot yet wes evill done as otheris thocht'. Guild also had the walls of the Snow Kirk, the parish church of Old Aberdeen, taken down to build the college dykes. Spalding laments the loss of fine buildings 'thrown down by despiteful soldiers, and then demolished by Doctors of Divinity.[1] But for all that we must regard Guild not as the iconoclast but as the perpetuator and preserver. After his death a house in the Castlegate that had come to him through his marriage, and known by its pious association as the Bursar's house, was mortified for the support of three craftsmen's sons at Marischal College.

1   Slezer's picture of Old Aberdeen, 1688, however, shows the Snow Church intact.

David Anderson's sister, Marjory, in 1585 became the wife of Andrew Jamesone, who later rebuilt the Bridge of Don at Balgownie and erected the new Bow Brig over the Denburn. The second son and third child of the marriage, George Jamesone, was born probably in 1588. George Jamesone, 'the Scottish Vandyck', was educated at the Grammar School and perhaps at Marischal College. There is, through loss of documents, no record of his attendance at college, and indeed we have far too few details of his life. He studied on the Continent, according to tradition in Antwerp in the studio of Rubens, when Vandyck himself was a pupil. He was back in Aberdeen about 1620 and very soon received lucrative commissions from the Scottish aristocracy. In 1624 he married a handsome girl of whom we know nothing save her name, Isobel Tosche, and her appearance from a family group painted by her husband. Three sons and three daughters were born to the couple. All the sons died before their father. When in 1633 Charles I visited Scotland, the magistrates of Edinburgh invited Jamesone to be present in a professional capacity. He executed a portrait of the King, made many new contacts, visited London, where he is said to have painted the Queen, and then crossed to the Continent for a tour of Italy. On his return he busied himself with a series of portraits commissioned by Sir Colin Campbell of Glenorchy, and it was about this time he acquired a piece of greensward by the Denburn, near the Well of Spa, approximately where the old Infirmary buildings now stand. Of this plot, known for long as the Playfield, from its having been the scene of the outdoor theatricals which were common in a less puritan age, Jamesone proposed to 'mak some policie and planting . . . for the publict vse and benefitt of the Toune'. The Town Council accordingly gave him the life-rent of the field at a yearly payment of three and fourpence Scots 'if the same be asked'. This first public park of Aberdeen, built up against spates and soundly enclosed, came to be known as the 'four neukit garden', and the 'Garden Neuk Close' in living memory was the name of a lane which ran along what was believed to be the original eastern wall. Jamesone's house, which he inherited from his father, was one of the most beautiful private buildings in Aberdeen, pulled down in 1890 during one of those attacks of vandalism to which the town is subject. It stood on the north side of the Schoolhill, over against the West Kirk and a little east of the line of the present Harriet Street. Andrew Jamesone may have built the house, next to a property belonging to his brother-in-law, David Anderson. Samuel Rutherford is said to have lived in it during his banishment, and in later years it came to be known as the manse of St. Nicholas. Jamesone divided the last fifteen years of his life between Aberdeen and Edinburgh, and it was in Edinburgh that he died in 1644. Where he is buried is unknown. His enduring claim to our remembrance lies in the fact that he was the first great portrait painter of native British stock.

By two branches of his family David Anderson, and through him the Guilds and Jamesones, were related to the most astonishing collection of academic prodigies that ever graced Scotland. David's daughter Janet married John Gregory, the minister of Drumoak, who died in 1651. They had amongst other children, James (1638–75) and David, whose progeny during two centuries were to be prominent in British university society. James showed the bent of his genius with his first book, on Optics, published when he was 24 and proudly informing the world on its title-page that its author was 'An Aberdonian Scot'. From 1668 to 1674 he was professor of Mathematics at St. Andrews, transferring in the latter year to the corresponding chair at Edinburgh on account of the hostility of some of his colleagues and the lack of equipment in the Fife seminary. Gregory demonstrated how the transits of the inferior planets could be used to provide a system for determining the solar parallax. He also was the first to distinguish between convergent and divergent series, and to give a systematic geometrical account of the differential and integral calculi. His fame during his lifetime was established as the inventor of the reflecting telescope, which Newton perfected, and he was regarded as Newton's equal in scientific eminence. In 1675, after showing his class the satellites of Jupiter, he was struck by sudden blindness and died three days later.

James Gregory had a son by his wife, George Jamesone's daughter, also James, born in 1674, the first of the medical Gregories, who became professor of Medicine at King's College in 1725. He died in 1731 and was succeeded by his son, yet another James, who may be called the third. He was the boy of whom Rob Roy, who claimed kinship with the Gregories, proposed, on a visit to his father in Aberdeen, to make a cateran. There is insufficient data as to James the third's medical charges to form an opinion as to whether the freebooter's suggestion would have been worth a trial. James the second, the first medical Gregory, is remembered as the man who cut a new channel for the Don, diverting it from its old outlet nearer the Broad Hill to its present estuary. This he did in 1727. James the third was succeeded in 1755 as professor of Medicine at King's College by his brother John who in 1766 moved to Edinburgh, where he became professor of the

9

Practice of Medicine and wrote, besides several philosophical works, 'A Father's Legacy to his Daughter', in which he warned the young lady, 'If you happen to have any learning, keep it a profound secret, especially from the men, who generally look with a jealous eye on a woman of great parts and cultivated understanding'.

John Gregory died in 1773 and his son James became professor of the Institutes of Medicine in Edinburgh in 1776 and of the Practice of Medicine in 1790. He died in 1821 and is perhaps unfavourably remembered as the inventor of Gregory's powder by those who were young up to fifty years ago. His son William, who died in 1858, was professor of Medicine at King's College from 1839 to 1844, and thereafter of Chemistry at Edinburgh until his death. William Gregory's cousin, William Pultenay Alison, held in succession three medical chairs in Edinburgh and died in 1859. This triple professor's brother was Sir Archibald Alison, author of the *History of Europe*.

The first James Gregory's elder brother Alexander was murdered in 1664 by an uncle of the Viscount of Frendraught, the Viscount himself being an accessory to the crime. Although the murder was truly atrocious, the jury acquitted the accused. James Gregory's second brother David inherited the estate of Kinairdy from the murdered Alexander and was remarkable for his virility in more ways than one. He had fifteen children by his first wife and fourteen by his second (some counts make it thirty-two by the two.) He invented a device, says his grandson Thomas Reid the philosopher, 'for improving the effect of firearms, of which he at least completed a model and sent it to his son David at Oxford that he might get the opinion of Sir Isaac Newton about it . . . . Sir Isaac persuaded the suppression of the invention as destructive to the human species and it was never brought to light.' Reid adds that Kinairdy was so certain of the efficiency of his invention that he contemplated making a campaign in Flanders all by himself. Kinairdy also studied medicine and 'being much occupied through the day with those who applied to him as a physician, he went early to bed, rose about 2 or 3 in the morning and after applying to his studies for some hours went to bed again and slept an hour or two before breakfast'.

His descendants were as notable as those of James. His son David (1659–1708), entered Marischal in 1671, and was M.A. Edinburgh 1683, M.A. and M.D. of Oxford 1692, and Fellow of the Royal Society in the same year, professor of Mathematics in Edinburgh 1683 to 1691 and of Astronomy at Oxford 1691–1708. David of Kinairdy's next son

James (1666–1742), also attended Marischal College, was M.A. of Edinburgh and professor of Mathematics first at St. Andrews and then at Edinburgh. Another son Charles was professor of Mathematics at St. Andrews from 1707 to 1739, and his son David succeeded him in that chair and died in 1763. A daughter of David of Kinairdy married the minister of Strachan and became the mother of Thomas Reid the philosopher (1710–96), who was a regent at King's 1751–64, and professor of Moral Philosophy at Glasgow thereafter until his death. He was the author of an *Inquiry into the Human Mind on the Principles of Commonsense, Essays on the Intellectual Powers*, and *Essays on the Active Powers*. The first mentioned was probably the best reply to Hume's theories that had been or could be made. Finally a great grandson of David of Kinairdy, Alexander Innes, was professor of Philosophy at Marischal College from 1739 to 1742. This gives a total of fourteen professors in the Gregory family in 200 years.

When the Protectorate was approaching its end, there passed out of Marischal in 1657 along with James Gregory another Master of Arts destined to fill a high place in British history. Gilbert Burnet, born in Edinburgh of a Mearns branch of the Leys family, was reared at Aberdeen. After graduation he studied both in Edinburgh and in Holland, returning to become (under the Episcopal dispensation) parish minister of Saltoun. The death of the patron, Sir Robert Fletcher, gave him his first opportunity to measure himself in letters by an elegiac discourse. In 1669 he became professor of Divinity at Glasgow but entered the Church of England four years later. Being a good Whig who had taken an active part in bringing over William of Orange, he was rewarded at the Revolution with the see of Salisbury, in the enjoyment of the emoluments and dignities of which he died in 1715. As the recorder of the Revolution of his own times (his personal recollections covered nearly two thirds of a century), Burnet must still be regarded as one of the primary historians of the country's development.

While James Gregory was making his way in the world, an earlier M.A. of Marischal, Robert Morison, born in Aberdeen in 1620, had reached the top in medicine and botany. In 1650 after a decade of study and practice in France, he had been appointed superintendent of the Royal Gardens at Blois and physician to the Duke of Orleans. The Restoration brought him back to England as physician to Charles II and royal professor of Botany, which was the penultimate step to the professorship of Botany at Oxford in 1659. He died in 1683 the leading botanist of his generation.

CHAPTER TWELVE

A Diversity of Creatures

During the third quarter of the seventeenth century 'the oy of a baxter' was the leading figure in the corporate life of Aberdeen, as well as one of the most energetic actors in the drama of national affairs. The third Alexander Jaffray of Kingswells, twice Provost of Aberdeen, friend of Charles II and Oliver Cromwell, a member of Barebone's Parliament, Presbyterian, Independent, Millenarian, Quaker, had more experience of the inside of prisons than most men. He is the only Provost of Aberdeen who has left us an autobiography, the now famous Diary which was found by accident in Ury House, Stonehaven. Its fault is that it contains far too much theologicial disquisition and far too little subjective narrative. Alexander Jaffray was only 59 when he died, but he lived at a rate which we, in our exciting and very fast days, never seem to be able to achieve.

Jaffray was born in Aberdeen in 1614, son of Provost Alexander Jaffray (1635-6, 1638, 1641) and Magdalen Erskine, daughter of the laird of Pittodrie. His parents, after the fruitful fashion of those times, had fifteen children, most of whom died in infancy. His father, Alexander's grandfather, also an Alexander, had been admitted a burgess of his craft in 1534, and this first Alexander's elder son, Alexander again, bought the estate of Kingswells in 1579 from Robert Arthur, whose father, John Arthur, had been the first feuar of the property under the ill-advised scheme which, in the 1550s, permitted the Town Council to dispose of the Freedom Lands.

The first Alexander Jaffray of Kingswells rose to be a baillie, married a niece of Burnett of Leys, and in 1613, fourteen years before his death, matriculated a coat of arms. The second Alexander of Kingswells, and the first Jaffray Provost of Aberdeen, despite his mother's breeding and his wife's social status, had a good deal of civic snobbery to live down. The first Sunday after he was made Provost by the Privy Council (in consequence of a dispute as to procedure), he found a pie in his seat in the kirk, a crude allusion to his grandfather's trade. But he had the virtue of good temper, and he 'miskenit all and never querrellit the samen', as Spalding, of whose friends he was not, is constrained to admit. He was an ardent Covenanter .. 'rigorouse', Spalding terms him .. and was one of the first to sign the Covenant in 1638. The establishment of the House of Correction seems to have been due mainly to him. In fact, his sound sense and practical nature were a godsend to the burgh during the very trying times when the Civil Wars were in process of incubation. He from time to time acted as Aberdeen's representative at the meetings of Parliament, General Assembly and Convention of Burghs. In 1639, when the Royalists under Viscount Aboyne were for a brief period in control of the town, during Jaffray's second provostship, there was a Head Court of the inhabitants to which the question was put whether the provost had been disloyal to the King. 'They all in ane voice, but (without) ony oppositioun or contradictioun, answered that they had no point of disloyaltie or miscarriage to say against him, or any brak of duetie in his office to lay to his chairge, but be the contriar, they give him thair approbatioun and applause that he has dischairgit and acquytted himself in his said office most dutifullie and honestlie, as one loyal and gude subject to his maiestie, and as a most cairfull and painefull magistratt for the weill and gude of the toune'. This conscientious character descended to his son.

The career of the great Alexander Jaffray is a seemly example of the life led in the seventeenth century by the better class of Scotsmen with brains and a capacity for public affairs. Despite complete lack of security they possessed dignity, and the courage with which they confronted misfortune won them liberty. Alexander Jaffray was several times imprisoned, many times harried and persecuted, often inconvenienced and for thirty years seldom out of range of the bright eyes of danger, yet the last thing he would have asked was a policy of social security for his friends or of safety first for himself. He was born in June 1614, educated at the Grammar School and Marischal College, the daughter of whose principal, Jean Dun, he married when he was 18, and by whom he had ten children in twelve years before she died in 1644. Three years later he married Sarah, daughter of his relative the celebrated Calvinist divine Andrew Cant, by whom he had eight further children.

Soon after his first marriage Jaffray was sent to Edinburgh by his father to the care of Robert Burnet, advocate (father of Gilbert Burnet, the historian) to learn 'not only some things of the law and practice of the Tolbooth, but some things as to the practice of holiness and charity'. He then paid a visit to France via London, and in Paris had his first narrow escape from death when a drunken sailor wounded him in the street. In 1636 he returned home, and two years later, we find him a leader of the Covenanting party in the town and a baillie, suffering in the execution of his duty at the hands of Sir John Gordon of Haddo, as already narrated. He fought against Montrose that year in the battle of the Justice Mills, where the Irish nearly slew him, and where he saved one of the Covenanting colours.

Montrose's victory sent Jaffray into temporary retirement at Dunnottar with the Earl Marischal. Soon after he was caught, with Andrew Cant and others, by a Royalist band and thrown into Pitcaple Castle (which Montrose also was to know as a prison) for six weeks of pretty humiliating confinement. But one day, when all the garrison but two (who were flaying an ox) were out of doors, Jaffray stole down and shut the great door and iron gate against them, and the prisoners prepared to withstand a siege. By this time Montrose had been routed at Philiphaugh, and the Covenanters were in the ascendant, so that in a few days Jaffray and his friends were relieved, and after a banquet to their rescuers, they set fire to the castle and went home. Alexander Jaffray, senior, also a Covenanter, was by this time dead, 'much reformed (says his son) and withdrawn from company-keeping in taverns before his death'. Alexander junior now became Member of Parliament for Aberdeen, and in 1649, besides being elected Provost for the first time, he was appointed one of the Scots Commissioners to approach Charles II, then at The Hague, with the offer of the Scottish Crown provided he would sign the Covenant. Then as afterwards Charles was perfectly willing to sign anything that promised advantage to himself, but Jaffray in later life was not very happy as to his own part in this embassy. 'We did sinfully both entangle the nation and ourselves, and that poor young prince; making him sign and swear a Covenant which we knew he hated in his heart — where, I must confess, to my apprehension our sin was more than his. I had so clear convictions of this that I spoke of it to the King myself, desiring him not to subscribe the Covenant, if in his conscience he was not satisfied.' But Charles never had a conscience and therefore signed as requested, came to Scotland and brought Cromwell north to overthrow him. Jaffray fought at Dunbar Drove in 1650, where his horse was shot under him, and he was four times wounded and taken prisoner.

Jaffray was carried before Cromwell, and his sterling sincerity must have appealed to the English Dictator, for his incarceration only lasted a few months, during which he held much profound theological debate with some of the Protector's highly religious associates, as a result of which he joined the Independents and from them graduated into the sublimer flights of belief among the Millenarians or Fifth Monarchy sect, who were convinced of the immediate reappearance of Christ upon earth. This radical conversion may have enhanced his personal worth in Cromwell's eyes, but the great Oliver did not appoint Jaffray in 1652 to be Director of the Chancery in Scotland or accept him as one of Scotland's five Commissioners to the first Union Parliament, known as the Barebone's Parliament, simply because he was rather too pellucid in his religious faith. Nor were these posts his by virtue of a readiness to say Yea to Cromwell's decrees, for Jaffray was one of the few in the Parliament who had to be forcibly ejected by Cromwell's troops. On the contrary, after that display of political contumacy, Cromwell offered Jaffray a judgeship in the Court of Session, which was refused, and saw that the Provost was reimbursed with the £1,500 of expenses incurred in the embassy to Charles II in Holland. In short, Jaffray was a big enough man to be deemed worthy of very high office and to refuse to accept posts for which he felt he was unfitted. Despite the vigour with which politics were conducted in that age, we must conclude that, judged by modern standards, Jaffrey's bump of self-interest was primitive and ill-developed. That he was honest with himself and others would doubtless not come into the reckoning.

Nor was his candour to Charles II remembered at the Restoration. He was once again thrown into prison for failing instantly to subscribe the bond of allegiance, and was held for four months, when he was released under surety of £20,000 Scots and because he was 'in ane Infirm and valetudinarie condition, his health much impaired and lyff endangered for want of his ordinarie helps and frie air'. On his return home he joined the Society of Friends, then a severely persecuted sect, and his own sufferings consisted of much abuse in Aberdeen and ten months' imprisonment at Banff. He died at Kingswells on 7 May 1673, and was buried in the Quaker cemetery he had established there, north of the old Skene road, a 'wise, pious and discreet man all his time' whose greatest legacy to his native burgh was the example of his own firm and fearless character, and who in addition performed for the town the valuable material service of getting largely repaid the debt it had incurred during The Troubles.

From the Restoration to the last Jacobite rising the most interesting in a line of exceptional provosts was George Fordyce of Broadford, whose family in two generations achieved almost as much distinction as the

Gregories and in a much wider variety of ways. He had the chair in 1718–19, 1722–3, and 1726–7, and at his death in 1733 it was said of him that 'his integrity in publick and goodness in private life left a better monument in the memory of the good and wise than can be raised to him by posterity'. His later life he spent at Eigie in Belhelvie. By his first wife he had five, by his second, a minister's daughter, sixteen children. Of those of the sixteen who survived to the adult stage, one was professor of moral philosophy at Marischal, one became a prominent preacher in London, and wrote elegiac verses on his friend Dr. Samuel Johnson, two (as well as a grandson) had medical practices in London, one of whom, William, was knighted and founded the Fordyce lectureship in agricultural chemistry at Marischal, of which he was Lord Rector. He wrote treatises celebrated in their day on fevers and sore throats and was a Fellow of the Royal Society like his nephew George, who also practised in London, was a lecturer on medical subjects, eventually was elected physician to St. Thomas's Hospital and was a member of the famous club of which Johnson, Reynolds, Goldsmith and Boswell were the leading members. The provost's youngest son, Alexander, became head of the London banking firm of Fordyce & Co., was like William Lord Rector of Marischal, purchased the estate of North Colpna (now Orrok) in Belhelvie, and married a daughter of the Earl of Balcarres. Excessive optimism in speculation led to the collapse of his bank, a failure almost as cataclysmic in the end of the eighteenth century as the failure of the City of Glasgow Bank towards the end of the nineteenth. One female member of the Fordyce family married, to the scandal of her relations, a pastrycook and poet (of sorts) who became Lord Mayor of London.

Of the many other noteworthy Aberdonians in this golden age of Aberdeen's culture two stand out pre-eminently. Arthur Johnston of Caskieben (now Keith Hall) born in 1577, and educated at Kintore parish school, at King's and on the Continent, in the seventeenth century took George Buchanan's place as Scotland's greatest humanist. He was professor of philosophy at Heidelberg and Sedan, M.A. of Padua, physician to James I and Charles I, and with Sir John Scot of Scotstarvet compiled and edited in 1637 the *Delitiæ Poetarum Scotorum*, besides writing a Latin Psalter of his own and many epigrams. Towering above him, thirty years his junior, was Sir Thomas Urquhart of Cromartie (1608–60), probably reared at Craigston, King-Edward, educated at King's and immortal as the translator of Rabelais. Urquhart's rendering, which unfortunately he never finished, is incomparable.

No one ever entered so naturally and whole-heartedly into the spirit of an author as Sir Thomas did into that of his original, and when as frequently, he expands him, he never betrays him. Urquhart was the author of many books, always in an English of his own creation, vivid, racy and unconventional. One of his best known essays is his sketch of the Admirable Crichton, and he himself has claims to be considered as the Admirable Crichton of the English language. The first shots of the Great Civil War were fired at his house of Balquholly, now Hatton Castle, near Turriff; he was taken prisoner after Worcester, and died of a laughing fit when he heard that Charles II had been invited back to his father's throne.

Other figures, literary and scientific and mostly academic may be more shortly mentioned. All were Aberdonians, of either city or county. Arthur Johnston's cousin, John Johnston of Crimond, born 1565, educated at the Grammar School and King's, in Germany and Geneva, became professor of Divinity at St. Andrews and made his reputation in the dissimilar subjects of physiology and poetry, being sometimes remembered by epigrams not quite so striking as Arthur's.

Aberdeen's achievement in medicine then was remarkable. John Craig, son of Sir Thomas Craig, was professor of Logic and Mathematics at Frankfurt-on-Oder, and wrote treatises 1577–8 opposing the astronomical theories of Tycho Brahe. He was a physician to James VI. Duncan Liddell, 1561–1613, whose monuments, apart from the Aberdeen University prizes bearing his name, respectively stand in the haughs of Pitmedden of Dyce and repose on the wall of St. Nicholas Kirk, went through the Grammar School and King's College to study and later to profess Mathematics and Medicine in several universities of Germany. Thomas Morrison, 1554–1604, another King's product and M.D. of Montpelier, wrote on metallurgy and Papists and practised medicine in Edinburgh. James Cargill, 1565–1614 ('buriet in the auld kirk befoir the pulpit, 20 September 1614, honorabillie'), like so many others was a product of the Grammar School and King's. He was an M.D. of Basle, and a very distinguished botanist. He practised medicine in Aberdeen, and left bursaries to his old school and to Marischal College. Another Aberdeen doctor and benefactor of Marischal College, David Chamberlane, was physician to Anne of Denmark, consort of James I. James Leith after teaching in the University of Paris, where he became Rector, had a medical practice there about 1620. Sir Thomas Urquhart states that he made a fortune, 'as the vast means possessed by his sons and daughters there as yet can testify'. A pupil of Liddell's,

Gilbert Jack, 1578–1628, published a much esteemed medical textbook, *Institutiones Medicae*, in 1624, was professor of Philosophy at Leyden, and was invited to be professor of Civil History at Oxford. Patrick Dun, another Marischal graduate and M.D. of Basle, was regent in 1610, Rector in 1619 and Principal in 1621 of his alma mater, and died in 1652. Alexander Reid of Banchory, educated at Aberdeen and in France, was a surgeon and the first London Lecturer in Anatomy. His brother Thomas Reid was Latin Secretary to James I. William Gordon, 1593–1640, who went from Aberdeen to take his M.D. at Padua, was Mediciner at King's in 1632 and was the first medical man to secure the corpses of criminals for clinical dissection. He rebuilt the Crown of King's when it fell in 1631. A contemporary of his, William Davidson, 1593–1670, went to Paris from King's, took his M.D., was appointed professor of Chemistry when the Jardin des Plantes was inaugurated, and became physician to Louis XIII. In 1650 he went to Poland and held a like office for the Polish King, John Casimir. Another Aberdeen graduate, Patrick Gordon of Braco (M.A. Marischal 1610), was Consul in Danzig in 1611 and later Mandatory of the British Crown in Poland.

Thomas Dempster, 1579–1625, had as hectic a career as Thomas Urquhart. Born at Muiresk, Turriff, his mother a Leslie of Balquhain, a triplet and twenty-fourth child of a family of twenty-nine, he made an unusual start. He wrote an account of his life which is chiefly romance, and his historical lucubrations are of the same nature as a rule. Yet his *Historia Ecclesiastica Gentis Scotorum* had a great vogue, while his own life, as professor of Oratory at Nimes and at Pisa, and in the Humanities chair at Bologna, with all its hairbreadth escapes and perilous persecutions, attests that in those years it was quite possible to combine the delights of academic concentration with the fascinations of living dangerously.

Dempster proved that the doctors were not the only learned men produced by Aberdeen, although the sole Aberdonian to be a familiar and correspondent of Lord Bacon, Thomas Morrison, was an M.D. of Montpelier. Walter Donaldson, 1570–1630, educated at King's and Heidelberg and in succession principal of the Universities of Sedan and Rochelle, was reckoned one of the most learned men of the century. John Fraser, a son of Philorth, finished his education at Paris and became Rector there in 1596. He wrote on theological subjects in English with quaint traces of the Buchan doric. Alexander Gardyne, 1580–1642, an advocate of Aberdeen, procurator fiscal of the county in 1629 and sheriff-depute in 1634, was an energetic author in prose and verse.

A Garden of Grave and Godlie Flowres. Sonets, elegies and epitaphs. Planted, polished and perfected by A. G., 1609, is his magnum opus. He also wrote *Characters and Essays* and left in manuscript 'A Theatre of Scottish Worthies' and a 'Life of William Elphinstone'. Sir John Skene, Aberdeen's greatest jurist, has already been mentioned. David Wedderburn, 1580–1646, for nearly forty years Rector of the Grammar School, was a consummate grammarian whose textbooks were in use in his native city for nearly a century after his death. William Barclay, 1570–1630, yet another M.D., who acquired his culture at King's, Paris and Louvain, and was professor of Humanity first at Paris and later at Nantes, was a pioneer in the good graces of my Lady Nicotine, and wrote *Nepenthes, or the Vertues of Tobacco.* Alexander Ross, born in Aberdeen in 1591, chaplain to James I and Charles I, and vicar of Carisbrooke, wrote many works, including *The Marrow of History*, an abbreviation of Sir Walter Raleigh's History of the World, and *Leviathan drawn out with a Hook*, a criticism of Thomas Hobbes's *Leviathan*. Patrick Copland, a native of Aberdeen and a graduate of Marischal College, whose Divinity chair he established, was a chaplain on board East Indiamen and founded Henrico College, the second university in America. George Dalgarno, born in Aberdeen about 1616, matriculated at Marischal College in 1631, died in 1687, was the inventor of the first composite universal language in his *Ars Signorium*, which may have inspired Sir Thomas Urquhart's *Logopandecteison*; he also specialised in shorthand.

Many other names no less famous in their day and even faintly remembered from time to time in ours might be added. Amongst them was John Leslie, 1527–96, Bishop of Ross at the Reformation after having been a cleric and a professor in Old Aberdeen, who ended his life in exile, and was the confidential agent and one of the leading champions of Mary Queen of Scots. His *Defence of the Honour of the Right Highe, Mighty and Noble Princesse Marie Quene of Scotlande and Dowager of France* probably did neither its author nor its heroine any good by its assertion of her claim on Elizabeth's throne; his *De Origine, Moribus et Rebus Gestis Scotorum*, 1578, is as good an early history of Scotland as we have in Buchanan's time from the Catholic side. A no less polemical historian was James Laing of Auchterless 1502–94, who was professor of Theology at Paris and wrote lives of Luther, Calvin, Knox and Beza, whom he presented as chiefs amongst the heretics. Another Catholic, James Hay of Delgaty, 1546–1607, a Jesuit, has claims to be considered the first bibliographer on the strength of his *Bibliotheca Sancta*. Yet another Catholic, William Barclay, 1546–1605, of the famous Towie-Barclay family, was educated at King's, Paris and Bourges, was professor of Law at Pont-a-Mousson and at Angers, and left a more famous son, John, 1582–1621, author of the *Argenis*. William when a boy was present at a stupendous hunt organised by the Earl of Atholl in Mar and Atholl in honour of Queen Mary, in which 2,000 men took part; and he wrote an account of the episode before his death. Another John Leslie, born at Crichie in 1571, was Bishop of the Isles and later of Raphoe and Clogher in Ireland. He left a manuscript treatise on the application of scientific mnemonics to Scripture history, and contrived to avoid dying until 1671. The most remarkable single family of the time was that of the Chalmerses of Fintray, of whom David made a name in theological controversy, George in poetry and William in philosophy. But of them all, the one whose words today we unconsciously repeat most was William Keith, whose rendering of the 100th Psalm, the Auld Hundredth, in metre remains one of the most popular of Scottish exercises in psalmody and devotion.

CHAPTER THIRTEEN

The Burgh Pump

For Aberdeen the seventeenth century opened auspiciously. For nearly forty years the annals of the burgh, with very occasional exceptions, are a chronicle of small beer, the most favourable sign of a profound peace that a community could desire. In 1600 James VI paid his last personal visit to the city and collected his customary cash present, this time for 3,000 merks, while his sweet tooth cost the Council in addition 550 merks for wine and spiceries. It was an expensive year for the citizens: only a month later Queen Anne made her first appearance in the burgh; and the bill was nearly £2,000. In 1601, the inhabitants, in common with the rest of the kingdom, spent 5 August[1] in expression of their thanksgiving for the deliverance of the King from the Gowrie conspiracy. The methods taken included a public holiday, 'singing of psalms and praising of God', the decoration of the market cross, wine and spiceries 'drunkin and spent, a number of glasses to be cassin and brockin', and the recital of a Latin treatise on his Majesty's escape by Thomas Cargill, master of the Grammar School, on whom the Council bestowed the sum of £20 for his literary effort. The Council was a generous patron of local merit. In 1643 John Row was granted 400 merks for compiling a Hebrew dictionary, in 1657 the Council paid for printing and binding a theological work by William Douglas, professor of Divinity at King's; in 1663 John Forbes, stationer, got 100 merks, for printing some songs; and in 1661 Master James Gordon had a still worthier propine which has been more fully mentioned elsewhere. These benefactions do not exhaust the list. A dedication to the Town Council worked wonders.

James seems to have been personally popular in Aberdeen. Certainly he was kind to the burgh after his fashion. He twice — in 1605 and 1617 — gave it a charter (although 4,000 merks had to be paid for the first one) confirming Aberdeen's ancient properties and privileges and,

1 James directed that his deliverance should be celebrated annually. He had had a bad fright, but not so bad as all that. After the Restoration we find the Council ordaining that 5 August should be a public holiday.

in 1605, specially ratifying the town's acquisition (at the Reformation) of the altarages of St. Nicholas Kirk. Perhaps his second charter was even more acceptable, for in it his Majesty settled a much disputed point in favour of the town by decreeing that the burgh maills or feu-duties payable to the Crown in terms of the Great Charter granted by Robert the Bruce should be calculated not in sterling as stated in the original warrant but in the vastly cheaper Scots money. The King's confirmation of his ancestor's munificence rendered it idle during many a year to come for any community or party or individual to endeavour to infringe Aberdeen's prerogatives in the Freedom Lands.[1] The people of Old Aberdeen had put forward alleged rights to pasturage in the barony of Murthill and the forest of Stocket in 1599, and they had been disposed of by a compromise that gave the Aulton a certain amount of grazing without undermining Aberdeen's superiority; but after 1605 even that concession might not have been made.

On 30 March 1603, came news that James was King of England, and immediate thanksgiving was ordained, with bonfires, clamour of bells, consumption of wine and spiceries, and the shooting of the town's artillery and of muskets till late at night, with 'all godlie mirrines and pastyme'. On the afternoon of 15 November 1605, on news of the Gunpowder Plot[2] being received, 'everie maister of houshold' was ordered to have bonfires before 'thair yettes and douris', and to pass with the magistrates and ministers through the streets, 'singing of psalms, and magnefeing the Lord for the said benefitt', to the mercat cross for the usual oblation of wines and spiceries.

When James left for England in 1603 he promised to visit Scotland every three years. In fact, he returned but once, and Aberdeen, although it made all preparations to receive him, did not see him. On 18 February 1617, the town was convened to hear the contents of a letter intimating that in the spring the King would visit the burgh and desiring 'that the ludgings in your toune be preparit in the most handsome, civile, and comelie order that can be, with goode bedding, weele washine and weele smellit naprie, and with goode cleine and cleir weshell, and of sufficient lairgeness that thair be sufficient provisioun

---

1   The Charter was even more potent than that. In 1634 the Council used it to plead exemption from assisting in hunting down the 'licht horsemen', a band of hellicat Gordon gentry who were terrorising the country. For failure to co-operate the Privy Council fined Aberdeen 5,000 merks, but after thirty months of protest on Aberdeen's part remitted the fine.
2   It may be of interest that the famous Aberdeen family of Vaus (now Vass) has the same surname as Fawkes, Vaux, Fowkes or Fox.

for viveris for men and horse, that your streets and vennels be kept clene, and that no filthe nor middingis be seine vpon the same'. These injunctions by deduction graphically describe the state of life in Aberdeen in those days. As it turned out, James never got farther north than Dunnottar, where he stayed to hunt. Some of his entourage came to the city, and were given its freedom to the number of twenty, including Archibald Armstrang, the Court jester, who may be the wisest man in the list of burgesses.

The accession of Charles I was greeted with the greatest enthusiasm in Aberdeen, and when he came north to Edinburgh to be crowned King of Scots — the last British Sovereign to do so — the citizens again had splendid entertainment, with plenty of shooting and drink and all that the heart of man could desire. But disaster and tragedy loomed ahead, and those exhibitions of civic loyalty, more especially those that followed at the Restoration, the accession of James VII, the Revolution and the Hanoverian Succession, lose their bloom by their inconsistency in all but the citizens' very evident determination to have a good time somehow, and the Council's equally patent eagerness to do 'the right thing'. The particulars of those celebrations in the Records are all couched in the same terms, and if the periods of Presbyterian ascendancy are reflected in the language of a profound piety, it is equally clear that the sermons in forenoon and afternoon had no effect in mitigating the horseplay and insobriety of the crowds at night.

Charles, for all his faults, tried to be a good friend to Scotland and especially to Aberdeen, which, almost alone among the burghs, stood by him, if vainly, in the hour of his greatest need. His rule had all the efficiency and logic of personal government, and had he been as true to others as he was to himself, he might have carried the country with him and his reign might have vied in history with the Age of Elizabeth or Anne or Victoria. He certainly interfered with the electoral rights of the burgesses, and alienated the support of many of them, but that mattered little in a community which, until the pressure of events and facts enforced a change of opinion, was remarkably devoted to his interests. He was not, after his own way, ungrateful. His chief contribution to the welfare of the burgh was a new Great Charter, the last it was to receive under the Great Seal, finally confirming all its privileges and powers and adding a few new ones. That is the description which all the historians apply to this document, evincing an unusual unanimity which seems to imply only one thing — that it had proved beyond their patience and application to read its tedious and unrelieved clauses through to the end. The harmony of these classic historians of Bon-Accord in this matter will not be disturbed by their humble successor, who is fortified in his decision to agree with them by the fact that modern bureaucratic practice has negatived the spirit, if it pretends to respect the letter, of all the venerable endowments bestowed upon Scottish local authorities. Two of his predecessors give the text — one in Latin and English (Kennedy) and one in English only (Thom) — of this interminable dead letter.

The strictly local politics of Aberdeen between the Union of the Crowns and the Restoration had little to distinguish them. There was, in James's time, one curious coincidence, that three successive provosts died in office — Alexander Cullen in 1610, Alexander Rutherford in 1614, and Sir Thomas Menzies in 1620.[1] In 1608 the pest appeared again. The usual precautions were taken, though nothing so drastic as the erection in 1585 of three gibbets, at the Brig of Dee, the Market Cross and the harbour mouth, to hang strangers and townspeople who gave them shelter; in 1608 the notable thing was the appointment of a man from St. Andrews as 'clenger' to burn the bodies of the dead.

About the same time leprosy, which for over a century had been endemic in the country, began to abate and quickly disappeared. The Leper-house or 'lazar-house' of Aberdeen, built by Parson Galloway of Kinkell in 1519, stood half-way between the Gallowgate port and Old Aberdeen. At the end of the sixteenth century the inmates were so starved and cold that they came into Aberdeen 'for halding in of thair lyves', and to keep them in their hospital King James ordained that they should have one peat off each cartload brought into the city. Aberdeen's last and worst visitation of plague was in 1647, when 1,600 people (out of less than 8,000) in the burgh and 140 in the adjacent villages of Futty and Torry fell victims. A gibbet on this occasion was erected at the court de guard in the Castlegate and communications between the town and the outside world almost entirely ceased. As late as November 1648, there were cases of pest in the burgh. The dead were buried in various places, in particular near the windmill on the Porthill, in the east slope of the Castlehill, and in the Links, whither the infected wretches were driven out of the way of their whole brethren.

In 1613 the town sergeants, five in number, were rigged out in the

---

1 Provost William Gray died in office in 1662, his successor Gilbert Gray in 1667, Provost Alexander Patton in 1705; Provost Alexander Aberdein, though not in office at his death in 1756, had his pall 'supported by six provosts', like ex-provost Robert Stewart at his funeral in 1749.

burgh livery — a juip of red staming with the arms of the town embroidered on it. In 1647 they were provided with red coats. About this time a certain amount of staid pageantry in municipal affairs was common throughout Scotland. In 1623 we encounter an ordinance that town councillors should wear their gowns at Council meetings and at church. More than a century later, in 1743, the Council decided that the provost, following the practice in other Scottish burghs, should wear a black velvet suit, that being esteemed 'a very decent habit', and that his suit should be 'mounted with a gold button or not, as the provost for the time should incline'. But this sartorial distinction was not long maintained. In 1622 a rule, more honoured in the breach than in the observance, was laid down that councillors absent from meetings without reasonable excuse were to be fined, and a vow of secrecy in regard to council matters, which we find reiterated in 1661, was imposed. In 1666 the Council 'for good considerations', ordered the 'high counsell house' to be enlarged and repaired for 'the better decorment of the toune and accommodatioune of those who happen to resort thairto'. In 1649, under the influence of Puritanism, the Council decided to open its sessions with prayer; previous to that the Council seems to have held its meetings on Wednesday of each week at 8 a.m. after morning prayers. The Council was punctilious in its religious observances: in 1637 it had a loft 'in most decent and comelie forme' built for its own use within the aisle of Greyfriars Kirk before the pulpit. In 1699 an order was sent to Hamburg for 'wainscot daills, clifts and trees' to construct a loft in St. Nicholas Kirk for the magistrates above the Council's seat. The Council continued to fence itself about with respect. In 1617 James Craighead, a flesher, was put in the Castlegate pillory crowned with a paper label and banished the town for saying of a baillie, 'My malediction I give to Baillie Gray, by all the baillies of Aberdeen! I am as honest and as true as any of his kin' — an imprecation which would not be esteemed so very dreadful in our age for all our fear of libel.

In 1651 there occurred the unusual incident of two occupants of the civic chair, Robert Farquhar of Mounie, then provost, and Patrick Leslie of Iden, whom Charles I had so disliked, being knighted by Charles II on his second visit to the town. Leslie was the son of a burgess and a man of wealth and standing, though what his occupation was does not transpire. Farquhar, a much less ardent Covenanter than Leslie, was a wholesale produce merchant and in addition a collector of taxes for the North of Scotland. He was one of the wealthiest men

of his time and a public-spirited citizen who used his wealth to relieve
the community. He gave free house to Major-General Monro during
his residence in Aberdeen during The Troubles. He supplied so much
food to the army that the Estates ended in his debt to the extent of
£180,859 Scots. As a collector of taxes he was probably no better than
he should have been, for on one occasion, just before the audit of his
accounts by the authorities in Edinburgh, he contrived to make the
preacher Andrew Cant accept a handsome velvet cloak, which inspired
a eulogistic testimonial by the cleric on the provost's behalf for presentation to the men who mattered and could make the audit a
formality.

The career of the diarist Provost Alexander Jaffray has been noted
elsewhere,[1] but while he was the most notable of the provosts between
the Reformation and the end of Scotland's civil wars, there were other
characters at the head of Aberdeen's municipal affairs. Robert Petrie
of Portlethen, who was provost in 1665 when the Convention of Burghs
met in Aberdeen, was appointed moderator on that occasion and seems
to have made a reputation for himself among his colleagues. In 1674 the
Convention had to deal with Charles II's interference with Scottish
burghal business, and the provost of Edinburgh, who was moderator,
being too timid to take a high line, Petrie was voted to the chair and
signed the Convention's protest to the King. Charles was annoyed and
Petrie was fined £1,000 Scots, a sum which he was unable or unwilling
to pay, for in January 1675, he entered Edinburgh tolbooth as a prisoner.
He remained there until April, when Aberdeen Council, having repudi-
ated his action at the Convention, agreed to pay his fine. He never
seems to have repaid the money. Occasionally, a provost would be too
high-handed in dealing with the elections. Thus in 1685 Baillie Walter
Robertson complained, on behalf of himself and other councillors,
of Provost Sir George Skene's methods in that year's election. The
Privy Council declining to arbitrate, the Duke of Gordon consented
to act as umpire, and having been conveyed to his lodging in the town
by a great number of burgesses and saluted by a salvo of cannon, he
pronounced Sir George's election valid, ordered Robertson to declare
that his complaint was not personal, and wound up by suggesting that
both parties should undertake not to interfere in the election of
magistrates for three years. To any citizen with a historical memory
the spectacle of a Gordon advocating compromise must have been
amusing.

1   See p. 250.

Skene's father was the miller at Potterton, Belhelvie, and he himself made a fortune as a merchant at Danzig. In 1666 he bought Wester Fintray and in 1687 the estate of Rubislaw, 'Cumberland House' in the Guestrow, which still displays his coat of arms being his town residence. He was provost from 1676 to 1684 and was knighted in 1681 by the Duke of York, later James VII and II. He died unmarried in 1707, and was succeeded eventually by a grand-nephew who was the ancestor of James Skene, the friend of Sir Walter Scott, who dedicated a canto of 'Marmion' to him. Another relative was Baillie Alexander Skene of Newtyle, mentioned elsewhere.

A more masterful provost than Skene was Robert Cruickshank of Banchory, who died in 1717 at the age of 94, and who by his robust methods for the complete restoration of the Presbyterian religion during his four years in the chair, 1693–6, probably raised a good deal of antagonism. He took his own way. When Ruthrieston bridge was rebuilt in 1693–4 he had built into the bridge a stone with his arms carved on it. In 1698 a Council unfriendly to him had the stone reversed and a record that the town had restored the bridge was chiselled on the new face. By 1705 opinion had quite swung round, the provost's arms were restored to view, and an addition was made that he had been provost when the bridge was rebuilt. Cruickshank's civic politics were equally high-handed. In 1696 he fought strong opposition to get the chair again. In 1697 he retired but put his son-in-law John Johnston forward as a candidate. To tie his hands, the opposition stayed away on election day, but Cruickshank, when he found no quorum present, brought in voters off the streets and his son-in-law was elected. On a protest being made to the Privy Council, the election was upset, Johnston deposed and the order given for a new election. As a result of this incident biennial provostships became the rule for many years, the Council declaring that no one should occupy the chair any longer at any one stretch.

The first biennial provost was Thomas Mitchell of Thainston, whose granddaughter marred Sir Andrew Mitchell, Britain's famous Ambassador at the Court of Frederick the Great. Provost John Allardes, as a baillie, one of the ringleaders of the opposition to Cruickshank, was Aberdeen's Commissioner — Aberdeen forming a constituency with Banff and Cullen — to the last independent Scottish Parliament. In 1739 his daughter-in-law presented to the Council the saddle-cloth, stirrups and bridle which the provost had used when he rode south to Edinburgh to hear 'the end of an auld sang'. The provost in 1706–7 was John Gordon, who had been a merchant at Campvere, the Scottish staple port in Holland. In October 1708, at the first election after the Union, he represented the constituency of Aberdeen, Montrose, Arbroath, Brechin and Bervie. He was so lacking in political ambition that he seems to have been elected almost against his will. He was, however, a fairly conscientious member, and for his attendance at two sessions of Parliament he received from the Town Council expenses amounting to £425 7s. 2d. sterling, which meant a great deal more than £1,750 a year and first class travel in 1970.

His son John Gordon was the central figure in the notorious incident[1] known as the Rabbling of Deer that brought about the Act of Toleration in 1712 favouring Episcopalian clergymen and the first violation of the Act of Union in the form of the Patronage Act, which in its turn was responsible for most of the dissensions in the Church of Scotland culminating in the Disruption. Young John Gordon, a Presbyterian minister, was ordained to the Church of Deer, a stronghold of Episcopacy, in 1711. The Episcopal minister refused to leave, and he and a majority of the congregation held the church successfully against the Presbytery and seventy horsemen. Eventually the Lord Justice-Clerk awarded the living to Gordon.

John Ross, provost 1710–11, bought the estate of Arnage when in office, left the then large fortune of £5,000 sterling, and had his house in the Shiprow.[2] James Morrison, Jr., of Elsick, provost at the beginning of the Forty-five, 1744–5, had a son, an army doctor, whose interest in the wells at Strathpeffer first made the reputation of that famous spa.

National organisation was, throughout the period, still rather primitive, yet there was a curious thread of loyalty to the national tradition.

---

1   It was reduced to farce by the Jacobite-Episcopalian satirist William Meston in his poem 'Mob Contra Mob'.

> About the ports of Aberdeen
> The Hotch-potch rabble did conveen
> Of different Hames and different Natures,
> Complexions, Principles and Features . . .
> Some were for this Kirk, and some for that Kirk,
> And some no mortal knows for what Kirk,
> Yet all of them their course did steer
> To storm and take the Kirk of Deer.

2   The house still stands; renovated and now the Aberdeen headquarters of the British Council. It is one of Aberdeen's few remaining examples of seventeenth-century architecture. Sir Frederick Leith-Ross, economic adviser to H. M. Government 1932–46, is a descendant of this Provost.

Thus in 1613, when a certain Startorius, a German, was prosecuted and executed abroad for an infamous libel against the Scots, the Scottish burghs shouldered the cost of the prosecution, Aberdeen taking its share of the total of £600. Again in 1637 it was reported that some men of Ayr had been captured by the Barbary pirates. The Council ordered the town's ministers to intimate a collection from the pulpits, and sent the four baillies to stand at the kirk doors to receive the contributions and note the donors' names, so that the absentees could be approached severally later. No less than a thousand merks was raised. There was also a spirit of good-neighbourliness. Stonehaven was burned during the Troubles, and Aberdeen voluntarily contributed a thousand merks to its rebuilding. Aberdonian cosmopolitanism is probably reflected in a gift in 1633 of 200 Scots merks to John Elsmer, 'ane destrest preacher in Polland, laitly come to this brught', although the payment two years later of £478 8s. 8d. Scots to Mr. John Elshinder, 'ane of the distressit Protestants in Polland', was made by direction of the Privy Council, the money having been raised by the burgh in 1628 at the instance of that august body on behalf of the Polish Protestant Churches.[1] In 1681 the Town Council decided to support at the town's expense two Polish students of divinity who had come to study in Aberdeen, the petition being made by one 'Patrick Forbes, merchant in Croco in Poland'.

When the Troubles ended in 1651, the public debt of the town amounted to £51,508 sterling. At the Restoration it stood about the same figure. The Council, therefore, solicited and got an Act of Parliament passed enabling the following dues and taxes to be imposed locally for eleven years: — 4d. per Scots pint of ale and beer; £50 per tun of wine; 2s. per pint of brandy, wine or whisky sold or consumed in the burgh; 13s. 4d. on the carcase of every ox, 12s. on every calf, and 6d. on every other animal brought to market for sale. These taxes were farmed out,[2] however, and did not prove very lucrative. In 1687 the duty on wines, spirits and ale only amounted to £195 16s. 8d. sterling. In 1695 another Act authorised the following taxes for at least thirteen years, and until the burgh's debt, by this time reduced to £10,000 sterling, should be wiped out .. 2d. on every pint of ale

---

1   To this sum was added £105 8s. 8d. Scots 'of annual rentis, accresat by the good improvement' of the original collection — a handsome return in interest in seven years.

2   One of the statutory duties of the town's bellman was to 'attend and serve the tacksman of the customs of the meal and meat markets in uptaking of the fruits and others belonging to the said office'.

and beer sold; £50 per tun of wine; £50 per butt of sack, Spanish or Rhenish wines; 2s. on every pint of imported brandy or of spirits distilled or sold within the town. In 1707 the time-limit was extended for another twenty-five years, by which time the burgh's public debt had happily disappeared. By 1712 the public debt was given as £3,450, but the ordinary revenue then being only £700 against an expenditure of £1,170, it is not surprising that the debt by 1716 has risen again to £5,763.

Until 1633, the water supply of Aberdeen was drawn from the Loch, which by that time was 'filthillie defyillit and corruptit, not onlie be gutteris daylie rynning in the burne, but also by litsteris and the washing of clothes and abwssing of the water in sindrie partis, with wther sorts of vncleanness'. The Council proposed, and the community agreed, that fresh spring water should be brought into the burgh from a spring about a mile out, and distributed by means of fountains. The scheme involved a tax or stent upon all inhabitants, and while the Guild brethren agreed to bear their share of the general tax, the deacon convener, on behalf of the Crafts, offered 1,000 merks Scots towards the work provided all the members of the Crafts were exempted from the tax. They were, however, ready to pay their personal shares in the cost of maintenance and upkeep once the system was in operation. The Town Council had to get an Act of the Privy Council passed to bring the Crafts into line with the rest.

The scheme appears, however, to have fallen through, despite a canvas of public opinion in 1683, and for a further period of seventy years Aberdeen resorted to natural springs within its bounds for drinking water and depended upon the Loch and burns to fill the casks of washing water which watermen hawked through the streets in low carts. In 1706 the water of Carden's Well was brought into the town, the principal distributing centre being the great fountain which until recently stood in the Green, but which was originally erected, in 1708, in the Castlegate, where it stood for a century and a half. Later the Carden Well supply was augmented from Gilcomston, the additional flow being conveyed to a great cistern in the Broadgate beside Greyfriars Kirk, and by smaller tanks elsewhere. William Lindsay, goldsmith, a burgess, after a year's trial at the job, was in 1708 appointed water engineer for his lifetime at a salary of £200 Scots, with the obligation to choose and instruct an assistant who would take his place 'after his decease, removeall, or non-residence as said is'. Lindsay also made and erected a brass statue on the fountain in the Castlegate for which he received £60 stg. Two years later the Council had to descend firmly on persistent bad habits by prohibiting washing at the wells and tramping in tubs on the streets and keeping casks at the fountain longer than the time required to fill them.[1]

1   This was as effectual as most public edicts against ingrained customs. It was repeated in 1726, no doubt to as little purpose.

CHAPTER FOURTEEN

Jacobite Escapades

'The Troubles' were the last serious bloodshed Aberdeen was to experience within its own boundaries. It was not that there were not other wars in Scotland, for strife during the hundred years that succeeded the defeat of Montrose at Philiphaugh was never far away in the northern part of Britain. In the Scotland of those years there were, not counting the Covenanters' risings in the South-West, four campaigns that find a place in the history books. Aberdeen was directly concerned in three of them and indirectly concerned with the other, yet no single life was spilled because of them within the Freedom Lands of Bonaccord.

The Restoration was received with extravagant rejoicing and apparent unanimity in Aberdeen, as indeed throughout the whole of the North-East. At the conference held by General George Monck at Dalkeith before he took the step of offering back to Charles II the crown of his fathers, Aberdeen had a representative in the person of Baillie Gilbert Mollyson. When the King enjoyed his own again the usual ceremonial celebration was held in the Castlegate after public thanksgiving in the churches. Principal Ross of Marischal College and two of the town ministers, Paterson and Menzies, delivered eloquent sermons, later published, which quite failed to fit the character of the Merry Monarch, the King's 'dease' in the West Kirk was adorned with tapestry, the magistrates drew up an address of congratulation which they entrusted to Irvine of Drum to carry to London, and on Gilbert Gray of Saphock being elected Provost at the Michaelmas elections, which were held with all due remembrance of the 'former practices of a few disloyal persons who prospered in their wickedness', one of his first functions was to take a second congratulatory address to the King in London. On his return, in February 1661, Provost Gray handed over the dismembered limb of the great Montrose, which had been lying in the West Kirk, to Harie Graham, the representative of the Marquis's family.

In 1664 occurred the affair of the Cruive Dykes. The Earl of Mar and several other riparian proprietors of the Don valley, finding the supplies of salmon in their stretches of river reduced by the operations of the salmon fishings in the lower reaches of the Don, of which the Town Council was the superior, assembled a force of 2,500 men at Hallforest Castle, Kintore, and marched to the cruives below Woodside. The Provost and two citizens hastened out to meet and mollify the irate lairds, but the Earl would listen to no pleas and set his party, unopposed, to the task of destroying the dyke. Although much indignation was expressed in the city at this outrage, no steps appear to have been taken for redress, nor, when the damage was made good, did the lairds return to cast the offending works down again. The passive nature of the citizens' reaction to an inroad on their liberties which would have provoked a battle a hundred years before may indicate that 'the Troubles' had taken the heart out of the lieges so far as fighting went. In our own time, while the cruives still prevent the passage of salmon upstream, riparian proprietors square the account more prosaically but also more effectually by being partners in the company that owns the obstruction.

In the Covenanting wars Aberdeen had no part, for the North-East was thoroughly Episcopalian in sympathy, and even the Earl Marischal, whose father had been a lion of the Covenant, supplied the dungeons of Dunnottar to incarcerate the wretched Whigs who were thrown into durance for their religious convictions. Doubtless Aberdonians felt scant sympathy for the sufferers, since the Tolbooth in the Castlegate was crammed full of Quakers in conditions little less miserable than those in the vaults of Dunnottar.

When in 1685 the news of Charles II's death reached the town, the Market Cross was hung in black and the day observed as one of communal mourning. But with the following sunrise the pall was removed from the Cross and its place taken by cheerful tapestry. The funeral visage of both city and citizens was wreathed with smiles as long life and happiness was drunk to King James the Seventh and Second, and a band in the Castlegate discoursed instrumental music which, according to a tradition mentioned by Kennedy, included the first public performance of the tune 'God Save the King'. Dr. Patrick Sibbald prayed 'most seriouslie and ferventlie' for the new sovereign, who was soon to prove himself past praying for, and the ships in the roadstead answered the bells of the city 'with shott of canones, and at night haveing lanthornes on there topmasts'.

It may be taken as evidence of the extent to which James had contrived, in less than four years, to alienate the affections of his subjects, that Aberdeen, which in February 1685 had so sumptuously welcomed him to the throne, should in January 1689 have accepted his successor and supplanter William III with scarcely a dissentient voice. In 1691 the Privy Council for some reason unstated, but probably because of his disaffection to the new regime, ordered the election of John Sandilands of Countesswells as Provost to be cancelled, but the incident is obscure, and was in any case an isolated one.

Dr. George Garden in 1689, one of the town's ministers (who in 1693 was deprived for not praying for the King and Queen) was sent to London with the civic address. But almost at once Aberdeen became involved in the little civil war with which the Bonnie Dundee of the Episcopalians and the Bloody Clavers of the Covenanters greeted the new era. General Mackay, after the rebels' Pyrrhic victory at Killecrankie, occupied the burgh, around which the Highland remnants of Dundee's army under General Buchan ravened and prowled. Finally the Highland host withdrew towards the west, where the surprise dawn attack immortalised in the ballad of the 'Haughs of Cromdale' ended their capacity for mischief. About the same time some of the better class of Dundee's followers, who had thrown themselves into Fedderate Castle, near New Deer, surrendered on honourable terms and made their way to Europe, where in the service of Louis XIV they covered themselves with glory by defeating Stirk's Germans at the Island of the Scots. As for Aberdeen, it suffered the usual fate of a community which has troops, whether hostile or friendly, quartered upon it. Much of the provisions supplied were never paid for and no bill for the incidental damage to property was ever settled. Anne's accession in 1702 was received quietly in Aberdeen as throughout the rest of the country, and there seems to have been no serious objection in the city to the Legislative Union.

The first armed Jacobite attempt of the century to restore the Stewarts was not much better than a demonstration off the coast in 1708 by some ships of the French Navy under Admiral Fourbin. The flotilla sailed as far north as Buchan Ness, and was doubtless seen from Aberdeen. The second Jacobite attempt was a much more serious affair and involved Aberdeen very intimately. The Union to begin with failed to come up to expectation in its consequential benefits. A series of bad years brought famine to the cities. The English were not effusive. There was a long tradition of mutual suspicion and active antagonism to break down. Matters were so unpromising that the Earl of Findlater, an original supporter of Union, came within three votes of carrying a motion for its repeal in the House of Lords. Before Queen Anne's death there were signs of popular dissatisfaction. In 1714 the Secretary of State, the Earl of Mar, had to communicate with Aberdeen Town Council about a seditious incident which had probably acquired a fictitious importance as the report of it made its way south to London. Some young men in the city 'did in the night-time under the guise of women's apparrell, proclaim the Pretender' and at the well in the Castlegate took water in their hats 'and drank to his health'.

That thoroughly despicable and dishonest character, Bobbin' John, Earl of Mar, made himself notorious to begin with by his fawning upon George I, but as the advisers of the Hanoverian king failed to appreciate the Earl of Mar at the earl's own high valuation, he took ship home and after various intrigues and consultations, and having obtained the Old Pretender's commission as Lord Lieutenant of the Kingdom, raised the standard of revolt at Braemar (where the Invercauld Hotel now stands) on 6 September 1715. Exactly a fortnight later the young Earl Marischal, whose mother was a Catholic, a woman of very strong will, and a relation of Mar's, with his brother James, the Earl of Errol and other country gentlemen, rode into Aberdeen and proclaimed 'King James VIII' at the Market Cross. The following day Marischal was entertained by the Incorporated Trades, who were strongly Jacobite. Riding home that afternoon to Inverugie Castle, he proclaimed the Pretender in Old Aberdeen likewise. On 28 September the Council election fell due, but no steps were taken to appoint a new Council. A proclamation, however, was made by the Jacobite authorities that on the 29th all burgesses would be entitled to vote for a new Council, in the New or East Church of St. Nicholas. Whether this invitation to a popular election was accepted by any burgesses either of Jacobite persuasion or not does not transpire, but a compliant Council was appointed with Patrick Bannerman, fourth son of the first baronet of Elsick, as provost.[1]

The position as regards the rebellion seems to have been that the majority of the better-class citizens were for the established

---

1   In 1832 when Alexander Bannerman, later knighted, Governor of New-
    foundland, and husband of Thomas Carlyle's first sweetheart, Margaret
    Gordon, was standing for Parliament, he remarked in a speech, 'It is a
    singular circumstance that the last *popular* election in this city was that of
    my great-grandfather, who was chosen the Chief Magistrate of Aberdeen
    upwards of a century ago. *He was not chosen by the self-elected Corporation
    but by his fellow citizens*'. This 'adaptation' of the truth of the 1715 election
    truly presaged a successful political career for the orator.

Government, while the lower orders favoured the Stewarts.[1] This reversed the state of opinion in the county, where most of the gentry rallied round Mar, but the common folk and tenantry could only be forced into the Jacobite army by the direst threats. Even Mar's own tenants required coercion. In the city resistance was useless. The old Council had taken precautions for defence, but the Government, blind to portents as most British Governments have been, actually ordered the Aberdeen magistrates, through the Lord Justice Clerk, to deliver up all the gunpowder in the town — there were 4,000 lb. of it — at a specified rate of £3 6s. 8d. per cwt. The result was that the Jacobite interest was able to establish itself in Aberdeen; but it should be admitted that the defenceless condition of the burgh probably saved it from a recurrence of the misfortune of the Civil War.

The Jacobite Town Council at once proceeded, after holding a head court, to levy a stent or tax of £200 10s. 9d. sterling upon the inhabitants to pay for supplies for Mar's army. On 1 October the Earl Marischal left to join the insurgents in the south, and was convoyed for some distance by the Magistrates and Trades, 'having all their swords drawn'. Two days later the Marquis of Huntly with seventy horse passed through on his way to Perth. That day also, after debate, the Council decided that the Presbyterians might use the East Church, but the West Church would be reserved for those of the true Episcopalian faith. Mar, in the meantime, was marching southwards at his leisure. Soon after the stent, Aberdeen being the only considerable source of wealth in the Jacobites' power, a contribution of £2,000 sterling, styled by the euphemism of a loan, was imposed, the first £500 being exacted immediately. Mar had also to be furnished with 300 Lochaber axes, the Marquis of Huntly with four cannon, and the Jacobite headquarters at Perth with the printing press and type belonging to the town's printer, James Nicol. A demand for the raising of a troop of thirty horse, however, significantly could not be complied with: there were apparently no volunteers.

The Jacobites met the Government forces under the Duke of Argyll

---

1 'The Magistrates having mett in the Counsel-house, about the toune's affaires, they were insulted by a mobb, who first mett in Mistress Hebbrun's and then came to the Counsel-house, and requeyred the armes and ammunitions belonging to the toun, with the keys of the Block-house, saying that they were not to regard the Magistrats any longer as Magistrats, for Earl Marischal had given command of the teun to Captn. Jo. Bennarman.' Contemporary Manuscript quoted by Joseph Robertson, *Book of Bon-Accord.*

(Red John of the Battles, Marlborough's famous lieutenant) at Sheriff-muir, near Dunblane, on 13 November 1715. Neither side could claim the decision, which as regards Mar's troops was not surprising, since some of them spent the period of the battle in looting the baggage of their friends who were fighting in front of them. But Sheriffmuir was a moral victory for Argyll, who remained at Dunblane whereas Mar, foiled in his attempt to break through to the south, withdrew to Perth again. On 22 December James landed at Peterhead, came to Aberdeen incognito, dined in Skipper Scott's house or inn on the Castlegate, and went on to the Earl Marischal's house at Fetteresso. There the Jacobite magistrates of Aberdeen, and several of the professors and regents of the two Colleges, including the poet of the Cause, William Meston. waited upon him with loyal addresses and personal homage. Mar was made a duke, Provost Bannerman a knight, and the ministers of Aberdeen were commanded to pray for James instead of George, an injunction to which they seem not to have paid scrupulous heed. From Fetteresso the old Chevalier passed to Perth and held court for three weeks in Scone Palace. But he was a feckless creature, Mar was incompetent if not a downright rascal, and soon, seeing the game was up, the two of them retreated to Montrose, where they took ship, ostensibly to be in Aberdeen to prepare for the reception of their men, actually to save their skins by flight to the Continent. They never returned.

The Jacobite Army wilted away thereafter. The remnant reached Aberdeen under the Earl Marischal and other nobles. There some of the leaders took ship for the Continent. Marischal, his brother who was to be Frederick the Great's field-marshal, Meston the poet and others more stubborn and hardy than the rest, took to the hills, and finally those of them who were attainted or proscribed got clear of the country. Marischal, Errol and several others forfeited their estates. So, not ingloriously though in an inglorious cause, the House of Marischal, which for a century and a quarter had been a benefactor and friend to Aberdeen, fell into ruin. The smaller fry of the rebellion were not harshly dealt with: the Government was not sure enough of its stability to be cruel. In Aberdeen the Jacobite Council demitted office and Provost Bannerman, though carried for trial to Carlisle, escaped the death sentence.

On 10 April a new municipal election was held, and Provost Stewart, whose two-year tenure of the chair had been interrupted, resumed office. In an address to King George I the Council declared: 'As it was our greatest honour to be among royall burghs on this syde of the Tay, who were most maltreated for adhering to the present Government, so being now restored to our office by your Majestie's order of ellectioun, we could not but take the first opportunitie of congratulating the wisest and best of Kings on the late great and happie turn of affairs in these northern parts.' A little fulsome, perhaps, for modern taste, and certainly exaggerated as regards the Council's sufferings and the King's wisdom and goodness; but nevertheless the address in its hyperbole reflects the relief of the community. All acts of the Jacobite Council were rescinded, all names of those connected with that Council were deleted from the burgess roll, and the town settled down to thirty years of unwonted placidity which the din of the Jacobite landing at Glenshiel in 1719 was too faint and distant to disturb.

For some time after the Fifteen, Argyll had troops quartered in the town, and on occasion afterwards there was a garrison. In 1729 Colonel John Middleton of Seaton received permission from the Council to add 'two wings or toofalls' to the big house in the Castlehill for accommodation of a whole troop of horse. The 'Big House' had been granted to Middleton some time before, and in it he had stationed a half troop of horse. The wings were to be stables for twenty-eight horses. The Council, rather surprisingly, considered that the presence of soldiers 'would tend to the great interest, benefit and advantage of the inhabitants of this place'. Thus was inserted a link in the long chain of military connection with the Castlehill.

The imminence of another Jacobite rising was no secret for long before Prince Charles landed in August 1745. In February 1744, the Council was warned by the Marquis of Tweeddale, one of the principal Secretaries of State, that an invasion backed by the French was intended 'in favour of a Popish Pretender'. As in 1715, so again when news of the Young Chevalier's landing was received, the burgh was at once put 'in a posture of defence'. The town was mustered, the lists taken up of the fencible men, their arms and ammunition. Four ex-Provosts were appointed majors in charge of the burgh's four quarters, and the inhabitants were divided into twelve companies, each led by a captain, a lieutenant and an ensign. On 11 September Sir John Cope, whom the Highlanders had evaded at Inverness, arrived in Aberdeen with 2,000 men and camped on the Dovecot Brae, now the Union Terrace Gardens. Cope demanded, and received, all the town's weapons, the cannon in the fort at the mouth of the harbour and the citizens' small arms, the general's argument being that if these weapons fell into the enemy's hands, 'the toun would lay themselves obnoxious to the Government and be made answerable for such conduct'.

Cope left by sea on the 15th. On the 25th, election day, the statutory meeting of the old and new Councils had just concluded, when Sir John Hamilton, chamberlain to the Duke of Gordon, and a hot Jacobite, appeared in the streets with horse and foot. Sympathisers among the citizens at once joined him. The Provost, James Morison of Elsick, a courageous man whose conduct on this day earned him the nickname of 'Provost Positive', was sought out along with two of the baillies, and 'carried down prisoner, with drawn swords and other weapons, to the town-house'. Thence the whole party mounted the platform on the top of the Market Cross. James Petrie, Sheriff-substitute of Aberdeen, read the Old Pretender's proclamation, and he was toasted as James VIII. The Provost refused to drink, and his captors poured the glass of wine down his breast. Soon after he and most of the supporters of the Government left the town. No one could be found to take their place on the Council, and control of Aberdeen devolved on Lord Lewis Gordon, whom Charles had appointed Lord Lieutenant of Aberdeen and Banff. The political atmosphere had quite changed in thirty years. In 1745 most of the nobility and gentry of the county were indisposed to come out, and the people both in town and country were indifferent. Lord Lewis was little more than a lad.

Money and men were sorely needed, but they were not forthcoming in adequate supply. Aberdeen was ordered to pay a year's cess, but compounded for a single payment of £1,000. The Jacobite recruiting officers 'came little speed', wrote a contemporary. Prospective recruits, complained a recruiting agent, were dissuaded by 'the diabolical lies' of the Presbyterian ministers. The boys in the streets cheered for King George and showed resentment when the masters of the Grammar School dropped the King's name from prayers.

Aberdeen never heard the sound of gunfire. The nearest skirmish befel at Inverurie, beside the parish kirk, where Lord Lewis on 23 December 1745, with about 1,100 of his father's tenants and Aberdeen men under Moir of Stoneywood, surprised and routed an equal number of MacLeods and Munroes who had been sent down from Inverness to relieve Aberdeen by the Hanoverian commander in the Highlands, Lord Loudon. The victors had more dead than the defeated Highlanders, but they caught several prisoners, including some Whig professors from Aberdeen, and their triumph was celebrated in rather pleasing doggerel by a ballad-mongering reprobate named Mussel-mou'd Charlie.

Until the turn of the year Charles was on the full tide of success. The victory at Prestonpans (where Aberdeen's cannon were captured after all), the occupation of Edinburgh, the invasion of England must all have loomed portentous in the public mind. But once the first shock was over the Government troops were well handled. Two armies threatening his long line of communication caused Charles to turn northwards again at Derby, and although he thrashed General Hawley at Falkirk, the rebels were becoming increasingly disillusioned and dissatisfied. On their retreat into the Highlands, one strong detachment of them passed through Aberdeen, with the Duke of Cumberland and the royal troops following at their heels on 27 February. George II's 'martial boy' spent six weeks in the town, whose affairs he put in charge of Provost Morison, five ex-provosts and six other prominent citizens. The only evidence that he behaved like a boor while in residence in the Guestrow mansion of Alexander Thomson, advocate, comes from Jacobite sources, and even they admit that he tipped the servants when he left. But no hint of misdemeanour comes from official records; on the contrary, he was made a Freeman during his stay, and his ticket, drawn up 'in the genteelest form', was sent him later in a gold casket. He had, however, some louts in his entourage. General Hawley was no soldier, but had all the instincts of a common thief. Being lodged in the town house of Mrs. Gordon of Hallhead, he cleared all portable articles of value off the premises and sent them to London.[1]

Culloden having caused the dispersal of the Jacobite host on 16 April 1746, the municipal proceedings of the previous September which had been suspended by the appearance of the rebels were resumed and on 9 July the old and new Councils met and held the customary elections. Cumberland had left a guard of 200 soldiers in the city who occupied the recently completed Gordon's Hospital (the central block of the College today) and threw up earthworks for defence which earned the building the name of Fort Cumberland.

There was a last echo of the Forty-Five that summer. When Cumberland went south, the Earl of Ancrum was left in charge of the troops in the North-East. On 1 August, he instructed the magistrates to have the bells rung and all the houses illuminated in honour of the King's birthday. Certain officers in the town, dissatisfied with the amount of

---

1   We should not give too much credence to Jacobite evidence, for accusations against Wolfe, who was one of Hawley's staff, have been proved false. On the other hand, the Presbyterian minister of the city, John Bisset, says the Jacobite soldiers behaved better than the Government regulars.

light in some windows, ordered soldiers to smash the inadequate panes. But Provost Positive's spirit was strong in the Council. Brushing aside pleas of military jurisdiction, the magistrates arrested one of the officers responsible, and their protests secured the removal of the garrison commander. The cost of the damage to the houses of the poor was recovered from the Government. The well-to-do forbore to claim. So, with dignity and firmness, Aberdeen closed the book of the Jacobite rebellions.

On to Reform. 1746–1860

If the period from the Reformation to the last of the Jacobite risings was one in which civil order was gradually restored out of what at one time promised to be chaos, the age which succeeded the Battle of Culloden and contrived to keep in character until the passing of the Reform Act in 1832 and its local authority counterpart the following year was primarily that of the gradual extension of control of civilised development by the scientist and the engineer. The effect of their researches and inventions upon every sector of human activity was irresistible as an explosive. All was bustle and expansion and novelty. The whole traditional style of life had to be adjusted to the new methods.

There were big wars — the Seven Years', American Revolutionary, French Revolutionary, Napoleonic — which exercised a considerable if delayed influence upon political practice, but which, compared with the twentieth-century's experience, passed the nation by for the most part, and Aberdeen, though the American war put an end to the port's transatlantic trade and the Napoleonic struggle cost the town's industry a substantial sum in lost exports, was not very seriously affected. The more permanent consequences of these conflicts began to become apparent after Waterloo in the form of unfamiliar industrial problems that involved a generation of hardship on the working population and tended to create a wider social gulf between the classes of the community. It may indeed be accurate to bracket the soldier with the engineer and the scientist among the builders of the great Victorian Age, and on the other hand with the politician and the civil servant among the principal contrivers of the Decline of the West.

For most of the Pre-Reform period the main features of Aberdeen's history are industrial; only in the last decade or two did the politico-social aspect begin to present itself. The final rout of the Jacobites was the signal for the release throughout Scotland of all the pent-up energies which had been restrained previous to the Union of the Parliaments by the dynastic and religious troubles of the Northern Kingdom, and for forty years thereafter by these influences and the uncertainty they created in the public mind. The independent intelligence so characteristic of the seventeenth century was carried forward far enough into the golden age of Scottish culture. If Edinburgh was the modern Athens, Aberdeen was the northern Corinth, its wits rivalling the philosophers of the capital. But when Reid migrated and Beattie fell into senile decay, Aberdeen retreated into the background, never again to emerge so far into the full light of cultural distinction as in those its palmy days.

Despite the lack of these cultural leaders in the second part of the century when the industrial revolution was acquiring momentum, Aberdonians continued to be prompt to learn and to follow good example. Consequently, the city was very little behind the first wave of the industrial revolution, to which it might claim to have made two not unimportant if vicarious contributions, in that Adam Smith's father was born at Mains of Seaton and James Watt belonged to a Kintore family. Until the middle of the nineteenth century Aberdeen's industry maintained its place in the van of Scots production.

The learning for which Aberdeen had been noted since the days of Bishop Elphinstone was pursued successfully, although its products no longer enjoyed the supremacy that the graduates of ancient King's and Marischal had won in the countries of Europe. For the loss of that great national faculty of cultural endeavour, the Union of the Parliaments was undoubtedly mainly responsible; for the English never had the cosmopolitan flair that characterised Scotsmen, and after the Union England stepped between Scotland and Europe, and Scotland came to be regarded by Europeans as an integral part of England. Englishmen were not wanted in the universities and colleges of the Continent, and so Scotsmen were seldom invited to take up residence in its seminaries. At the same time, the Union gave Scotsmen the entry to the universities of Oxford and Cambridge, entailing less travel and expenditure on higher education than residence at Paris or Leyden had previously involved. It was natural enough, therefore, that the Scottish scholar who had been wont to wander learning and teaching over the face of Europe should cease to exist. There was indeed to be one exception later but his designation as 'The Wandering Scholar' is proof of how nearly absolute was the rule.

The contribution of Aberdeen to the world of what for several centuries had been its principal export, human brains, was continued, but with the qualifications that have already been noted as applying to its students. Its soldiers, instead of serving with Gustavus Adolphus and Louis XIV, fought under Abercromby and Wellington, its business men transferred their attention from the Low Countries and the Baltic to colonial expansion and English markets. The readjustment of Aberdeen to the outside world was in fact complete and it was carried through principally in the first half of the nineteenth century with a smoothness and rapidity which are as much a testimonial to the adaptability of the Aberdonian as to the efficiency with which power machinery was incorporated in the city's industrial fabric. The only difference was that the change-over from manual to power industry was attended with widespread hardship, whereas the reorientation of Aberdeen's outlook took place without harm to the feelings or prospects of any Aberdonian.

Insensibly these radical industrial changes altered men's ideas of how business should be run. The industrial revolution wiped out the independent craftsman working by and for himself and substituted the big firm and the mass of employees compelled by circumstances over which they had no control to serve or perish together, without individualism and without the incentive to excellence in their work which the individual craftsman had to have if he was to survive. This retrograde development in the individual's status in the community was soon accomplished, but the craftsman's pride in his work took longer to destroy. At the same time the enormous expansion of business created economic forces which became in themselves a threat to the business out of which they had sprung, and towards the end of the period under review, although still on a small scale, we see tentative endeavours by individuals and by the community to diminish these forces by various devices. The era of municipal enterprise, as distinct from, but not yet in opposition to, private enterprise began. Some individual firms which found themselves in parlous circumstances sought to strike an agreement with stronger firms of the same kind.

In Aberdeen public enterprise had been experimented with before, as we have seen, at the beginning of the seventeenth century. Subsequent developments arose partly as the result of the extension of the community's direction of social services, such as hospitals and education, water supplies and watching. The cumulative effect of these new methods in public and private combination was to lessen still further the opportunities open to the individual citizen, but this diminution of human dignity was not to any great extent obvious within this period. After the Reform Act, however, there began to be evident an encroachment of the central Legislature upon the local authority. As long as law-making was minimal, this development was hardly perceptible, and it did not in fact assume serious proportions until after the years with which we are concerned here.

Part 4

The Burgh Crosses Its Rubicon

CHAPTER ONE

Modern City Making

During the century that followed Culloden Aberdeen experienced two developments that were almost explosive in character. One was topographical, the other sociological. The former, while later in point of time than the second, may be given precedence of treatment because it altered the image of the burgh and was the recognisable basis of the Aberdeen that we know today.

The burgh of 1746 was still substantially the burgh of Gordon's map in 1661; and so it remained for nearly ten years longer. In 1755 the lands of Gilcomston stretched westwards from the city in an untidy waste, which probably did not differ from the prospect in Robert the Bruce's time save for the presence of three miserable crofts, two of whose tenants had gone bankrupt and only one of which wrested enough produce from the soil to be able to boast a farmhouse. The lands of Gilcomston, purchased for the benefit of the Bridge of Dee fund from the Menzies family in 1674 for £1,500, were in 1750 turned over at the purchase price to the city treasurer — or, in modern terms, to the Common Good. They were then divided into twelve lots and feued out, the annual income, in addition to an initial lump sum paid to the treasurer by the feuars, being close on £200. Next, the Council sold back the feu-duties to the Bridge of Dee fund at the enhanced value of forty-years' purchase and by means of the whole deal made a profit of over £2,000.

The lands, on being feued, were promptly taken in hand by their new owners. 'On the morning of the day of the roup', it was recorded, the three farms were about £80 sterling rent; in the afternoon the rent was £225 sterling, besides all the money paid down by the feuars. In the next thirty years, following Provost Alexander Robertson's pasture-making experiments in the Lochlands, acres were cleaned up, tilled and manured. The ground was still raw material, but it had rich possibilities. It was worth clearing of stones, for they could be sold in the town for building purposes, and as much as £25 was realised from the stones gathered from a single acre, and the purchaser paid the cost of transport. The cleared ground was then dunged with 'fulzie' from the still prolific burgh middens, lime was added, and turnips put in which were sold to the 'Aberdeen cow-feeders for about eight pounds the acre'. Barley was next sown as a nurse crop for rye grass and clover, and the ensuing pasture fetched from £7 to £9 the acre.

A distillery had been erected on the site of a lint mill on the north side of what is now Baker Street in 1760 — it was converted into a brewery six years later, with buildings on the southside of the line of Baker Street; the first dwellinghouses were built in 1755 where now are Northfield Place, Loanhead Terrace and Jack's Brae (mentioned in 1758); by 1773 there was a meal mill (now Strachan's) at the junction of Jack's Brae and Leadside Road; and before 1800 the suburb, for such it then was, could count a thousand inhabitants, with a church — built in 1770–1 — to accommodate them ministered to by the re-doubtable Irishman Dr. James Kidd, who near the turn of the century had succeeded the Rev. James Gregory, the first incumbent. North of the area Craigie Loanings, as Crag's Loanings, had been known since 1461 as a rural, and no doubt green, lane.

South of Gilcomston the town also began about 1775 to burst through its ancient boundaries, and, crossing the Denburn, moved up the Windmill Brae until the Hardgate came to rank as a suburb. Another bridge was constructed south of the Bow Brig to link up with the feus of what is now the Crown Street area. The southerly approach was still, however, the narrow and awkward one down that venerable highway of the Windmill Brae to the Bow Brig, through the Green and up the Shiprow; and it was not until 1799 that action was taken to improve matters in that respect. Towards the harbour, down the slope from the Castlegate, not then congested as it soon became, a building scheme was pushed rapidly ahead in 1767–8, the Trinity burn being diverted, Virginia Street[1] laid out along its former course, and Marischal Hall with its garden purchased by the Council so that the bridge over Virginia Street, the foundation of which was laid on 15 March 1768, might be erected. It cost £950. By 1785 the whole of the Shorelands, which had been reclaimed in the middle of the previous century, when the old quay was prolonged towards Futty

1   So called because until 1776 the buildings connected with Aberdeen's trade with Virginia were in that area. A group who seceded from the East Parish Church about 1757 worshipped in a tobacco warehouse, which still stands in this street, hence Chapel Lane. This congregation later moved to Correction Wynd and then built Melville Church at the north end of Rose Street.

village, was a very much built-up area. In 1782 Commerce Street was constructed, and in view of present-day opinions upon unemployment relief it is interesting to note that improvements were carried out upon it in 1816 to provide work for the workless.

In 1754 the Aberdeen Lodge of Freemasons secured the Castlegate site which half a century later was to be the corner of King Street, and there they built their headquarters, combining it with a hostelry which during all its fourscore years of existence was known as the New Inn. This house no doubt was rendered all the more necessary inasmuch as the burgh's older inn, Skipper Scott's, a little farther east in the Castlegate, was about this time acquired by Francis Peacock, the dancing-master, who had come to Aberdeen from Edinburgh in 1747, and after conducting his classes in one of the buildings of the old town house of the Earls Marischal and subsequently in Mealmarket Street, had settled in the close that bears his name. The New Inn lodged many a famous traveller — Dr. Johnson and Boswell stayed there, and Robert Burns on his only night in Aberdeen — and arrangements were being made to extend it when the young North of Scotland Bank bought the property in 1839 and erected the head office which still stands very much architecturally as when Archibald Simpson designed it.[1] The New Inn abutted upon the Castlegate end of Lodge Walk, which was named after the Freemason Lodge.

To the north the Lochlands — in Parson Gordon's time 'a fen or puddle' — which about the time of the last Jacobite Rebellion had been the scene of Provost Robertson's experiment, and were now drained, began to be feued out, and by 1790, in 'the only quarter where the town can be extended to any great degree', as one contemporary town planner believed, a beginning had been made with the layout of George Street. John Street and Jopp's Lane come into the picture in 1783. By the end of the century the extent of the Loch corresponded with the present Loch Street. Between the thoroughfare of the Broadgate and the then still intact crofts upon the Links, there were made the Longacre, Barnet's Close, Littlejohn Street and Lodge Walk. Between the last of the rebellions and 1800, the burgh acquired other ten new streets — Virginia, Tannery, North, Marischal, Belmont, Queen, James, Carmelite, George and St. Andrew. Some of these are already memories. The Schoolhill was at the same time prolonged, and private dwellings

1   The original, but temporary, head office had been 'the old Bank' in Broad Street, once the Aberdeen Bank's habitation, and in the twenties and thirties of the present century the St. Katherine's Girls' Club. It was demolished in 1945.

sprang up on the Woolmanhill. In 1802 Charlotte Street was constructed in honour of George III's Queen. In 1768–9 the Gallowgate and Justice Ports were demolished.[1] The Netherkirkgate port, the last of the six original 'bows', or city gates, to be taken down, was bought over for £140 by the Council and removed in 1793.

'I had an agreeable ride yesterday forenoon', wrote Francis Douglas in the summer of 1780, 'to see the late improvements in the neighbourhood' of Aberdeen. He then proceeds at great length to describe the environs of Aberdeen within the marches of the Freedom Lands. The burgh itself was still at that date to all intents and purposes bounded on the west by the Denburn, but the immediate hinterland was changing radically during the second half of the eighteenth century, as Francis Douglas discloses.

North-East of Gilcomston lay the village of Loanhead, situated on what is now the Rosemount ridge, the prospect from which may have suggested the 'Belvidere' titles that were later associated with it. Says Douglas, 'there is a fine prospect of the town, the harbour, the sea, Old Aberdeen and the adjacent country. From the Bridge of Dee to the river mouth, the country seems one continuous village.' On the Loanhead slopes there were 'many decent houses', and well cultivated fields won back from their primeval state of rocky desolation. One crofter called his holding there Bergen-op-Zoom, after the Dutch town which British troops had found a tough nut to crack when they besieged it. Beyond Loanhead there stretched to the north and north-west the former common pasture of the town, by Douglas's time feued out and broken up by bleachfields. The slopes of the Stocket were under cultivation, and no doubt Oakbank's name today has some connection with the large wood that was planted with Scots fir about 1750 — since it is a persistent Aberdeen habit to name a place after a tree that never grew there. Once over the summit of the ridge, 'an extensive but wild prospect opened up to the west and south-west in which little was to be seen but heath and moor, except in one place to the north (no doubt in the Foresterhill direction) where the observer was astonished by the grass and grain produced in a great many fine enclosures'.

Out the old Skene road agricultural developments had been less fortunate, the farmer being too far from the manures and the markets provided by the city. Swinging round to the north-east from Dykeside

1   There is a reference in the Town Council records of 1787 to a wall of the Justice Port which, as the gable of a house, was still protruding into the street. But it seems clear that the Port itself had ceased to exist some twenty years before.

and its douping stane ('a term which cannot be rendered into English'), Douglas came to Sclattie, taken in and farmed by Dr. John Chalmers, Principal of King's College, who had bought the property after farming Cairntradlin, in Kinellar, part of the College endowment. All around Sclattie the country was very wild, but on both sides of the north road land had been taken in and residences built. On the Doupin' Stane, during the official Riding of the Marches, which used to take place annually on the last Saturday of August, those who rode the marches for the first time were forcibly bumped thrice in the posture indicated by the title of the stone. The annual peregrinations became quin-quennial at the beginning of the nineteenth century, but were dis-continued after 1810, and only occasionally revived thereafter. On both sides of Old Aberdeen the land was fertile and well-tilled. and 'the advance of rent within the past forty years is almost incredible', some lots having risen from 8s. to as much as £4 per acre. In the Spital there were many market gardens 'raising every kind of common root and vegetable', the consumption of coleworts and cabbage in Aberdeen being much greater than in the south and west of Scotland, where more meat was eaten. Broadford (known as 'the Provost's mire' from having belonged to Provost George Fordyce, who farmed an acre or two there before he became tacksman of Eigie), Barkmill, and Clerkseat, the lands which covered the present Berryden and Elmhill area, were well drained and the fields, as elsewhere around Aberdeen, were marked by stone fences.

The mansion house of Clerkseat, belonging then to Mr. Innes, the Commissary-Clerk, 'the richest man that ever held office, being the happy father of six sons and eleven most amiable daughters', was overshadowed as a show place in 1780 by a neighbouring villa in pos-session of Mr. Leslie, a druggist, and Mr. Douglas spends three pages in describing its pleasance and policies, its shrubberies and walks, its obelisk and bathing-pool, its hermitage and all the other embellish-ments of its five and a half acres. Mr. Douglas envied Mr. Leslie. 'He enjoys, on a small scale, all that a man of sense would value in a retreat from the noise and bustle of a town; fine air, pure water, rising shelter; his fields produce bread-corn, his garden roots; and his milk pails overflow. In his morning walks, while the ascending vapour is just seen on the mountain top, he inhales fragrance; herbs innumerable emit the treasures of the atmosphere, and flowers of a thousand dyes reflect the golden ray.' All this, remarks the panegyrist in wonder, but half a mile from the Cross of Aberdeen.

As regards the city itself, Douglas mentions the elegant single-arch bridge over the Denburn, the entry to the town, the close-built character of the burgh, the generally 'reasonable breadth' of the well-paved streets, especially the Broadgate, which 'would have been a fine street had it been quite straight and in all parts equally broad'. The weather cock on the spire of the Townhouse was 120 feet above the street. Marischal Street had recently been made, 'a fine new street', the town having paid £800 for the Earl Marischal's old house and garden. At the east end of the Castlegate a record office, 'a large and not inelegant building', had also been recently built, the sheriff-clerk's office with many valuable papers having been burnt about 1724.

Behind the Townhouse stood the large poorhouse: in Drum's Lane was the 'maiden hospital' for old unmarried women. East of the poor-house was the butcher-market, 'sufficiently large, but unworthy so fine a town' where 'beef and pork are sold by the Dutch pound, about seventeen ounces and six drams; veal, mutton and lamb are commonly bought by the eye'. Douglas adds that the beef 'is in general inferior to that killed in the south and west of Scotland',[1] but the 'mutton and lamb are excellent, especially the first'. He mentions 'excellent, well-fed poultry'. North of the Castlegate was the meal market, the boll being eight stones Dutch. The Castlehill still carried 'the remains of a small fort built by Oliver Cromwell'. There were four public breweries, that at Gilcomston being 'esteemed among the largest in Scotland'. In the Broadgate under the large water reservoir were kept the fire engines. These engines were paraded and used in practice every municipal election day, when the fountains and water pipes were inspected by the Council.

1   This was before the Aberdeen-Angus breed had been developed.

CHAPTER TWO

Over the Denburn

Aberdeen at the end of the century had grown into too busy and great a town to be approached by devious and crooked paths like that which crossed the Den Burn by the Bow Brig or wound from the Brig o' Balgownie over the Spital brae and the Porthill to the Castlegate. In 1796 Charles Abercrombie, a road engineer and surveyor, suggested a scheme for the opening up of the city from both north and south. This led to the most decisive event in Aberdeen's later civic history, comparable with Davie do A'thing's clearing of the harbour channel two hundred years before — the crossing of the Denburn. At the very end of the eighteenth century the Town Council with the support and probably at the instigation of the ratepayers meeting under the chairmanship of the provost of the day, Thomas Leys of Glasgoforest, decided to open out the Castlegate to west and north by the great new arterial roads which we now call Union and King Streets. When that decision was taken, Aberdeen sloughed its medieval skin and when the project was substantially carried through the burgh stepped forth as a modern city. The alignment of Union Street involved the bridging of the Denburn, and Aberdeen in very truth crossed the Rubicon. Because Leys died early and his contemporary and business partner James Hadden of Persley was several times provost at critical periods of the scheme's development, Hadden has by posterity been given most of the credit for the great venture. Hadden during his terms of office was the main instrument in driving the scheme to its completion, thus earning the title of 'father of the city'. But Provost John Dingwall of Ardo and Rannieston, laying the foundation-stone of Union Bridge on 7 July 1801, paid tribute to 'the exertions of my worthy predecessor Mr. Leys, who has by his perseverance and zeal contributed so essentially to bring this work to its present advanced stage'. Provost Dingwall's father, it may be noted, had 'established the manufacture of knit stockings' in the burgh.

The decision to make new entrances to Aberdeen was that of the ratepayers, convened for the purpose of considering the problem by

Provost Leys. Estimates were produced of £6,493 6s. 8d. for the building of Union Street up to and including a bridge over the Denburn,
with smaller bridges spanning Carnegie's Brae and Correction Wynd;
the south end of King Street was to cost £625 3s. 4d. Buying up the
property between the Castlegate and the Denburn was at first estimated
to cost £20,000, but that figure soon rose to £30,000, and as the feus
on the line of the new thoroughfare were expected to fetch £27,000,
the town was left with £3,000 to find on that account. Parliament passed
the necessary legislation with a promptitude that we today may well
envy, and the task of clearing away the jungle of houses that stretched
between the east end of the Netherkirkgate and the north end of the
Shiprow was put in hand in a matter of months.

The town's credit was pledged to make the improvement possible,
and a body of trustees was established under the Act to carry the scheme
through. The design of a Glasgow architect, David Hamilton, was
adopted out of seven submitted. It provided for a street entering the
west-end of the Castlegate, sixty feet wide, and involving the levelling
of St. Katherine's hill, whose slope interposed between the Castlegate
and what is now St. Nicholas Street, and the levelling up of the ground
to the west of that to provide a basis for the new bridge over the
Denburn. The Union Street, like the King Street, entrance to the
Castlegate was opened in 1801, and the street got its title to commemorate the legislative union between Great Britain and Ireland, a
parliamentary feat which has proved much more expensive and less
durable than Aberdeen's main thoroughfare, costly though the latter
turned out to be. For the Union Bridge, John Rennie, the engineer who
was at that time building the Aberdeenshire Canal to Inverurie, was
called in as adviser. Hamilton's design, already mentioned, was for a
bridge of three arches, the aggregate span being 124 feet. The contract
provided for the work being completed by 1 July 1802, but early in
that year the contractors found they had made a mistake in their estimates and had to abandon the job, all that had been done being the
foundations and the piers to carry the arches.

The superintendent of the work, a young assistant of Rennie's named
Thomas Fletcher, eventually proposed a single-arch bridge of stone and
lime with 130 feet of span. Provost Hadden submitted this design to the
greatest of living engineers, Thomas Telford, who approved it with
modifications that, under modern conditions, did not improve it.
For example, he reduced the space between the keystones of the arch
and the roadway from 3¾ to 2¾ feet, which was not helpful when gas-

pipes came to be laid on the street, and which provided less room for the insertion of material to prevent water from the roadway penetrating to the arches and weakening the adhesive power of the mortar. Fletcher also proposed to increase the width of the street from 60 to 70 feet. The bridge itself later proved too narrow for traffic at 40 feet and it was widened to 60 feet. With that alteration, the bridge on completion had a central arch of 130 feet, with a rise in the arch of 20 feet, and a height from ground level to carriageway of 46 feet. It cost £13,342 altogether and was completed on 5 August 1805, although it had been open to the public since 4 June. Abercrombie's plan as we saw, estimated the cost of all Union Street at £6,393 exclusive of the purchase of property. As Putachieside bridge over Carnegie's Brae alone absorbed £3,634, the three bridges required three times as much to erect as their first fond imaginer contemplated for them and the whole street.

King Street outpaced Union Street, and about the same time St. Nicholas Street was driven through from George Street to link up the Inverurie road with the main thoroughfare of Union Street. King Street was connected with the Broadgate and Gallowgate respectively by Queen Street and North (now West North) Street, whose northern end had been known as the Back Butts or the Back Causeway. The space between King Street and Lodge Walk was the Poultry Market. The first important building to be erected in King Street was St. Andrew's Chapel (now Cathedral) in 1817, to a £6,000 plan by Archibald Simpson, Aberdeen's greatest architect. He was also responsible in the following year for the Medico-Chirurgical Society's Hall opposite, done with a portico of four Ionic columns and costing £2,000. The Hellenic motif was retained by John Smith, the architect of the North Church, when he built its portico in 'the Ionic order after the proportions of that of the temple of Minerva Polias at Athens'. The church, erected in 1820–31, cost £10,500. In 1833 what was originally the County Record Office, south of the Medico-Chirurgical Hall, took shape even more emphatically Hellenic, with its frontage supported by four pilasters on the model of the Choragic Monument of Thrasyllus.

Off King Street Frederick Street was built, being distinguished by the erection in 1807 of a 'conventicle' for the accommodation of 'Independents understood to be in connection with the Congregational Union of Scotland'; and in 1835 by a school for 600 pupils, conducted on the Madras system, the subjects taught being English, reading and grammar, writing, arithmetic, the elements of geography, plain needlework, knitting, and each pupil paying a weekly fee of three halfpence.

Wales Street contained the butcher market, built in 1806; while Constitution Street 1807, named in celebration of the King's refusal to sanction Catholic emancipation, cut across the croft of Fill-the-Cup and eventually and ironically held the Roman Catholic School, built in 1832–3, then with about 120 pupils; and the Banner Mill at the eastern end.

At the south-west corner of the Castlegate, in a part of Exchequer Row that no longer exists, there was built in 1803 a library and reading room called the Athenaeum, which in 1822 was transferred to a position where the name remains although the pabulum has altered. Off the north-west corner of the square there was Concert Court, so called because the Aberdeen Musical Society held their entertainments there. The Society of Advocates built a meeting place for themselves at the corner of Back Wynd, which on their leaving it became a restaurant known as the Queen's Rooms, until it was converted into the second cinema to be opened in Union Street; the Electric Theatre (now the Capitol) being the first. The Society of Advocates, on quitting the Back Wynd premises in the middle of last century, made their home in their present Hall in Concert Court.

Once Union Bridge was built, housing development beyond the Denburn began to extend. Union Terrace, Golden Square, and the streets Silver, Diamond, Skene, Chapel, Gordon and Dee[1] were laid out before 1818, followed in the next twenty years by Crown Terrace, Crown Street, Marywell, Affleck[2] and Huntly Street, and Archibald Simpson prepared Bon-Accord Square, Terrace and Crescent, his own house being 13 Bon Accord Square, although he removed to 1 East Craibstone Street later, where he died. A few residences facing south already stood on the line of Union Street and were known as Union Place, while Alford Place and Wellington Place were still unaware of Babbie Law. Probably owing to the high price of the sites, the ground at the eastern end of Union Street was slow in being taken up; another reason given is interference with builders' plans by the local authority. First the houses between Shiprow and what is now Market Street appeared, with the Athenaeum newsroom to the east of them. In 1811 came Archibald Simpson's first effort, Union Chambers,

1 Dee Street was then New Dee Street, to distinguish it from the older Dee or Lower Dee Street that ran across the site of the Joint Station. When the Station was built, Lower Dee Street disappeared.
2 Affleck Street was named after Deacon-Convener Affleck, who in 1824 presented George Street U.P. Church with the first gas lamp in Aberdeen.

comprising Lipton's shop and McCombie's Court pend. Between St. Nicholas Street and Union Bridge on the north side there was a blank for nearly twenty years. This gap was accentuated by the rough vacant space — vacant except when occupied by menageries and circuses — which yawned between the southern boundary of the kirkyard and the line of the street. In 1830 the burial-ground was extended to incorporate this plot and the well-known façade by John Smith, city architect, was constructed. Fifty years ago there were still people who could remember the dilapidated hovels that littered the street line west of Union Bridge.

The opening up of the road to the south was mainly, though not wholly, responsible for Aberdeen's greatest municipal financial crisis. For many years the administration of the burgh treasury had been lax as well as secretive, and those methods loosened the foundation of the burgh's credit. Upon this insecure basis was imposed the immense weight of the Union Street and King Street Improvement Scheme, costing in all £114,000. This substantial sum, added to £57,000 representing unpaid interest, brought the public debt of Aberdeen up to the then colossal total of £226,000. In February 1817, the City Treasurer had to suspend payment of interest on money borrowed by the town, and a few weeks later the Council conveyed all the burgh's property to a board of twenty-one trustees, representing the Corporation's creditors. The close of the Napoleonic Wars, however, and the steady progress of the application of machinery to industry together imparted such buoyancy to trade, that in 1825 the trustees found that the interests of their clients could be held to be adequately safeguarded if the city's property were restored to the Council, and accordingly this was done.

From 1800 scarcely a year passed but a few new streets were added, Union Street, King Street and George Street having opened up the adjacent crofts and fields. In 1801 Drum's Lane connected the Upperkirkgate with the Loch area, running beside the grounds of the home for indigent women established by the Drum Mortification of 1633. In 1806 came Young Street, named after Provost Young, and the beginning of Catherine Street. In 1807 Nelson Street (in honour of Trafalgar) and Hutcheon Street were added. Gerrard Street (it is misspelt), named after a Professor of Divinity, belongs to 1810. In 1816 among other streets there were constructed Wellington Street (in gratitude for Waterloo), York Street, Prince Regent Street, and in 1817 Hadden Street after one of the Provosts that great family gave to Aberdeen, and Shoe Lane, made by the Shoemaker Craft.

In 1842 the ancient and noisome Vennel was cleared away to make room for St. Paul Street. Thistle Street and Rose Street, Victoria Street and Albert Street and Albert Terrace came into being during the effervescently loyal late thirties and early forties, while on either side Albyn Place and Carden Place stretched steadily out like twin tentacles towards what was long before the end of the century Queen's Cross. In the forties the Woolmanhill district was still almost a village separate from Aberdeen, and its older inhabitants clustered of a summer evening for smoke and chat round the Corbie Well in a quietude that was undisturbed by shunting locomotives and had not yet been turned into Union Terrace Gardens with their pleasance of parterres and tree-shaded walks. An Act of 1846 abolished the ancient trading privileges of the guilds and incorporated trades. In that year the foundation stone was laid of a new Trades Hall at the east end of Union Bridge, the opening ceremony being held on 6 November 1847. The old Trades Hall had to be taken down and its site was covered over when Guild Street and Exchange Street were made in 1844, but the gateway, erected soon after the old Hall was restored in 1632, was built into the wall of the new building on the Denburn frontage. John Smith's son William was architect for the new Hall, which contained some priceless relics of Aberdeen's early civilisation, in particular a set of venerable oak chairs which are unique.

In 1818–20 the Sheriff Courthouse was built as it still stands, and in 1829 in Lodge Walk the East Jail, which should be distinguished from the old Tolbooth at the mouth of the street, and from the Bridewell, a sumptuous house of durance erected in 1809 in Rose Street. At that time Rose Street was a cul-de-sac, the half of the present thoroughfare terminating in the imposing gateway of the Bridewell, about opposite where Harrott's factory is now, and the northern half, connecting with Skene Street, being called (after Provost George Henry, 1784–1867) Henry Street, with a joinery works, belonging to the Garvie family that are now best known for their threshing-mills, backing on to the Bridewell. Female prisoners went to the Bridewell with its 109 cells; males to the East Jail, which had but sixty cells. In 1838 the numbers of persons committed to prison was 252, of whom 220 were incarcerated for the first time. Of these forty-two could not read and 124 could not write; thirty-four were regular church-goers; 131 attributed their lapses to drink, seventy-eight to idleness and bad company, and ten to want. The proportion of females to males was about one to three, and about one-fourth of the males were under seventeen, and one-seventh of the females. The Bridewell was closed down in 1868. The adjacent Summer Street had been Summer Road in 1771.

Opulent public buildings began to be erected at the end of the eighteenth and during the early years of the nineteenth century. Castlehill Barracks were built in 1792 at a cost of £16,000 on the site of St. Ninian's Chapel which was pulled down to make way for the military cantonment; the site was granted by the Council on condition that it should revert to the town if the barracks were removed. The new Bridge of Don costing £26,000 was built in 1827–30, and opened the same year as Wellington Suspension Bridge. In 1842 a widened Bridge of Dee was ready for service. The Militia Barracks, now the Transport Department's garages, went up in 1863 to William Smith's design. These barracks took the place of the older Militia barracks in Farmer's Hall Lane and Kintore Place the quaint old mess house of which is opposite the new printing works of Aberdeen University Press.

In the same year, on 30th April, the New Market buildings, one of Alexander Anderson's innumerable schemes, were formally opened; and by a coincidence, exactly forty years later, on 30 April 1882, they were destroyed by fire, being reopened after restoration in a much less pretentious form the following year.

The burgh's population was swiftly mounting. At the Parliamentary Union of 1707 it was 6,000, in 1801 a little more than twice that reckoning only the inhabitants within the old burgh limits of the four quarters of the parish of St. Nicholas. From 1755 Old Aberdeen and Gilcomston were also included in the count. In 1841 the census gave the town over 63,000 souls. An analysis of the 1811 returns shows 6,556 families occupying 1897 houses, with 20 houses under construction within the old burgh and, significantly, ten in Gilcomston. The males at 10,213 were outnumbered by 14,997 females. There were eighty-one families employed in agriculture, in trade and manufactures 3,797 families.

CHAPTER THREE

All the Years Round

The second great expansion, cultural, economic and financial, occurred on the morrow of the Jacobite rising. No sooner had the town returned to normal after the departure of the garrison of 'Fort Cumberland' in 1746 than the citizens began to be agitated concerning many matters pertaining to their own and their community's affairs. There was excitement over the founding of the first Aberdeen bank, of the first Aberdeen newspaper, of a linen factory on the Porthill, and over the first (and last) coal mine in the district. In 1751 John Gorsach received from the Town Council three nineteen-year leases of all coal and metals on the lands of Torry, which he would work at his own charges, paying as rent to the Council one-fourteenth of the coal and one-twelfth of the metals. It appears that he found neither, for no further mention is made of the undertaking, although ten years later the Council and the Governors of Gordon's Hospital in concert sank a shaft for a coal mine at Findon.

Alexander Livingstone of Countesswells, a Rotterdam merchant who was provost 1750–1, was responsible for the eighteenth-century reconstruction of the Town House and was a central figure in several Corporation squabbles. During the provostship of one of his associates, William Mowat of Colpnay, the West Church of St. Nicholas was reopened on 9 November 1755, after thirty years of neglect and disuse. It was in 1732 that the nave of the old church became unsafe, and for over twenty years thereafter the congregation worshipped under their own ministers in Greyfriars. In 1751 an Edinburgh mason and Edinburgh carpenters undertook to build a new West Kirk to the plan of the London Aberdonian architect James Gibbs. The price in all was £4,600 stg., paid out of funds belonging to the Church. The building was 100 feet 6 inches long, 66 feet broad, the nave 25 feet wide. The basement was of granite, the rest of freestone. There were three galleries on either side and one at each end. The east gallery was the Corporation's, with a canopy raised on four Corinthian mahogany pillars with gilt tops, and the town's arms cut in front of the canopy, above the space reserved for the Provost's Chair.

A century later it was the turn of the East Kirk, the fabric of which had become unsafe, so that in 1835 it had to be taken down, the new church being opened for worship in 1837. The southern end of Drum's Aisle was altered and made the main entrance. When the old building was being demolished it was discovered, too late to save them, that the walls and arches were as sound as the day they were built. In 1828 the parish of St. Nicholas was divided into six parts, to serve which, in addition to the four existing town's kirks, the South Church was built in 1830 and the North in 1831. Like every part of Scotland, Aberdeen was greatly agitated by the Non-Intrusion controversy which shook the Church of Scotland to its foundation in the second quarter of the nineteenth century. When the Church finally split in twain at the Disruption of 1843, all the ministers in Aberdeen — and there were fifteen of them — went out, and the six parishes had to be declared vacant. By a majority of more than two to one the Council refused to pass an expression of regret that the town's ministers had left the Establishment. Ten free churches were immediately built in Aberdeen, and in 1850 the Free Church Divinity Hall at Babbie Law.

In 1754 a dispute arose over the psalmody in the Kirk, where the Council had engaged a music master, with his pupils, to improve the singing. As this individual used a pitch pipe the ministers and kirk session smelt idolatry and attempted to dictate the manner of the singing. The presbytery, however, found that the session were exceeding their rights. In 1756–7 a new Grammar School was built west of the old school, on the site covered by Gray's School of Art until 1967. In 1760 when William Davidson was elected Provost, it was resolved that the provost should wear a gold chain, and the chain was purchased that was worn by the chief magistrate until Sir Andrew Lewis substituted a less cumbersome jewel in 1928.

The rejoicings at the coronation of George III in 1761 showed some alterations from previous festivities arising out of the same cause. The town's bells rang on the auspicious day and bonfires were lit in the streets. There was a forenoon concert of vocal and instrumental music in the Marischal College hall, and what Kennedy calls 'an elegant collation' in the town-hall afterwards. Thereafter, on an amphitheatre created east of the Cross in the Castlegate, the gentlemen of the civic party drank various patriotic toasts, punctuated by volleys of musketry. The Incorporated Trades marched in grand procession through the streets in full regalia, and entertained the magistrates and principal citizens to a banquet in their hall at night. All the houses were lit up in the evening, and the magistrates staged a feast for the people in the town hall.

In 1768, on a rumour of famine, a mob broke into a meal-dealer's store and stole much of his stock in trade. The military had to be called out and fired, one person being killed and several wounded. Some of the mob's leaders were caught, one was banished and another transported. In 1769 the Council amended a 300-year old regulation and permitted women to inherit property held of the Council.

In 1771 the Council gave ten guineas to encourage a fisherman from Hartlepool who proposed to establish a trawl fishing for flat fish. In 1773 we find the Council refusing to grant the usual gratuity of a guinea to the trumpeter at the Circuit Court on the ground that it was an improper application of the funds of the town. On 23 August 1773, Dr. Samuel Johnson received the Freedom of the Burgh and remarked, 'What I am afraid I should not have had to say of any city south of the Tweed, I found no petty officer bowing for a fee'. Johnson was Aberdeen's most distinguished visitor since William Harvey, the discoverer of the circulation of the blood, in 1642.

The Dean of Guild in 1774 estimated the cost of keeping the streets in repair and lighting them and of supplying water to the town at an assessment of a shilling in the pound of house rent. In 1780 and 1781 there was talk of a new road running over the summit of St. Katherine's Hill, and linking the Castlegate and the Green to form an arterial road to the south. Thus imperfectly was foreshadowed the great improvement, already described, that was to be Union Street some twenty years later.

There was a great scarcity of food after a bad summer in 1782. Harvest was not over by the middle of December. Aberdeen at the end of October had not two weeks' supply of cereals, and a meeting of the principal citizens was called at which it was decided to raise a relief fund for the purchase of corn. Immediately the sum of £1,719 17s. 6d., including 300 guineas from the Town Council, was raised, and the Aberdeen Bank and the Bank of Scotland both offered to advance £3,000 free of interest for twelve months. With these funds grain was purchased on the Continent and in England. On Christmas Eve a meeting of the landed gentry met in Aberdeen to consider the food situation, and it was computed that 220,000 bolls of corn would be required, over and above the harvest, to feed the people of Aberdeen and Aberdeenshire. A part saving was effected by a cessation of the malting of bere. The committee's action saved the town from famine,

and when the accounts were cast up it was found that the relief fund
was short by only a few pounds of the total net expenditure. In 1784
and 1785 the town was exercised by a discussion of burgh reform, and
a committee of burgesses demanded auditing of the accounts and
inspection of the records, which the Council described as an attempt
'to create and stir up groundless jealousy, division and discontent among
the citizens'. The troubles in France and in 1794 the outbreak of war
with the Revolutionary Government put an end to this agitation.

In 1790 horse-racing on the Links was inaugurated by the members
of the Northern Sporting Club, and a year or two later the Council
presented a purse of £30. The races were discontinued in 1829 and
restarted in 1843 for five years. In 1755 the plainstanes, a raised pavement beside the Cross opposite the Town House, was made for gentlemen to walk for the discussion of business. The plainstanes were removed in 1842, when the Cross was set back to its present position at
the east end of the Castlegate. In 1795, thanks mainly to the exertions
of John Ewen, jeweller, author of 'The Boatie Rows', an Act was
passed in Parliament 'for the better paving, lighting, cleansing and
otherwise improving the Streets, Lanes, and other Publick Passages of
the City of Aberdeen, . . . for the better supplying of the Inhabitants
with fresh water, and for the removing and preventing all obstructions
and annoyances within the said City and Royalty'. A Police Board was
appointed to carry out many of these civic duties. It published accounts
of revenue and expenditure. The same year the Baillies, Dean of Guild
and Treasurer got their chains of office.

The King's birthday in 1802 saw one of the most lurid events in the
later history of Aberdeen. The barracks were occupied by a unit called
the Ross and Cromarty Regiment, whose officers were invited to the
Town House to drink the King's health. There they got drunk, and as
they crossed the Castlegate to their quarters some dirt was thrown at
them by a crowd of boys playing in the street. The officers called out the
troops, a step which exasperated the public. Shots were fired, and
four people were killed and several wounded. The magistrates then
got control of the situation, and the regiment was immediately withdrawn from Aberdeen. Some of the officers were arrested on a murder
charge but were conveyed to Edinburgh and liberated by the Sheriff
of Midlothian. Leading Aberdeen citizens then combined to defray
the charges of a fresh prosecution in 1803 before the High Court of
Justiciary, when two of the officers were found not guilty, the complicity
of two sergeants was found not proven, and an ensign who absconded

rather than thole his assize was outlawed. The public-spirited Aberdonians thus found themselves saddled with an expenditure of £900 without the satisfaction of seeing the responsible officers punished.

In 1801 there was called to the civic chair one whose personality and ability put him on a plane with Aberdeen's great provosts of the past — the Menzies, Rutherfords and Jaffreys. James Hadden of Persley — 1758–1845 — was descended on both sides from well-known Aberdeen families. The Grammar School and Marischal College saw to his education, and he at once became a partner in his father's woollen firm of Alexander Hadden and Sons and of the great linen firm of Leys, Masson & Co. Afterwards he helped to found the Commercial Banking Company, the Aberdeenshire Canal Company and the Aberdeen Life Assurance Company, so that when he entered upon his first term as Provost in 'the year one' he was a very important man in the life of the burgh. His first term saw the preparations for the new lay-out of the city, Union Street and King Street, well advanced and Union Bridge built; in a second term, 1809–10, the works under the Harbour Act of 1810 were put vigorously in hand; in a third, 1813–14, powers were secured to build a new Court-house and offices, and to erect what came to be known as the Bridewell or West Prison. His last term was 1830–1, and he retired from the chair to contest the city in the 'Reform' election as a Tory against Alexander Bannerman. He withdrew before the poll owing to public opposition to his policy, but when after 1832 a democratically elected Town Council came to scrutinise his administration, it was found that far from having indulged in jobbing and corruption, as his opponent had alleged, he deserved the title of 'father of the city'. His brother, Gavin Hadden of Union Grove, 1770–1857, a much less powerful character, was also four times provost.

In 1806 the first feus on Union Street were sold at £1 11s. 8d. per foot of frontage. In 1813, as in much more recent years, coals were bad, and the Dean of Guild Court had a measure adopted, capable of holding fifty-two Aberdeen pints of water, which when filled with good coals contained a weight of nine stones Amsterdam, but of inferior coals nine and a half. The measure was, therefore, preferred to weight for the selling of coals, since the greater quantity of bad coal in the measure made up to some extent for its badness. On 13 August 1816, the town had an earthquake which set the house bells ringing. The last previous shock had been recorded on 8 September 1608.

The Reform Act of 1832 gave Aberdeen a Member of Parliament to itself. The Burgh Reform Act of 1833 extended the period of office of provosts from two years to three, polling day was fixed as the first Tuesday of November (in place of Michaelmas in the old system), the election of Dean of Guild on the Tuesday before polling day, the election of magistrates on the Friday immediately after the Council election. Until 1860, however, no one could be a member of the Town Council who was not a burgess of the burgh. The contest before the Reform election and the excitement when the Bill became an Act led to rejoicings and demonstrations of the most extravagant character in Aberdeen, as elsewhere throughout the country. James Blaikie of Craigiebuckler was the first Reform Provost, and in the last month of his three year term he dropped dead in the vestibule of the Town House.

James Blaikie's brother, Thomas Blaikie, 1801–61, Sir Thomas from 1856, was another of Aberdeen's outstanding provosts, serving two consecutive terms of office, 1839–46. In his last year he presented to the Council, which approved, and to a Head Court of the citizens, which rejected, an ambitious scheme for the improvement of the city and its administration. He proposed a new Board, consisting of three members of the Council, two from the Incorporated Trades, two from the Police Commissioners, and six elected by the public. This board was to abolish the Bell and Petty Customs, acquire the Newmarket, buy up the United Gas Company's works, build a new slaughter-house and cattle market, and lay out new streets. A tax of 4d. in the £1 on owners and 2d. on occupiers was included in the plan. The Council, in giving approval, withheld consent to the acquisition of the gasworks and the erection of a municipal cattle market as being the proper domain of private enterprise. Sir Thomas Blaikie died suddenly in Union Street.

In 1847 the Town Council advanced its hour of meeting from 6 p.m. to 3 p.m. and in 1848 admitted the public to witness its deliberations. That same year Queen Victoria first passed through Aberdeen, landing at the harbour from the royal yacht, and being met by the civic dignitaries headed by the Provost, George Thompson, later of Pitmedden, who was called 'Jr.' all his life. As Provost, George Thompson saw the first train enter Aberdeen and he conferred the freedom of the city on the Prince Consort and Sir Robert Peel. When he left the Council he became M.P. for the city from 1852 to 1857. He died at the age of 81.

In 1848 the Council decided that 'the procession of the magistrates attending church be dispensed with in future', but one sturdy individualist, Councillor Torn, dissented, appeared at the Town House next Sunday, called out the town sergeants, halberds and all, marched up behind them to the West Kirk and seated himself in the magistrates' pew in solitary splendour. In 1869 the ancient custom of a Town sergeant attending service in the West Kirk in full dress every Sunday forenoon was discontinued. In 1849 the custom of calling the hours by the night-watchman was dropped, except for half-past four, five and half-past five. In 1851 the old Bow Brig was taken down, its components being used later in the construction of the grotto in Union Terrace Gardens. In 1852 the big well was shifted from the Castlegate to the Green.

Distinguished visitors to the city, in addition to those already mentioned, included Robert Southey the poet, who came with his friend Thomas Telford the engineer, and Charles Dickens. Others who received the Freedom of the City were the Rev. George Whitfield, the Methodist leader, in 1741; George Colman the younger, later famous as a playwright, who was sent to Aberdeen by his father to be educated and left some amusing reminiscences of his stay, 1781; Sir John Sinclair, founder of the Board of Agriculture and inspirer of *The Statistical Account of Scotland*, 1795; Walter Scott, 1796, because his father was the town's agent in Edinburgh; Sir Ralph Abercromby, 1799, and Sir David Baird, 1806, distinguished Scottish soldiers; Lord Brougham, 1834, and Rowland Hill, the Postmaster-General with the penny stamps, 1844. Amongst local luminaries who received the civic accolade were Principal Campbell in 1761, Dr. Beattie five years later; John Skinner the poet in 1790; and Sir James McGrigor, founder of the Royal Army Medical Corps.

CHAPTER FOUR

Industrial Enterprise

It was in 1709 that a visitor to Aberdeen, the Rev. Edmund Calamy, D.D., saw there 'the finest knit worsted stockings anywhere to be met with', whose higher qualities could only be seen through 'a glass' and the best kinds of which cost five guineas a pair, with two guineas quite a common price. Half a century later, an Aberdeen Town Council with its weather eye on business showed its regard for one of Aberdeen-shire's most famous men by presenting Frederick the Great's field-marshal, James Keith in Potsdam, with a pair of stockings at the higher price and fine enough to be drawn through a thumb-ring. No doubt the hose were a good advertisement for Aberdeen wares in Prussia. With modern methods we can produce nothing like them, for in one pound of the wool there were twenty-four miles of thread.

The textile manufacture which became important in Aberdeen about the beginning of the eighteenth century was to expand in many ways before the century's close. The making of stockings was for long essentially a home weaver's job, and in 1770 there were no fewer than twenty-two Aberdeen merchants who bought wool from the south and distributed it amongst thousands of women in the countryside to be converted into stockings and ladies' gloves. By 1790 this system had begun to lose ground, the change being hastened by the introduction into the district the previous year by Charles Baird of two carding engines and four spinning jennies. Baird later started a wool mill of his own at Stoneywood which does not seem to have survived long. It was the firm of Alexander Hadden & Sons, for many years associated with the old hand-knitting methods already mentioned, who put Aberdeen's woollen manufactory in a sound state. This firm built their famous mill in the Green in 1798, driving the machinery by means of two steam engines, and producing for both the home market and for export large quantities of stockings, gloves, cloth and clothes. They also had a mill opposite Grandholm, the Gordon's (wool) Mills. Another firm, at the Barkmill, about where the Royal Mental Hospital now is, commenced in 1781 the manufacture of carpets. Messrs. Crombie,

Knowles & Co., later J. & E. Crombie, who had a mill at Cothal, opposite the old Kirk of Dyce, about 1790, eventually brought their heavy tweed-making to Grandholm in 1859 when that mill was vacated by the great linen firm of Leys, Masson and Co. The first Crombie was born at Fetternear on the Don, became associated with a wool firm in Old Deer run by a family of Kilgours, a name still familiar in Aberdeen textile circles. Over 2,000 persons in Aberdeen at the beginning of last century were employed in woollen manufactures.

In linen textiles Aberdeen must have been a pioneer town in Scotland, for Taylor the Water Poet, who visited the North-East in 1618, mentions home-made linen from home-grown flax along with the home-made hose among the several objects, which included whisky, of his admiration. It was, however, the firm of Leys, Masson & Co., originally Leys, Still & Co., which in 1749 established Aberdeen's linen industry upon a broad basis. Manufacturing linen cloth and threads, the firm's great mill was at Grandholm, the main building seven storeys high with 386 windows, and equipped with an iron foundry and a bleachfield. Their town premises were in Putachie-side, where the Douglas Hotel now stands. Leys, Masson & Co. were Aberdeen's grandest textile firm, with Thomas Leys the Provost and his friend James Hadden as the dynamic force within it. When Dundee was producing about 5,000 spindles of flax yarn per week, the Grandholm establishment with its 240 frames was turning out 10,000 to 12,000 spindles a week. Although by 1882 Dundee had nine times Aberdeen's output, yet in 1850 the four Aberdeen linen mills could still supply nearly one-ninth of Scotland's production of linen. There was something majestic about the Leys, Masson organisation even in its final years of decay and collapse. Up to 1828 it had expended £100,000 on land, buildings and machinery for its business, including the construction of a canal a mile long, a bridge over the Don, and its bleachfield of 80 acres, and in the forties of last century it maintained a works canteen for its thousand employees at a charge of three halfpence a head per meal. Leys, Masson & Co. closed down in 1848, re-opened with only 300 hands in 1850, and was wound up in 1859.

Another linen firm was Milne, Cruden & Co. of Spring Garden, the original Cruden a provost of the city and uncle of 'Alexander the Corrector', compiler of the classic Concordance to the Bible. Milne, Cruden in 1763 commenced business in the Porthill Mill, at Seamount, at the top of the Gallowgate, which had been built in 1752 by another company that failed. Later the firm built the Spring Garden works, secured other premises on the Windmill Brae, and at the Gordon's Mills that became a paper works afterwards they installed a spinning mill and made a bleachfield. Tape was made by the Aberdeen Tape Company in a shop at the west end of John Street. In 1854 Milne, Low & Co's tape-works had 100 hands and made 20 million yards per annum. Maberly Street commemorates the meteoric Englishman John Maberly who in 1810 purchased the Broadford Works recently erected by Scott, Brown & Co., and commenced linen manufacture there. He introduced power-loom weaving in 1824. Maberly was an educational enthusiast and took a leading part in a society founded to promote education by mutual tuition. He also started a bank in 1818 and got into Parliament, but the bank failed and he deserted politics in 1832, and in 1835 his Broadford Mill was sold to Richards & Co. In twenty years the Richards establishment had so expanded that it was giving work to 622 male and 1,614 female workers and manufacturing a yearly output of 2,500 tons of flax. From 1860 to 1898 the proprietors were another Englishman, Wilmot Holland, and his son. In the latter year it was taken over by a group of local people and this firm, now Richards Ltd. which in the early thirties of the present century came very near to the same end as the much younger Aberdeen Jute Company, has happily survived to enter a new lease of prosperity. After 1833 Dundee almost wholly deserted linen for jute, and it is interesting to compare the 1867 statistics for Aberdeen's jute industry — one factory, 16,814 spindles, 428 power looms, 2,175 employees — with Dundee's seventy-two factories, 202,466 spindles, 7,992 power looms and 35,310 hands. It may be added that while in 1808 Aberdeen's output of linen was over 300,000 yards worth £31,000 and of linen thread nearly 600,000 spindles of yarn which brought £35,000 to the women alone who were employed in the spinning of it, by 1830 the plight of the weaver was miserable, and the average wage of the 1,400 men in Aberdeen who still followed the trade was only from 3s. 6d. to 5s. 6d. per week for a 14-hour day. In 1843 things were better. Three firms employed 7,600 hands, weavers making 7s. to 20s. a week and girls 2s. 6d. to 8s.

Gordon, Barron & Co. introduced cotton manufacture into Aberdeen in 1779. They had a mill and bleachfield at Woodside and a handloom weaving shop in Schoolhill at the corner of Belmont Street now occupied by the 'Free High' Church. William Thom the poet was employed there. About 1780 another firm, Forbes, Low & Co., constructed a factory on the Denburn at Poynernook, on the site lately occupied by Pirie Appleton's works. By the time of the Battle of Waterloo, those two concerns and some smaller ones employed 2,500 adults and 1,500 children of from 9 to 15 years. The men's earnings were 9s. to 25s. the women's 5s. to 10s., and the children's 2s. to 5s. per week. These wages, with the immensely decreased purchasing power of our money, compare not so unfavourably as might be thought with the apparently much higher remuneration today. In the early thirties Thomas Bannerman & Co. built the Banner mill, but sold it in 1850 to Robinson, Crum & Co. who in 1857 had the only cotton mill left; they then employed 645 operatives. They disappeared in 1904 at the same time as Hadden's Mills.

Paper-making, like so much else, had been started on a serious scale as soon as the Jacobites were out of the way. The first mill — apart from a short-lived one at Gordon's Mills opened in 1696 — was at Culter, at the Waulkmill of Craigton, in 1751. This mill employed six men in 1795. It was owned in 1811 by Lewis Smith, who employed fifty hands and kept his machinery going night and day, 'being only stopt occasionally to oil or wash different parts of the machinery'. In 1820 the mills were sold for £4,000, and after other changes were taken over by the Stoneywood concern, but became independent again in 1865 and their subsequent prosperity is one of Aberdeen's economic romances. Stoneywood Mill, opened in 1771, belonged to Alexander Pirie, and by the middle of the century had nearly 1,000 employees and was using 2,500 tons of rags for special writing papers every year. By 1900 the mills covered 35 acres, burnt 25,000 tons of coal and consumed 15,000 tons of raw material. The Mugiemoss Mill, begun by Provost Dingwall, passed into the hands of Charles Davidson & Sons in 1821. By 1871 there were altogether five paper mills in and about the city employing 2,500 workers. Pirie's had commenced to use esparto grass in 1864 and had built a school and paid a staff to teach the children of their employees.

By that time also the city was developing the chemical industry. In the thirties the engineering firm of Barry, Henry & Co. was making bone manure, as well as machinery, and in 1871 Sandilands was producing 27,000 tons of manure and 300,000 gallons of oils and spirits annually. William Paterson & Sons, the pharmaceutical manufacturing chemists, commenced in 1842. The combworks of John Stewart, established in 1830 with forty hands, by 1854 was turning out 9 million combs in a range of 2,500 to 3,000 styles and sizes and employing over 700 men, boys and girls. In 1904 the output of combs was 25 million a year. At the same time five provision firms gave work to 600 people and processed £250,000 worth of preserved food in the year. A match factory had 180 hands. In the fifties the Aberdeen Quill Manufactory made several million quills annually.

At one time or another many other trades were tried. There were rope works, a nail factory, sail-making, tanneries, soap and candle works, a straw-hat factory, pin-making, paint-works, and the various industries connected with agriculture, such as those of the blacksmith and the cartwright. Of several breweries the first after 1745 was that opened in Gilcomston in 1768 and the most famous was the Devanha Brewery of William Black & Co., whose porter was in demand as far away as London in the early days of the nineteenth century. The Industrial Revolution naturally saw the rise of the engineering industry, and there were foundries like those of James Abernethy & Co at Ferry-hill and of Barry, Henry & Co., while William Mackinnon started an engineering shop in 1798 whose products have gone very far afield in more recent years.

Most characteristic of all Aberdeen's industries was granite-quarrying and processing. There was a quarry in the Freedom Lands in the seventeenth century which supplied stone for doors and windows, but before the Forty-five the first thoroughly up-to-date quarry was opened by James Emslie at Loanhead, and in the last two decades of the eighteenth century the London market for setts and paving-stones was brisk enough to give employment to 600 Aberdeen quarriers. To begin with the Adam family of architects in London had the stones they required hewn from the rocks at Nigg, but soon they found it better to buy their wants from the quarry-owners. In 1817 there were sent to London 22,167 tons of stones valued at £23,275. The new Aberdeen became at the same time the Granite City. Union Bridge was made of the native stone, and whereas before the eighteenth century most of the public buildings, like King's College, were of freestone, and even the West Church of St. Nicholas, when it was rebuilt in 1750–5, was mainly in freestone, the tendency after the Jacobite Rebellions was to concentrate upon granite for both public and private buildings. One of the oldest Aberdeen quarries, Dancing Cairns, opened about that time and later supplied the portico of the Music Hall and the block for the statue of the Duke of Gordon, 14 tons in weight, in the Castlegate, now in Golden Square. Rubislaw, opened at the beginning of last century, sent much of its product to build great undertakings in London and the south.

Granite polishing by hand was known in Aberdeen as early as 1770. About 1830 the trade received a tremendous and quite fresh impetus from the invention by Alexander Macdonald of machinery for the dressing and polishing of the stone. In 1810 granite was said to have 'brought gold to Aberdeen', but when the full effects of Macdonald's invention were felt, the native quarries were for a time a veritable Golconda. Sixty polishing yards were kept busy, of which the largest, Alexander Macdonald's own, employed 150 men. By 1864 the various firms, with 1,000 workers, were dealing with 8,000 tons yearly; in 1892 £67,000 of polished and dressed granite was exported, the U.S.A. being the principal market; and in 1898 the other side of the industry had its innings when 747 new buildings worth £500,000 were constructed, while about a million tons of stone were quarried in Aberdeenshire.

Before the introduction of steam for propulsion and the discovery that iron could be used for construction, ship-building at Aberdeen was in an exceedingly active state. In 1817 there were half a dozen ship-building yards in constant employment on the building of new and the repair of old vessels. Three were big — Alexander Hall & Co., founded 1790; J. Duthie, Sons & Co., and John Vernon & Sons; the others were John Duffus & Co., which later absorbed Blaikie Bros., Nicol & Reid, and Ronald and Shepherd. Walter Hood & Co. was established in 1839 and survived until 1881. These yards in the former year launched twenty-two vessels of an aggregate displacement of 3,300 tons, one ship, the *Castle Forbes* of 439 tons, being the first Aberdeen-built ship to be destined for the India trade. In 1820 when the Glasgow Association of Underwriters and Brokers instituted a register of shipping, it was found that Scotland boasted 2,851 vessels of 273,453 tonnage, the principal centres being:

Aberdeen	374 boats of 51,852 tons
Greenock	338 boats of 44,107 tons
Leith	213 boats of 24,874 tons
Port-Glasgow	118 boats of 18,511 tons
Glasgow	89 boats of 6,842 tons

In 1818 the port employed 2,000 seamen and was exporting over £80,000 worth of the city's manufactures to the Continent. In 1814 the first sea voyage was made by a steamboat; Aberdeen's first steamboat was launched from Duffus & Co's yard in 1829, but the first to sail from the port of Aberdeen was the *Velocity* in 1821. In 1827 the first Scottish iron ship was launched; Aberdeen's first was built in 1837 by John Vernon & Sons. In 1839 Alexander Hall & Co. put out the first Aberdeen clipper the *Scottish Maid* for the London coastal trade, and in 1845 the Aberdeen-built *Torrington* was sent to challenge the fast American vessels in the Chinese opium trade.

In 1859 Aberdeen was responsible for three of the swiftest of the wooden tea clippers, the *Stornoway*, the *Chrysolite* and the *Cairngorm*, the last a particularly fast and famous ship whose speed and superior workmanship enabled its tea cargo to be delivered in better condition and eliminated the Americans from the China trade. The fifties and sixties were, however, the golden age of the clippers. For George Thompson & Company's Aberdeen White Star Line trading to Australia, Hood & Co. built an entire fleet of magnificent clippers of which the *Jerusalem* and *Thyatira* were masterpieces and the *Thermopylæ* was unrivalled, while Hall & Co. were responsible for the *Yangtse*, the *Fychow*, and several others. The *Thermopylæ*, of 947 tons, could do the voyage to Melbourne in sixty days, and to Foochow in ninety, and her greatest day's run, a record for all sailing ships, was 380 miles.

The least publicised but probably the most interesting of the clipper-building firms was that of the Duthie family, known latterly as John Duthie, Sons and Co. Founded in 1816, the then head William Duthie ran the first mercantile service between London and Australia and was the first owner to send ships to South America for guano. Amongst their great ships were the *Australian*, one of whose voyages in 1869 was described by a Melbourne newspaper as comparing 'favourably with anything accomplished by the tea clippers'; the *Ann Duthie*, according to her skipper, twice beat the *Cutty Sark*; the *Ballarat*, which is said to hold the record for a fast passage by sail between Australia and the United Kingdom; the *Brilliant*, which over a period of eighteen years made the fastest average passage of eighty-one days; and the *Rifleman*, reputed to be the fastest Duthie clipper of all. Many of the Duthies commanded the ships their firm built, and one of them, Alexander (1824–97) designed the most celebrated of all their boats, the iron four-masted clipper *Port Jackson*, which was built by Alexander Hall & Co. She was the last ship to fly the Duthie flag, was sold as a training ship in 1907, about the time the firm itself was taken over by Hall, Russell & Co.

Aberdeen's final tea clipper, the *Caliph*, left the stocks in 1869; and the reason for the passing of the wooden vessels was that in 1867 Hall Russell & Co. had commenced the building of iron ships. In 1860 Aberdeen had fewer ships — 275 was the number — but of a much higher tonnage — 76,489 — than in 1820, and was turning out about a dozen vessels annually of an aggregate displacement of some 6,000 tons. In 1870 there were 2,000 workmen employed by five shipyards. The Thompson Line and the Aberdeen Line of John T. Rennie & Sons trading to South Africa kept the Aberdeen yards busy on steamships.

In 1752, a company of commercial men and landed gentry raised capital to the extent of £8,000 to undertake the whaling business. Two whalers, the *Saint Ann* and the *City of Aberdeen*, each of about 500 tons, went to Greenland the following year, and returned with five and two whales respectively. In the next year one caught nothing and the other two as before; and that was the end of the venture. The company lost the most of its capital. In 1783 another company sent out the *Hercules* and the *Latona*, and with such good results that by 1817 there were five companies engaged in the industry, with fourteen ships, four at the Davis Straits and the rest at Greenland, of an aggregate tonnage of 4,379, which in that year caught 48 whales and 668 seals, and thus produced 688 tons of oil and over 35 tons of whalebone. About 700 men were employed on the boats themselves, to say nothing of shore-hands. Gradually, however, the whale fishing interests departed to Peterhead or Dundee. By 1837 only two whalers were left in the port; in 1856 Aberdeen's revenue from the whaling was only £12,500 compared with £70,000 at Peterhead; four years later the whaling revenue was insignificant.

Salmon had been Aberdeen's first staple fish crop. In 1789 there were exported to London, whence a great proportion, salted, went on to the south of Europe, 1890¼ barrels, 4 cwt. each, of Dee salmon and 1,667 barrels from the Don. That was an exceptional year, and the average was 1,000–1,200 barrels from the Dee and 800–1,000 from the Don. Kennedy explains that 'the fishings in the Dee are distinguished by the names of cavels, in each of which there are six shares, called half nets'. The town's fishings were the Stellis, the Rake, the Midchingle, the Pot, the Foords, and a half share near the bridge. Of the Don fishings, several were fished by the owners themselves, while the proprietors of the Cruives at Gordon's Mills paid a yearly sum to the owners of the fishings farther up the river.

Before it was discovered that salmon could be kept fresh on ice, they used to be salted in barrels for the continental market or pickled in vinegar for the London market and packed in kits. Fresh at the plentiful time of year, in April and May, the salmon sold in Aberdeen at 1s. 6d. the lb., and grilse in summer at 4d. White trout and finnock fetched

2d. the lb. These prices are for the year 1818. At the beginning of the second quarter of last century, the average export was 869 barrels of 4 cwt. each. By the middle of the third quarter it had fallen to 360 barrels. It may be added that at the beginning of last century Dr. Skene Keith said not one salmon was eaten in the country for forty exported. In 1792 or 1793 a great quantity of eels went up the Dee. According to the first *Statistical Account*, 1795, 'this procession took place between the middle of May and the middle of June. The eels kept near the bank and near the surface of the water. They proceeded in regular rows, close to each other, and seven eels in a row. The arrangement and movement of the whole seemed to resemble that order which is the effect of discipline. They continued running three days. . . They returned from August to October, and then were considerably larger than when they went up.'

During these hundred years Aberdeen's commerce suffered many vicissitudes, but steadily expanded, even if, after the Napoleonic Wars, it failed to maintain its lead over that of other ports. The character of the trade, too, changed, and as the Clyde ships went overseas, Aberdeen's developed the coastwide trade. No doubt this tendency was strengthened by the privateering activities of the French and Americans during these wars, which accounted for no fewer than thirty-two Aberdeen vessels. But Government regulations and interference, then as now, were heavy shackles upon enterprise, and the navigation laws, by restricting trade, and the Navy's press-gang, by shanghai-ing seamen, cut down activities at and from the port substantially. The American War of Independence practically disposed of Aberdeen's very considerable carrying connection with that part of the world, and by the time it could be resumed other circumstances were operating to prevent its reopening. Smuggling also, which was widely and systematically engaged in, cost the authorities much money in lost dues, and no doubt greatly reduced the visible volume of commerce.

The coasting trade was conducted by the Aberdeen Steam Navigation Company, as it came to be called, which had instituted a service of smacks to London in 1707; and by the North of Scotland, Orkney and Shetland Steam Navigation Co. (originally the Leith and Clyde Shipping Co.) which commenced operations just before 1800. In 1837 the Aberdeen Commercial Company appeared in the field (or rather the waves) and in 1881 special attention was extended to the Moray Firth trade by the formation of the Aberdeen, Leith and Moray Firth Steam Shipping Company.

Agricultural produce was, and is, one of Aberdeen's principal exports, but the harbour returns under this head have naturally shrunk greatly since the city was first connected with the south by rail in 1850. The extent of the trade may be gauged from the fact that in the twenty years to 1849, no fewer than 150,000 cattle, valued at £3 million were exported from Aberdeen. In 1849 itself 7,800 cattle and 687 tons of meat were loaded at Aberdeen harbour. On 3 May 1850 the first railway consignment of 190 head of cattle left the town, and in December of that year the first weekly cattle mart was opened at the railway cattle station. In 1852 at the King Street market 17,695 cattle and sheep were sold. After the railway opened the consignments of cattle, sheep and dead meat doubled in six years. In December 1854 the Aberdeen Corn Exchange was opened in Hadden Street.

While all those important commercial and industrial undertakings were being developed, there was naturally much financial activity in the city. Aberdeen was the first town outside Edinburgh to possess a bank of its own, when in 1749 four merchants — Livingston and Mowat (both Provosts), Bremner and Dingwall — founded the Aberdeen Banking Company. The capital, which was only £600, was rather slender as a backing for the issue of notes, and in 1753 the united efforts of the Bank of Scotland and the Royal Bank, the two oldest Edinburgh banks and save in this respect deadly rivals, forced it into voluntary liquidation. All the company's debts were paid, although not without destroying Livingston's fortune made in the Low Countries and considerably restricting Mowat's credit. In those days, however, local patriotism was strong, and after the Town Council had warned the citizens not to accept the notes of some of the banks in the south, a second Aberdeen Banking Company was floated in 1766 with a capital of £72,000 in £500 shares, of which £200 was paid up. This Bank was an amazing success. It maintained a dividend of 8 per cent, and paid bonuses which raised its £30,000 of issued capital to £200,000 in 1836, with a reserve fund of £50,000. Its shares in that year were worth £3,000 each. But it fell a little later upon evil days. By 1848, when its capital of £300,000 came to be resubscribed in accordance with its founding articles, only £7,048 was forthcoming, and the Bank was taken over in 1849 by the Union Bank, which offered 44s. in shares of its own for each share of the Aberdeen Banking Company. The Aberdeen Bank head office, on the site of the Earl Marischal's house, remained the Union Bank's principal office in Aberdeen until it was merged in the Bank of Scotland in recent times.

The success of the Aberdeen Bank led in 1778 to the establishment of a rival local concern, the Commercial Banking Company of Aberdeen. Its shares were of the value of £500 and its prosperity such that they were worth £12,000 each in 1826. But it predeceased the Aberdeen Bank and was taken over by the National Bank of Scotland in 1833. In 1780 the Bank of Scotland, after several vain attempts to attain a foothold in Aberdeen, started a branch in the city which has had an uninterrupted existence since. In 1825, while banks were booming owing to low rates of interest, a third local bank, the Town and County, was founded with a capital that within a few months stood at £750,000 in 1,500 shares of £500 each, £100 paid up. It had a prosperous and uneventful career until 1908, when, with a paid up capital of £252,000, a reserve fund of £135,000, and a net profit that had been over 30 per cent since 1875, it was amalgamated with the youngest of the Aberdeen banks, the North of Scotland, which had been founded in 1836 by Alexander Anderson. The capital of the North Bank was fixed originally at £1 million in 50,000 shares of £20 each with £5 paid up. It could not be expected that much respect to convention would be paid in the conduct of a bank whose operations were inspired by a man of such daring as Alexander Anderson, and in 1848 the Bank was seriously, almost fatally involved in the hectic railway finance of that time. It emerged safely minus a great part of its capital and Alexander Anderson, and it survived more easily the great herring-curing crisis of 1885–7, when the careless methods of the curers in regard to their contracts for the season's supplies of herring ended in irretrievable ruin for many of them. At the amalgamation with the Town and County Bank, the North Bank's paid up capital was £400,000, its reserves £222,000, its general business 25 per cent greater than the other's, and its net profits, with the exception of the years of the curing crisis, had not been less than 40 per cent and had eventually climbed to 62 per cent.

There was one branch of commerce in which Aberdeen gained an unenviable notoriety, although other Scottish seaports participated in the traffic. This was the kidnapping of children and the selling of them into slavery in the North American plantations. In the early part of the eighteenth century Aberdeen had considerable communication with North America, several of her ships and merchants being engaged in the transatlantic trade. In order to augment the gains accruing from their legitimate dealings, some of the merchants — including several baillies and the town clerk depute — organised a system of enticing and kidnapping, their victims being usually but not always young lads, and very often those lads were from the country and therefore the more easily imposed upon by the temptations of the town.

In the five years preceding the outbreak of the Forty-five, it had been estimated that no fewer than 600 unfortunate beings were thus shang-haied into a slavery from which very few ever emerged. On being decoyed into the merchants' power, the lads were herded in a barn which stood in Rennie's Wynd off the Green, or in the cellars of the house in the Green, built by Andrew Aedie (grandfather of Mary Jameson's third husband), who died in 1604, which occupied the site that is now a vacant space on the east side of the steps leading from the Green to Union Street. When those places were full, the victims were put in the burgh workhouse or even in the tolbooth, until the time came for their ship to sail. Their parents might know that they had been trepanned and even came and gazed at them through the windows, but the kidnappers, by virtue of their position, were too powerful to be assailed and indeed one aggrieved father who attempted to raise an action could not find a sheriff's officer in Aberdeen who would under-take to cite the defendants.

Although the traffic was a matter of common knowledge, retribution was not exacted from the offenders until many years after the scandal had ceased. In 1758 there appeared in Aberdeen a discharged soldier, by name Peter Williamson, a native of Hirnley in Aboyne, who as a 'rough, ragged, humle-headed, long, stourie, clever boy' had been kidnapped in 1741. He had lived a life of amazing adventure since he was enslaved, and on being discharged from the army he had contrived to have his experiences printed at York in a chap book which he pro-ceeded to hawk through the streets of Aberdeen. The magistrates, considering this a libellous aspersion upon the fair name of Bonaccord, had him apprehended and sentenced to be imprisoned, fined and banished from the burgh. But Peter was a tough sow to take by the lug. In Edinburgh he enlisted legal sympathy and aid, raised an action in 1762 against the baillies, in which he was awarded £100 damages and £80 costs, the defenders to be personally liable for payment. The magistrates, however, persuaded Lord Findlater, who was then the patron of the town, to use the salvage money accruing from wrecked vessels of which account had to be made to him as Lord High Admiral of Scotland, to pay the damages and costs. Williamson next raised a civil action against the baillies who had kidnapped him and in 1768 was awarded £200 damages and 100 guineas costs. The defenders tried every possible ruse to evade the sentence. They pretended to agree to an arbitration by the sheriff-substitute of Aberdeenshire and then filled that functionary so drunk that they induced him to give an award in their favour which, however, the Court of Session set aside.

This limb of the law deserves a paragraph to himself, for he was greater than Falstaff in Falstaff's greatest occupation. The day before he gave the award he 'sate close drinking, as the phrase is in that part of the country, *helter-skelter*, that is copiously and alternately, of different liquors till eleven o'clock at night, when, being dead drunk, he was conveyed home by his two maid servants'. By nine the next morning he was at it again, 'a large dose of spirits, white wine and punch was administered to him, with cooling draughts of porter from time to time'. In the afternoon, having dined, he played cards, 'drinking at the same time, *helter-skelter*, a bottle and a half of Malaga, a mug of porter, two bottles of claret, a mutchkin and a half of rum made into punch'.

Peter Williamson prospered in Edinburgh, where he settled down as a banker — he issued bank notes; a wine merchant — he styled himself in the sign over his tavern door 'Peter Williamson, Vintner from the Other World'; a publisher — he produced Edinburgh's first directory; and a postmaster — for to him belongs the honour of having established the penny post in the Scottish capital, which in his case flourished so well in the city of Edinburgh that eventually the General Post Office took it over on payment of an ample solatium.

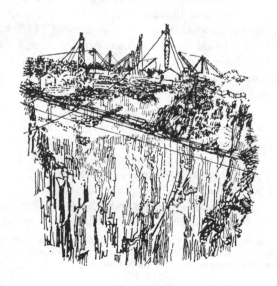

CHAPTER FIVE

The Harbour

In 1809, which is a convenient date for fixing the division between the old and the modern port of Aberdeen, the appearance of the harbour area was very different from that which it presents today. The most striking feature of change is in the course of the River Dee. Above Wellington Bridge its channel was as now, but immediately below the bridge it ran due north for half a mile, to a point opposite the railway goods yard behind Upper Quay today. There it took a sharp right-angle bend due east, through what is now the Albert Basin, past what is now Provost Matthews' Quay, into what is now the tidal harbour opposite the south-east end of No. 3 Pontoon Dock, and thereafter out to sea by the present-day navigation channel.

Opposite the pontoon dock the river was joined by a spillage channel or 'little water', as it would be called up-river. This stream wandered back through what are now the dock gates and skirting what are now Waterloo, Regent and Trinity Quays, received the waters of the Pow Creek that ran through the town from the Powis area, of the Millburn from the Loch area and beyond, and of the Denburn,[1] and swept round southwards at what is now the junction of Market Street and Guild Street to a broad lagoon opposite but about 200 yards east of South College Street between Marywell Street and Portland Street. This spillage was in fact equivalent to Aberdeen's original harbour.

Between the river and the spillage channel lay an extensive expanse of mudbanks, shoals, and inches, in shape somewhat like a man's foot seen from the side, threequarters of a mile long from east to west and a quarter of a mile broad from north to south at its widest part. It covered the whole of Victoria Dock, the quays on the south side of it, the Upper Dock, the Upper Quay and the railway goods yard. The biggest piece of dry land not submerged by the spring tides was a pear-shaped inch stretching south-westwards from the foot of Marischal Street to a point behind A. R. Gray's buildings in the south-east corner of the goods

1 The Denburn in 1661 had entered the harbour about Palmerston Road. A century later it debouched from a marsh where the Joint Station now stands into the harbour north of its old mouth.

yard. There was another inch from Regent Road along the line of Commercial Quay to beyond Black's Lane.

On the south side of the Dee in 1809 the whole Albert Basin area from Point Law to Poynernook Road was liable to tidal inundations, which might extend as far south as Wellington Bridge and over the line of what is now South Esplanade West. A large fig-shaped inch above the tidal level lay between the junction of Poynernook Road and Stell Road and a point in the present river channel 200 yards north of Craiginches prison. A small water ran from the southern point of this large inch north-eastwards to Clyde Street, where it had a backwater stretching 300 yards due west to Stell Road. The small water rejoined the river at Albert Jetty No. 2. Another small channel extended from Albert Jetty No. 4 to what is now Torry Harbour, which was then a shoal, like most of the area north of Greyhope Road.

The successive additions and alterations which transformed the aspect of the harbour may be briefly detailed, on a topographical rather than a historical survey, proceeding from the north side of the harbour entrance round to the South Breakwater. Some account of the general schemes of improvement which embodied the various pieces of construction will be given later.

The North Pier from what is now the south-east end of the Lifeboat Jetty for a stretch east and east-north-east of 1,200 feet, was built between 1775 and 1781. At its most westerly part the pier is 20 feet wide at the base, 12 at the top and 16 feet high, but farther east it broadens to 36 feet at the base, 24 on top and 30 feet in height. The stone is granite. A further 800 feet was added in 1810–16, the time taken being due to damage caused by storms, which even before 1800 on the much shorter and less exposed pier had been responsible for almost incessant repair work. It cost nearly £7,000 to keep the pier serviceable between 1827 and 1831. The final extension, made practicable by the construction of the South Breakwater, added a further 500 feet or thereby, built in 1874–9. This part of the pier has a base width of 120 feet, in 15 feet of water at low tide. The foundation was composed of 40-ton bags of half-liquid concrete and reached to within 2 feet of the surface at low tide. Thereon were deposited the concrete foundations in blocks of 600 tons weight. The pier is built of Bay of Nigg stone and gravel and Hill of Balnagask sand, there being a prejudice (puzzling to the modern economic theorist) in favour of using as much local material as possible. The pier is surmounted by a parapet at either side and rounded off with a lighthouse and fog bell at the extreme tip.

Abercrombie's (first called Smeaton's) Jetty, its present name commemorating the surveyor in charge of its construction, was built 50 yards out into the navigation channel in 1789. In 1820 it was curtailed to a stub of 20 yards, on which there is now a light. A capstan was mounted on the stub to enable ships to be warped up-channel against the wind. The Lifeboat Jetty and House were built in 1889. Pocra Quay, some 200 yards long, was constructed in 1826–31, a jetty, known as the Lower Jetty, at its south-eastern end, being removed in 1832. In 1886 a wharf was built for coping with the Canadian cattle trade, and a cattle sale-ring was provided behind the quay in 1890. The pontoon dock, No. 3, at the north-western extremity of the quay, was constructed in 1911. There was a dock for building and repairing ships before 1661 at the spot where Hall, Russell and Company (founded 1865) have their shipyards today. The first Dock Gates, substantially on the present site, were erected in 1844–8. In 1879 it became necessary to renew the gates, which had been damaged by sea fauna and general wear and tear. New hydraulic gates were erected in 1883–8, the cill of the south entrance being deepened to give 26 feet of draught at high water.

The wall of Waterloo Quay was begun in 1811 and by 1834 the quay had a continuous wharf. Between the end of Canal Terrace and Commerce Street lay, until 1853, the rectangular terminus of the Aberdeenshire Canal. The Canal Company first took shape in 1795, and by three Acts of Parliament in 1796, 1801, and 1809, authority was obtained to raise sufficient money to meet the cost of the canal, £44,000. The canal was 18¼ miles long, and extended from just inside the bend of the Don at Inverurie, the village of Port Elphinstone being created by the undertaking, to Waterloo Quay, just east of the beginning of Regent Quay. The canal's course through Aberdeen from Haudagain followed the line of Great Northern Road through Woodside (which was then not a village but a few houses west of Deer Road or Barron Street) to the Boathouse, two miles from the terminus, where passengers had to alight. Thereafter to the sea there were many locks, especially alongside Elmbank Road. At Mounthooly there was a wharf. At Nelson Street there was a bridge and a site for repairing barges. Beyond King Street green sloping banks to the canal were used for bleaching and drying clothes by conscientious housewives, and for the stealing of textiles by their less provident sisters.[1] These slopes were also communal wash-

1   These socialistic ladies had their Communist left wing who even took the clothes off the little girls who were sometimes set to watch their mothers' washing.

places. The clothes were placed in tubs and tramped in the water there by women with their skirts kilted — the Aberdeen variety of the wine-press.

A bridge crossed the canal at Park Street, called the Thieves' Briggie, but not the authentic bridge of sighs of earlier days which led to the gallows and which lay a furlong south spanning the Powcreek burn. Thence by three final locks the canal descended to the harbour rim. Alongside the canal's terminal lay the Lime Basin, covering what is now the south end of Waterloo Station, where ships discharged cargoes of limestone, then much in demand by farmers throughout Aberdeenshire. The Lime Basin was filled up in 1835, a year after the Canal was joined to the harbour by a sea-lock. In 1853 the canal was given over to the Great North of Scotland Railway Company, and Waterloo Station, eventually for goods only but at first a general purposes terminus, was built where the canal ended.

Waterloo Quay was variously improved, widened and strengthened in 1848 and 1868, for the excavation of the later-named Victoria Dock in 1829–34 and the filling-in of the old harbour greatly enhanced Waterloo Quay's importance. It was in 1848 that Queen Victoria and the Prince Consort made their first visit to Aberdeen, travelling in the royal yacht. It was at Waterloo Quay that the august vessel was moored, and it was claimed that in no other harbour in her dominions at that time could her Majesty have landed without the intermediary of a boat. Other improvements of the quay were made in 1884 and 1914–17.

The frontage of Regent Quay was completed in 1834 after the old Regent Bridge had been built in 1832. A bridge had been planned at this point much earlier in the century, but instead a wooden bridge was erected at the foot of Shore Brae spanning the old harbour and enabling horse traffic to cross over to the Inches and dump earth and rubble there from the town. There was further work on Regent Quay at the end of last century and in the first decade of this.

Trinity Quay had originally stretched from Shore Brae in a wide, long arc round to Poynernook. In 1827–34 it was completely recast over its whole length. In the process an interesting discovery was made in 1832 about the end of present day Exchange Street, where the Trinity Hospital stood, of an old oak tree a few inches below the surface of the soil, the trunk 6 feet in length and 20 in girth and two branches respectively 23 feet 6 inches and 9 feet 7 inches long. This may have been one of the trees[1] brought down from Drum by the earliest boat-builders

1   There is another theory that the tree had been washed down by a spate and cast up where or near where it was found by the flooded Dee.

to whom the Town Council at the beginning of the seventeenth century gave Trinity Monastery's burial-ground as a shipyard. The tree, after being set up for some years on the Inches, was removed to Duthie Park.

Like its neighbour, Trinity Quay has been much altered since its big remodelling, but its character was changed altogether by the building of Market Street in 1842. Three years later, when the Aberdeen Railway Act was passed, it was seen that much readjustment would be required west of the Trinity Quay. That Act, which applied to an east coast railway from the south, embodied a terminus in Hadden Street, 80 yards west of Market Street, with some intention of using the Newmarket buildings as the station. The whole of the area between Market Street and Guild Street was bought for this purpose, and Trinity congregation purchased the Marischal Street theatre for their church. The line of railway was to cross Trinity Quay by a bridge and run through the Poynernook area of the old harbour.

In 1831 the Raik dyke which prevented water from the Dee from flowing past Torry was opened up. This caused a considerable fall in the volume of the main stream and greatly facilitated the making of the Victoria Dock, which cost about £122,000 to construct. Provost Blaikie's Quay was built in 1834 and much improved in 1850 and 1907–10, Provost Matthews' Quay in 1885–8 rounded off the point of what had now become a solid promontory in place of shoals and mudflats. Provost Jamieson's Quay was erected in the early eighties, Upper Quay being already in existence and South Market Street having been driven south-east to the new (present) channel of the Dee which had been diverted in 1870–3.

Victoria Bridge was opened for traffic on 2 July 1881. The building of the bridge had been enforced by a dreadful disaster on 5 April 1876, one of Aberdeen's black days. The day was a Fast Day and regarded as a general holiday. The easiest means of crossing the Dee was by ferryboat from Point Law at a spot still marked by Ferry Place. The boat, whose normal load was thirty persons, was hauled across on a wire rope. On this day sixty people crowded into the craft, their weight tilted the boat in midstream and she was swamped. Thirty-three people were drowned.

The new Fish Market stretching along Commercial Quay for half its length was opened in 1889 and extended along Palmerston Quay in 1892 and into the line of Albert Quay in 1894. The first of the Albert Quay wharves were constructed in 1873–5, forming the southern wall of Albert Basin, which took the place of the old channel of the Dee.

The existing frontage for the most part and the four easternmost jetties belong to 1932–3, but the two pontoon docks were made in 1899 and 1908. The basin itself was redone in 1907–9. As its northern side the great graving dock built in 1882–6 at a cost of £50,000 was removed in 1924–7.

The tip of Point Law was removed in the early years of this century, during which Provost Mearns's Quay was built. As that improvement was being completed, the Blockhouse Jetty across the river was built, and then Provost Maitland's Quay, enclosing the River Dee Dock No. 1, was made in 1909–15. Beside it the ship-building yard of Messrs. Lewis opened in 1916. To the east of it Torry harbour had been trimly enclosed by its quay since 1898.

In 1812 a commencement was made with the building of the first or old South Breakwater, which extended 800 feet northwards to within 250 feet of the end of the North Pier then. It cost £14,000 and was complete in 1815. But the contemplated further extension of the North Pier required that the South Breakwater be sited farther east and accordingly in 1869 the present breakwater was begun. At the land end the foundation was of concrete blocks in frames, but where the base ran under water great spars of Oregon pine costing £55 apiece were set up to form a staging along which wagons carried mammoth sacks of semi-liquid concrete and dropped them in place within the area of the staging. In 1872 80 the old breakwater was removed as far back as low-water mark. In 1874 the new breakwater, of a total length of 1,050 feet and having cost £78,000, was complete save for the light-tower at the tip, which was in position by 1877.

The only important part of the harbour not due to local effort or initiative is Girdleness Lighthouse, which was built by the Commissioners of the Northern Lights and first sent forth its rays at sunset on 15 October 1833. To begin with the lights were fixed, but in 1890 the revolving light, giving two flashes every 20 seconds and visible in normal conditions at 19 sea-miles, was substituted.

Such in brief outline is the tale of the physical expansion of Aberdeen harbour, and the map of 1746 printed by G. and W. Paterson, which shows the layout at the end of the Jacobite Rebellions, differs as much from Parson Gordon's plan of 1661 as from a modern map of the port. These great changes in the harbour's aspect were brought about by a series of improvement schemes of which we have the first beginnings in the appointment in 1751 of a harbour overseer, forerunner of the harbour engineer and harbour-master, to control the practice of dumping ballast and to regulate the berthing of ships. In 1742 the fish market was removed from the Laich Cross in the Castlegate to the top of the harbour.[1] But during the eighteenth century the usefulness of the harbour was steadily curtailed by the shifting northwards of the channel of the Dee, and the narrowing of the waterway in consequence, and the loss of depth[2] due to the constant intrusion of sand and silt from both sea and river.

In 1770 the Town Council, still the proprietors of the harbour, approached John Smeaton, the most distinguished harbour engineer of his day, to inspect and report. He it was who in due course recommended the construction of the North Pier to ward off the sand thrown into the harbour entrance by north-east winds. His scheme was authorised by an Act of Parliament of 1773. Another harbour bill was carried through in 1797 after consultations with John Rennie, architect of the London Docks, but nothing much was done about it and several years of abortive planning followed. In 1810 the great engineer, Thomas Telford, submitted an extensive scheme which had a difficult passage through Parliament but achieved the distinction of inspiring the most celebrated dinner in Aberdeen between that which King Malcolm gave to the Viking Sweyn in the twelfth century and the gargantuan repast served to members of the University by the first Lord Strathcona in 1908. The harbour dinner of 1810 cost £2 19s. 6d. a head — well over £20 in our degenerate days — and the most doughty opponent of the scheme, who attended the function, took three months to recover from its effects. Telford's recommendations resulted in the extension of the North Pier by 800 feet and the deepening of the channel at the harbour entrance to 20 feet. The first South Breakwater was initiated in 1812 by John Gibb, who was appointed resident harbour engineer.

The building of Market Street in 1842 and its extension as South Market Street brought to an end an earlier attempt to expedite the work of the city by bringing the quays to industry rather than the products of industry to the quays. Trinity Quay had been produced southwards by two wharves, forming a kind of double ellipse or crescent, stretching as far as Poynernook. One of these curves, running through the site of what is now the railway goods yard nearly opposite the east end of the Joint Station, discharged coal for the adjacent gasworks. The other fronting the claybank that rose between what are now Portland and Affleck Streets, afforded facilities for the loading of the bricks fired by

1   For its subsequent history see p. 450
2   Opposite the Weigh House the depth of the harbour actually fell to 7 feet.

the Clayhills brickworks. These extensions were surrendered to the Aberdeen Railway Company after the passing of the Aberdeen Railway Act of 1845. In 1843 a plan by the harbour engineer James Abernethy, for the development of the harbour at its western end, went through Parliament, but the Railway Act of 1845 clashed with the scheme, since the railway company intended to have its terminus in the corner between Market Street and Guild Street. When this intention was altered and the Aberdeen Railway fixed upon the present station site, the Harbour Commissioners, who had come into existence through an Act of 1829, had to resist a proposal which would have extended the railway's jurisdiction over part of the inches and the harbour also. Eventually a compromise was reached. The western limit of the harbour was the line for the newly built Upper and Market Quays, and the Commissioners, in return for the loss of the land beyond, were left in complete possession of the inches.

Until the end of the eighteenth century the management of the harbour was vested in the Town Council who were the proprietors. In 1810, however, the Act embodying Telford's scheme also incorporated a new method of administration. Although a demand by the political party of the Left in those days, the Radical Reformers, that two-thirds of the Committee of Management should be directly elected by the citizens was turned down, the magistrates agreed to the appointment of seven auditors with large revisionary powers over the Town Council's administration of the harbour. In 1828 the Radicals succeeded in throwing out a harbour bill which did not provide for a majority of directly elected members. In 1829 a new Act changed the whole system. Nine members of the Council, five Guild burgesses and one representative of the Incorporated Trades were designated the managing body.

CHAPTER SIX

Public Institutions and Services

On the eve of the last and most ambitious of the Jacobite insurrections, an institution was built upon George Jamesone's Four-Neukit Garden in Woolmanhill which has had a numerous progeny and a splendid history. It was in 1739 that the idea, and in 1740 that the structure of Aberdeen Infirmary first took shape. For some time the Town Council had been toying with unwontedly humanitarian thoughts. Their chief worry for centuries had been disease. On many occasions when plague threatened, the Council had taken control of the community and regulated the burgh like a beleaguered city, closing and guarding the ports, hanging or banishing visitors and their hosts, and segregating the afflicted in miserable hovels on the links.

Apart from provision against plague and leprosy the care of the sick had devolved upon the Church. Many of the monasteries before the Reformation had hospitals attached, and the Reformed Church, whose funds, after the Crown and the lairds had their pickings, were much less ample, had done what it could. But as civilisation ages, both diseases and its awareness of diseases increase, and by 1739 it was imperative that Aberdeen, like other big towns, should have a capacious hospital of some kind. To begin with the Town Council's scheme envisaged a combination of poorhouse and poor's hospital, and in fact the Earl of Aberdeen's old house adjoining the Townhouse was purchased in that year and converted into a hospital for the indigent. Its master, appointed in 1742, was a clever, capable and industrious person, but 'small in stature, of mean appearance, a peevish temper, and parsimonious habits', Thomas Man by name (1700–61), who is today remembered, if at all, for far other reasons than his post in the Castlegate. To his hospital he did indeed bequeath the residue of his estate, £95, but his *Memoirs of Scottish Affairs*, of which only one section of 72 pages was ever printed, but more is in manuscript in the National Library, is his enduring monument amongst antiquarians, whilst his temerity in challenging Thomas Ruddiman the grammarian's classical attainments brought down upon him the vituperation of that worthy son of Banff-shire and the laughter of his contemporaries.

It was immediately clear that the Castlegate institution was not to be sufficient and the larger and more permanent project of the Infirmary was at once put in hand. After Man's death the Poor's Hospital was closed, and its inmates and their successors in need received a small sum monthly in their homes. The Council contributed its patronage to the Infirmary property, the site for the building and a garden — in which a cow was kept for long to provide milk for the patients — and the promise of an annual subscription. Subscriptions from benevolent citizens and country gentry made up the £500 needed to build the hospital. The foundation stone was laid on New Year's Day 1740, and the first patients were admitted in August 1742, the managers then having scarcely enough funds to meet the charges of five or six people. Dr. James Gordon, Professor of Medicine in Marischal College, was appointed physician and surgeon at a remuneration of 10 guineas a year, with a mistress of the household at a salary of £4 to watch over the creature comforts of the four patients who were first to be admitted. There were twenty-one patients in all in the first year. Between August 1742 and November 1750, when it became necessary to make the first extension of the building, 228 patients were received of whom 160 were cured, 52 sent home as incurable and 16 died. In 1748 the managers approached the Synod to assist in raising contributions, and the ministers of the parishes in the surrounding counties spoke from their pulpits, and so not only helped the Infirmary's income then, but also established a connection which continued with great mutual benefit down to the darker days of Beveridge and Bevan.

The first extension, a wing with sixty additional beds, was completed in 1755 and cost £500. This wing contained an operating room. In 1758 a second wing was added at a similar cost. In 1773 a royal charter was obtained. Three physicians attended at the institution, while a house surgeon doubled the duties of his branch of medical science with that of an apothecary and compounded the medicines prescribed by the physicians. The affairs of the Infirmary were administered with great prudence and economy and considerable funds laid aside in capital account. On the professional side, proof of its efficiency is shown in the figures of 923 patients, 51 operations,[1] 623 complete cures, and only 42 deaths in 1816. By 1839 the Infirmary, despite new buildings in 1818

---

1 Four patients out of five cut for the stone recovered. 'The fifth after the danger of the operation was over, and after the lapse of five weeks died of inflammation of the stomach.' Even then the operation could be successful yet the patient died!

and 1833, was both too small and out-of-date, so a completely new building was erected on the same site by 1840, at a cost of £16,700. Even that accommodation had fallen behind the times in 1887 when Queen Victoria's Jubilee was utilised to collect £30,000, with which the hospital was expanded to 240 beds and otherwise improved. These additions were opened by Princess Louise (then Marchioness of Lorne) on 4 October 1892. A convalescent home was started at Lochhead in 1873, later transferred to Cults.

When the Infirmary was opened part of it was set aside for lunatics, who were incarcerated, if violent, in stone-paved cells, and taken out to have their heads soused under the water falling below the lower mill of Gilcomston. In 1798 it was apparent that the two institutions should be separated, and with a timeous legacy coming in, a piece of land was feued at the Barkmill, the site of the present Royal Mental Hospital, and a building of sorts run up. This shanty was replaced by the older part of the existing building, accommodating fifty patients, in 1819. Elmhill, for wealthier patients, was built in 1860.

In 1781 the work of the Infirmary was taken outwith the actual institution by the appointment of a physician to attend the sick poor in their homes. In this connection it was deemed expedient to erect a dispensary which could deal with patients whose ailments did not demand their admission to the Infirmary. For a few years the dispensary subsisted on allowances from Infirmary funds, but in 1786 it also was placed upon direct private munificence. The physician attended at stated hours to examine and prescribe for patients, who received medicine gratis. At the beginning of the nineteenth century the original dispensary was passing through annually between 600 and 700 patients, and two other dispensaries were dealing with even greater numbers. Besides these, a vaccine institution was set up in 1803 to vaccinate children against smallpox, and in a dozen years no fewer than 5,000 children were submitted to its ministrations. In 1823 a 'General Dispensary, Vaccine and Lying-in Institution' was founded which had several homes in the town before it finally came to rest in 1870 in Provost Abercrombie's house in the Guestrow, along with Provost Walker's house adjoining. The latter was for a short time used for maternity cases. In 1828 the 'Honourable The County Club' of Aberdeen, which flourished from 1718 to 1876, gave £21 to assist the funds of the Ophthalmic Institution, and every year thereafter until the Club itself closed down, except 1833 and 1834, 5 guineas went to the same cause. The promoters were Drs. Skene, Moir, French and Dyce, and it would seem that Sir James McGrigor was also active in the foundation. The first surgeon was Dr. Cadenhead, who had had London experience, and served in the Institution until 1862. It had several homes, and was in 1854–63 at Crown Court, Upperkirkgate in the Dispensary premises. An Asylum for the Blind, founded on a bequest of £7,000 from Miss Christian Cruickshank, a member of a well-known Aberdeen family, was opened in 1843, and in Huntly Street found training and work for a hundred persons thus afflicted. The Asylum turns out about 12,000 mattresses a year and many other articles of upholstery and in basket-making and kindred crafts.

The provision of an operating theatre in the Infirmary was a boon to medical students, who to begin with paid two guineas a year for the privilege of being present with the physicians and surgeons. At that time little instruction in medicine was given at either college, and the students themselves had made arrangements to study anatomy extra-murally in discreet houses. In 1831 they feued a piece of land and built an anatomical theatre in St. Andrew Street, where they dissected human remains procured by means best known to themselves. The neighbours were aware of their activities, for the building was popularly known as the 'Burkin' Hoose', Burke and Hare still being fresh in the public memory, but the students were not interfered with until a dog was found at the back of the premises gnawing a piece of a human body. A mob broke in, found three more cadavers, which were taken to Drum's Aisle, and the Burkin' Hoose was forthwith committed to the flames.

When the Poor's Hospital in the Castlegate was given over and the indigent received small subsistence allowances at home, there was initiated a rudimentary form of public assistance. By the beginning of the nineteenth century over 900 people were receiving £400 monthly, while the care of orphans was absorbing £200 a year more. At that time the orphan boys were accommodated in the old workhouse, being admitted when eight years old, taught the three R's and the principles of religion, and kept there until they were thirteen years of age. Forty boys were in the house at a time and cost about 5 guineas each annually. In 1815 a soup kitchen was established which provided at the outset for nearly 500 daily recipients.

Among other and later institutions of the kind was the Female Orphan Asylum which was founded in Albyn Place about 1840 by an Aberdeen lady, Mrs. Emslie, who spent £16,000 upon her benevolence in her lifetime and left to it ample funds at her death. About fifty girls were trained in it at a time, mostly as domestic servants, and it performed a useful function for about half a century. In 1892 the building was disposed of to the School Board, and it became the nucleus for the High School for Girls, which until then was located in Little Belmont Street.

Of a somewhat different type and under municipal auspices was the Bridewell, which was erected under Act of Parliament, the magistrates and landed proprietors of the county being designated commissioners and powers being granted to levy a rate to defray expenses. Sums of £7,000 and £5,000 were borrowed to build the institution in Rose Street, which was completed in 1809. It was intended as a house of correction for petty delinquents, the object being to give them a fresh start in life by removing them from evil associations and by training them in useful industry. The main interest in the place today, apart from the modernity of its conception, lies in the sumptuousness of its architecture and the advanced character of its equipment. With its imposing entrance from Union Street, its elegant gateway, porter's lodge and guardhouse, and its 14-foot wall enclosing a garden and exercise grounds, it was perhaps the first example in Aberdeen of the extravagant elaboration in rate-supported institutions which is today a commonplace. The Bridewell had five floors, the topmost being a hospital, while the rest contained eleven rooms for working and fourteen dormitories, the whole being warmed by steam, probably the first appearance in Aberdeen of central heating. The building and equipment cost £10,000, the annual expenditure was £420, the annual assessment (which also covered interest and sinking fund in the building debt) £1,116, divided equally between town and county, and during a year some 120 prisoners would be catered for, who earned about £2 a head towards their own maintenance.

Two cognate institutions, both of which survive, one in its original character and the other absorbed into the corpus of the Welfare State, originated in the 1830s. One was a House of Refuge for old people at Oakbank and the other a Reformatory for delinquent youths at Oldmill. Subsequently they exchanged their functions. Both owed their inception to Alexander Anderson, later Aberdeen's great provost, administering the estate and carrying out the wishes of his uncle, Dr. George Watt of Old Deer, who after a lifetime of general practice left a fortune of about £40,000, some of which no doubt launched both Anderson and his cousin George Smith ('Chicago Smith') on their remarkable careers.

Closely connected with the physical and moral health of the public are two other aspects of local administration which have been retained for the most part under municipal control — water supplies and sewage. In the early days the water supply became a matter of importance to the Town Council because the frequency of famine compelled the community to equip itself with mills for the provision of its essential stocks of meal, and those mills depended for their efficiency upon an adequate flow of water to drive them. The location of many medieval mills in Aberdeen determined the general lines of the earliest water supplies. The first water supply, used probably to drive mills where Stafford Street now is and also at the junction of the Guestrow and Netherkirkgate, came from the West or Gilcomston burn and perhaps the Spital burn. Traces of the course of a channel have been found which ultimately crossed the line of Union Street and Exchequer Row and dropped down the brae to the line of Virginia Street, where the Denburn used to run. This water-course was no doubt quite open, and ran down the sides of streets in Aberdeen's early days.

Some time before 1438 a second supply of water was required, and found in the Denburn, from which an open channel was taken at a point where the Gilcomston dam was later formed. This stream was partly open as late as the middle of last century, and drove the wheel of a wool mill in Leadside Road, opposite where Grosvenor Place now issues. It then ran down by Jack's Brae (named after John Jack, farmer at Gilcomston in 1750) through Gilcomston village to Baker Street, past the end of Gilcomston Steps (so called after the series of large stones in a mill lade there), and it still runs under the first house in Skene Square and crosses the railway in an overhead pipe. At Loch Street it widened into a dam which was separated from the original Loch by a bank. On its further journey southwards it drove a mill at Barnett's Close, the Upper Mill of the town, which was still functioning in 1865, and an iron plate where the Netherkirkgate and St. Nicholas Street meet denoted the site of the Little Bow Brig over the burn. Near here the stream divided. The west branch ran by Correction Wynd and was used in the Correction House there; it rejoined the east branch, which had meantime driven the Mid Mill, standing in the middle of Union Street opposite the Commercial Bank but at a lower level, before flowing down to Exchange Street to drive the Nether Mill. The presence of the stream was the reason for the building of the first house in Union Street between Market Street and Union Bridge; it was erected by a druggist over the burn so that he could use the water for power to grind drugs.

In 1632 the need for still more water was felt, but both then and fifty years later when the subject came up again circumstances prevented a scheme from being undertaken. One of the difficulties was the reduced population and its inability to stand additional assessments, owing to the depredations of war and plague. In 1706, however, it was decided to bring water from Carden's Well, which still exists on the east side of Carden House,[1] and which used to be known as the 'Tea Wallie', because water used to be carried from it to make tea when that beverage was still novel enough to be considered a luxury. The water, which the well supplies at three gallons a minute, was carried in a pipe down to a point opposite where Black's Buildings were, then to the east end of Schoolhill where there was a stone cistern; there the water was divided between two pipes, one of which went up the Upper Kirkgate to supply a well at the south end of Broad Street, and the cistern well in the Castlegate. The other pipe supplied a cistern well at the head of Carnegie's Brae in the Netherkirkgate, whence the 'Wallace' or 'Wellhouse' Tower, and went down to replenish other wells in the Green and at the Shore.

The needs of the city expanded so rapidly that yet another augmentation of the water supply was found necessary in 1742. A spring where 37 Desswood Place now stands was brought into service, and gave five gallons a minute which were carried by pipe to the Carden's Well cistern. Fountainhall House took its name from this spring. In 1766 more water was taken from the now non-existent Gilcomston Burn which rose in a well on the south side of Morningfield Road and cistern houses for this supply were built, among other places, on the south side, near the east end, of Carlton Place, where a skating pond was later formed; and another on the north side of Desswood Place, which was shifted in 1905 to the Duthie Park. This supply was conveyed by pipe to the Broad Street cistern in front of Greyfriars Kirk, and it increased the total produce of water for the burgh's use to twenty-six gallons a minute. In 1769 the Broad Street cistern was converted into a large reservoir, which formed the upper part of a waterhouse that was not demolished until 1902. This house had a pediment gable and a clock (which in 1902 was removed to the City Hospital), and the lower part of the house, which came to be used to store workmen's tools, was

1 It is most unlikely that Carden takes its names from Cardanus, the famous Italian physician of the sixteenth century, who is conjectured to have visited Aberdeen. As there is another Cardenwell and several Cardens in Aberdeenshire, the name most likely had a Gaelic derivation.

separated from the upper by a couple of wooden floors a foot apart. The story is that a workman, observing the reservoir floor to be leaky, gave it a coating of tar, which gave Aberdeen's water a fine flavour for a few days, but which failed to seal the leak; and a second floor was therefore made.

Towards the end of the century many other smaller schemes were employed to increase the supply. A spring called the Gilcomston between Baker Street and Calton Terrace provided several additional gallons, and by lowering the outlet pipe past the well that addition became still greater. Hazlehead's capacity was canvassed, eventually more water was taken from the Denburn, while after the opening of the Aberdeen-Inverurie Canal in 1805, water was got there for washing for one district of the town. About the same time all the new houses west of Union Bridge were being built with pump wells of their own or common to a group of residences. There were also the Angel Well on the site of Hanover Street School; the chalybeate Firhill Well, issuing from a sandhill, now demolished, off Sunnybank Road and College Bounds; the Corbie Well, in Union Terrace Gardens, of much repute for its cooling draughts the morning after before the age of Seidlitz powders; St. John's Well, shifted in 1885 to a place under the stair leading down to the Hardweird; St. Mary's at the foot of Affleck Street; and the almost classically famous Well of Spa, chalybeate like the Firhill, which originally issued on the west side of Spa Street 50 to 100 yards from the Upper Denburn, was buried by a spate in 1650, rebuilt with an inscription by Baillie Alexander Skene in 1670, over-whelmed a second time when its supply was cut off by the building of the railway, and at last transferred to the east side of Spa Street and fed by a pipe from the Gilcomston Well at Calton Terrace. These devices together raised Aberdeen's available supply to 100 gallons a minute.

Two circumstances connected with those developments deserve mention. In 1791 the Superintendent of Edinburgh Waterworks was asked to report upon a new supply, and advised the use of wooden pipes as being cheaper but likely to last thirty years, and because they were used in London and Edinburgh. Aberdeen Town Council was, however, unimpressed by the fashions of the two capitals, and insisted upon iron. The second circumstance is that the Town Council's Bill for a water supply in 1794 was opposed by the citizens themselves on the ground that if the water accounts had been kept properly, it would have been shown that previous water debts had already been paid, whereas the Bill assumed that they had still to be wiped off. This salutary scrutiny of Town Council administration prevailed and the Bill did not pass.

After the dry summer of 1826 the Water Commissioners, who since an Act of 1795 had been responsible for the burgh's water supply, began prospecting again, and after considering the Loch of Skene, the Culter Burn, and even the Aberdeenshire Canal at Stoneywood, decided to use the River Dee. An Act of 1829 gave the requisite authority, and a well was sunk, 660 yards above the Bridge of Dee, in the haughs on the north bank. A house was erected over the well and a tunnel driven along the riverside for 200 yards westwards to collect filtered water. The house, well and tunnel still remain, although the first crude Dee water system has vanished. It supplied a thousand gallons a minute at the new Waterhouse in Union Place (now 478–484 Union Street). It brought to Aberdeen not only water but baths and water-closets. The water had to be pumped up to a height, at the highest part of the town, of 160 feet, and this cost £1,200 a year. At first only six hours' pumping a day was required to supply the needs of the town, but the demand increased so sharply that by 1855 it took twenty-three hours out of every twenty-four to send up the 1,125,000 gallons that early Victorian Aberdeen required.

For many years the local water resources of the city were used to wash away the city's impurities, when rain was not forthcoming in sufficient quantities to act as the cleansing agent. Many of the houses had cesspools in their backyards, or under the pavements. Where there was plenty of space behind the houses there might also be ashpits there, but there seldom was much space and the streets were the great communal middens, with which we have already made acquaintance more than once in this history. In addition to the noisome solids of the midden, however, there were also the equally odoriferous liquids of the gutter. These ran full, summer and winter, down the braes of the Gallowgate, the Kirkgates and the Shiprow. The largest of those streams was known as the Braid Gutter, which carried off the foul waters that flowed down the Gallowgate round the north-eastern end of Marischal College to West North Street and into the Powcreek Burn. Another classic cloacal channel was the Foul Gutter, which crossed the Castlegate from Broad Street and took its course at first no doubt down the Shiprow, but was later enclosed more decently in a square wooden pipe which discharged its burden through Exchequer Court and down the brae into the Denburn which in those days ran at the foot of that slope. For the other parts of the city the Denburn and the Holburn were the chief receptacles of liquid refuse. There was also a sewer carrying off the contents of drains in the Shorelands. But it was more than a decade into the second half of the century before a proper sewerage system was undertaken.

Gas supply is another service introduced by private enterprise which was taken over by the Corporation. The first Aberdeen Gaslight Company was formed in 1824, but the gas was made from oil at a price that was prohibitive to most private houses. In 1828 coal began to be used and at a tariff of 15s. per thousand feet the gas came into more general use. The gas works were at Poynernook, where the Joint Station now stands, and there was a storage gasometer in North Charlotte Street. The company, however, abused its freedom from competition and its high charges at last became intolerable. In the end of 1843 a new gaslight company prospectus was issued from the office of Adam and Anderson (Alexander Anderson's firm), announcing a flotation of a £50,000 concern in £5 shares, the statement being made therein — but unhappily the promoters could not foresee the future of a century ahead — that the 'days of all monopolies' were numbered. This Company's gasworks was in Cotton Street. By the summer of 1845 the new company was advertising gas at 4s. per thousand cubic feet, and the older company, protesting that this was below cost of production, had to follow suit. Anderson's tactics, however, were to smash the old company and this, by further sharp price-cutting, he finally succeeded in doing, and the concerns were amalgamated. In 1871 the company was taken over by the Corporation and the present gasometer was erected in the early nineties.

CHAPTER SEVEN

Schools and Colleges

We left Aberdeen's educational development at the point where Robert
Gordon's Hospital had been founded and built but was still untenanted
save as the lodging of Hanoverian troops, mostly invalids, under the
alias of Fort Cumberland. The inception of this great school, although
the bequest was written in 1729 and the fabric was completed in 1739,
properly belongs to our new and modern period which begins in 1746.
The academic inauguration of the existence of Robert Gordon's
Hospital was, indeed, the principal event in Aberdeen's educational
history during the eighteenth century.

Robert Gordon, the founder, was a man of great business acumen
and extraordinary tenacity of purpose, and his foundation was the last
and greatest gift of his family to Aberdeen city. His grandfather was
Robert Gordon of Straloch, the map-maker; his uncle Parson Gordon
of Rothiemay the delineator of Aberdeen; his great-grandfather had
represented Aberdeenshire in the Scottish Parliament; his great great-
grandfather fell at Pinkie. Robert Gordon himself was born in Aberdeen
in 1668, son of Arthur Gordon, who had been an advocate in Edinburgh, and Isobel Menzies, whose father owned the estate of Balgownie. Robert's birthplace was in Huxter Row, where the back rooms
of the Townhouse now stand. He became a burgess of guild in 1684,
having succeeded to his father's effects in 1680, the estate amounting
to about £1,000. Deciding to try his luck abroad, Gordon established
himself as a merchant in Danzig, lending out some of the profits of
his business to Aberdeenshire lairds on the security of their land. In
1720 he returned to his native burgh, and having conceived the idea of
founding a school for poor boys, and feeling that his not inconsiderable
fortune was insufficient to realise all his ambition, he devoted the last
decade of his life to augmenting it by the favourite Scottish method of
'studying economy'.

The inventory of his effects quite disproves the legend that he lived
in poverty, but he certainly did deny himself some of the social amenities
and pleasures that his industry entitled him to enjoy. His estate amounted

at his death on 28 April 1731 to £10,000, which was vested in a trust of which the main direction was in the hands of the Town Council.

> 'Be it known to all Men by these present Letters, Me, Robert Gordon, Merchant in Aberdeen, only lawful Son in Life, to the deceast Mr. Arthur Gordon Advocate'

so runs the deed of mortification of 1731. It goes on to relate how 'I have deliberately and seriously (for these several Years bygone) intended and resolved, and am now come to a full and final Resolution and Determination, to make a pious Mortification of My whole Substance and Effects, presently pertaining resting and owing to Me . . . and that towards the building of an Hospital, and for Maintenance, Aliment, Entertainment and Education of young Boys, whose Parents are poor and indigent, and not able to maintain them at Schools, and put them to Trades and Employments'. The Provost, Baillies and Town Council and the four ministers of the city churches were named sole executors. The hospital he directed to be built 'upon any fit Place, within the said Burgh of Aberdeen, where the Patrons and Governors shall think fit, or upon the Piece of Ground called the Black-Fryars, lying upon the North-Side of the School-Hill'.

This ground was part of Jean Guild's Mortification of which the Town Council were trustees, and so in 1732 they granted a feu-charter to themselves in respect of it. More land was required for the hospital, however, and the Marischal College authorities were persuaded to give a little of the adjacent ground belonging to them — the first alienation but one of the original property of Marischal College; but they charged a rent, 20 bolls of bere, which was considered ample recompense. The architect was William Adam, Edinburgh, first proprietor of Blairadam, and father of the celebrated John and Robert Adam who built the now demolished Adelphi, off the Strand in London. The school, 'a very neat building of three stories, with pediments projecting in front and on each end', and with dimensions '86 feet long and 33 feet 9 inches wide over walls', stood 'at the north extremity of an extensive garden', and the ground included or reached to the sites of Blackfriars Street and St. Andrew Street, then non-existent. Next to the garden on the east side was the Grammar School, behind it on the north-east the Loch. The present playground was enclosed in 1828. The Governors at various times from 1805 to 1923 gave off ground for the laying out of St. Andrew Street (till 1831 called Hospital Row) and of Blackfriars Street, the Education Society of Aberdeen's Lancastrian School being erected in 1823 on what is now the site of the Woolmanhill Drill Hall. Up to the late 1820s the ground in front of the Hospital was cultivated by a market gardener named Saunders Sheriffs, who laboured the land on both sides of the approach from Schoolhill, which was on the same line as at present. Part of this garden was laid out as a bowling green, and the gardener was under obligation 'not to suffer boys or prentices who incline to play', and he had to report and exclude as disorderly persons any who were found 'cursing or swearing in the garden or bowling-green'. The green was becoming less popular in 1818.

The occupation of the Hospital by 200 of the Hanoverian troops when the Duke of Cumberland marched in pursuit of the Jacobites took place in April 1746 and seems to have lasted several months. The soldiers made the desolation that all soldiers make: 'the garden walls were taken down, and some fortifications erected in the gardens, and many other necessary alterations were made therein.' A year later the Town Council petitioned the King for restitution, the damage being computed at 'two hundred and ninety pounds and upwards lawful money of Great Britain'. With an expedition and honesty unknown in Government Departments of more advanced civilisation, the damages were discharged by the payment of £300 within six months.

In his Deed of Mortification, Gordon instructed that the Headmaster should be 'an unmarried man of Good Respect and free of the Burden of Children, or a Widower who has no Children or whose Children are all forisfamiliate'. 'His principal Care shall be to see that the Children and Servants be brought up and instructed with Fear of God'; he had to be a Protestant, and 'he shall not be any Night out of the Hospital, without leave of the Praeses, or at least two of the Governors'. There were to be one or two schoolmasters, to teach English, Latin, writing, arithmetic in all its parts, 'Book-keeping, and the common Parts of vocal music', and if the resident masters were unable to instruct in the four last-mentioned subjects, then some person or persons from outside had to 'come to the Hospital at certain Hours' for the purpose. In these particulars Gordon gave his school a praiseworthy initial advantage over the Grammar School, where the only subjects then taught were Latin and a little Greek, so that the Grammar School pupils had to go to other schools in the afternoon for non-classical instruction. Other officers provided in the Mortification were a steward, a cook, and two or more men-servants. No woman was included, but within a month or two of the opening of the school we find mention of payment of 8s. a week to 'the woman who comes every morning to comb the boyes heades'; soon after she was engaged at 1s. 6d. per week and her 'dyet' to act as nurse when required; by the summer of 1751 the Governors had decided to employ women servants, and at the end of that year Isobel Marsh was chosen as Mistress of the Hospital.

As many boys were to be admitted as the revenue was able to maintain, preferences being given to those of the name of Gordon or Menzies, or 'of any other surname who are my Relation', but all had to be sons and grandsons of burgesses of Guild of Aberdeen; and when all these had been taken in, if there was room, sons and grandsons of tradesmen of Aberdeen might be accepted, again with the above-mentioned preferences. Ages at entry had to be between 8 and 11, and 'proper certificates of their indigent circumstances' had to be produced. At the date of their departure from the Hospital, which had to be between the ages of 14 and 16, they were to receive £10 sterling as apprentice fee to a merchant or £5 if to a tradesman; and if they fulfilled their apprenticeship diligently they were to receive a further bounty. Fourteen boys were admitted when the Hospital was opened on 10 July 1750 and were provided with a tailed coat and waistcoat of blue cloth with yellow metal buttons, knee breeches, and leather caps (which were soon replaced by blue woollen bonnets). The knee breeches lasted longer, being replaced by corduroys in 1793 as 'a cheaper and more frugal wear'. At the end of 1752 there were thirty-six boys in the school, the first eight of whom departed in November 1754, as apprentices two to merchants, two to square wrights, one to a wright and cooper, one to a saddler, one to a watchmaker, and one to a silversmith. Everyone, of course, lived in.

Gordon provided in his Disposition for the acceptance of other endowments to his Hospital, but the only very substantial one was bequeathed in 1821, when the lands of Crichie and Easter Barrack were conveyed under the will of Alexander Simpson of Collyhill in trust to the four ministers of Aberdeen and the Principal and Professors of Marischal College for the maintenance of boys in the Hospital. An additional building was built and it was arranged that twenty-six further boys should be admitted. In 1835 there were 126 boys in the school, in 1865 the Collyhill allocation rose to forty and the total to 140, and in 1881, when the Hospital became the College and changed over to a day school, the number was reduced to 120. The property of the Hospital by that time had a capital value of £184,416, and the net income for 1879, including £1,332 from the Collyhill Trust, was just over £7,000.

The tenor of the Hospital's existence was even. During the 130 years to 1881 it turned out 2,500 boys, many of whom did very well in a wide variety of professions and occupations, and one, Peter Gray, is regarded as the pioneer of modern actuarial science. Of the headmasters up to that time, the Rev. George Abercrombie became minister of Forgue after nine years; the Rev. Alexander Thom spent thirty-six years in the Hospital before accepting the charge of Nigg — he introduced the system of Censors, some of the more prudent boys being selected to superintend the others while at prayer; and during his mastership the school began to provide the main part of the choir of the West Kirk, the precentor there being also the music master at the Hospital; Robert Simpson, 1826–9, became minister of Kintore and went out at the Disruption, while his successor. James Robertson, 1829–32, became minister of Ellon and founded the endowments scheme of the Church of Scotland and was one of the leading opponents of Secession, besides, outside theology, being a pioneer in the introduction of artificial fertilisers. Robertson was succeeded by George Melvin (at a salary of £100 a year), only brother of the great James Melvin, rector of the Grammar School. By that time the Hospital was much enlarged, but Melvin had not the temperament for his post, and was dismissed in 1841. He became schoolmaster of Tarves and left his money to build the Melvin Hall there. When Melvin went the salary was doubled and Andrew Findlater appointed in his stead with furnished apartments in the Hospital. He got £25 to open a workshop for the boys, and so may be regarded as the founder of the Technical College. After nine years he went off to a literary career and became editor of *Chambers's Encyclopedia*. While he was headmaster a Pole, John Jazdowski, was appointed teacher of drawing in the Hospital, and in 1852 he became teacher of French.[1] The Rev. W. D. Strachan then reigned until 1872, and the last Head under the old dispensation was the Rev. Alexander Ogilvie, who had been schoolmaster at Monymusk, and who commenced at a salary of £260 with free unfurnished house, living-in and celibacy on the part of the master having by this time been abolished.

During those years the Grammar School had a somewhat more chequered history. Its traditions were made and it could afford to take its ease. After the new regulations of 1700, nothing very important happened until a new school was built, almost on the old site, in the

1   About that time, 1834, another Pole, named Ostroski, advertised classes in fencing, gymnastics, etc., in Brown's Hall, 137 Union Street; applications were to be made to Mr. Kowalewski, Union Terrace. There was a small Polish colony in Aberdeen then, composed of refugees, who then as now were Poland's principal export.

Schoolhill in 1757. The new building, says Kennedy, 'forms three sides of a square, having a belfry in the centre of the main building, and contains the public hall where the boys assemble, and four teaching rooms, all upon one side. The area in front is enclosed by a low wall, with an iron rail on the top of it.' By Kennedy's time two additional wings had been built at the back of the house. The 1757 building cost £400. By 1818 the number of pupils was 220, the plan of education was completely classical, and there were examinations in October at the annual public visitation and by the class-masters in presence of the whole school. After the public examination prizes were distributed until one year in the mid-eighteenth century a pupil, dissatisfied with his award, cut his book prize in two with his penknife, threw it at the person presenting the prizes, and walked out. This caused a suspension of prize-giving until 1773.

Much attention has been given to the Grammar School of the late eighteenth century because of Lord Byron's attendance from 1795 to 1798. The Rector then was Dr. James Dun, who had joined the staff in 1732, succeeded James Milne as Rector in 1744 at a salary of 600 merks, and remained in that position, although he ceased to teach in 1791, until his death in 1798 at the age of 90. Education thus regulated could hardly be of much account, and indeed when in 1795 the recently appointed Joint-Rector disappeared from the town, an inquiry disclosed that one of the ushers or class-masters had not discharged his duties for over twenty years. In 1796 Andrew Dun was appointed Joint-Rector, but a considerable time elapsed ere the school supplied instruction in a sufficient number of subjects besides the classics to be able within its own walls to give an all-round education to its pupils.

The man who, without seriously altering the scheme of instruction, raised the Grammar School to the standard of a great educational seminary was James Melvin, LL.D., Rector from 1826 until his death in 1853. He has been bracketed with Buchanan, Johnston and Ruddiman in Scotland's quartet of supreme humanists. Born in Aberdeen in 1794, and a citizen of it nearly all his life, he should have been, and if he had not been a Tory would have been, Professor of Latin in Marischal College. Fortunately for the Grammar School, 'Grim Pluto', or 'Grim' as he was nicknamed, was spared to it. His parents were poor, but he entered Marischal College as First Bursar. After a short spell at Udny, he became undermaster to Ewen Maclachlan in Old Aberdeen Grammar School, and than Maclachlan Aberdeen then had no more elegant humanist. In 1822 he became a master in the Grammar School and four years later, when the rectorship fell vacant, he won the post in public competition. The salary was then £250, and in addition he was Lecturer in Latin at Marischal. Melvin not only gave his pupils good Latinity, he supplied them with academic self-respect, the school with status and reputation, and the North-East with a real enthusiasm for classical learning and with many of the pedagogues who could minister to that enthusiasm.

He was succeeded by W. D. Geddes, who left two years later to become first Professor of Greek at King's, and later Principal of Aberdeen University, and for all time 'Homer' to the intellectuals of the north. After Geddes, at a short interval, came an Irishman with a Welsh name and the unseemly English pronunciation of Latin and Greek; but Aberdonians, men and boys, having some respect for themselves and their own institutions, saw to it that he did not remain more than a few months. There was no one else of importance until Dr. James Moir became Rector in 1881. In 1863 the older part of the present school was opened in Skene Street West, the belfry of the Schoolhill building being incorporated in the new.

Among the Grammar School's old boys who rose to fame in the eighteenth and nineteenth centuries were several of the ubiquitous Gregories; Dr. James Beattie, who married Dr. Dun's daughter; James Gibbs, the architect who designed Radcliffe Library at Oxford, St. Martin's-in-the-Fields in London, and the West Kirk of St. Nicholas, Aberdeen; Lord Byron; Sir James McGrigor, founder of the Army Medical Service; Sir Alexander Anderson, greatest of Aberdeen's provosts, who indeed was responsible for the building of the modern school; William Dyce, R.A.; David Masson, editor of Milton's works; Alexander Bain, famous for his logic, his psychology, and his English grammar; the illustrious teaching Ogilvies; George Croom Robertson the philosopher, and Robert A. Neil, one of the greatest of modern scholars. The list could be extended much further without reducing the standard by much. The classical training of Melvin is obvious throughout the latter portion of the tally.

Byron is his correspondence mentions several of his Aberdeen teachers, including 'Bodsy Bower', teacher of English in Longacre to both sexes, whose son John, after teaching in Robert Gordon's Hospital, was minister of Maryculter from 1812 to 1866; James Ross, minister of St. Nicholas 1795–1824, son of James Ross, teacher of writing and arithmetic; and William Duncan, who forsook the mastership of the Writing School for the Chair of Natural Philosophy at King's and was succeeded by George Cruden, whose salary from the town was £25 sterling. Kennedy mentions as recently founded in 1818 a school 'of public institution' commenced 'by the incorporated artificers' for the teaching of English etc., and up to his day there were many other small private seminaries and two schools of industry, besides 'the new system for the education of children' introduced at Aberdeen in 1815. In 1824 the Mechanics' Institution was founded, and until the evening classes in connection with Gordon's College put an end to its activities, it was a virile education centre at its Market Street headquarters, built in 1845, with its library of 16,000 volumes.

The Forty-five, unlike the Fifteen, affected King's and Marischal but little, and within a few years of the rebellion we find both in the throes of an academic revolution. At King's Principal John Chalmers, who had succeeded his namesake George, and who was to reign until 1800, had the Senatus draw up in 1753 'an abstract of some statutes and orders' by which the session was extended from the first Monday in October until May, and the smaller bursaries were amalgamated on account of the consequential increase in cost of residence to the students. This enactment was repealed in 1760. Bursars were warned that their tenure of the bursaries was dependent upon their proficiency, and it was insisted, by no means for the first time, that 'for the future all the students should lodge in rooms within the College and eat at the College Table during the whole session'. Two college servants were appointed to attend upon them at the students' expense. . . . Besides instruction in the Classics and Philosophies, there were classes taught by visiting pedagogues in 'those Parts of Education which are not commonly reckoned Academical, such as Dancing, Writing, Book-Keeping, French, etc.' Regenting, which had been abolished in the other Scottish Universities before 1750 and at Marischal in 1753, was continued at King's until 1799, when it was done away with after seven years of anxious deliberation and experiment by the Senatus. Its survival at King's in the middle of the century was due to the powerful influence of Thomas Reid, founder of the Scottish School of Philosophy, exponent of the doctrine of Common Sense, and David Hume's only serious rival in metaphysical polemics, who had become a regent in 1751. Another of Reid's victories is reflected in the decision of the Professors of Philosophy to devote less time to 'the Logic and Metaphysics of the Schoolmen' and 'to employ themselves chiefly in teaching those parts of Philosophy which may qualify men for the more useful and important offices of Society'.

Marischal College in 1754 adopted a 'Plan of Education' corresponding in broad outline to the recent decisions taken at King's, drawn up
by Professor Alexander Gerard, author of an *Essay on Taste*. At
Marischal, however, there had ceased to be collegiate life, and all the
students, no doubt because the homes of most of them were in town,
boarded out. Apart from that there was not much to choose between the
two institutions, especially in the laxity of their methods. In 1765 the
custom of combining graduation with disputation on a thesis was abandoned for the even simpler method introduced by the genius of Professor James Beattie, author of the *Essay on Truth*. The aspirants to a
degree were set a series of Latin questions in Logic and Rhetoric, both
questions *and answers* being dictated to the candidates by the Professor
of Moral Philosophy, who heard the candidates repeat these first to him
alone and later in presence of the Faculty. The questions and answers, it
should be added, varied as little from year to year as did in more recent
times the lectures of certain professors who shall be nameless.

At King's in 1789 the Mediciner, William Chalmers, instituted what
has been described as the first Medical degree paper in the history of
the College of Aberdeen — for at Marischal at that time Medicine can
scarcely be said to have been taught at all, since no lectures on the subject were delivered there until 1823, and the medical students of whom
a leader was James McGrigor, later the great army surgeon, had to
found for themselves in 1789 the society then called the Medical and
today the Medico-Chirurgical Society, at which doctors and surgeons
in the town gave lectures. Professor Chalmers's first degree paper
contained four questions:

(1) What are the principal peculiarities in the structure of the fœtus,
    and are there any impediments to seeing or hearing at birth?
    What are they?
(2) In how far may Acrimony be considered as existing in the system,
    and what are its effects?
(3) In what proportion of our present diseases may Debility be sup-
    posed to take place, and how may it be effectually obviated?
(4) What are the advantages resulting from the Brownonian doctrine?

Chalmers had some drive, and in 1792 had secured permission for the
foundation of a museum and the giving of weekly lectures, fee one
guinea, on anatomy and physiology, when he died. His successor, Sir
Alexander Bannerman, whose remote ancestor had been physician to
David II and whose medicine was probably as advanced as that of his

progenitor, never ventured to lecture. Marischal College in 1780 through the efforts of the energetic Patrick Copland, Professor of Natural Philosophy 1780–1822, secured an observatory. In that year the Town Council voted £20 to purchase instruments (on the excellence of which Kennedy enlarges, including 'a very fine scale' of the like of which there were only two others in existence), and in 1781 a site on the Castlehill. This observatory was levelled in 1795 when the barracks were being built, and a substitute was erected at the west wing of the College buildings, where in 1694 a square tower had been raised to function as an observatory but had probably never been furnished. Kennedy also mentions that Copland was responsible for amassing a remarkable collection of models of the then modern industrial machinery, including Arkwright's spinning machines, steam engines, saw-mills, cranes, threshing machines, oil-mills and a multitude of other mechanical devices, no doubt considered then to be as emphatically the last word as our contemporary inventions are today.

Collegiate habits at King's in the eighteenth century are illustrated by some information about food. The students were accommodated in 1753 at two tables, the second for the poorer class, whose supper consisted of 'sowens or bread with ale or milk', and the first table, where the rich were regaled on 'eggs, or sowens, or roots, or pancakes, or bread and butter, or ox cheek, or Finnan haddocks and ale'. When in 1763 the students complained of their food, the Senatus replied by substituting boiled beef and broth for the Saturday's dinner of roast beef, being declared to be 'better for the students and easier for the Economist'.[1]

The principal event in the history of the two colleges between 1800 and their union in 1860 was the creation of a Joint Medical School in 1818. This step, taken at the instigation of the authorities of Marischal College, which even then was directing its main attention to medical studies, failed in its full effect because of lack of enthusiasm at King's, whose Mediciner simply refused to lecture. The conditions imposed on every candidate for the degree of M.D. were strict indeed, involving that he should be 25 years of age, in possession of an M.A. degree, and should have attended a very full course of medical lectures. However desirable all of those provisions may have been, they discouraged

---

1   Arguing on a curiously modern note the College authorities of 1763 contended that the students were better fed communally than at home (what else is the basis of the schools meal scheme today?) and that they 'were never so healthy'.

the students, and between 1826 and 1839 only four graduated in Medicine at King's and twenty-five at Marischal. In the latter year, a twelvemonth after the Medical Society had celebrated its jubilee with some justifiable exultation, King's College Senatus broke away from the sister institution on the ground that it was 'inexpedient and even dangerous to maintain further intercourse with Marischal College'.

Before the joint school collapsed William, the last of the Gregory professors, had succeeded Bannerman as Mediciner at King's and he proceeded to infuse new life into medical teaching at the older College. In fact, he carried the war into the Marischal camp, and a medical school was fitted up at Kingsland Place, Broadford, to teach a curriculum consisting of Materia Medica, Institutes of Medicine, Botany, Chemistry, Surgery, Midwifery, Anatomy and Medical Jurisprudence. This range of instruction compared favourably with Marischal's Chair of Medicine and lectureships in Anatomy (established 1802), Midwifery (1811), Surgery and Materia Medica (1819) and instruction in Botany and Medical Jurisprudence. In 1849 King's sought to get State sanction for several new Medical Chairs, but in vain. Gregory in 1844 went off to Edinburgh as Professor of Chemistry there.

There was little further of great interest on the administrative side in either college. In 1826 a Parliamentary Commission made certain recommendations that raised the standard of the teaching and the frequency of the lectures, which hitherto had not been either regular or very numerous, and encouraged the award of prizes by examination. At King's in 1824–7 the Chancellor and Senatus attempted to secure that the Civilist should teach law, the Mediciner medicine and the Principal divinity, as they were supposed and paid to do. It was in vain. On various pretexts the three evaded their obligations with complete success, except the Civilist, who gave less than a dozen lectures and then desisted on the plea of ill-health. At Marischal a Latin Chair, founded in 1839, was assigned to John Stuart Blackie, 'a boy in commonsense, a very child in talents, a very infant of the Classics'. He refused to sign the Confession of Faith except in his 'public professional capacity', and when the Presbytery held that his contumacy invalidated his election, he appealed to the Court of Session, who found in his favour. In 1853 it was enacted that the Test Act, ultimately repealed in 1889, did not require acceptance of the Confession of Faith where professors of lay subjects were concerned.

In 1825 Beattie's degree examination system was discarded in favour of a real test, which resulted in five out of thirty-three candidates being debarred from graduating, since they could not 'answer the simplest question'. One of the 'failed M.A.s' approached the then rector, Joseph Hume, the Radical politician, who held a Rectorial Court, the first since 1738, at which, true to the traditions of his kind, he gave a decision that sought to please everyone. Next year the distinguished Aberdonian Sir James McGrigor ousted Hume. In 1833 the new Marischal chair of Church History was bestowed on Dr. Daniel Dewar, described as 'sitting in a vehicle drawn by two horses, Ambition being the name of one, and Avarice that of the other'. The same pen, that of a divinity student of the period, is responsible for the statement that Principal William Laurence Brown, of Marischal, who taught Divinity, was never heard by its owner during his four years' attendance at the Divinity Hall to pronounce the name of Jesus Christ.

In matters not strictly academic there has to be recorded a big domestic change at King's during the first quarter of the nineteenth century. By 1826 there was not a student in residence, and in 1836 the office of Economist, which had long been held by a woman, was abolished. In 1811 a bequest by Dr. Alexander Murray of Philadelphia, a King's graduate, enabling a course of lectures to be delivered in the College Chapel, became available, the chapel was put in a habitable state, the gallery in the Cathedral where the students were wont to sit was given up, and in exchange the Cathedral authorities bestowed Bishop Stewart's pulpit on the Chapel, where it is still in use. The Chapel services commenced in 1821, the General Assembly giving its sanction on condition that the Murray lecturers be Established Church clergymen. In 1854 the students of King's regained the power of electing their rector. In 1836 the average entrance age of students at King's was 14 and at Marischal 12, and King's had 235 students, while Marischal had 225 in Arts. By 1860 there were 145 Medical students, and in 1893 there were 367. In Arts the average age of entry had risen to between 17 and 18.

In 1824–5 the west front of King's College, with Archibald Simpson as architect, was built at a cost of £7,000, and at the same time the old living rooms of the College were converted into classrooms. Between 1836 and 1845 Marischal College was completely rebuilt after long negotiation. An attempt was made in 1818 to get a site on the Castlehill when the scheme of the barracks was mooted. In 1824 Archibald Simpson submitted a plan for rebuilding on the Broad Street site and another for a location in Belmont Street, while there was also talk of moving the college to ground between the Denburn bridge and the present line of Crown Street. The existing College Street may commemorate this project or simply embody the fact that Marischal College held the land through which the street runs. The cost of the new Marischal College was £30,000, of which the Government found, with accrued interest, £21,000.

In 1854 there were initiated, at the instance of King's College, which in the past had been oftener inimical to union than otherwise, the proceedings which ended six years later in giving Aberdeen a single university. There had been many abortive attempts since the days of the short-lived Caroline University. In 1747 the union of the two St. Andrews' colleges, St. Salvator's and St. Leonard's, inspired a similar project in Aberdeen. In 1754 the question was up again. Both these were wrecked on the stipulation that the university should be in Aberdeen itself. In 1770 and 1784-7 proposals were made which came to nothing. The Royal Commission of 1826 advised union, Alexander Bannerman, M.P. introduced a Bill in 1835, and in 1836 the Government got a Bill of its own as far as the committee stage. In these endeavours a division of faculties and classes between the two colleges was fundamental. The King's plan of 1854 provided for Arts and Divinity there and Medicine and Law at Marischal. A Marischal minority blocked the scheme. There was another abortive Bill in 1856, then in 1857 a Commission was appointed that reported to Parliament, which thereupon empowered a new Commission to unite the two universities. This was finally done on the basis of the original King's scheme of 1854, except that the Natural History Class, which should have remained with Arts at King's, was assigned to Marischal.

In 1860 the fusion was completed; the chancellorship was held jointly by the Duke of Richmond and the Earl of Aberdeen; the Rev. Peter Colin Campbell, the Principal of King's, became the first union principal; the students chose Edward F. Maitland, afterwards Lord Barcaple, the Solicitor-General for Scotland, as rector. Six new chairs were added — Biblical criticism (Milligan), Physiology, Midwifery, Botany (Dickie), Materia Medica, and Logic-English (Alexander Bain). The most serious loss among the professoriate was James Clerk Maxwell, who was the junior of the two exponents of Natural Philosophy, and who took his genius to Cambridge. New degree courses were introduced, and the University Court was established to administer the property of the University.

CHAPTER EIGHT

Doctors Learned and Medical

It is a fact which finds, naturally, little favour in the twentieth century that the mind of man reached its highest development as an intellectual instrument in the eighteenth. That century has been justly termed the Age of Reason, and its fruits were gathered in France and England and to a remarkable extent in Edinburgh, which in that period when human reason was so triumphantly enshrined earned the supreme epithet of 'The Modern Athens'. Aberdeen during the century was conspicuous also, and three of the great leaders of contemporary thought had their homes in Aberdeen when they wrote their chief contributions to the philosophy of their time. When the dust of the Forty-five had settled down and the strife of peace was substituted for the violence of war, the first intellectual battle to be fought was opened by David Hume, whose *Treatise of Human Nature*, published in 1739, had been a serious enough challenge to the orthodox, but whose *Philosophical Essays* of 1748 were a regular bombardment of conventional religion and established faith. One of the most iconoclastic and resented of the essays was that on Miracles, in which Hume elaborated the argument that witnesses of miracles are more likely to lie or be mistaken than miracles to occur.

This challenge to a cherished Christian belief was accepted by the Rev. George Campbell, Professor of Divinity and Principal[1] in Marischal College, who replied (somewhat belatedly, but those were stately and unhurried times) with his *Dissertation on Miracles*, 1763. Campbell, son of one of the ministers of St. Nicholas, was born in 1719, learned Latin in the Grammar School and Greek under Thomas Blackwell at Marischal College, served an apprenticeship to a lawyer in Edinburgh, but turned by personal preference to Divinity. Licensed in 1746, he became minister of Banchory-Ternan in the following year and in 1756 he succeeded the Rev. John Bisset as minister of the East Church of St. Nicholas. His appointment was the cause of the secession which

1 Campbell insisted on the use of the hard 'C' in Latin and was accordingly known as 'Prinkipal' Campbell. Is this the origin of the term still used at King's for the executive head of the University, 'the Prink'?

is elsewhere mentioned. While at Banchory, Campbell, who was a little man and quiet, married one of the Farquharsons of Whitehouse, a vigorous emphatic lady. When they removed to Aberdeen they rented at 46 Schoolhill a house which still stands west of the Back Wynd: and there one day while she was busily running about the house preparing for a party, she ran into her husband. 'Oot o' the wye, ye bodie! Ye're aye in the road in a steer' was her sharp admonition, to which the meek philosopher replied, 'Weel, Gracie, if I were oot o' the wye, maybe there wouldna be sae muckle steer!'

Campbell's reply to Hume, which with much adroitness and fertility of argument sustained the orthodox attitude to miracles, he sent to his opponent in manuscript and accepted certain deletions and alterations that did not commend themselves to David's self-esteem. When the dissertation appeared Hume wrote Campbell in hearty congratulation, and readers with a taste for reminiscence will remember that it was Campbell's *Philosophy of Rhetoric* that James Boswell found Hume reading on the morning of 7 July 1776, a few weeks before the philosopher's death. This book on Rhetoric was a text-book for many years and kept green for that term the memory of a good man and a scholar who has been almost wholly forgotten despite those once famous books and his *Translation of the Gospels* and his *Lectures on Ecclesiastical History*. In the last work, published after his death, he showed little sympathy for the Scotch Episcopalians and aroused the ire of Bishop Skinner, 'Tullochgorum's' son, who replied in a 'Vindication' that was described in the free polemics of those candid days as an example of the living ass kicking the dead lion. Campbell died in 1796, having been Principal of Marischal College 1758-95. For those who believe in the *mens sana in corpore sano* fallacy, it may be added that he was never robust and was given up for lost in tuberculosis when he was a youth.

A greater than Campbell was Thomas Reid, Professor of Moral Philosophy at King's College from 1752 to 1763, when he was transferred to Glasgow and the chair of Natural Philosophy there. Reid, born at Strachan in 1710 and a graduate of Marischal College, was of the same family on his father's side as Thomas Reid, Latin Secretary to James VI and I, and Alexander Reid, physician to Charles I, and his mother was a niece of James Gregory. He could, therefore hardly escape being intelligent. He entered literature with a critical examination of some of the theories enunciated by Professor Francis Hutcheson of Glasgow, who remained during the eighteenth century the most popular of its philosophers. But in 1764 Reid sought a higher quarry, assailing the tenets of Hume in his greatest work, *Inquiry into the Human Mind upon the Principles of Common Sense*. In this treatise and in subsequent books, Reid pursued the inductive method of philosophy, and established a reputation for himself in metaphysical reasoning which still preserves for him a place among the great minds of a great century. Hume was by 1764 becoming bored by clerical animadversions upon his theories and when he heard that Reid was preparing a book he wished 'that the parsons would confine themselves to their old occupation of worrying one another'. When he read the *Inquiry*, however, he was frank in his praise. His conversion was not unlike that of the parishioners of Newmachar, who, Reid being imposed upon them as their minister by the patron of the parish, 'fought against Dr. Reid when he came, and would have fought for him when he went away'. He died in 1796, leaving his native country and generation the legacy of a character of 'intrepid and inflexible rectitude' and 'a pure and devoted attachment to truth'.

Third and least important of the professorial luminaries of Aberdeen at that time was James Beattie, son of a small shopkeeper in the then small hamlet of Laurencekirk, where he was born in 1735. He entered Marischal College in 1749 and achieved the distinction of being the best student in the Greek class. In 1758 he was appointed an usher in the Grammar School, and in 1760 to the Chair of Natural Philosophy (which he at once exchanged for that of Moral Philosophy) in his Alma Mater. In the same year appeared in London his *Original Poems and Translations*. In 1865 he met Thomas Gray the poet, and the friendship thus formed ended only with Gray's death in 1771. In 1767 he married the only daughter of Dr. Dun, the rector of the Grammar School, and finished his *Essay on the Nature and Immutability of Truth*, which, when published in 1770, made him famous in a day.[1] In 1771 appeared

1 That frank and primly scandalous recorder James Bruce, in his 'Eminent Men of Aberdeen', writes with ill-concealed glee of what has been called 'the pious fraud' that gave 'The Essay on Truth' to the world. Beattie was parsimonious — as his papers still at King's College attest — and he would be at no expense to publish the essay. He gave it to Sir William Forbes the banker and some other friends to find a publisher, but no one would look at it except at the author's charges. So Forbes and the others offered Beattie 50 guineas which they pretended was a publisher's offer and which they knew he would accept. They then became partners with the author in the venture and guaranteed the price of printing. The book went into a second edition within a year, and says the caustic Bruce, 'the devisers of the scheme do not appear to have regretted that it was by a temporary sacrifice of truth that they were enabled to establish its eternal immutability'.

the first and in 1774 the second part of *The Minstrel*, suggested by the prefatory essay by Bishop Percy to the *Reliques of Ancient English Poetry*. By this poem, more remarkable for its sweetness of expression than for the strength of its thought, he came to be chiefly remembered, until our own day, when he is altogether forgotten. He became a frequent visitor to London, the lion of several noble houses, the friend of Johnson, the subject of one of Sir Joshua Reynolds's most celebrated pictures; yet to his credit he resisted the most flattering offers to accept an Edinburgh chair and a living in the Church of England. In 1787 his elder son James Hay Beattie was associated with him in his chair as assistant and successor, but the young man died at two-and-twenty in 1790, and his younger son did not reach even that short age. His wife inherited mental infirmity from her mother, and Beattie's own reason, under that succession of domestic afflictions, succumbed at least partially. He died in 1803 and is buried in St. Nicholas churchyard.

Alexander Cruden, compiler of the *Concordance to the Bible*, was the son of an Aberdeen baillie whose existence and residence are still commemorated in Cruden's Court, Broad Street,[1] and having been born in 1700 and his great work first published in the thirties, he may be regarded as belonging to the earlier period of this history. He came to fame, however, only about 1761, when, the first edition of the *Concordance* having been with difficulty disposed of, a second edition met with a readier appreciation. It has been pointed out that the first *Concordance* ever compiled afforded employment to 500 monks, whereas Cruden made his infinitely superior specimen alone and unaided; but he was an Aberdonian, a Protestant, a fanatic, and more than a little mad. The trials and tribulations, mostly encountered and endured in London, whither he went in 1732, of Alexander the Corrector, as he called himself, have nothing to do with the history of Aberdeen. It is sufficient to remark that when he died in 1770 Cruden had established for himself a familiar reputation which has proved far more enduring than that of any of his contemporary compatriots, although that reputation does partake more of the 'household word' quality which is usually accorded to vendors of commercial articles than to the creator of books.

While these were names of more than ordinary eminence during the

---

1   When Miss Edith Olivier, Cruden's last biographer, called on the present writer to ask for information, he was able to assure her that they were conversing in the room where Cruden was, if not born, at least accustomed to eat his meals and read the Scriptures.

eighteenth century, there were many more whose contributions to knowledge, to learning, the arts, and human progress were little, if at all, less distinguished. But as the decades go on, the numbers of the illustrious increase, and where so many are (or were) important, each loses somewhat in stature. Of medical men who passed through King's and Marischal, Sir James McGrigor remains one of the most famous, but it is not unfair to remember that while he was building up the Army Medical Service of the great Empire of the West, a contemporary Aberdeen student, but of King's not Marischal, Sir James Wylie (1768–1854), was director of the medical services in the army of the Empire of the East and physician to the Tsars Paul and Alexander I.

Greatest names of all in the long record of Aberdeen doctors born between 1746 and 1850 are those of Sir Patrick Manson (1845–1922), Francis Adams (1796–1861) and Charles Creighton (1847–1927). Manson, born at Oldmeldrum, was founder and first principal of the London School of Tropical Medicine, and it was his discovery of certain facts about the mosquito that made possible the researches which have enabled science to conquer malaria and to open up the tropics to modern civilisation. Francis Adams, of Lumphanan, was an extra-ordinary compound of classical and medical erudition who, in the scanty leisure that falls to the lot of a medical practitioner in a wide country district, translated and descanted upon the works of the ancient Hellenic doctors, commented on Greek prosody and grammar, and compiled a paper on the birds of Banchory-Ternan for the British Association conference at Aberdeen in 1859. Creighton, a native of Peterhead, possessed as powerful a brain as ever was produced by the North-East, but his intellectual gifts were marred by suspicion of the motives of others and a combativeness that was unnecessarily energetic. Skilled in languages and an expert both in pathology and anatomy, he gradually drew aloof into his task of writing his monumental *History of Epidemics in Britain* (1891–4), in which he records the visitations not only of plague and other forms of 'the pest' but also of famine from 1664 to 1893. Worthy to be mentioned along with these three was Sir Alexander Ogston (1844–1929), the great surgeon, and professor of that subject in Aberdeen University, who in 1881 discovered the pus organism which had been responsible for so much of the mortality and morbidity in wounds and sores, and who thus opened up the way to safer surgery.

Other medical pioneers who can only be mentioned were the fashionable London physician, Sir William Fordyce (1724–92), who left his fortune to endow a lectureship in Agricultural Chemistry that formed the nucleus of the North of Scotland College of Agriculture; George Fordyce, his nephew (1736–1802), who was a noted authority upon materia medica and wrote upon fevers; Sir Walter Farquhar (1738–1819), the Chapel of Garioch boy who went through King's and became physician to the Prince Regent and Charles James Fox; Alexander Gordon of Strachan (1752–99) whose researches[1] were the first steps in a campaign which finally conquered puerperal fever; Neil Arnott (1788–1874), author of *Elements of Physics* and one of the founders of London University; Sir James Clark, Cullen (1788–1870), physician to Queen Victoria, upon whose advice the Royal Family settled on Balmoral for their Scottish residence; Francis Ogston (1803–87), father of Sir Alexander, one of the earliest experts upon medical jurisprudence, of which subject he was professor at Aberdeen; William Pirrie, Huntly (1807–82), Professor of Surgery, who, with Sir John Struthers, Professor of Anatomy from 1863 to 1889, laid the foundation of the fame of Aberdeen's medical school; James Matthews Duncan (1826–90) the obstetrician; Sir Andrew Clark (1826–93), W. E. Gladstone's doctor; Sir Arthur Mitchell (1826–1909), who made a professional name for himself by his advanced views upon lunacy and who, out of his hobby, as an antiquarian, wrote *The Past in the Present; What is Civilisation?*; Sir Andrew Leith Adams (1827–82), an army surgeon who contributed substantially to our knowledge of fossils; and George Bidie, who reached the rank of surgeon-general, and did good work in India on the not unconnected subjects there of sanitation and botany.

In the sciences, taking economics to be included in that term, Adam Anderson (1692–1765) was the author of the exhaustive *Historical and Chronological Deduction of the Origin of Commerce*. James Burnet (1714–99), raised to the bench of the Court of Session as Lord Monboddo, mingled his wrestlings with legal cases with speculations upon the kinship of man with the animals,[2] while Sir James Mackintosh (1765–1832) abandoned medicine for the law and for politics, a bent disclosed by his part in the foundation of the students' 'Hall and Mackintosh Club' to discuss philosophy and by his famous and not ineffective reply, *Vindiciae Gallicae*, to Edmund Burke's animad-

1 These researches were a link between him and the author of *The Professor at the Breakfast Table*.
2 He anticipated Darwin, explaining the hole in the centre of the three-legged stool as being meant for the insertion of the tail!

versions on the French Revolution. The Rev. Alexander John Forsyth of Belhelvie (1769–1843) combined the pastoral duties of a parish minister with a zeal for scientific investigation that led him to the discovery of the percussion cap. Napoleon offered him £20,000 for his invention, but Forsyth would hand the secret only to the British Government, whose experts with typical caution failed to recognise its value till the urgent need for it had passed. Another parish minister educated in Aberdeen, Dr. Robertson of Ellon, a Moderator of the Church of Scotland (1803–60), cultivated more peaceful sciences and introduced the earliest forms of phosphatic fertilisers to Scottish agriculture. Yet another, perhaps the most versatile of them all, George Skene Keith (1752–1823), minister of Keith-hall and finally of St. Cyrus, not only wrote that invaluable book, *A General View of the Agriculture of Aberdeenshire*, but was also a specialist on grasses, in distilling and in surveying. Patrick Copland (1749–1822), already mentioned in another connection, Professor of Natural Philosophy at Marischal College from 1775 to 1779, of Mathematics from 1779 to 1817, and of Natural Philosophy again from 1817 to 1822, deserves commemoration as the founder of the University's Natural History Museum.

James Mitchell (1786–1844) did a great deal of sociological research that led to the factory legislation of the second and third quarters of last century; Alexander Gerrard (1792–1839) and his brother James Gilbert (1795–1835) rank high amongst the early climbers and explorers of the Himalayas and Hindu Kush; Hugh Falconer (1808–65) introduced the culture of tea and quinine on an extended scale to India; and James Augustus Grant, a soldier by profession and a botanist by preference, accompanied Speke in his explorations of the Nile area and wrote an international book *A Walk Across Africa*. Robert Brown (1773–1858), a Marischal man who came to be recognised as easily the leading botanist of his generation, had worthy Aberdonian successors in William MacGillivray (1796–1852), Professor of Natural History at Marischal College and author of a *History of British Birds* and *The Natural History of Deeside*, and George Dickie (1812–82), Professor of Botany from 1860 to 1877.

CHAPTER NINE

The Fourth Estate

The cultivation of literature and the liberal arts in Aberdeen, of which we saw the beginnings in John Barbour, Parson Galloway, Walter Cullen, the Sang Schule, and George Jamesone, was continued with a fair amount of persistence during The Troubles and the Jacobite disturbances. But like everything else, culture took its greatest leap forward once the Jacobite threat was finally disposed of at Culloden. Disregarding the pale shade of a news-sheet said to have been printed by the Forbeses about 1660, Aberdeen had its introduction to journalism if legend may be credited, as a direct result of Culloden itself, for it is averred that James Chalmers, the town's printer first issued a newspaper in order to retail the news of the famous battle.

There are details in the story which rather cast doubts upon its authenticity, but there is tangible evidence of the formal birth of the *Aberdeen Journal* newspaper with its first issue on 5 January 1748.[1] From that day to this no week has passed without the appearance of the *Journal*, now the oldest Scottish newspaper. It began as a small four-page foolscap news-sheet, the first to be published in Scotland outside Edinburgh, and in contrast to its reputation a century later of carrying more advertisements than any other Scottish weekly newspaper, it presented only one advertisement, dealing with the disappearance of some banknotes the return of which would be rewarded with 2 guineas and 'no questions asked'. News in those days consisted mainly of extracts from London papers and periodicals, but life moved more sedately then than now, and the public were perfectly content to wait a week or even more for the latest tidings of the great world.

That slow transmission of topical information did not lessen the appetite for news is indicated by the appearance in October 1752, of the *Aberdeen Intelligencer*, whose rivalry appears to have been inspired mainly by Jacobite opponents of the Whig regime of which James Chalmers was a staunch upholder. The proprietors of the *Intelligencer*

1 When celebrating the 150th anniversary the proprietors of the *Journal* published a facsimile of the first issue, which is often mistaken for the original number. Its first title was *The Aberdeen's Journal*.

were Francis Douglas, an Aberdeen baker turned bookseller, and William Murray, a druggist, who in partnership had set up a printing-house and so gravitated into journalism. In 1757 at a meeting of Commissioners of Supply for the County of Aberdeen, the suggestion was made that if there were but one newspaper those who had goods for sale would save half the expense of advertisement. Accordingly, the proprietors of both papers were approached, and the publishers of the *Intelligencer* were glad enough to leave the field, for a consideration, to the *Journal*. Francis Douglas in 1761 commenced the first series of the *Aberdeen Magazine*, the earliest of our Aberdeen periodicals; but it also was discontinued within the year, one number only being known.

The next rival to the *Journal* was a sheet in 1770 that died very soon. The next was fathered by Andrew Shirrefs, a literary man like Francis Douglas who started with some others the *Aberdeen Chronicle* in 1787. It lasted no time at all, but before it disappeared Shirrefs was trying a more important venture as part-proprietor and joint editor with one Alexander Leighton of the *Caledonian Magazine*. This was an excellent publication which gave room to the best work of several contemporary local writers, but Shirrefs had to close it down in 1790. All the while John Chalmers, son of James, was running his series of the *Aberdeen Magazine*, which began in 1788 and ended in 1791. Yet another *Aberdeen Magazine*, published by Burnett and Rettie in the Netherkirk-gate, appeared from June 1796 to December 1797. In 1806, John Booth, a merchant, founded another *Aberdeen Chronicle*, a newspaper with a tendency to Reform, which enjoyed a considerable public for many years, and especially once the Napoleonic Wars were ended. In 1832, however, it also was discontinued, although not altogether because Reform had been achieved. Towards the close of the *Chronicle's* existence, the Tory philosophy was expounded by the *Observer* founded in 1829. The *Journal* supported the Reform Bill, but later turned Tory.

In September 1832 appeared the first number of the Liberal *Aberdeen Herald*, and under the tremendously virile editorship of James Adam, who came from the south-west of Scotland and was put in charge of it in 1834, it speedily became a power in the North-East. Adam was not only an able journalist, he was also an indefatigable controversialist, at all times prepared to uphold his case and to vindicate the independence of the Fourth Estate. He attacked sheriffs and procurators-fiscal with the same glee and resource as he belaboured his political opponents, but it was characteristic of him that when the rival *Journal* celebrated its centenary with the reigning Chalmers in the chair, the croupier was James Adam. While William Forsyth edited the *Journal*, he and Adam used to spend the evenings before their respective weeklies were issued in a Guestrow howff together, and together they penned the next day's editorials. Forsyth, William Thom, William Cadenhead, William Anderson and Alexander Taylor all contributed to the poets' corner of the *Herald*, and in that line Aberdeen never produced anything better.

The *Observer* gave place in 1837 to the *Constitutional*, a politically conservative and theologically Moderate paper, which just managed to survive the Disruption and expired in 1844. One of its sub-editors was John Robertson, who became a well-known London art critic and the father of that fine actor Sir Johnston Forbes-Robertson. Among its contributors was Joseph Robertson, the antiquary, and greatest of all Aberdeen's historians. Arrayed against the *Constitutional* and (curiously enough) the *Herald*, which supported patronage, was the *Banner*, founded in 1842, whose advocacy of Non-Intrusion was reinforced (even more curiously) by the *Journal*. For some years the editor of the *Banner* was David Masson, who later went to Edinburgh and became Professor of English there and distinguished for his massive edition of Milton. The paper was discontinued in 1851. Yet another Liberal organ, the *North of Scotland Gazette*, appeared in 1847, eventually under the editorship of William McCombie, who in the spring of 1853 substituted for it the *Aberdeen Free Press*, its first number appearing on 6 May. The *Free Press* absorbed the *Herald* in 1876.

The journalistic activity displayed in the weekly Aberdeen newspapers of the first half of the century was not exhausted by the topical publications. *The Inquirer* and *The Intruder* each lived for but a few numbers in the early 1800s. The fortnightly *Aberdeen Censor* in 1825 was a much more intelligent effort than either, and can still be read, by anyone who possesses some knowledge of the Aberdeen of those days, with pleasure and even excitement. Its principal writers were William Ferguson, son of a druggist in the Gallowgate and himself a teacher, who eventually emigrated to America; John Jaffrey, a minister, who was put in charge of the business of the Free Church after the Disruption; Alexander Milne Mowat, a lawyer; and John Ferres, son of a mason, who served his time in an advocate's office and finally emigrated to Australia. In 1826 Messrs. Robert Cobban & Co., 35 Guestrow, published 'a weekly, literary, political and commercial journal', the *Aberdeen Star*, which existed for eighteen months. The same printers produced a virulent monthly, the *Aberdeen Independent*, which was extinct within a year, and a sixpenny medical paper, the *Aberdeen*

Lancet. In 1831–2 there first appeared Lewis Smith's *Aberdeen Magazine,* whose contributors included John Stuart Blackie, John Hill Burton, John Ramsay[1] (for some time editor of the *Journal*), Joseph Robertson, and John Ogilvie, who reached a wider fame later with his dictionary. Then in 1832, Cobban produced Aberdeen's first true comic paper, *The Squib.* It was something new in a host of newspapers that had become commonplace, for from 1748 to 1829 there had been no fewer than twenty-three papers in Aberdeen, while between 1830 and 1840 a further batch of thirty-one was added. The thirties were Aberdeen's most fertile decade, the next being the eighties when twenty-eight papers were published. To return to 1832, that year also saw the arrival of *The Pirate, The Mirror,* and the longest-lived comic of all, *The Shaver,* published by John Anderson, printer, which did not expire until 1839.

Another Guestrow printer, John Watt, had started a Radical sheet, the *Scots Champion and Aberdeen Free Press,* in 1832, as well as Aberdeen's only dramatic paper, the *Theatrical Reporter.* In 1834 he issued a rather well-done magazine, *Letter of Marque,* which John Ramsay of the *Journal* edited, and then in quick succession the *Radical Artisan,* the *Aberdeen Monitor,* and finally an avowed rival to the *Shaver,* entitled the *Quizzing-Glass.* In 1837 the one and only number of the *New Shaver* appeared from the press of William Edwards at 35 Broad Street. The *Aberdeen Review* was another short-lived magazine published in 1843, and run by John Mitchell, a bookseller who had begun life as a shoemaker. The Aberdeen Young Men's Literary Union tried to express themselves in 1854 through *The Tyro,* but I know of only one number.

Of the Bards of Bon-Accord we need concern ourselves only with those who were actual natives or for long inhabitants of the city. James Hay Beattie, eldest son of the author of *The Minstrel,* died in his early twenties, in 1794 already a professor but not a poet although he wrote various pieces, including the long, rather incoherent *On the Excellence of Christianity.* The Rev. John Ogilvie, although he lived to be 80, was as stilted and pompous in verse to the end of his days as the young Beattie; he wrote *The Day of Judgment* and *Providence* among a lot of other things of the same kind. Francis Douglas, already mentioned for

---

1 Ramsay died of a painful disease. When on his death-bed he was visited by one of those ladies who thrive in every age upon the worst traits of human nature. She explained to him that his sufferings were due to his sins. 'Madam', said Ramsay, 'it's whom the Lord *loveth* that he chastiseth.'

his share in the *Aberdeen Intelligencer*, wrote, printed and published his *Rural Love, a Scottish Tale*, in 1754; and, unlike his newspaper, it was thought good enough to be stolen and reprinted as one of the poems of Alexander Beattie in 1832.

Andrew Shcrrifs (born 1762, date of death unknown), was the son of a deacon of the Incorporated Trades, a pupil at the Grammar School, a graduate of Marischal College. His *Poems, chiefly in the Scottish Dialect*, 1790, have made him perhaps rather more famous than their intrinsic merit warrants, for the book was published in Edinburgh at a time when Edinburgh badly wanted a vernacular poet to balance the achievements of a certain Robert Burns from the south-west; and Sherrifs therefore struck a lucky moment. He was keen on plays and wrote several, but apart from the song, 'A cogie o' yill and a pickle aitmeal', nothing came from his pen that is very memorable today. William Beattie, a flax-dresser, whose *Winter's Night* appeared in the little volume, *Fruits of Time Parings* in 1801, was a much better poet, and the already-mentioned Alexander Beattie (1780–1840), a native of Inverurie, 'borrowed' the most of his verses. William Brown, brother of the Alexander Brown who was Provost 1822–3 and 1826–7, eventually became editor of the *Edinburgh Weekly Journal*, and was the author of some racy pieces.

Alexander Watson (1744–1831) a tailor, was the author of *The Kail Brose of Auld Scotland*. John Ewen (1741–1821) who hailed from Montrose, was a jeweller in Aberdeen, where the Athenaeum Restaurant now is, for forty years, a member of the Musical Society, and a town councillor who helped to improve the condition of the streets of Aberdeen. He wrote 'The Boatie Rows' and (according to George Walker) the chapter in Walter Thom's History on 'Literature and the Arts'. The Rev. John Longmuir (1813–83), minister of 'the sailors' kirk', wrote *The College and Other Poems*, and *Ocean Lays*, as befitted his associations. John Imlah (1799–1846), born in North Street, became a pianoforte tuner, migrated to London, emigrated to Nova Scotia and died in Jamaica, leaving for his enduring monument the version of 'Where Gadie Rins' that comes nearest in beauty to the old traditional lines.

But the Aberdeen poet who gained the greatest celebrity in his life-time and is still, whether deservedly or not, the best known of the Bards of Bon-Accord was William Thom. Born towards the end of the eighteenth century into the humblest circumstances, sent to a cotton factory at the age of 10, and eventually a weaver to trade, who picked up a precarious living through the countryside, he had a poem accepted by Adam of the *Herald*, which appeared on 2 January 1841 and, under the title 'The Blind Boy's Pranks', made its author's fame at once. Before that year was out he was the guest of honour at complimentary dinners in Edinburgh, London, and Aberdeen, and until 1844 he luxuriated in the sunshine of public approbation, which presented him with many a hundred guineas and no doubt helped to inspire some of his best verse. In 1844 appeared the first edition of his *Rhymes and Recollections of a Handloom Weaver*, other editions following in 1845 and 1847. He lived and wrote and traded in Dundee, Inverurie, Peterhead, London, and when eventually his funds dried up and his friends deserted him, in Dundee again, where on 20 February 1848 he died in penury. Thom, so far as he has anything to say, is an exceedingly slender and often blatantly sentimental poet, but on the gentle, whimsical themes that accorded best with his genius, like 'The Blind Boy's Pranks' and 'The Wedded Waters', he was a more exquisitely musical singer than any writer the North-East has produced.

After William Thom came four other Williams, all of whom attained considerable eminence among the verse writers of their day. William Anderson (1802–1867), born in the Green and apprenticed first as a cooper and then as a weaver, joined the harbour police in 1849 and the city police in 1860, reaching the rank of lieutenant. His poems are contained in his *Rhymes, Reveries and Reminiscences*, 1851 and 1867, which are in fact two separate volumes although the latter professes to be the second edition of the former. The best work he did was in his friendly 'flyting' with William Cadenhead, each speaking for an Aberdeen well and dealing faithfully with the pleas and pretensions of the other. The competition had the effect of bringing out also the best work of Cadenhead (1819–1905), who rose to the position of overseer of Broadford Works, and whose talent was for light, slightly convivial verse.

William Forsyth (1818–79), although a native of Turriff, lived most of his life in Aberdeen, once he was compelled by ill-health in 1841 to give up the study of medicine. After being sub-editor on the *Herald* he was for nearly thirty years editor of the *Journal*, but when the newspaper became a daily his health again broke down. He contributed to such national periodicals as *Punch*, *Blackwood's* and the *Cornhill*, won a public competition in England with his *Martyrdom of Kelavane*, 1861, took a firm seat amongst local writers with his *Midnight Meeting*, and strengthened both reputations with his *Idylls and Lyrics*, 1872. He had a fine sense of rhythm, and a good heart, and like all the singing Wil-liams, he loved his Aberdeen. William Carnie (1824–1908), born like Anderson in the Green, began as an engraver, became interested in music, joined the ranks of Aberdeen journalists and in 1861 was ap-pointed treasurer of the Infirmary and Asylum. He wrote several excellent songs, such as 'My Neighbour the Miller', and 'There's aye some Water whaur the Stirkie Droons', and his 'Daavit Drain o' Hirpletillim' was considered good enough to be included in the best of all Scottish anthologies, John Buchan's *Northern Muse*.

These were the singers. By the plain prose-writers, setting aside the academes, who are mentioned in the account of the University, and others already alluded to, much good literary work, mainly in history, was done by Aberdeen writers. Before 1800 the only attempts at writing Aberdeen's history, apart from incidental references in descriptions of the burgh, were the very imperfect contemporary records made by Walter Cullen and John Spalding. In 1811 Walter Thom wrote a two-volume *History of Aberdeen*, rather rudimentarily economic and sociological in character, which Joseph Robertson is never weary of castigating and which George Walker describes in the sentence, 'Thom is a good condenser of what was put before him'. In 1818 William Kennedy (1768–1836), an Aberdeen advocate who had indexed the municipal records, published his two-volume *Annals of Aberdeen*, a work which, while its imperfections are many and it con-tains numerous inaccuracies due to inadequate information, yet possesses a soundness that is impressive and a charm that grows with closer acquaintance. In 1822 Robert Wilson issued his *Historical Account and Delineation of Aberdeen*, with a number of line engravings, and so provided the basis for James Rettie's somewhat disappointing *Aberdeen of Fifty Years Ago* of 1868.

Joseph Robertson (1810–66) has been described, not unfairly, as a 'quarrier rather than a builder'. His *Collections for a History of Aberdeen and Banff* and his *Illustrations of the Topography and Antiquities of Aberdeen and Banff* are indeed quarries to which all subsequent students of the history of the North-East have had to resort. His *Scottish Abbeys* and his *Reformation in Scotland* are written, like his delightful *Book of Bon-Accord*, with an unexpected lightness of touch. From time to time his Episcopalian leanings impart a somewhat rabid tone to his historical opinions, but few men knew more about their subject than he.

John Hill Burton (1809–81), a graduate of Marischal College and a member of the Scottish Bar, soon gave himself up to the study of history. His *History of Scotland* and his *History of the Reign of Queen Anne* are the chief supports of his reputation, his once famous *Political and Social Economy* being now considered out-of-date. But these more ambitious works have not the grace and charm of his *Narratives from Criminal Trials in Scotland*, his *Book-hunter*, his *Cairngorms* and his *Scot Abroad*. He received an office in the Civil Service in 1854 and his *History of Scotland* won for him the post of Historiographer Royal. William Forbes Skene (1809–92) Burton's successor as Historiographer-Royal, belonged to the family of Skenes of Rubislaw. He was a lawyer, with a lawyer's analytical mind that stood him in good stead when he wrote his *Celtic Scotland*. His successor in turn was David Masson, another Aberdonian. The office of Historiographer-Royal since Masson's death has been held by a fourth Aberdonian, Sir Robert Rait. George Grub (1812–92), also a lawyer and eventually Professor of Law in the University of Aberdeen, wrote *The Ecclesiastical History of Scotland*, which is now less esteemed than it should be. John Mackintosh (1833–1907), a merchant, demonstrated by his *History of Civilisation in Scotland* that the historical sense was not confined in Aberdeen to members of the learned professions, and his *Historic Earls and Earldoms of Scotland* and his *Valley of the Dee* attest his ability to specialise in an age when specialisation was less common than it is now.

Two other local historians deserve mention out of quite a group of their kind. In 1893 there appeared William Robbie's *Aberdeen: Its Traditions and History*, a work which, although much less exhaustive than Kennedy's, is in all material respects a better history. It is selective and it is reliable and it is exceedingly readable. Of quite a different stamp, but yet containing almost as much detail as any history of the burgh, is William Walker's *Bards of Bon-Accord*, 1884, whose author (1840–1931) was the son of the last handloom weaver and the secretary of the Chartists in Aberdeen. William Walker's application was such that he rose to be managing director of the Equitable Company, while he acquired among students of traditional minstrelsy throughout the world a reputation not excelled save by Gavin Greig, New Deer. *The Bards* is the most companionable book ever written in Aberdeen.

Amongst miscellaneous writers whose work has brought lustre to Aberdeen there should be mentioned Alexander Chalmers (1759–1834), the first man in this country to produce an adequate dictionary of biography; Alexander Bain (1818–1903) son of a weaver, Professor of Logic and Rector of Aberdeen University, founder of the modern study of psychology, founder and inspirer of *Mind*, and one of the leading philosophers of the century; and William Minto (1845–1903), Bain's professorial successor, who wrote that classic of criticism, *Characteristics of the English Poets*. In modern Biblical criticism William Robertson Smith (1846–94), if he did not lead the field, certainly set the pace. Deposed on account of 'heresy' from his chair in the Free Church College at Aberdeen, he lived to see his theories, as expounded mainly in his *Essays on Biblical Criticism*, accepted by a great body of theological scholars. He was also editor of the *Encyclopedia Britannica*.

The Aberdonian's innate fondness for journalism was signalised very early in the modern history of the Fourth Estate. James Pirie or Perry (1756–1821) graduated at Marischal College, but his father having died penniless he became a draper's assistant and then joined the theatrical company of Booth, the famous actor. Later he secured a post as a manufacturer's clerk in Manchester, took an active part in debating and other societies, went up to London in 1777, made a name for himself as a reporter, became editor of the *European Magazine* started in 1782, and eventually editor and part proprietor of the *Morning Chronicle*. His contributors included Charles Lamb, the Campbell who became Lord Chancellor, and William Hazlitt, some of whose critical articles Perry had the temerity in turn to criticise, and he offered Robert Burns a well-paid job. Nelson stood godfather to his daughter, the greatest of English Greek scholars, Porson, was his brother-in-law, he died worth £130,000, and to the end of his days 'he never quite lost his retail manner' that he acquired behind the draper's counter. A contemporary of his, John Scott (1783–1821), whom Bishop Heber called 'the ablest of the weekly journalists', and who was a schoolfellow of Byron, became editor of the *London Magazine* in 1820, and by his attacks upon the filibusters of *Blackwood's Magazine*, Christopher North and John Gibson Lockhart, arrived at the point of a duel with the latter, who, however, called off, but on his place being taken by another Aberdonian from Turriff, Jonathan Henry Christie, shots were exchanged, and Scott was mortally wounded.

James Gordon Bennett (1795–1872), though a native of Newmill, near Keith, was educated for the priesthood at the Roman Catholic School in Constitution Street, Aberdeen. He emigrated to America in 1819, and after a precarious career in several occupations, began to lecture in New York on political economy and to write for the press. In 1835 there appeared the first number of *The New York Herald*, price one cent, which was printed in a cellar and of which he was proprietor, editor and circulation and advertisement manager. Like Perry, he was an innovator, he published the first Wall Street financial article, the first telegraphed full report of a political speech, led the way in the use of illustrations and maintained a large staff of correspondents during the American Civil War. He was editor of the *Herald* almost to the day of his death.

There was another great journalist whose fame is more localised, but whose abilities were no whit less than those of the men who followed their careers in London. William Alexander (1826–94) came from Pitcaple to accept a post on the staff of William McCombie's *North of Scotland Gazette*, from which he passed to the *Free Press*. From the beginning he had the feeling that he must write a book about his own people, and his ideal took shape first as articles and sketches and then as the great Doric classic of Aberdeenshire country life, *Johnny Gibb of Gushetneuk*, 1871. This was followed in 1875 by the volume of short stories, which some regard as an even higher achievement, *Life Among My Ain Folk*, and in 1877 *Northern Rural Life*, a description of the manners and customs of the county, completed the trilogy. The vernacular has never been more masterfully handled than in *Johnny Gibb* and the short stories; the phrases have come to be quoted as a classical scholar quotes Virgil or Homer; and the characters, even without the magnificent portraits that George Reid gave them in aftertime, are strong and life-like to a degree that is not often encountered in Scottish imaginative literature.

CHAPTER TEN

Concert, Stage and Studio

One of the most virile as it was one of the most interesting and character-istic associations in Aberdeen came into being shortly after the Battle of Culloden. Its inception was due to Andrew Tait, organist of St. Paul's Episcopal Church, last Master of the Song School, composer of the psalm tune, 'St. Paul's', and life and soul of this famous association, the Aberdeen Musical Society. Tait's birth-date and birth-place are unknown, but the name is an Aberdeen one and he appears to have had some degree of kinship with the rather younger Charles Tait, Sheriff-substitute in Aberdeen, who married into the same family and whose burial ground adjoined Andrew's in St. Nicholas churchyard. He first appears in Aberdeen on his appointment to St. Paul's Church in 1734. In 1740 James Chalmers, the printer and original publisher of the *Aberdeen Journal*, was appointed precentor in St. Nicholas Kirk (a post traditionally conjoined with that of Master of the Song School) on condition that he found for the Song School a competent teacher of instrumental music. He found Andrew Tait, whose task there was to teach 'Singing, the Spinet, Harpsichord, Violin, German Flute and Common Flute, Italian Music, Church Music, Scots Music' and so on. The Song School was finally closed in 1755.

Despite the Song School's end, Aberdeen at that time was intensely musical. In 1748 Chalmers printed a little book of *Psalm Tunes* dedi-cated to the Provost, Baillies and Town Council, in which the tune of 'St. Paul's' appeared for the first time. Many years later it was assigned to Nahum Tait,[1] but a century earlier than that it was known in Edin-burgh as 'Aberdeen or St. Paul's' which pretty clearly fixes its origin. In the year that 'St. Paul's' was first printed there was founded the Aberdeen Musical Society of which Andrew Tait was an original if not

1 There was a long discussion on the authorship of 'St. Paul's' in the *Aberdeen Journal* in which an argument against Tait's claim was that John Rose, organist and composer, and his 'son-in-law', left the composer's name a blank when he printed 'St. Paul's'. But John Ross was the son-in-law not of Andrew but of Charles Tait, the Sheriff, who was not born until two years after Andrew came to St. Paul's.

indeed the original member, and of which for more than a quarter of a century he was the clerk and manager. From 1748 until he retired in 1775 'he copied out the music for every instrument, had charge of all their contracts for halls and housing.'[1] Although a comparatively poor man, his fee was the proceeds of one concert a year for all this.

During his lifetime the Society attracted all that was best in the population of town and county. Provosts and professors, earls and lairds, barons and baronets, colonels, merchants and artists and Francis Peacock the dancing master, were members and many of them, like Dr. John Gregory and Professor Beattie, were performers at the concerts. After Tait's retirement, the practice grew up of letting the honours go round by making frequent changes in the directorate, with the result that the Society steadily declined in energy and in 1806 was practically moribund. It was finally wound up in 1838 and all its books and instruments sold by public roup for the benefit of the Girls' Hospital then being founded. During its long career the Society had given frequent concerts — weekly at one time — always of the best music (not excluding Scots music) in the city, and the standard it attained may be gauged by its bill in 1792 of 117 guineas in fees to professional performers, equivalent in our values to well over £1,000.

Aberdeen's interest in music, however, was by no means extinguished with its Musical Society. The first musical festival in the town, a three-day affair, was held in 1828 as part of a campaign to revive the Musical Society, and cleared £40; but a second venture in 1834 cost the promoters £150. The 'Messiah' was first performed in Aberdeen on that occasion. In 1847 an orchestra, the Euterpean Society, was founded, but survived only for a year or two, being merged in the Haydn Society, which introduced subscription concerts. In 1849 William Carnie, later precentor of the West Kirk and editor of *The Northern Psalter*, founded the Harmonic Choir which eventually included ladies in its membership and lasted until 1860.

Medieval Aberdeen we have seen as foremost for its interest in the crude pageantry that then passed muster for acting. The Crafts whose members staged the Halyblude plays were discouraged from these activities after the Reformation, but one fragment of pageantry persisted in the form of a New Year's Day procession. Each craft had its champion, fully armed in 'mail', which often was no stronger than tin or leather, and its chaplain, complete with Bible, Geneva gown and bands

1   From a Manuscript history of the Musical Society, by the late William Walker, in the present writer's possession.

and flowing wig. The Hammermen had Vulcan grasping a thunderbolt and seated in a chariot, while St. Crispin, patron saint of shoemakers, led his Craft with a crown and a crowd of acolytes. Fancy dress was frequently worn. In 1785 an attempt was made to stop the procession and several participants were arrested but had to be released on bail as their friends had smashed all the Tolbooth windows. On the passing of the Reform Act in 1832 the ancient pageantry was for once revived, Crispin on this occasion being flanked by Earl Grey and Lord Brougham, while Lord Althorp and Lord John Russell rode in a hackney coach and the Archibishop of Canterbury walked amidst the insignia of cobblery.

Aberdeen's first playhouse was a wooden building in the Spital, where about 1751 a company of actors from Edinburgh performed for a short season. It was in the Spital, too, in 1773, to the south of the churchyard that the celebrated Edinburgh actor, West Digges, built a small playhouse, but nothing much seems to have been done about it or in it. Like its immediate successors, one about 1780 in a Queen Street inn and another in Chronicle Lane, it was a small affair. The Chronicle Lane place was known as 'Coachy's playhouse', its owner being a coach proprietor. The Queen Street theatre was, curiously enough, converted into a church in 1780. The mellowing influence of the Moderate element in the Church of Scotland was still hardly strong enough in Aberdeen to soften the community's heart to the fascinations of the stage. But the atmosphere was changing nearer the end of the century. In 1789 the building was commenced of the Theatre Royal (later to become a church and still later a dance hall) at the south end of Marischal Street. Financial difficulties, however, suspended the work until 1794, and it was only in December 1795 that the house opened under the management of Stephen Kemble, an English actor-manager whose acting and physique may be imagined from the criticism that 'his sole qualification for acting Falstaff was his being able to do it without stuffing'. His wife was an actress, a Miss Satchell, with a beautiful voice and a turn for sentiment but with a vicious temper — once while playing Lady Randolph in *Young Norval* and bending over her son, Henry Johnston, with the words 'my beautiful, my brave', she nearly bit a piece out of his shoulder in sheer spite.

Kemble stayed in Aberdeen only a few months. The lessees who came after him had a sore struggle to find the rent. One of them, Mrs. Mudie, engaged in 1811 the first 'star' turn Aberdeen ever saw in the person of Mr. John (or Jack) Bannister, described as 'the prince of comedians of his day' and 'favourite pupil of David Garrick'. Bannister played the parts of Colonel Feignvill in the comedy *A Bold Stroke for a Wife* and Dr. Lenitive in the farce, *The Prize, or 2, 5, 3, 8.* He also sang the comic song, 'The Tortoiseshell Tom-cat', stated to have been disposed of at an auction in London for 233 guineas—the cat, not the song.

The Theatre Royal could seat 600; the prices of admission were boxes, 3s.; pit, 2s.; gallery, 1s. The house was worth about £65 full, and it had cost £3,000 to build. An English visitor in the middle of last century thus described it:

The check-taker looked like a worn-out bum-bailiff; the woodwork of the interior looked as if it had been made out of old orange boxes and ruined market stalls. The tragedy was a farce; the comedy was downright murder; and the music sounded like an accompaniment to toothdrawing. But the scanty audience very evidently enjoyed the whole thing; and so did we. It was so gloriously ill-done that it was impossible not to be pleased with it. And I question whether the fingering of Sivori, or the baton of Julien, could have delighted us half so much as the comical antics of the sordid wretch who misled the orchestra of three split fiddles and a hoarse cornopean.[1]

The theatre had a very difficult time until 1827, when Corbett Ryder took it over and ran it capably until his death in 1842. After a short interregnum, his widow married John Pollock, a member of the stock company, and carried on until Pollock died in 1853, after which Mrs. Ryder held it until 1862. In 1828 Ryder brought Edmund Kean to Aberdeen to play Richard III. The prices were doubled and the receipts on the last night of the run were £160. William Charles Macready was also in Aberdeen, where he found his wife, Katherine Atkins,[2] daughter of a scenic artist. Amongst the notables who played their parts at the Theatre Royal were Daniel Terry, the comedian; John Philip Kemble, the tragedian; Charles Mackay, who created the part of

1   It can hardly have been so bad as all that. Joseph Robertson says it was quite comfortable, and two such enthusiastic playgoers as William Carnie and William Walker were not so censorious as the English visitor.

2   I know not whether in the state of girlhood
        Or womanhood to call her. 'Twixt the two
        She stands, as that were loth to lose her, this
        To win her most important. The young year,
        Trembling and blushing 'twixt the striving kisses
        Of parting Spring and meeting Summer, seems
        Her only parallel.

So Sheridan Knowles of her. Apparently quite a girl!

Bailie Nicol Jarvie; Sheridan Knowles, the playright; Charles Kean and his wife; John Vandenhoff; G. V. Brooke; Miss O'Neil (immortalised in *Pendennis*) Helen Faucit, Miss Braddon, the novelist; Corbett Ryder himself, said to have been the best Rob Roy there ever was and Mrs. Ryder, whose maiden name was Jeannie Fraser, a very fair actress and an excellent coach. Ryder's son by his first marriage, Tom, described as a first-rate comedian and good singer, was an outstanding member of the theatre's stock company.

Not only were there visiting 'stars' and the home repertory actors, the amateurs were frequently able to show their faces on the boards. Officers from the barracks, the local Freemasons, and the workers at Broadford and the Combworks were all wont to present the plays they liked. Great singers of the day also appeared — such as Madame Catalini, the prima donna, Sinclair the tenor, John Wilson, the Scottish singer, and Sims Reeves. Ryder himself seems never to have been at a loss to keep his patrons interested by a variety of entertainment. In 1830 he ran a Masquerade. In 1834 when the Highland Show was at Aberdeen, he supplied a Music Festival presented by the local Musical Society, oratorio being given in what is now St. Andrew's Cathedral and the songs and instrumental music in the theatre.

Mrs. Ryder lived for thirteen years after relinquishing control of the theatre, and in her retirement was presented with her portrait in the character of Lady Macbeth, which, along with Helen MacGregor in *Rob Roy*, was her favourite and most impressive part. From her the husband of her daughter Jessie, A. C. M'Neil, took over. M'Neil was also a good actor, much approved as Rob Roy and as the Badger in *The Streets of Aberdeen*. In 1867 he took over the Princess's theatre, Edinburgh, and was succeeded by his brother-in-law, Edward Price, husband of Emma Ryder, herself a great favourite as Jo in *Bleak House*. Price's best part was Mr. Micawber in *Little Emily*. In these later years notable players in the theatre were Osmond Tearle and Wilson Barrett, the latter of whom won his wife Miss Caroline Heath, 'The Queen's Reader', while playing in *East Lynne*. The titles of these plays indicate the sentimental cast that came over the theatrical taste in Aberdeen during the middle Victorian years.

Aberdeen's first considerable portrait painter after Jamesone was John Michael Wright, who seems to have had some tuition from Jamesone, became a prominent member of the artistic circles in Florence, and on returning home did many portraits of Restoration celebrities. But the nineteenth century was Aberdeen's golden age in art. The eldest of the important painters was James Giles (1804–70), of whom William Carnie reported that 'his name was the first to be mentioned when Aberdeen living painters were the subject of conversation'. His father was a calico-printer's blockmaker, and he himself began life as a teacher of drawing. After a tour of continental art schools, he came home and took up painting in earnest. He is reputed to have suggested, through his patron Lord Aberdeen, to Queen Victoria that Balmoral would make a suitable Highland residence. For Lord Aberdeen he did the remarkable collection of North-East castles some of which the Third Spalding Club published in what is the most attractive of its volumes. He was specially appreciated by his contemporaries for his animal studies, sometimes with a landscape background; and it used to be said that one could dine off his salmon. At his death some sixty oils and a hundred water colours were sold in his Bon-Accord Street studio. A dozen of Upper Deeside scenes were purchased for the Queen.

Amongst Aberdeen's greatest artists was William Dyce, R.A. (1806–64), who belonged to a slightly different social class from his contemporaries, his father being a doctor in the city and he himself a product of the Grammar School and an M.A. of Marischal College. After some years in Rome, he set up his easel in Edinburgh, but migrated to London, where in 1843 he was appointed headmaster of the New School of Design at Somerset House, and some years later, professor of Fine Art at King's College, his interests in art being very wide, and embracing music, to which latterly he devoted a great deal of skilled attention as well as painting. He was one of those selected to embellish the Parliamentary buildings and executed some of the frescoes in the House of Lords, being thus indirectly responsible for its 'tee-name' of 'the painted chamber'. The frescoes were unfinished when he died. In 1848 he became an academician and would had he lived have been President of the Royal Academy. He specialised in Scriptural and mythological subjects, and he also did portraits and a few landscapes, mostly in his earlier years. Before his death he became deeply interested in church music. When a group of Aberdeen art lovers — Alexander Macdonald, John Forbes Whyte, Alexander Walker, George Reid amongst them — commissioned Daniel Cottier to execute the famous Artists' Window in St. Machar's Cathedral to Aberdeen's three greatest painters, Dyce was set beside George Jamesone and John Phillip.

John Phillip, R.A. (1817–67), was the son of a shoemaker born at 15 Skene Square (where, amazingly for Aberdeen, a tablet was put up to signalise the connection), apprenticed to a house painter at the

Wallace Tower corner of the Netherkirkgate, got a little coaching from James Forbes of Peterhead, a portrait painter of some ability, and was taken up by Major Pryse Gordon and Lord Panmure, both of them with influence in quarters where influence could help. For Lord Panmure Phillip twice painted an Aberdeen-Angus bull of his lordship's breeding. Panmure 51, that does not look very impressive on canvas but gave a helping boost to the breed in its formative stages. Phillip's career naturally falls into two parts, before and after 1851, the year in which he first made acquaintance with Spain. Much of his earlier work involved study of the working classes and the ordinary run-of-the-mill people with whom his lot had been cast. These impressions, less vivid than his later work, are nevertheless characterised by a delicate and subtle colour sense that may not be outlasted by the more intense and flamboyant of his Spanish canvases. In 1852 two of his Scottish pictures 'A Scotch Washing' and 'A Scottish Baptism' won him more than passing notice in London, one of them being sold at £300, a very respectable price for a production of an unknown young artist. Even when Spain was making his fortune he often reverted to subjects from his Aberdeenshire recollections, notably such compositions as his 'Lowrin Fair' (mistakenly called 'Aikey Fair' in the catalogue of the centenary show of his works). The sunshine and richness of the Spanish atmosphere evoked a new talent and the man who had only a few years before paid his sea passage from Aberdeen to London by his brush was commanding sums of four figures. It was said that for one of his portfolios he received no less than £20,000, the Scottish National Gallery at second-hand paid £5,000 for 'la Gloria', the Queen commissioned the canvas of 'The Wedding of the Princess Royal' and the Speaker that of 'The House of Commons'. But it probably is as 'Spanish Phillip' or 'The Scottish Velasquez' that he will be most generally remembered.

James Cassie, R.S.A. (1819–79), born in Aberdeen, practised in many styles of composition, but the verdict of one critic at the Royal Scottish Academy Exhibition of 1864 that 'there is no artist in the Exhibition who can be compared to James Cassie as a marine painter' pays tribute to his flair for bold coastal scenes, upon which latterly he concentrated after his first penchant for animal studies; he illustrated the now very scarce volume upon British cattle breeds for which Professor William Macgillivray wrote the descriptions. In natural alliance with his sea pictures were studies like his 'Aged Fisherman' which also won him a reputation.

Two brothers, Andrew Robertson (1777–1845), and Archibald Robertson were prominent as miniaturists, the former in London, and the latter in U.S.A. where he had Washington among his sitters. It is fitting that here a word should be said of Aberdeen's great photographic pioneer George Washington Wilson (1823–93). He belonged to Forglen, was apprenticed to a joiner, then studied art in Edinburgh and Paris, and began to paint miniatures. In 1849 back in Aberdeen, he was struck by the possibilities of calotypes, built himself a camera and began to 'take' photographic portraits. He was commissioned in 1855 to make a portrait of Queen Victoria and by 1856 he had no equal in Scotland as a photographer. He constructed a travelling dark room and toured the country photographing everything he saw of beauty or interest. He took the first snapshots, which in 1862 gained awards at the London International Exhibition. His son Charles who died in 1958 at the age of 94, was associated with his father, and left his priceless stores of negatives to Aberdeen Public Library. About the same time as Wilson, in Australia the son of a Culter blacksmith, John Smith (1821–85), a graduate of Marischal College and for a time lecturer there, became the first professor of Chemistry in 1852, and besides providing Sydney with a safe water supply, he pioneered photography in what was not then a British Dominion.

Sculpture was popular with Aberdeen artists. Sir John Steell, R.S.A. (1804–91), son of an Aberdeen wood carver, spent most of his life in Edinburgh which he embellished with his statues of Allan Ramsay, 'Christopher North', Lord Jeffrey, Dr. Chalmers, and other eminent Scotsmen. For Aberdeen he did a marble statue of Provost James Blaikie, and his 'Head of Minerva' surmounts the entrance door to the Art Gallery. William Brodie, R.S.A. (1815–81), born in Banff, began life as a plumber in Aberdeen, but his extranean work came to the notice of some influential people, with the result that he was commissioned by Queen Victoria to do marble busts of royalty for Balmoral and elsewhere. Eventually he settled in Edinburgh. His bust of John Phillip is one of his best pieces. His brother, Alexander (1829–67), born in Aberdeen, executed the marble statue of Queen Victoria which the Prince of Wales unveiled in 1866 at the south-east corner of St. Nicholas Street, but which had to be removed to the shelter of the Town House in 1888 on account of deterioration by the weather.

In the first half of the nineteenth century Aberdeen had its first major break-through by native practitioners in the most utilitarian of the arts, architecture. The period saw the creation of many fine examples of building and civic planning, which continue to add grace, dignity and variety to the modern city. It was a Glasgow man, David Hamilton, who was responsible for the lay-out of Union Street and King Street. Others, both native and imported, are still represented by extant buildings in the city, but for the first half of the century two architects dominated the scene in more senses of the word than one — Archibald Simpson and John Smith. The former, born in 1790, son of an Aberdeen merchant and nephew of a master mason who may have had a hand in the making of Marischal Street, studied his art in London and in Italy. His first essay was Union Chambers in 1811, his last completed work in Aberdeen the three Free Churches and their lovely brick spire at the corner of Belmont Street and the Schoolhill in 1844 (he died in 1847). His memorials in the city are too numerous to mention and, like those of John Smith, they are remarked from time to time in these pages. Both men designed mostly in granite and usually in the classical tradition. What is regarded as Simpson's greatest creation was the North Bank head office at the corner of King Street and the Castlegate, the unique terracotta emblem of Demeter which surmounts the portico being the design of James Giles. St. Andrew's Cathedral, the frontage of the Music Hall (the large hall itself was the work later of Simpson's pupil and successor James Matthews), the old Royal Infirmary, some lovely private houses such as 28 Albyn Place, once occupied by Sir John Marnoch, the surgeon, now the Conservative Club, and the layout of numerous streets of which those that command the admiration of the experts particularly are Bon-Accord Crescent, the unfinished Marine Terrace and Victoria Street. Simpson was also responsible for the southern end of Albyn Place, but the gracious gardens and their background of terraces owe their origin to James Skene of Rubislaw, the friend of Walter Scott, in whose patrimony the solum lay. Other notable buildings attributable to Simpson are the old Marischal College at the east end of the present quadrangle, comprising the lower part of the Mitchell Tower with the Picture Gallery and the adjacent wings; and the very difficult frontage to the New Market which survived the fire of 1882 but has recently succumbed to the vandalism of Big Business as licensed by the Town Council.

A similar fate from the same Philistine combination has befallen John Smith's first work in Aberdeen and the first house to be built west of Union Bridge, Sir Alexander Bannerman's town residence at 204 Union Street, afterwards the second home of the Royal Northern Club, which was demolished in recent years to make way, as is the fashion of those modernising schemes, for something resembling a cross between a broiler house and an upright garden frame. Other of Smith's notable productions are the old North Church in King Street, now the Civic Art Centre; the Grecian screen to the St. Nicholas Kirkyard; the delicious little gem in Little Belmont Street built in 1841 as the Town's Schools, later occupied by the High School for Girls and after that it was part of Aberdeen Academy. Smith was the first official City Architect, and rejoiced as much no doubt in his nickname of Tudor Johnnie from his affection for styles Elizabethan as his father William Smith, a builder who was responsible for houses on the west side of Marischal Street, must have enjoyed his cognomen of Sink-'em Smith.

CHAPTER ELEVEN

Sodality in War and Peace

During the century between the crushing of the last Jacobite Rising and the eve of the Crimean War Great Britain was involved in many conflicts, and on at least four occasions the authorities had their apprehensions lest invasion might occur. War, however, continued to be in the main the affair of the professionals, and if the Navy was recruited by the kidnapping methods of the press gang, the Army had to depend for its strength mainly upon those who voluntarily adopted the career of the mercenary soldier. The armed forces, when war broke out, were never sufficient for all the demands of offence and defence, and in consequence there were always opportunities for the citizen soldier to combine with his daily work the discharge of the civic duty of defending his country.

Whenever danger threatened, the citizens spontaneously offered their services in arms, and the authorities of the War Department manifested with equal regularity a reluctance to entrust these arms to the masses. Thus in 1746, as soon as Lord Lewis Gordon and his Jacobites were withdrawn, a militia 360 strong was mustered, but the men were 'vastly discouraged for want of arms'. In 1759 in Pitt's war with the French, Aberdeen raised 500 men, and the Provost was instructed by the Council to borrow or buy 200 or 300 stands of arms and four 12-pounder cannon. He apparently succeeded in this commission for we hear of these weapons many years later. In 1778, during the American War of Independence, Aberdeen's offer to raise volunteers was declined by the Government, and the arms acquired in 1759 were called in, to the intense indignation of the city. The result was that four years later, when the Government realised the situation and formulated a plan to raise local levies, a public meeting called in Aberdeen to consider the scheme was attended by no one but the town's drummer, who had failed to persuade a single citizen to present himself.

In 1794, after the French Republic's declaration of war, when the 'Gallant Ninety-Twa' were raised, Aberdeen subscribed 300 guineas in defence subscriptions. In 1798, along with a scheme for volunteers,

Aberdeen Town Council voted 500 guineas for the Government's defence needs, while Provost Leys gave 100 guineas, two other citizens a like sum, and the Society of Advocates, Robert Gordon's Hospital and the Shipmasters' Society 200 guineas each, and farmers offered their men, horses and carts to increase the mobility of the home defenders. A 3 guinea bounty was made available, twenty firelocks were assigned to each company of sixty, the remaining forty men to serve the 'great guns', and eventually the city had a further 400 volunteers under the command of Alexander Moir of Scotstown, scion of a famous Jacobite family. This pre-Napoleonic Home Guard drilled from 5.30 to 8 a.m. and had a social as well as a martial bent, for we read of a performance, on 15 September 1795 'by desire of the Corps of Gentlemen Volunteers', of Shakespeare's *Merry Wives of Windsor*. In the same year they were issued with ball cartridge to suppress riots, while the ladies of the town presented the regiment with colours, and the sergeants were enjoined 'in particular to watch over the morals of the drummers' who were presumably the most susceptible of the corps to the temptations that assail the artistic temperament.

In 1796 the Volunteers were indeed called upon to show their mettle in quelling a mob, which they did very efficiently. Soon after this Moir retired from the command and was succeeded by Thomas Bannerman, whose grandfather Patrick had been Aberdeen's Jacobite Provost in 1715–16, and who was himself the father of Sir Alexander, Governor of Newfoundland. In 1797 a band was formed and John Ewen the watchmaker and author of 'The Boatie Rows', who was a captain in the force, wrote a song, 'The Aberdeen Volunteers', which John Ross, the organist of St. Paul's Church, set to music. About the same time the Incorporated Trades, which twenty years before had subscribed £400 to the Government 'to put down the rebellion in the colonies', raised a corps, the Royal Aberdeen Light Infantry Volunteers, of which Captain Alexander Dauney, of the Aberdeen Corps of Volunteers, Professor of Civil Law at King's, and uncle of Archibald Simpson, was appointed Lt.-Colonel. Old Aberdeen had also its Light Infantry Volunteers under Lt.-Colonel the Rev. Professor Gilbert Gerard.

All these corps were disbanded at the Peace of Amiens in 1802, but the respite did not last long, and in 1803 the citizen soldiers were re-embodied as the Aberdeen Volunteers or Finlason's Fencibles, so called from their colonel, nearly 800 strong who, in 1808 were transferred to the Aberdeen Militia. The pay per diem on duty in this corps for the permanent staff was — adjutant 8s.; sergeant 1s. 6¾d.; corporal

1s. 2¼d.; private 1s. In 1801 the adjutant received only 3s. 6d. The Royal Aberdeen Volunteers, successors of the Aberdeen Volunteers, were 480 strong, under Provost Thomas Leys as colonel, with another in the city's list of provosts, James Hadden, as lt.-colonel, and yet a third, Alexander Brebner of Learney, as major. In addition, there were the Gilcomston Pikemen[1] 150 in number, under Captain James Chalmers of the *Aberdeen Journal*, and the Aberdeen Pikemen (raised in Footdee), to the number of 400, who were led by Lt.-Colonel Alexander Tower of Ferryhill and Logie, son of a convener of the Incorporated Trades. In 1807 the pikemen got muskets and the whole organisation faded out as the menace of Napoleon receded.

Philosophic

Two of the enthusiasts who appear prominently in the records of the Aberdeen Musical Society played a leading part in a contemporary organisation intended to cultivate another interest of the mind. The Philosophical Society in Aberdeen, popularly known as 'The Wise Club', was founded in 1758, the principal members at the outset being Professor Thomas Reid, Principal George Campbell, Professor Alexander Gerard, Dr. David Skene, and the two musician-academes, John Gregory and James Beattie. The Society met in Aberdeen and the Aulton alternately once a fortnight, on the second and fourth Wednesdays of the month, in a hostelry, and after partaking of dinner (then an afternoon meal), at each alternate meeting there was a discourse or dissertation of not more than half-an-hour on a subject of which notice had been given at the previous meeting. This paper was then discussed by the other members, and the sederunt had to be ended according to the rules by 10 o'clock. The cost of the entertainment was limited to 8d. a head, and the substance of it consisted, besides the meal, of 'red-port', punch, porter, 'paips and tobaco', Reid for one being both a snuffer and a smoker. The other meeting of the month was usually devoted to a further talk upon the paper of the previous session. In this bracing atmosphere 'Sweet-bleedit' Campbell tried out the discoveries that eventually crystallised into his *Philosophy of Rhetoric*, Reid expatiated upon lines that became more widely known through his *Inquiry into the Human Mind*, Gerard rehearsed his *Essay on Genius*, Beattie his *Essay in Truth*, and the Society were the first to make acquaintance with Gregory's *Comparative View of the State and Faculties of Man*

---

1 It is not true that their discarded pikes were those issued to the Home Guard of 1940–1, but at least in 1803 there was no pretence about the pikemen's status, and they were not likely to face tanks and machine-guns.

with those of the Animal World. The end of the Society came in 1773, but during the fifteen years of its existence its members debated upon over 120 subjects, many of them topical as well as philosophical, and the range of their interests and fertility of their fancy are a tribute to the inspiring qualities of a diet of punch and haggis.

A second Aberdeen Philosophical Society was established in 1840 in the house of Professor William Gregory, a grandson of that Professor John Gregory who had been one of the founders of the first. The majority of the original members of the second society were professional scientists — they called themselves the 'Cultivators of Natural Science' to begin with — and included George Dickie the botanist, and Dr. Francis Ogston, father of Sir Alexander, Professor of Medical Logic and Medical Jurisprudence. Gradually the character of the membership became more general, lawyers and teachers, ministers and men of business being elected during the first ten years, and the scope of the papers increased in liberality from the severely scientific aspect of the first session.

In 1846 the Society was responsible for a series of twelve public lectures upon the then popular topic of mesmerism. In 1861 it undertook a survey of the ocean currents and other phenomena of the Arctic regions, but found the project beyond its powers. In 1852 a committee was appointed to draw up a glossary of the Aberdeenshire vernacular. That and similar schemes by other institutions have long evaded achievement. In 1883 a committee of the Society co-operated with the School Board in an investigation of school ventilation, and the same year 10,000 copies of a paper on Free Libraries read to the society by J. D. Milne were circulated in Aberdeen and were understood to have helped in persuading the burgh to adopt the Free Libraries Act. Conversaziones, the Victorian counterpart of the neo-Georgian coffee morning, were several times organised by the Society, and a feature of the sessional business was a summer excursion. The papers covered a wide range of subjects, those scientific possessing today mainly an antiquarian interest, those cultural in the old sense of the term being still valuable as befits the observations of minds like Bain's, Blackie's and Geddes's, while those on local subjects have become more useful with the passing of the years.

Medical
The Medico-Chirurgical Society, founded as the Medical Society, arose in 1789 out of the absence or inefficiency of the academic

instruction purveyed in medical science by the two colleges. It originated among medical students, led by the son of an Aberdeen merchant, James McGrigor, later and otherwise much more famous. Beginning as a debating club in the rooms of its members, the Society soon required the use of a hall, which was provided by Dr. Livingstone, the Professor of Medicine at Marischal College. In 1811 it assumed its present name, and the next year a new constitution providing for two sections, one for students admitted by examination which disappeared in 1870, and the other for fully-fledged physicians and surgeons who were elected to membership. The energetic founder continued for many years to watch over it 'with the anxiety of a parent', as he himself put it. In 1806 he suggested the building of a hall and forwarded 50 guineas for this object, a sum which by 1813 he had augmented by £300 out of the pockets of Army officers, who then, like those of Cromwell's army of occupation in the 1650s, were either better off or more inclined to learning than their modern counterparts. The handsome hall in King Street was built in 1820, and the Society has ever since been the focus and the inspiration of the medical profession in the city.

Eupeptic
In 1839, after a short-lived experiment in 1828–30, there was founded, two years in advance of any similar body in the United Kingdom, the Aberdeen Society of Apothecaries, Chemists and Druggists, today the Aberdeen Pharmaceutical Association.[1] The principal object of this society, which indeed grew out of a meeting of chemists and druggists held at the request of their staffs, was the welfare and education of the assistants and apprentices of the apothecaries' profession. The first achievement of the society was the founding of a library, and the second the institution of lectures, which were for many years conducted by the first secretary and librarian, Charles Davidson, who had then a business at 1 Exchequer Row, but had previously been of the firm of P. Williamson & Co., 10 Gordon Street. Rooms were secured in St. Nicholas Lane and there the library was housed. Shop hours in the forties were 7 or 8 a.m. (according to the season) to 9 p.m., except Thursdays and Saturdays, when the closing hour was optional, and on Sunday when the shops were closed during church hours. Some years later the shutters were kept up throughout Sunday but business was attended to on request.

1   For full particulars of this interesting institution see the *Aberdeen Pharmaceutical Association, 1839–1939*, by Alexander Keith.

In 1868 the Pharmacy Act introduced examinations qualifying for professional status. After the Pharmaceutical Society of Great Britain (which the Aberdeen Society members had joined individually in 1853) had proved typically metropolitan in its refusal to be generous in assistance to the local effort, the Aberdeen pharmacists took matters into their own hands, and in 1871 established the Aberdeen School of Pharmacy in rooms in the old Girls' Hospital, 56 Gallowgate, with Dr. Beveridge as principal lecturer at a fee of 25s. In 1873 assistants and apprentices were admitted as associate members. In 1874 the Society returned to St. Nicholas Lane, in 1879 a pharmaceutical museum was formed. In 1881 Gordon's College provided evening classes in Botany and Chemistry which the Society encouraged the apprentices to attend. In 1882 country chemists were admitted. In 1885 the Society took rooms in 21 Bridge Street for a laboratory, museum, lending and reference library, and there classes were conducted until 1898, when the arrangement was made with the Governors of Robert Gordon's College which ended shortly in the establishment of the Pharmacy School there.

Historical
The year in which the apothecaries founded their Society saw also the birth of a body of a very different kind. Historical research, thanks in large measure to the influence of Walter Scott, had become an intellectual hobby with many Scotsmen, and in the autumn of 1839 two Aberdonians, John Stuart, advocate, 3 Queen Street, and Joseph Robertson, journalist, about to become editor of *The Constitutional*, had the idea of providing for Aberdeen a society 'for the publication of the Literary, Historical, Genealogical and Topographical remains of the north-eastern counties of Scotland'. On 23 December 1839 a meeting was held in the Royal Hotel with the Lord Provost in the chair at which the Spalding Club (called after Aberdeen's first historian) was launched with the Earl of Aberdeen (the Premier Earl, 'the travell'd Thane, Athenian Aberdeen') as President and John Stuart as Secretary. The Club was wound up on its birthday in 1870, after having spent £13,000 on thirty-eight volumes of local history, some of them having cost over £500 to produce, the great two-volume edition of *The Sculptured Stones of Scotland* requiring almost £3,000 and *The Book of Deir* nearly £800. These two books, the two-volume edition of Spalding's *Memorialls of the Trubles*, and the five volumes of the *Collections and Illustrations of the Shires of Aberdeen and Banff* are the most important of a very fine shelf of work emanating from the Society. John Stuart

edited thirteen of the set, while Robertson, Cosmo Innes and George Grub had each several to their credit. When the Club was wound up a memorial was erected over Robertson's grave in the Dean Cemetery, Edinburgh, while Stuart was presented with a piece of plate and his portrait by George Reid.

Forensic

The advocates of Aberdeen have long enjoyed among their brethren of the lesser breeds a reputation for an acquisitive power not easily distinguished from rapacity. Actually no association of legal men is governed by a code of ethics more humane and friendly than the Society of Advocates, which was probably embodied in 1633, formulated rules in 1764, instituted a generous benevolent fund for the widows and orphans of its members, and was granted three Crown Charters, in 1774, 1799 and 1862. From 1549 to 1912 the number of Aberdeen procurators or advocates is put at 613, several of whom have risen to eminence in their profession. Seventy-four were the sons of advocates, seventeen the sons and grandsons of advocates, and one the son, grandson and great-grandson of advocates. No satisfactory solution has been discovered to the conundrum, why is an Aberdeen solicitor an advocate? Nor has there been any revelation as to the condition of the members in 1838 when, at the dinner annually held after the Annual Meeting, a toast list of no fewer than fifty-three sentiments had been honoured.

Athletic

Golf is believed to have been played in Aberdeen about the time of the Union of the Crowns, because in the Town Council records of 1625 a muster of citizens for weapon practice is mentioned 'in the principall pairt of the links betwixt the first hole and the Quenis hole'. Gordon in his description of 1661 mentions golf, with football, bowls and archery, as being played in Aberdeen. In 1780 a Society of Golfers was formed, not to exceed more than twenty-five town members, though no limit was placed on the number of county members. Aberdeen Golf Club was founded in 1815 with William Kennedy the annalist as secretary, and as its first captain William Black, in 1828 captain of the great Blackheath Club. In 1828 a uniform of scarlet coat and gilt buttons was adopted, a black velvet cap some time later displacing a lum hat for headgear. Entry money was raised in 1827 to two guineas, with an annual subscription of 5s. In 1867 a clubhouse on the Links was opened, and in the account of a club dinner about that time when twenty-four members left eighty-two 'dead men' behind them, 'those present recollect nothing that happened'.

Agricultural

In 1758 in Old Aberdeen there was instituted the Gordon's Mill Farming Society, with several prominent members of the staff of King's College taking a more or less active part. Principal John Chalmers, who farmed the College farm of Cairntradlin in Kinellar and became proprietor of the estate of Sclattie, then a rural expanse at Bucksburn, was a noted agricultural pioneer. He and Thomas Gordon, Professor of Humanity and father of Anna, later Mrs. Brown of Falkland in Fife and source of many of the best ballads in Scott's *Minstrelsy of the Scottish Border* and Robert Jamieson's *Popular Ballads and Songs*, was secretary of the Club. Sir Archibald Grant of Monymusk and Robert Barclay of Ury, both important in the field of agriculture, sometimes attended, as did Professor Thomas Reid, better known as the philosopher of Common Sense, and Dr. John Gregory. Outside the University Francis Douglas, author of the *Description of the North-East of Scotland* and for the nonce farming in accordance with the best theory and at a heavy loss at Drum, Sir Alexander Gordon, the contemporary Fordyce of Eigie, and the minister of Kintore were among the members. J. H. Smith who has edited the minutes thinks there was an agricultural society in Aberdeen before the Club was founded, and in fact there was in 1759 a Farmers' Society of Gilcomston, which continued until 1837, whereas the Gordon's Mill Club closed down in 1764.

In 1843 Anthony Cruickshank, a haberdasher in Union Street, and partner with his brother Amos in the Scots Shorthorn herd at Sittyton, Newmachar, founded what is now the Royal Northern Agricultural Society, along with Captain Barclay of Ury, Grant Duff of Eden, and other breeders of pedigree cattle. For many years the Royal Northern's Show was greater than that of the Highland Society, its classes attracting competitors of the highest standard from all over the United Kingdom. In 1963 the Society, whose shows, for long at a stance in Kittybrewster now occupied by a housing scheme, and later at Hazlehead, having purchased the farm of Bankhead, near Bridge of Don, laid out a showground which was not inferior to any in the country. Departmental regulations and financial pressure have of late unfortunately severely limited the showing of stock, and even the display of agricultural requisites from which the Society drew a considerable part of its income being curtailed by the pressure of financial circumstances, the annual summer show was discontinued and the show-ground sold.

Masonic

While the first clear records of a Freemasons' Lodge in Aberdeen date to 1670, Masonry had been active for perhaps as long as two centuries before that. The Mark Book of Lodge 1 belongs to 1670, when there were forty-nine master and eleven apprentice masons in membership. About 1680–2 the rules of the Lodge were printed. To begin with the Lodge appears to have met in the open 'in the Parish of Nigg at the stonies at the poynt of the Ness', but in 1700 the Croft of Futtiesmyre, more or less where the gas works now are, was purchased and let for £78 Scots (£6 10s. sterling), to the father of James Gibb or Gibbs, the architect who was responsible for the eighteenth-century fabric of the West Kirk, as well as many famous buildings in England. In 1743 the Lodge of Aberdeen got its charter, counting No. 3 in Scotland.

In 1755 the foundation stone of the New Inn, immediately east of the Tolbooth was laid with Masonic honours to be the headquarters of the Lodge, but the move produced a split from which in 1781 the Operative Lodge was formed. Already, besides the original unit, there were three lodges in the burgh, St. Nicholas 1763, St. Andrew 1768, and the now extinct St. Luke 1777. Old Aberdeen, or St. Machar, founded about 1749, came in from the Aulton to a house 41 Queen Street some quarter of a century later. The extinct St. James followed in 1787, St. George in 1794, Neptune in 1856, St. Machar Woodside, 1826, Bon-Accord 1882, St. Clements 1883, Saltoun 1888. In 1821 the Aberdeen Province was erected into a dependency, with Thomas Burnett, a lawyer, as first Provincial Grand Master. By 1865 the house 41 Queen Street was the headquarters of most of the lodges and the premises were purchased in 1895.

The Age of Limited Liability. 1860–

The introductory chapters to the four preceding parts of this record marked a fairly clear division between phases in the development of the nation and of Aberdeen. There was the emergence into the light of history, followed by the War of Independence, the Reformation, and the last Jacobite rising. The cleavage was surprisingly clean-cut: neither the nation nor Aberdeen was quite the same after these decisive occurrences had fulfilled themselves. But the introduction to the fifth and last section is, as an Aberdonian would put it, like a mids in the sea. It has no clear location, no discernible place, it is fluid and intangible. Neither the 1832 Reform Act with, as subsidiary, the local government reform of 1833, nor the coming of the Victorian age, neither the great revolutionary year of 1848 nor the taking over of the administration by the business middle classes from the aristocracy, neither (in the case of Aberdeen) the provostship of Alexander Anderson in 1860–6, nor the union of the city's two universities in the earlier of these years, marked a well-defined period of development. The age of the Industrial Revolution merged insensibly into the era of the limited liability company and so on to 'rationalisation' and 'consolidation' and 'centralisation', to the take-over bid and the merger, eventually revealing in the first attempt at municipalisation and then nationalisation the tip of the iceberg of socialism throughout the activities of the community.

In the period of roughly one hundred years which the final section covers two great wars, especially the first, deprived the State of a high proportion of its best brains and masculine initiative. Aberdeen, like every other city in the kingdom, perhaps as much indeed as any, suffered this loss of brains and character, which in itself was responsible for the blurring of regional qualities and the reducing of civic individuality to a dull and soulless uniformity. Nothing in fact is more apparent to the historian of the city than the essential change that came over the nature of the community in the last two centuries. Much was achieved in that time, much that was admirable and in keeping with tradition as well, but especially in later years there crept into the schemes and efforts of the town an amateurishness, a woolliness of texture that are, or should be, at variance with the proficiencies of professional administrators, and the allegedly higher standards of education. Only in the private sector do we here and there catch a glimpse of the old flame of independent thinking and planning upon which Aberdeen's fortunes were founded.

The ascendancy of steam gave way to the dominance of the internal combustion engine, first on the ground and then in the clouds, just as the community's control of its destinies slipped from the hands of its own competent and experienced leaders into the flaccid fingers of politicians, knowing nothing of local needs and conditions, politicians whose ideas began by being earthy and ended in the air. The City Fathers who pioneered social service in Aberdeen's House of Correction would have been amused, amazed and disgusted at the waste and inefficiency of the Welfare State 350 years after their time. There would have been no Aberdeen had the hardy Saxons and Flemings of the burgh 700 years ago let the ownership of their flat-bottomed undecked boats pass into alien hands as has happened with Aberdeen's merchant marine today.

The loss of the nation's best young brains in the Kaiser's War gave an opening to the politicians, whose principal attribute is opportunism in the interests of their own order, and they proceeded between the wars, using the depressive weight of the civil service to reduce the country to a sombre uniformity of conduct. Towards this process in Scotland the Tory–Lloyd George Education Act of 1918, strengthened by the Tory legislation in the same sector of 1929, went a very long way towards dulling the public recognition of what was happening. In no part of Scotland was the revolution more destructive than in the North-East area, which both in town and country had during some fifty years built up an educational structure which enabled its youth to face any kind of competition anywhere requiring intellectual training and disciplined skill. The process of deterioration is still at work, and the decline in, for example, the achievement of Aberdeen's university products to which Theodore Watt drew attention forty years ago, had not been halted in the middle of the century.

But it would be misleading to present too doleful a picture. In the last hundred years Aberdeen has enjoyed three great boom periods in commercial reputation — with her clippers, her beef cattle and her white fish. She had clearly not forgotten, at least up to 1900, how to make money. In the same span of years many of her sons — and daughters — have made a name for themselves in many callings and in many lands. The traveller will find once he is beyond these shores that to be an Aberdonian is to be a complete cosmopolite equipped with the password that gives entry to whichever magic cave he wishes to explore or exploit. Those who deplore the 'drain' of emigration from Aberdeen do not seem to be aware that it has been going on for over 400 years, that actually it is nowadays lower in proportion to population than for generations, probably at any time, and that nothing has done more to maintain the city's reputation or given its resident business men more scope and opportunity to sell their produce. It has commercial links with every country whose needs are worth supplying and whose credit is good. 'Scotsmen, damned Scotsmen, and Aberdonians' is no more a jocular phrase. The Aberdonian abroad soon learns that for good or ill repute, for work or for play, he is regarded by the *cognoscenti* as the superlative Scot. The rest of Scotland does not like the comparison but the Aberdonian does not mind.

And so, in this final phase of the survey, Aberdeen remains, a little the worse of the wear perhaps, a little less dourly individualist in its outlook, a little more prone to go with the tide in business and organ-isation and opinion, but still recognisably a community on its own feet and in its own right, and both prepared and able to adjust itself at least as well to whatever exigencies the future may hold as any other city of its size. It is still the fair city by the sea that the Vikings knew 800 years past and its indigenous inhabitants are still the self-reliant characters that Dr. Johnson found them to be when he called in a couple of centuries ago.

Part 5

Aberdeen's Efforts to Keep in Step

CHAPTER ONE

The Town Within Living Memory

In the last decades of Victoria's reign the upward surge of population was being accommodated through the enterprise of private builders by the erection in all parts of the burgh of flatted tenements, almost all of them with only the most rudimentary sanitation, and in the west-end and other so-called residential parts of private dwellings, two-flatted or semi detached, terraced or detached, some of them built to elaborate and even grotesque designs, the smaller sorts neat and prim and unpretentious, but all of beautifully dressed granite, grey, pink and red, and often with pleasant ornamentation and relief. The building of the Viaduct westwards from Schoolhill opened up Rosemount in 1883, just as the opening of Victoria Bridge in 1881 made the south bank of the Dee available, and the formation of Sir Alexander Anderson's City of Aberdeen Land Association provided large areas in the Torry and Rubislaw districts for development, and as the tramways stretched outwards north and west and south, areas in Holburn, Ferryhill, Mannofield, Rubislaw, King Street and Gilcomston blossomed with single houses and little side streets like branches and buds upon a tree.

Even so, it was well after the commencement of the new reign and new century ere the changes became very marked. In Torry especially, as the trawling industry prospered, skippers and other well-paid key men both afloat and ashore built their houses along Victoria Road, for example, within smelling if not visual range of the element that kept them in comfort. Farmers who retired from the land while the going was good established themselves on the high ground north of Kitty-brewster and above Woodside, within easy reach of their friends and familiar scenes of the agricultural marts. About the same time the possibilities of Rubislaw den as the place for mansions with some se-clusion and the unusual amenities which the shallow wooded valley of the Denburn afforded were recognised, and the little glen was engrossed in the select complex that was taking shape with two arms, north and south. Refugees or retired people mostly from the valley of the Dee sought the rather less expensive neighbourhood of Mannofield, and the excellent houses of Great Western Road and its adjacent streets gradually filled the southern area.

Within the ancient boundaries considerable changes were taking place. Much that was old, but not all of it necessarily rotten, was coming down, and much that was modern but not all of it seemly, was going up. The erection of the new Town House, which included the county sheriffdom buildings, created almost as much of an upheaval at the west end of the Castlegate as the laying out of Union Street sixty-five years before. In 1867 when the new (and curiously Flemish-looking) municipal headquarters had taken shape, what remained of Huxter Row and Narrow Wynd disappeared, carrying much history and many ghosts with them. Mrs. Ronald's hostelry, 'The Lemon Tree', was there, Robert Gordon of Gordon's College had been born in Huxter Row, and the city police office, the city tax office, the weights and measures office, and the offices of the city and county procurators-fiscal, in short every limb of the establishment had been located in that narrow and withdrawn lane. Almost on the site of Huxter Row there took shape the Concert Court familiar today, with its elegant Society of Advocates hall. The lawmen migrated thither from their habitation at the south-west corner of the Back Wynd, their rooms becoming the Queen's Restaurant, superseded in turn about 1910 by the Queen's Cinema. The advocates in building their hall dispossessed the *Free Press*, which in 1872 flitted to Broad Street, whence it was driven by a fire in 1895 to the island site on Union Street east of St. Katherine's Wynd. Concert Court itself owed its name to the celebrated eighteenth-century Musical Society, whose fortunes have already been related.

The building of the Sheriff Court-house encroached upon the Laigh Tolbooth, which might easily have shared the fate of the remnants of Huxter Row and Narrow Wynd. It had already been altered rather to its detriment in 1820, and now the frontage and lower reaches of it were interfered with and refaced without much regard to the preservation of a harmonious aspect, only a small portion of the original wall of the tower, facing along Lodge Walk, remaining of the 1629 building. Behind this venerable edifice stood its attendant High Tolbooth, otherwise the East jail, which had been for generations the headquarters of Aberdeen City Police. Beside it was the rather temporary resting-place of the *Aberdeen Journal*, an old silk-mill to which the newspaper had migrated from what had at one time been the printing-house of Edward Raban, Aberdeen's first printer. The Town and

County building operations sent the *Journal* on its travels again. It eventually found a home in the office of the recently defunct *Northern Daily News* in Broad Street. It is now in very modern offices at Lang Stracht, Mastrick.

The Raban house was the one in which Robert Burns met Bishop Skinner, son of John Skinner the poet, in the sanctum of James Chalmers the printer, and they adjourned for a dram to the New Inn, where Dr. Johnson and James Boswell had lodged a few years before, and which formed the lower portion of the building erected by the Aberdeen Lodge of Freemasons (whence Lodge Walk). The *Journal* had to move when in 1839–42 the New Inn came down and the North of Scotland Bank built its head office. The High Tolbooth or East Jail was, as already noted, a men's calaboose, while the women were confined in the West Jail or Bridewell, half way along Rose Street. The governor of both jails from 1825 to 1862 was A. W. Chalmers, the maternal grandfather of one of Aberdeen's greatest latter-day characters, the Rev. James Smith of St. George's-in-the-West. The present police headquarters were opened in 1895. Craiginches Prison took over in 1891 from the High Tolbooth, which for some twenty years had been used for women as well as men.

On the east side of the Castlegate in 1893–6 when the Salvation Army Citadel was built to present a nondescript front to the line of Union Street, two houses had to come down, the residences of Francis Gordon of Kincardine o'Neil, the other of Principal William Laurence Brown of Marischal College, who was followed by James Cassie, R.S.A. North of them was the old Record Office which later became the burgh police court until 1891, when Justice Street was widened and improved. On the south side, west of the Aberdeen Bank, taken over in 1849 by the Union Bank and now the Bank of Scotland, was what was known as the Bursar's House, which had belonged to Dr. William Guild, but in more recent times had become a public-house, the Bursar's Hotel. It was engulfed in the demolitions of a slum clearance scheme that was intended to mop up Exchequer Row, but which remained an open space for over half a century until occupied by a supermarket. At right angles to the Bursar's House were buildings of Archibald Simpson's design and made into a newsroom by Provost Alexander Brown. The venture did not pay. The Athenæum as he called it, which had cost him £12,000 he sold to the newsroom attendant for £5. In 1888 James Hay, a butler with excellent ideas, bought the place and converted it into an eating-house whose fame as 'Jimmy Hay's' spread throughout the Seven Seas and the Five Nations. Its reputation was ably sustained when in 1908 John Mitchell, owner of the now defunct County Hotel (later and until a few years ago the Gordon Highlanders Club) in King Street, took it over. Mitchell was a Cabrach man who earned a triple reputation as a doric poet, a good business man, and as Mine Host superb.

Beyond the north-east corner of the Castlegate Albion Street, which connected the end of Justice Street with the Links, and was known as the Bool Road, presumably because it led to the place where bools were played (though there are other suggested derivations), was the scene of an experiment in social service. There in the early forties was established Dr. H. Wilson's Ragged School for poor children, the first of its kind in Scotland. A Ragged Kirk built of wood followed in 1848-9, which became the Albion Street Congregational Chapel in 1855. Under Wilson's successor Dr. John Duncan, the congregation so increased that a new church, Trinity Congregational, had to be built in the Shiprow in 1878. The labours of Wilson and Duncan had by that time completely changed the atmosphere of the Bool Road (its original name, Albion Street, being the title arbitrarily imposed upon the thoroughfare by the Police Commissioners in 1830). The former in 1847 had termed it 'the most debased and neglected part of the City, a special haunt of dissipation, a very hot-bed of profligacy and vice'; the most abominable of its 'dens of inquity', to quote another scandalised observer, being known as the Bool Road Theatre or Penny Rattler, a penny being the admission charge to the enjoyment of its unsavoury entertainments. Thirty years later the squalor had vanished and the district was notable for its good works, its temperance society, penny savings bank, and the Park Street day school for 150 children who were taught the three R's for a penny a week.

On the south side of the Castlehill the Hangman's Brae, so called probably because the hangman who operated on the adjacent Heading Hill at one time resided there, disappeared when Castle Terrace was built in 1865. It led into Castle Lane. The later Victorian decades also saw the setting up of the Sick Children's Hospital and the Maternity Hospital in Castle Terrace. Since the turn of the century far-reaching changes have taken place throughout the whole area to the east and to a lesser degree to the south of the Castlehill. Much of Cotton Street, Commerce Street and Virginia Street has disappeared. The Bool Road with its sins and Wales Street with its butchers have been swept away to make elbow-room for the wide Beach Boulevard which the Queen

Mother opened in May 1959. Off Justice Street Chapel Court may survive in name but the Templars have long gone and Peacock's Close does not even evoke snatches of ribald song or thoughts of light fantastic toes, while at its northern-end the bulk of East North Street has become a daily resting-place for motor cars except on Fridays and Saturdays when the neck of bare land between it and Justice Street accommodates what is left of the stalls and the spirit of the ancient Castlegate market. Farther east the area of the Links and the various industrial works abutting upon them have had as much of a face-lift as green sward and the exigencies of gas, fertiliser and feeding-stuff manufacture will permit. The fine Beach Esplanade from Dee to Don goes to the credit of the Victorian city fathers, but the amenities of the sea-front itself, the shops, the Beach Dance Hall and the fun fairs, have been added mostly since 1918. Not least of the attractions is the great concrete glacis which now protects the esplanade from Don to Dee from the sea. The Links themselves are as ever the place of amusement and recreation and all manner of games are played as of yore but with more obvious regimentation upon them.

Down on Trinity Quay yet another ancient monument disappeared when the Weigh-House was demolished in 1883 to make way for the handsome Harbour Offices opened in 1885. The balcony which ran along the front of the weigh-house was floored with timbers off an Amsterdam galley wrecked on the Balmedie sands in 1707. In the Ship-row, despite the threats to extend to its precincts the slum clearance that operated in Exchequer Row, there was not a great deal of change until after the First World War apart from disturbance at the south-west end caused by the construction of Market Street. The Exchequer Row demolitions, however, did affect part of the eastern side and just before the Second World War what remained of St. Katherine's Hill was lopped off to make way for a cinema which the outbreak of war caught in an unfinished state. Fortunately Provost Ross's house — a little gem — and one or two other quaint old properties survived.

The transformation of Broad Street by the building of the great new front of Marischal College and the suppression of the west gable of Greyfriars Kirk has been related elsewhere. But there are those, in some hundreds if not thousands, still alive who can more or less dimly re-member the east side of the street before the time of reconstruction. A pend with the small coat of arms was all the access Marischal College and Greyfriars Kirk then enjoyed. The coat of arms was sculptured in free-stone and was mouldering when taken down. Next door southwards was the Water House built in 1766 and discontinued exactly 100 years later when Queen Victoria turned on the city's new and sumptuous Cairnton supply. The fire engines were kept in the Water House, which became after 1866 William Pyper's stores. The clock and bell with which it was surmounted found their way to the City Hospital. Next but one, No. 68 Broad Street, was the house on whose first floor Mrs. Byron with her hirpling son took up her abode about 1790 after short periods lodging in Virginia Street and thereafter at No. 10 Queen Street. Afterwards the floor became a printing-house. Underneath was the general merchant's shop run by that extraordinary character John Mackintosh, LL.D., whose writing of his *History of Civilisation in Scotland* and other works was accomplished at his desk, with interruptions to serve his customers. His son John Mackintosh, also a historian, edited the third volume of Aberdeen University's Roll of Graduates.

Actual history had been made behind Mackintosh's shop. Arthur Dingwall Fordyce (mentioned elsewhere) had, on his offer of making an access to Greyfriars Kirk through some Broad Street property of his being turned down, constructed such a passage nevertheless which got the name of Long Acre, off which in turn were situated Henderson's and Jopp's Courts. There on 14 November 1784 Bishop Seabury of the United States had been consecrated by Bishop Skinner — the Church of England to which Seabury belonged not then, on account of the American Revolution, being on speaking terms with anyone American. The actual house had been taken down in 1795 and an episcopal chapel built which, when the congregation migrated to St. Andrew's in King Street, was taken over by the Wesleyan Methodists. When demolition came it was a warehouse. A plaque commemorating the consecration is affixed to the wall of the College. There was little of interest on the west side, which has gone the way of its easterly counterpart. The North of Scotland Bank had its first office there which later became the St. Katherine's Club for Girls, and at the corner of Ragg's Lane leading out of the Guestrow opposite Queen Street a grinning face in stone, on the pavement edge of the gable, one storey up, was understood to be a quondam tenant's defiance of some neighbour who had offended him.

The gradual erosion of the west side of the street in the fifties and sixties of the present century laid bare the already almost wholly levelled Guestrow, which, whether it had housed guests or ghaists in its original form had been occupied by tenants very much of the character of those with which the novelist of *The Garden of Allah* peopled the street called Straight. But all their tenements had by this time gone, nothing remaining save the Corporation Lodging House, once the mansion of the Skenes of Rubislaw and the (fortunately temporary) abode of the Duke of Cumberland, and the buildings of the old Dispensary and a few stubs at either end of the street. Happily the Skene house has been saved, its quaint rooms turned into a museum and its painted ceiling revealed, but its environs instead of being bright and spacious, are now darkened and dominated by the ungainly towering architecturally speaking amorphous structure that now houses the administrative side of the municipality, latterly balanced by an equivalent monster at the corner of the Upperkirkgate, the whole of whose south side had been torn down years before. On the opposite side the Aberdeen University Press, in extending its premises beyond Clark's Court, which was too small for the printer's need, into the adjoining Ross Court, while it did not indeed retain the salient features of the two houses involved built respectively in 1680 and 1730 each for a provost, the one for Provost George Leslie, the other for Provost Robertson, at least preserved their dignity and paid some respect to the architectural climate of the street. The Leslie house, which abutted on the street, had its new frontage modelled on that of the Scots College in Paris, the then proprietor of the University Press being a staunch Catholic. He cut the initials of the first proprietor and his wife on the central pair of the four dormer windows. While operations were in progress behind these two houses a bronze pot containing over 12,000 small silver coins of many countries and many reigns, but chiefly from 1296 to 1346, was unearthed. The treasure trove was believed to have been some of the pay for Edward III's army when it was in Aberdeen about the latter year. The pot is now in the Aberdeen Art Gallery, it and some of its contents having been returned by the authorities in Edinburgh, no doubt in a moment of aberration, as they are not in the habit of relinquishing anything committed to their care or custody.

Principal Sir William Geddes was of opinion that the Gallowgate of his day, from the sixties of last century, could if imaginatively handled be made on a smaller scale as romantic and picturesque as Edinburgh's High Street. No doubt it was too much to expect, and Geddes should have remembered his history, not of Aberdeen merely. Now a hundred years later the street is a shambles and irretrievable. In 1897 the Town Council ordained the demolition of the house at the summit of the Gallowgate brae on the west side known as Mar's Castle, traditionally

believed to have been built by some unspecified Earl of Mar either in
1494 or 1595, for both dates were ascribed to it by reputable commentators. The Corporation decided to level it, as part of a general scheme for
improving the neighbourhood — the intention appears the more
mephistophelian the longer we contemplate the sequel. It was officially
described as no longer fit for human habitation, and ruinous, and it was
claimed that its removal would improve the amenity. In 1894 Aberdeen
Ecclesiological Society characterised it as 'the only picturesque structure
in the whole length of that dreary and dismal thoroughfare'. Down it
came, and a little later was followed to dust by its very plain neighbour,
the old meeting-house of the Society of Friends. In subsequent decades
the local authority and German raiders have combined to wipe out
the ancient street after a half-hearted attempt at its 'improvement',
and today instead of the near-royal half-mile, of Sir William Geddes's
dream, we have a congeries of harled concrete boxes, some longi-
tudinal like Greyfriars House, others vertical battery houses like the
multi-storey domiciles at the Mounthooly end.

The whole Seamount, Porthill and West North Street area once so
prominent in the burgh's history has been transformed since Hitler's
war mainly by being denuded of houses and assigned to the service
of the motor-car. Causewayend U.F. Church was the northern limit
of the houses in that district in the seventies. Causewayend has been
rather less drastically handled but Canal Road has been largely stripped
of residential buildings. At the northern end of Causewayend, the little
house Split-the-Win' with the larger building at right angles to it as a
base gave place in 1895 to the handsome Powis Church designed by
A. Marshall Mackenzie, upon which has descended the old and expres-
sive nickname. The radial streets between Causewayend and George
Street suffered much from the big German air raid of April 1943, and
the gaps then formed have been enlarged by Corporation policy, nearly
whole streets having been removed in conformity with the plans for
large development schemes which so far do not seem to have progressed
much beyond the blue-print stage, but which could be capable of
substantially improving the aspect of that rather dull area of the city —
but the shade of William Geddes can be observed to shake its head in
disbelief that such a miracle is possible.

King Street, which was opened in 1800 with high hopes which are
reflected in the various public buildings of Archibald Simpson and
John Smith at its southern end, and which were to some extent sustained by the substantial tenement and flatted houses that accompanied

them, has failed to maintain the promises of its youth. It is no doubt, as we know it today, a good deal more tolerable than it was a century ago. Geddes inveighed against it as 'the general deposit of the refuse of Society both moral and material. Dung carts and sewage, a poorhouse, a churchyard — with a hideous barrack and powder magazine — these form some of the attractions planted by way of adornment to the road'. Perhaps because of his animadversions, delivered in lectures to the then influential Philosophical Society, private builders, who for several generations thereafter had a near monopoly of the construction in the street, avoided anything that offended the eye but equally shied away from anything that showed originality and aesthetic taste, with the result that King Street is one of the dullest thoroughfares in the town, so utterly without character that it is difficult for the passing motorist to differentiate it from the approaches to any other town in the United Kingdom. Fortunately, the Corporation housing schemes are off the main line, otherwise one might with good cause add to the United Kingdom the Republic of Ireland, with Dublin as an awful example. It may here be interposed that the most seemly of the municipal housing schemes are those on the line of Great Northern Road some furlongs before it reaches North Anderson Drive at Scatterburn.

Like its twin, the Netherkirkgate has sustained a great deal of rough usage during the period under review and its predecessor. It is, of course, quite unsuited for vehicular traffic, and even before the southern exit was closed a few years ago, few people cared to take a car into its precincts, and only the hardiest motorist braved Carnegie's Brae as a short, if tenebrous, cut to the Green. The old mis-named Wallace Tower, town house in the eighteenth century of the Keiths of Benholm, was transhipped stone by stone to Tillydrone by the Don within recent years, while before that date there had passed away a monument not perhaps quite so venerable but certainly regarded with equal veneration especially by the womenfolk of the North-East, Morrison's Economic Stores, a veritable mine of bargains in good articles for the wise house-wife. These radical alterations, sponsored by Marks and Spencer, have been carried through with the most commendable regard for amenity and public benefit, and however much the disappearance of material and mercantile landmarks may be regretted, it must be admitted that seldom is such abolition combined with a replacement which represents the modern spirit in its best aspect. The Marks and Spencer development, combined with the Commercial Bank building at the opposite side of the street before the Second World War has made practicable and indeed inevitable a complete re-alignment of St. Nicholas Street which when accomplished will remove a tiresome bottleneck from the busiest channels of the city's business.

Schoolhill saw a great deal of activity, which may not be completed yet. In the eastern portion the biggest change was the disappearance of that fine specimen of sixteenth-century building, George Jamesone's house, with its 50-foot frontage halfway down the slope, its turreted windows, and its great garden stretching back to the borders of the Loch where Loch Street now is. Sentence was pronounced upon it and in 1886 it gave place to a presentable building for Wordie the carting contractors, designed by Matthews and Mackenzie (which guaranteed its quality) and set back from the old line to enable the street to be widened. Immediately opposite, the houses which then stood between the Back Wynd and the North gate of St. Nicholas churchyard came down in 1884–5, and the porter's lodge of Gordon's College was transferred to the gateway, along with the gate itself, the railing and the lamp pillars. About the same time the Sang School house in the corner of the Back Wynd was done away with. Beyond the Back Wynd the first houses belong to the last years of last century, then come some dwellings a hundred years older and before Belmont Street, the Central School, now Aberdeen Academy, buildings which are comparatively recent.

Further west, on the north side, the pend which gave access to Harriet Street was thrown open, and the disappearance of the Grammar School, when the new school by James Matthews was ready in Skene Street in 1863, opened the way for the building of the dignified complex that now occupies the space between Harriet Street and the gateway of Robert Gordon's College, the site of the old Grammar School being partly occupied by Gray's School of Art. The College governors had purchased the building for £1,000 in 1864 and they owned the whole of that enclave of the Schoolhill by this time. Gray's School of Art within the last few years migrated to Garthdee House, to share with the School of Architecture (originally opened in 1914) the splendid accommodation presented by Tom Scott Sutherland in 1957. The increasing range and complexity of the courses conducted under the auspices of Robert Gordon's Technical College has filled most of the ground between the original school and Schoolhill with classrooms and, of course, the handsome hall presented by the MacRobert Trustees and the swimming pool given by three public-spirited citizens. Gray's School of Art, which included the screen or façade bounding the

Gordon's College campus went up in 1883, and in 1884 the Art Gallery took shape, a feature of its architecture being the base of pink Corennie granite, a variant of Aberdeenshire's native stone whose delicacy of tint entitles it to a more extensive use. The whole complex in this charming corner of the city was completed when on 29 September 1925 the noble hall provided by the first Viscount and Lady Cowdray and the city's War Memorial forming its frontage was unveiled by King George V. From Harriet Street to Blackfriars Street there is no more delectable precinct in the city, and its effect is enhanced by the triangle in front of the theatre-public library line and the vista which the hollow of Union Terrace Gardens affords from Union Bridge. In this blend of Schoolhill and Rosemount there are three statues — General Gordon of Khartoum fame, Sir William Wallace, and the Prince Consort while Union Terrace presents Robert Burns and King Edward VII. Aberdeen's other two statues are Queen Victoria now at Queen's Cross, and the Duke of Gordon, 'the Duke', removed from the Castlegate to the centre of Golden Square. The only flaw in the above prospect is the perpetuation of the old entrance to the Schoolhill suburban station and waiting room (now a cafe), which presents the appearance of a superannuated ridotto, and could with advantage be made to conform to the dignified architecture of its neighbours; that and the quite modern glasshouse erected north of the Cowdray Hall on the line of Blackfriars Street could well be replaced by more gracious substitutes.

The face of the Denburn valley has also been altered substantially since the linking up of the G.N.S.R. and Caledonian Railways at the Joint Station in 1867. The Bow Brig was taken down in 1857, and its arch eventually became one of the arches supporting Union Terrace, and one of the obelisks on it stands at the north end of the gardens. At the north end Mutton Brae, which linked the top of Woolmanhill with the Denburnside was wiped out when the railway works were commenced in 1867. Mutton Brae was the locus of the St. James's Lodge of Freemasons, and there also resided such worthy citizens as Feel Peter, Feel Jamie and Beau Aiken. Further down the valley Wapping Street contained the Gas office. It was James Matthews who about 1875 suggested the laying out of the gardens, and this was done in 1877. In 1892 Union Terrace was widened to 102 feet, extending over the gardens on the arches, in one of which there is preserved the Corby Well, one of the best loved of the burgh's old springs. Above the gardens the Doocot Brae had long disappeared. The Northern Assurance building stands where the doocot stood. This corner house was originally the town bouse of Harry Lumsden of Belhelvie Lodge, grand-father of Lumsden of the Guides. A son leased it to the Northern Club in 1854, from its window Queen Victoria in 1863 unveiled the statue of her beloved Albert at the corner of Union Bridge, and in 1874 the Club, now Royal, migrated to the town house of the laird of Crimonmogate, where it remained until 1954, when it entered into possession of its present premises at 9 Albyn Place. On the other side of the street, Bridge Street was built in 1865–7 and the Palace Buildings, with Pratt and Keith's shop on ground level and the railway hotel above, opened in 1873.

Above the Bow Brig there stood in the valley a large basin or trough for watering horses. The burn was confined in a 10-foot channel which dropped down to this basin in several little falls of 18 inches, and to help those who wished to cross a succession of flimsy so-called Chinese bridges were thrown over the burn. Half way up there was a bathing-room. Such was the foundation upon which the Corporation moulded the very attractive pleasance of today. Across the valley, in Belmont Street, the unprepossessing Trades Hall in 1864–5 impaired the view of Archibald Simpson's three Free Churches at the end of Schoolhill. The Union Bridge was widened in 1906. At its south-east end the new Tarnty-Ha' was opened in 1847, the ornamental gateway from the old hall being built into the wall on Lower Denburn. From there it had to be removed but the scroll work was preserved within the hall. The great fire of 1874 which consumed the wooden steeple and much of the East Parish Church fortunately left Drum's Aisle and other precious areas of the building substantially unharmed. As recently as 1837 Archibald Simpson had rebuilt the church, and now William and John Smith piously re-erected it in accordance with Simpson's conception, but building the tower and spire of granite. They also restored Collison's Aisle. The work was completed in 1876. When the Bow Brig was removed the Denburn valley was considered a nuisance and was to be covered in, but the railway scheme saved it. In 1852 the 'Mannie' that had supplied generations of water to the Castlegate was brought into the Green. In 1904 Hadden's Mill at its western end near where the Bow Brig had stood closed down.

Another consequence of the building of the railway from Kitty-brewster to the Joint Station was the sweeping away of a cluster of hovels known as 'the Rotten Holes' between Gilcomston Steps and the west-end of John Street. Milne, Low & Company's tape factory was there and John Macpherson & Company's Gilcomston comb works.

These the railway and to a certain extent the expansion of the Royal Infirmary in 1891–2 swept away, along with the east side of Spa Street, while further extensions encroached upon Sim's Square, on North St. Andrew Street, or as it was formerly termed, Shuttle Street, being a populous area of weavers. This corner of Gilcomston had the distinction of being the original of Ilkastone, a community described in a novel *The King of Andaman*, by James Maclaren Cobban, a native of the district. Gilcomston dam, lying a furlong or two to the west of the present-day steps was filled up in 1907 after some litigation because even then it provided water for a mill below. Several quaint streets in the neighbourhood such as Hardweird, the Galleries, Black's Buildings and Jack's Brae have gone out of commission, in the last few decades and even in the past few years. The gaps created by wholesale demolition have not been filled by anything more permanent than parked motor vehicles. Skene Square on its eastern side has been levelled, while at the northern end the bottle neck of Caroline Place has been removed by a generous widening.[1]

Union Street crept slowly westwards to link up with Union Place, Aberdeen's Harley Street, where the doctors resided and whence they issued forth on their rounds in carriages of varying grades of opulence from the brougham downwards. Most of the houses not only in Union Place but in Union Street as far east as the bridge had areas fenced off with railings, and with steps leading to the front door. The houses themselves are well described in Lachlan Mackinnon's recollections 'substantial, well designed, and comfortable, with ample entrance hall and staircase and spacious rooms'. But as like as not there was neither bathroom in the house nor hot water in the kitchen, and sanitation consisted of perhaps a cesspool under the kitchen window and a dry closet and ashpit at the end of the garden. Moreover, until the sixties there were grain crops along the line of the street at various points and other stretches were littered with shacks and hovels. On the north side of Union Place a former water house rendered obsolete in 1866 was occupied by William Bain Limited, a firm of horse and carriage hirers, that conducted its operations until well after the Kaiser's War, and when in 1888 it was proposed to double the line of tramways, the parliamentary bill prepared with that end was fought by the hiring firm with great pertinacity and much though unsuccessful resource. Although it was in 1885 that Babbie Law disposed of her

1   Plans for the development of the Upper Denburn are at the time of writing being put in operation.

licensed shop wherein the carters of granite setts from Rubislaw were wont to quench their thirst, the corner still goes by her name. The Divinity College, now Christ's College, which the pious liberality of Francis Edmond the advocate had made available to the Free Church in 1849–51, was designed by James Matthews and Thomas Mackenzie who at the same time were responsible for St. John's in Crown Terrace.

In the city itself Union Street and its adjacent thoroughfares have suffered a change of face. Just before the First World War, the Picture House and La Scala cinemas[1] had been built and the present Joint Station constructed. After the 1918 Armistice there were built Poole's Palace (on the site of the old Palace Theatre), the Regent (now the Odeon), Capitol, the Picture Playhouse, the Astoria at Kittybrewster, the Majestic (where La Scala was) and several other cinemas. Other Union Street alterations were the Commercial Bank of Scotland at St. Nicholas Street corner, and Burton's at the opposite side at the top of Market Street, where the Italianate colonnade had been taken down some years previously, its opposite number on the other side of the street having been demolished about a generation earlier, Investment House in Union Row, Amicable House, T. C. Smith's building in Bon-Accord Street, the Savings Bank at Holburn Junction; Falconer's Arcade and Esslemont and MacIntosh's conversion of the old 'Free Press' building. The new U.F. Church at Torry raised by the sub-scriptions of its congregation after the Church Union of 1927, the Elphinstone Hall[2] at King's College; the new wings of Gordon's College; the Gordon Highlanders' (later the Highland Brigade) Barracks, costing £150,000, at Bridge of Don; the Northern Hotel at Kittybrewster; the Douglas Hotel in Market Street; the Gloucester (formerly the Forsyth) in Union Street, the George in Bon-Accord Terrace, brought variety and modernity into their surroundings. The development of the sea-front with dance hall, pavilion, restaurant and shops at a cost of £53,000 was commenced in 1927. The new Bridge of Dee, opened by the King and Queen and named the King George VI Bridge, in 1942, involved the making of a new arterial road — Great Southern Road — from Holburn Street to the river. In 1929 the first

1   Aberdeen's first cinema, omitting Dove Paterson's in Belmont Street, was the Electric Theatre — where the Capitol now stands — opened in 1910, seats being 3d. and 6d., the latter price including a cup of tea and a cake; and the Queen's Cinema at the corner of Back Wynd, occupying the floor where the Queen's Restaurant had been.
2   New King's, opened in 1913 by Professor (later Sir) Herbert Grierson, was the University's first sign of expansion in the Aulton.

turf was cut of the outer Ring Road, Anderson Drive, from the old Bridge of Dee to the Aberdeen-Inverness turnpike at Haudagain, the cost being estimated at £140,000. The great joint medical services scheme, including the Sick Children's Hospital, the Maternity Hospital, the Royal Infirmary and the Medical School at Foresterhill constituted the biggest undertaking of all.

As at the New Year 1860 there were no houses west of Albyn Place or north of Carden Place, apart from isolated cottages and buildings. To the north-west, one or two houses in Rosemount excepted, the town did not extend beyond Mount Street on one side or Short Loanings on the other. Peacock the dancing master built Villa France — 156 Hamilton Place today is partly on its site — as a country residence remote from the bustle of the town, and it was to this villa and another called Honeybrae further west that the child Byron used to be taken to 'country lodgings'. Fountainhall House, now 138 Blenheim Place, has seemed strangely out of its element since the modern house-building caught up with its isolation and surrounded it. The last of the several 'fountain' houses that did duty in that area in connection with the pre-1866 water supply was removed from Desswood Place to the Duthie Park in 1903 to play the part of a well. The Duthie Park itself, after its owner Arthur Dingwall Fordyce died in 1834 had been a 'royal garden' or recreation ground until it came into the possession of Miss Duthie who presented it to the community in 1873. Arthur Dingwall Fordyce, grandfather of the first Dingwall Fordyce laird of Brucklay and himself tacksman of Eigie, Balmedie, was a notable Aberdonian in his day. He built the square called Dee Village on the site of the old Potter's Hamlet by the mill burn which gives the name to the site of the Hydro Electric Board's headquarters now. Fordyce's burgess ticket, his LL.D. diploma, and his commission as a notary public were presented by one of his descendants in Canada to the museum in the Duthie Park which had been his house, Arthur's Seat.

Rubislaw House, the house of the Skenes of Rubislaw, was taken down in 1886, and in its place John Morgan, a prominent builder and public man who had much to do with the laying out of Union Terrace gardens, the building of the Public Library, and the creation of the town's great fish market, reared to the plans of J. B. Pirie that amazing baroque edifice No. 50 Queen's Road. A sun-dial there that had belonged to the Earls Marischal was purchased by J. B. Keith the banker for his house at the top of Rubislaw Den North which he called Keith House. In the late twenties after his death it became the home of the first Marchioness of Aberdeen and Temair and was known as Gordon House. Later it became a hotel and is now a university residence. The sun-dial was purchased by Lord Catto and is at the House of Schivas. Rubislaw Den South was 'the new road' in the last quarter of the century. The central part of that impressive thoroughfare was at that time (as has been noted) the croft of Hirpletillim, the chief house of which coincided fairly nearly with the site of No. 6. In what is now the North Den there was for many years a Glenburnie Distillery, 'about 100 yards north of the Rubislaw toll bar'. It was discontinued in 1857 and the buildings were then for some years occupied by George Washington Wilson, Aberdeen's photographic pioneer. It disappeared from the directory in 1867. Another fairly lonely house was Loch-head, on the edge of what is now Westburn Park. The Rev. Alexander Munro, M.D., minister of Westhills, Skene, for many years, became a convert to hydropathy, bought and extended Loch-head and took in as many as seventy patients. In 1804 he went to Forres as superintendent of the hydro there. Loch-head was converted into dwelling-houses, but in 1873 the Infirmary Board purchased it, and used it until the Convalescent Hospital was opened at Pitfodels in 1895, when the Board of the Royal Asylum took it over. In 1903 part of the policies were incorporated in the Westburn Park.

Apart from the examples given there was really little expansion compared with what was to come, before 1914. A curious little dispute that flared up in 1887 near the Bridge of Dee might be taken to indicate a certain amount of new building in that area, but actually it arose from the fondness of the public, which even the modern developments in transport have done nothing to eradicate, for straying upon land that does not belong to them. In that year the Ruthrieston Trustees attempted to block access to the historic old bridge there and began to raise a wall to obstruct the public's access. The Town Council however intervened, asserted the right of way and demolished part of the offending structure, and the trustees acquiesced. They were less fortunate, or perhaps had a less pliant local authority to deal with than Francis Edmond the lawyer, who owned Kingswells House (the old Jaffrey and Quaker house), and who, being plagued by the traffic on the public road which ran past his door built a cottage across the highway (it may still be seen at a bend on the Countesswells-Clinterty road on the slope of Cloghill).

A glance at the Ordnance Survey map as revised in 1927 will convey better than many paragraphs an impression of how the city has burst its ramparts, as it were. In the late twenties and thirties the idea was canvassed in the Town Council of an industrial suburb at Tullos. Nothing much was done then, but by the time Hitler's war commenced a good deal of municipal housing had been erected on the Kincorth slopes; but even so the Church of Nigg and one tall lone house that belonged to the most senior of the Elder Brethren of Trinity House, Harry Birnie, stood in that corner in a rural setting. Streets in Kaimhill were taking shape, and Mannofield was built up to and slightly beyond the parish church by 1918, where a few years before Friendville, the residence of the man after whom the district was named, and Thorn-grove, where Mr. Jackson just before the turn of the century displayed to a wondering public Aberdeen's first motor-car, had lorded it in splendid and almost complete isolation. In 1918, too, building stopped short of the Rubislaw quarries, except for a stray cottage or two like the strange looking and strangely named Zoar on the northern spur of Springfield Road, and nearer the quarries the Angusfield preparatory school. King's Gate had not yet climbed the hill, Raeden House on the Stocket Road, Maryville on what is now the Ring Road, and all beyond were in virgin country, with dairy farms behind Maryville and at Mastrick and green fields and cultivation where today the unwary visitor can easily be lost in the maze of streets that stretch from Summer-hill and Woodhill houses away along the Lang Stracht from the Cocket Hat to near Maidencraig, around Springhill House to Sheddocksley and the salubrious neighbourhood of the ash-tip at Cairncry, and on to the confines of Bucksburn farm and the dormitory suburb built by the County Council on the Newhills slopes. Between Woodside, that was an independent and physically separate community until nearly the end of last century, and the Denburn to the south and the Don on the north there arose in the former area between the wars and in the latter mostly after 1945 a veritable forest of municipal houses, and further east much of the lands of Seaton were engulfed, while across the lower Don another satellite suburb arose. In the Torry area the older streets with their solid granite houses were submerged in numer-ous corporation housing schemes. Finally, when slum clearance and other factors had operated to clear away many of the purlieus of the old burgh, and when conventional building methods had proved insuffi-cient to supply the demand for homes, multi-storey piles began to rear their heads here and there throughout the area, presenting to the observer from a distance a curious impression of a kind of inverted troglodytism.

Not least in the alterations of Aberdeen's face has been the recent development of the university area of Old Aberdeen. Besides the pre-first war New King's, the Science complex, the Taylor Law and English Building, a great number of renovations of old houses, and notably the very charming group of dwellings by Robert Hurd on the site of the old 'Barn' or Grammar School in School Road, have been not unworthy successors to some of the historic houses that have now vanished from that area, and that despite the rather grotesque appearance of some of the Science departments and the surrender to modern ugliness in the College of Agriculture monster and in one or two of the later halls of residence. The restoration of the Old Town houses, of which the University owns about sixty, was made possible by a generous grant from the MacRobert Trustees, who have also assisted in other contiguous building.

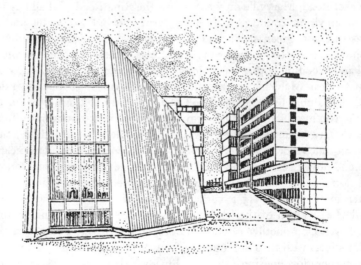

CHAPTER TWO

A New Deal for the Burgh

The Reform Act of 1832, and even more Disraeli's 'leap in the dark' of 1868, released aspirations and ambitions which were soon to make their influence felt in Aberdeen, as in other communities, with surprisingly little delay. Gladstone's Education Act of 1872 and Disraeli's 'sanitas sanitatum' were to impinge upon the ordinary life and meddle with the savings of the citizens in ways undreamt of by their sponsors. At the same time, scientific inquiry and discovery and philosophical speculation introduced new ideas and forces into industrial and commercial activities, and these became manifest in events and trends hitherto unknown and in striking contrast with the older and conventional style in historical records.

In 1868, apparently on the initiative of Charles Wisely, secretary of the Aberdeen branch of the Associated Carpenters and Joiners in Scotland, Aberdeen Trades Council was formed. From 1846 there had been a committee representing one of the trades, but it had confined its interest latterly to arranging the summer holidays. This earlier body had connections with the Chartists, whose local secretary was the father of William Walker, author of *The Bards of Bon-Accord*, and had been called a 'Delegated Committee of Sympathy', the sentiment being for joiners and bakers affected by a strike in that year. The Trades Council, at its first general meeting, elected a mason, Alexander Kidd, as president and a slater, Alexander Rennie, secretary. By 1884 the Council had become so important that the Trades Union Congress held its annual conference in Aberdeen. The Council in its early years was active in advocating the municipalisation of the gas works and the establishment of a public library, and persuaded the Town Council to embark in 1896 on its first essay in municipal housing with the erection of artisans' dwellings in Urquhart Road. Its representatives also had the standard wages clause written into all public contracts and, following success in its gas works transfer, campaigned for the municipalisation of the tramways. The start of nursery schools is rather less credibly ascribed to the Trades Council's advocacy. The Council also in association with Aberdeen Chamber of Commerce, established in 1853 but unlike the Council a non-political body, set up a conciliation board to settle district disputes by round-table talks.

In 1884 two Labour members were returned to the Town Council — James Forbes, shoemaker for St. Machar, and George Macconnochie, a compositor, for St. Andrews. Within a decade Treasurer Bisset, Baillies Glass and Johnston, Dr. A. T. Gordon Beveridge and Woodside's first Socialist, William Cooper, had seats in the Town Council; on the Aberdeen School Board were the blind John Keir, its chairman, and two others; and the Parish Council had also three Labour members. On the Parliamentary side Aberdeen since the Reform Act had been in both its divisions consistently Liberal. In 1892, however, H. H. Champion bore the Labour standard in South Aberdeen, and although he was at the bottom of the poll in a three-cornered contest, his 991 votes out of 6,272 was his party's best showing in Scotland. Not until 1907 did Labour run its own candidate again in South Aberdeen, Fred Bramley securing 1,740 out of 8,931 votes cast. The Liberal member for the constituency, James (later Viscount) Bryce, was an intellectual aristocrat and was less successful in attracting Labour votes than Dr. William Hunter in North Aberdeen, who was never opposed by a Labour man, being regarded in his day as very far to the Left, although he was never convinced that the advent of Socialism would be equivalent to a re-opening of the gates of the earthly Paradise.

In 1871 the Town Council was increased from nineteen to twenty-five members under the Aberdeen Municipality Extension Act of that year. The whole council had to retire. In 1883 under another Extension Act the wards were rearranged, and the old four, relics of the medieval quarters, became eight — St. Clements, St. Andrews, St. Machar, Greyfriars, St. Nicholas, Rosemount, Rubislaw and Ferryhill. In 1871 also the gasworks were municipalised — the first step on what nowadays some people regard as the Gaderene slope. The Police Board disappeared in that year; the School Board first met in 1873. The first trams — horse-drawn, of course — appeared in 1874 and the Channel Fleet lay in Aberdeen Bay for public inspection.

In 1891 the burgh of Old Aberdeen amalgamated with Aberdeen. Created 'a city, university and free burgh of barony' in 1498, the burgh had survived many, though mostly small, vicissitudes until the 1715 Rebellion completely upset its communal economy. In 1719 and 1729 the government of the burgh was laid upon certain citizens — baillies, councillors, deacons and conveners of trades — by Royal Warrant.

The merger was inevitable. The union of the colleges greatly diminished the status of the burgh. The Town House was built in 1702, but later in the century the ground floor of the building was converted into the cistern for the burgh water supply, the first floor was given over to meetings of the Town Council and the Incorporated Trades, and the second floor did duty as a prison. At the end of the century the building had to be restored at a cost of £350. There were then 1,100 people in Old Aberdeen, whose aggregate rent amounted to £540 15s., and a tax of a shilling in the pound was imposed to keep the streets paved and lit. But as the nineteenth century advanced it became impossible to support the essential communal services on the limited resources of the burgh and in 1887 Old Aberdeen agreed to amalgamate with its larger neighbour.

There are still a few relics of old Aberdeen's independent existence in the Aulton. Mitchell's Hospital was a group of little cottages on the west side of the Chanonry presented in 1801 by a native of the burgh to house five widows and five unmarried daughters of burgesses of Old Aberdeen. One was to be governor of the institution, and among the provisions, the inmates were to have beef and vegetables three times a week so long as beef was not more than 4d. a lb. There are now four modernised cottages in the block. The Bede House in Don Street was built for the bedesmen who had been housed in Bishop Dunbar's Hospital that stood till the end of the eighteenth century about where the Seaton gate now adjoins the north side of the Cathedral churchyard. The hospital was intended to cater for twelve poor men who got 18 merks a year and a merk to buy a coat of white undyed wool. The Bede House was built in the seventeenth century.

At the beginning of the nineteenth century Aberdeen had about thirty streets, at the end 500. The first valuation, struck in 1855–6, was £178,167; at the century's close it was £750,000. The population in 1901 was 153,503 compared with 34,600 in 1811 and 63,000 in 1841. It may be added that in 1893 the area covered by the city was next in extent in Scotland to that of Glasgow.

The 1914–18 war seems to have inspired Scots with an unwonted and unwanted docility to the fashions and the dictates of England. Thus, before the century opened, in 1895, when the English Labour leaders carried a resolution at an annual conference of the British Trades Union Congress that Trades Councils should be excluded from Congress membership, Scotland revolted at once. On the invitation of Aberdeen, the nine Scottish Trades Councils of those days met and eventually instituted the Scottish Trades Union Congress in 1897, whose second conference was held in Aberdeen the following year.

This expression of independence was administrative and idealistic rather than industrial and economic. Scotland participated in the railway strike of July 1911 and in the coal strike in the spring of 1912. In that year Aberdeen had a painters' strike, and the thing was so catching that the Aberdeen Branch of the British Medical Association favoured a doctors' strike. Broadford workers, granite workers, coachbuilders, coopers, carters, fishworkers, all struck work, but the war put a stop to such effervescence for a time and during the first eighteen months of the first struggle with Germany the only sign that Labour could still be thoughtless was a Trades Council protest against the replacement of some workers by women. It was not until the end of January 1916 that a serious stoppage occurred amongst the dockers and the painters followed in March for three days.

Once the nation got clear of the foreign strife, it had more time to fight at home. In the first weeks of 1919 the shipyard workers voted for a 40-hour week but took no other action in the matter. The Broadford employees came out shortly after and the epidemic soon spread to the Army, 200 Gordons at Balnagask refusing to be absorbed in the Camerons and sent to India, though whether it was the Camerons or India they objected to was not quite clear.[1] A prolonged fishing dispute which lasted seventy-two days caused the laying-up of over 200 boats. A railway strike in September paralysed the country for nearly a week. In May 1920 sawmillers, rivetters, and dressmakers in Aberdeen — especially the dressmakers — suspended their labours.

By this time the unemployment situation had become oppressive. Less than three months after the Armistice there were 2,300 people out of regular work in Aberdeen. Munitions production had summarily ceased, and no provision had been made for a gradual switch-over from peace to war, the Government indeed — Haig being the only man who knew better — having braced itself for a 1919 campaign when the Germans began to collapse suddenly in October 1918. At the beginning of 1921 there were 6,150 unemployed in the city, and the Town Council,

1 How times change and lions lie down with . . . lambs. After the Second World War, the 51st Division was for a time amalgamated with the 52nd, and the 92nd or true Gordon Highlanders were annihilated — a stroke of the War Office pen thus effecting what all the legions of Napoleon, Ludendorff and Hitler had failed to accomplish; and the Gordon Barracks were made over to the Royal Regiment of Artillery. Not one of these arbitrary acts evoked a single public protest.

as a partial means of alleviating the distress, approved the making of a new road from Woodside to Old Aberdeen at an estimated cost of £23,850. This was big money for those days though the undertaking had had a precedent. But the trade union leaders themselves were uneasy and bewildered, and as they became more nervous strikes increased in frequency. In March there was trouble amongst the barbers, the vehicle-builders, the granite-workers, painters, joiners, butchers, carters. Some 2,400 came out. On top of that the miners struck work on 1 April, coal and lighting had to be rationed, a thousand citizens volunteered to carry on essential services, the price of coal jumped to £7 10s. per ton, the roll of unemployed swelled to 10,500, and after eighty-nine days of a strike the Government paid 10 millions of the taxpayers' money to ease the inevitable wage decreases that unrest and world upheavals had earned for the coal industry. Before the end of the summer the Town Council were working out relief schemes to the tune of £112,000, and wages were tumbling in all trades by the end of that calamitous year.

The following year was quiet, apart from a scandal about 2,000 unemployed Aberdonians spending £1 a head to attend a football match at Dundee. It was appropriately played on All Fools' Day. In the spring of 1923, so ineffectual were communal relief projects in absorbing the workless, it had to be admitted that Aberdeen's schemes would employ only 700 out of 7,000 unemployed. Very slowly conditions improved. Corporation workers received an increase of 2s. a week in 1925, and were put on a system of retirement at 70. But the great miners' strike[1] that commenced on May Day 1926, followed on 4 May by the week-long fiasco of the General Strike, set back the clock for at least a decade. The coal strike cost Aberdeen Harbour £5,800 in revenue alone. By 21 May practically 9,000 persons had to apply for unemployment benefit at the Labour Exchange. Before the end of May domestic coal was rationed at a hundredweight a fortnight, and the trawling industry, almost wholly dependent upon steam, was crippled. In June Aberdeen granite manufacturers instituted a five-day week of seven hours a day. Even when the miners had gone back to work and the black year was near its end, there remained 6,600 names on the books of Aberdeen's Labour Exchange.

As for the General Strike, it was the chief evidence that the Scottish worker's docility was the only thing about him that was not capable of

[1] It should be mentioned that one of the less obvious but most compelling causes of the miners' strike was the return to the gold standard in 1925.

being subdued. Very few indeed of the workers in Aberdeen wanted to come out, but when the order went forth they obeyed meekly. Only the small hooligan element that had come to be much in evidence at political meetings in those days welcomed the stoppage. They thought they would get their opportunity of power, or perhaps merely of plunder, in the troublous times. But they soon found that they had not the strength or the intelligence. An Emergency Committee of the Town Council was immediately set up under the chairmanship of Treasurer William Edwards, to whom experience of the turbulent Rand made the apprentice efforts of the Aberdeen rowdies seem insignificant. Volunteers came forward in great numbers to run essential services. Before the end of the strike 2,220 had been enrolled and many others were taking the strikers' places without formal enrolment. In the first days some buses driven by students were attacked but the students gave at least as good as they got. A tram conveying defective children to school also attracted the attention of the wilder spirits, the police made several baton charges, and two rioters received sentences of sixty days imprisonment. All Corporation employees got notice to report for duty before noon on 12 May or leave the municipal service. By that time the strike was over. The workers returned to their duties, but a large number of firms refused any longer to recognise the trade unions. During the General Strike the *Press and Journal* produced a series of typewritten bulletins until the middle of the week, when a sufficient number of mechanical staff had reported for work to enable a small paper to be issued.

The Town Council of 1919 had eight Labour members. In 1920, on the day of the municipal election, there was a local veto poll for and against prohibition of the sale of alcoholic liquor. All ten Labour candidates were defeated, as was the attempt to impose prohibition. The following year Labour lost two seats and gained one; in 1922 all six Communist candidates were beaten. In 1923 Labour was defeated in all wards and another local veto poll left matters as they were. Labour had one gain in 1924 and two, besides three in the Parish Council, in 1925; in 1926 after the General Strike Labour lost a seat on balance, a third local veto attempt being at the same time frustrated, while in 1927 five Labour aspirants all failed to secure election. Thereafter, however, the Socialist element very slowly gained in strength, and in 1938 after the last pre-war election, the Council, which had been increased to thirty-seven members by the Conservative Local Government legislation of 1929, consisted of twenty non-Labourists and seventeen Labourists. In the first post-war election of 1945 Labour for the first time achieved a majority in the Council. During all the Parliamentary elections of those years South Aberdeen was strongly Conservative, and North Aberdeen uniformly Socialist except in 1931 when on the financial debacle of Ramsay MacDonald's Ministry a Conservative was returned, the same party's South Aberdeen majority on that occasion being the record one of 37,000.

The most violent of local controversies in modern times was that aroused by the latest of Aberdeen's water supply schemes. In 1909 the Town Council adopted the draft of a Provisional Order for the supply of water from the river Avon. The scheme was based on a volume of 20 million gallons a day and the cost was to be £1,400,000. All sorts of interests opposed the plan, and although the municipal election results showed that the citizens as a whole were at least not unfavourably disposed, Parliament threw the Bill out. It was, however, only then that the fun began in earnest. Water had to be got, and the alternative to the Avon could only be the Dee. Engineers were asked to estimate the cost of extracting a further 10 million gallons from the Dee. Some experts said £777,000, others (who had advised the Avon) put the figure at £850,000. Then the microbes were called in. Opponents of the Dee waxed lyrical over the purity of the Avon and endeavoured to freeze the marrow of the citizens' bones by horrid tales of the character and organic contents of Dee water, the protagonists of the Dee followed the less picturesque line of doubting the Avon's capacity. The battle was fought with the most amazing virulence and fertility of argument, families were riven, brother against brother, old friendships destroyed, but eventually the Dee won — and none of the epidemics so darkly foreshadowed has visited Aberdeen. By this time Aberdeen had a population, as established by the 1911 census, of 163,000.

There seems to be an unwritten law that sovereigns of Great Britain visit Aberdeen on ceremonial duty once during the period of their reigns. Queen Victoria came in 1863, as we have seen, to unveil the statue of the Prince Consort, her own statue being unveiled in 1866 by the then Prince of Wales, who at the same time was enrolled as an honorary burgess of the city. The coronation of King George V in 1911 was made the occasion for a great pageant in memory of the Battle of Harlaw fought in 1411. King Edward's ceremonial visit was in 1906, when he drove through the city from Ruthrieston suburban station to Marischal College to open the extensions there. King George V's visit was on 29 September 1925 when he opened the extension to the Art Gallery, the Cowdray Hall and the Museum. On the forenoon of the same day the Moderators of the Church of Scotland and of the United Free Church, Dr. John White and Dr. James Harvey, had dedicated the city's War Memorial, which is incorporated in the frontage of the Cowdray Hall. The first Lady Cowdray, to whom and whose husband's generosity this handsome architectural addition to the city's amenities was due, gave a treat to the children of Aberdeen that day, and during the week-end some 20,000 people visited the Shrine of Remembrance within the Hall. Queen Mary paid a visit to the city in 1930 when she was laureated LL.D. at Marischal College.

King Edward VIII, who as Prince of Wales, had laid the foundation stone of the new Infirmary Buildings at Foresterhill, was approached to perform the opening ceremony in September 1936, but was unable to do so. The Duke of York, about to be King George VI, undertook that duty.[1] He had already opened a school in the city, and in the early days of the war in August 1914 he was one of a number of naval invalids landed in Aberdeen. His Royal Highness was taken to the Northern Nursing Home, where he was operated on for the removal of his appendix by Professor (later Sir) John Marnoch. King George VI's ceremonial occasion was in 1942 when he declared open the new bridge over the Dee and bearing his name which was intended to be the principal entry to the city from the south. His consort Queen Elizabeth paid several visits to Aberdeen, including one in 1946 when she attended the Mod of An Comunn Gaidhealach, and another in 1959 when she opened the Beach Boulevard and the newly widened Bridge of Don and received the Freedom of the City.

There were many distinguished visitors to the city. Winston Churchill made his first appearance in 1904, his last in 1946, when amid scenes of unprecedented public enthusiasm, he was presented with the Freedom and was laureated LL.D. of the University. In 1907 the fine new Post Office in Crown Street was opened with considerable pomp by Sydney Buxton, the Postmaster-General.[2] Less welcome were the attentions of the suffragettes, not all of whom were local protagonists of votes for women. In December 1907 they waylaid the then Chancellor of the Exchequer, H. H. Asquith; in May 1913 they set fire to Ashley Road School; and in February 1914 they interrupted a service in the West Kirk. Much more congenial was a visit from Ellen Terry in

1 King Edward, however, as it happened, was in Aberdeen on a different errand that day.
2 It is interesting to observe that the Sunday delivery of letters ceased on the last day of January 1909.

November 1911 to give a recital. In the summer of 1914 the British Medical Association held its annual meeting in Aberdeen, and returned in the summer of 1939 — not, therefore, for Aberdeen a body of altogether good omen. Many notables were in the city during the war years, but kept their business private. In 1919 the stormy petrel of Australian politics, the then Premier of the Commonwealth, the Rt. Hon. W. M. Hughes, addressed the Chamber of Commerce, and with Lord Alness (with whom he differed outspokenly on Free Trade) a public meeting in the Music Hall.

In the summer of 1919 Field-Marshal Sir Douglas Haig received the Freedom of the City and (along with Admiral Sir Roger Keyes) the LL.D. from the University. Service guests of a different kind were treated in 1924 when the battleships *Resolution, Royal Oak* and *Royal Sovereign* visited Aberdeen and 900 of their ratings were entertained at Hazlehead. This style of reception was repeated a year later, when Aberdeen's own Regular battalion, the 2nd Gordon Highlanders, had dinner at Hazlehead. The same year the British Chambers of Commerce held their annual conference at Aberdeen, in the same week as the opening of the Cowdray Hall; and in the middle of October the famous evangelist, the late Gipsy Smith, preached for the first time in his life from a cathedral pulpit in St. Machar's Cathedral.

Lloyd George had spoken in Aberdeen several times, but his last appearance was in the election of 1924, when in course of a peregrination Gladstonian in extent though not in effect, he addressed a meeting from the Wallace Statue. Stanley Baldwin was in the city on political business and to make a speech in the late autumn of 1925, but the two most effective exercises in political oratory were those of Lord Birkenhead on the Zinovieff Letter in the 1924 election, and of Robert Smillie the miners' leader (once, very long before, a well-known visitor to the city) on the 1923 Coal Commission. For his numerous and great benefactions the Town Council decided to give the first Viscount Cowdray the Freedom of the City, but two days before the date fixed for the ceremony he died, and the scroll and casket were presented privately to his widow some months later. Sir Robert Williams of Park and Sir Thomas Jaffrey of Edgehill, who with the 1st Lord Cowdray had been conspicuous for their generosity to every important public fund raised in the city for more than a decade, also were admitted to the Roll of Burgesses.

Dearer, because more familiar, to good Aberdonians than their honorary burgesses and temporary indwellers were the 'worthies' or 'characters' for which Aberdeen was famous. Alexander Ross, or Statio Ross, the Flying Stationer, had a portable stand which he erected daily in the Castlegate for the sale of his pictures of famous personages and events, and for his squibs and slipsongs. A libel on the colonel of a regiment stationed in the town led to Sandy being imprisoned and his stock in trade burnt by the hangman. On his release he circulated an appeal for aid which was very effective, and which began:

> Stern winter now — with cruel, ruthless hand,
> Has spread his chilly carpet o'er the land.
> So very high the price of beef and coal,
> And whisky too! the comfort of my soul.
> Indeed, my friends, I'm now come to death's door —
> Help, or your Flying Stationer's no more.

Willie o' the Wall had a stall near Statio Ross, selling with his wife's aid all sorts of wares from pins and needles to garters and mirrors, razors and banners:

> Willie o' the Wall and Sawnie i' the Meen,
> Wha gaed up the Castlegate and ran doon the Green.

Deaf Joe, Jacob Blackwell ('Lemon-cakie'), Feel Peter, Hielan' Geordie ('Red Tappie'), 'Pizzie' Grant, 'Piddlie' Guyan, 'Ginger Blue', 'Forty Piggies', Blin' Bob, Sawdust Calder, Buttery Willie Collie, Jean Carr, Lazarus Myres, Morrican Roum, Turkey Willie, and Hallelujah Thomas were the numerous Victorian successors to men like Mussel-Mou'd Charlie, the packman and penny-rhymester, whose 106 years spanned the eighteenth century, and who was credited with the elegant quatrain:

> I bocht a wife in Edinbury
>   For a bawbee
> I got a farthing in again
>   To buy tobacco wi'.

This disreputable citizen was present on the Jacobite side at the Battle of Inverurie, and was said to be an illegitimate member of one of the county families.

Fire gave Aberdeen during both war and peace its greatest and most frequent moments of excitement. A description of all the fires in Aberdeen since 1901 would make a very full chapter in itself, but only the larger ones can be mentioned now. In January 1902 there was a

£20,000 outbreak in Loch Street; in 1904 the Aberdeen Distillery was burnt, the damage amounting to £80,000. Less costly was the £14,000 blaze at Grandholm Mills in 1905. In 1910 an outbreak at the Farmers' Supply Stores cost £10,000 and one in Gordon's timber yard over £7,000. In 1917 Miller & Sons' timber yard at Blaikie's Quay and Spencer's oil factory suffered. Just a month before the war ended Garvie & Sons' premises valued at £9,000 in Canal Road were burnt. The greatest blaze of all consumed the Aberdeen Commercial Company's oilcake mill, valued at £100,000, on 11 June 1920. The bakery of Mitchell & Muil in Harriet Street was burnt out in 1923. In March 1925 the destruction caused by a tremendous blaze at William Davidson & Son's Palmerston Road warehouse was estimated at between £30,000 and £40,000. A month later there was an £8,000 outbreak at John Bissct & Son's sawmills in Back Hilton Road. Fiddes's sawmills had one of their worst visitations in March 1926, nearly £25,000 damage being done. During the Second World War the Palace Hotel was rendered unfit for occupation by an accidental fire; the shell was levelled and the present Telephone House built after the war. Ogston & Tennant's stores in Loch Street and Kilgour & Walker's factory in Berryden Road were gutted by enemy action. Not a fire, but a rushing, mighty wind was responsible for the collapse in November 1927 of the Hardgate distillery chimney stalk, which was to have been felled the day after nature took matters into her own hand.

This elemental intervention was characteristic of the strange outbursts of meteorological moods that seemed, oddly enough, to play a larger part in Aberdeen's interests than formerly. The increasing delicacy of the machinery of civilisation has made the vagaries of the weather more capable of upsetting routine and comfort than in days or in districts less dependent upon the complex modern inventions. On 12 August 1906 phenomenal rain was recorded at Aberdeen. On 28 December of that year there was the great snowstorm which occasioned the Elliot Junction railway disaster. In 1908 at Christmas there was an even severer snowstorm. 9 July 1911 was recorded as memorable for a thunderstorm, 13–19 January 1912 for a great gale in which the steamer *Frederick Snowden* was lost off Port-Erroll with thirteen hands. March 1915 saw a bad storm, and at Christmastide the trawler *Empress* was lost off Aberdeen with her crew. After heavy snowfalls the eleven days, 10–20 March 1916, had one and a half hours sunshine. On 6 May there was snow and thunder.

A prolonged snowstorm introduced 1918, while 12 June 1919, saw the end of the most protracted drought since 1868. On 14 November 1919, there were 22 degrees of frost, but in March 1917, there had been 26 degrees; on 14 January 1922, the worst snowstorm for years was experienced. In an influenza epidemic there were thirty-four deaths in one week, a much higher rate than in previous outbreaks. Just before the Armistice in 1918 there had been an epidemic which had resulted in eleven funerals to Allenvale Cemetery in one day, and again in February 1919 influenza was so prevalent that the Infirmary had to be closed to visitors. No doubt the severity of those epidemics was caused partly by the reaction from the war and the low vitality of the community that had been living for too long on suspense and what the Government considered was sustaining food. On 26 July 1945 there was a terrific thunderstorm and on 9 October 1926 a gale blew down many trees. On 14–15 October of the same year there was an excellent display of the Aurora-borealis, although it was surpassed on Burns Night 1939. On 24 January 1927 Aberdeen had the unusual experience of an earthquake shock; its previous one had been in 1816.[1] This was followed by a tremendous gale in which several citizens were injured. The greatest gale of all was on 30 January 1953, when Hazlehead wood was levelled, one of scores so destroyed in the North-East. On 24 July 1940, in a tremendous thunderstorm, the Grammar School was struck by lightning. In January 1942, in one of the heaviest thunderstorms of modern times, an early morning train took half-an-hour to make the half-mile journey between Craiginches and the Joint Station. Aberdeen had seen nothing like it since 1908.

Miscellaneous events indicate the widening of the community's range of activities. In 1901 the Macdonald collection of pictures was handed over to Aberdeen and was on view when the Art Gallery was reopened in 1905. Balnagask Golf Course came into being in 1905 also. In December 1907, the new His Majesty's Theatre in Rosemount Viaduct was opened with the pantomime 'Red Riding Hood'; the new Palace Theatre had been opened in 1898, and the Tivoli was ready as a music-hall in 1910. In 1908, following upon the Haldane army reforms, Aberdeen held its Volunteer Farewell celebrations, and the next year saw the first combined parade of the Territorial units in the city. The widening of Union Bridge was completed in May 1908. In November

---

1   This may be true, but in either 1900 or 1901 (impossible now to date it) the present writer sleeping with his father was awakened by the vases rattling on the bedroom mantlepiece, and remembers his father saying, 'That's an earthquake'.

a motor-car made a non-stop run to London, taking most of the twenty-four hours[1]; in 1926 the 547 miles were done in 12½ hours. In 1909 the Forbesfield roller-skating rink was opened only to close down in 1910. That form of sport died out, but before the 1939 war rinks upon which orthodox skates could be used had become much frequented.

The first official wireless message was received in Aberdeen on 22 May 1910. On 3 March 1923, wireless broadcasting commenced from Glasgow but Aberdeen heard nothing. On 10 October, 2BD, Aberdeen's own station was opened. In 1922 the *Daily Journal* had photos of the Derby brought from London by air in 4¼ hours. It was possible by 1929 to fly from Aberdeen's own airport at Dyce, and there was a time when it seemed likely that a second aerodrome might be opened at Kintore. In 1911 the Masonic Temple in Crown Street was consecrated by Lord Tullibardine (later Duke of Atholl) and in 1927 was celebrated the centenary of the Aberdeen Provincial Lodge of Freemasons, Lord Blythswood, G.M.M. of Scotland, being present at a special service in the West Kirk. St. Andrews' Episcopal Church was made a cathedral in 1914. In July 1914 a Peace Brotherhood was formed rather belatedly, and in the same month some Germans attended the unveiling of the Harlaw Memorial near Inverurie. Aberdeen Rotary Club first met in April 1916. In 18 September of the same year the Town Council sitting lasted five minutes, a record not likely to be lowered nowadays. Mixed bathing had begun in the summer of 1913; in 1917–18 the Bathing Station revenue, due perhaps partly to that and partly to the numbers of servicemen on leave, was £4,636, against an average of £2,890 for the previous five years. In October 1918 Aberdeen saw its first and only authentic baseball match at Pittodrie, the players belonging to the U.S. Air Force.

Reactions from wartime restrictions began to be manifested very plainly in the summer of 1919, when Glasgow Fair brought 15,000 visitors to the city, and Aberdeen Holiday Week sent 20,000 Aberdonians away for a change.[2] The Aberdeen Music Festival restarted in April 1920. In 1919 Professor Harrower made an experiment of staging a Greek play, the 'Antigone' of Sophocles, in the Music Hall, the English blank verse translation being his own. He followed this up with 'The House of Atreus' in 1920 and the 'Oedipus Tyrannus' in 1922, but the public (and probably the undergraduates) were becoming less disposed

1 One of the motorists was Malcolm V. Hay, the laird of Seaton, and later a noted historian.
2 By July 1927 the influx had risen to over 54,000 in two week-ends.

to such departures from theatrical and filmland conventions, and as Harrower's health declined, there was no one else to carry on the endeavour. In 1923 horse-racing at Seaton, a revival from Victorian days, was started, but it faded out after a few years and after the course had been removed to a field on the Ring Road near Mastrick Farm. In the Seaton district a new attraction for some time was an air circus at which the public saw feats of airmanship and could enjoy both plain and purled flights themselves. On 14 September 1923, Pittendrigh Macgillivray's statue of Byron was unveiled at the Grammar School, and in the following February two busts by Epstein, whose work in London had raised acrid controversy, were exhibited in the Art Gallery, for which they were purchased. In 1927 it was announced that the Art Gallery had about £65,000 in hand with which to buy pictures. Its principal benefactors had been Sir James Murray, who in that year sold off his private collection, which realised almost £70,000, and Sir Thomas Jaffrey.

The new rifle range at Black Dog, where the wapinschaws were resumed, was opened by Major-General A. E. Ritchie, commanding the 51st Division, in April 1924. In 1925 the Aberdeen branch of the Scottish Country Dance Society was instituted. In the autumn the Town Council's proposal to have licensed premises at the Beach was vetoed by the Scottish Secretary as 'without precedent in Scotland'. A few months later the magistrates granted the Palais de Danse permission to open on Sunday for music and light refreshments, a licence which was violently but vainly assailed by the Aberdeen Presbytery and other bodies. The same year a series of special Sunday evening services in picture houses was given, and several ministers, mainly of the United Free Church, began to hold open air Sunday evening services in the Castlegate and elsewhere. In May 1927 a corporation motor bus service was inaugurated on the Bridges route. In July Hazlehead Golf Course, which had cost £20,000 — or nearly twice the estimate — to lay out, was formally opened by a match between Dr. William Tweddell, formerly of Aberdeen University and then Amateur Champion, and J. H. Taylor, five times Open Champion. In September the new Aberdeen lifeboat, the *Emma Constance*, was named by Lady Maud Carnegie.

CHAPTER THREE

The Victorian Lord Provosts

The third great 'explosion' which projected Aberdeen finally into the modern age was engineered by one man, Sir Alexander Anderson, a controversial figure in the city both before, during and after his double term as Lord Provost, but in retrospect unanimously regarded as the greatest of the civic heads of Bon-Accord. He was a native of Strichen, son of the parish minister there, a member probably of that amazing family descended from the 5th Earl Marischal's Skipper Anderson of which some account will be given later. After some years at Strichen School, he came in to the Grammar School, graduated at Marischal College and joined the legal firm in the city which soon became 'a household word' as Adam and Anderson. His flair for doing the right thing (though perhaps not always in the conventional way) for the public interest was first illustrated by the founding, already mentioned, of Oldmill and Oakbank. His driving force found outlet when he became treasurer of the Dispensary, then in a semi-moribund condition, which he speedily revitalised.

Anderson next turned his attention to the sector of private enterprise. In 1836 he promoted two most successful ventures which established themselves firmly in the proud esteem of Aberdonians, though both, alas! have succumbed to the contemporary craze for size before service — the Northern Assurance Company and the North of Scotland Bank. The next year he indulged, in company with his cousin George ('Chicago') Smith in what proved to be an unpleasant gamble for all those connected with it save Chicago Smith and the band of young men from Aberdeen and district whom he took out to the United States to staff the concern, which was known as the Illinois Investment Company, later joined by the Wisconsin Marine and Fire Insurance Company. In these two projects hopeful Aberdonians lost about £100,000 of their hard won cash. Anderson returned to local and more respectable undertakings in 1838, when he founded the Aberdeen Market Company, under whose aegis Market Street was made and the first Newmarket built in 1842. In 1844, as recorded in an earlier chapter, he launched a gas company which within three years displaced the existing concern.

Then came his intervention in the great railway boom. In 1844 he floated the Aberdeen Railway Company with a capital of £900,000 in £50 shares to build a line from Aberdeen to Forfar that would link with the existing line from Forfar to Arbroath. This Aberdeen Railway which reached Aberdeen in 1850, became the northern section of the Caledonian Railway system. In February 1845 appeared the prospectus of the Great North of Scotland Railway originally intended to link Aberdeen with Inverness. The capital was put at £1,100,000 in £50 shares and the issue was subscribed seven times over. The first operating section of the Great North, between Kittybrewster and Huntly, was opened in 1855. The Deeside Railway, at first only between Ferryhill and Banchory was running in 1853. These and subsequent railway developments affecting Aberdeen will be related in a more appropriate context. By the time these railway facilities were available to Aberdeen, Anderson had retired into the background. He had even dropped out of the board of the North Bank in 1849, and for a time his reputation appears to have been under a cloud. Crudely put, he had used the North Bank till to finance his railways, and for once the end may be said to justify the means.

Ten years later he was approached to enter the Town Council and did so as a representative of the third ward. Such was his prestige (and such perhaps was the state of torpor into which the Corporation had fallen) that he was at once elected Provost, but within a few months after a flaming row in the council chamber he resigned, fought his seat again, was returned with a majority that left no doubt as to whose side the electors were on, and resumed his place in the chair. He at once began to put his ideas into action. The first thing was to increase the town's water supply to meet the needs of an expanding population. In 1862 the Police and Waterworks Act sanctioned the Cairnton scheme which Queen Victoria opened on 16 October 1866. In 1861, when the Prince Consort died (under an Aberdeen doctor!), Anderson at once proposed in a public meeting of the citizens the erection of a statue, which was forthwith commissioned and executed by a foreign sculptor named Baron Marochetti, who was understood to be popular at Court. As William Carnie says, 'everyone knows the result'. The statue of the seated Prince, now in its parterre behind the towering Wallace statue in Union Terrace, was originally set at the north-west end of Union Bridge where King Edward VII's statue now stands. By means best known to himself, the Provost persuaded the Queen, who had withdrawn into seclusion on the death of her husband, to perform what was believed to be the first public engagement of her widowhood. On 13 October 1863, in a day of pouring rain, Her Majesty unveiled the statue, the ceremony being performed from the first floor of the building at the opposite corner of Union Terrace then occupied by the Northern Club (of which Anderson had been one of the founder members and which by this service to the Queen received the additional epithet 'Royal' to its title). After pulling the cord the Queen knighted the Lord Provost. It was in 1863 that the term Lord Provost was introduced. The Queen's own statue was in marble, unveiled three years later by the Prince of Wales who received the freedom of the burgh on that occasion.

In addition to the Cairnton water supply, Anderson put in being a new sewage scheme which was at least as necessary as the other. He pressed forward the building of the new Grammar School in Skene Street which was completed in 1865, and he was responsible for the decision to erect the new Townhouse for which permission was obtained in an act of 1866 and the city's portion of which became habitable in 1871. After his retirement, Sir Alexander (who as baron baillie to Lord Saltoun was Provost of Fraserburgh and had modernised the harbour to make it Scotland's premier herring port) founded the City of Aberdeen Land Association, whose members to this day praise and magnify the memory of the founder. This association purchased great areas of land on the perimeter of the burgh, particularly in Rubislaw and Torry. The association eventually became owners of Torry Farm, which Sir Alexander and James Milne of Kinaldie — owner of the Inver line of coasters — had purchased for £15,000. Disputes clustered round Anderson's head like bees round a honey-pot. When the diversion of the lower reaches of the Dee came to be undertaken, entailing the certainty of a residential development south of the river, the Town Council could have had the whole 115 acres of the farm for £28,000. Two Lord Provosts, Sir Alexander's successor Alexander Nicol, and William Leslie after him, both contested the owners' valuation, which James W. Barclay, who was shoremaster and incidentally related by marriage to James Milne, regarded as a reasonable figure and a good investment. After endless haggling, arbitrations, litigation and volleys of calumny, thirty-one acres were purchased by the town for some £20,000, and in 1901, when more of the land was required for harbour expansion, the harbour commissioners had to pay £56,500 for 7½ acres.

Thus the community, through misplaced thrift, refused to spend £28,000 on 115 acres and got 39 acres for £76,500. Sir Alexander died in 1887 at the age of 85. His portrait was painted by Sir George Reid, and his son Andrew Anderson left his house, with his books and its other contents and an endowment, to secure the Library at Strichen, an institution which is unique in itself and rich in everything but ready cash. As a result of its lack of the latter, it has been (1968) taken over by the County Council, and will, of course, lose its identity before long.

The setting of men and events in which Alexander Anderson fulfilled his vital reforms was characteristic of early modern Aberdeen. Before him in the provost's chair had been his two friends, Sir Thomas Blaikie (1839–46 and 1853–5), already noticed, founder and partner in an engineering firm famous in its day, knighted in 1856, prominent in many of Anderson's great ventures, and George Thompson, Jr., of Pitmedden, founder of the Aberdeen Line whose name is still to be seen in Australia (if not in its native Scotland) and whose ships were noted the world over for their comfort and efficiency. The emus in the policies of Pitmedden House, Dyce, were evidence until the First Great War of its owner's connection with the Antipodes. From 1850 to 1852 George Henry, senior partner in the Coffee Company, was in the chair and in his praepositial capacity he had the no-doubt stimulating experience of attending the celebrations in Paris in 1852 of Louis Napoleon's emergence as the Emperor Napoleon III. Provost Henry on his return was subjected to some sabbatarian criticism for having attended fetes on the Lord's Day. He survived until 1867. He probably belonged to the same family as John Henry, father of the orator of the American Revolution, Patrick Henry, 1736–99 ('Give me liberty or give me death!') He was the last Aberdonian to wear hair-powder. Sir Alexander's immediate predecessor was John Webster of Edgehill, who was largely responsible for the visit of the British Association in 1859 when the Prince Consort was present as President of the Association. Webster was Liberal M.P. for the city from 1880 to 1885.

An event which occurred soon after Anderson became Provost upset Aberdeen because of its unusual nature and of the standing of its principal actors, and must have deeply disturbed the Provost himself who had close business associations with one of those involved. The legal firm of John and Anthony Blaikie were sequestrated with liabilities of between £200,000 and £300,000, a fantastic sum in those days. One member of the firm died, the senior partner disappeared. The crash was attributed to railway speculation and similar vagaries.

When Sir Alexander Anderson stepped down, Alexander Nicol, a shipowner and owner of Aberdeen's first clipper, the *Scottish Maid*, took his place for a term. He had been Provost of Old Aberdeen. He assisted in promoting the Association for Improving the Condition of the Poor. His objections to the purchase of Torry Farm cost him his municipal seat in 1869, in which year William Leslie, the architect of Dunrobin Castle and partner with Alexander Macdonald the granite merchant, had been elected Lord Provost. He held office from 1869 to 1873. In 1871 the city boundaries were extended to include Ferryhill, Mannofield, and Kittybrewster, the Police Commissioners disappeared and their functions were assumed by the Town Council, which was increased from nineteen to twenty-five members. The city's first public park, the Victoria Park, was laid out. In the same year the burgess ticket was presented to W. E. Gladstone, and Leslie in 1874 got the Council to offer a similar honour to Benjamin Disraeli, who accepted but never found time for the ceremony. The Provost during his term of office bought the estate of Nethermuir, near New Deer. He was one of the founders of the Aberdeen Jute Company, which collapsed in the early twenties of this century under the combined pressure of bad trade and Government interference. George Jamieson, wholesale merchant, was next in order of the Provosts and acted for two terms until 1879. A quay was named after him in recognition of the good work he did for the improvement of the harbour. The rebuilding of the East Church of St. Nicholas after the disastrous fire of 9 October 1874 was promptly undertaken at a cost of some £6,000 plus a few hundreds to remedy peripheral damage to the West Kirk. The Victoria Bridge was begun to span the Dee, the new Post Office opened at the foot of Market Street, a fund was raised for the relief of those ruined by the failure of the City of Glasgow Bank, and in 1879 Sir Thomas Blaikie's vision of the abolition of the bell and petty customs came true. In 1875 races on the Links were resumed, and for the first time since 1781 Aberdeen had a maiden assize. A memorable snowstorm at the beginning of 1875 blocked the railways and brought almost all traffic and social gatherings to a standstill. The rail trip to London took thirty-three hours.

Peter Esslemont, founder of the firm of Esslemont and Macintosh, was Provost for only one term, 1880–3, but he was a remarkably active chief magistrate. In 1881 additions to Cairnton water works were put in hand. In 1881 also Miss Charlotte Duthie of Ruthrieston, sister of Alexander Duthie, an Aberdeen lawyer who had been a member of the firm of Adam & Anderson, presented to the town part of the lands of Polmuir in Ferryhill to be a public park on the south side of the city. The Town Council purchased the adjacent estate of Arthurseat, which had belonged to and was so named by Arthur Fordyce Dingwall, Commissary of the Consistorial Court for the County, owner from 1783 until his death in 1834 of the estates of Eigie and Balmedie, and grand-father of the first Dingwall Fordyce, laird of Brucklay. These Ferryhill lands had earlier belonged to Principal Blackwell of Marischal College who had done some planting there, and adjoined the grounds of the residence of John Ewen the jeweller. Dingwall built the house. The Duthie Park was opened on 27 September 1883 by Princess Beatrice. The Victoria Bridge was put in commission in 1881. With the demoli-tion of the old weigh-house, new harbour offices were put in hand in 1882, as was the Art Gallery building, which was completed by the School of Art gifted by Councillor John Gray, a partner in the engineering firm of William McKinnon. Rose Street and Esslemont Avenue supplied a new access to Rosemount. Several other streets were made in various parts of the town and the burgh boundaries further extended in the Rubislaw, Pitmuxton, Stocket, Old Aberdeen and Bridge of Don directions, the area of the city being increased to 2,681 acres. Mr. Esslemont did not seek re-election, but in 1885 became Liberal M.P. for East Aberdeenshire until December 1892 when he was appointed chairman of the Scottish Fishery Board. He died in 1894.

Another architect, in the person of James Matthews, a pupil of the great Archibald Simpson, and a partner of A. Marshall Mackenzie succeeded Mr. Esslemont. The Grammar School, the Free Church College, the Town and County Bank Buildings at the corner of St. Nicholas Street, the large hall of the Music Hall, Her Majesty's Theatre in Guild Street, the Palace Hotel buildings, and many country resi-dences such as Ardo and Brucklay Castle were his work. During his provostship Rosemount Viaduct was constructed and with it Union Terrace Gardens in 1883. Riverside Road was made, the library of the Mechanics' Institute with its building in Market Street was handed over to the town as a public library and the British Association was for a second time in conference at Aberdeen in 1885. Lord Rosebery received the Freedom of the City. A banker, and since 1850 a partner in the Thompson shipowning firm, for which for some years he acted as London director, was the next civic chief. William Henderson, a native of New Aberdour, was knighted in 1893. He was responsible for a £30,000 extension to the Royal Infirmary to mark Queen Victoria's

jubilee, the commemorative service for which he attended in Westminster Abbey wearing the distinctive dress which the Council had
decided in the summer of 1887 should be provided. A ward in the new
surgical wing was named after him. Two statues were presented to the
city during his term, those of General Gordon and Sir William Wallace,
both in 1888. Sir William, before he entered the Town Council, was
President of Aberdeen Chamber of Commerce in 1874–5, and in
common with about a dozen other Lord Provosts of the city, he was a
director of the North Bank.

During his tour of office the last Riding of the Marches of the burgh
took place on 4 September 1889. A skit on the event was commissioned
and written, with illustrations by Robert Brough, but the Riding proved
to be a sad event for Aberdeen. Previous ridings had been held in
1840, 1848 and 1861. The 1889 parade was instigated by one of the
ablest and most popular personalities that have ever been in general
practice in the city. Dr. Maitland Moir was the son of a merchant.
Not only had he an extensive practice, but he was one of the keenest
members of a coterie of witty and intelligent people — journalists,
versifiers, artists, and well-read manufacturers and merchants — that
kept the town in touch with all that was worth knowing in the arts and
letters and contemporary affairs. In the course of the Riding intending
burgesses of guild were expected to be 'douped' or forcibly seated on a
big march stone, No. 31, on Wyndford farm on the slopes of Brimmond Hill, which was known as the Doupin' Steen. This initiation
ceremony was performed on Maitland Moir, who was a big, strong,
heavy man and who with his love of fun made a great fuss of the affair
so that considerable force had to be employed to bring his dorsal aspect
in contact with the stone. At the subsequent luncheon in a marquee
on the farm of Tulloch, the doctor remarked with a laugh that he had
suffered a good deal in consequence of the heartiness of his initiation,
but he added 'That's all past, and there's nothing lost'. Unfortunately,
there was a great loss in store. The discomfort becoming worse, he was
found to have sustained a fracture of the pelvis, and he died in a week
or two, to the profound grief of the whole community.

The double triennium of Sir David Stewart (he was knighted in
1896) was notable for civic expansion. Head of the combworks firm,
a former President of the Chamber of Commerce, and with varied
experience of public life, he gave much thought to the terms of the
Aberdeen Corporation Act of 1891. The burgh boundaries were pushed
outwards to include Old Aberdeen, Woodside and Torry. In the 1881

extension the ancient four wards had, we saw, been succeeded by eight, and now the 1893 Act added Woodside, Ruthrieston and Torry, the last-named ward being allotted only one member, and the membership of the Council being thus raised to thirty-one, plus the Dean of Guild. The extension more than doubled the city's area to over ten square miles or 6,694 acres.

An Act of 1893 dealt with the extension of the municipal gas works and with the storage and purification of the water supply. The Public Library buildings were opened in 1892, the burgh court-house and police buildings in Lodge Walk three years later. The Provost's wife (Lady Provosts at that time had not been invented) switched on the electric lighting for the city on 27 February 1894, and in that summer the Stewart Park was opened in Woodside and named after the Provost. Various other activities and events marked an exceptionally busy provostship. While statues of Robert Burns (1892) and Queen Victoria (1893) added to the city's population of permanent but silent burgesses, H. M. Stanley in 1890 and Andrew Carnegie in 1892 were rather glamorous additions to the roll of freemen. The big development that took place at the harbour and in the university, in both of which the Provost was active, will be related in their appropriate contexts. Sir David, when he retired in 1895, was asked to contest South Aberdeen, but despite his manifold services, his rosette was deemed to be of the wrong shade, and his distinguished Liberal opponent, James Bryce, who never did much for the constituency was re-elected.

Sir David's successor, Daniel Mearns, whose main interests were in shipping and fishing and consequently in the welfare of the harbour, paid close attention to street development and particularly to the improvement of the slum conditions in the Shorelands, the first of Aberdeen's slum clearance schemes which brought the corporation into the ranks of house proprietors. Mearns Street is his monument there. He did valuable work in preparing for the new fish market, and in his time, apart from many harbour reforms, he put in hand the fire station in King Street at a cost of £16,500 and a model lodging house in East North Street, costing £11,000, while he saw the bathing station completed at the beach. He also initiated the magnificent esplanade between Dee and Don, which was built up on city refuse, and it was in his provostship that the tramways were acquired by the municipality. Most approachable and humorous of men, his 'off-taking' manner was perhaps partly intended to screen the extremely shrewd brain behind it. He may be said to have been the Harbour Board, on which he served long and in every possible position, so that as he said himself he 'went in at the hawse pipe and came out at the cabin window'. Besides the Fish Market and many other projects he took a leading part in arranging for the clearance of the dangerous reef that lay athwart the navigation channel. When he joined the Council in 1876, the burgh valuation was £351,794; when he retired in 1898 it was £750,000. To him also fell the pleasure of being provost when the burgh records reached their 500th year. No more popular personality than Danny ever presided over the burgh — and in his triennium he took the chair at over 2,000 meetings, besides attending innumerable extraneous boards and functions. He deserves to be remembered as one of Aberdeen's really great Lord Provosts. In 1899 he was appointed a member of the Fishery Board. He died in 1913. There is a marble bust of him by D. W. Stevenson.

The last Lord Provost of the century and the Victorian Age was John Fleming, a native of Glentilt who came to Aberdeen as a timber merchant via Dundee. He entered the Town Council in 1893, was asked but refused to run against Danny Mearns in 1895, and succeeded him in 1898. During his time the burgh was accorded the status of a county of a city, which involved the conferment of Her Majesty's Lieutenancy upon the Lord Provost. During his time the main pre-occupation of the Council was with the extension of Marischal College, which raised the very difficult question of the future of Greyfriars Kirk, one of Aberdeen's noblest ancient monuments with its wonderful seven-windowed west gable, and, of course, the only complete pre-Reformation Church left in the city. Provost Fleming succeeded in keeping the controversial problem well under control, and his LL.D. was a measure of the University's gratitude.[1] It was not then the practice to laureate every Lord Provost. Provost Fleming was asked to serve for a second term, and did in fact remain in the chair for an extra year. In 1917 he stood as a Liberal for South Aberdeen and was returned to Parliament, but at the 'coupon' election of 1918 he refused to bow the knee to Baal and went down in the company of quite a number of honest men. He died during a trip to South Africa in Pretoria in 1925. There is a stained glass window by J. M. Aiken to his memory in what was Beechgrove U.F. Church.

1   The solution, with Greyfriars frontage equated with that of the new Marischal, did not please everyone, even in the University itself. Years later H. J. C. Grierson in one of the most famous of his many celebrated digressions in his English lectures used to inveigh against the 'municipal vandalism' that ruined the old church.

CHAPTER FOUR

Twentieth–Century Lord Provosts

———

To the student of history — and in this case of local history, despite
Aberdeen's well-earned reputation for 'going it alone' — few things
are more intriguing than the reaction from the *fin de siècle* atmosphere
which in public life as in the world of the arts takes place at the turn of a
century. It is not, in this particular case of Aberdeen's civic leadership,
that the last years of Victoria's reign were characterised by administrative decadence — Danny Mearns alone would have made such a
conclusion unthinkable. Rather, there was a definite shifting of the
concept of civic development and a re-thinking of the attitude of those
who occupied the chair to the development of the community's activities.
There began then what can only be described by the modern phrase,
a movement to the Left, and although a majority of the Lord Provosts
between 1902 and the end of the Second World War were not politically of that persuasion they were in the schemes which they introduced
or carried through influenced by a tide in the affairs of men, a current
in the slant of public ideas, that carried them on, not perhaps altogether
to fortune, but at least towards and into a very new age compared with
its predecessor.

There was nothing in the provostship of James Walker of Richmond-
hill, who was Lord Provost from 1902 to 1905, to indicate that the city,
like the nation, was passing into a new era. The coronation of King
Edward VII (strictly speaking, he should have been Edward I, being
the first of his name to reign over the United Kingdom, though the
resurrection of that medieval rascal's name would not have been very
welcome in Scotland), was celebrated in due form, though perhaps with
more decorum than in a neighbouring and more ancient royal burgh,
which set out barrels of beer for the delectation of patriotic citizens
and ended the day with a homicide. James Walker, whose portrait was
one of those painted by Sir George Reid for the Townhouse collection,
was a successful business-man in the fish trade who had been a member
of the deputation to southern fishing ports that recommended and
advised upon the creation of the present Fish Market. He had, in

public life, been upon the Police Board since 1869, and he had seen the population doubled, the burgh boundaries twice extended, and the public parks — Duthie, Victoria, Stewart, Westburn (part of which was acquired in his provostship), and Walker (named after and opened by him in 1903) — laid out. Provost Walker also took part in the planning of some of the great developments carried through by his immediate successor.

This was Alexander Lyon, of Garioch farming stock but born in Footdee in 1850, son of the founder of the hide and tallow business in George Street which still flourishes and still maintains premises in Footdee. A man of great energy and many interests — he was a good shot, a golfer, a keen gardener, a member of the Cairngorm Club, and like so many of the more progressive of Aberdeen's Provosts, a Free, or about this time a United Free, churchman — he became leader of what was known as 'The Young Party' in the Town Council in the late eighties. The old hands were cleared off the bench, he organised a campaign against diseased meat, he brought campanologists from Louvain to attend to the bells of St. Nicholas Church, he took a leading part in the laying out of the Stewart, Walker and Westburn parks and of Union Terrace Gardens, in the reorganisation of the fire brigade, in the development of the tramway system, in the clearing away of the less salubrious areas of the Gallowgate and Exchequer Row, in the widening of Union Bridge and of College Street, and in the improvement of the amenities of the beach. He first joined the Town Council twenty years before, in 1905, he was elected Lord Provost, and to him it thus fell to receive and escort King Edward and Queen Alexandra when they, on 27 September 1906, visited the city for the delayed quater-centenary celebrations of the University and to open the new buildings of Marischal College. The Lord Provost met the royal train from Ballater at Ruthrieston station and was on duty the whole day until, after a civic luncheon and the presentation of a loyal address, he was knighted. His memorable and constructive spell of office ended in 1908, when he retired from the Council. He died in 1927.

During the whole of Sir Alexander's provostship a controversy was alternately simmering and boiling up over the extension of Aberdeen's water supply. His successor, Alexander Wilson, a lawyer born in Drumblade who had entered the council as recently as 1902, had been prominent on the water committee and led the party which favoured the tapping of the Banffshire river Avon as the new and main source of supply instead of the existing Dee works. In 1909 Lord Provost Wilson in the crucial council debate moved the adoption of the Avon scheme, but his motion was defeated, and the following year a Bill authorising the use of the Avon was thrown out by the House of Lords. What would have been the consequences at the present time had the Avon party been successful is now only too obvious. Provost Wilson started the Aberdeen Juridical Society and was really the founder of the Aberdeen Society of Solicitors, besides playing a leading part in the building of the Masonic Hall in Crown Street and giving for many years valuable service on the board of governors of Robert Gordon's College. He was associated with Sir James Murray, John Forbes White, Sir George Reid and others in the provision of the Hall of Sculpture in the Art Gallery. He retired from the chair and council in 1911 and died in 1933.

Adam Maitland, who took over from Lord Provost Wilson, was a member of the family that had farmed Balhalgardy, near Inverurie, since before the battle of Harlaw. Another U.F. Churchman, a Liberal, a social worker and prominent supporter of the Y.M.C.A. movement, he had started life in Aberdeen as a book-keeper in the *Aberdeen Journal* and at the age of 20, in 1878, gained a similar position in the builders' merchant firm of J. & W. Henderson, of which he became a partner ten years later. He entered the Town Council in 1895, and as convener of the relevant committee he presided over the building of the great Girdleness sewer. In his time the public house closing hour was brought back to 10 p.m. He was a supporter of the Dee party in the great water controversy, but actually was not a member of the Council during most of the time. He returned to the Townhouse in 1911 to become Lord Provost and retired in 1914. He was active in various projects for the redesigning of the city's lay-out, the most notable being a new road from King Street to the Links and another from Back Wynd to the Joint Station, neither of which matured.

It is curious that Aberdeen's two war-time Lord Provosts were facetious fellows. James Taggart, who took the chair in 1914, was like his predecessor a Donside man, born at Coldwells, Inverurie, in 1849. He came to Aberdeen in 1865 as an apprentice stone-cutter, emigrated as so many of his trade did to U.S.A., but returned to Aberdeen and in 1879 set up as a granite merchant, first in partnership and in 1883 on his own account in Great Western Road, where the business he founded continues under other ownership. He entered the Town Council in 1899 and served several times on the bench and as a convener of committees, always with competence although never spectacularly. No sooner was he Lord Provost, in November 1914, than he set to recruiting and raised a brigade of artillery which came to be known as 'Taggart's Own', his right-hand man being a worthy companion of his own waggish kind, a member of the Church Militant, the Rev. James Smith, minister of St. George's in the West Church of Scotland. Taggart's main contribution to the city's welfare was probably his inexhaustible capacity for heartening the public and diverting its mind from the more critical phases of the war. Once it was over he applied his energies to raising funds for a new Hospital for Sick Children, in which he was very successful. He had the list headed by a contribution from the first Lord Cowdray, whom he found, according to the story that went around, in a not too pliable frame of mind. When the Provost had explained what he was after, his lordship demanded, 'Well, how much do you want?' to which, with a face as unemotional as the granite in which he traded, Taggart replied, 'How much have ye got?' He was the first president of the Aberdeen Rotary Club, president of the Aberdeen Burns Club, the Scottish Cyclists' Union, and the Home for Widowers' Children. He was knighted in 1918.

After the war it was he who presented the Freedom of the City to Douglas Haig, in connection with which ceremony another typical anecdote took shape. Haig and Sir Roger Keyes, the daring leader of the raid on Zeebrugge, had earlier in the day been laureated by the University, and it may have been association of ideas, when Haig had signed the Burgess Roll, for Keyes to step forward to do likewise. But the arm of the Lord Provost was stretched across his chest, and the Donside voice warned him, 'Na, na nae you! We've got to draw the line some wye!' His fame as a story-teller resulted in his appearing on several platforms with the first Marquis of Aberdeen and Temair in an exchange of anecdotes, most of which were just the kind of flat jests that can be told from the platform and were not at all the rich humorous commentary upon life and manners that Taggart loved to indulge in. He died in 1929. His portrait was twice painted, by Ambrose M'Evoy (in Aberdeen Art Gallery) and by Allan Sutherland. When he retired from the chair he received the rather unusual gift in such circumstances of a canteen of cutlery with a brooch for his wife.

For the next Provost the Town Council went back to the harbour, electing its Treasurer and former Dean of Guild, William Meff, a fish salesman, son of a trawler-owner. He had entered the Harbour Board in 1892 and the Town Council in 1894, and in all his assignments in these bodies showed himself a sound, if cautious, man of business. As convener of the tramways committee, for instance, he carried through a complete revision of the fares, while as Dean of Guild he persuaded no fewer than 200 canny citizens to become burgesses, thereby so augmenting the funds of the Guildry that the various annuities could be raised, in some cases almost doubled. During his provostship the Labour representation on the Council became much more powerful and vocal, and as his virtues did not include meekness or patience, there were several scenes and ejections. The post-war mentality in the higher regions of politics had imposed various unaccustomed duties upon local authorities, notably in housing, to which those who were habituated to traditional ideas did not react kindly. This problem, which will be studied elsewhere, was one which sharpened the exchanges in which the Provost indulged with the so-called opposition. Despite the civic storms, however, Meff's rule was not unappreciated, he received King George V and Queen Mary when His Majesty on 29 September 1925 opened the War Memorial and Cowdray Hall in Schoolhill, and he served for two terms, retiring in 1925, having received a knighthood for his pains. He died in 1935.

The same problems were prominent during the three-year reign of Andrew Lewis, another harbour personality who, having taken over an engineering-cum-trawling business on the death of his father, had in 1916 added to it by establishing a shipyard on the Torry bank of the Dee. A business man of great foresight and tremendous energy, he managed a whole chain of enterprises ancillary to those three industries still vigorous and extended under his son, Andrew, and he carried his flair into his public work. His apprenticeship thereto he commenced in 1910 on the Harbour Board, of which he remained a member until 1948. He entered the Town Council in 1919. He was not long in the chair when the city was threatened with complete disruption of its services by the General Strike of 1926. An emergency committee, presided over by Treasurer William G. Edwards (another granite merchant) was successful in maintaining order, and in fact there was little attempt at rash action by the strikers. During the earlier twenties a movement was gathering momentum for a completely new and modern Royal Infirmary, which was approaching the end of its second century. The city Medical Officer of Health, Matthew Hay, had broached the idea, the Professor of Medicine, Ashley Mackintosh, had won over the medical profession, but unless the very substantial sum required to finance the scheme was forthcoming, the new hospital was likely to remain a dream. Andrew Lewis was persuaded that the design was an essential one, and he devoted himself during almost the whole of his provostship to its realisation. For months he laid his plans, then in April 1927 he launched his appeal for £400,000, the amount then regarded as the minimum to build and establish the new Infirmary. He got it. When the appeal was finally closed £407,000 had been subscribed. Aberdeen and its hinterland got their magnificent hospital, but, unfortunately, the other achievement implicit in the money-raising effort was not appreciated by politicians, namely the lesson that it does not require the State with its wasteful and eventually uncontrollable expenses to supply the community with the services it needs. When he retired from the provost's chair, Andrew Lewis was knighted. He died at the age of 77 in 1952.

James R. Rust, who followed, was like Meff the City Treasurer, and like Taggart began as a stone-cutter and was President of the Granite Manufacturers' Association. He belonged to Lower Donside, having been born at Danestone in 1873, he was a member of the United Free Church, and in fact he had most of the qualifications usually associated with occupants of Aberdeen's civic chair. When he was 30 he had become a partner in the business, still run by his son and grandson, of Charles McDonald Ltd. He was elected to Aberdeen Parish Council in 1907, and was responsible for the grant of an increase to the allowance given to the outdoor poor. In 1914 he was returned to the Town Council, succeeded Meff as Treasurer, and in that capacity put through a succession of real estate deals which greatly enhanced the amenities of the city and provided the necessary acres for its physical expansion. In 1920 Hazlehead Estate was purchased for £40,000, and subsequent transactions included the lands of Kincorth for £45,000, Hilton and Rosehill for housing schemes, £24,000 of property elsewhere for slum clearance, and the Music Hall for £31,000. In his term as Lord Provost, improvements were made to the water supply, the fish market was extended, Hazlehead golf course was laid out, and Torry housing scheme advanced. Several municipal departments were housed in Broad Street property that had been acquired, and there was a grading of municipal staff. National legislation which involved the absorption of the Parish Council's responsibilities by the Town Council and the transference of educational administration from the Education Authority to the Town Council added considerably to the anxieties of Provost Rust's term, which were already intensified by the great recession round the early thirties and the uncertainty caused by the substitution of a Labour for a Tory Government. In his term the first woman Town Councillor, Miss I. Burgess, took her seat. Provost Rust's triennium, coupled with his work as City Treasurer, made a memorable page in the burgh's history. He died in 1945.

Henry Alexander, who became Provost in 1932, had been engaged while on the Council in working out a design for town and country planning. A journalist and son and grandson of journalists, he had edited the family newspaper, the *Aberdeen Free Press*, until its amalgamation with the *Aberdeen Daily Journal* in 1922. Born in 1875, a Grammar School boy and graduate of Aberdeen University, he was the first Master of Arts for many years to preside over the city's affairs. Like Sir Alexander Lyon, he was an enthusiastic mountaineer and had written an excellent book, *The Cairngorms*, on Scotland's highest group of hills. Chairman of the Aberdeen and District Joint Town Planning Committee from 1928 to 1933 and of the Scottish Housing Advisory Committee, his ideas and researches greatly helped to form the fabric of the town planning legislation that reached the Statue Book seven years after his death in 1940. For that legislation his report was in many respects the basis. The Aberdeen and district scheme covered the planning, construction and improvement of roads, the provision and maintenance of open spaces, the development of housing areas, and the preservation of historical and ancient monuments, buildings and other subjects. In terms of the plan the Kincorth suburb of Aberdeen was laid out and the ring road, Anderson Drive, was built to carry traffic from the Donside to the Deeside trunk road. He was knighted in 1938.

Edward W. Watt, who succeeded him, had been editor of the *Evening Gazette*, the afternoon paper of the *Free Press*, and a colleague for many years in the journalistic world. He was an Arts graduate of the University, took a prominent part in the affairs of the Boys' Brigade, was a keen Territorial and commanded a reserve battalion of the Gordon Highlanders in the Kaiser's War, and was the first chairman of Aberdeen Juvenile Court. He was Lord Provost when in September 1936 the new Royal Infirmary at Foresterhill was opened by the Duke of York. Provost Watt made an appeal for £100,000 to complete the equipment of the Royal Infirmary. He died in 1955.

When in 1938 the time for the election of a new Lord Provost came round, the shadow of the Munich Agreement behind and of inevitable war ahead made the prospects of the city, as of all civilisation, gloomy in the extreme. There was a close contest for the chair, between George Duncan, a leading lawyer, chairman of the Education Authority and convener of the Education Committee of the Town Council, and Thomas Mitchell, a master baker who had for three years been chairman of the old Parish Council and had served on the Town Council since 1928, about the same length of time as his rival. In the event and by the smallest of margins the latter won. As has been mentioned, he was a facetious fellow, and, while his long provostship — he presided until 1947 — was, mainly because of the war, not fruitful of much municipal advancement, he contrived to keep up, like Taggart a generation before, the spirits of the community by his quips and vitality. Thus, soon after the war was declared, a complaint was made at a Town Council meeting that the tramcars to the various districts of the city, instead of being at sensible intervals of time, were bunched together so that while the first would be reasonably full the rest would be more or less empty. The Lord Provost accepted that it was so but added, 'We're following the convoy system'. When at the opening of the New Bridge of Dee by King George VI on 10 March 1941, he was reading the loyal address, he discarded his paper with the remark, 'Ach, I've lost my place'. The response of the citizens to the numerous air raids upon it — Aberdeen was said to have had more alerts than any other town, its first visit from German planes being on 7 March 1940, and its worst on 21 April 1943, when ninety-seven people were killed and 235 injured — was to subscribe gladly to appeals made by the Lord Provost for money to build Spitfires, of which four received names appropriate to the city and to the country of the Gordons and the Keiths. When the war was over he received into the Burgess Roll Sir Winston Churchill, Sir Jan Smuts, J. G. Wynant the American diplomat, Wellington Koo of China, and Sir Peter Fraser, the Premier of New Zealand. He was knighted in 1943 and became a great favourite with the Royal family, the Queen Mother visiting him when he was in a nursing home shortly before his death in 1959 at the age of 90.

The first Labour Lord Provost, Duncan Fraser, a native of Rothes, was elected in 1947. Born in 1880, he had been a commercial traveller in Glasgow who came to Aberdeen as a drapery store manager in 1903, and in 1912 opened his own shop in Schoolhill. In 1944 he was chairman of the Aberdeen Food Control Committee. He was awarded the C.B.E. in 1950 and became a Chevalier of the Legion of Honour in 1952. By this time the Town Council, like other local authorities, was increasingly becoming a rubber stamp to endorse in its own area the policy of the central government. In education, housing, health services and the other branches of local administration it was basically a national programme that had to be put into operation and while Aberdeen changed during Provost Fraser's term in these respects to a very great extent with a proliferation in particular of new municipal houses and a start to the creation of the Welfare State so-called, it could not be said that the local initiative or responsibility for the basic ideas was much in evidence. Provost Fraser retired in 1951 with the satisfaction of knowing that he had been a popular salesman for his party in the chair. He died, much respected, in 1965.

The last non-Labour Lord Provost for at least twenty years was his successor, William D. Reid, a native of Peterhead, member of a legal firm in Aberdeen, and a member of the Town Council since 1934. Lord Provost Reid had been convener of the watching and lighting committee and during the whole of the Hitler war controller of civil defence and the city's emergency committee. He was the first Aberdeen lawyer to be vice-president of the Law Society of Scotland, which like most organisations with headquarters south of the Tay has little knowledge of Scotland beyond that river. He was a well-known bridge player and a supporter of cricket and art. A redistribution of local authority seats having necessitated a 'clean sweep' of the Town Council at the municipal election of 1952, he was Lord Provost only for a year, Labour being returned in control. He died in 1964.

Four subsequent Lord Provosts have all been Labour men — Professor John M. Graham who filled the chair from 1952 to 1955, and again from 1961 to 1964; George Stephen, who served two consecutive terms from 1955 to 1961; Norman Hogg, from 1964 to 1967; and Robert S. Lennox elected in 1967.

CHAPTER FIVE

Harbour and Fish Market*

There is one part of Aberdeen's organism that is never far from the thoughts of the citizens and their representatives. The railway may come (and go), road services for people and goods may escalate, air transport may become the popular method of long-distance travelling and dispatching, but always the mind of the Aberdonian returns to remember the sea and to consider the state of the harbour. One of its notable periods of improvement was inaugurated by an Act passed in 1868 which repealed the 1843 and 1844 measures and consolidated their provisions.

In terms of the 1868 Act the first work was the building of the new South Breakwater. It extended 1,050 feet from high-water mark and 700 feet from low-water mark of spring tides, and it cost £78,000. Next Trinity Quay was widened, costing just under £5,000. Then came the diversion of the Dee. This affected the salmon fishers who had to be bought out to the tune of £38,000 or a little more than the cost of the actual work of diversion. Some interesting relics were discovered below the chain bridge — dressed sandstone blocks and oak beams joined together, which some wiseacres speculated might have formed part of a bridge for which Robert the Bruce's engineer, John Crab, left a bequest. The old breakwater and south pier were removed except for stubs, and the navigation channel widened to 300 feet. After the completion of the south breakwater in 1873, the North pier was extended by 166 feet by the autumn of 1877. By the Act the management of the harbour was vested in a Board consisting of the Lord Provost and Baillies, the Dean of Guild, the City Treasurer, ten members of the Town Council, and twelve men elected by the harbour ratepayers.

In 1879, more money being required, another Act was obtained, and a policy of steady repair and improvement was followed. In 1895 the borrowing powers were raised to £535,000, and in 1899 to £735,000. By the end of the century the annual revenue was £68,000 and the

* This chapter deals in more detail with events in the development of the harbour after 1850 already mentioned without much elaboration.

ordinary expenditure £62,000, but the work of providing new quays, wharves, repair docks and buildings, and of keeping the navigation channel clear for the increasingly deep-draughted vessels that sought the port made the Board's borrowing powers very necessary. During the century close on £1,700,000 was expended on various enterprises and developments connected with the harbour. In 1810 there were 150 vessels of a tonnage of 17,131 belonging to the port. At the end of the century the tonnage was 120,000.

The harbour had at this time become almost a cesspool of refuse from the city. There are many testimonies to its unsavoury character. Under the 1879 Act by the end of the summer in 1880 the whole of the old river bed west of Market Street had been filled in and laid out in streets, and the portion east of Market Street became the Albert Basin. Commercial Quay ran along the north of the basin on the side of the present Fish Market, while Jamieson's Quay ran along the south of the Upper Dock. That cost £15,000. Then a graving dock was formed near the eastern end of the Albert Basin at a cost of £48,000. It was opened in 1885. The dock gates were renewed, controlled by hydraulic pressure, in 1884. Matthews' Quay running along the north side of the Albert Basin to the graving dock was constructed in 1885. As already noted the old weigh-house was taken down and harbour offices raised on the site at a cost of £9,000. Canadian cattle imports were provided for by a wharf at Pocra (Powcreek) Quay.

In 1895 another Act — the most formative of all — was obtained and in 1899 yet another. Among the alterations and improvements consequent upon these measures, old Regent Bridge was displaced by a new, wider bridge operated by electricity. Part of Point Law was taken away and a wharf erected. Various other changes mostly on the existing lay-out took place which are not likely now to be recognised save by very old people. The opening of the new Fish Market in 1889 and the fantastic expansion of the trawling industry had, while substantially increasing the harbour income, greatly added to its problems. But the Board manfully kept pace. The entrance channel was deepened by methods which would have evoked much interest and as much wonder in that ingenious mechanic Davie do A'thing; wharves were erected along the Dee, quays widened, the tidal harbour enlarged; a new dock constructed at Torry, and three pontoon docks provided. Such was the equipment of the harbour by the outbreak of war in 1914. To that date from 1895 the expenditure on the harbour (not counting the cost of normal repair and maintenance work) was £1,800,000. Trade kept on expanding until 1913 when 1,260 foreign ships came in and 442 took out cargo. But the number of vessels owned by the port steadily declined; in 1855 there were 234 of a tonnage of 58,230; in 1911 there were 86 and the tonnage was 83,143. By the end of the Hitler war there were only 16 of 12,885 tons. Trawlers are not, of course, included.

As in Davie do A'thing's day, the paramount anxiety of the harbour authorities was to keep the entry to the port clear, as the constant expenditure on the dredging of the navigation channel over many generations testifies. The fact that the roadstead and the river Dee were intimately connected had a great deal to do with this problem, as the river was constantly bringing down mud and silt which the contrary pressure of the tides tended to build up about the point where the sediment reached the sea. The controlling of the Dee's course, which reclaimed a goodly stretch of land and made the modern lay-out of the harbour possible, and the eventual straightening out of the last few hundred yards of the river, which built up a stronger current to act as a bore to flush out the sediment from the navigation channel, both tended to improve the condition of the harbour. As ships became larger, the navigation channel's clearance, the provision of deep water berthing facilities and the handling of equipment were priorities that were constantly under review. The navigation channel, half a mile long, with a designed maximum depth at high water of spring tides of 34 feet, and 110 feet wide absorbed £60,000 when it was deepened by 2 feet.

The Commissioners were succeeded under the Aberdeen Harbour Order of 1960 by a Harbour Board consisting of seven nominees of the users, four of the Town Council, two representatives of the Chamber of Commerce and two of organised labour. It should be emphasised that despite the inevitably large and constant expenditure upon improvements and new facilities — some £960,000 was spent between the end of the Hitler war and 1959 — the harbour had not cost the ratepayers of the city one penny although its status as a municipal asset is at the truest computation as high as that of any of the municipal services which impose a burden of more than a pound per pound of valued rent upon the citizens, not to mention a proportion of direct and indirect taxation that seems never to be counted. Moreover, the fact that up to 1961, for capital works costing almost £3¼ million loans had been required to the extent of £1,174,000 indicates what can be done in local administration when control is in the hands of business men with a direct and practical knowledge of the subject.

In recent years the pattern of the trade of the port has shown contacts with all countries of West Europe, the Baltic, the Iberian Peninsula, Russia, North Africa, North America (although this three-century old traffic has been somewhat seriously reduced by the withdrawal from the port of the Ellerman-Wilson Shipping Company's transatlantic services), and even places as far away as Nauru Island in the Pacific. Despite the passing of the control of the coastwise shipping lines from Aberdeen to London, the business with the main British ports is kept up even though in many cases the carrying medium is foreign tonnage, and although cargo-liner services between Aberdeen and Newcastle, Hull and Liverpool have been dropped because of competition by road. In 1959 the revenue was £387,000, the port was used by 1,980,000 net registered tons of shipping, and 1,400,000 tons of cargo were handled. Principal imports were fertilisers, esparto grass, wood pulp, china clay, fish, maize, flour, coal and oil, cement and timber; exports included, besides bunker coal and oil, ore, paper, preserved provisions, cereals and manures. Among the comparatively recent improvements made and facilities added have been two deep-water berths, high speed electric cranes, coaling plant, a new herring market at North Esplanade East, a new jetty, the replacement of the old bridges at the east end of the Victoria dock (built in 1848), the replacement of one of the three pontoon docks, a fitting-out berth, the modernisation of Pocra Quay, and of the Round House, now usually termed the hailing station, at the harbour mouth; and the demolition of old and the erection of new sheds and buildings. Hoppers, cranes (there are now twenty-four) and grabs (twenty-one) have greatly speeded up the turn-round of the vessels. In 1945, when the Board purchased the old property known as Findlay's Buildings, at Pocra Quay, a tablet on the wall recording that this in 1477 was the site of a fort and later of a blockhouse was put in a safe place near-by when the buildings were pulled down.

The harbour area is 370 acres with some 20,000 lineal feet of quays. Transit sheds have a floor space of over 12,000 square yards. It extends westwards from the tidal basin in two arms with a kind of basic third arm through which flows the Dee. The most northerly branch consists of the Victoria and Upper Docks, separated by Regent Bridge, the middle arm is the Albert Basin with the fish market extending along most of its northern and part of its western boundaries. The Harbour Board has now some 300 employees and its pay bill annually amounts to over £200,000. The Town Council owns the Fish Market, which has of late years been ever more insistently demanding repair and modernisation (in 1967 a large section, 600 feet, had to be closed for attention). The haulage and rolling stock on the quayside railway, seven miles in extent, belong to British Railways, although the lines themselves and the streets on which they run belong (like the solum of the fish market) to the Harbour Board. Since the Second World War over £1 million has been spent on capital works.

With the passing of the brave and graceful clippers, the glory departed from Aberdeen as an independent seaport. The Aberdeen White Star Line and the Rennie Line, that had carried the name and fame of Bon-Accord to the ends of the earth, disappeared. George Milne's Inver Line, having conducted a busy coastal trade up to the First World War, also faded out. Other Aberdeen coasting lines have suffered a similar fate. In 1870 the Leith and Clyde Shipping Company amalgamated with the Aberdeen, Dundee and Leith Shipping Company to form the Aberdeen, Leith, Clyde and Tay Shipping Company which in time became the North of Scotland and Orkney and Shetland Steam Navigation Company. In 1829 the Aberdeen Steam Navigation Company, which had originated over a century before, long ere steam was dreamt of, bought the first Aberdeen-built steamer the *Queen of Scotland* from Duffus and Co. The North of Scotland Company, which was operating eight smacks in 1820, brought, as already stated, the 200-ton paddle steamer *Velocity* to Aberdeen. Later they and the Aberdeen Steam Navigation Co. worked in co-operation to maintain a daily service between Aberdeen and Leith. In 1837 the Aberdeen Commercial Company was formed and collected a fleet of vessels. In 1881 the Aberdeen, Leith and Moray Firth Steam Shipping Company commenced operations with the Moray Firth ports, later extending their services to Liverpool, their fleet increasing from one small to five large steamers. These companies have either disappeared or have no longer their controlling offices in Aberdeen. The last Aberdeen-built sailing ship was the *Alexander Nicol*, to the order of the Aberdeen Lime Company in 1876. By 1909 only twenty sailing vessels, of which but three were home-built, were registered at the port. It may be added that the Aberdeen Line, before the century ended, had about a score of ships, of which the 4,000-ton *Australasian* carried the famous English historian James Anthony Froude, the biographer of Thomas Carlyle, to the Antipodes in a style which earned for the ship and its owners a gratifying tribute from the V.I.P.

Up to the end of last century Aberdeen could be said to be in regular direct contact with North America and the Continent of Europe, particularly with the Baltic; up to the Second World War in regular contact with the Baltic and in frequent contact with North America — all in Aberdeen-owned bottoms. Today while its harbour is busy indeed, all the coastwise and trans-ocean commerce (apart from coal and other consumer commodities for a handful of local firms) is carried by foreign or English-owned boats.[1]

For a community by the sea, Aberdeen was oddly dilatory in making the most of the sea's bounty. It is true, as we have seen, that from the very earliest recorded times of the burgh's history it had done a trade in fish cured in the rough and ready manner of a non-scientific age. But although Aberdeen fish were known and presumably appreciated in the Low Countries and the Baltic and in England, the export possibilities, though they can hardly have failed to be discerned, were not seriously exploited. Fishing of a kind went on for hundreds of years without a sign of expansion. The Dutch with their busses nosed along the coast picking up what they could, but specialising in herring, and it was through this poaching — as it would be regarded today, that a Peterhead man of the name of Harper threw his lot in with the Netherlands and became the father, grandfather and great grandfather of three Dutch seamen of the name of Tromp who were to remind the English several times that there were other sea-lions besides those who sailed from Plymouth and Tilbury.

Several times the Aberdonians tried to muscle in on what was almost a Dutch monopoly. A Dutch boat with skipper and crew was tempted to come over and teach the Aberdonians the trick of it, but for once the Aberdonians proved unwilling pupils. Yet it was the herring fishing that was indirectly responsible for the start of Aberdeen's trawling industry, which brought to the burgh the last great wave of abounding wealth, as had been done by woollen manufacture in the sixteenth and seventeenth centuries, by wool and linen in the eighteenth, and by granite in the early nineteenth. About 1870 some herring fishers were attracted to the port and did pretty well, their catches finding a ready market — later to be taken over by Peterhead and Fraserburgh — in the Baltic. The temporary herring boom attracted fishermen from farther afield, particularly the north-east coast of England. In the seventies there was for the first time what deserved to be called a

---

1 Glasgow has had the same experience. No Glasgow-based line now serves the North Atlantic trade. The clammy hand of London, whether the right hand of private capital or the left hand of departmental regulation, effectively strangles local development and enterprise.

trawling fleet at Aberdeen. In 1836 a 70-foot vessel had been procured to attempt the deep-sea fishing, but the fishermen of Futtie, accustomed to keeping inshore in their small boats, would not co-operate. Another attempt to break out in 1860 also failed despite backing from Town Council and Harbour Commissioners. Indeed, the Council soon after the battle of Waterloo had rebuilt Futtie for the fishermen — North and South Squares are still evidence of that interest — and provided a fish market at the foot of the Shiprow, but notwithstanding these attentions only forty-three boats aggregating 227 tons were fishing from Aberdeen and Torry in 1855, compared with 105 boats of 777 tons in the four nearest coastal villages to Aberdeen. In 1865 a few fishermen bought a smack of seventeen tons, the *Cruiser*, with a crew of seven for the deep-sea fishing, but once again enterprise was frustrated, this time by the theft of their gear, and they desisted. In 1868 there were two small decked steamers, 112 open boats for the white fishing and 124 for the herring fishing, employing 970 in crews.

As stated, the first trawlers began to work from the port in the seventies, but they were only sailing boats. It was the *Toiler*, the first steam trawler, a converted tug purchased by a deputation of Aberdeen fish trade pioneers from Dublin owners for £1,550 in February 1882 that set the ball rolling. William Pyper deserves to be remembered as the father of Aberdeen's trawling industry. He was managing owner of the *Toiler*, the manager was Robert Brown, the skipper William Watson, and the engineer the Dubliner J. O. Connor. She made the first commercial trip with trawl gear on 23 March 1882 and came into harbour with a catch of three boxes of haddocks, which were sold for £1 17s. The buyer, Thomas Davidson, also deserves to be recorded. She fished in Aberdeen Bay from Donmouth to Collieston and from Girdleness to Muchalls. Her first auctioned catch amounted to £2 11s. 6d., her first month's catch to £207 1s. 4d., and at the end of six months her gross earnings were £1,772 1s., expenses £1,002 17s., leaving a net profit of £769 4s., which enabled the fortunate partners to enjoy a dividend of 100 per cent for the year, while the six members of crew pocketed over £500. It is interesting to note that the cost of ice for the first six months was 22s. 6d. Such was the beginning of Aberdeen's greatest industrial romance.

The *Toiler*, old when she arrived, and wooden at that, could not long stand up to the hard strain of trawling, and after three years she was sold. In 1887 she sank in the Moray Firth, which was not then closed to British trawlers, and by a curious chance her immediate successor in Aberdeen trawling happened to fish up her oak trawl beam, which was brought to port and erected at the home of one of her eleven owners. They, nothing daunted by the strenuous opposition of the line fishermen, who even went so far as to approach the Town Council to intervene, had constructed for them by John Duthie Sons & Co. the first Aberdeen-built iron steam trawler, the *North Star*, with boilers and engines by Hall, Russell & Co. She was launched in September 1883, and after a trial trip that was remembered for many a day, she settled down to business and between the end of September 1883 and May 1891 she brought £46,591 worth of fish into the port. An hour later than the *North Star*, a second steam trawler, the *Gipsy*, took to the water. Aberdeen's trawling industry was finally afloat. In 1883 a Commission, of which the great T. H. Huxley was a member, sat at Aberdeen to investigate the complaints by line and drift-net fishermen that trawling was damaging their interests. The Commission found favourably to the trawlers. In the years that ensued the names of Daniel Mearns, John Brown and Thomas Walker, who had led the fishermen's deputation to the Town Council but seen the light, came to be very familiar as leaders of what rapidly expanded into Aberdeen's most important industry.

Many developments followed the trawler. In 1886 the Aberdeen Ice Company (still in business) was formed with a 20-ton-a-day plant. In 1890 the North-Eastern and in 1891 the Bonaccord Ice Companies came into being. Ship chandlers and similar supply stores sprang up on the quay. The otter trawl was introduced to Aberdeen soon after its invention in 1894, completely superseding the beam trawl, which was cumbrous and liable to easy damage, and revolutionised the whole industry by greatly increasing the catching power of the trawlers equipped with it. Whereas in 1882 the value of the fish landed was only about £10,000, by 1888 that figure had risen ten-fold as the price of a total catch of over 181,000 hundredweights, and by 1893 the aggregate haul of 414,251 hundredweights fetched £263,957.

The great expansion in the catch necessitated drastic measures with the Fish Market. To begin with, trawlers discharged at a wooden jetty at Point Law, where the fish were exposed in mud or dust according to the weather. The fish market, which stood at the foot of Market Street, which thus got its name, was moved across to the site of the L.M.S. goods station when about 1868 the Post Office acquired the Market Street site. But the new market had no roof, and dust and mud, as at Point Law, were the twin familiar conditions of the floor.

Accordingly the present market was built at the Albert Quay in 1889, after visits to great markets in London and the south by a deputation consisting of Daniel Mearns and James Walker, another Lord Provost to be, John Morgan a builder, and the inevitable William Pyper. They have been described as 'the most frugal four that ever went from good old Bon-Accord at the call of civic duty'. The improvement paid from its inception. In 1882–3 the dues of the Fish Market were £131 10s., in 1888–9 they were £297 7s. 11d.; in 1889–90, the first year of the modern market, they were £1,313 15s. 5d. At the end of the century there were nearly 200 trawlers employing 1,800 men with 4,300 curing-yard hands and 500 engaged in the ice, rope and net business, and a wage bill of about £1 million sterling. Not the least striking evidence of the bonanza was that between 1882 and 1902 the three shipyards of Alexander Hall & Co., John Duthie Sons & Co., and Hall Russell built no fewer than 267 trawlers, and in the latter year were employing 2,000 workers. The average cost was £4,500. Nor was the industry even then at its peak.

Landings and earnings steadily rose during the early years of the present century, but before glancing at that halcyon age a word must be said of a serious crisis which broke upon the fishing industry in the eighties, mainly upon the herring curing branch of that industry which in consequence only in part affected Aberdeen, although it had by that time become a substantial herring port. The cause of this sudden break-through in a sector which had hitherto resisted Aberdeen's effort to exploit it was that in the sixties the herring fishing in the Moray Firth waters fell away, and a number of substantial curers from the coastal communities of Banffshire and Morayshire transferred their stations to Aberdeen, whither naturally the fishermen from these places followed them. The cured herrings from Aberdeen found a market in the burgh's old traditional trading opposites, the seaports of the Hanseatic league from Hamburg to Danzig. The cure from other Scottish east coast herring ports, like Lerwick, Wick, Fraserburgh and Peterhead (of which today only Lerwick and Fraserburgh have been able to maintain a fishing of any size) went to Germany and Russia, both of them to prove financially, and the latter socially, vulnerable after the Kaiser's War. In 1885 the herring fishing brought in two-thirds of the value of Scottish fishing, and no fewer than 50,000 fishermen owning boats with gear valued at £1,750,000 made a living out of it. Of the 1884 catch one-half was landed within fifty miles of Aberdeen, and 750,000 barrels was the combined cure of Aberdeen and Aberdeenshire, eleven-twelfths for the foreign destinations indicated. But three years of bumper catches, a certain over-supplying of the cured market, and hopes too rosy for the continuance of these good times which encouraged curers to offer drifter crews too generous a bargain in advance not only of the catch, but also of the overseas sale, led to a tremendous smash the extent of which may be gauged by the fact that the North Bank, which was almost alone in financing these widespread operations, lost in a couple of years no less than £233,000. Actually it was the Bank's loyalty, and good sense, in meeting the deficiencies and, within the bounds of prudence, supporting the industry that rounded off the edge of the crisis so that by the summer of 1889 the herring fishing was, if the figure may be permitted, on its feet again, although it took its good fairy, the Bank, about fifteen years to get its balance sheet back to the figures of 1885. To be over and done with the herring fishing from Aberdeen, it may be mentioned that the port became the largest herring trawling port in the United Kingdom, its catch which was 190,800 hundredweights in 1938, being still 152,100 hundredweights in 1950, with herring stocks being depleted and foreign fishing competition increasing all the time. The use of the trawl as opposed to the drift net for fishing, and of dye and any kind of chips instead of oak chips for kippering have not improved the quality of the food the herring presents, but then mostly all foods, what between so-called scientific methods, and popular fancy, have tended to decline in the scale of epicurean desirability.

Until the Kaiser's war the white fish industry enjoyed a progression of almost unalloyed prosperity. In 1907 1,785,000 hundredweights valued at £882,000 were landed by 258 steam and motor vessels with crews of 3,000 men, giving shore employment to 6,000 persons, and the boats and gear estimated at £1,250,000. By 1913 the figures were up to 2,677,330 hundredweights in quantity and £1,469,580 in value, of which 521,430 hundredweights worth £174,180 were landed by foreign trawlers. These were even before the First World War posing serious problems, as they were fishing waters and landing qualities of fish that the Aberdeen fleet regarded as beneath their standard, and the distinction is reflected in the lower value of the foreign catch. Before Hitler's war the Aberdeen fish salesmen took drastic measures discriminating against foreign landings which reduced them from 885,033 hundredweights, one-half of the port's catch, and worth £366,220 to 107,473 hundredweights valued at £100,419 in 1938. By the latter date the total landings were 1,668,541 hundredweights worth £1,673,000, of which three-quarters had been caught by steam trawlers operating the otter trawl, which had been long in use but improved in design and function. In that year there were 253 trawlers fishing out of Aberdeen. By 1950, when landings were at 1,744,005 hundredweights after a rise to 2,213,356 hundredweights the year after the war, there were only 159 trawlers, besides thirty-four steam and six diesel great line boats landing about 240,000 hundredweights of the total. At the outbreak of the Hitler war it was calculated that 40,000 men, women and children were dependent upon the fishing industry in Aberdeen.

During the twenties Aberdeen lost its pride of place amongst Britain's fishing ports, first to Hull and then to Grimsby. It remains third on the list. After the first war, for a year or two Aberdeen shipyards were busy on the repair and reconditioning of trawlers, then from 1920 until the eve of the second war only one new trawler left the stocks at Aberdeen. That fact helps to explain how the mechanics of the industry changed. By 1950 out of 196 operational Aberdeen trawlers, 173 were over twenty-five years old, 11 over twenty, and only 8 under ten years of age. Whereas the Hull landings went up between the wars by several hundred per cent, Aberdeen's actually dropped by one-fifth. Some of the disparity was believed to have been due to the fact that in Hull more than half of the firms owning the boats had over nineteen vessels, and only 11 per cent had less than five, whereas the corresponding figures for Aberdeen were 9 per cent and 41 per cent. Since the last war this distribution at Aberdeen has been drastically altered, and the total numbers have been no less drastically reduced. Twenty years, even ten years ago, a man overlooking Aberdeen bay on a Monday forenoon expected to see a considerable fleet of trawlers issuing from the harbour mouth and fanning out across the sea to north and north-east. Now it will be only by chance that he sees one and these 'single spies' leave and return at any time of the week. The old insistence at Aberdeen Fish Market on quality fish and the trawlers' preference for the 'continental shelf' in the nearer waters like the Orkneys and Shetlands, the Faroes, Iceland, and perhaps Bear Island off the north coast of Norway, where those superior classes of fish were expected to be found, are now less pronounced, and the fleet are going more frequently and more automatically to distant waters like the Grand Banks of Newfoundland and the Greenland seas, whither a different type of vessel had sailed at the beginning of the nineteenth century when for a short spell Aberdeen was a whaling port.

The trawling business has given rise to a variety of industries and occupations, some of which in the comparatively short period during which their style of fishing has been in existence have disappeared or changed, in cases almost beyond recognition. The fish, having been caught, must of course be sold, and having been sold they must be consumed either at once or at some not too remote date. The selling involves salesmen, in association or singly, and the buying implies merchants who may as wholesalers pass on the fish to retailers or to processers, some of whom are themselves part of the many merchanting concerns. The processers fillet and cure either lightly or less temporarily. Curing implies drying or salting, or kippering, or smoking or canning, or freezing, or part cooking with some accompanying products like tomatoes. There is in fact a remarkable choice of flavours and consistencies for those who prefer their fish to be in some way or other preserved. There are finnan haddocks, smokies, speldings, the great dried cod that used to be cut up by frugal housewives and then teased out to form one of the two important constituents in the dish that was known in older and more economical but still good-living days as 'hairy tatties', and, of course, the herrings provide kippers and pickled herring.

A great deal of honest work and ingenuity — which are not perhaps associated so often as they might be — `has gone into the process of making the denizens of the deep, as they have been called, attractive to human palates. This is well understood in the fish trade. Unfortunately, it is not at all understood by the politicians and the civil service. In 1949 under an impulse which has never been quite credibly explained in its official context, Whitehall, in the shape of the Ministry of Agriculture, Fisheries and Food, established an experimental factory in Aberdeen's suburb of Torry, convenient for the supply of fish, meat and vegetables. The staff of this factory working on the lines of the dehydration of food in very short time developed what was known as accelerated freeze drying, applying to the preservation of foodstuffs techniques that had before then been reserved for pharmaceutical and biological substances. The Government promptly closed it down. Fortunately a small factory in Aberdeen had been working in touch with the experimental establishment, so that, while the chief fruits of the Aberdeen discoveries went to overseas manufacturers, and in particular to a place in Cork, Aberdeen's break-through was not altogether divorced from Aberdeen.

The experiments at this establishment are not to be confused with the steady haul of work put through since 1929 at the Torry Research

Station on the general subject of the preservation of fish. Working as a section of the Department of Scientific and Industrial Research, and with a branch laboratory opened at Hull in 1952, the Torry Research Station has hunted out and certified a long list of facts concerning the chemical changes that take place in fish after capture. This has led to a wide range of discoveries and suggestions for the quick-freezing and cold storage of fish both afloat and ashore, and since what has been frozen must be brought back to practicable temperature before consumption, for thawing also. The findings at Torry have been in great measure responsible for the building of the large factory trawlers that are rapidly becoming a dominant feature of the industry. The problems of kiln smoking have also been under consideration and the Torry mechanical kiln is the result. Yet another research station, the Marine Laboratory of the Scottish Department of Agriculture and Fisheries, has been located at Aberdeen since 1899. Costing half a million a year, compared with some £770 little more than half a century ago, its function is to study everything that can possibly be ascertained about fish life — habits, locations, environment, migrations, mortality, birth-rate, diseases, enemies and the effect of fishing itself, to mention a few aspects of a many-faceted subject. A fleet of research vessels feeds the laboratory at Torry with facts; on board experiments are made with, among other things, different brands of catching gear and advice is given on different meshes for nets and similar technical matters, while the laboratory has frogmen and underwater cameras and a varied array of both staff — 160 strong, 100 of them scientific workers — and equipment for the observation of fish, which term includes shellfish and plankton and the strange and sometimes minute fauna that lurk in the rocks and the deep. The Marine Laboratory which was housed in modern premises in 1955, naturally acts on an international level as well as assisting the White Fish Authority and the Herring Industry Board, the two British bodies that strive with a rather greater amount of success than they get credit for, to keep the fisheries viable.

The occasional gluts of fish and the inevitable percentage of almost every daily catch that is below commercial size have to be used in preference to being thrown back into Aberdeen Bay, although that drastic solution has not been unknown. From white fish unwanted for food, fish meal is manufactured as a valuable animal food stuff; from unwanted herrings in an up-to-date fish-meal factory opened in 1928 at Point Law, fish manure is made. There is a variety of other by-products, including the halibut liver oil which is used by the medical profession and which has been on the list of Aberdeen products since 1932. Cod liver oil is also made, and fish glue and lacquer. These industries are at the issuing end of the trawling complex. At what may be termed the entrance are the ship chandlers, net makers, ice-manufacturers, and the purveyors of all kinds of ship supplies and fishermen's equipment. Box-making, partly for the end product and partly for the fishermen, is rather less extensive than it was, other containers and methods of packaging having come to compete with it. Most recently prominent among these new methods are the polystyrene boxes for fish and other foods, produced from a factory established at Tullos in 1965.

CHAPTER SIX

Ups and Downs in Business

The Victorian era so far as Aberdeen industry was concerned opened not inauspiciously. Once the hungry forties were out of the way, the Repeal of the Corn Laws made living easier for the employed classes and in various ways directly promoted the prosperity of most kinds of business. At mid-century, however, there was a financial crisis which arose partly out of unduly optimistic ideas of what money could be made to do, and which, as already related, resulted in disaster to one venerable Aberdeen bank and one great Aberdeen industry and in near-disaster to another of the city's banks and an industry related to that which was irremediably stricken. Later on in the century the collapse of the City of Glasgow Bank, which had considerable repercussions both in business and to individuals in the city, and in the eighties the recurrent malady of undue financial optimism which scattered bankruptcy and dismay throughout the herring curing industry and obliquely inhibited for a time the development of other and quite different industries curbed the advance of the city industrially and commercially.

Aberdeen enjoyed a quiet and sound prosperity as a whole from 1850 to the turn of the century, and in some respects rose to its grandest heights in manufacturing activity. To an extent that is not perhaps generally recognised, this healthy expansion was due to the rise of agriculture as an urban industry. It was the opening of the railway to the south in 1851 that imparted the first impetus to this new departure. A cattle market was started first of all near the railway terminus, and later, when the Great North was running through to Waterloo from Kittybrewster, in King Street which was the forerunner of a complex which in Aberdeen and its hinterland is today responsible for an over-turn of about £500,000 a week. In the city there are annually sold some 40,000 fat cattle, 60,000 fat sheep, 100,000 store cattle, 150,000 store sheep, 50,000 pigs and a quarter of a million poultry. Between 1877 and 1882 four auction marts were opened in the city, with a large number of branches in the surrounding country. In the Combworks' old premises in Berryden Road the Aberdeen and Northern Marts Ltd., which is a co-operative and embodies the four original agricultural marketing units, handled many millions of eggs under the Egg Marketing Board as well as the livestock already mentioned.

The amount of business, not merely agricultural but of a general retail character and so assisting wholesale food marketing is very substantial, as a long outbreak of foot-and-mouth disease, which restricted the normal influx of country people into town in the autumn of 1960, emphatically disclosed. The involvement of the industry within the town is not confined to livestock. The Aberdeen Commercial Company, the Aberdeen Lime Company, founded to bring lime from the Howe of Cromar and distribute it through the area, and the Northern Agricultural Company, the North Eastern Agricultural Co-operative Society, Seggie & Company, James Wilson & Son, Gavin and Gill, after the First Great War Scottish Agricultural Industries, and various other public and private concerns conducted a thriving trade from their respective Aberdeen headquarters (the N.E. Agricultural Co-operative Society occupied the Bannermill when the former textile firm departed in 1904) in fertilisers, feeding stuffs, grain, potatoes, and farm seeds. The 'sheds' which the three first-named of these built at railway stations to facilitate distribution of their stock in trade were until the 1930s a familiar feature of the rural scene. Barclay, Ross & Tough (later Hutchison), George Sellar & Son, not now in Aberdeen, the now defunct Allan & Son, Charles Taggart & Company (now taken over by Barclay, Ross) and R. G. Garvie & Sons, all manufacture agricultural machinery. Nurserymen such as William Smith and Son, Benjamin Reid and Son, Reid and Leys, George Bruce and Company, Springhill Nurseries, Anderson's Rose Nurseries and James Cocker and Sons deal in shrub-species, roses and seeds, trees and implements for garden and farm.

A massive feature in this *rus in urbe* landscape is the manufacture of fertilisers. This branch of chemical production seems to have been started as a sideline with the engineering firm of Barry, Henry and Cook. But it was the Rev. James Robertson, erstwhile headmaster of Robert Gordon's College and parish minister of Ellon, who about 1840 tested the theories of the German scientist Baron von Liebig on what were then known as 'dissolved bones', applying the equivalent of superphosphates to crops on a field scale. Robertson, who was eventually Moderator of the General Assembly of the Church of Scotland and the leader in the regeneration of the church after the Disruption, had as colleague in his fertiliser trials the schoolmaster of Tillydesk, near Ellon, William Hay, who as a collector of folk-song made a name for himself in another field. From Robertson's inspiration there came the Sandilands factory of the Miller family and the Dyce factory of John Milne, as well as the fertiliser works of Nalco at Waterloo Quay and of the North-Eastern Agricultural Co-operative at Bannermill.

At the opening of the present century, granite continued its boom in export of monuments and the building of houses, but the textile trades were hard hit, and the closing down of Hadden's Mills (whose site in the Green was bought over by the Great North of Scotland Railway) and of the Bannermill, both in 1904, not only meant the loss of two great factories but put an end to the association with Aberdeen of two names — Hadden and Bannerman[1] — that had bulked prominently and long in the life of the burgh. The white fishing experienced an unwonted depression, and some trawlers had to be laid up. A reduction in 1904 of £65,000 in the deposits of the North of Scotland Bank reflected the prevailing uncertainty, but perhaps a secondary cause lay in the decision of the Scottish banks — but, be it noted, against the wishes of the two Aberdeen Banks — to discontinue paying interest on current accounts. In 1908 the North of Scotland and Town and County Banks amalgamated.

This depression, however, proved to be only temporary. The building trade revealed a decrease of output, it is true, in 1908 — 268 houses costing £184,850 compared with 747 and £514,013 in 1898. But in the monumental yards pneumatic tools — particularly surfacing machines and hammers — brought increased output and decreased costs of production, and 65,000 tons of causeway and building stones and dressed granite were exported in 1906 from Aberdeen. This was slightly lower than in 1901 but far better than any years in the previous century. Granite from Aberdeen was even sent to help build Chinese pagodas and Japanese temples. Paper and book-making were no less prosperous, and when the First World War broke out, Aberdeen was in a thoroughly sound way of business industrially. During the war the city's various factories were feverishly busy on unaccustomed projects, granite alone being hit in a fashion that could not be recouped from belligerent production, but so many men were away that the orders trickling in kept the trade going.

Between the wars, Aberdeen, like most other considerable centres of population, was extensively affected by the policy of combining business concerns which was stimulated by difficult economic conditions and

1 Actually the Bannerman name vanished in 1857 when Robinson, Crum & Co. took over the mill. See p. 310.

encouraged by fashionable economic theory. To begin with, the idea of amalgamation was not favourably received. A proposal to merge certain Aberdeen, Dundee and London shipping interests (which in the last few years has been accomplished as regards Aberdeen and London) evoked a protest from the Chamber of Commerce, and fell through when turned down by the Aberdeen company. In 1928 the North of Scotland Bank was affiliated with the Midland Bank, and in 1949 with the Clydesdale Bank, still later losing its name. It had signalised its centenary with a history and a sumptuous dinner in the Music Hall presided over by the chairman of the Midland Bank, Reginald M'Kenna. In 1924 the Grandholm Wool Mills were bought by Salts (Saltaire).[1] In 1927 the Donside Paper Mills amalgamated with the Inveresk group. In 1922 the Great North of Scotland Railway and the North British Railway became part of the newly formed London and North-Eastern Railway. In that year Pirie & Sons amalgamated with Wiggins Teape, and the *Aberdeen Daily Journal* and the *Aberdeen Free Press* amalgamated as the *Aberdeen Press and Journal*, the *Evening Express* absorbing the *Evening Gazette* and the *Weekly Journal* remaining the weekly issue of the united paper. In 1928 the amalgamated concern was taken over by Allied Newspapers, and a few years later became a unit in the chain of Kemsley Newspapers. During the same period Scottish Agricultural Industries (a branch of Imperial Chemical Industries) fused four Aberdeen firms, the Aberdeen Commercial Company, John Miller & Co., Sandilands, John Milne & Company's Dyce Chemical Works (recently closed), and Barclay, Ross & Hutchison, which, once again independent, has taken over Charles Taggart & Company. In the early thirties two other Aberdeen agricultural supply companies, the Aberdeen Lime Company and the North Agricultural Company amalgamated as Nalco. After the Second World War the Angus Milling Company absorbed several agricultural businesses. J. and W. Henderson were another firm to link up with national interests: they entered the Cement combine, but later reverted to an independent existence. Ogston and Tennant's soap works were taken over by Unilever. The four cattle auction mart companies in the city have been reduced to one, trading as a co-operative, the Aberdeen and Northern Marts. Hall Russells during the second war was merged in the Burntisland Shipbuilding Co., which in turn was acquired by London interests in 1951, but survived when the Burntisland firm collapsed.

The same coalescing tendency was evident amongst the big retail

1   Several of these mergers are noted elsewhere.

businesses in the city. Many well-known and long-established firms disappeared altogether — such as Pratt & Keith, Sangster and Henderson, Peter Beveridge, R. K. Smith, Hay and Lyall, Saint the draper, Anderson and Thomson, Philip and Cooper, Porter and Leighton, Raffans and Lorimer, bootmakers; Steele the hatter, John Spalding, Hampton the picture-dealers, Stephen the picture framers; Johnston & Laird, the Crolls, and Garden and Raeburn, Lockhart and Salmond (all bakers); Brown & Co., A. & R. Milne, Murray, all booksellers. Some of them were absorbed in other businesses that still remain. Others, still in existence under the old name, have become part of larger concerns with a national basis. Multiple firms appeared in the principal streets, after Woolworths opened on 17 October 1919. During the Second World War, the Scottish Co-operative Wholesale Society began to buy up all and sundry businesses, including a meal-mill, an undertaker's, a couple of taxi-hirers and a laundry.

Aesthetically, the most splended achievement of Aberdeen's manufacturing industry was the clipper sailing-ships, whose period falls athwart this section of the town's history and its predecessor, and is accordingly dealt with in the latter. But such expert shipbuilding could not be expected to cease with a type or a fashion, and the shipyard industry went ahead after the clipper era in more pedestrian but not less significant progress. Coincident with the launching of the last of the clippers in 1869 Alexander Hall sent down the slips Japan's first warship built for herself. The *Jhoshu Maru* was an armour-plated corvette with a powerful ram and equipped with pivot guns called bow and stern chasers on her fighting deck and carriages for muzzle-loading cannon. Although essentially a sailing vessel, carrying a vast spread of canvas on tall masts, she was equipped amidships with an auxiliary steam engine and she was actuated by a propeller. This (to modern ideas) remarkable vessel was ordered by the Japanese Government, it is said on the recommendation of Thomas Blake Glover, a civil engineer resident in Nagasaki, who is credited along with another Aberdonian named Annand, with having introduced railways to Japan. His father, Thomas Berry Glover, had been Superintendent of Coastguards at Bridge of Don when his son was born in 1838. The younger Glover, with a brother, appears to have established a large trawling business in Nagasaki, and he is reputed to have been the original of Pinkerton in Puccini's opera 'Madam Butterfly', although his own domestic life hardly supports the suggestion. He had gained the ear of the authorities in Japan and no doubt the common knowledge of the excellence of the Aberdeen clippers reinforced his arguments and brought the *Jhoshu Maru* and a later consort upon Alexander Hall and Company's order-book.

The eagerness with which steam trawling was adopted at Aberdeen naturally created a tremendous demand for fishing-boats in that category. In the twenty years to 1902 the three yards of Duthie, Hall and Hall Russell had built 287 trawlers at an average cost of £4,500. They were doing a certain amount of miscellaneous work also. But as the century drew to its close the smaller yards began to shut down. Walter Hood and Co., for instance, went in 1881. At the beginning of the new century, the Duthie yard was opened at Torry in 1904, but it did not long survive, and in 1916 John Lewis & Sons took up the running but not the yard. By that date only Alexander Hall & Co. and Hall, Russell and Co. remained of the half-dozen that had been busy forty years before. Aberdeen's first motor boat had been launched in 1907, and the then largest ship to leave Aberdeen stocks was the *Intaba* of 4,720 tons. During the Kaiser's war the yards specialised each in its own type of vessel for national service, and rather outwith the conventional scheme of things, a start was made towards the end of the war in the building of concrete ships.[1]

Once the war was over, Hall and Company began to build dredgers and tugs, turning out between 1923 and 1935 no fewer than thirty-three dredgers and thirty tugs. Hall, Russell built Aberdeen's own merchant ships — the *Thrift, Spray, Redhall, Ferryhill, St. Magnus* and *St. Sunniva,* some of them lost in Hitler's war, and amongst the firm's productions for foreign owners was a steel sailing yacht for France, the first constructed in Britain under the ocean racing rules. Up to 1935 Messrs. Lewis launched forty-six cargo boats, including several for Australia and the Far East. During the Second World War the three yards produced fourteen vessels — frigates and corvettes, mine-sweepers and tank-landing craft, besides a constant stream of repairs. Since 1945 the size of the ships built has been steadily increasing. The *Intaba* would bulk small indeed beside the 8,000-ton cargo freighters that Hall Russell turns out.[2] Lewis's with less ample accommodation

---

1   It was said that after the war a prominent Aberdeen business man who had been mainly responsible for the concrete ship innovation received an Admiralty cheque for £46,000 in respect of his output, followed a week or two later by a duplicate cheque which he returned. It was, however, passed back to him and — so the story went — he handed it over to charity.

2   In 1969 it was announced the firm had won an order for a ship of over 10,000 tons.

make the most of their skills and have been pioneers in the adoption of several important inventions, not only as applied to Admiralty craft during the war, but in the modern techniques of long-distance fishing since. Both Aberdeen yards — for Hall Russells having bought the whole share capital of Alexander Hall in 1953, later absorbed it altogether — do not, of course, stick the one to cargo boats and the other to trawlers, but enter each other's fields and other fields besides. At the half-century mark shipbuilding employed some 3,000 and marine engineering 1,000 hands.

This record of triumph over constant adverse factors would have been more brilliant had the great Aberdeen shipping lines of the nineteenth century been able to resist the pressure of economics and take-over bids; but that as we have seen was not to be.

Engineering, always in the modern era a favourite occupation in Aberdeen, is pursued by over thirty firms great and small. A few have dropped out in the last half century or so — great names like Blaikie, Abernethy and Harper have vanished from the roll, although in some cases their business continues under other names. The biggest firm of all, J. M. Henderson & Co., has withstood the blasts of competition and enemy action, and several of its achievements, such as the great lifts at Kowloon and Hongkong and its contributions to the successful construction of dams and barrages in Portugal and Egypt and of varied enterprises from Shanghai to South Africa and from Australia to Jamaica have something of the romantic quality about them.[1] Their senior but smaller neighbours, Barry, Henry and Cook, have acquired a high reputation with a wide range of machinery, and that other veteran William McKinnon and Co., the oldest of them all, have for many decades specialised in plantation machinery, for the milling and grinding of sugar, coffee, rice and cocoa, and this trade, mainly with the Far East but also with East Africa, accounts for some 90 per cent of the firm's production, a proportion of exports which few concerns in the United Kingdom or elsewhere can equal. Firms such as C. F. Wilson, and George Cassie and Co., who took over Harper's shop in Wellington Road, as well as a branch of the Consolidated Pneumatic Tool Company from Fraserburgh keep Aberdeen's variegated machine production going at a satisfactory rate. This branch of industry employs about 5,000 people.

Largest (after the fishing industry) in the numbers of its employees

1   Taken over by the English firm, Mitchell Construction Co., they survived its fall.

is the paper trade, carried on in five establishments within Aberdeen's bounds or the immediate perimeter and in one mill fifteen miles out. With the exception of the last one, which is locally owned, all these are part of southern combines, but enjoy a varying amount of local control. Between 1910 and 1939 the mills doubled their aggregate annual output. They produced together some 60,000 tons of paper valued at £2 million, consuming in the process 80,000 tons of raw material and 85,000 tons of coal, thus creating a traffic amounting to 225,000 tons annually, part of which represented a salient portion of Aberdeen's seaborne trade. The numbers employed are in the region of 5,000. The largest mill, that at Stoneywood, was owned by Alexander Pirie and Son until 1922 when it became part of the Wiggins Teape combine. It has built a school and employed a staff to teach the children of its workpeople. The works today are an impressive sight, conveying a sense of spaciousness as well as efficient industry, surrounding by smiling housing schemes and ample playing fields, and with a well-stocked river running past from which the visitor may have the good fortune to see an angler take a salmon or one of the brown trout for which the Don is world famous.

The oldest mill, whose name has cropped up several times in this narrative, at Peterculter, although only about half the size of Stoney-wood, long enjoyed a period of prosperity which for length and height could well be the envy of any of its competitors. During most of the present century, under the inspired management of the Geddes family, of whom William Geddes and his son J. Fraser Geddes have been outstanding, it maintained its place as a producer of very high-class utility papers as well as other lines, amongst which cigarette cartons have not been decried, and steadily expanded its business at home and abroad. Like Stoneywood, the Culter Mills Paper Company has been attentive to the social welfare of its workpeople, and indeed throughout the whole of Aberdeen's paper industry the labour relations are excellent. Latterly it amalgamated with a third Scottish concern.

Next door to Stoneywood is the Mugiemoss mill of Charles Davidson and Son, which concentrates mainly on paper-board, Kraft paper, and wrapping paper, and which conducts a wide-reaching collection of waste paper for the purposes of its production. A mile down the Don at Gordon's Mills, the Donside Paper Mill functions in what, for some time before 1890, was the meal and flour mill of John Forbes White. In 1893, when it came into the possession of John Laing and Co., it received the name by which it is now known, in 1927 it became part of the Inveresk Paper Company, and it has more recently changed hands again. It was reputed to be the largest producer of newsprint in the kingdom but about 1960 it turned over to the production of coated fine papers, millions of pounds having been spent upon the transition. The fifth mill, a part-subsidiary of Stoneywood, is Pirie, Appleton and Co., whose Union works west of the Joint Station produce a very large proportion of the envelopes used in this country.[1] Amongst them, Aberdeen's paper mills in the last few years have spent something like £12 million on modernisation of plant.

In the second half of the nineteenth century there was nothing very much in Aberdeen's textile trade to report apart from the already mentioned immigration of the Crombie woollen firm to Woodside in 1859 to take over the great Grandholm mill of Leys, Masson & Co. Aberdeen's three branches of the textile industry, wool, linen and jute became so exceptionally busy that some firms had to engage outside mills to cope with their orders. But when the Kaiser's war was over and the slump began in 1920, almost without exception all the textile firms suffered. Government interference in the form of controls and a long succession of labour troubles arising out of the national reaction of the trade unions to falling wages, curtailed and in some cases crippled production. The activities of trade boards were harmful: Aberdeen Jute Works permanently closed down from this cause, after a temporary stoppage in 1921 that threw 400 workers idle. The bespoke tailoring trade was grievously damaged by the rise of great mass-production firms, and the boot and shoe-making industry disappeared from Aberdeen.

Crombie's of Grandholm has become a name 'to conjure with' the world over. James Crombie was head of the firm in 1859 and the production of the mill at once greatly expanded. After his death in 1878 and until 1893 members of the Crombie family kept the direction in their hands, but in the latter year Alexander Ross, who had started in the mill as a junior, became managing director. He died in 1923, and his son John A. Ross and a grandson of James Crombie, J. E. Crombie, sold the whole of the shares to Salts of Saltaire while themselves remaining in charge. During their lives they were noted philanthropists, especially to the University of Aberdeen, of whose Court they were in turn members. John A. Ross played the most active part in the firm almost to the end of his very long life and it was to his father and himself, with the loyal assistance of the able men they gathered round them, that the firm's pre-eminence is due. Their success was not

1   This firm has now migrated to Dyce.

merely in trading, but in the social welfare of the community of Wood-side, which depended and depends, as in the days before the Crombies came, upon the prosperity and goodwill of Grandholm.

The site of Kilgour & Walker, whose woollen mill was burnt out in the April 1943 air raid, is now occupied by Glen Gordon, Ltd., producing knitwear. Harrott & Co. was founded at the beginning of the century by a manager of Hadden's Mills. It also produces woollen wear. Richards Ltd. of Broadford, the largest firm in the city, has already figured prominently in our story. Its more modern experiences since the days of Mr. Maberly have been almost as exciting as those when it was under his direction. The manufacture of linen has long been practised in the burgh, but never with more success or with more invention. Nearly half of the output of canvas fabrics of many kinds from artists' canvas to fire hoses goes for export, and at the Garthdee bleachfield the firm dyes and proofs cloth woven at Broadford itself. Garthdee is the centre for synthetic fibre production, one of the great expansionist developments promoted by the firm in recent years. The massive red rectangular building at Broadford was erected in 1911, and in 1914–18 no fewer than 3,000 hands were employed. About the period of the great de-pression the firm fell on evil days and only the energetic intervention of a small group of local business men saved what appeared to be a hopeless situation.[1] Since then, in war and peace, the firm has gone ahead in an abounding prosperity.

Granite, popularly regarded, quite erroneously, as Aberdeen's principal industry, has suffered a sea-change since 1900. Up to that date its fortunes were followed in a previous chapter. The 'great divide' between ancient and modern came in 1895 with the introduction of pneumatic tools. Neither of the wars did the industry any good, and after the Second World War the spiralling of wages and prices led on the one hand to the appearance of new methods of construction and on the other discouraged the longer processes of working granite both for building and ornament. The trade, however, set itself to solve the problems that confronted it. Many, indeed most of the quarries either closed down or resorted to the crushing of stone into aggregate — granite aggregate being a first-class cement base — or dust, while those that remained, in conjunction with the processors of building stone,

1   Shares in the company were actually offered (and taken) at 1d. each. The equivalent value today is 35s. It was even rumoured that one prominent Aberdeen business man with a large holding was so convinced of the im-pending ruin (the shares were then partly paid) that he offered his shares not merely free but with a gratuity of 9d. each.

adopted the practice of slicing the granite blocks into cladding to act as a facing material to bricks and concrete. Since the last war substantial orders have been won for this kind of granite slabs, for buildings in London, Manchester, Edinburgh and elsewhere — but not with any great enthusiasm from Aberdeen.[1] One of the London contracts negotiated in the later fifties was believed to be the largest ever to be won by Aberdeen. Granite rolls for paper-making and other purposes keep one establishment going. On the monumental side the increasing popularity of cremation naturally limited the demand for funerary stone, and for other ornamental purposes coloured stone such as Aberdeen quarries could not provide led to large imports of granite from Scandinavia, Argyll and Cornwall. The monumental masons, however, tenaciously clung to their public by producing a great variety of exceptionally attractive coloured granite articles, among which coffee and occasional tables figured prominently.

The Combworks, deprived of the traditional horn by the fashionable polling of cattle, fortunately found the recently discovered plastics as a substitute after the Second World War. Their products at the same time became more diversified, including tableware and similar lines as well as their accustomed stock-in-trade. They also in the fifties were taken over and energised by a Glasgow firm. Box-making by 1939 had developed into a huge business employing about 2,000 people and producing 5 million boxes annually. Paint has been made in Aberdeen for well over a century. Farquhar and Gill (founded 1818) invented mixed paint in 1864 and produced many kinds of paints, varnishes and enamels until absorbed by Isaac Spencer & Co., a younger firm, which had built up a reputation for synthetic paints and enamels and compositions for painting.

Ships' hulls, fishing tackle, photographic appliances, sweets, aerated waters, bedding furniture, and many other so-called light industries have their exponents in the city. Roses are a product of the burgh that flourish in more senses than one. Half-a-dozen nurseries, some of them of national and even international celebrity, grow hundreds of thousands of bushes between them which can be depended upon to sustain the worst encroachments of cold or stormy weather. Forest trees, shrubs, herbaceous and alpine perennials all enjoy a brisk demand, and beautiful rotational vegetable growing may be seen in the several large market

1   The ultimate abomination befell when, for such 'pedigree' stone as was required for the new Aberdeen Town House administrative building, marble got the preference over granite.

gardens within and adjoining the town's boundaries. Since the Second
World War a number of interesting new industries have either been
started or found their feet after a beginning before the war. Precast
concrete, glass fibre, and plastics are used in the manufacture of an
astonishing variety of articles.

Printing has since the days of Edward Raban been a much respected occupation in the city. The standard of work done has
always been high, and in contemporary circumstances this means
steady employment despite the fairly active competition from all parts
of the kingdom. Singling out firms for special mention is never other
than an invidious measure, but is unusually so in connection with an
art-trade or skilled craft like printing. The larger firms may, however,
be recorded without prejudice to their smaller and less well-equipped
but not on that account less competent brethren. The Aberdeen University Press, its oldest component founded in 1840, its name given to it
by its very vigorous second proprietor John Thomson (1840–1911),
a public company since 1900, merged with Theodore Watt's Rosemount
Press (formerly the job-printing associate of the *Aberdeen Free Press*)
in 1932. Now embodying John Avery & Co. printers, and the book-
binding works of William Jackson, it is the largest establishment of its
kind, enjoying a widely-spread connection in the south with publishers,
libraries and learned societies. The Central Press also specialises in
book printing. Middletons, rehoused at Abbotswell after a disastrous
fire at their Rose Street premises, has a country-wide calendar market.
The Waverley Press in Crooked Lane has developed 'reprographics'.
The Langstane Press, Alex P. Reid & Son (successors to W. W.
Lindsay in Market Street) and Taylor & Henderson in the Adelphi are
in general business. Henry Munro, printers of the now defunct *Bon-
Accord* newspaper, continue in Union Row as a branch of George
Outram of Glasgow. Charles Siddon's bag-making facilities serve shopkeepers throughout the north of Scotland. G. Cornwall & Sons, the
oldest of all the city's printing firms, have a strong lithographic side,
serving markets far removed from Aberdeen.

One industry which has developed out of all recognition in the present century is contracting in every form of constructional work. In
this respect Aberdeen is, if not absolutely in the lead, right in the
forefront of Scottish enterprise. William Tawse, Ltd. founded in 1896
by the manager of the Kemnay quarry of John Fyfe and Son, has grown
into a far-flung concern whose activities cover the whole of the northern
half of Scotland in an expansion which most appropriately reflects the

commercial genius and vision of its second head, William Tawse, whose too early death in 1940 deprived modern Aberdeen of one of its greatest characters. Admiralty and other Government work during both wars, many hundreds of miles of roads, dams and reservoirs for the North of Scotland Hydro-Electric Board, bathing and swimming pools, bridges, barracks, a great multiplicity of structures culminated, as some think, in the magnificent two-mile long breastwork or glacis from the Dee to Don that protects Aberdeen beach and esplanade from the encroachment of the sea and the no less perilous wear-and-tear of many human feet. Wm. Tawse, Ltd. is now one of the key firms in a consortium of over thirty allied concerns handling all kinds of building and civil engineering construction and controlling interests south of the Forth as well as in their native north. Of this consortium another pillar is Alexander Hall and Son. Great housing contracts are supported in this firm's order book by important constructional work of more individual kinds, by delicate rebuilding and renovation, such as that performed at Inverary Castle, St. Leonard's Chapel at St. Andrews, and the venerable Town Hall of Berwick-upon-Tweed. The firm maintains a task force of experts where special speed in construction is required. It incorporates G. W. Bruce, Ltd., concrete specialists, and a number of general contracting firms including W. J. Anderson, who built the George VI Bridge over the Dee and whose founder was a one-time foreman with Tawse. Not least picturesque of the group's assets was the 700-foot deep and 230-year-old Rubislaw Quarry, recently closed.

Behind all those industrial undertakings, financing them, and reflecting the prosperity created in their deposits were the banks. Aberdeen's own bank, the North of Scotland, had in 1919 deposits of £20,811,000, and gave advances of £6,451,000. In 1935, on the eve of its centenary, it recorded £29,159,000 of deposits and gave accommodation, the lowest figure for twelve years, of £7,083,000. During the 1914–18 War it was calculated that Aberdeen had found £15 million of loan money for the Government. In 1926 the balance due to depositors in Aberdeen Savings Bank, which had been founded in 1815, was £5,676,473, but during and since the Second World War that balance has been equalled almost every two years and at the end of 1946 the total funds amounted to some £30 million with 180,000 open accounts in the books. At November 1970 the total funds amounted to £83,270,410, the amount due to depositors being £81,718,153, an increase of nearly three and three-quarter millions in the year. Some 23,000 new accounts were opened in that period, and the bank now consists of fifty-two offices throughout the North-East and North of Scotland, twelve of them in the city. The great prosperity of the Bank was founded by Sir Thomas Jaffrey, and developed by James R. Fiddes (later knighted when he had become actuary of Glasgow Savings Bank); and his successors the late Oliver Horne, who wrote a history of the savings bank movement, the late A. E. Walker and Mr. A. J. Miller.

CHAPTER SEVEN

Railway Mania and Decay

England's first railway was opened between Stockton and Darlington in 1825, Scotland's first, the Monklands Railway, a year later. In 1837 a route was surveyed between Aberdeen and Perth, but it was not until 1844 that, out of three competing projects, one called the Aberdeen Railway emerged, aiming to connect Aberdeen, Stonehaven and Laurencekirk with the already existing Arbroath and Forfar Railway at Friockheim, with branches to Montrose and Brechin. Alexander Anderson and his usual group of fellow-adventurers in Aberdeen business development subscribed the prospectus, the capital was fixed at £830,000, the length of the line at 66 miles, Parliamentary sanction was secured in 1845, and an arrangement made with the Arbroath and Forfar Railway to lease it at $5\frac{1}{4}$ per cent of its capital for five years and then absorb it.

The original intention was to build the terminus at the angle of Guild Street and Market Street, and there was talk of taking over the New Market buildings for the station until the New Market Company put an end to the idea by demanding £50,000 for their place. Eventually the station was fixed at Ferryhill. Piers for the arches of a viaduct between Guild Street and Ferryhill were built, those in the northern half being later taken down, while those in the southern half were arched over, and the bridge over Riverside Road and the Dee, of seven arches of 60-foot span on granite piers was constructed. While the viaduct was being built in 1846 several arches collapsed and seven workmen were killed.

From the autumn of 1847, when trains were running between Friockheim and Dubton, the Aberdeen Railway Company got into low water financially. An offer by the Edinburgh and Northern Company — which later became part of the North British — was turned down, but money was eventually raised in London and in April 1850 Aberdeen heard its first train whistle when the Aberdeen Railway reached Ferryhill, over a million and a half having been spent. Ferryhill was for several years the terminus, while negotiations were going on with the Harbour Commissioners and other bodies, which ended by the terminus being transferred to Guild Street in 1854. In 1850 the Aberdeen Railway amalgamated with the Scottish Midland Railway as the Scottish North-Eastern, and in 1866 it was acquired on a perpetual lease by the Caledonian Railway Company.

The advent of the railways meant a big change for Aberdeen's travellers. At the end of the eighteenth century there had been a great spurt in road-making and better roads encouraged the enterprising to embark on coaching ventures. In 1794 the only coach between Aberdeen and the South was the Aberdeen and Edinburgh Fly, which took thirty-four hours to do the journey to Edinburgh for a fee of 2 guineas. When the roads improved a Royal Mail coach did the same journey in twenty-two hours, at 3 guineas fare. The Royal Mail took six passengers, its rival the Telegraph carried sixteen, but took thirty hours at a £3 fare. In 1808 'The Fly' went on the road to Huntly, doing the journey one day and returning the next. The following year 'The Caravan Coach' started carrying more than the three passengers that were the maximum load of 'The Fly'. It made the return journey within the day. In 1811 'The Union' to Perth began, and other coaches set out daily for Huntly, Ellon, Peterhead and Montrose, with two Royal Mail diligences to Inverness. By 1821 there were eleven, by 1830 there were sixteen four-in-hand coaches operating from Aberdeen. In 1830 Captain Barclay of Ury started 'The Defiance', which with two coachman, four passengers and a guard made Edinburgh in twelve hours. In 1838 there were twenty-four coaches, seven of them carrying mails. Twelve years or so later there was none.

One of the original railway projects linking Aberdeen and the South had for title the Great North of Scotland Railway. This name was given in 1845 to another scheme, connecting Aberdeen with Inverness, and promoted by Alexander Anderson and his friends. The same group at this time or later projected the Deeside railway to Aboyne, the Alford Valley Railway from Kintore to Alford, and the Eastern Extension (or Formartine and Buchan) Railway from Dyce to Peterhead and Fraserburgh. The Great North Act passed through Parliament in 1846, but owing to the drying up of subscriptions after the bursting of the railway speculation in 1848 and to the heavy cost of promoting the necessary legislation, work on the line did not commence until 25 November 1852 — by which date the Morayshire Railway, Elgin to Lossiemouth, had been functioning for three months. In the interval another Act provided for the amalgamation of the Great North with the Aberdeen Railway, but as the former could not raise its stipulated capital within the prescribed time-limit, the fusion never took effect.

The Great North bought up the Aberdeenshire Canal Company, and to keep the canal in operation as long as possible, the Huntly-Inverurie section of the line was first constructed. The lawyers had not completed their job of transferring the canal when the contractor brought the line to Inverurie. He at once cut the canal bank at Dal-weary, near Kintore, thus drying the canal from Port-Elphinstone to Stoneywood, and stranding all the barges. The bank had to be filled up again to let the barges reach home. On 19 September 1854, Huntly and Kittybrewster were linked by a single line of rail, and the Great North was left without money to reach Keith on the one hand or Aberdeen on the other. Within a few days, the first fatal accident occurred, when an incoming engine ran into a stationary passenger train at Kittybrewster and one woman was killed. By 24 September 1855, the railway had made its way along the canal bed to Waterloo where a goods and passenger station was opened.

A railway to Banchory was constructed in 1853, opened on 7 September, and extended to Aboyne on 2 December 1859. Powers were obtained to carry the line to Braemar, but Queen Victoria, who objected to the intrusion on her privacy at Balmoral (not foreseeing the motor traffic of the twentieth-century Sunday) bought up the land on the route under consideration, and so the eventual terminus was Ballater, opened on 17 October 1866.

Two other schemes Anderson had in mind. His Alford Valley Railway, from Kintore to Alford, was in reply to a plan by an Aberdeen advocate, John Duncan, for a line from Drum to Alford. Duncan was chairman of the Caledonian, of the Deeside Railway and even in the long run presided over the Board of the Great North itself. Over the Alford scheme, Anderson won, getting Parliamentary approval by midsummer 1856, and the line opened on 25 March 1859. The other big Anderson idea was to open up his native Buchan. Originally he thought of breaking off from the Great North at Inverurie, from which burgh a branch to Oldmeldrum was opened on 26 June 1856, but in 1855 Dyce came to be preferred. The Formartine and Buchan Railway was to be a Dyce-Peterhead affair to start with. Immediately Duncan put up the Aberdeen, Peterhead and Fraserburgh Railway project, the route envisaging a line crossing the Aberdeen Links, sacred ground to every right-thinking Aberdonian. Duncan, however, succeeded in persuading the relevant Committee of the House of Commons to pass his Buchan scheme and reject Anderson's. Anderson at once brought up all the heavy artillery of Aberdeen Town Council, under his friend and fellow rail director, Sir Thomas Blaikie, and the following month the House of Lords threw out Duncan's scheme, although Duncan brought in support a petition signed by 11,000 names against 9,000 for the other side. Throughout 1857 there was a terrific war of words and figures throughout Buchan, from which Anderson and his friends emerged victorious with the more plausible arguments and calculations, if not the most accurate statements. And so in May 1858 Parliament accepted the Anderson and rejected the Duncan scheme flatly and finally.

It was during this battle royal, conducted not only by speeches, but to the greater profit of the local newspapers by advertisements, that Duncan committed the indiscretion that led to one of the juiciest Aberdeen cases ever to come before the Court of Session. By 1857, although Anderson had resigned from the North Bank Board in 1849 along with George Thompson and other two directors with big railway interests, Duncan got it in his head that the Bank directors were still as in 1847 behind Anderson's railway schemes. Actually at that time four of the Board were in one way or another connected with the G.N.S.R. while Duncan, as a director of the Aberdeen Bank before it crashed, was familiar with the unconventional Aberdeen method of handling bank finances and with contemporary frauds by a London bank in connection with which a member of the Macgregor clan had been prominent. He, therefore, alleged that to find the necessary deposits for presenting the Buchan and Formartine project to Parliament these four directors, with the connivance of the rest of the board, had put their hands into the bank till and taken out £36,000. There was, he declared, 'a nest of Macgregors' in the North Bank, and he went on to allege that in 1846 several of the directors juggled with the bank funds to provide the G.N.S.R. subscription contract monies.

The Board of the Bank, of course, could not take that sort of thing as a compliment. The Bank at once raised an action for damages, while the four directors personally impugned followed suit. Duncan employed all the resources of casuistry which the law on desperate occasions can command to defend his case. First of all, he claimed that the Bank as a corporate body had no reputation to lose and, therefore, couldn't claim for slander. He lost that round right away and also an appeal. In the next round he defended his allegations as one might say by metaphysical argument, but that did not avail. Then when Sir Thomas

Blaikie's action against him came up he asked, on thirteen counts, the Court's permission to inspect all the North Bank books from 1845 to 1857 that might bear upon the matter in dispute. The Court unanimously refused diligence. Then Duncan appealed for a postponement of trial because his counsel had been briefed for the Madeleine Smith murder trial. That also was refused. The four directors were awarded £250 damages each. The Bank action for £10,000 was then settled out of court, Duncan withdrawing his charges and paying the Bank's expenses of £250. Several years later Anderson and Duncan were in opposition again. Anderson had been elected to the Town Council and the civic chair, had resigned over a dispute and stood for re-election when Duncan was put up to oppose him. Duncan lost. But in 1867 he was chairman of his great rival's G.N.S.R. He died in 1874, Anderson, always the survivor, in 1887.

Railway finance intensified the great financial crisis of 1848, when the Aberdeen Bank collapsed, and the North Bank lost over £250,000, the sum of its reserve fund and more than half of its paid-up capital. The Aberdeen Bank's downfall and part of the North Bank's losses were due to a considerable extent to the failure of the great linen firm of Leys, Masson and Co., and James Hadden and Son, the woollen manufacturers, and partly to share gambling in the stock of so-called exchange companies which had sprung up about that time. But it was the railway mania which bore most hardly upon the North Bank. Five of its directors and its manager (who got the sack over the crisis) between them held £82,500 of local railway stock and the bank itself, through Alexander Anderson's legal firm as intermediary, had lent the Great North £73,350. There was actually a debt — an overdraft in modern phraseology — of some £100,000 standing against Adam and Anderson. It should be added that eventually it was repaid all but a small fraction which was written off.

We now move back from the counting-house to the marshalling yard. While the Buchan line was getting underway the directors of the railways to south and north and the citizens of Aberdeen began to be much exercised by rival schemes to link up the systems, whose termini were at Kittybrewster and Waterloo, Guild Street and Ferryhill. The Scottish North-Eastern Railway, in which the Aberdeen Railway had been merged, finding the Great North directors unimpressed by a proposal to carry a line down the Denburn Valley to link up with the southern system at Guild Street, projected a line from Limpet Mill just south of Muchalls, to Kintore, with a spur to Culter and with a separate line between Kintore and Oldmeldrum. The Deeside Railway Board, however, at the instigation of the chairman, John Duncan, gave the Great North Railway a lease of their line which rather nullified the North-Eastern Board's scheme. His action won him a Great North directorship. The Town Council opposed the Limpet Mill proposition, only to be confronted by a Great North fantasy (it could hardly be described otherwise, although it secured Parliamentary sanction) nicknamed the Circumbendibus. This extraordinary conception, which some knowing individuals believed to have been concocted to force the North-Eastern Board to accept the Great North's terms for a junction line, was to run from Woodside via Stockethill, Queen's Cross, the south side of Albyn Place eventually through Hadden's Mills to Guild Street, with several tunnels on its course, and the irretrievable ruin of Aberdeen's carefully laid out west-end in its wake. At the municipal election in November 1862 the Circumbendibus proved to have few friends, but it had influential support for all that. Alexander Anderson, from the Provost's chair, regretted that his own scheme of a joint station at the top of what is now Bridge Street had been made impossible by the North-Eastern Board's conditions, and declared that the public would have to choose between Limpet Mill and the Circumbendibus. This scheme that Anderson favoured with the terminus where the Palace Hotel eventually was built and where Telephone House now stands, had been suggested in 1850 by an Aberdeen architect named James Henderson, all of whose plan, save the actual site of the station building, eventually took shape. With his brother, Henderson was the founder of the builders' merchants firm of J. & W. Henderson, today one of the most prosperous of Aberdeen concerns with branches throughout the country. James Henderson was responsible among other professional work in Aberdeen for that very gracious cul-de-sac Westfield Terrace, and he also laid out Broomhill Road and the approaches to the Duthie Park.

Tempers may have been as excited as over the Duncan version of the Buchan Railway, but good sense and Scottish economy supervened, and the Circumbendibus project was suspended while the North-Eastern company promoted a parliamentary bill for the construction of the Denburn Valley line, for which the Great North was to provide £125,000, and the North-Eastern £70,000. As the latter had originally offered £30,000 the Circumbendibus diversion justified its short existence. The bill was passed in June 1864. The line took longer to complete than had been expected, one of the two tunnels, 270 and 275 yards long, that at Hutcheon Street having held up proceedings through part of its roof falling in. But on 4 November 1867 the Joint Station and the Denburn Line were opened, the goods traffic of the Great North continuing to use Waterloo and that of the North-Eastern Guild Street. Guild Street itself, which had hitherto been the designation of the thoroughfare from Stirling Street to Trinity Street, now extended from Market Street to College Street (once called Wapping). In 1889 the Schoolhill Viaduct, resulting in the obliteration of the Mutton Brae between the East and Belmont Churches and the site of the viaduct, was built, along with Schoolhill Station. The centenary of the opening of the Denburn Line was celebrated on 4 November 1967, by members of the G.N.S.R. Association, which conducts a kind of permanent wake over the remains of Anderson's far-flung project, by a tour from Guild Street goods station to the old Great North terminal at Waterloo, complete with steam engine and rail coach — not, it should be mentioned, without some dislocation of what modernists might term more sophisticated traffic.

The salient features of the Great North's history may be briefly recounted, while for the systems to the south it may be recalled that in August 1895 there began the great race from London to Aberdeen between the East Coast and Midland systems which cut the time by two-and-a-half hours, resulting in trains leaving London at 8 p.m. pulling into the Joint Station at 6.30 a.m. The Great North co-operated so that a London passenger could reach Inverness at 11.5 a.m. The race was shortly discontinued and the timing relapsed by an hour to begin with, but on the Great North in the following summer the run from Aberdeen to Elgin at 1 hour 58 minutes for 80¾ miles was one of the fastest in the kingdom. In 1886 a sorting carriage was put on the main Great North line; it was withdrawn in 1916. In July 1887 the suburban service to Dyce was opened and in the summer of 1894 that to Culter, and for some years there were twenty trains each way on both. The suburban services were closed on 5 April 1937. Sunday trains had been tried from 1928 to 1930, with in addition two each way to Elgin.

In 1891 the Palace Hotel, built on the site of Alexander Anderson's chosen location for the central station, was acquired, the covered way and lift were installed connecting the hotel with the station, and for some years uniformed porters from other hotels were denied access to the platforms. After the Cruden Bay branch, from Ellon to Boddam, was opened on 2 August 1897, with the golf course ready for play, the Cruden Bay Hotel, with its electric tramway to the station was built and open for guests in February 1899. It never managed to pay its way, it was requisitioned for hospital use in the Second World War, handed back to the railway in 1945 about the same time as the branch line itself was closed, and it was finally demolished after 1947. The Palace Hotel was closed after a fire on 30 October 1941, never reopened and demolished some years after the war. The Station Hotel, purchased in 1910, and requisitioned during the war, was remodelled, extended, and modernised when it was restored to the railway. In 1894 the main offices of the Great North were transferred from Waterloo to Guild Street in the same block as the Station Hotel.

In 1896 an independent company projected a light railway to Echt and the Great North Board, besides putting forward a rival scheme, proposed a light railway to Newburgh. Both schemes required or entailed the use of the town's tramway system, which was not regarded as very practical, and the projects were dropped. But the idea persisted in the minds of the Great North directors, and in 1904 they enrolled themselves amongst the pioneers of road services by introducing among other bus systems services from Ballater to Braemar, Alford to Bellabeg, Aberdeen to Cluny, Culter to Echt and eventually to Aberdeen. In 1907 a special service to Newburgh was added. The bus bodies were built at Inverurie, whither between 1898 and 1905 the railway workshops hitherto at Kittybrewster had been transferred and the housing scheme (locally known as the Colony) built for employees. The terminus for goods and passengers by bus was Schoolhill, steam wagons with 3-ton trailers having been built for the carriage of goods. By the summer of 1914 there were thirty-five buses and fourteen lorries operating over 150 miles of road.

Within thirty years of its opening the Joint Station was becoming incapable of coping with its traffic. After many delays a complete reorganisation scheme was put in hand, the first part in 1907, the main part in 1913, and in July 1914, nine new platforms, 11,340 feet of them, were working. The scheme involved the building of what was known as the suburban station at the south-east corner of Bridge Street, and the whole job, necessarily held up by the First World War, was completed in 1920, the presiding genius having been the Great North. engineer James A. Parker (incidentally a doughty mountaineer who, besides ascents in the Rockies, the Alps and the Dolomites, had climbed every mountain of 1,000 feet and over in the British Isles). In the early months of 1898 the Great North directors held a series of four receptions for their employees with their families. The receptions were held in Aberdeen, a lantern show, concert and display by a team of Gordon Highlanders amused the guests, after which there was supper with dancing, and special trains to convey the happy revellers home at the Board's expense. In 1922 a restaurant car to Inverness was tried and in 1923 a sleeper-coach to Lossiemouth was added, both being discontinued in 1939.

On New Year's Day 1923, the Great North was merged with the North British in the London and North-Eastern Railway. After the Second World War, the larger unit was itself swallowed up in British Railways. The 'Great North' earned during its nearly seventy years of independent existence the affection of its public. The fusion of 1923 was the end of yet another auld sang to which the public loved to dance. Now they have to pay the piper.

No sooner was Aberdeen connected with the south by the speedy agency of the railway than the local exporters took advantage of it. Within a few months of the first train reaching Ferryhill, live cattle were being trucked for the southern markets. Immediately before 1850 they had been sent by sea, and before about 1835, when drill sowing of turnips was becoming general and cattle could be fed through the winter at home, the cattle trade with England had been confined to store animals driven in large convoys by the drove roads to the big fairs such as Falkirk Tryst in the Scottish Midlands. The coastal shipping lines to Orkney and Shetland were, of course, the conveyers of all the store cattle of the islands to Aberdeen, but the railways until the end of the First World War were the main channel for all kinds of cattle, lean and fat, alive and dead, to the south. But after the war was over the scene began to change. In 1921 there were less than a score of road haulage firms, all small, operating out of Aberdeen. By 1948 there were forty-five, some of which owned 100 vehicles. In 1938 there were 1,400 commercial vehicles licensed, while in 1948 there were 2,515. By the middle twenties most farmers had realised that if they drove their fat cattle on foot to the nearest mart or railway station they lost half a hundredweight in weight compared with their condition when a float called at the farm and carried the animals all the way to their destination. The same argument, *mutatis mutandis*, applied to personal travel. It saved effort and time and often a mile or two of walking to make a journey by bus instead of by rail; and equally in the transport of goods, the internal combustion engine brought the lorry to the workshop or warehouse door and took its load to its ultimate address.

Accordingly, while railway traffic at Guild Street in 1947 amounted to 194,992 tons of all kinds of goods forwarded, and 281,497 tons received, by 1950 the respective totals were 152,139 and 186,529. The disparity between 1950 and any year previous to 1947 was increasingly greater the further back the comparison is carried. Statistics for road transport, both passenger traffic and goods, are not so far as quantities go ascertainable. It is simply a fact that over the last forty years both personal and goods traffic has been progressively attracted from the sea and from rail to the roads. This movement has been stimulated partly, as regards rail, by strikes and occasional mistakes in delivery as well as by increased charges, and by the upward tendency in fares and freights by sea, one of the consequences being the discontinuance of the carrying of passengers on the Aberdeen-London sea service. The other influences which hastened the drift to the roads have already been indicated.

It may be that the great railway amalgamations and the increasing regulation of railway activities from London obscured from the directors, even before nationalisation, the realities of the situation. London's surface traffic congestion which gave underground electric and other railway services in the metropolitan area a distinct advantage in the minds of the commuting public, may have been taken as representative of conditions throughout the country. That such parochial thinking is typical of London control, whether through the civil service or head offices of nationalised concerns or private enterprise, is a commonplace in the experience of all who have to deal with such complexes. At all events, the railways failed to wake up to the facts confronting them until it was too late. As a consequence passenger traffic both north and south of Aberdeen has dwindled to almost nothing except perhaps during the public holidays. The Deeside and Alford railways have gone, the Buchan line is reduced to goods and not very much of that, the Cruden Bay and Oldmeldrum branches are memories, the Macduff connection is non-existent, and even the main Great North line to Inverness maintains what is little more than a skeleton service. To the south there is now only one route, which seeks to make the best of what used to be two worlds, and executes a circumbendibus round by Dundee on its way to Perth and Glasgow.

Latterly British Railways endeavoured to counteract the drift to road and air by a few devices, though the ultimate test, the reduction of fares to woo back passengers, has not been and in the present economic climate of nationalisation is not likely to be tried. On the goods side, Aberdeen in 1966 became a terminus for freight liner services which offered certain advantages to consigners of large loads, and these services link up with Glasgow and on to the great English centres, the 536 miles to London being, on time-table, covered in eleven hours.

Aviation as a commercial proposition in the realms of transport came to Aberdeen when Eric Gandar Dower developed the Farburn area south of Dyce, commencing about 1927, and eventually sending out passenger flights from the airport there in all directions. Amongst other innovations was a route to Scandinavia. The Hitler war, when the airport was taken over and civil flying very strictly controlled, put what it was hoped would be only a temporary stop to a valuable experiment that was bound to become a real asset to the Aberdeen area. But after the war the private operator was ousted by nationalisation and, incidentally, very badly treated. Characteristically ignorant and contemptuous of local connection, traditions and potentialities, the metropolitan planners did not trouble and never have troubled to resume the Scandinavian service, although Aberdeen is the most available point of departure for that part of Europe. Nor for some time was much enthusiasm shown for Aberdeen's possibilities as part of a British internal air network. The city's strong European contacts, however, as well as its wealth and its long continued habits of keeping in close business and social touch with the south gradually penetrated the dense official mind. The airport is now, for the population of the area it serves, one of the busiest in the kingdom, and since it got a chance to prove its mettle, has paid its way—which is more than can be said for most routes. The services have in consequence been greatly improved, increased and speeded up, and not only are there well patronised flights to London, and connections can be made to nearly one hundred centres in the world, but a surprising weight of goods is carried in always expanding quantities.

Aberdeen is, of course, the airport for Wick, Orkney and Shetland, and operates regular services thither and thence both for passengers and goods. But it is characteristic of the mental processes of a nationalised industry whose activities are concerned with more than one distinct nation, of which one is predominant in wealth and population, that B.E.A. publicity for Aberdeen is meagre and curt compared with that for centres elsewhere approximately the same size.

CHAPTER EIGHT

Education: Medical Services: Welfare State*

Aberdeen's first School Board election under the Education Act of 1872, which made instruction of the young compulsory between the ages of 5 and 13, was held in March 1873, and was hotly disputed between the two great bodies of the Scottish Presbyterian Church. Judged by the number of ministers who came out at the Disruption, Aberdeen was preponderantly Free Church, and there was a strenuous contest now to decide who was to shape the educational destinies of the city's youth. The result of the election was to leave pretty much a balance between the two denominations, and the good sense of the Rev. W. R. Pirie, who became Principal of the University in 1876, and got a sound apprenticeship as chairman of this first School Board, enabled the new body to accomplish its work with decorum and practical ability.

When the School Board commenced to function there were thirteen public schools in existence apart from the Grammar and Robert Gordon's College or Hospital and the Aberdeen High School for Girls. About 3,000 Aberdeen children had no opportunity of attending school. Within ten years Commerce Street, Middle, Causewayend, Ferryhill and Skene Street Schools had been built, which, in conjunction with the schools taken over and enlarged, provided places for nearly 8,000 pupils, about double the 1872 capacity. At the end of twenty-one years there were twenty-two elementary schools, King Street, Rosemount, Ruthrieston and Ashley Road schools having been added since 1882, and there were 18,905 elementary pupils on the roll, besides 561 (as against 1,095 in 1873) in industrial and hospital schools, 274 (as against 2,166) in low-fee schools, 430 (as against 1,550) in high-fee schools, 1,752 (as against 269) in the Grammar, High School for Girls and Gordon's. Walker Road and Kittybrewster schools were built before the end of the century, and the School Board offices were re-

---

* Those who wish fuller information, analytical tables, statistics and similar *notabilia* of the Welfare State will find it in *The Third Statistical Account* of the City.

moved in 1898 from King Street to Union Terrace. At the outset the school rate was 3d. in the pound; in 1900 it was 1s. 1¼d., by which date the Board had borrowed over £327,000, carried an outstanding debt of £265,000, was catering for an average daily attendance of close on 20,000 children, whose percentage of attendance had risen from about 80 in the seventies to 87·7, and employed 716 teachers whose salaries amounted to £51,000.

As a part means of providing the teachers there were two Normal Training Colleges, Church of Scotland (established in 1873) and Free Church (1875) in the city. In 1906 the colleges were merged in a single Training Centre with a demonstration school to provide practical training in the art of teaching, the pupil teacher system being abandoned about that time and temporarily replaced by a system of junior student trainees. Eventually the Aberdeen Training Centre became the focus and finishing seminary for the Junior Student centres in the North-East. The name had again been changed in recent years to College of Education without much alteration in its purpose.

In general educational administration, two fundamental changes took place at the close of the First World War. In 1919 the School Boards were supplanted by Education Authorities, an alteration which meant much in the rural districts, where parish school boards were lost in a county authority, but less in a city like Aberdeen, where the change was mainly one of name. Very little interest, however, was shown in the first Education Authority election in Aberdeen in April 1919, only 12 per cent of the electorate troubling to vote. Mr. George Duncan, advocate, became the first and (as it proved) only chairman of the Authority, worthily maintaining the efficient and progressive standards established by his School Board predecessors, the Rev. Gordon J. Murray, John Keir (the blind manager of the Aberdeen Asylum for the Blind), and George Mackenzie. It was a tribute to Mr. (later Dr.) George Duncan's status in the educational organisation of Scotland that the first annual congress of the Association of Education Authorities should be held at Aberdeen in 1925. But the cost of providing education, which did not noticeably surpass that of later Victorian times in quality, rose steeply. In 1909–10 it was £5 13s. 3d. per pupil; in 1929 it was £11; in 1930 it had advanced to £16 under the town.[1] In 1930 the Education Authorities disappeared, their place being taken by the Education Committees of the Town or County Councils, a

---

[1] In 1969 about £237 was spent per pupil and Scottish education had ceased to be better than that of its rivals.

step whose retrograde character is now only too obvious. Dr. Duncan was succeeded as convener of this committee by John D. Munro, who from the commencement of the Authority's existence had been prominently identified with the financial side of the work.

Gradually the schools took all manner of subjects under their jurisdiction. By 1950 there were fifty-seven schools under the Education Committee catering for 25,926 pupils instructed by slightly over 1,000 teachers. The schools themselves had expanded into a great variety of special establishments — nursery schools, originating in 1933 in a movement sponsored outside the Committee but incorporated from 1937 in the official structure; schools for handicapped children, including one for the deaf and dumb; a residential school outwith the city boundary at Tertowie House, originally intended for youngsters who wished to go on the land, but later with more emphasis on community-living and what might be termed in the language of those who work on the land, out-wintering. Elementary or primary, and junior and senior secondary schools were for some years the descriptions of styles that changed almost kaleidoscopically after the education committees ceased to be *ad hoc* and the paternal rule of the dominie in each school gave way to the Director of Education with an office staff and civil service ways, and auxiliaries like psychiatrists and other specialists to assess the progress and guide the destinies of the pupils. Pre-apprenticeship courses, much more appropriate with the school-leaving age at 15, form an introduction to further training for learners in the principal industries and trades of the city, while holiday camps and instruction in what in earlier days would have been regarded as frivolous games perform a parallel pre-adult guide to the life of leisure that is the ideal of modern politicians. Under the Labour majority in the Town Council, both the Grammar School[1] and the High School for Girls were made non-fee paying, and their primary departments abolished despite very strongly expressed public disapprobation. Neither school would appear to have gained much by the change except in floor space — the Girls' High having been greatly enlarged on its present Albyn Place site, formerly a school for orphan girls called Mrs. Emslie's Institution, to which it had been transferred in 1893 from the charming little Grecian building in Little Belmont Street, later part of the Aberdeen Academy, in which it had succeeded what was called the English School in 1874. Mrs. Emslie, a member of the Calder family

1   The Grammar is now Rubislaw Academy and the Girls High is Harlaw Academy.

who for long were wine merchants in the city, founded the orphanage in 1840, built it at a cost of £16,000, and endowed it amply; it trained girls to be domestic servants and had usually fifty on its roll.

Outside the ambit of the Education Committee are several independent schools, the Albyn School for Girls, St. Margaret's School for Girls, the Convent of the Sacred Heart, and St. Nicholas School, a fee-paying but not profit-making institution now located in what used to be the public school buildings at Bridge of Don. Most important of all the schools in this category is Robert Gordon's College, which not only provides a full academic course up to university standard in the traditional subjects but whose curricula have been greatly extended as the result of a series of provisional orders secured round about 1880. It has taken under its wing as Robert Gordon's Institute of Technology the Technical College, based upon Gordon's College itself and the old Mechanics' Institute which was such a boon to ambitious young men in early Victorian days. There are courses in Engineering (in conjunction with the University), for which in 1925 a scheme costing £100,000 was preferred, Chemistry, Navigation, Domestic Science, and Art including Architecture, the College having taken under its wing Gray's School of Art, which in 1968 was translated to Garthdee House, to which the School of Architecture was moved in 1959. Linked with Gordon's College in its work was the Aberdeen Educational Trust. By an Act of 1882 a group of benevolent institutions which need not be specified separately were placed under the charge of the Trust, whose headquarters in King Street had been the premises of the Boys' and Girls' Hospital. At the end of the century, with an annual revenue from capital of about £5,000, the Trust supported a Girls' Home and School of Domestic Economy in addition to the Hospital with 200 boys and girls; and provided bursaries and scholarships for pupils proceeding to the Grammar School or Gordon's College or studying at evening schools. There was thus by the nineties of the last century a complete framework for the present educational fabric. This school is now in Queen's Road.

It is almost impracticable in this history to follow the various branches of educational activity in the city, or even to go into details of the courses in adult education which are a valuable solvent during the winter months of the tedium to which so many town dwellers are subject. Nor can the ramifications of physical education be followed with the numerous playing fields and other loci outside and indoors for indulgence in sports and pastimes.

But vocational education and Old Aberdeen's schools require some attention. In 1875 the Education Committee of the Free Church took over an institution in Charlotte Street with an interesting history, and converted it into the Aberdeen Free Church Normal Practising School, providing practical training in teaching for over 1,200 students. Since 1845 this school had been under the care of the Free South Church, before which it was managed by the Aberdeen Education Society. The Society was founded in 1815 following a visit by an eminent educationist, Joseph Lancaster, who advocated the monitorial system in schools. In 1816 the Society opened a school for boys in Harriet Street: Thomas Edward the naturalist entered it in 1819 as a child of five. In 1821 a new school building was opened, capable of accommodating 700 pupils, in Blackfriars Street; one master was expected to supervise 450 pupils, at a salary of £50 and half the fees of a penny a pupil a week. In 1828 the Charlotte Street establishment was opened by the Society as the Lancastrian School for Girls. In 1838 it was divided into two class-rooms, one being allocated to the boys from Blackfriars Street school, which was then closed.

In 1904 the 'Normal' was removed to John Street and in 1907 came under the Aberdeen Provincial Committee for the Training of Teachers as a demonstration school, the Charlotte Street college becoming the Training Centre at which, when the pupil teacher system was swept away under the 1918 Education Act, the junior students throughout the North-East were 'finished'. In 1922 Dr. George Smith was succeeded as Director of Studies by Mr. George A. Burnett, who two years later went to Glasgow centre, and was followed by Dr. W. A. Edward. In January 1928 a Training College Hostel costing £81,000 was opened at Hilton.

In 1846 a Ladies' Boarding and Day School was opened by a Miss Stephen. Ten years later it was moved to Union Row to the premises that were to be occupied by the 'Bon-Accord' printing department. In 1889 the School was transferred to Union Grove House and in 1900 it occupied the present premises in Albyn Place of St. Margaret's, the name then chosen for the school.

Old Aberdeen Grammar School, whose history went back to the Pedagogium or Preparatory school which stood at the gate of King's College, was situated by 1831 in School Road, 'a long low-roofed building, built in the cottage villa style'. It had succeeded the older grammar school in the previous century. For long it consisted of one room, but wings for younger pupils were added eventually. The complement of older pupils, from twelve years upwards, was forty. Ewan Maclachlan, the Gaelic Poet and King's College librarian was rector for years. Thomas Davidson, 'the wandering scholar' from Old Deer who founded the Fabian Society and introduced Classical culture of a sort to the U.S.A., was rector when, it was not quite accurately said, there were only two pupils, one of them his own brother; and then Dr. Dey and Mr. Fyfe greatly increased the efficiency and reputation of the school, sending out a number of distinguished pupils, of whom the latter rector's son, Maxwell Fyfe, attained to high Parliamentary and political distinction.

Even more spectacular was the achievement of the Gymnasium or 'Gym', located in the angle of School Road and The Chanonry now occupied by the Cruickshank Botanical Garden of the University. The school was founded by the Rev. Alexander Anderson, a Presbyterian minister who had 'come out' at the Disruption, but whose views on baptism were too advanced for the Free Church and he joined the Baptist communion. Both his family and his school might be described as overflowing the land. The record, both academic and commercial of his pupils both at home and abroad fill a substantial volume, and as for his family, a member of it still alive has compiled this list, which formidable as it is, happens to be far from complete:

A Chief of the Imperial General Staff, a First Lord of the Admiralty, an Ambassador to the United States, a President of the Royal Society of Water Colour Painters, a chairman of the South Wales Coal Owners' Association, a principal woman factory inspector, a Master of Gonville and Caius, a fellow and tutor of Balliol, a Fellow of Trinity College, Cambridge, a Regius Professor of Botany, one of the earliest woman M.P.s, a Director of the Bank of England, an M.P. for the City of London, a Colonel Commandant of Engineers, two millionaires. The Crown has awarded at least thirty-five honours to the family.

Actually there ought to be added one of the classic medical historians and the head of one of the great British shipping lines. All are descended from the skipper who four hundred years ago took the Earl Marischal of Scotland to Scandinavia as proxy wooer for James I; and some of them carry the blood of Nelson's surgeon at the Battle of Copenhagen.

Aberdeen, like the rest of the country, has to thank Disraeli for its contemporary health services. In the short Tory administration of 1867-8 a bill was passed giving Scottish local authorities certain powers to deal with infectious diseases which led to the building in 1877 of a fever hospital, now the City Hospital at Cuningarhill at the east-end of Constitution Street. Two years later the Town Council set up its health department, the Tory Act of 1875 having given local authorities powers to deal with housing congestion and a variety of sanitary and health services. J. R. Simpson (later knighted) who became M.O.H. for Calcutta in 1886 was followed a year later by Dr. Matthew Hay, who was to organise and lead the department until 1923, as well as filling the chair of Forensic Medicine at the University from 1883 to 1926. Having reorganised and restored in public opinion the work and the reputation of the City Hospital, which was being almost boycotted, he then proceeded quietly but efficiently to build up his department, using the City Hospital to supplement the work of the Infirmary.

At the end of the Kaiser's war, however, the pressure on all the hospitals was such that the Town Council took over from the Parish Council the buildings at Oldmill, the nucleus of which had been a boy's Reformatory, later, in 1907, turned into the poorhouse of the Aberdeen urban area, and taken over by the authorities as a Services hospital during 1914–19, the name being changed to Woodend and the premises considerably extended. The Parish Council retained the right to send its sick poor there for treatment. When the functions of the Parish Council fell to the Town Council on 16 May 1930, the hospital was greatly developed, and by the end of the Second World War, nearly 400 beds were available for medical, surgical and particularly tubercular cases. The City Hospital again reverted to infectious diseases, covered an area of ten acres, wherein was sited the Public Health laboratory. In 1930 the Town Council and Aberdeen County Council and within a few months Kincardine County Council became partners in a Regional Medical Services Scheme. The take-over of Woodend was the work of Dr. J. Parlane Kinloch, Matthew Hay's successor, who reorganised the municipal hospital services, pushing them indeed into the field then operated by the voluntary agencies in a way that aroused a certain amount of resistance. He was in 1928 appointed Chief Medical Officer to the Scottish Department of Health.

During the early twenties a dynamic movement in Aberdeen's health services was gathering momentum. Kinloch's schemes of hospital amalgamation had had their genesis in Hay's brain, but while Kinloch's persuasiveness was to fail to make much headway, his mentor had already developed another scheme which commended itself much more congenially to the medical profession and the general public. Matthew

Hay suggested the building of a hospital to embrace all the branches of hospital care, plus a medical school, and he pointed to the Burnside-Foresterhill slope as the appropriate site. He propounded his plan in 1920 to the Medico-Chirurgical Society, whose President, the Professor of Medicine, Dr. (later Sir) Ashley W. Mackintosh, sponsored it at a conference at which the Society, the Corporation, the University Court, and the governing bodies of the Royal Infirmary and Royal Hospital for Sick Children were represented. Approval having been gained there, the financial foundations had to be laid. The Sick Children's Hospital had been collecting subscriptions for a new hospital in 1914. The pre-war plan was scrapped, seventeen acres of the land for Matthew Hay's joint scheme allocated, another campaign started for subscriptions, and in 1928 Lady Cowdray opened the new hospital with 134 beds. It had cost £115,000, the site had been presented, and the total subscriptions amounted to £140,000.

The Royal Infirmary part of the project was a much heavier undertaking. The scheme was presented to the public in 1927 by Lord Provost (later Sir) Andrew Lewis with an appeal for £400,000, of which nearly £200,000 had already been promised. The money was subscribed with amazing readiness by rich and poor alike and when in 1936 the Duke of York, later King George VI, formally opened the great, new, gleaming white buildings on the hillside below Ashgrove Road West, the cost of £525,000 had been fully met by the generosity of the public. There were 500 beds. Later the Maternity Hospital and the University Medical School were added to form a massive modern centre of healing and teaching. When the State took over medical services in 1948 the great institution, built by voluntary effort and run by the free liberality of the public — and as such a proof that the State's intervention was a work of supererogation — the Royal Infirmary, physically part of Aberdeen, ceased to be an Aberdonian project and became merged in the anonymity of a Civil Service concept. The hospital has expanded to keep pace with the increasing valetudinarian condition of the community under the depressing burdens of the new civilisation.

One interesting result of the realisation of the scheme was the partial desertion after nearly three and a half centuries of 'the toun's colledge'. With the majority of the Medical classes transferred to Foresterhill, many of the other classes shifted elsewhere, Marischal for a time had a deserted look.

Aberdeen opened a day nursery in October 1913, its Children's Centre in 1925, a birth control clinic the following year, and a home for (defective) babies was provided at Thorngrove House in 1933. There was a joint nursery school and child welfare centre for 120 children at Torry. In 1947 the Eye Institution had more cases than ever in its 128th year, the Dispensary and Vaccine Institute were still at work, and an orthopaedic centre was opened just before the outbreak of war in 1939.

Associated with the Royal Infirmary, Woodend and the Casualty Centre in Woolmanhill under the Board of Management for the Aberdeen General Hospitals, itself a committee operating under the North-Eastern Regional Hospital Board, was Morningfield Hospital for cases of incurable diseases founded in 1857 by the Trustees of John Gordon of Murtle's Charitable Fund and under the auspices of the Aberdeen magistrates, housed originally at Belleville in Baker Street with six patients, and removed in 1884 to Morningfield with accommodation for fifty-five patients. There was also a convalescent hospital at Cults and the Watson-Fraser Nursing Home, once at 3–5 Albyn Place, now incorporated in the Royal Infirmary building. Under another Board of Management came the once voluntary Royal Asylum now called the Royal Cornhill Hospital, with the Ross Clinic beside it; the publicly-owned Kingseat Hospital, opened in 1904 with 500 beds at a cost of £125,300, and now extended to take several hundred more patients; a Rehabilitation Centre in the city; and Woodlands Hospital, Cults. A third Board of Management, for the Special Hospitals, became responsible for the City and Sick Children's Hospitals; also for the Maternity Hospital, transferred to Foresterhill in 1937 from Castle Terrace, which with three smaller hospitals at Fonthill, Queen's Cross and Summerfield, deals with practically all Aberdeen's 4,000 confinements yearly; and Tor-na-Dee at Milltimber four miles out. By 1971, reorganisation reduced the number of Boards of Management to two.

When the Parish Council's functions were vested in the Town Council in 1930 such social services as the former had performed were naturally transferred. They mostly related to poor relief, and in a very short time much of these responsibilities were lifted on to the broader shoulders of the State to a very considerable extent. The transfer made no difference to the burden of housing which since 1918 had been weighing with ever greater pressure upon the Corporation.

The population explosion in the last third of the nineteenth century did not result in a lack of housing accommodation. At this time municipal housing was almost non-existent. After a Corporation Act of its own in 1881, Aberdeen did indeed embark on a programme of slum clearance, which before the outbreak of war in 1914, chiefly in the Gallowgate, Exchequer Row and the Castlehill area, had condemned nearly 2,500 houses, although only three out of every four were taken down. It was not until the end of the century that fourteen tenements, representing 131 dwellings, were erected by the Town Council at Urquhart Road and Park Road. It was private enterprise building that kept pace with the population to an extent that both municipal and private building — the latter inhibited by rent restriction and other legislation — together cannot achieve even in circumstances of a much slower population increase. Needless to say, the Victorian level of housing was much lower, in comfort and sanitation and such respects, indeed in everything but solidity of construction, than the standards of the years after the Second World War.

After the 1918 Armistice the building trade gradually came to depend to an increasing extent upon local authority orders. Building trade wages for masons rose from 8d. to 2s. 3d. an hour, but the slump after 1921 brought them down thereafter to 1s. 6d. Under the Addison Housing Act of 1919 Aberdeen Town Council built 242 houses, although by 1925 it was stated that only 228 of the 4,000 houses required were completed. Under the Wheatley Act of 1924 no fewer than 1,300 were constructed before 1928, but the number was proportionately lower than in any other large Scots city. Under later Acts 1,894 houses were erected, making up to the year 1935 a total of 3,436 houses costing £1,273,500, while private enterprise had built 3,159 houses at a cost of £2,600,000, towards which the Council had advanced loans amounting to £187,784. Cheap and dear bungalows were built for sale at from £450 to £2,000, while municipal houses were let at from £17 to £32 10s. The first post-war municipal housing scheme was at Torry. Then the Hilton estate was acquired by the Town Council, and at Hilton and Cattofield extensive areas were eventually built up at a cost of £390,000. In the later twenties the Mansefield Road district of Torry and the Pittodrie and School Road parts of the northern end of the town were laid out, and a new technique in town-planning began to be employed which was the harbinger of the pioneer work in that direction undertaken during the provostship of Henry Alexander. At the same time a commencement was made with the Augean task of clearing away the slums in the older parts of the town, and 327 decrepit condemned houses in Guestrow, Longacre and Shuttle Lane were first demolished, the Denburn, Young Street and Berry Street being partially attended to thereafter, and the dispossessed tenants sent to low-rented houses in Seaforth Road, Sunnybank Road, Errol Street, School Road and Torry.[1]

Outside municipal schemes, the town bulged over its previous boundaries with houses, villas and bungalows in all directions. In the Westburn Road, Rubislaw, King's Gate, Duthie Terrace, Bridge of Don and other districts houses were built by private enterprise very rapidly. In 1918, for example, there was only an old-fashioned cottage or two and one lonesome flatted house between Kepplestone and Oldmill. New streets were piled one beyond the other up the hill of the Stocket. All these expansions meant more schools — and larger ones took shape at Torry (made of the stones of Pitfour House in Buchan), Hilton, Linksfield and Powis. New churches were built at Hilton, King Street and Seaton. In 1926 the Duchess of Fife inaugurated an extension of Cairnton waterworks.

In the thirties, as Scotland was plunged deeper and deeper into industrial depression, Aberdeen took a lead from the conception of the Hillington estate near Glasgow, where special attractions were given to firms seeking factory space, and bought the lands of Kincorth, on the rising ground on the south side of the Dee. The intention, to which Hitler's war put a temporary stop, was to create a satellite township there, with houses and all their communal and social amenities as well as factories. Nothing much, however, was done. One big factory was erected south of the Dee, but many people looked with some dubiety upon the assumption by the Town Council of responsibilities that brought it directly into control of business. After much money and valuable space were absorbed in constructing garden cities and similar styles of lay-out, it was found desirable to revert to tenements, and, in South Mount Street, on the site of what had been Morton's provision works, there was begun (and completed at a snail's pace during the Second World War) a housing development on the Continental model which had become especially popular in Austria and Holland. After the Second World War and the short era of the pre-fabs, there was a slow progress — if that is the word — towards the modern style which has culminated in the multi-storey flats.

With Sir Henry Alexander as convener, in 1928 a committee drafted an ambitious scheme of development not merely affecting the land within the city boundaries, but also specifying large areas adjacent to the city and enclosing it in a belt 'eight or ten miles deep which could

1   The result in part at least was that the slums moved outwards. One of the housing developments was significantly nicknamed 'Dartmoor'.

not be developed otherwise than in conformity with the regulations laid down by the committee. This innovation, whether for good or ill, has since been followed on a much wider scale elsewhere and incorporated in legislation.

Between the wars Aberdeen built 11,409 houses, of which 6,434, two-fifths of them tenements, were constructed under the aegis of the corporation. At the same time almost 3,000 were demolished or converted to purposes other than residential. The bulk of the 5,000 houses privately built were to be owner-occupied, the Rent Restriction Act and similar regulations being still in operation and discouraging private building for letting. In 1938 there were still some 27,000 dwellings without separate sanitary closets. There were still seventy dry closets. After 1945 the Corporation built some 7,000 new houses (and completed twenty-five new schools) in ten years. Private builders constructed less than 500. From the First World War onwards the municipal housing schemes came to be scattered all over the city area and eventually crept out beyond it across the Dee, over the Stocket Forest, and along the right bank of the Don to Bucksburn, whilst private enterprise shook a pepper-box of bungalows and villas along the North Deeside Road to Culter, and Aberdeen County Council erected 'dormitory suburbs' at Bridge of Don and in the Bankhead-Bucksburn-Newhills area.

The tramways system began in 1872 when a private company got parliamentary sanction to give Aberdeen this new form of transport. The first lines, which cost £18,240 to lay and equip, from Queen's Cross to the North Church, and from St. Nicholas Street to Kittybrewster — a single track of about three miles with passing places — were opened on 31 August 1874. The seven cars were drawn in relays by eight horses each, working in 3½-hour shftis. Although the first year's revenue was £5,535, it was four years ere the first dividend was paid. It rose steadily from 4 to 5½ per cent. In 1880 the tramways were extended to Woodside, to King Street Cattle Market, and to Mannofield and in 1888 the Union Street line was doubled. By this time the revenue was £16,000 on a capital outlay of £54,500.

Bridge of Don was reached in 1892, Bridge of Dee in 1894, and Rubislaw in 1896. Albyn Place line and that from Loch Street to Kittybrewster were doubled. The total length of line reached was eleven miles with a capital expenditure of £85,000 and revenue of £26,000. There were no Sunday services, wages were 24s. a week for drivers after the first year, they worked 14¼ hours per day with an hour off for breakfast and another for dinner and an extra shilling a week in lieu of tea-time; and all employees had three nights off after 5 p.m. Horses cost 11s. a week for upkeep and their average life was five years.

In 1896 when the question of electrification came up, the Company felt disinclined to find the additional capital, and the Corporation bought over the concern at £15 per share and extinguished a mortgage — a total price of £103,785. The date of transfer was 25 August 1898. On 23 December 1899 the first electric tram ran from St. Nicholas Street to Woodside, and by July 1902, when Sunday services were instituted, the whole system had been electrified at a cost of £156,000. The Beach line was laid in 1901, the Ferryhill and Torry lines in 1903 making 12 miles of track, 8¾ being double. Woodside had the first halfpenny fares, which were introduced in Union Street in 1903. By that time the revenue was £50,986 on a capital outlay of £259,597, a ratio which probably carries a sufficient explanation why the original company decided to sell out. In 1907 the Corporation transport carried 17,676,008 passengers; in 1939 it travelled 6,709,157 miles with 77,175,353 passengers; and in 1950 the mileage was 8,373,874 and the passengers numbered 113,292,042. By then there were 105 tramway cars in service.

But even then a new power was discernible in the realm of urban transport. With the steady increase in private and commercial internal combustion vehicles, the rigidity of the tram, its distance from the kerb which had boarding and descending passengers open to accident from passing traffic, the character of the road surface which the presence of a tramways system demanded, and the cost of laying new lines on new thoroughfares as the town expanded, all combined to portend the doom of the tram. The first buses appeared in 1921. The Torry and Ferryhill routes were in the city the first to go, in 1931, bus services being substituted. But they were not the first in the area. In 1904 a Suburban Tramway Company had commenced a service from the Fountain at Woodside to Bankhead and from Mannofield to Bieldside. Here the bus conquered as early as 1926. After the war, buses took over on the Mannofield route in 1951, in 1954 the Rosemount and ·Circular routes went, Woodside in 1955, Hazlehead in 1956, and last of all the Bridges route linking north and south of Aberdeen in May 1958. The halfpenny fare which had been introduced in 1903 disappeared in 1941, the ordinary fares steadily rose until they were, allowing for shorter stages, nearly ten times the pre-1914 levels. Season tickets were discontinued in 1954. Before the trams were wholly off the streets there were 139 buses, mostly double-deckers. In 1925 privately owned motor buses were running in competition with those of the Corporation, but were gradually eliminated by economic causes. In 1914 the Town Council bought the old Militia Barracks in King Street, and when the war was over they were converted into the Corporation workshops, which had hitherto been located in Dee Village Road. Tramcars were also accommodated there, and at Queen's Cross, while at Canal Road in 1926 and at Mannofield in 1947, there were bus depots. About the same time an R.A.F. hangar in Advocates' Park was used to house buses pending permission from St. Andrew's House to develop that open space beside Advocates' Road as a central bus depot, which has now been done. The 1956 figures for the transport department gave an annual mileage of 8,160,917, passengers carried 104,656,753 and revenue £1,078,600. Before the war both the Corporation and private companies had begun to run bus and charabanc tours which remain a recreative feature.

The intrusion of local authorities and of the State into the domains that used to be considered the preserves of private enterprise has given a communal character to a great deal of industrial activity. Thus in the thirty years before 1939 Aberdeen's municipal gas department had increased its scope and output by more than 125 per cent, although the town's population had remained almost stationary. In 1914 the gas department introduced vertical retorts on the continuous carbonisation system, the first in Scotland to do so. In 1910 the department converted some 70,000 tons of coal — at 15s. 3½d. per ton — into 795 million cubic feet of gas: the revenue for gas was £92,445, for coke £15,498, and for tar and other by-products £10,543. Twenty-five years later 113,857 tons of coal at 21s. 9d. a ton were converted into 1,765 million cubic feet of gas that fetched £180,515, besides £37,690 for coke and £14,419 for tar. The price of gas had been considerably reduced to over 51,000 users. Electricity made as spectacular an expansion. In the quarter century Aberdeen's electric cables lengthened from 48 to 190 miles, the capacity of the generators rose from 6,200 horse power to 47,000, the number of sub-stations from three to fifty-five, the units sold from 5,436,000 to 46,000,000 and the horse-power of industrial motors driven by the current from 4,400 to 35,000. During those years almost £1½ million of capital expenditure was incurred, and when the war came the use of electricity was extending into all kinds of houses from west-end mansion to tenement.[1] Nationalisation, whatever else it did, stimulated their will to charge.

1   By 1948 both these thriving municipal concerns had vanished into the maw of nationalisation.

Electricity, the supply of which was secured to the Corporation by the Aberdeen Electric Lighting Order in 1890, and for which Professor Kennedy was appointed consulting engineer in December 1892, was first turned on, by the wife of Lord Provost Stewart, 27 February 1894, when ten public arc lamps were switched on in Union Street and Castle Street. The first thirty-five consumers were connected on 7 March 1894. The first generating station was in Cotton Street, and equipped with five small non-condensing steam engines driving direct current dynamos of an aggregate capacity of 257 horse-power. After the turn of the century several parishes on the perimeter and Woodside were taken into the area of supply, which by 1948 covered 97¾ square miles. In 1901 a temporary station, which became permanent in 1903, was opened at Milburn Street, on the site of the old Dee Village, and there the headquarters remain. By the mid-fifties there were almost 700 miles of distributing cables, the Aberdeen station generated only about one-tenth of the power required for the whole of the North of Scotland Hydro Board, which, when it took over, found some 114,000,000 units being sold at an average price of 1·14d. per unit to over 48,000 consumers. All these figures are now much below the present levels.

The 113-year-old Aberdeen gas undertaking was taken over by the Scottish Gas Board in 1948, being like the town's electricity 'in one red (or perhaps more accurately pink) burial blent'. The Electricity Department's Cotton Street depot was taken over as the Gas headquarters in 1905. Prepayment meters were introduced in 1900, gas was supplied to some 190,000 consumers, and at the time of nationalisation over 150,000 tons of coal were used to produce 2,366,000 cubic feet of gas, which was distributed by 286 miles of mains at from 2s. 1½d. to 3s. 6½d. per thousand cubic feet, the department's total revenue, including the sale of coke, being some £570,000.

By 1855 with the population at 75,000, using sixteen gallons of water per head, extension of the supply again became imperative. The expert, a London civil engineer this time, called in to advise, made four suggestions: (1) a 20-mile aqueduct from Paradise on the Don ending at Hilton; (2) a slightly longer aqueduct from Brig of Potarch on the Dee, ending at Springbank, costing £112,530 and yielding 5 million gallons daily; (3) a 19-mile aqueduct from Cairnton on the Dee to Springbank, costing £110,860 and giving the same yield; and (4) a direct supply from the Dee above the Bridge, pumped to elevated reservoirs and a filtering plant at Springbank, costing £107,200 and yielding one-half of the Cairnton flow. He preferred the Cairnton scheme, and a public meeting of the citizens gave approval to the proposal, which was embodied in a Bill and passed in 1862. Work began in 1864, and the waterworks at Invercannie were opened by Queen Victoria on 16 October 1866. A brick aqueduct conveys the water, over a course of 19 miles with a fall of 2 feet in the mile, to Mannofield, and at Cults hydraulic rams force the water up to a height of 400 feet. The settling reservoir at Invercannie had a capacity of 18 million gallons. The Act also gave the Town Council power to make all house-owners introduce water for a sink and a water-closet wherever there was a waterpipe within 10 yards of the house.

Even this vastly augumented supply could not keep pace with the mounting demands of a steadily increasing population. By 1885 the population was almost twice that of 1861, and the consumption had risen from 16 to 55 gallons per head, entailing a daily drain of 6 million gallons, which was the amount authorised by the Act of 1862. Accordingly in 1885 a new Act was secured giving power to take 8 million gallons daily from the Dee, and a second reservoir at Mannofield, twice the size of the first enabled 18 million gallons to be held there. At Cattofield on a lower level a reservoir to contain 2,500,000 gallons was provided, and at over 300 feet, at Slopefield, yet another reservoir with a capacity of six million gallons for the higher parts of the town. At the same time meters were installed where branches joined the mains, by which exceptional consumption could be detected and waste remedied. By this means the consumpt was reduced from 55 gallons in 1889 to 44 in 1891 and 42½ later.

Since the 1885 developments various additions and alterations have been made. In 1926 Princess Arthur of Connaught opened a new intake at Invercannie, where the two reservoirs, the original one circular and a newer one rectangular between them can store 36 million gallons. In 1930-2 the old aqueduct built in 1865 was reinforced and now carried 8 million gallons a day, while a new aqueduct laid 1922-6, carried about 12 million gallons. Since the beginning of Hitler's War the water is chlorinated to the extent of about half a part per million. Six reservoirs, at Airyhall, Slopefield, Pitfodels and Fernhill and two at Mannofield held in all 38 million gallons. There is a subsidiary reservoir at Cattofield, and the grand total storage at 1955 was over 40 million gallons equal to four days' supply. The citizens use about 53 gallons per head per day. The cold water tap, reluctant hot water systems and the flush closet between them levy a heavy toll compared with the pump, the kettle and the earth closet. In addition to domestic, commercial and industrial consumers, some 10,000 ships in the harbour use the supply.

Fairly early in the nineteenth century there were sewers running eastwards along Union Street, down the steep slope of what is now Union Terrace Gardens north of Union Bridge and discharging into the Denburn which was still an open stream. Bon-Accord Terrace had a sewer to the Ferryhill Burn, and both Crown Street and Dee Street had sewers. All these, however, were private, made by the municipality at the request and at the expense of the feuars in the areas served. It was not until 1862 that Parliamentary powers were obtained to make provision for a proper sewerage system in the burgh, and not until 1865 that steps were taken to prepare a scheme. At that time there were only 9 miles of sewers in 30 miles of streets. The completion of the Cairnton water supply in 1866 made it possible to undertake at long last the sewerage project. Its character illustrates how economically practical were the views of the local authority at that time, but how lacking they were in the facilities for carrying them through in an equally practical manner.

It was decided that the sewage of the city should be carried to an irrigation farm on the east side of King Street, north of St. Peter's Cemetery. The area of the farm was originally 14 acres, later expanded to 47. The initial rent was £250 a year for the sewage, but as time went on it was so weakened by dilution that the proprietor of the farm would not pay more than £100. Finally in 1899 the sewage farm idea was abandoned. For over thirty years, however, the town's waste was used, or intended, for the fertilisation of a substantial piece of ground that was to cover 230 acres.

The burgh was laid out in four sewage areas. One covering the south-western district, had its effluent collected in a sewer that crossed Rosemount Viaduct at Schoolhill and struck north-eastwards to the farm. The second sewer, serving the north-western district, joined the first sewer at the south-end of Blackfriars Street and became the Leper's Croft (now corrupted to Leiper's Croft) sewer. The third, draining the area south of the first district and west of the railway, joined the harbour sewer in Regent Quay and discharged its contents into the tidal waters. It is called the Footdee High Level Sewer. The sewage of the old burgh and the ancient streets followed a devious course from the top of the Porthill down to Broad Street, Longacre and Lodge Walk, then west to St. Katherine's Wynd, by Netherkirkgate to Flourmill Lane, across Upperkirkgate and along Loch Street to enter the main sewer at St. Andrew Street. By 1883 there were 50 miles of sewers.

When in 1899 the Town Council, to which control of sewage had been transferred in 1871, discarded the irrigation farm, many drastic changes in the sewage plans were made. For example, the Seamount sewer now turns down Littlejohn Street, crosses King Street, and enters one of the main sewers at Jasmine Terrace, which ultimately has its outfall at Abercromby's Jetty. The Broad Street area sewage follows the fall of the ground to Jasmine Terrace also. The north-eastern and northern districts are drained by a sewer that runs along to Westburn Road, Hutcheon Street, over to Nelson Street, across King Street to Urquhart Road and so into the Links sewer which discharges at Abercromby's Jetty. By the 1899 Act all the sewage of the west-end of the city as well as of Torry is carried under the Dee at Point Law by a tunnel 342 feet and 8½ feet in external diameter at a depth of 62 feet below high water mark, and is discharged, after passing by another tunnel through St. Fittick's Hill, into the sea at the Bay of Nigg. The last part of the track had to be blasted through rock, about 40,000 tons being shifted. An old quarry where the outfall sewer begins had been the source of the stone that built Girdleness Lighthouse. It now contains the chamber which encloses the two penstocks or portcullisses that regulate the flow of the sewage ascending to the height of the tide. The outlet sewer stretches 190 yards beyond this chamber into the sea and is 21 feet below mean high water of ordinary tides. The total length of the Girdleness main sewer, which took from 1900 to 1907 to build, is 3 miles. The cost of the 1899 scheme was £187,000, the sewers varying in diameter from 12 inches to 7 feet 6 inches.

In 1935 Parliamentary powers were secured to add substantially to Aberdeen's network of drains and sewers so as to cope with the rapidly expanding areas of municipal and private housing. The scheme, providing for 14 miles of sewerage, of which 1¼ miles were tunnelled, was estimated to cost £450,000 and finally ran out at over a million, an escalation (at the ratepayers' expense) which has become a common-place feature in all expenditure of public money.

A remarkable, but perhaps not surprising, development in the present century has been in food research. The College of Agriculture was, of course, engaged in such work after a fashion that was empirical rather than on an inductive basis — perhaps wisely so. In 1910 the first Lord Strathcona gave £10,000 towards the endowment of a Chair of Agriculture, and in 1911 the Town Council gave £1,000 and the County

Council £2,000 towards the purchase price of the estate of Craibstone as an experimental farm. Since then field trials have been a feature of the College's activities, the most energetic spirit in these, under Professor James Hendrick, who resigned from the principalship and chair in 1943, being Mr. William Findlay, part of whose work is described in his posthumous volume *Oats*, but whose most valuable contribution was to grassland farming. In 1912 an Institute for research on animal nutrition had been founded by the Development Commission, but it had no local habitation until 1920, when John Q. Rowett, a successful American rum-runner, set aside from the profits that had accrued from the business of evading the Nineteenth (Prohibition) Amendment £10,000 for the endowment of the Institute, which thereupon acquired his name. The Institute buildings at Bucksburn, with laboratory and offices, were opened in 1922. The Duthie Farm was bought and equipped in memory of William Duthie, 'the Shorthorn king', by his nephew J. Duthie Webster, who at his own death left other farms to be applied to the uses of the Institute. A library was gifted by Dr. Walter A. Reid, chairman of the Governors of Robert Gordon's College, in 1938. It contains the Commonwealth Bureau of Animal Nutrition. Strathcona House owes its existence principally to the munificence of the second Lord Strathcona, who provided one half of the necessary capital. It was opened in 1933 as a hostel for overseas research workers and students.

In 1943 the College of Agriculture and the Institute were temporarily amalgamated, the late Sir John (later Lord) Boyd Orr, director of the Institute, becoming principal of the College and Professor of Agriculture. He resigned these posts in 1945 to become the first head of the International Food Organisation with headquarters in Washington. A later addition to the agricultural science resources of Aberdeen area was the Macaulay Institute for Soil Research, to accommodate which Craigiebuckler House and fifty acres were purchased in 1930 from funds gifted by the late Thomas B. Macaulay, a former president of the Sun Life Assurance Company of Canada, and son of a native of Fraserburgh. This Institute, besides conducting pioneer work in the reclamation of land, undertakes soil surveys for farmers. Its first director, Dr. (now Sir) William G. Ogg, became Director of Rothamsted Agricultural Institute in 1943, and on retiring from that post, was elected chairman of the North of Scotland College of Agriculture. In 1968 at the junction of King Street and School Road, an imposing multi-storey building was erected to house the College. At Craibstone a school of agricultural domesticity, as it might be termed, for girls was closed down in 1966.

Fish research is of considerable importance in Aberdeen, and there are two institutions for that purpose, serving the whole country, in the city. One is the Marine Laboratory of the Fishery Board for Scotland, which maintains a specially equipped trawler for the investigation of fishery problems and has gathered a great mass of evidence regarding the habits of the herring, haddock, plaice and other fish. The second establishment is the Torry Research Station, opened in 1929, which deals with the problems of the fishing industry once the fish have been caught. There was a third research centre, the Ministry of Agriculture, Fisheries and Food Research Establishment, dealing with dehydration and other methods of food preservation. This factory, an extension opened in 1953 containing a library, darkroom, and four more laboratories making ten in all, and a suite of storage rooms reproducing temperate, jungle and desert conditions, was of great assistance in leading to the threshold of a remarkable break-through, at which point in 1961 the Government then in power closed down the exercise.

The Post Office, or its municipal counterpart, dates back in Aberdeen to 1590, when the baillies established an official post to Edinburgh carried by a man on foot clad in a special blue uniform with the town's arms in silver on the sleeve. In 1667 the postman got a horse. By 1763 an almost daily mail service by relays of horses linked Aberdeen with Edinburgh and London. The mail coach, introduced by John Palmer of Bath (a freeman of Aberdeen) in 1784, reached Aberdeen in 1798. The Post Office service, however, was not all that good. An *Aberdeen Journal* posted to Forgue in 1810 with news of the Peninsular War, took two days to reach its destination. For several years from 1819 onwards the mail coach leaving London on Monday did not reach Aberdeen until Thursday afternoon. During a great snowstorm in 1822, it took eleven days for the trip. Alexander Bannerman, later M.P. for the city and Governor of Newfoundland, rigged up a coach and took it out to the Brig of Dee, whence he drove it at full gallop to the Castlegate, hoaxing the public into thinking the mail had arrived so that they streamed down for news.

The Post Office with very small beginnings of which the most memorable is the Market Cross in the Castlegate, followed by the Adelphi, in the middle of last century reached the top of Market Street. In 1876 it took over the site of the old Fish Market, where a branch office and the Labour Exchange now are. The handsome building in

Crown Street was opened by the Postmaster-General, Sidney Buxton, in 1907; it cost over £55,000. The very modern extension whose lay-out and equipment make Aberdeen's one of the finest post offices outside London, was opened in 1966, having cost altogether £290,000 to build and equip. Aberdeen is the Head Office of 153 subsidiary offices, thirty-seven in the city, over an area of about 1,500 square miles. In 1966 nearly 36 million letters were delivered and 41 million were posted in the area.

The city was linked with the south by telegraph in November 1854. The first telephone in Aberdeen was installed in the Town and County Bank head office on 22 September 1881.

There is a multitude of agencies for what used to be called charitable work — a Lads' Club, a Girls' Club and many more for the instruction and entertainment of youth; the Royal Asylum for the Blind and the Society for Teaching the Blind in their homes are an expression of corporate assistance to those who require aid through no fault of their own; the Aberdeen Association for the Prevention of Cruelty to Children, formed in the twenties as the outcome of an Aberdeen suspicion that the Royal Scottish Society required too much of Aberdeen's sub-scriptions for the maintenance of administration in Edinburgh; and the Aberdeen Association for the Prevention of Cruelty to Animals founded in 1870, William Pyper being a prime mover, which is on terms of thorough co-operation with the Royal Scottish Society with the same purpose.

CHAPTER NINE

The University United

═══

There were several exciting, and some revolutionary episodes in Aberdeen's educational history from the middle of the nineteenth century. We left the universities of King's and Marischal at the moment of fusion as Aberdeen University in 1860, in much better shape to face the future than for a couple of hundred years before, save that it had shed James Clerk Maxwell in the achieving of that happy condition. But the fusion and reorganisation, involving half-a-dozen new chairs, mainly at Marischal, created new problems of accommodation, which, of course, meant finance. Change rather tentatively at first, but much more emphatically than ever before, was becoming the order of the day, although the mid-Victorian apostles of 'progress' would not in their wildest dreams have credited the scope and speed of the upheaval that was to come. The Universities (Scotland) Act of 1858 constituted in each University a University Court and a General Council, the latter composed of the graduates, certain alumni and members of the Court and of the Senatus. The Council had the right to elect the Chancellor, and (by an Act of 1868) to return in conjunction with Glasgow one Member of Parliament. In 1876 Dr. William R. Pirie, of the chair of Church History, succeeded Campbell as principal, and on his own death in 1885 was succeeded by the professor of Greek, W. D. Geddes.

The Universities (Scotland) Act of 1889 raised the membership of the University Court from six to fourteen and made it the supreme body in the university except in the spheres of teaching and discipline, where the Senatus remained in charge. The Students' Representative Council (established 1884) was officially recognised. In 1883 the students had launched their own weekly paper, *Alma Mater*, the first of its kind in Scotland. The Faculty of Science was created, liberty was given to women to study (one had done that already before the union) and to take degrees. The Arts curriculum, which in 1858 had been based on a four-year course of fixed subjects — Greek, Latin, English; Mathematics, Greek, Latin; Natural Philosophy, Mathematics, Logic; Moral Philosophy, Natural Philosophy, Natural History — was thrown open to options by means of which the students could graduate, it was calculated, in 617 different combinations.[1] The Medical course was extended from four to five years. These and many other changes still further strained the already inadequate housing resources of the University, and a large extension scheme was initiated in 1891.

By an Act of 1892 the Treasury doled out the sum of £72,000 a year to the Scottish Universities, of which Aberdeen's share was £14,400. This in practice — and as is usually the case with State benefactions towards objects in Scotland — proved both unfair to Aberdeen and inadequate for the purposes intended. To a certain extent this disparity was met by a generous grant from Andrew Carnegie. But financially there was no room for manoeuvre, still less for the physical expansion that the changes mentioned had rendered absolutely imperative. Just before 1891, with the aid of a Treasury grant of £6,000, the south wing at Marischal had been enlarged to accommodate the Natural History and four Medical classrooms. When the University Court specified its requirements, the Treasury offered to make a grant up to a maximum of £40,000 conditional upon the raising of a like sum locally. It was appreciated that even so large a sum (as it was in those days) was unlikely to be sufficient to meet all the costs, for apart from the actual new building, the whole of the east side of Broad Street from Queen Street northwards, had to be bought and levelled, and Greyfriars Church, according to the final plans, would have to be practically redesigned and rebuilt. In the event almost £75,000 had to be spent on that aspect of the scheme, absorbing both Treasury grant and its local equivalent.

Happily, Aberdeen has never found the people a-wanting in times of difficulty. The money was forthcoming. An alumnus of the University, Charles Mitchell, principal of the Newcastle ordnance firm of Armstrong, Mitchell & Co., offered sums amounting in all to £20,000 to build a graduation hall, a students' union and an Anatomy Department, and to heighten the central tower to 235 feet — a bountiful bequest commemorated to this day in the titles, Mitchell Hall and Mitchell Tower. On Mitchell's death in August, 1895, on the eve of the opening of the hall and the union, his son, Charles W. Mitchell made himself responsible for a further sum of £6,000 towards additional extensions in the south wing provided the university raised £10,000 more. Concurrently with the building operations at Marischal a sum

1   Robert Walker ('Functions'), University Librarian, Registrar, Clerk to the General Council, describe these options as 'no fewer than six hundred and seventeen pathways to a degree in Arts.'

of £3,000 had been raised through the efforts of the Rev. Professor Milligan and Principal William D. Geddes to install the fine organ which still graces the praise in the chapel.

Even with that assistance, the means persistently lagged behind the need, but in 1900 Lord Strathcona, delivering his Rectorial address, intimated his subscription of £25,000 provided the University could raise £75,000 within a certain time (a donation which was subsequently modified to the University's advantage), while the following day the University Court heard from Charles W. Mitchell that he was prepared to take over the existing debt on the buildings, 'provided it does not much exceed £20,000'. With another appeal to the public in the spring of 1901 and certain outlays on municipal phases of the scheme by the Town Council, the ambitious extension dream was translated into reality. The only casualties of consequence were old Greyfriars Church (although the freestone tracery of Master Alexander Galloway's pre-Reformation east-gable window has been preserved) and the house 64 Broad Street, in which Byron as a boy lodged with his mother. Charles W. Mitchell (died 1903) and Principal Geddes (died 1900) did not see the consummation of their wishes in the soaring and sparkling pinnacles of A. Marshall Mackenzie's Marischal College 400-feet frontage, which the stodgy conservatism of some art critics finds so repellent to such sense as they possess, while the wider culture of the educated man rejoices in the capture, in such intractable mould, of the aspiring quality of the cloud-capt towers of Prospero's vision. The coats of arms over the quadrangle doorway are from north to south, those of Lord Strathcona, the burgh of Old Aberdeen, Bishop Elphinstone the founder of King's, Aberdeen University itself, the 5th Earl Marischal, founder of the toun's college, the burgh of Aberdeen, and Charles Mitchell — a noble group of worthy benefactors, friends and institutions of Bon-Accord. The buildings of the college extend backwards for some 600 feet.

For various reasons which are of no consequence today the Quater-Centenary celebrations in connection with the University were not held until the autumn of 1906. On that auspicious occasion, and largely thanks to the always ready liberality of Lord Strathcona, by this time Chancellor of the University, the occasion was honoured on a scale thoroughly worthy of the best traditions of Aberdonian ceremonial and hospitality. The celebrations continued through four days. On the first there was a reception of delegates and University guests, of whom no fewer than 374 had accepted invitations, followed by a Town Council banquet in the Music Hall. Next day the degree of Doctor of Divinity was conferred upon seventeen and of Doctor of Laws on 102 distinguished men. In the afternoon there were sports at King's and a University reception in King's College Library, and in the evening a reception in the Art Gallery and a Students' ball in the Music Hall. On the third day, Thursday, 27 September, King Edward VII, accompanied by Queen Alexandra, inaugurated the new buildings at Marischal College.

After the Hall of the Incorporated Trades had been opened to the visitors during the afternoon the Chancellor gave his banquet in the evening in 'the Strathcona Hall', a tremendous if temporary structure erected for the occasion in the vacant ground on the Gallowgate north of Marischal College. This Hall, designed by Marshall Mackenzie, could seat 4,740 and dine 2,500, and it cost £3,400. The banquet itself, worthily described by Neil Munro as 'this gigantic feast where all the culinary resources of the South had been requisitioned to give the North one evening with Lucullus' was a terrific affair, an unforgettable milestone in the minds of those present, and now almost a legend in the tales of the Aberdeen that is gone.

It was not for nothing that Sir Frederick Treves, the Rector, the following day expatiated on 'the extraordinary immunity that that community appeared to possess against the effects of alcohol'. The menu of the dinner, greatest of all Aberdeen's banquets, and not likely to be paralleled now that we have entered into the twilight of the dwarfs, although the final seal of perfection would have been set on it, had the Roti contained Aberdeen-Angus beef, cannot be omitted from a history of the city. It reads thus:

Vins
Sherry
Gonzalez, Byass & Co.
Royal Pale

Hock
Rudesheimer Bosenberg, 1895
(J. B. Sturm)

Champagne
Heidsick and Co.
Dry Monopole, 1898

Hors d'Oeuvre
Melon Cantaloupe Glace

Potage
Tortue Claire
Poissons
Darne de Saumon — Sce. Ravigotte
Filets de Soles Bagration
Mayonnaise de Homard
Entrees
Chaudfroid de Cailles Lucullus
Perdreau Souffle Souvaroff

Relever
Cotelettes de Pre-Sale Jardiniere
Roti
Poulards de Surrey
Langues de Boeuf Epicurienne

Claret
Chateau Ducru Beaucaillou
1896

Jambon d'York
Balotine de Pigeon
Salade de Saison
Legume

Port
Warres Finest Old

Asperges en branches
Sce. Vinaigrette
Entremets

Liqueurs
Mineral Waters
Apollinaris, Perrier
Schweppes

Charlotte Russe
Timbale de Fruits Parisienne
Gateau fouree Mascotte
Marrons Chantilly
Dessert

Cigars — Villar y Villar (Regalia de Paris), Cabana (Regalia).
Cigarettes — Quo Vadis, State Express.

The last day of the celebrations was Students' Day, when many of the distinguished visitors gave the undergraduates a taste of their wisdom and their wit.

For nearly a decade after the alterations at Marischal the University Court had a respite from building cares. But the pressure steadily increased for more accommodation, and in 1913 what was called New King's, built on the north side of Regent Walk, was opened to house the English, History, French and German Departments — the two latter brought over from Marischal — the inaugural lecture being delivered by Professor Grierson on 'The Background of English Literature'. In 1913 a bequest of £29,000 from William Robbie, a Finzean-born Australian, and in 1920 a legacy of £20,000 from Miss Agnes Maclennan were put to good use. The Church reunion of 1927 carried the Divinity classes of the Church of Scotland at King's to the U.F. College, renamed Christ's College, at the west-end of Union Street. In the twenty years between the wars a certain amount of expansion — timid indeed in comparison with the explosive growth in the fifties and sixties — brought Botany to the site of the old 'Gym' in the Cruickshank Botanic Gardens at the south west corner of the Chanonry, and the building north of the Cromwell Tower of the Elphinstone

Hall opened on 5 June 1931, with its suite of reception and larger rooms, part of the stones coming from Castle Newe which had succumbed to taxational strangulation. On 3 September of that year Marischal College was floodlit for the first time.[1] A replica of the Elphinstone tomb was placed before the west-end of the chapel and other less noticeable changes were made. The Hitler war again interrupted extensions but the building of the new Royal Infirmary at Foresterhill foreshadowed the transference of many medical classes and the clinics to that part of the city, while the moving of various mainly Arts classes to Old Aberdeen actually for a time raised speculation on the sale of Marischal College to the Corporation. Before the war the University authorities had committed themselves to a policy of real civic statesmanship by unostentatiously buying up property in Old Aberdeen. As a result, when the resumption of development became possible the Aulton was in truth a university precinct and Aberdeen was spared the not very seemly wrangles between Town and Gown that St. Andrews experienced and the controversies over the destruction of historical amenity that resulted from Edinburgh University's desire to find elbow-room.

After the war, amongst various blessed words that bourgeoned in politics, Education took a prominent place, and higher Education, which had never received much attention south of the Border began to acquire an almost mystical significance particularly in the realms of Science and Technology. A rash of 'red-brick' establishments which broke out in England eventually and to a limited extent spread to Scotland, but the four old Scottish universities were too full of tradition and character to be converted into training colleges, and their share of the consequences of the new crusade was to absorb more students. Aberdeen's undergraduate population which in the early days of the century had been from 600 to 800 had doubled by the late thirties and by the fifties was at or over 2,000. But even that was not enough to drain off the ever increasing numbers of those who aspired to a university degree of some sort. The figure talked about in governmental quarters in the early fifties was 2,750, which rose by the end of the decade to 4,000 or more and looked forward by the end of the sixties to

1   To show that Aberdeen is no laggard behind Oxbridge in 'double-column news', it may be recalled that on 11 December 1931, a medical student, Charles Ludwig (killed in the war while serving with the R.A.F.) climbed the Mitchell Tower and crowned the spire with an article of domestic china which subsequent hygienic fashion has tended to make obsolete.

6,000. Such numbers involved not merely a prodigious building programme in the shape of class rooms, laboratories, reading rooms, all the paraphernalia of modern study, but also — because for various reasons the corps of Aberdeen landladies who had taken charge of students for well over a century could no longer cope — of halls of residence with all their auxiliary suites, of car parks and other amenities. The Court's quiet buying in Old Aberdeen now paid sumptuous dividends, but even so there was not room enough and in the long run the former policies of Seaton House which had been converted into a public park at the south end were leased for playing fields from the Town Council, and at the north end for a residential development, Hillhead of Seaton was acquired where modern building techniques have, fortunately, not been permitted irretrievably to spoil one of the most lovely reaches of the river Don which is probably unique in the country as an example of *rus in urbe*.

The first big building scheme was for the Chemistry Department on the old Market Stance north of Meston Walk. There the wonders of modern architecture arrest the artistic eye much as the iguanodons and pterodactyls on the plateau of the Lost World attracted the biological scrutiny of Dr. Challenger. It was in 1952 that Chemistry moved from Marischal to its new home. A variety of other buildings gradually took shape in Old Aberdeen and at Foresterhill, notably the Taylor Arts Building linked to what so comparatively recently had been designated as New King's and now seemed part of the older structure. The Students' Union which had migrated from the eastern end of Marischal quadrangle before the War to the corner of the Upperkirkgate and Gallowgate, was extended and eventually it and certain university offices absorbed the former home of the Aberdeen University Press. Across the road from King's the Crombie Hall, the first Hall of Residence in the United Kingdom in which students of both sexes found rooms, was reinforced by the Johnston Hall in the old grounds of Powis Lodge, and the Dunbar Hall was later built to the east of the Cathedral. Not only was the gracious hall of the King's Library turned into a reading room, but a false ceiling was inserted to provide a second floor with numerous alcoves opening off it. Whereas there were at the end of the Kaiser's War but two libraries, at King's and Marischal, by the mid-sixties there were eight, the staff had increased from six to sixty, and the annual expenditure on books from £5,000 to over £40,000. The bill for the building expansion both erected and in the course of erection, stood by the later sixties at almost £9,000,000.

Just after the Second World War the Agricultural Department purchased the mansion house of Tillycorthy, near Udny, with three farms of close on 600 acres as an experimental and demonstration unit. When the headquarters at Craibstone of the North of Scotland College of Agriculture, a kind of Cyprian handmaid to the University, were destroyed by fire, a new lecture and headquarters building was erected — and completed in 1968 — at the north end of the University playing fields in King Street. In 1955 a property at Newburgh on the estuary of the Ythan was purchased for ornithological purposes, a field study centre for geologists, geographers and similar students near Muir of Ord north of Inverness was bequeathed to the University, and a house at Farr on the north coast of Sutherland was purchased as a botanical field centre.

This is not a history of Aberdeen University, in respect of which an elaborate presentation of detail would be out of place here, but the progress of Aberdeen as a civilised community has been so interwoven with the academic fortunes of its two colleges, both before and after they became one, and the mutual services as between Town and Gown have been so various and so valuable to both that some record of the character of the modern university cannot be omitted without impairing the truthful presentation of Aberdeen's story. In the hundred years, or rather more, that have elapsed since the Fusion, the University has, like the Burgh, changed almost beyond recognition, the only constant factor in both, and perhaps the only dependable quality in both, being the natural genius of the people born in the Aberdonian area and those bred (as the old idiom had it) at Aberdeen's University. So far as the latter is concerned, that change has presented itself in four different but quite separate ways. These changes were, and still are, welcomed and deplored, according to the habit of mind of those who saw them in the making and have observed them as they developed. It seems to be relevant to our story to give some consideration to these issues.

The first and probably the most fundamental change, was the substitution, already referred to, of a wide selection of courses for the four-year all-round Arts degree. The old dispensation was a marmoreal affair, that demanded exact knowledge, a sternly disciplined mind, and an infinite capacity for hard work in those who successfully toiled through it. The Arts graduate who emerged was a well-educated man (there were no women then to take it). He had a thorough grounding in those basic subjects which have already been mentioned, and a number of the students actually found the time and energy to add a modern language or some other non-curricular subject to their tally.[1] The formidable array armed the Aberdeen graduate for successful combat in any intellectual armageddon anywhere. It was essentially a cultural training and as practically everyone passed through it who intended to proceed to other faculties, not the least of its benefits lay in its presenting the community with doctors, scientists, lawyers, clergymen, who were not simply narrow technicians in their own profession. When the old curriculum was superseded, it was still possible, and indeed common practice, to take a course which contained a backbone of the former curriculum, but the temptation of soft options grew, not only amongst students but with educational legislators, until between the wars a desperate effort, which eventually proved impracticable, to firm up the Arts course took the form of a compulsory two-year attendance at Mathematics and Natural Philosophy.

Second perhaps in importance in the change has been the vast distension of the University. Until the First World War there were fewer students than there now is staff, while the student body has quadrupled and will within a few years be at least ten times as numerous as it was before the entry of women in the nineties. It is no doubt beneficial to the State that the virtues of education should be as widely disseminated as possible, but reform even when (which is by no means always the case) it makes for progress inevitably involves some loss. In this case the loss is the close relationship which existed between students and professors. It is impossible for the latter today to have much personal contact with and therefore precise knowledge of the capacities of their students, except, of course, their honours people. When students were few several professors had the members of their class in batches for an evening in their houses. In classes where there was clinical, experimental or practical work, and in a system which depended to a certain extent upon oral sessions there was bound to arise a closer relationship between the rostrum and the benches which grew into something more genial if there was a promising response among the occupants of the latter. No one in fact who in ordinary class displayed reasonable ability escaped the notice of the professor. The result was that every man who matriculated and who applied himself became in a very short time a member of a fraternity which included the professoriate

1   This is perhaps extraordinary today, but it was quite common before the Kaiser's War to extend voluntarily the range of the curriculum. We knew one First Class Classics man (killed at Loos) who took eight classes in his final year.

as elder brethren, while to be an undergraduate was to enjoy a privileged position in the eyes of the professors whatever their faculty.[1] Such a relationship is, of course, quite impossible now. Its passing is regretted by many professors but its existence is unknown to the acolytes, the extension of the imported tutorial system, which does provide a link between staff and students, having actually tended to interpose a barrier between professor and undergraduate.

The great revolution is in the character of staff and students alike. Aberdeen University is regarded in Scotland as enjoying a happy proportion of overseas and English undergraduates to its aboriginal or at least indigenous students. But the expansion of staff has resulted in the number of Aberdonians or Aberdeen-bred professors, lecturers, readers and so on being submerged in those hailing from other universities, from south of the Border, and even from other lands. Again this is no new phenomenon in Aberdeen, although it was never so pronounced before. King's was founded by a Glaswegian (or a Spanish Borgia!), its first Principal, many of its Chancellors, several of its most illustrious later principals and professors were not Aberdonians, and even Marischal, the toun's college, which preferred its own fish, knew eminent exceptions, the last one of all Clerk Maxwell being the most renowned. He would be a bigoted Aberdonian who would suggest that 'foreigners' have been responsible for any lowering of the University's aims or achievements, except in one particular. Across the seven seas the great advantage an Aberdeen man finds he possesses is being an Aberdonian. And that quality was reinforced by the rigour of the training conducted by Aberdonians who were inspired not at all by what they would have regarded as the nonsense of the equality of man and the virtue of specialisation.

Which leads to the last major point of difference between the old and the new. Until the 1918 Education Act all Scottish education, whether at school or university, was directed by the belief that the foundation of knowledge was general intelligence and that by training of the mind in such subjects as most thoroughly induced accurate thinking, the pupil or student could in the fullness of time and at will apply his mental powers successfully to any subject or section of a subject that he fancied. In the half-century that has elapsed since the impact of that in many ways

1   These statements contradict a passage in the Introduction to the 'Fusion' Centenary Number of the *University Review* from which it is to be gathered that (before 1900 at least) the gulf between professor and student was not bridged. There is, however, much evidence the other way, even in the Victorian epoch; certainly in the years after 1890.

calamitous legislation, the opposite view has gained control, and the early specialisation which has for long been a feature of the English style of education, in performance much inferior to the traditional Scottish style, has tended to take its place. This concentration upon a single topic — which puts the student much in the position of the hound at the dog stadium which chases an electric hare hemmed in by the walls of an alley — may be regarded as accentuating the deficiencies of the optional courses in the faculties. The emphasis, in other words, is on training instead of education.

The stresses created by these changes did not become serious until the twenties. During the sixty-five years or thereby that elapsed between Fusion and that date, the University reached the apex of its academic achievement. Its two constituent parts had had their moments. King's men round about the Union of the Crowns, Marischal products just after the time of the French Revolution had carried Aberdeen's name far beyond the marches of Scotland; while Marischal in the mid-seventeenth century and King's a hundred years later had been notable for the eminence of their professors. But from Fusion onwards to the mid-twenties Aberdeen University excelled its components singly or together (except perhaps, but only perhaps in the international celebrity of its graduates, where the standard was the King's men 300 years before). Whether, in those years to 1925 it out-topped the period since then will not, of course, be clear for some time to come.

It is out of the question in short compass to present the achievement of Aberdeen University men in the professions, in business, in the British Empire and in the wider world. It is possible only to present some evidence indicating the nebulous limits of their spheres of influence. In the decade 1858–67 five Senior Wranglers at Cambridge hailed from Scottish universities, four of them from Aberdeen; and it is interesting to observe that three of these had gone to the English University before Fusion in Aberdeen, and all four of them had come out of King's.[1] One family, the Nivens, had four Wranglers — Senior, third, eighth and fifteenth — and ranks in intellectual eminence almost with the Gregories and Fordyces and equally with the four educational Ogilvie brothers, who became respectively the headmaster of Gordon's College, the headmaster of George Watson's Edinburgh, the director of the Church of Scotland Training College, and H.M. Inspector of

---

1   This offers an odd commentary on the unquestioned eminence of Clerk Maxwell: he was less successful than Thomson or Fuller in fitting out men for scientific distinction.

Schools for Scotland. On a par with these were the six Dunbar daughters of a Banffshire shepherd who graduated between 1905 and 1914 and the five members of a grocer's family, four of them girls, who collected a Cambridge fellowship and a knighthood, while one was in M.I.5. Between 1856 and the First World War, just on eighty graduates or alumni of the University were successful in entering the Indian Civil Service by the stiffest of all the Civil Service tests, 'planned without relation to Scottish candidates and conducted by English scholars'. One barony and four knighthoods were won and the Aberdonians provided four Governors or Lieut-Governors of provinces, five members of the Governor-General's Council and one each of the Council of India and the Council of the Secretary of State, four Chief Secretaries to Provincial Governments, two members of provincial executive councils, chief commissioners and commissioners and high court judges in quantity. As a pendant it may be recorded that the first place in the first two competitions for entry to the Indian Medical Service were filled by Marischal men, and in the next three years Aberdeen recorded a second, a third and a fourth. Until Britain left India, the Aberdeen Roll of Graduates was peppered with the names of I.M.S. Colonels. A further significant feature of the Roll was the number of native Indians in it who came to occupy responsible posts in both official and civil life.

Curiously suggestive in the Rolls are the Sinhalese from Ceylon and the Dutch from South Africa who crop up from time to time. Five graduate members of one family emigrated to South Africa, where they rose to positions of trust, epitomising the fact (which happens to be truer than history as it is written) that the inconspicuous contributions of Aberdonians to the development of that great country have been more constructive and more rewarding to the inhabitants of whatever colour than anything done by Milner or Kitchener or even for that matter Rhodes, who depended a great deal more than he admitted on his Aberdonian associates and whose opportunities for unhappy intervention in the politics of the Cape would have been considerably curtailed had not fate intervened to thwart the prospects of an Aberdonian born near the verge of Rubislaw quarries. The link with China is also remarkable. Several Chinese are graduates, one of them very eminent indeed in recent Chinese history; while several Aberdonians have maintained a long connection with the country and acquired such facility in the language and knowledge of the race as to be advisers thereon to British Governments. In South America the Aberdeen graduate has confined himself mainly to business interests, in which also in North America many names occur in high positions which are to be found in the Roll of Graduates. One graduate fell at Isandhlana, one was murdered along with Cavagnari at Kabul, one has been adviser on the Congo — surely one of the trickiest of political assignments — to the secretary of the United Nations, another the U.N. technical administrator in a succession of South American Republics; one was a companion of Speke the African explorer, another in the Antarctic wastes has an island named after him, one has gone into history as 'the Father of Tropical Medicine', another was the founder of the Royal Society of Tropical Medicine and Hygiene, one was the administrative head and governor of six colonies in succession, another of four; the Royal Botanic Gardens at Calcutta have had several Aberdeen superintendents, and missionaries and moderators are a commonplace in the Roll. One Scottish lawn tennis champion and a British Open Golf Champion are perhaps the most outstanding in sport, but heavy-weight athletes, association footballers and Rugby internationalists are numerous.

The distinctions gained at Oxford and Cambridge have been frequent, there are many fellows of the Royal Society and more of the medical and surgical colleges both of Edinburgh and London; there have been seventy-four knights, three baronets and two barons, twenty-five principals of colleges and 123 professors; five M.P.s, twenty-five editors, one field-marshal, two lord justices of appeal, several heads of departments in the civil service, and one Senator in the College of Justice which is generally regarded as an Edinburgh preserve. The contributions of graduates and alumni to the public services and the still more vital economic, industrial, commercial and social life of the North-Eastern community will emerge elsewhere. It should be said, however, that while the University has drawn its students from all classes, professions and trades, there has been a special loyalty to it amongst the middle classes of the city of Aberdeen itself and the so-called working classes of its hinterland. The only section of the population that has not availed itself of the higher educational facilities at its door has been what is termed the landed class, the ancient (and not so ancient) proprietorial families, whose scions (with, we believe, only two exceptions in recent times) have by-passed the University which their forebears helped to found, almost invariably attended, and never ceased in their peregrinations over the western world to honour.

It has already been pointed out that this is not a history of Aberdeen's University, and these remarks are, therefore, far from completely descriptive or adequate to a most fascinating subject. Something of the historical work done in the past on the development of this renowned and dignified school of learning obtains mention elsewhere. This short and inadequate analysis of the more recent achievement of its sons and daughters requires the addition of a brief appendix. The University's Roll of Honour for the First World War contains the names of 341 of its graduates, alumni and students who lost their lives in that disastrous struggle, in the course of which 2,852 served in the armed forces or performed work of national importance. Eleven knighthoods, ninety-four companionages, and seventy minor orders, 250 decorations for gallantry, 501 mentions in dispatches, ninety-three foreign orders and decorations, and in all, with certain other recognitions, 1,066 distinctions fell to the University's family.

The academic achievements that have been mentioned owed, of course, something, perhaps more than a little, to the professional competence of the university staff. It is invidious to single out individuals for special mention, since many a professor was an inspired teacher yet has left no permanent memorial of his skill in the way of books or discoveries through research — although ability to turn out such evidence does not actually qualify as testimony to his gifts in the classroom. Nevertheless, if a complete picture of the united university is to be presented, some attempt has to be made to assess the staff, or at least those members of it who best lend themselves to such portrayal. The period to the mid-twenties was extraordinarily rich in professorial personalities, whose character and idiosyncracies and even prejudices impressed themselves as emphatically upon the college community as their various talents.

The first two Principals after Fusion, Peter Colin Campbell and William Robinson Pirie, devoted themselves mainly to the administrative side of their duties. But with Sir William Duguid ('Homer') Geddes in the last fifteen years of the century Aberdeen University began to spread its wings. Geddes was a most powerful inspiration not only to the staff but to the students — a Hellenist, a poet, a scholar, with a clear sense of what the purpose and end of university education should be. His successor John Marshall Lang is remembered on two counts. One was his welcome, delivered without a note, to the distinguished company assembled in the Strathcona Hall for the Quatercentenary celebrations. The other was the procreational schizophrenia that enabled him to beget a Moderator of the General Assembly of the Church of Scotland and an Archbishop of Canterbury. On Lang's death in 1909 there was appointed George Adam Smith, theological scholar, scientific historian — he had sat, like Saul at the feet of Gamaliel, before William Robertson Smith — orator, preacher, whose services to his country during the First World War in presenting the British case to a somewhat sceptical America that still remembered the burning of Washington, thoroughly earned his knighthood. During the full quarter-century of his incumbency he gathered around him a devoted band of professors and kept in touch with undergraduate life through his Sunday afternoon gatherings at Chanonry Lodge, recreating the atmosphere of *le gai savoir* that had characterised the Geddes regime. By the time of his retirement in 1936 (he died in 1940) the period we have elected to discuss came near to an end. His immediate successor, Sir William Hamilton Fyfe, whose wife was the daughter of a first bursar and notable Grecian of Marischal, John Forbes White, manfully wrestled with indifferent health, failing eyesight, the exacting trials of the Second World War, and the little less distracting conceptions of the immediate post-war Government of the functions of education until 1948. Sir Thomas Murray Taylor, the third Aberdeen-reared Principal since Fusion, had a distinguished career both in classics and law. Upon his head descended the building problems of the great expansion, so that he was driven to complain that he accepted the post of Principal of a University only to find he was a clerk of works.

For a University with traditions resting principally upon the Classics and Mathematics, it may superficially seem odd that Aberdeen's major achievement, in the main cultural faculty of Arts, should have been in English, a department that did not achieve independence until 1894 after twenty years as a sub-division of Rhetoric and thirteen as a partner of Logic. But the explanation is simple. From 1860 to 1938 English was imparted by, in succession, Alexander Bain, William Minto, Herbert John Clifford Grierson, and Adolphus Alfred Jack — the first three Aberdeen graduates — and their cumulative influence produced a remarkable sequence of critical and creative writing quite capable of standing comparison with the output in the same genres of any contemporary university, Scottish or otherwise. Edinburgh had during approximately the same period Masson, Saintsbury, Grierson and Dover Wilson — the first and third Aberdeen graduates — but while their personal production was formidable, that of their school has been less notable.

Humanity had Sir William M. Ramsay, the eminent archaeologist and a magnificent teacher; then Alexander Souter, expert in 'silver' Latin, who was succeeded by Peter Noble, later Principal of King's College, London, now a knight — all Aberdeen men. Greek, on 'Homer's' elevation to the principalship, had his son-in-law John Harrower, another inspired teacher, for nearly half-a-century, to such purpose that the University now has a Harrower chair of Greek Art and Archaeology. To Bain and Minto in Logic there succeeded William Leslie Davidson, Bain's particular disciple, and a logician and philosopher outstanding in his day. He and Harrower were also Aberdeen graduates. James Black Baillie, Hegelian and most mellifluous of lecturers, eventually became the highly successful Principal of Leeds University. John Laird, who followed him in Moral Philosophy, had a European reputation. Charles Sanford Terry, an Englishman, was responsible for establishing the department of History on a footing firm enough for it to compete with the older chairs; he was, and remains, the great authority on John Sebastian Bach. Hector Munro Macdonald, for over thirty years to 1935 the Professor of Mathematics, was Smith Prizeman and a Fourth Wrangler. Charles Niven, Senior Wrangler, and reputed to have passed a wireless message between Marischal and King's before Marconi came on the scene, was in the chair of Natural Philosophy for forty-two years. He was succeeded by George Paget Thomson (now Sir), one of the world's leading nuclear scientists today. French and German during most of the period were only lectureships. Political Economy, elevated to a Chair in 1921 by the munificence of Sir Thomas Jaffrey, attracted to Aberdeen another blithe spirit in Alexander Gray, later knighted, who until 1934 when he passed to a similar chair in his alma mater, Edinburgh, contrived to keep the dismal side of his subject sternly under control.

There was one feature of Aberdeen University education during the last four decades of the nineteenth century which was unique in that it operated outside the University and depended upon the genius of one man. David Rennet came to Aberdeen about 1856 and set up as a mathematics coach. His success in that capacity year after year with all kinds and conditions of men was beyond the comprehension of lesser mortals belonging to a subsequent age. With the broad doric into which he so frequently lapsed, with his amazing capacity for expounding and expiscating a difficult problem in mathematics or physics, with his uncanny appreciation of the character of each student who presented himself to his ministrations, and with as a background to all his technical expertise the broad culture and sterling individualism which constantly lightened and diversified his observations, never did rarer spirit steer aspirant and often erring humanity. It has to be pointed out that the students who laboured under his eye in Golden Square worked out their calculations with skylie upon slates, and that, the absence of cuffs being no doubt general, his injunction for the memorising of an important subject to 'pit it doon on yer thoom nail or ony wye whaur ye'll no forget it' was as practical as the more conventional parts of his teaching. 'Water that's drumlie is nae aye deep' was his judgment of certain areas of Teutonic philosophy in which he was no doubt influenced by his strong Francophile opinions. 'A pint o' licht hits A an' syne stots aff to B' more easily describes one natural phenomenon than conventional English could hope to do. As John Harrower said, to do justice to him would call for the co-operation of a syndicate for the men of all faculties in those days presented themselves at his footstool so that he dealt with Classics and Mathematics pure and applied, Philosophy, and the whole gamut of subjects, and coached for all the examinations from that for the Indian Civil Service downwards. When he died in the autumn of 1914 a lamp brighter than those which had been quenched three months before over Europe went out in Aberdeen University. He was the fulfilment of the pious founder's hope that King's would be the Lamp of the North.

The distinction which the four preceptors of English had in their sequence given to Arts was imparted to Medicine most spectacularly by three colleagues. John A. ('Daddy') MacWilliam (Physiology 1886–1927), Sir John Marnoch (Surgery 1909–32), and Sir Ashley W. Mackintosh (Medicine, 1912–28) stamped their dynamism upon all who came in contact with them. MacWilliam probably had the widest reputation for his researches into cardiac functions. Marnoch was noted for what the *cognoscenti* in these matters called 'the beauty' of his operations. Ashley Mackintosh had the most distinguished academic career ever registered in Aberdeen University. He entered as First Bursar, took his Arts degree with a double first, in Classics and Mathematics, took his M.B.,C.M. with first-class honours, and his M.D. with first-class honours. He died on 14 October 1937. His main interest as a consultant was with nervous disorders, but he took all illness for his portion, and it was recorded that one who had consulted him and went on to Sir Morell Mackenzie was told by that acknowledged head of his profession that he was no court of appeal from Mackintosh.

But, of course, both before and contemporaneously with the trio there were notable men — in Surgery Sir Alexander Ogston (1882–1909); after MacWilliam in Physiology J. J. R. Macleod (1928–35), whose name is associated with insulin; the succession in Anatomy of John Struthers (1863–89), Robert W. Reid (1889–1925), and Alexander Low (1925–38). Last but far from least Matthew Hay (Forensic Medicine, 1883–1926) to whom Aberdeen's magnificent Joint Hospitals scheme owed its inception. As a result of Matthew Hay's conception, Aberdeen was able, in professional opinion, to challenge Edinburgh's supremacy in the medical schools of the United Kingdom, its smaller size and wealth of exceptionally competent instructors making for more personal teaching.

In the Science side the most prominent name is that of one whose stay was all too short, spanning almost exactly as it did the First World War from the outbreak to the signing of the Peace Treaty, Frederick Soddy, whose researches into radio-activity made him as Professor of Chemistry a fitting complement to Paget Thomson in Natural Philosophy. In the natural sciences James William Helenus Trail, (Botany, 1877–1919) followed in the great tradition of MacGillivray and George Dickie, and although a pedestrian lecturer, turned out a constant stream of first-class systematic botanists as it was his job to do. Sir J. Arthur Thomson (Natural History, 1899–1930) rivalled Grierson as the University's most exciting lecturer, and by his books and his readiness to give lectures extra-murally spread the knowledge of and interest in zoology far and wide. One whose career faithfully illustrated the Aberdonian spirit was the University's lecturer in Statistics, James Fowler Tocher, a country chemist who followed up his 'Major' degree by taking his B.Sc. and D.Sc. at Aberdeen, and attaining a national reputation as an anthropometrist and as an analytical chemist. He died on 29 October 1945.

The two schools of Divinity that existed in Aberdeen from shortly after the Disruption in 1843 were merged soon after Reunion in the late twenties. At King's Henry Cowan (Church History, 1889–1924) and George David Henderson who succeeded him (1924–57), William Milligan (Biblical Criticism, 1860–93), and James Gilroy (Hebrew, 1895–1932) are best remembered. The Free Church College, whose disconnection with the Establishment perhaps made for more speculative adventures in Theology, enjoyed the ministrations of William Robertson Smith, Principal Iverach, and later Principal David S. Cairns and James A. Robertson, both of whom came into the united

College. In Law the second occupant of the Chair, George Grub (1881–91), made the greatest impact, but Law was most fortunate in its subsidiary lecturers on Roman and Constitutional Law, who were wont to be practising advocates in the city with a leaning towards these subjects. Indeed in all the faculties the university had been enriched and enlivened by the ability of its lecturers.

One other and almost legendary figure of those days must be mentioned, though more will be said of him elsewhere. Peter John Anderson, who came from Inverness and who as a bajan 'sat' (actually stood) for Sir George Reid's painting of King's with a togaed student, became to the great gain and glory of the University the Librarian in 1894 and clerk to the General Council. In many respects the College community when he died in 1926 regarded him as the University, for which he lived and worked and had his being. His successor, and occupant of the post for the next forty years, William Douglas Simpson, nobly emulated his wide research work, though in a different line of country, and his sudden death in 1968 deprived the North-East of one of the most devoted of its sons.

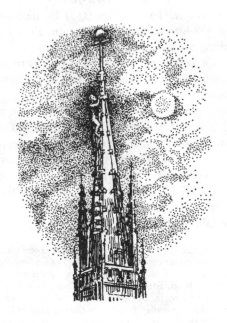

CHAPTER TEN

Townsmen in Arms

In 1859 in the unsettled state of Europe the Government sanctioned the formation of individual companies of volunteers and an Aberdeen Volunteer Rifle Corps was embodied in the summer of that year, consisting of two companies, whose rifles later were handed over to Her Majesty's Theatre and used to arm 'supers' on the stage. A further company, the City of Aberdeen Merchants' Rifles, was commanded by Captain William Stevenson, a provision merchant, whose martial enthusiasm called forth what is probably the first published work of that great artist, George Reid, himself a member of the unit and then a lithographer with Keith and Gibb. This apprentice effort, a thin quarto volume entitled *Ye Nobell Cheese-Monger*, consists of a score or two of stanzas of doggerel verse illustrated by half-a-dozen or more drawings of the Volunteers and their captain. Reid drew and wrote out the whole thing for lithographing, and he may have had a hand in the verses.[1] At the same time the artisans of the town provided the Artillery Rifle Corps, in three companies, one of which was drawn from the railway servants.

All the infantry volunteers were fused into a single regiment under Lt. Col. Napier Turner Christie of Corsee House, Banchory, who held the command for about a year, when he was succeeded by Major Thomas Innes of Learney. The regiment was then known as the 6th Aberdeen Royal Volunteer Corps, and had at one time 762 actual strength. In 1861 a Highland Company, nicknamed the Drovers, was raised and put into trews, and soon after another company was formed which wore the kilt. Both companies had pipe-bands. Unfortunately,

1 The writer's copy, the only one he has seen, was given him by Dr. William Kelly, who also had never come across another complete copy. It contains a pencilled sketch of Stevenson's head and some additions in pencil to one of the pictures, all by Reid. Stevenson's warehouse was at 5 Belmont Street, and his house Burnieboozle, but he is called 'of Viewfield'. Another of the characters in the skit, 'Drouthy John', was the assessor of lands and heritages for the burgh, and the leader of the band who figures in one of the cartoons was probably James Wood, a photographer at the top of Crown Street.

an inspecting officer animadverted on the appearance of the trews, and a sergeant of the Drovers inserted an advertisement in the local press criticising the critic. Such insubordination had to be treated with dismissal, but the incident rankled with the Drovers, and one of Innes's first jobs was to strike them off the roll. He was succeeded by Lieutenant-Colonel Henry Knight Erskine of Pittodrie, under whom the kilt was discarded and the whole regiment got a green uniform. In 1862 a headquarters in Blackfriars Street in the old militia depot was set up. Later the corps feued ground there and built the Woolmanhill Drill Hall.

In 1862 also there was held, mainly by the energy of Colonel Thomas Innes of Learney, in forming the Aberdeen Rifle and Artillery Association, the first of the modern wapinschaws. The site was in the Links north and east of the Broadhill, about half way to Donmouth, near where the 'Magazine' used to be in our day. It lasted for three days, from 7 to 9 July, and there were forty company and 700 individual entries. The highest scorers were Corporal James Tytler, later a well-known C.A. and Private Harvey Hall who became President of the Society of Advocates, both from the office of Lachlan Mackinnon. The Ladies' County Brooch was won by Corporal Alex. Mackie, landlord of the North Hotel, opposite St. Andrew's Free Church, and the Aberdeen Shooting Badge by Private George Wilken, Ellon.[1] On the second day there was a grand review of troops, 180 regular, 718 militia and 1,631 volunteers, the line stretching from the foot of the Broadhill to beyond the Beach fort at the Ropeworks. The first of the Royal Reviews of Victoria's reign had been held on 7 August 1860, in the Queen's Park, Edinburgh, when 464 officers and men of the 6th Aberdeen Rifle Volunteers and thirty-eight of the 4th Aberdeenshire Artillery were on parade. In 1881, at the famous Wet Review, Aberdeen's contingent numbered 647 from the 1st Aberdeen Royal Volunteer Corps under Colonel Jopp, who had succeeded Erskine in the command in 1862, and only resigned in 1890 to make way for Colonel Douglass Duncan, and 480 Artillery and 127 Engineers. In 1863, it should be added, 331 of all ranks received the Queen on her arrival in Aberdeen, and

1   It is interesting to note, as illustrative of the diversity of Aberdonians' activities, that one of the units on parade was commanded by Colonel Cosmo Gordon of Fyvie, in whose black polled herd originated the Fyvie Flower family that formed the basis of the breed in New Zealand, where 90 per cent of the beef cattle are Aberdeen-Angus; and that George Wilken, who became tenant of Waterside of Forbes at Bridge of Alford in the first five years of the 1880s exported 1,000 Aberdeen-Angus to North America and bred Waterside Matilda 2nd, a multi-champion of the breed.

Volunteers took part in the pageantry or street patrols on all Her Majesty's subsequent visits.

In 1859 four artillery corps of a total strength of 361 officers and men were raised, and were amalgamated in 1874 as the No. 1 Battery, 3rd Aberdeenshire Artillery Volunteer Corps. The name of this unit seems to have been one of the most serious problems exercising the War Office in those days, for it figures in 1880 as the 1st Aberdeenshire Artillery Volunteer Corps, next as the 1st Aberdeenshire Artillery Volunteers, and in 1891 as the 1st Aberdeenshire Volunteer Artillery. The headquarters were for long in the Gymnasium, Queen Street, and Lieutenant-Colonel Youngson was in command for nineteen years. He was succeeded by Colonel James Ogston of Kildrummy. In 1878–80 a movement was set on foot which ended in the latter year with the founding of the 1st Aberdeenshire Engineer Volunteer Corps under Lieutenant-Colonel William Hall and 172 strong. The Engineers put in a lot of practice, their first feat being to throw a barrel-pier bridge across the Dee. Lieutenant-Colonel R. N. Anstice succeeded Colonel Hall in 1889. The previous year the War Office sanctioned the formation of an R.A.M.C. unit which had already been brought together, 101 strong in 1886 under Surgeon Alexander Macgregor.

All the while the infantry were going ahead. In 1880 they exchanged their green uniform for red coats and Gordon tartan trews, and in 1895 a kilted company was again permitted, and gradually the kilt became the garb of the whole battalion. In 1883 ambulance lectures and gymnastics were introduced, as well as sword exercises for officers. In 1884 the Government adopted the system of linking volunteers to their local territorial regiments, and in conformity with this Aberdeen's infantry became the 1st Volunteer Battalion Gordon Highlanders (the 4th Battalion belonged then to Donside). In 1890–1 a cyclist section was attached to the unit, and in 1898 there was a rearrangement of companies and U Company, first commanded by Captain W. O. Duncan, came into being for the University. It was Captain Duncan who took out the relief draft to the City Service Company that joined its Regular battalion in the Boer War, this company being originally under Captain J. B. Buchanan and Lieutenant Frank Mackinnon. At Doornkop the company had three killed and thirteen wounded. An engagement of a very different kind was on 18 November 1900, when under the guidance of Charles Murray, the author of *Hamewith*, and the real founder of the Transvaal Scottish, whom he garbed in the Murray tartan and of which unit he was the first recruit, visited Cecil Rhodes's farm.

Captain Duncan was a kind of general servant of the battalion, for he took twenty men to help line the route in London of the Diamond Jubilee procession.

In the 1860s there was a rifle range for the militia at Nigg, and there about 1865 Lachlan Mackinnon saw the Aberdeen Rifle Volunteers practising with muzzle-loading Enfield rifles. The range had to be closed when bullets dropped into the navigation channel and on to the north pier. After 1867 the Snyder needle-gun was issued. The marking was done by flags held out by the marker from the shelter of an iron butt, The bull's eye was 8 inches, the centre 2 feet in diameter. The original uniform included a shako for full and a glengarry for un-dress, officers wearing the 'pill-box' and chin-strap. The uniform carried bronze ornaments with the thistle, and the city arms and 'Bon-Accord' on the waist-belt buckle. The officers had black gloves and to begin with their undress uniform jacket was fitted with braid tabs with long free ends, which the War Office later prohibited as encroaching on the uniform of a cavalry unit.

After 1884 the men got the 'long rifle' of army pattern but had to drill with it as if it were the 'short rifle'. The volunteer had to carry it vertically at his side instead of shouldering it, and was not permitted to fix bayonets when marching past but had to carry his rifle at the trail. At the Wet Review, at which greatcoats were not allowed, uniforms to the value of £700 were ruined. The *Scotsman* commented that 'along with certain of the Glasgow battalions and the Queen's Edinburgh brigade, the Aberdeen men carried off the palm'. After 1906 the officers — it might have been thought the experience of the Boer War would have taught the authorities to know better — were authorised to wear the feather bonnet to distinguish them from other ranks.

In 1890 and until 1900, the period during which Colonel Douglass Duncan was in command, the battalion was thoroughly reorganised and a wide variety of training measures introduced. In 1895, for instance, the battalion was the first volunteer unit to spend a week-end in the country. In 1896, in the course of training, there was a surprise parade of all the volunteers in the city, the summons being given by rockets. In 1900 Colonel George Cruden took over, being succeeded by Colonel Lachlan Mackinnon, whose spell of command, owing to business commitments was curtailed to two years, 1904–6. In 1902 the battalion had been at Aldershot for what was a completely wasted week, during which they did and learned nothing and where some of the more out-spoken officers are understood not to have concealed their opinion of

the Regular Army's organisation and ideas. At the 1905 Review
Colonel George Milne was in command of the Royal Garrison Artillery
unit, Colonel W. S. Gill led the Royal Engineers, the R.A.M.C.
detachment was under Major J. Scott Riddell, and of course Colonel
Mackinnon had the 1st V.B.G.H. Colonel D. B. D. Stewart succeeded
Colonel Mackinnon in the command. W. O. Duncan became Hon.
Lieutenant-Colonel in 1907.

The excitements of the South African War — the disasters at
Colenso, Spion Kop and Magersfontein, the relief of Ladysmith[1] the
relief of Mafeking and the end of the war in 1902 were soon seen to be
mere ebullitions of childish feeling when the First World War broke
upon the country on 4 August 1914. In all respects except perhaps its
political and social consequences, it was a much worse war than its
successor of twenty-five years later. Civilisation in 1914–18, however,
still had a fabric strong enough to stand the strain, and a sufficiency of
people survived with intelligence robust enough to bear the tension of
those four years of strife and their immediate aftermath.

When war broke out Colonel J. Scott Riddell was at once appointed
Red Cross Commissioner in the North-East, and the first hospital
train, bearing 100 casualties, steamed into Aberdeen on 25 September,
the next on 3 October. Within a few days of the outbreak, Aberdeen's
Territorial infantry battalion, the 4th Gordons, had joined the big
camp at Bedford, while most of the other units belonging to the city
were established in training centres throughout the country, their
barracks in Aberdeen being occupied by second line recruits, of whom
over 800 had joined within a month. On 25 September came the first
'black-out', on 21 November the first Red Cross flag day, which realised
£946 7s. 8d. Bread rose to 7d. for the 4lb. loaf on 23 November, and
within six months had risen to 9d., while meat had gained 2d. a lb.
While the disaster which sent several hundreds of 1st Gordons from
Le Cateau into German prisoner-of-war camps hit Aberdeen, there

1   Aberdeen had a special stake in the Ladysmith affair for the little town's
defender, General Sir George White, V.C. was Colonel of the Gordons
and as such was entertained in Aberdeen with much splendour when on
August 23, 1902, he opened the Gordon Highlanders' Institute in Belmont
Street (formerly the Deaf and Dumb Institution) as a memorial to Lieutenant-Colonel Dick-Conynham, V.C. and the officers and other ranks who
fell in the Great Boer War. Captain H. V. Brooke of Fairley was president
of the Gordon Highlanders Association at the time — one of his sons became secretary of the Aberdeen Territorial Force Association between
the wars, and another was Captain Brian Brooke (Korongo) V.C. — and
the Secretary of the Institute Club was another Gordons V.C., Lieutenant
and Quarter-Master Robertson.

was a feeling of greater imminence of danger in the loss of the trawlers *Crathie* and *T. W. Irvin* blown up in the North Sea.

By the end of July 1915, twenty-nine of Aberdeen's fishing fleet had been sunk by enemy action, direct and indirect. At the beginning of this year Aberdeen's two Victoria Crosses were won by Gordon Highlanders, Lieutenant Colonel J. A. O. Brooke, who was subsequently killed, and Drummer, later Drum-Major, W. Kenny. On 10 March there was a stirring parade of 4,500 garrison troops, and the City of Aberdeen Brigade of Artillery, raised by Lord Provost James Taggart, and the Rev. James Smith, St. George's-in-the-West, was nearly 700 strong. The sinking of the s.s. *Aberdeen* with sixteen of its crew was a severe blow and so also were the casualties inflicted by a U-boat raid on trawlers on 2 May, four being killed and fourteen wounded. The men who remained at home were beginning by this time to undertake part-time war work. A year after the war began Aberdeen had 300 special constables, and by the end of 1915 an Aberdeen association had been formed to co-ordinate voluntary war work in the city. The Hooge battle early in summer and Loos in September cost the city's territorial infantry a woeful casualty list, and the flower of the brains of the North-East, the University lads who had joined U Company, was cut down.

Lieutenant-Colonel Thomas Ogilvie took the 4th to Bedford and to France. He left in February 1916, having been on leave for a period in the summer of 1915 when Major Alexander Lyon was twice in command. After Colonel Ogilvie came home, in the intervals of command by regular officers, Major Lachlan Mackinnon, Jr. and Major C. D. Peterkin were several times in charge, and in spring and summer 1917 Major Lyon was back. The battalion got a bad mauling in the March 1918 retreat, when Major James Gordon, then C.O., was wounded; he returned to take over after the armistice for a spell.

The 1st Highland Brigade R.F.A. on the outbreak of war was commanded by Colonel Macbeth Moir Duncan. The three batteries of the brigade were under John Everard Rae, James William Garden and Frank Fleming, the C.O. and the first two battery commanders being lawyers and the third a timber merchant. Shortly after mobilisation Major J. E. Rae and Captain F. W. Kay were promoted and returned to Aberdeen to raise the second line brigade. Rae's place at the 1st Battery was taken by Thomas Davidson, of Mugiemoss Paper Works. Eventually Colonel Duncan was invalided out, his successor being Colonel Fleming who brought the brigade home.

The Sappers went to France under Colonel Harry J. Kinghorn with Major Alexander B. Robertson in command of the Signals company, which was not separated from the Royal Engineers until 1921. Robertson was the first Aberdeen Territorial officer to be appointed to staff colonel. He was badly gassed in the March 1918 retreat, and Kinghorn was wounded earlier, being succeeded by Angus Mitchell, while Colonel T. P. E. Murray, who was A. B. Robertson's second-in-command, was in charge in 1953 when this unit became the 51st Highland Signals. As a result of their distinguished conduct at the front Colonel M. M. Duncan, Colonel David Rorie, R.A.M.C., and Colonel Sam Macdonald of the Gordons, later a Sheriff-Substitute at Aberdeen were promoted to the equivalent rank in their respective services of Brigadier-General.

In the first year of the war volunteer training corps were raised to take the place of the regulars and territorials if and when they went overseas, this home defence organisation being filled by men who by age or imperative civil duties could not be expected to undertake active service. Colonel Lachlan Mackinnon, Sr., was the first C.O. of the Aberdeen unit which ultimately mustered over 1,000 men. He was succeeded in 1916, when he became County Commandant of the Volunteers, by R. W. Walker. In 1917 the Aberdeen Volunteers were inspected by Lord French, by which time they included an artillery section and a transport section. In 1916 a military tribunal was set up. When the war ended the volunteer battalion was under Major A. H. C. Mackinnon.

At the beginning of 1916 the street-lighting regulations provided for the black-out at 10 p.m. Aeroplanes could not fly from Germany to Aberdeen then, and the main precaution was to prevent the betraying of the position of the city to a naval force, but on 2 May Aberdeen almost had an air raid, when a Zeppelin, losing touch with a force that had attacked Edinburgh, lost its way and, misled by an avenue of private lights, bombed but failed to hit the ancient Gordon stronghold of Craig Castle.[1] A recruiting tribunal was set up in February; an early-closing order for certain classes of shops came into force at the end of October. Meanwhile, by May 1916, the cost of living had risen 40 per cent on August 1914. Whisky was 6d. a glass and 7d. and 8d. for special, while pale ales were 3s. 6d. the dozen and strong ales 4s. 6d. the dozen for off consumption. This increase (whisky was soon 400 per cent up since the war) may have predisposed Aberdeen Town

---

[1] In 1929 a German balloon with three men in it, which was sent up at Leipzig, drifted to Dover, made its way up the North Sea and finally came to ground at Torphins on 11 January.

Council at their first meeting in 1917 to favour total wartime prohibition. By Christmas milk was 5d. a quart and meal from 3s. 8d. to 4s. per stone.

Restriction and stringency grew during 1917. There was a potato famine in the spring with potatoes themselves at 1s. 9d. the stone. Someone began to think others should be 'digging for victory', although the public mind in 1917 was hardly so childish as to need slogans to energise it. That spring 173 plots were allocated to ready gardeners; a year later there were 2,300. In the autumn cattle prices were fixed at 74s. in September, 72s. in October, 62s. in November and December, and 60s. in January, all per live hundredweight. Milk went up to 2s. a gallon. The sale of new baps and 'buttery rowies' was discontinued. On the other hand, Aberdeen's rates, although they showed an increase of $4\frac{3}{4}$d. on 1916, were only $26\frac{20}{32}$d. on occupiers and $16\frac{24}{32}$d. on owners.

In the spring of 1917 Aberdeen witnessed some wild political trouble, issuing from a profound spirit of principle which, if maintained, might have warded off endless misfortunes later. Some Socialist extremists came to town to speak. Ramsay MacDonald was howled down and pelted with assorted vegetables one night, the following evening Pethick Lawrence held a meeting which evoked street rioting that required a baton charge to quell, and a night or two later some Gordons raided the same gentleman's platform in the Trades' Hall. In June when the Russian Socialists were trying to smother down the war by talking to any who would listen, Messrs. Ramsay MacDonald and Jowett set off from London to make for Stockholm by land and sea. They were to embark at Aberdeen, but the Sailors' and Firemen's Union were in the city before them, and the innocents bound for abroad were accosted as they left the station and made clearly aware that whatever boats might leave Aberdeen, they would not travel by them.

At the beginning of 1918, thanks to the last gamble of the final U-boat campaign, food became scarcer and prices rose further. The 4 lb. loaf rose to $9\frac{1}{2}$d., flour to 2s. 1d. per stone, eggs from 3s. to 3s. 4d. a dozen, potatoes to £5 10s. a ton. In January two meatless days were introduced, on 7 April meat rationing arrived with a weekly ration of 1s.; and ration books made their appearance on 15 July. Aberdeen's first Tank Week raised £2,501,000, and in summer 360 boys went from Aberdeen schools to assist in the harvest. Finally, almost suddenly, came the Armistice, solemnly acclaimed in Aberdeen by a church thanksgiving, a parade of discharged servicemen and a students' torchlight procession. On 12 November the lights went on again, but no longer on the scenes of yore.

Peace hath her tribulations no less renowned than war. On 3 February

1919 coal rationing was added unto us, and by midsummer coal was up 6s. a ton with the miners beginning to talk of the New Elysium. Milk reached as high as 3s. 4d. a gallon. In April 1920 the 4 lb. loaf was 1s. and the city, despite the boom, had already 1,700 unemployed. Coal rose by 14s. 2d. in May and the 4 lb. loaf to 1s. 1d. In September coal went up another half crown thanks to a 100 per cent increase in railway rates. Nevertheless local food control was abolished on 25 June 1920. The immediate consequence was that meat rose by 8d. per lb. only to drop again at once. The loaf rose to 1s. 4d. but by the beginning of 1921 had fallen to 1s. 2d. and by October to 1s. In the middle of the year food prices were 17s. 5d. against 22s. 7½d. in December 1920. City rates for 1920 were very inflated, 6s. 1¾d. for owners and 8s. 7d. for occupiers, but by 1921 they were lopped by 3s. 11½d. During 1922 coal was at 48s. and the loaf was at 8d. in 1923. In 1921 the licensing hours were fixed at 10.30 a.m. to 2.30 and 5.30 to 9.30 p.m.

The Second World War, much better conducted (after a shaky start) both in the field and the cabinet so far as the United Kingdom was concerned, soon put a stop to all conventional social practices except perhaps that of drinking. On 1 September the Territorial Army was mobilised and window-darkening decreed, but it was not until 5 October that the 4th Gordons, under Colonel William Philip and R.E. Signals under Colonel T. P. E. Murray left Aberdeen for their training areas in the south. The Gordons went to France that autumn, but after Dunkirk they remained in this country as a motorised battalion for the rest of the war. Colonel William Philip took them to France; Colonel Alex. Milne was C.O. till the war's end. The so-termed phoney war which supervened until Hitler invaded Denmark and Norway did not extend to the sea. On 28 November Aberdeen's s.s. *Rubislaw* was sunk and thirteen drowned. On 9 January 1940 a ship was bombed and sunk off Girdleness, on the 21st the *Ferryhill* was sunk and on 7 March a German plane flew high over the city without dropping anything, and was chased and shot down by a couple of planes from Dyce, where the civil airport had been almost entirely commandeered by the Air Ministry. On 15 April citizens had the unusual experience of seeing a brigade embark on the *St. Sunniva* and other steamers for Norway, the authorities in London having for once realised that Aberdeen is the natural port for British communication with Scandinavia or did they think their opposite numbers in Berlin would never guess that so unlikely an embarkation point as Aberdeen would be selected?

The invasion in May of the Low Countries and France suddenly brought home to both Government and public the hitherto scarcely realised fact that Hitler meant business. On 30 May the Local Defence Volunteers were instituted, later to be known as the Home Guard, and as it consisted for the most part of the men who had thrashed the Germans in 1914–18 it probably was as great a deterrent as any to plans for the invasion of Britain. Aberdeen had three battalions, the 4th or City, the 6th or Post Office, and the 7th or Works. Eventually the first and third of these units were entrusted with the perimeter defence of the city in place of the regulars. The 4th was commanded by A. S. Anderson, the 7th by R M Ledingham. Their crowning achievement was on 31 May 1942, when two battalions of the 52nd (Lowland) Division and a Recce company attacked the city's Home Guard defences. Despite the fact that the umpires whom the Army had undertaken to supply to the defenders failed to turn up, the 'Battle of Bon-Accord' ended in the elimination of the attackers in the judgment of their own umpires, the predominately ex-51st Division of the Home Guard having been specially concerned to teach their old rivals a lesson. When, more than two years later, the 52nd so competently mopped up a German town as to earn special publicity, the Aberdeen Home Guard found complacent satisfaction in pointing to the education the repulse had imparted in the 'Battle of Bon-Accord'. Apart from the citizen soldiers, Aberdeen had for defence a battery of 3.7 guns at Balgownie and another of 4.5s at Balnagask, and — after air raids had ceased — a spectacular array of rockets beneath the Broad Hill.

The Air Force at Dyce was kept pretty busy. Its first alert was a curious one. On 3 August 1939, the Graf Zeppelin, looking for all the world like a small rain-cloud above the horizon, appeared off Aberdeen, no doubt on a reconnoitring expedition. A Dyce plane went out and photographed it, but it was some time before the German Embassy in London retracted its original denial of its presence and pleaded a navigational error or something of that kind in extenuation of what came very near to an invasion of Britain's air space. On 26 June 1940 a house at Tullos was bombed. On 30 June Walker Road School was burnt, on 12 July in a very bad raid when a bomb just missed Old Machar Cathedral, another smashed a granite yard off King Street, and yet another fell on the Neptune Bar at Footdee, crowded with shipyard workers in their lunch-break. The casualty list, dead and wounded, was over 100. The raider, chased by Spitfires from Dyce, crashed in flames over the Ice Rink in Anderson Drive South. On 28 August there was a bomb on Forbesfield Road, and the next day a raider bombed Oscar

Road in Torry. On 4 November three were killed in Wellington Road and on the 14th the s.s. *Highlander* was sunk off Aberdeen. The first visitation in 1941 was on 13 February when Ogston & Tennant's soap factory was burnt out and the Loch Street Bar hit, with casualties, in a snowstorm. On the 19th a beached leave ship, already badly damaged and from which corpses for many days were washed ashore at Balmedie, was bombed off the Bridge of Don. July was a pretty interrupted month, with on the 24th three 'alerts' in one night. On 5 August Poynernook Road was the main target. J. M. Henderson's engineering works was bombed on 27 April 1942, and there were seven casualties in a raid on 7 August. The biggest raid of all was on 21 April 1943, when the 'double-red alert' lasted from 10.26 to 11.21, the worst hit area being George Street and its adjacent streets and in the newer housing districts in the northern quarter of the city. The 'tartan kirkie', St. Mary's Episcopal in Carden Place, was badly damaged and bombs fell but failed to explode in Westburn Park near the Royal Mental Hospital. The raiders were lucky as their first bomb upset the predictor on the eighteenth green at Balgownie which put the 3.7 battery temporarily out of action. The official casualty list was 97 killed and 235 wounded, but there may have been more, as a squad at the barracks was wiped out and army casualties of that kind were not separately identified. The last aerial visitation of consequence came in 1944, on 22 April, when a German plane was shooed away by gunfire. Thereafter the Civil Defence volunteers who had served most nobly during the four preceding years, were free of worry, and the fire-fighters at the various works and shops and in the street groups could sleep out their period of duty without disturbance. The Royal Observer Corps and the other Women's Voluntary Services, the War Comforts Fund which financed parcels to the troops and the Prisoners of War Fund performing a like service to the prisoners in enemy hands, the cadets, male and female, and a host of other organisations, mostly nation-wide in structure, had all their branches in Aberdeen. The National Fire Service volunteers had had their share of excitement, and had their organisation ruffled as a by-product of the scandal at the city crematorium involving the disposal of coffin lids and other trappings of mortality and affecting a member of the Town Council and probably being connected with a change in the fire service direction. All in all, while life in the city as elsewhere was dull enough until Hitler collapsed in the summer of 1945, Aberdeen had sufficient excitement to be able to claim a high if not the premier place in the Kingdom in the number of its 'alerts'.

CHAPTER ELEVEN

The Art of Writing

In 1872, responding to the increased tempo of the age, to better facilities for the collection of news, and to the greater demand for news, the *Free Press* became Aberdeen's first daily newspaper, but the weekly edition was continued. The *Journal* followed suit in 1876, and in 1879 laid new foundations of prosperity by commencing an afternoon paper, the *Evening Express*, which had a three years' lead over the *Free Press* afternoon paper, the *Evening Gazette*, and never lost the ascendancy it then acquired. In 1886 the Irish Home Rule controversy convulsed the country, both *Free Press* and *Journal* professed Liberal-Unionist views,[1] and in consequence the Gladstonian Home Rulers in the area felt that they should have a medium to express their opinion. The *Northern Daily News*, first appearing on 13 May 1891, was the result, but it never paid and was suspended before the end of 1892, an afternoon successor, the *Northern Evening News*, being no more fortunate and coming to an end in March 1893. In the last quarter of the century there were a good many light periodical publications, the best and most enduring example being the *Bon-Accord*, which, with a break during the First World War, continued until a strike closed it in 1959. A vivacious weekly of the same style in 1922, *The Aberdonian* came to an untimely end. Amongst many other effusions of the kind, in which wit and good draughtsmanship were conjoined, *Holloa!* deserves mention for its quality, although it only produced a few numbers.[2] *The Meteor*, of which No. 1 appeared in December 1884, may have been the only issue of a rather smart sheet published by D. Macpherson, bookseller. Between the wars the local Labour Party tried a short-lived sheet, the *Citizen*. Up to the end of the nineteenth century 160 newspapers and periodicals had appeared in Aberdeen.

1 Of the Alexander brothers who conducted the *Free Press* group of papers, Henry, who edited the *Free Press* itself, was a Liberal-Unionist, but William, the author of *Johnny Gibb*, was a Home Ruler.
2 The 'manager' was C. A. Wilson, son of the famous pioneer photographer, G. W. Wilson.

In 1922 the *Aberdeen Daily Journal* and the *Free Press* amalgamated as the *Aberdeen Press and Journal*, the *Evening Gazette* being discontinued. The *Fishing News*, which the *Free Press* had conducted for some years, continued publication in London. In 1927 the Aberdeen papers were taken over by Allied Newspapers, and a few years later became part of the Kemsley Newspaper Group. In 1959 the whole group was purchased by Mr. Roy Thomson and became part of Thomson Newspapers. The *Aberdeen Almanack*, reputed to be the oldest periodical in Europe, came to an end in 1955/6 and the *Aberdeen Weekly Journal* in 1957. No account of Aberdeen periodicals is complete without mention of *The Aberdeen Book-lover*, published at irregular intervals from 1913 to 1931 by D. Wyllie & Son, and edited by Robert Murdoch Lawrance, who subsequently had his essays individually reprinted and tastefully bound. They numbered several dozen.

Of the Aberdeen journalists who remained at home, the greatest, William Alexander, the author of *Johnny Gibb*, is dealt with in another connection than his newspaper life. The pride of place in metropolitan journalism which Aberdonians had achieved in the late eighteenth and early nineteenth centuries was not lost in later decades. Of the Victorian journalists perhaps the most spectacular was the celebrated war correspondent Archibald Forbes (1838–1900) whose remains now lie in Allenvale Cemetery. A native of Boharm, where his father was minister, he attended Aberdeen University, enlisted in the dragoons, left the army for journalism in 1867 and first made his name in the Franco-Prussian war by his telegrams from the front to the *Morning Advertiser* and the *Daily News*. He entered Paris with the Prussians, was nearly drowned as a German spy, and reported the Commune.[1] He then was with the Carlists in Spain, at the Schipka Pass and the siege of Plevna in the Russo-Turkish war, reported the second Afghan War (in which another Aberdeen alumnus was murdered in Kabul) and the Zulu War. In the latter campaign after the Battle of Ulundi he rode 110 miles in twenty hours and 170 miles in thirty-five hours to find a telegraph office with his report. He refused a war medal. Aberdeen University conferred upon him its LL.D.

No Aberdonian exercised greater responsibility in London, and indeed in international journalism in the present century than William

---

1 Another Aberdonian, Miss A. M. Davidson, then at school in Paris, witnessed the burning of the Tuileries Palace during the Commune. Sixty odd years later she had the curious complementary experience of finding herself in a Bavarian inn while a gentleman named Adolf Hitler was addressing his supporters in the adjoining beer-cellar.

Lints Smith. Born in humble circumstances in Aberdeen, he began life as a clerk in the Combworks, joined the *Aberdeen Daily Journal*, became editor of a small local newspaper in the English provinces, held various other reportorial posts, and on the day the First World War broke out was appointed by Lord Northcliffe as Associate Manager of *The Times*. He became manager in 1920 and for the next seventeen years he wielded the great authority of that arduous office with outstanding ability. 'During this period *The Times*', says the official history of the newspaper, 'under his commercial direction and with the benefit, it is just to emphasise, of the delayed results of Northcliffe's reorganisation, rose to a degree of prosperity it had not known for half-a-century. Printing-House Square had been extremely fortunate in having, during its immediate post-war Northcliffe period, the services of a Manager with sound commercial instincts who also possessed varied editorial experience.' He retired in 1937.

William Will, a Huntly native who also trained in the *Daily Journal*, had a somewhat similar career, filling reporting positions, editing an English local paper, entering London newspaperdom as manager of the *Daily Graphic*, from which he graduated into managing director of Allied Newspapers, during which time he was mainly instrumental in the take-over by that group of the Aberdeen Journals Company, and latterly of Kemsley Newspapers. He was a keen Burns enthusiast, wrote *Robert Burns as a Volunteer* and *William Murdoch the Tutor of Robert Burns* as well as an inquiry into the life of the Doric, *Our Persistent Speech*, and a short history of the Kincardineshire Volunteers. He was very prominent in the work of the Royal Caledonian Society of London and its various charitable activities.

For some time editor of the *Daily Graphic* and later literary and dramatic editor of Allied and then of Kemsley Newspapers, John Malcolm Bulloch (1867–1938) bulked large for many years in the estimation of Aberdonians. A graduate in 1888 of Aberdeen, he went to London after serving his journalistic apprenticeship in the *Free Press*. His great feat in London was as a theatre first-nighter, his collection of programmes being unrivalled. He wrote assiduously first of all bright facile verse as a student, when also he helped found the student magazine *Alma Mater* and was the Aberdeen representative on the committee of the four Scottish Universities that was responsible for that excellent musical anthology, *The Scottish Students' Song-Book*. Thereafter he turned his attention to the Gordon family, and a succession of studies of Gordon cadet families and estates streamed from his pen, the solid keep of the whole structure being his three-volume *House of Gordon* which was published under the aegis of the New Spalding Club. He also wrote a history of Aberdeen University, of which he became an LL.D. in 1921. He was a son of John Bulloch, author of *The Pynours* (otherwise the Pioneers), the old name for the Aberdeen Shore-Porters Society whose recorded history goes back to 1498, and certainly antedates the exploits of Christopher Columbus, and which gives its name to Poynernook Road. J.M.B.'s brother William, also an LL.D. of Aberdeen, was Professor of Bacteriology in the University of London and an F.R.S. He died in 1941.

Contemporary with Bulloch was Howard Alexander Gray, who graduated in 1888 and was trained on the *Free Press*. He was assistant editor of the *Birmingham Daily Post*, editor of an evening paper there, leader writer on the *Pall Mall Gazette*, assistant editor of the *Observer* under J. L. Garvin from 1928. The corresponding post on the other big Sunday paper the *Sunday Times* was held by a product of the *Aberdeen Journal* J. Brodie Fraser. A little later than these came James D. Symon (1867–1925) who graduated in 1892, trained in the *Free Press*, was last editor of the *English Illustrated Magazine* before it was sold in 1901, and thereafter was principal assistant editor of *The Illustrated London News*. He wrote an excellent book on the young Byron entitled *Byron in Perspective* and a readable history of newspapers, *The Press and its Story*. Another Aberdonian, William Hutcheon, whose brother James was manager of the North Bank, was the first non-Oxbridge creature to be admitted to a cell in the celebrated editorial corridor of the *Manchester Guardian*, from which he went to London as foreign editor of the *Morning Post*. On its staff he had for a colleague Ian D. Colvin, another product of the *Free Press*, the very Rupert of polemical artists, who as leader-writer under H. A. Gwynne slew the Amalekites with wounding words from the Bible and *The Pilgrim's Progress*. His political eccentricity became rather too much expressed in fancy in *The Unseen Hand in British History*, 1917, which was a pity because before the war he had written a set of political satirical verse better than anything since the *Anti-Jacobin* or perhaps even Dryden. Hutcheon wrote a semi-autobiographical *Gentlemen of the Press* which is still breezy reading to newspapermen.

These names do not exhaust Aberdeen's contribution to the major journalism of those days. An *Aberdeen Journal* trainee, Robert Bruce, became editor of the *Glasgow Herald* and a knight. Morley Brown, once caseroom foreman on the *Journal*, ended as editor of the *Sunday*

Referee. Charles Innes Beattie, a graduate of 1896, after being chief-sub-editor in the *Free Press*, became a sub-editor in *St. James's Gazette*, chief-sub-editor on the *Observer*, joined the *Daily Mail*, became a director first of Associated and then of Northcliffe Newspapers and editor of the London *Evening News*. Robert Donald, yet another of the *Free Press* young men, became editor of the London *Daily Chronicle*, which chair he filled until the paper was amalgamated with the *Daily News* under the somewhat dubious auspices of Mr. Lloyd George. Frank Low, chief reporter of the *Free Press* when it was merged in the *Press and Journal*, went to Bombay and became editor of the *Times of India*, receiving a knighthood for his advisory part in the final grant of independence to what used to be called 'the sub-continent'.

Of journalists on the staffs of local newspapers, Alexander Mackintosh, London representative of the *Free Press*, was over several decades the chief support of the paper in an intensely political community, his 'London Letter' being a daily feature eagerly looked forward to, although when he embodied his recollections of the great Parliamentarians, whose friend he was, in book form they seemed to lose their vividness and his pen its racy power. A chief sub-editor of the *Free Press* who became editor of the *Journal*, Robert Anderson, was a mine of information on Aberdeen and its history and hinterland, wrote a book on Deeside and edited the fourth edition of Dr. Pratt's *Buchan*.

Many others fared forth to America, South Africa, Australia, South-East Asia and made names for themselves within the Fourth Estate, but one other member of the fraternity, but a member with a difference, deserves a paragraph to himself. William Robertson Nicoll (1851–1923) was the son of the first Free Church minister of Auchindoir, who amassed a library of 17,000 volumes and who became the subject of his son's biography *My Father*. Nicoll graduated at Aberdeen in 1870, and while still a student and later during his ministry at Dufftown and Kelso he dabbled in journalism beginning with the *Aberdeen Journal*. On retiring from Kelso through ill-health he became associated with Hodder and Stoughton the publishers, for whom he edited several books, wrote others, and from 1884 until his death edited *The Expositor*. In 1886 the *British Weekly* was founded with Nicoll as editor. His contributions were 'The Correspondence of Claudius Clear', one of the most vivacious causeries in all journalism, articles by 'A Man of Kent' and those over his own initials, and he gave their chance to Barrie, Crockett, Ian Maclaren, Joseph Hocking, and others, although one clerical author whom he offered to assist replied, 'I am as God made me;

I have no wish to be nicoll-plated'. He founded *The Bookman* in 1891 and *The Woman at Home* in 1893 and was recognised in the period of Liberal ascendancy from 1906 to 1914 as the most reliable of political prophets, though as a bosom friend of David Lloyd George he did not escape calumny. He was knighted in 1909 and made a Companion of Honour in 1921. Amongst his many books was a life of another distinguished Aberdeen journalist, James Macdonell of *The Times* (1842–79).

The *Aberdeen University Review*, the organ of the graduates of the University, was not instituted until 1913, almost thirty years after the students' periodical. It was to begin with issued three times a year, and coming as it did so near to the outbreak of the First World War, it became the natural medium for the presentation of the university's Roll of Service, eventually revised and collected in book form. But the *Review* was not by a long chalk Aberdeen's first university magazine. The first attempt in that direction, which appeared in 1836 was not properly speaking a magazine but an extended pamphlet published to combat the Fusion proposal put forward by Alexander Bannerman, M.P. for Aberdeen at that time. A twopenny effort of 1846 *King's College Miscellany*, and the much larger *Aberdeen Universities Magazine* of 1849–50 derived from the Mutual Improvement Movement which originated in the village of Rhynie and spread far and wide particularly in the country places. The *Aberdeen University Magazine* of 1854 which was a graduates' production, and *The Student* of 1857–8 from Marischal, were the last attempts at an academic periodical before the Fusion. After 1860 there came *The Aberdeen Medical Student*, 1872–3, and on the same professional lines the *Aberdeen University Gazette* 1873–4; while *The Academic* of 1876–7 represented the only Arts response until the founding of *Alma Mater*.

It was after William Thom's death and in the second half of the nineteenth century and subsequently that Aberdeen became a nest of singing birds. They were not all nightingales or even mavises, and some may have been as imitative as starlings, but at least they were doing something which was from time to time and more or less readable. The Williams of that time have already been glanced at, but so far as Doric poetry went the greatest of the lot was a lawyer's clerk named Alexander Taylor, a native of Stonehaven who in the later forties went to Edinburgh, where he enjoyed a double-barrelled reputation as a rhymester and as an astronomer. His first effort — and it is very impressive indeed — appeared in the *Aberdeen Herald* in 1857 and is entitled 'Lummie'. Lummie purports to relate the tragic history of the then farmer of Lumgair, near Laurencekirk, whose reputed devotion to John Barleycorn was heightened and intensified by Taylor into a tragedy related with gusto and superb effect. Adam of the *Herald* thought, not unreasonably, that it was the best thing since Burns's 'Captain Grose's Peregrinations'.[1]

William Forsyth might with some justification be described as the first of the Aberdeen University wits of the Victorian era — although there were other graduate rhymesters before him of less account. A disparate collection of versifiers, some of them worthy of the name of poet, brightened the academic quadrangle of King's and Marischal from 1870 on. There was Duncan Macgregor, later minister of Inverallochy,[2] whose vivacious squib, *The Scald*, 1874, was written in Alexandrines of all things, the whole 650 lines of it. There was Principal Sir William Geddes himself and his *Flosculi Graeci Borealis* which illustrated the Hellenic equipment of his Greek class and was to a certain extent balanced by the *Musa Latina Aberdonensis* edited by William Keith Leask, himself both Grecian and poet of no mean order. There was George MacDonald, LL.D., the novelist whose *Scotch Songs and Ballads*, 1893, are not as well-known as they deserve. There was Alexander W. Mair, the infant prodigy who won the Liddell Latin Prize four years running and of whose Greek verse Sir William Ramsay declared he 'was the best Greek poet since the last Greek poet of the Anthology died'. He became Professor of Humanity at Edinburgh, but his heart never left Old Aberdeen and his 'King's Revisited', the first poem in the volume piously selected and edited by Herbert John Clifford Grierson, is the loveliest thing ever created about King's since the Crown and Chapel took shape.

Ronald Campbell Macfie, a doctor, who earned the rather equivocal distinction of being singled out, with another Scottish medical man, as the only Scottish poet of his time by a publicist of the self-styled Scottish Literary Renaissance, began with a collection of lyrics entitled *Granite Dust*, 1892, and went on to much more serious and pretentious themes, *War: an Ode* being one of the best of his productions. In 1894 William Andrew Mackenzie, who had forsaken medicine at

1   The only copy, a reprint for the author's use of the *Herald* verses, is in the possession of the present writer. The farmer of Lumgair was the father of the Rev. Dr. W. S. Bruce of Banff, author of *The Nor'-East*, and so grandfather to the Rev. Bruce McEwen, minister of the second charge at Oldmachar between the wars.
2   He, and his son, were central figures in a fascinating true spy story of the First World War which brought him a decoration.

Marischal to become a journalist on *Black and White*, published *Rosemary* containing the classic 'Shon Campbell', which immediately was acclaimed as the perfect and tragic figure of the poor Scottish student. The same year the irrepressible John Malcolm Bulloch, almost as versatile (except in the Classics) as the somewhat earlier Andrew Lang of St. Andrews, issued *Certain College Carols*. Ten years later Rachel Annand Taylor, a niece of the great heavy-weight athlete Donald Dinnie, ventured first into print with her *Poems*. She had been one of Grierson's first women students and he used to insist his best. She did not take a degree, but was laureated LL.D. in 1943. Her very precious Renaissance type of mind produced jewelled verse written in a medieval Italianate hand. She died in 1960.

The First World War deprived the University of several promising poets like J. W. Shanks and R. H. Middleton. After it George Rowntree Harvey, with *Green Ears* and *The Shepherds* (a Scriptural drama), Nan Shepherd, with *In the Cairngorms*, Eric Linklater with *A Dragon Laughed*, and others supplied a kind of verse obligato to the novels of the period — Dr. Shepherd's *The Quarry Wood*, Eric Linklater's shelf of vivid and boisterous tales with *Juan in America* as a centrepiece; Agnes Mure Mackenzie supplementing her really exciting history of Scotland with stories like *The Half Loaf*; Alan Mackinnon supplying a Florentine flavour in *Love by Halves*; Lesley Storm with her bright plays and many others have contributed to diversify the reputation of Aberdeen University. Sir Robert Sangster Rait, the third Aberdonian — John Hill Burton and David Mather Masson preceded him — to be Historiographer Royal for Scotland, amongst his many excursions into the history of Scotland found time to write *The Universities of Aberdeen*. John R. Allan has probably more certainly written a classic of country life than any graduate of the university in *Farmer's Boy*. But again it must be asserted that this is not a history of the university and a halt must be called to the enumeration of the *flosculi boreales*.

In 1893 there appeared in a limited edition of a dozen copies *A Handful of Heather* (Lewis Smith the publisher), which was the true harbinger of a Scottish literary revival and the first effective shot in the revolt from the domination of Scottish verse by the shade of Robert Burns. The author Charles Murray, who had served his apprenticeship as a civil engineer in Aberdeen, was by this time in South Africa. In 1900 Messrs. Wyllie published a revised and extended volume with the title *Hamewith* which straightway became the most fashionable house-name in the North-East of Scotland. In 1909 a new and still larger *Hamewith* was published in London by Constable and Co., with an introduction by Andrew Lang and two illustrations by Douglas Strachan. His war poems, *A Sough o' War*, appeared in 1917, and *In the Country Places*, containing some of his best work in 1921. All these were collected in 1927 as *Hamewith and Other Poems*. Occasional pieces were published in newspapers and periodicals, one of them 'There's Aye a' Something', which appeared in the *Aberdeen Press and Journal* in 1938 having such a sale that several reprints of the newspaper were required to satisfy the demand. An almost similar public appreciation was given to J. C. Milne's posthumous *Poems* in 1963 which sold three editions at a guinea in a few days. Milne, an Aberdeen graduate was a lecturer in Aberdeen Training College.[1]

Several other poets in Murray's time were busy in Aberdeen. Dr. David Rorie's 'Lum Hat Wantin' a Croon' came to be sung wherever Scotsmen gather, and his *Auld Doctor and Other Poems* had an appreciative audience. He was a doctor in the suburbs. Professor Alexander Gray, though an Angus man by birth and Edinburgh University by education, in the three lustra spent in Aberdeen fully assimilated the Aberdonian philosophy of life and half-a-dozen volumes of verse, some of sparkling quality and many with the quiet atmosphere of the ballads and lieder he enjoyed added to the cultural riches of the city. Marion Angus, with her *Tinker's Road* and other highly mannered verse could impart to both Scots and English an elfin grace, with something of the elusiveness of 'Kilmeny' set in a rich jewellery of words. John Mitchell's *Bydand* and *Tibby Tamson o' the Buck* were real evaluations of rural character.

The prose writers were even more active than the versifiers. First and foremost came William Alexander, eminent among Aberdeen's journalists, whose novel *Johnny Gibb of Gushetneuk*, 1871, bears to Aberdeenshire prose the relation that Murray's poems do to its verse. There is not much action in the novel; its twin virtues are its character-drawing and its beautiful language, presenting with Murray's pieces the full splendour of the doric tongue. *Life Among My Ain Folk* consists of four short stories, very powerful studies that anticipate by a full

1   It is a common complaint in Edinburgh and the south that the public won't buy poetry. The complainants overlook the possibility that this could be the fault not of the public but the poets. For the last thirty years of his life Charles Murray never had less than £1 a week in royalties from *Hamewith*, and his centenary celebrations in which a dozen of his pieces were presented in a sylvan setting, drew 500 people. In 1969 of his *Last Poems*, 2,000 sold in three weeks.

generation the questionings that succeeded to the decadence of the fin de siècle. Neil Maclean's *Life at a Northern University*, 1874, led the way for a long succession of reminiscences, interpretations and impressions of university life.

Outside the university some excellent work was being done. William Walker's *Bards of Bon-Accord* was the work of a man who left school at the age of eight and in his adult life combined success in business with expertise in literary criticism, particularly in relation to the popular ballads and traditional music of Scotland, in Professor Francis J. Child's great edition in which he gave varied and valuable assistance. He also wrote several local studies, the most considerable being his vindication of Peter Buchan the Peterhead ballad collector and his edition of David Melville's *Commonplace Book*. William Carnie in three volumes of *Reporting Reminiscences* gave what amounted to an eyewitness account of the town during the second half of the nineteenth century. John Mackintosh, a general merchant and like William Walker an early school-leaver, wrote a three-volume *History of Civilisation in Scotland* while standing at his desk in his shop. He also was responsible for the *Historic Earls and Earldoms of Scotland* and a book upon Deeside. The University gave him the LL.D., and his son John, a graduate, wrote a history of contemporary affairs just before the Second World War and edited the third volume of the *Roll of Graduates*, *1926–55*, the first having been compiled for the period 1860–1900, and the second, 1901–25, by Theodore Watt, LL.D.

A. W. Robertson, Aberdeen's first Public librarian, in 1893 issued a *Handlist of Bibliography of the Shires of Aberdeen, Banff and Kincardine*,[1] extending to 133 pages of about fifty items each, a fact which is a sufficient deterrent to any attempt to indulge in a quick survey of local literature. A few may, however, be mentioned besides those already noted. William Robbie in 1893 published his *Aberdeen: Its Traditions and History*, in many respects the best history of the town. He was the author of two local novels, *Mains of Yonderton* and *The Heir of Glendornie* now quite forgotten. From 1871 to 1902 Alexander Walker, who was for many years Dean of Guild, wrote at least fifty books and pamphlets, of which the most important are his *List of Deans of Guild*, 1875; *Robert Gordon and his Hospital*, 1886; *Mary Queen of Scots*, 1887, and

---

1   The writer has the interleaved copy handed by the compiler to William Walker for the latter to insert any additions that his profound knowledge of Aberdeen literature might suggest to the addenda already written in by Robertson. Robertson died before he could revise his list. The additions amount to several hundreds.

Knights Templar in and Around Aberdeen 1887. George Walker in 1897 produced a volume of miscellaneous and delightful sketches, *Aberdeen Awa*. Ebenezer Bain wrote the history of the Incorporated Trades in his *Merchant and Craft Guilds*, 1887. A. M. Munro, the City Chamberlain, amongst several other useful books of local importance wrote his *Memorials of the Aldermen, Provosts and Lord Provosts of Aberdeen* in 1897. G. M. Fraser, the city librarian, contributed much valuable information in his *Historical Aberdeen*, 1904–5; *Aberdeen Street Names*, 1911; the *Bridge of Dee*, 1913, and other studies. Dr. John Milne, a celebrated educationist at the turn of the century, in his *Aberdeen, Topographical, Antiquarian and Historical Papers*, 1911, propounded many novel ideas and unearthed many curious facts about the city. Col. Lachlan Mackinnon wrote what is probably the best book of Aberdeen personal reminiscences in *Recollections of an Old Lawyer*, 1935, which extended over the best part of a century. One of the most noteworthy of specialised studies is J. P. Edmond's *The Aberdeen Printers* which appeared in the eighties. Edmond was for a good many years chief librarian to the Earl of Crawford and Balcarres when that noted bibliophile's *Bibliotheca Lindesiana*, published by the Aberdeen University Press in 1910, was being compiled. Another highly specialised work was the *Bibliographia Aberdonensis* of James F. Kellas Johnstone, 1929–30, an account of books relating to or printed in the three North-eastern Counties from 1472 to 1700, which contains, in addition to exact bibliographical data, an extraordinary accumulation of historical and biographical facts. In the early stages of the work A. W. Robertson, already mentioned, was associated with Kellas Johnstone.

Two historians, fit to rank with Aberdeen's greatest, Joseph Robertson, between them dominate the Aberdeen literary scene from 1880 to the present day. Peter John Anderson the University Librarian issued his first publication in 1880, and thereafter year after year he contributed something to some aspect of local history, not always of the university. As regards the University itself, his three-volume *Selection from the Records of Marischal College* and his *Officers and Graduates of University and King's College*, his quater-centenary *Studies in the History and Development of the University of Aberdeen* and his *Record of the Celebration of the Quater-centenary*, his *Notes on Heraldic Representations at King's and Marischal Colleges*, his *Aurora Borealis Academica: University Appreciations* — these and many more volumes or pamphlets or papers, in conjunction with his labours as general editor of the New Spalding Club attest his piety to his Alma Mater and the vigour of his enthusiasm, while his studies like the *Aberdeen Friars* show that he was prepared to give the town a share of his loyalty to the gown.

His successor in the Library, William Douglas Simpson, became the leading authority in Scotland on castellated architecture and history, commencing in the early twenties and continuing until his sudden death at his desk in 1968. His *Origins of Christianity in Aberdeenshire* brought the work of the early Roman missionaries and their identities into a more realistic perspective and cleared up several dubious problems that acceptance of Columba as the pioneer had created. His *Early Castles of Mar* gave a coherent strategical as well as historical picture of the system of medieval and Norman fortifications based upon the Don valley. There was scarcely a castle in Aberdeenshire that he did not survey and describe, the books on those of Kildrummy, Kindrochit, Huntly and Dundarg being of especial importance. He did not, however, confine himself to Aberdeenshire but ranged over the whole of Scotland and dealt in addition with strongholds on the Continent. He was general editor of the Third Spalding Club.

CHAPTER TWELVE

Pursuits of Peace

In 1852 there was instituted the Aberdeen Musical Association which gathered many of the leading citizens of Aberdeen and their womenfolk into its membership, adding an orchestral branch called the Philharmonic Society in 1857, and fell a victim at last to domestic quarrels, its swan-song being sung in the early months of 1866. For its lifetime the Association was conducted by Richard Latter. In 1853 the Choral Society was formed, consisting of working men trained by a self-taught musician, James Melvin, a moulder. It expired in 1855. But a stronger body was in existence to take its place. In 1854 William Carnie lectured on psalmody to an audience of 2,000 in the Free West Church and in the same year the Aberdeen General Association for the Improvement of Psalmody was formed. One of the memorable feats of this association was to raise a mixed choir of 160 voices which was first heard in a special service of praise in the East Church. Another was a public class for the practice of tunes which was sometimes as large as 900 members. A third was Carnie's great 'Choir of a Thousand Voices' which used to perform in the Music Hall. By 1856 this remarkable association had accomplished its aim, and Aberdeen possessed 'one general, three denominational and twenty-six congregational associations with meetings for practice, eight societies for the practice of vocal music, six schools in which music is taught, five schools where singing is practised, and at least five or six special classes for teaching music'.

From this tremendous enthusiasm there sprang in 1858 the Aberdeen Choral Union. Latter at once became its conductor, and an examining committee which auditioned candidates recommended after a fortnight's work seventy ladies and 107 men. Soon an orchestral section was added. The Union's first public appearance was at the opening of the Music Hall by the Prince Consort on 14 September 1859, when a music festival was held, and the singing of 'Lord, Thou alone art God', from *St. Paul*, by 250 voices of the choir created a deep impression. A secular concert in 1860 netted £40, and the same year the Union commenced to study *The Messiah*, following that with *The Creation* the next year. All the great oratorios were performed and a series of Saturday evening concerts was given each winter for many years. After Latter's departure for London, the Union had many vicissitudes with its conductors, including a touching gentleman from England named Annesley who made a moonlight flitting with a lot of Aberdeen money, and a meteoric Frenchman named Guyan whose unexpected tenacity almost defeated the efforts of the committee to dislodge him.

Trials and tribulations arising out of the susceptibilities of the artistic temperament from time to time threatened to wreck the Union, and these were also probably the most frequent cause of the Union's occasional financial crises. But with the appointment in 1880 of John Kirby as conductor and the following year of J. B. Keith as secretary the organisation began to flourish again, its recovery of poise being assisted by the dissolution as a separate entity of the instrumental branch. The standard of musical erudition required by candidates was very high. They had to be 'familiar with musical signs, note value, and the various kinds of time' and be 'able to sing intervals and major and minor, and chromatic scales, as well as a passage selected from an oratorio chorus and one from a standard vocal work', besides giving satisfactory evidence of a good voice and ear. Among many distinguished vocalists who visited Aberdeen under the Union's auspices were Anna Williams, Barrington Foote, Edward Lloyd, Antoinette Sterling, J. W. Turner, Joseph O'Mara, David Hughes, Ben Davies, Fanny Moody, Charles Manners, Foli, Charles Santley, Durward Lely, Ellen Beach Yaw ('the Californian Lark') and Madame Albani.

Twice in the early thirties Sir Thomas Beecham conducted the London Symphony Orchestra in the city, Kreisler played to what was said to be the biggest audience ever seen in the Music Hall on 11 February 1932, and Cortot the pianist appeared a little later, all four appearances being sponsored by Will Jamieson, a well-known Aberdeen bookmaker. After the Second World War the Scottish National Orchestra included Aberdeen in its itinerary.

The city's musical tradition in what may be termed the direct line of succession was continued in more recent years by the Aberdeen Choral Society with David Henderson as conductor and its regular concerts and annual performance of *The Messiah* attesting to the enthusiasm and artistic achievement of its members. In the earlier part of the century the shipyards, Hall & Co. and Hall, Russell's, had their excellent male voice choirs, as had the railway employees. There are an Orchestral Society, Chamber Music Club and in connection with the University there is a great deal of musical activity. Indeed, in the arts there has been much the same 'explosion' though it occurred at a rather later date than in sport.

In 1872 the Theatre Royal closed down, its place being taken by a new theatre in Guild Street, opened on 19 December that year, as 'Her Majesty's Opera House' and today still functioning in a different fashion as the Tivoli. The name was changed after a few years to Her Majesty's Theatre. The first lessee was William Gomersal, creator of the part of Napoleon in *The Battle of Waterloo*.[1] He continued the repertory traditions, specialised in parts like Wah-no-tee in *The Octaroon*, and sang duets like 'When a little farm we keep', and 'ABC' with his daughter, and his second wife, Miss Elsie Maisey. In the spring of 1880 he took a theatre in Worcester, and Miss Annie Baldwin succeeded him as lessee, but she was not so lucky and in October 1881 the theatre, which had been shut down, was reopened by William M'Farland, who had for many years been manager of the adjacent Alhambra Music Hall, into which Trinity Church had been converted when that area was scheduled under the Aberdeen Railway Act.

M'Farland was lessee for ten years. The stock company had practically disappeared in Miss Baldwin's time, for in 1880 Robertson's *Caste*, the Beatrice Company and the Carl Rosa Opera Company all visited Aberdeen. Dr. W. N. Hodges, manager to Professor Anderson, 'the Wizard of the North', was M'Farland's first manager, and both he and Reginald Hare, the next, died soon. Finally John Cavanah and his son Henry C. Cavanah carried on until the local company was absorbed by Arthurs Ltd. and Robert Arthur, destined to be a name for long familiar in Aberdeen theatre circles, took over control.

During the final years of Her Majesty's in Guild Street there were many distinguished names on its bills. In 1891 Mrs. Langtry made her only Aberdeen appearance, and, her visit coinciding with a maiden police court, the white gloves were presented to her. She had already parted an Aberdeenshire laird, Abington Baird of Strichen, from £100,000 of his fortune. Wilson Barrett, John Hare and Olga Nethersole were in Aberdeen in 1892; E. S. Willard, with *The Professor's Love Story* of J. M. Barrie in 1895, and Toole and the Carl Rosa; in 1896 and 1897 the Kendals; in 1898 Ellen Terry, Sir Henry Irving being prevented by illness. There were two big opera engagements in 1899, the Carl Rosa and the National Opera Company with Robert

---

1 At Astley's every night, the play of Moscow's fall; Napoleon, for the thousandth time, by Mr. Gomersal. *Bon Gaultier Ballads*.

Cunningham as director; and amongst the actors there was Edward Terry. Miss Nethersole returned in 1903, Ellen Terry, Beerbohm Tree and Henry Irving made 1904 triply memorable. Other companies were the Compton Comedy and the Turner Opera Companies. In truth, Her Majesty's, Guild Street, had a rich record.

Aberdeen's own output of actors has not been large, Sir Johnston Forbes-Robertson and Matheson Lang being Aberdonians, as it were, at one remove. But there were a few who enjoyed a substantial if not supreme celebrity — James Gibson (1842–7), his daughter Brenda Gibson; William Lowe, author for Mr. Gomersal of *The Yellow Dwarf* in 1879; Campbell Gollan, well-known in America; Lester Thomson, Leopold Profeit. In our own day Miss Lois Obee (Sonia Dresdel) has won high tributes from the London critics. Andrew Cruickshank besides many stage triumphs became one of the most familiar of T.V. troupers. Of actor-managers, Mackay Robertson in Victorian days was not very successful, but Stephen Mitchell in our time is one of the country's leading impresarios, and Alan Melville, at one time a B.B.C. producer in Aberdeen, is both playwright and producer in London. Sir Harry Lauder sang his prentice songs in Aberdeen and John Henry Anderson, the Wizard of the North, whose grave is on the Schoolhill side of St. Nicholas Kirkyard, was an even more famous showman in his heyday than Walford Bodie. One of his greatest feats was at Balmoral where, under the noses of the Royal Family, he produced out of his 'Magic Scrap Book' plates, glasses, birdcages, hats, a live goose, goldfish in bowls, and his own son in Highland garb, so that 'Her Majesty lifted her hands in reverential awe and the Prince Consort cheered heartily'.

Across the Denburn on the slopes of Windmill Brae that began to be developed with the extension of the railway there arose another centre of entertainment which for half a century enjoyed a considerable celebrity. Alfred Eugene Cooke and his two brothers brought their famous circus from a site opposite the old Fish Market to Bridge Place, somewhere in the mid-seventies, succeeding Newsome's Circus which had been popular there for several years.[1] Within wooden walls and a

1   The suggestion that the site of the circus was also the 'theatre' of the Aberdeen Crafts players who used to perform the *Halyblude* morality at Corpus Christi, is based on confusion as to the whereabouts of the city's Windmill. It was at the head of the Gallowgate. The windmill which gave its name to Windmill Brae was built in 1678, long after the craft plays were discontinued. The Porthill was the place where the *Halyblude* was originally performed.

canvas roof the Cookes presented their varied performance to an audience that slowly declined in size and which indeed sank to nothing
while a permanent structure was being built towards the end of the
eighties. In 1891 George (Jolly Little) Lewis opened a variety entertainment in the Jollity Vaudeville Theatre, which closed down in July
1893, and the following month the Livermore brothers opened the
People's Palace. Closed temporarily in 1896 it was reopened on 21
September and on 30 September was devastated by fire which cost the
lives of seven people, thirty-six being seriously hurt when the audience
stampeded.

Eventually the Palace, rebuilt at a total cost of £15,000, was opened
for business again on 24 October 1898, and for the next thirty-three
years functioned mainly as a theatre of varieties, presenting the greatest
artistes of the music hall stage. Harry Lauder from early in his career
to the height of his popularity, Charles Coburn, Walford Bodie, the
Aberdonian G. W. Fyvie, Florrie Forde and Harry Tate, May Moore
Duprez, Dan Leno, Bransby Williams, Hackenschmidt the wrestler,
whose erstwhile opponent Mahmont the Terrible Turk had been seen
at the Guild Street house, and among many others there is a vague
hint of a visit of a youngster named Charles Chaplin in that cleverest
of all Music Hall clowning, Fred Karno's Mumming Birds. In 1902
there seems to have been a cinematograph in the Palace, and in 1931,
after the theatre became the property of Jack Poole, it was turned into
a picture house. Just before the transformation it had, however, enjoyed an Indian summer of Thespian glory when the Arthur Hinton
Dramatic Company presented a series of barn-stormers, such stuff
as nightmares are made of, like *Maria Monk, The Stranglers of Paris*,
and other exercises in blood and thunder, softened from time to time by
the introduction of such local favourites as *Mill o' Tifty's Annie*.
Eventually the Palace was taken over by the Rank Organisation. From
a club in more recent years it became a dance-hall. For many years as
secretary and manager Walter Gilbert, whose son W. L. Gilbert became business manager of H.M. Theatre, was in charge at Bridge
Place, and maintained its high reputation as a home of vaudeville and
dramatic entertainment. He had been Nanki Poo in *The Mikado*, and
in his youth as a choir boy been noted for his singing of 'The Holy
City'.

On 3 December 1906, there was opened with the pantomime of
Red Riding Hood Aberdeen's last and most distinguished playhouse,
His Majesty's Theatre, its striking yet dignified design by Archibald

Frank Matcham fitting in with the viaduct, the South Church and the Public Library, and emphasising the yawning gulf on its eastern flank that bordered what was then Black's Buildings and the Schoolhill railway halt. The Robert Arthur Theatres Company were the proprietors (which perhaps explains the metropolitan architect when Aberdeen had several highly competent practitioners of its own) and H. Adair Nelson was then and for almost a quarter of a century the manager. In 1933 when theatrical fortunes were at a low ebb, His Majesty's at a lucky juncture for Aberdeen came into the possession of the Donald family, already well-known in the city in a variety of activities, and from father to son and on to grandson, it has provided the North-East of Scotland with a programme which no town of Aberdeen's size in the United Kingdom has been able to emulate. In war and peace, in bad times and good, H.M. Theatre has furnished its patrons with all that is best in current stage productions. Drama from Shakespeare to pantomime, grand opera, light opera, musical comedy, ballet, with occasional vaudeville and revue, all are at the disposal of Aberdeen's audiences, while local amateur companies both dramatic and musical from time to time have the opportunity of testing themselves on as large and modern a stage as is available anywhere. The theatre is for Aberdeen's size a large one and admirably appointed, and in an age when so many playhouses in provincial centres are closing down, Aberdeen perhaps does not give the management enough credit for the continuity of its performances.

In the years since 1906 there have been few companies and few actors who have not found their way to the Schoolhill. The Carl Rosa, the O'Mara, the Moody Manners, the D'oyly Carte, the Sadler's Wells and Scottish National Opera Company, great Shakespearian actors like Frank Benson, Wilson Barrett, Osmond Tearle, Edward Compton and his daughters (the Compton Comedy Company), Alex Guinness, Ellen Terry, Sybil Thorndike, Vivien Leigh; all-rounders like Martin Harvey (who even tried Greek tragedy, some years before Professor John Harrower presented in the Music Hall his versions of *Antigone* and *Agamemnon*), Matheson Lang, Oscar Asche, Robert Donat, Emlyn Williams, Robert Morley, H. B. Irving, Ivor Novello, Owen Nares, Anna Neagle, Julie Neilson, Zena Dare, those splendid troupers Cicely Courtneidge and Jack Hulbert, John Clyde in *Rob Roy* just after the New Year for many a year, the cream of the country's comedians Gracie Fields, Florrie Forde, Vesta Tilley, Bebe Daniels, Alice Delysia, Harry Lauder and George Robey — Aberdeen theatre-goers have supped full of many a dish, nourishing, dainty and stimulating in His Majesty's Theatre.

The vitality of the cultural life of Aberdeen and the North-East in the seventh and eighth decades of the nineteenth century cannot be better illustrated than by reference to a remarkable society that called itself the Academy of Deer. This company was wont to meet in the manse of Old Deer, in Buchan, the incumbent, the Rev. James Peter, acting as chairman and host with the title of the Abbot. Some idea may be gathered of the extent of 'the Academy's' influence from short notes on its members. The Rev. James Peter (1823–86), lover of good talk, good books, good art, good wine, and good company, had been responsible along with some of his ministerial brethren and with Dr. Alexander Gavin of Strichen, for the resuscitation of the Club of Deir originally founded by a group of landed proprietors and ministers at the time of the French Revolution, and still flourishing in its second incarnation.[1] Peter's brother George, parish minister of Kemnay, was also a member. Dr. Gavin, son of Nelson's surgeon at the Battle of Copenhagen who was reputed to be the author of the lovely lyric 'Mormond Braes' that has been absorbed into the folk-music of Scotland, was like Peter an exponent of the art of good and cultured living.

Sir David Gill (1843–1914), son of an Aberdeen watchmaker, after being in charge of Lord Crawford's observatory at Dunecht, was appointed director of the Cape of Good Hope observatory in 1879 and was responsible for a great deal of astronomical research and observation in the southern hemisphere. Professor William Robertson Smith (1846–94), a native of Donside, was Professor of Old Testament Exegesis in Aberdeen Free Church College when his article 'Bible' in the Ninth Edition of the *Encyclopaedia Britannica* led to his deposition from the chair in 1881. He later became editor-in-chief of the encyclopaedia and Professor of Arabic and university librarian at Cambridge. He was the nephew of Margaret Robertson (born in Deer parish), author over the pseudonym of John Haberton of the American classic *Helen's Babies*, and mother of Ralph Connor the Canadian novelist. John Kerr was an inspector of schools who in two volumes of reminiscences produced a lively picture of life in the North-East in those days.

1 The occasion for the resuscitation was the sale of a deceased Church of Scotland minister's effects, which included some excellent claret purchased by the clerical brethren mentioned and sampled at a lunch convened on the spot. At the time of writing, the club has celebrated with fully appropriate pomp and circumstance, the centenary of its second founding.

John Forbes White (1831–1903), First Bursar at Marischal at the age of 13, outstanding classical scholar, a meal miller, and a thoroughly experienced connoisseur of the arts, was one of those principally responsible for the Aberdeen Art Gallery and its later embellishment the Sculpture Gallery. He was president of the Hellenic Society, and he bought the first Corot to come to Scotland. He lived at Seaton Cottage, Bridge of Don, part of it designed by Collier, and his town house, where he kept his pictures, was at the corner of Union Street and Bonaccord Street, later occupied by Pratt and Keith, the drapers, and more recently by Andrew Collie & Son.

One of the clerks in White's office was Sam Reid, brother of George Reid (later Sir George and President of the Royal Scottish Academy but by some lapse without mention in the *Dictionary of National Biography*) and of Archibald D. Reid, also an R.S.A. Sam, who was a member of the Royal Society of Water Colour painters, was not a member of the Academy of Deer, and he was a less gifted artist than his brothers. Archibald, who was a member, was particularly successful with his landscapes, some of them pastels and quite a number in a style reminiscent of pastel work, which is also seen in, for example, an impression of King's College by J. L. Logan. George Reid (1841–1913), whose versatility was equalled by his astonishing skill as a draughtsman, deserves to be ranked with his two almost contemporaries, Dyce and Phillip, to form Aberdeen's trio of great artists of the century. His range was wider than even Dyce's, though he may have lacked the colour sense of Phillip. His etchings, in illustration of such books as the *River Clyde* and the *River Tweed* and Charles St. John's *Natural History and Sport in Moray*, his pen-and-inks in innumerable local books reproducing architectural and similar features, land or seascapes like his massive *Dunnottar Castle*, brilliant flower pictures like the *Roses* now in the boardroom of Aberdeen Chamber of Commerce, and his magnificent series of portraits of characters in *Johnny Gibb of Gushetneuk* establish him as an interpreter of Scottish scene and character with few equals in the history of Scottish art. Beginning life with a seven-year apprenticeship to Keith and Gibb, lithographers, he took art lessons from a pupil of James Giles, then in Utrecht from Alexander Mollinger, in Paris from Yvon and at The Hague from Josef Israels. He first made his mark with a portrait of George Macdonald, the Strathbogie novelist, but he felt, and many of his admirers have suspected, that the demand for portraits was detrimental to more sensitive and imaginative work in which he could have excelled. To the end of his life his eye retained its phenomenal clarity and his pencil its sureness of touch. His association with Peter inspired him to design the fine tower that adorns the parish church of Deer and upon the front of which the Buchan Club in 1961 placed a plaque commemorating the Book of Deer, the first Gaelic writing in Scotland which was inscribed in the monastery on the site of the parish church.

Other two artist members of the Academy were James Cadenhead, R.S.A. (1858–1927), an Aberdonian whose reputation was not commensurate with his abilities, and George Paul Chalmers, R.S.A. (1833–78), a most gifted painter whose accidental death in 1878 in his thirties was a blow to Aberdeen and Scottish Art. According to White, Chalmers's weakness was in not knowing when his canvases were complete, and he would spoil them by elaboration. On one occasion White and George Reid tied Chalmers to a chair, and holding a red-hot poker under his nose compelled him to promise not to put another stroke on a picture which they regarded as complete in itself and worth saving.

Robert Brough, A.R.S.A. (1872–1905), a Ross-shire man who lived a good deal in Aberdeen may be regarded as the most 'modern' of the artists of the later Victorian Age in Aberdeen, showing the influences of the post-Impressionists with a decided character of his own which could have carried him far had he lived. Of his contemporaries Alec Fraser (1868–1939), while more conventional, produced especially upon small canvases some landscape gems, and in character study excelled with his fisher folk. George Russel Gowans, R.S.W. (1843–1924), was excellent in his favourite role of water-colourist, in which medium John Mitchell (1838–1926) was at his happiest in sea and Deeside scenes; William Smith (died 1941), who did a good deal of book illustration, also found his inspiration in Aberdeen itself in street scenes and the like, as well as on Deeside; Leslie Thomson, R.W.S. (1851–1929), did most of his best work in the Broads of East Anglia; George Fiddes Watt, R.S.A. (1873–1960), who made his name by his interiors and groups, came to concentrate upon portraiture; John M. Aiken, R.S.A., was notable in landscape and portraiture; Thomas Bunting (1851–1928) did his best work in water colours. W. Jackson Simpson worked in oils and water colours, and produced etchings and drypoints, and by his example and his teaching did much to foster artistic appreciation and amateur art in the city.

In a very different category was Douglas Strachan, H.R.S.A. (1875–1950), who began with sketches and crayons, went on to oils and portraiture, but eventually found his true metier in the assembly (if that is the word) of stained glass windows, in which esoteric accomplishment he had few rivals and no superiors. A fine example of his work is the triple-light memorial window in King's College Library to the three great Scots Humanists — George Buchanan, Arthur Johnstone and James Melvin. His friend James Cromar Watt (1862–1940) who re-discovered the Renaissance secret of enamelling on metal, the medium in which he preferred to work with such success that he attained a world-wide reputation, equalled by his fame as a practical botanist, for his exquisite aesthetic sense was combined with an uncanny ac-quaintance with rare species of plants. He lived as much in his cold greenhouse at the foot of his tiny garden in Dee Street as in his studio; he specialised in rhododendrons, of which he had under glass and along his garden wall a choice selection of species, and in auriculas of which he had a small border that he tended with perpetual care. The city owes to him its magnificent collection of rhododendrons in Hazlehead policies and to him also some of its most enviable pieces of china and porcelain in the Art Gallery.

In close contact with Aberdeen during their formative years were two artists who attained to considerable celebrity. James McBey (1884–1959) began life in the North Bank in Aberdeen, took up etching with plumber's sheet metal for his plates and a small mangle for a printing-press and in 1910 decided to try his fortune in London. He was official artist with the Egyptian Expeditionary Force during the 1914–18 war, producing a series of studies that won tremendous applause — 'Strange Signals' and 'Dawn Camel Patrol Setting Out' are two of the most notable, but his evocation of north-eastern scenes, like 'Gamrie' and 'Sea and Rain, Macduff', vie with his wider subjects in their economy of line and their memorable quality, which was more difficult to achieve than in his bull-fights and Moorish pictures. Later he turned to water-colour and did for good measure a portrait in oils of the General Manager of the North Bank, James Hutcheon.

James Pittendrigh MacGillivray, R.S.A. (1859–1938), born at Port Elphinstone, devoted himself to sculpture and poetry. He did busts in bronze of a number of distinguished Aberdonians including Sir George Reid and Dr. William Alexander, and in Aberdeen Art Gallery are several of his more imaginative conceptions — Atalanta, The Gipsy Queen, a Pieta. He did the Byron statue in the grounds of the Grammar School and there is an interesting bronze figure of Robert Burns in the Gallery. He was appointed King's Limner for Scotland at the beginning of the century. As a poet in the old Scots tongue he wrote amongst other things the volume *Bog Myrtle and Peat-Reek* which contains 'Mercy o' Gode', that is a certainty for modern Scottish anthologies. Born in the gracious shadow of Bennachie, he named that delectable mountain's Mither Tap the Fujiyama of Aberdeenshire. A near contemporary of MacGillivray was William Macmillan, R.A., like him an artist very much in the classical tradition. The Northern Arts Club exists mainly for the encouragement of local artists and holds an annual exhibition. In recent years some of the younger aspirants have held an open-air show in summer in the forecourt of the West Church of St. Andrew in Union Street.

In 1886, at a public meeting with Lord Aberdeen in the chair, the New Spalding Club was founded. It died during the first war with Germany, after adding almost as many books to the library of local history as its predecessor, the original Spalding Club. The standard was perhaps less high, although the Secretary and principal editor, P. J. Anderson, the University librarian, deserves to be bracketed with Robertson and Stuart for width of interest and accuracy of knowledge. The most sought-after of the New Spalding publications is probably John Malcolm Bulloch's *House of Gordon*. But many other studies enriched Aberdeen's store of historical fact. The two-volume *Cartularium Ecclesiae S. Nicholai Aberdonensis* by the Rev. Dr. James Cooper; P. J. Anderson's *King's College Officers and Graduates* and *Records of Marischal College and University* in three volumes; Dr. James Moir's edition and translation of Boece's *Bishops of Aberdeen*; A. M. Munro's two-volume *Records of Old Aberdeen* — these are a fairly representative selection of its products.

The Great War really killed the Club, with two of its major projects unaccomplished. One, a collection of folk-song of the North-East undertaken by Gavin Greig, a Buchan schoolmaster, has never been fully published. The ballad section was issued by the Buchan Club in 1926, Greig having died during the war, and the rest of the material, the largest and richest local collection of folk-song in existence, still lies in King's College library. The other undertaking, a bibliography of Aberdeen books to 1700, was begun by the city librarian, A. W. Robertson, and taken over by J. F. Kellas Johnstone, who, however, had not completed the work when war broke out and the Club suspended operations. But in 1928 the Third Spalding Club was formed, took over the *Bibliographia Aberdonensis*, which it published after Johnstone's death, in 1929 in two volumes. W. Douglas Simpson, the University librarian in succession to P. J. Anderson, also took up his mantle as

Spalding Club editor. The third club paid more attention to county family history than to urban subjects, which in consequence scarcely figure in its tally of some thirty titles. Printing costs and declining interest in the bare bones of local history led to the winding up of the Third Spalding Club in the mid-sixties.[1]

Mainly during the eighties there was a spontaneous upsurge of enthusiasm for sport of all kinds. Golf, of course, was already familiar, and the Links course, on which the Aberdeen Club played, was in 1875 the scene of a remarkable feat, when W. G. Bloxsom, a Lothians man who was a member of the club, played twelve rounds between 6 a.m. and 9.30 p.m. with scores ranging from 76 to 90, and topped this up by walking eleven miles along the Deeside road. In 1872 the first 'artisan' club, the Bon-Accord, was founded with John Doleman as captain, in 1877 the University Golf Club took shape, in 1879 the Victoria, the Caledonian and Northern following a little later. In 1880 an amateur tournament was held on the Links, in 1888 the Aberdeen Golf Club crossed the Don to Balgownie, and in 1903 it received the title 'Royal'. Deeside, Balnagask, and Murcar and between the wars a second municipal course at Hazlehead enhanced the city's golf facilities.

Cricket seems to have been an early favourite with Aberdeen's young men, for as far back as 1853 there were complaints that the pitches were encroaching upon the sacred Links territory of the golfers. The Aberdeenshire Cricket Association, founded in 1884, has a club membership that has risen from sixteen to nearly a hundred, and its matches are catered for on many pitches both private and public. The Aberdeenshire Club itself with its own Mannofield ground has several times won the Scottish Counties championship, and has been host to several overseas visiting clubs, including the first Australian side after the Second World War, when Don Bradman delighted a large crowd with a sparkling 123 not out.

Aberdeen Football Club was founded by a merger between three existing clubs in the city in 1903 — Aberdeen, Orion, and Victoria United. Aberdeen itself had taken shape in 1881. The club has won the Scottish Cup (in 1947 and 1970), the League Championship (in 1955). It also has the distinction of having drawn, with Celtic in the Scottish Cup final at Hampden Park, the Scottish record crowd of 146,433, its

---

1 By that time only the general editor, Dr. Simpson, the secretary Benjamin W. Gunn, and two members of the original committee, Lyon King of Arms Sir Thomas Innes of Learney and the present writer had survived.

home record at Pittodrie Park being 45,061 against Hearts in the fourth round Scottish cup-tie in 1954.

There are numerous other association football clubs in the city, despite the banning by the Town Council's Education Committee of any football but the alien Rugby from the senior schools. But the development not merely of football in both its styles and of the other outdoor and indoor sports is a subject rather for a statistical account (the latest of which does indeed deal with these activities) than a history of this nature.

But one or two bodies whose main arena is outdoors and who could be described as being addicted to sport with a difference, deserve special mention. The Aberdeen Boat Club, started in 1870 by some students under the leadership of David Manson, brother of Patrick who defeated malaria, endured for half-a-century with a curious reputation for a blend of social and sporting distinction. Although the Club's crews had for their chief rivals in many doughty contests of oarmanship the workers in the ship-building yards, membership of the club was very much 'west-end' and to enter it was a considerable feat for a young man whose parents were not 'better-class'. The Cairngorm Club, founded in 1889 to enjoy the grandeur and hazards of Scotland's main mountain massif, which had already inspired the historian John Hill Burton's classic and was to be the subject of excellent studies by Alexander Inkson M'Conachie and Henry Alexander, had no segregation — to use the modern political jargon — in its philosophy. Every sincere lover of the hills was welcome. From 1893 the Club has published, under M'Conachie's editorship for many years, the *Cairngorm Club Journal*, a fascinating library of information about the great mountain range. One of the most enthusiastic members of the Club, James A. Parker, the engineer of the G.N.S.R. who had climbed every hill over 1,000 feet in the British Isles, besides conquests in the Alps, the Dolomites, the Graians and the Canadian Rockies, initiated with the Aberdeen advocate George Duncan during the First World War a hillmen's club which in the twenties, under the vigorous and imaginative direction of the Aberdeen constructional engineer William Tawse became known as the Life Preserving Society, and from January to mid-July explored each Saturday some part of the area, the highlight being the ascent of Ben Avon on Midsummer's Eve to see the sun rise. After Tawse's death in 1940 efforts were made to keep the society going, but when the war was over changes in personnel and habits caused it to lapse. Yet another institution that belongs in part to the same category is the Deeside Field Club, founded in 1920 in emulation of the Buchan Club which in turn was born of the Banffshire Field Club. The Deeside Field Club has a valuable magazine, *The Deeside Field*, originally edited by a Gramma r School master, J. Bentley Philip, and meets frequently in summer to visit places of interest and in winter for lectures.

Epilogue

Here, so far as this exposition is concerned, ends this strange eventful history. Many more tales might have been told of curious events and achievements not so much in Aberdeen itself as by Aberdonians the world over. But the emphasis has been rather upon acts and facts than on personalities, otherwise something would necessarily have been said of the Mutton Brae's most distinguished daughter, Mary Slessor, not unworthy to be bracketed in missionary history with David Livingstone, or of that colourful personality of the world of grand opera, Mary Garden, whose eminence on the stage was balanced by her shrewdness in the box-office. An excursion, unusual for Aberdonians, into music was made by Lilias Mackinnon, whose interpretation of Scriabin has earned her a high reputation as a pianist on both sides of the Atlantic.

Not being a literary history, there are lamentable gaps in the preceding pages in the record of Aberdeen's contribution to letters polite and otherwise. That sweet singer John Skinner of Linshart is represented by his son the bishop of Aberdeen who consecrated the first bishop of the American Anglican Church. Worthy in every respect of comparison in range and exactness with Creighton's *History of Epidemics* is Colonel William Johnston's *Medical Officers in the British Army*, covering the centuries from 1660 to after the Boer War, upon which the author was still engaged at his death in 1914, the compilation being completed by Colonel Alfred Peterkin. Johnston was of the same family as the elegant Latinist Arthur Johnston, and was in fact heir presumptive to what just missed being the senior of the Nova Scotian baronetcies. Missing also is that sound and reliable *History of Aberdeen and Banff* by William Watt, which succeeds in doing for the county what this present work attempts to do for the city. Nor should we forget Colonel Johnston's relative Alexander Johnston's analysis of the most successful piece of financial skulduggery not only of Aberdonians but of British and American tycoons, the *Inquiry into the Illinois Investment Company*, the abundant fruits of which were engrossed by 'Chicago' Smith and his nephew 'Silent' Smith.

These things are of the past. The future for Aberdeen, all unknown, promises to be more revolutionary than anything in its past. The steady and rapid deterioration in the city's physical appearance we have only to look about us to see. The general backwash of the growth of a permissive and affluent society elsewhere has now reached Aberdeen and begun to influence its moral and cultural outlook. In a year or two the reorganisation of Scottish local government will upset what for seventy years has been the communal balance of the burgh and will ensure that the permanent official instead of the elected representative will set the pace and call the tune. And over and above all loom the derricks and the rigs of North Sea oil, elevating Aberdeen to an economic precedence it never in its palmiest days knew amongst the burghs of Scotland and converting it, as the journalistic soothsayers describe it, into the Texas of this country.

For a final paragraph, and a prophecy that is as likely to prove true as any, an anecdote that used to be related by Charles Murray may be quoted, in the hope that it will relieve the horror of the prospect with a grin. A Scots minister was exhorting his flock. 'The day will come, my brethren, when ye'll raise piteous hands to heaven and cry, "Oh, Lord, Lord, we never thocht that hell would be like this." And the Lord, in His infinite mercy and compassion, will look doon on ye and say, "Weel, ye ken noo".'

Indexes

CHRONOLOGICAL LIST AND INDEX OF

Aldermen, Provosts and Lord Provosts

Firms and Industries

Persons

Places

General